Lecture Notes in Computer Science 13454

More information about this series at https://link.springer.com/bookseries/558

Savvas Papagiannidis · Eleftherios Alamanos ·
Suraksha Gupta · Yogesh K. Dwivedi ·
Matti Mäntymäki · Ilias O. Pappas (Eds.)

The Role of Digital Technologies in Shaping the Post-Pandemic World

21st IFIP WG 6.11 Conference on
e-Business, e-Services and e-Society, I3E 2022
Newcastle upon Tyne, UK, September 13–14, 2022
Proceedings

Editors
Savvas Papagiannidis (iD)
Newcastle University Business School
Newcastle upon Tyne, UK

Suraksha Gupta (iD)
Newcastle University Business School
Newcastle upon Tyne, UK

Matti Mäntymäki (iD)
University of Turku
Turku, Finland

Eleftherios Alamanos (iD)
Newcastle University Business School
Newcastle upon Tyne, UK

Yogesh K. Dwivedi (iD)
Swansea University
Swansea, UK

Symbiosis Institute of Business
Management Pune
Pune, India

Ilias O. Pappas (iD)
University of Agder
Kristiansand, Norway

Norwegian University of Science
and Technology
Trondheim, Norway

ISSN 0302-9743   ISSN 1611-3349 (electronic)
Lecture Notes in Computer Science
ISBN 978-3-031-15341-9   ISBN 978-3-031-15342-6 (eBook)
https://doi.org/10.1007/978-3-031-15342-6

This Springer imprint is published by the registered company Springer Nature Switzerland AG
The registered company address is: Gewerbestrasse 11, 6330 Cham, Switzerland

Preface

This book presents the proceedings of the 21st International Federation of Information Processing (IFIP) Conference on e-Business, e-Services, and e-Society (I3E), which took place in Newcastle upon Tyne, UK, during September 13–14, 2022. The annual I3E conference is a core part of Working Group 6.11, which aims to organize and promote the exchange of information and cooperation related to all aspects of e-business, e-services, and e-society. Considering the nature of the conference and the interest of the community, the I3E conference series is an interdisciplinary one, welcoming contributions from both academicians and practitioners alike.

Given the restrictions imposed due to the pandemic, the 21st conference was the first in-person one since 2019. The COVID-19 pandemic is arguably one of the most defining crises our societies have experienced in the past 50 years, both in terms of the global reach and its impact on numerous levels. In a very short time SARS-CoV-2 has created havoc across continents, effectively halting social and economic activities. In such unprecedented times individuals and private and public organizations had to respond with unprecedented measures, which had a similarly unprecedented impact. The scars of COVID-19 will be deeply felt for a long time. Not surprisingly, information and communication technologies had a vital role to play. Social distancing meant that online applications became critical in ensuring the continuity of personal and business services. An online meme asking "Who led the digital transformation of your company?" with COVID-19 as the chosen answer perfectly captures the urgency with which existing digital services were extended and new ones were rolled out, often in haste. IT managers had to react quickly to a rapidly escalating crisis and come up with innovative solutions to ensure business continuity.

Although everyone is eager to return to "normal", the post-pandemic business-as-usual is likely to be different to that which individuals and organizations were accustomed to before the pandemic. Understanding the changes that have taken place and their impact in the future is a pressing priority, if we are to thrive in such a turbulent environment. To this end, I3E 2022 invited submissions that aimed to offer topical insights into areas of interest. More specifically, the theme encouraged authors to consider the role that digital technologies can play in shaping a post-pandemic world. However, in line with the inclusive nature of the I3E series, all papers related to e-business, e-services, and e-society were still welcome.

We accepted submissions in two main categories: full research papers and short research-in-progress papers. Each submission was reviewed typically by three knowledgeable academics in the field, in a double-blind process. The conference received about 72 submissions, with half of them making it to the proceedings, subject to the authors' consent. The final set of papers included in the proceedings were clustered into eight groups, as listed below. Each group features conceptual, empirical, and review papers, covering each theme from a number of different vantage points.

- Artificial intelligence: a topical group of papers that consider a wide range of AI applications and contexts.
- Careers and ICT: papers on the role that ICTs can play in supporting careers but also ICT as a career choice
- Data and Analytics: papers considering different aspects of collecting, analyzing, and using data for research and practice purposes.
- Digital Innovation and Transformation: this group of papers includes research that examines how organizations can innovate and transform themselves and their products/services using digital technologies.
- Electronic Services: this group features studies considering different aspects of developing and offering services underpinned by digital technologies.
- Health and Wellbeing: papers examining how digital technologies can support health systems and promote the wellbeing of users.
- Pandemic: this group of papers offers insights into different aspects of user and organizational experiences when facing the challenges that COVID-19 has created.
- Privacy, Trust and Security: these papers consider how regulation could affect users and how privacy might impact adoption.

The 21st IFIP I3E Conference was the outcome of collective work over a period of much uncertainty. Despite restrictions being relaxed, we appreciate that we are not back to "normal" and traveling to a conference is not as easy as we would have hoped. This especially applies to international conferences like I3E, which aspires to welcome colleagues from around the world. We hope that the 21st conference will become a stepping stone on this ongoing journey towards the new normal.

We would like to thank the authors, reviewers, the Program Committee, our keynote speakers, Springer LNCS as the publisher of these proceedings, and everyone who contributed to the success of I3E 2022. We are grateful for all the energy, time, and dedication put into making this conference a success. Last but not least, we would also like to thank Newcastle University Business School for hosting, supporting, and sponsoring the conference.

July 2022

Savvas Papagiannidis
Suraksha Gupta
Eleftherios Alamanos
Yogesh K. Dwivedi
Matti Mäntymäki
Ilias Pappas

Organization

Conference Chairs

Savvas Papagiannidis   Newcastle University Business School, UK
Suraksha Gupta   Newcastle University Business School, UK
Eleftherios Alamanos   Newcastle University Business School, UK

Program Committee Chairs

Savvas Papagiannidis   Newcastle University Business School, UK
Suraksha Gupta   Newcastle University Business School, UK
Eleftherios Alamanos   Newcastle University Business School, UK
Yogesh K. Dwivedi   Swansea University, UK
Matti Mäntymäki   University of Turku, Finland
Ilias Pappas   University of Agder and Norwegian University of
                                    Science and Technology, Norway

Keynote Speakers

Eivor Oborn   Warwick Business School, UK
Paul Watson   Newcastle University and National Innovation
                                    Centre for Data, UK
Paul Wealls   IoTNorth, UK

Program Committee

Pamela Abbott   University of Sheffield, UK
Muhammad Ovais Ahmad   Karlstad University, Sweden
Nisreen Ameen   Royal Holloway, University of London, UK
Spyros Angelopoulos   Durham University, UK
Masoud Barati   Newcastle University, UK
Khalid Benali   Université de Lorraine, France
Edward Bernroider   University of Vienna, Austria
Patrick Buckley   University of Limerick, Ireland
Simos Chari   University of Manchester, UK
Crispin Coombs   Loughborough University, UK
Dinara Davlembayeva   University of Kent, UK
Carina De Villiers   University of Pretoria, South Africa
Hassan Dennaoui   University of Balamand, Lebanon

Sachin Modgil	International Management Institute, Kolkata, India
Bashir Mustapha	American University of Nigeria, Nigeria
Rennie Naidoo	University of Pretoria, South Africa
Olabode Ogunbodede	University of the West of England, UK
John Oredo	University of Nairobi, Nigeria
Panos Panagiotopoulos	Queen Mary University of London, UK
Niki Panteli	Royal Holloway, University of London, UK
Thanos Papadopoulos	Kent Business School, UK
Emmanouil Papagiannidis	Norwegian University of Science and Technology, Norway
Sofia Papavlasopoulou	Norwegian University of Science and Technology, Norway
Elena Parmiggiani	Norwegian University of Science and Technology, Norway
Douglas Parry	Stellenbosch University, South Africa
Sobah Abbas Petersen	Norwegian University of Science and Technology Trondheim, Norway
Ariana Polyviou	University of Nicosia, Cyprus
Tania Prinsloo	University of Pretoria, South Africa
Peter Saba	EMLV Business School Paris, France
Aly Salama	Northumbria University, UK
Brenda Scholtz	Nelson Mandela University, South Africa
Eric Seeto	Lingnan University, Hong Kong
Konstantina Spanaki	Ecole Supérieure de Commerce Audencia Nantes, France
Tahir Abbas Syed	University of Manchester, UK
Chekfoung Tan	University College London, UK
Devinder Thapa	University of Agder, Norway
Cristina Trocin	Norwegian University of Science and Technology, Norway
Yanika Tueanrat	Newcastle University Business School, UK
Corné Van Staden	UNISA, South Africa
Polyxeni Vassilakopoulou	University of Agder, Norway
Arturo Vega	Newcastle University, UK
Yichuan Wang	University of Sheffield, UK
Josepha Witt	University of Hohenheim, Germany
Hiroshi Yoshiura	University of Electro-Communications, Japan
Tuan Yu	University of Kent, UK
Efpraxia Zamani	University of Sheffield, UK
Hans-Dieter Zimmermann	Eastern Switzerland University of Applied Sciences, Switzerland

Contents

Electronic Services

Health and Wellbeing

Pandemic

Privacy, Trust and Security

Artificial Intelligence

Artificial Intelligence Adoption for FinTech Industries - An Exploratory Study About the Disruptions, Antecedents and Consequences

Hitesha Yadav$^{(\boxtimes)}$ ⓘ, Arpan K. Kar ⓘ, and Smita Kashiramka ⓘ

Department of Management Studies, Indian Institute of Technology Delhi, New Delhi, India
hitesha1902@gmail.com

Abstract. Artificial Intelligence (AI) with its highly cognitive features has been increasingly adopted by FinTech firms. With increasing market and economic fluctuations during the unprecedented times of Covid-19, AI offers high computational and easily accessible personalized financial solutions. During the Covid-19 pandemic, customers showed keen interest in AI-assisted financial services. AI in the FinTech industry is now gaining a lot of traction in terms of customer engagement and business prosperity. But with the benefits of availability of consumer data and automation for offering customized and personalized services, the black box effect of AI has a potential dark side affecting both consumers and employees. Lack of human intervention has questioned the accountability and transparency of these financial wealth management solutions that are susceptible to security threats and biased decisions. The purpose of this empirical study is to better understand the adoption of AI in the disruption of the FinTech ecosystem. A mixed approach of focus group and interviews for the purpose of data collection, and qualitative content analysis using natural language processing (NLP) for data analysis have been used to conduct this exploratory study. The findings of the study help to develop an understanding of the social, ethical, and economic consequences of strategic AI adoption for both consumers and businesses.

Keywords: Artificial Intelligence (AI) · Technological innovation · FinTech · Finance · Survey · Natural language processing (NLP)

1 Introduction

Computational technologies play a vital role in the transformation of modern financial services. Rapid advancement in the digitization and adoption of innovative technologies has been observed to improve financial solutions for investment, insurance, and the banking industries. Recent advances in AI, cloud computing, and machine learning (ML) have empowered us with capabilities to make sense of huge amounts of digital data from internet and mobile usage [5, 9].

The past decade has witnessed rapid progress in the adoption of technologies such as AI, Internet of Things (IoT), cloud computing, blockchain, and big data analytics [21]

S. Papagiannidis et al. (Eds.): I3E 2022, LNCS 13454, pp. 3–12, 2022.
https://doi.org/10.1007/978-3-031-15342-6_1

in many industries such as healthcare, manufacturing, retail and finance for the purpose of decision making and strategizing the business process [13]. In recent times FinTech has been growing fast, enabling the financial market services with the introduction of speedy online payments, crowdfunding, and services for managing personal finances. An immense transformation in financial businesses is evident where the processes are digitized, direct dealings with the customer are promoted, less human intervention, customized and intelligent services, decentralization of governance, and increased attention toward information security [19]. Unlike physical cash and banking processes, FinTech was just about digital payments and online banking services. With the availability of rich customer-centric data, a lot more digitally enabled personal financial management services such as portfolio optimization, fraud detection, algorithmic trading, and insurance have emerged [15].

Technology and digitization have brought about lots of positive business transformation but then these advantages are teamed up with challenges to the financial institutions such as regulatory reforms, fewer profits, financial crisis and collapsing public trust [3]. Industry and academic researchers believe there are a lot more hidden insights in the FinTech revolution that needs further assessment. FinTech firms are technological organizations dealing with financial services whose fundamental task is to provide infrastructural facilities to other financial institutions by digitizing their processes with improved risk management and customer experience [6, 18].

Vast internet use and bizarre advances in technological trends has led to an abrupt advancement in the financial system. It has completely transformed the way financial sector functions, while providing opportunities to the investors in the FinTech industry. The widespread technological revolution in FinTech has no geographical boundaries forcing the regulatory and policy makers to wisely propose the strategic adoption of FinTech solutions [10, 24]. New media participation leads to a complex information environment making it difficult for FinTech institutions to have an equilibrated strategy and restrain excessive innovation to maintain public reputation in long run [27].

The worldwide economy has suffered greatly due to the COVID-19 epidemic and challenges for traditional systems in the financial sector makes it more important to understand the role of digitization and technological adoption in financial business services. Hence, it has become very crucial to develop an in-depth understanding of innovative collaboration by technological firms and financial institutions in strategizing the financial services based on the historic consumer data and past financial behaviors.

Although there have been studies focusing on how the financial services especially the banking sector are undergoing changes in their business processes through technology adoption. But there is a void in the literature that discusses the creative and innovative digital disruption caused by AI to various financial services and the FinTech industry. Prior research discusses the technological, economic, political, legal, organizational, and ethical challenges of AI integration with financial big data, while a positive influence has been found between the technology adoption in the form of robo-advisors with the perceived usefulness and attitude of the customers [2]. However, there exists a gap in how AI plays a role in disrupting FinTech to provide the best possible financial solutions to their customers. Hence, to identify the various aspects surrounding the adoption of AI, its consequences in the FinTech industry, and customers' attitude toward this technological disruption, our study aims to explore the following research questions:

RQ1. What are the drivers of AI adoption in the FinTech industry?
RQ2. What are the positive outcomes of AI adoption in the FinTech industries?
RQ3. What are the adverse outcomes of AI adoption in the FinTech industries?

The rest of the article is organized into six subsections: introduction, theory development, research methodology, findings, discussions and conclusion.

2 Theory Development

Industrial revolution in the finance industry has opened up opportunities for FinTech institutions to launch automated financial products so as to ease the stress of indecisiveness amongst the financial service consumers (end-users) as well as service providers (banks). Innovative technological solutions by the startup FinTech firms as well as banks have made customer's life easier in terms of speedy, accurate, and efficient service irrespective of their geographical location, especially during the lockdowns of the Covid-19 pandemic. But there are always the two sides of a coin, with so many advantages comes the challenges and adverse effects of AI proliferation into the financial sector. Therefore, the authors try to understand the nuances associated with this paradigm shift of AI adoption in FinTech industry through the following research questions using inductive methodology:

RQ1. What are the drivers of AI adoption in the FinTech industry?
Unlike past, recently a lot more investment from both banking and non-banking organizations is visible in the FinTech industry. The strategy of automatic intelligent behavior of AI-driven solutions is one of the most impressive strategy that has gained attention amongst the practitioners and researchers in the AI field [7, 22]. Hence, research question one tries to identify various drivers of the adoption of AI in the FinTech Industry from the end-user point of view.

RQ2. What are the positive outcomes of AI adoption in the FinTech industries?
Literature highlights significant contribution of AI applications to knowledge creation and management, controlling the buyer perception and crisis management [14]. To gain better customer satisfaction, the automated channels empower firms to reach out to the consumers irrespective of the geographic location or platform of their usage [6]. Rigorous use of technological solutions by financial institutions has been observed, therefore research question two tries to capture the advantages the users of digital products gain over the traditional financial services.

RQ3. What are the adverse outcomes of AI adoption in the FinTech industries?
Robots with AI capabilities are expected to have a significant impact on the service industry for both customers and staff. Potential negative outcomes such as lack of trust, security issues, and deteriorated service experience on the consumer end [16, 23]. However there is a need for more empirical research to identify the consequences of long-term usage of automated machines on actual behavior, well-being and potential

inconveniences for the customers and the employees. So to identify the adverse outcomes associated with the AI adoption by FinTech industry research question three was proposed.

Using above mentioned research questions authors of the study try to explore various themes surrounding each research question with an aim to gain factual insights attributing to AI adoption by FinTech institutes from the consumer perspective. These inputs may provide valuable information that may be useful to the industry and the research society.

3   Research Methodology

A mix method of qualitative research methods has been adopted for conducting this exploratory study. Adoption of mixed methodologies contributes toward reducing methodological biases and offers improved validity and reliability of the outputs of the research [11]. A mix of qualitative and quantitative methods i.e. focus group followed by interviews has been adopted for the purpose of data collection [4]. Methods of big data analytics such as NLP and ML [12] have been used for deriving valuable insights from the responses collected through the interview.

3.1   Data Collection

The study attempts to develop deeper insights on adoption of AI in the FinTech industry through a mixed methodology approach of focus group followed by structured interviews for data collection. A group of five members including PhDs and working professionals in the BFSI sector PAN India was invited to participate in a focus group discussion for developing a rough definition of the research questions addressing the research gaps. The primary topic of discussion was surrounding the technological advancements in finance for providing automated financial services to banking and non-banking organizations. AI was found to be the top most widely used technology used to enhance the business processes in the finance sector. Based on the discussions, an open-ended questionnaire was prepared to conduct further interviews having an agenda to gain in-depth insights into various factors associated with AI adoption in the FinTech industry.

An open-ended structured questionnaire constituting 4 questions was prepared for capturing their real-life experiences and knowledge during the interviews. The first question captured the demographic profile of the participants and rest of the questions tried to capture the opinion of respondents towards AI in terms of financial services and customer engagement.

In this study, participants for the interviews were targeted using purposive sampling technique depending on the accessibility and time availability of the respondents [25]. The interviews were conducted amongst the members attending a short two months program on AI for finance at a business school in Delhi. The attendants were qualified professionals, majority of them worked in the domain of IT consulting and business analytics in the BFSI sector. Responses corresponding to each of the five questions through a structured questionnaire were collected in a natural environment. The responses indicated a thematic saturation post 46 responses, hence the sample size was restricted to 51 responses [17]. Out of these 51 respondents, 12 were female and the rest 39 were male respondents. The respondents were of different age groups with different educational qualifications. The average work experience of the respondents is 4.8 years and the maximum work experience is 13.5 years.

3.2 Data Analysis

Methods of unsupervised learning from NLP have been used to derive insights from the interview responses. The first step involved pre-processing and cleaning the text data. The text was converted into lowercase and removal of numeric values, special characters, punctuation marks, and extra spacing in between the text was done. A list of stop-words was created, revision of which was done repeatedly for analysis of separate research questions. Finally, word2Vec with n-grams and Latent Dirichlet Allocation (LDA) methods of unsupervised learning were used to extract key features and hidden topics in the responses [8]. Wordcloud has been used to showcase the popular topics against each research question. Sentiment mining was conducted to derive the polarity of sentiments of participants towards the AI adoption in the financial industries.

To enhance the trustworthiness and reliability of the study findings, methods of inter-coder reliability and face validity were adopted. A consensus of more than 86% was achieved to formulate the final themes for each research question whereas topics where consensus was not achieved, were dropped off the list [20]. The team consisted of three members with a minimum of ten years of work experience in research and industry, two were PhD holders working in the FinTech area, and one from industry in the field of AI and finance.

4 Findings

4.1 Drivers of AI Adoption in the FinTech Industry

Many industries including healthcare, travel, retail, and finance are exploring the best ways to exploit AI and ML for their businesses. The BFSI industry has also observed a paradigm shift due to this technological evolution. Themes corresponding to the drivers of AI adoption are financial data availability, accelerating technology with rapid digitization and automation, increased financial literacy, personalized and customized services, reduced operational costs, big tech companies entering into the FinTech landscape, and Job creation.

The sentiment analysis for RQ1 indicates that most of the respondents possess positive sentiments, some with negative sentiments, and very few neutral sentiments. This is an indication that the majority of the respondents are strongly convinced by the importance and benefits of AI for financial dealings in the FinTech industry as it caters to the demand of the changing economy as well as changing consumer behavior towards technology adoption by providing personalized and consumer-friendly financial services. The negative notion in a few of the respondents may be because AI is in an experimentation phase that lacks human intervention in contrast to brick-and-mortar financial service providers. Sentiment analysis and Wordcloud based on *RQ1* are shown in Fig. 1.

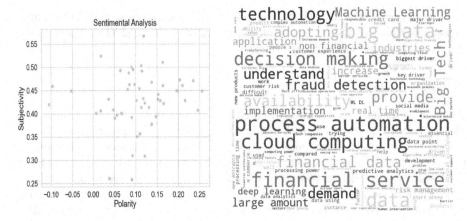

Fig. 1. Sentiment analysis (left), Wordcloud of n-grams (right) for RQ1

4.2 Positive Outcomes of AI Adoption in the FinTech Industry

AI provides notable contribution to FinTech institutions by facilitating cutting-edge solutions for financial service organizations. It is transforming the consumer engagement and business processes of the financial institutions by extracting useful insights from massive amounts of customer data. Sentiment analysis and Wordcloud for positive outcomes of AI in the FinTech industry are represented in Fig. 2. Major themes of the advantages of AI adoption in the FinTech industry are customer satisfaction, increased productivity and better efficiency, multiple technology collaboration, precise decision making, enhanced fraud detection, enhanced security, employment generation, and competitive edge.

Sentiment analysis graph as shown in Fig. 3 demonstrate positive notion in all the responses and no negative sentiments while discussing the benefits of AI in financial decision-making. This clearly indicates that respondents were optimistic about the changes in the FinTech industry processes due to technological advancements such as big data, cloud computing, ML algorithms, etc. to make predictions and offer the best financial services to their customers.

4.3 Adverse Outcomes of AI Adoption in the FinTech Industry

AI offers various advantages by revolutionizing the financial industry, but these solutions can spawn various unintended problems and daunting trends. The themes associated with the adverse outcomes of AI adoption in FinTech industry are lack of accountability, biased solution, and breach of privacy, cyber-security issues, monopolies, unemployment/ threat to jobs, disrupting business model, high cost, algorithm selection, and narrow focus.

A lot more negative sentiments have been found when participants discuss the adverse effects of AI adoption in the FinTech industry. The negative polarity in the sentiments may be due to a threat to one's privacy with zero accountability of the AI services and the threat to loss of jobs in the finance sector. Few responses possess neutral and positive sentiments that may be indicative of the hope and trust in advanced and more responsible AI solutions

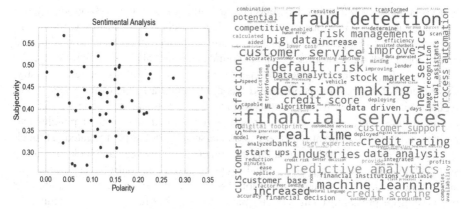

Fig. 2. Sentiment analysis (left), Wordcloud of n-grams (right) for RQ2

for proposing efficient and safe-to-use financial products protecting sensitive customer data, mitigating the fraud and offer more transparency. Sentiment analysis and word cloud of keywords associated with *RQ3* are shown in Fig. 3.

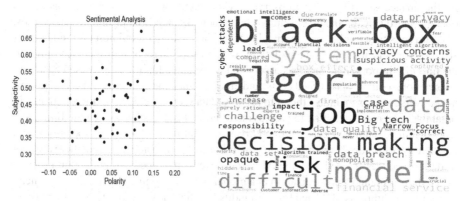

Fig. 3. Sentiment analysis (left), Wordcloud of n-grams (right) for RQ3

5 Discussion

Currently, due to COVID-19 pandemic, the world economy and society are undergoing a lot of challenges in terms of business strategy, policies, regulations, and many more. A drastic change in people's psychology and approaches has been observed when working from home [1, 26]. From the findings of this study it was observed that with the increasing availability of real-time big data, automation with less human intervention, and advanced data analysis algorithms having high computational power has enabled FinTech institutions to deliver multiple solutions and offer personalized financial services. With a lack of accountability and transparency, biasness and minimal human intervention AI has a dark side that leads to serious issues such as data breaches, risk to privacy, fraudulent services, threat to employees, inequality, an unhealthy competitive environment, and many more resulting in various social, economic and political harms to the society.

This study provides valuable information for finance as well as the tech industry. Combined with its ubiquitous effects AI has a potential dark side over society. If not regulated in a time then it may lead to serious social, political, and economic issues/ harms to the society. Hence there is an utmost need to strengthen their policies and regulations so that the threat to privacy and data security could be mitigated. Through sentiment analysis, it is well evident that consumers are quite keen and look forward to such technological innovations that give them more power and control over their actions and autonomous financial decisions. A lot of effort and understanding are required for overcoming the prevailing challenges, the participants in the FinTech ecosystem must not rush to achieve their target profits but make a slow and efficacious wealth management system accessible to everyone without bias.

6   Conclusion

Over the past decade, tremendous technological advancements surrounding AI solutions for the finance sector have been observed. AI is changing the way financial businesses operate and the way consumers think about their financial management capabilities. The current study tried to derive insights from the customer's opinion on the need for AI adoption and its impact on society as well as the FinTech industry. According to the findings, important advantages associated with such adoption is increased customer satisfaction, reduced operational costs, and efficient financial solutions. Whereas, prominent adverse effects include a threat to privacy, data security breaches, drastic change in organizational processes, risk to employment, lack of transparency, accountability, and responsibility, and bias in AI-generated financial solutions. A lot more associations with negative impacts have been found than positive ones. This is indicative that there are a lot of dark aspects associated with the AI-based systems that needs urgent action in terms of regularization and standardization at a global scale for controlling the social, ethical, and economic impacts of AI-led FinTech industry. The study contributes significantly to the AI and finance literature and opens up directions for future research. Since this topic is naïve in the field of finance, a lot more research needs to be conducted to explore this arena completely.

References

1. Alipour, J.V., Fadinger, H., Schymik, J.: My home is my castle–the benefits of working from home during a pandemic crisis. J. Public Econ. **196**, 104373 (2021)
2. Belanche, D., Casaló, L.V., Flavián, C.: Artificial Intelligence in FinTech: understanding robo-advisors adoption among customers. Ind. Manag. Data Syst. **119**(7), 1411–1430 (2019)
3. Boot, A., Hoffmann, P., Laeven, L., Ratnovski, L.: FinTech: what's old, what's new?". J. Financ. Stab. **53**, 100836 (2021)
4. Bryman, A.: Quantity and Quality in Social Research. Routledge (2003)

5. Chang, R.M., Kauffman, R.J., Kwon, Y.: Understanding the paradigm shift to computational social science in the presence of big data. Decis. Support Syst. **63**, 67–80 (2014)
6. Cheetham, W., Goebel, K.: Appliance call center: a successful mixed-initiative case study. AI Mag. **28**(2), 89 (2007)
7. Flavián, C., Pérez-Rueda, A., Belanche, D., Casaló, L.V.: Intention to use analytical artificial intelligence (AI) in services–the effect of technology readiness and awareness. J. Serv. Manage. **33**(2), 293–320 (2021)
8. Hannigan, T.R., et al.: Topic modeling in management research: rendering new theory from textual data. Acad. Manag. Ann. **13**(2), 586–632 (2019)
9. Herath, H.M.K.K.M.B., Mamta, M.: Adoption of artificial intelligence in smart cities: a comprehensive review. Int. J. Inf. Manag. Data Insights **2**(1), 100076 (2022)
10. Jiao, Z., Shahid, M.S., Mirza, N., Tan, Z.: Should the fourth industrial revolution be widespread or confined geographically? A country-level analysis of FinTech economies. Technol. Forecast. Soc. Change **163**, 120442 (2021)
11. Kar, A.K., Dwivedi, Y.K.: Theory building with big data-driven research–moving away from the "what" towards the "why." Int. J. Inf. Manage. **54**, 102205 (2020)
12. Krippendorff, K.: Content Analysis: An Introduction to its Methodology. Sage Publications, Thousand Oaks (2019)
13. Kumar, S., Mookerjee, V., Shubham, A.: Research in operations management and information systems interface. Prod. Oper. Manag. **27**(11), 1893–1905 (2018)
14. Kushwaha, A.K., Kumar, P., Kar, A.K.: What impacts customer experience for B2B enterprises on using AI-enabled chatbots? Insights from Big data analytics. Ind. Mark. Manage. **98**, 207–221 (2021)
15. Lomotey, R.K., Kumi, S., Deters, R.: Data trusts as a service: providing a platform for multi-party data sharing. Int. J. Inform. Manage. Data Insights **2**(1), 100075 (2022)
16. Lu, V.N., et al.: Service robots, customers and service employees: what can we learn from the academic literature and where are the gaps? J. Serv. C Pract. **30**(3), 361–391 (2020)
17. Marshall, B., Cardon, P., Poddar, A., Fontenot, R.: Does sample size matter in qualitative research? : a review of qualitative interviews in IS research. J. Comput. Inf. Syst. **54**(1), 11–22 (2013)
18. Mogaji, E., Nguyen, N.P.: Managers' understanding of artificial intelligence in relation to marketing financial services: insights from a cross-country study. Int. J. Bank Mark. (2021)
19. Muthukannan, P., Tan, B., Gozman, D., Johnson, L.: The emergence of a FinTech ecosystem: a case study of the Vizag FinTech Valley in India. Inf. Manag. **57**(8), 103385 (2020)
20. Nili, A., Tate, M., Barros, A., Johnstone, D.: An approach for selecting and using a method of inter-coder reliability in information management research. Int. J. Inf. Manage. **54**, 102154 (2020)
21. Palmié, M., Wincent, J., Parida, V., Caglar, U.: The evolution of the financial technology ecosystem: an introduction and agenda for future research on disruptive innovations in ecosystems. Technol. Forecast. Soc. Chang. **151**, 119779 (2020)
22. Pillai, R., Sivathanu, B., Mariani, M., Rana, N.P., Yang, B., Dwivedi, Y.K.: Adoption of AI-empowered industrial robots in auto component manufacturing companies. Prod. Plann. Control, 1–17 (2021)
23. Rana, N.P., Chatterjee, S., Dwivedi, Y.K., Akter, S.: Understanding dark side of artificial intelligence (AI) integrated business analytics: assessing firm's operational inefficiency and competitiveness. Eur. J. Inf. Syst. **31**(3), 1–24 (2021)
24. Riikkinen, M., Saarijärvi, H., Sarlin, P., Lähteenmäki, I.: Using artificial intelligence to create value in insurance. Int. J. Bank Mark. **36**(6), 1145–1168 (2018)
25. Rowley, J.: Using case studies in research. Manag. Res. News **25**(1), 16–27 (2002)

26. Zhang, T., Gerlowski, D., Acs, Z.: Working from home: small business performance and the COVID-19 pandemic. Small Bus. Econ. **58**(2), 611–636 (2021). https://doi.org/10.1007/s11 187-021-00493-6
27. Zhou, X., Chen, S.: FinTech innovation regulation based on reputation theory with the participation of new media. Pac. Basin Financ. J. **67**, 101565 (2021)

The Role of Organizational Culture on Artificial Intelligence Capabilities and Organizational Performance

Katja Bley[1,3]([⊠]) [iD], Simen Fredrik Brunvand Fredriksen[2], Mats Eide Skjærvik[2], and Ilias O. Pappas[1,2]

[1] Department of Computer Science, Norwegian University of Science and Technology, Trondheim, Norway
{katja.bley,ilias.pappas}@ntnu.no
[2] Department of Information Systems, University of Agder, Kristiansand, Norway
simen-f@sf-nett.no
[3] Business Information Systems, esp. IS in Trade and Industry, TU Dresden, Dresden, Germany

Abstract. In recent years, artificial intelligence (AI) has become increasingly relevant for organizations to exploit business-related databases and remain competitive. However, even though those technologies offer a huge potential to improve organizational performance, many companies face challenges when adopting AI technologies due to missing organizational and AI capability requirements. Whereas existing research often focuses on technological requirements for the application of AI, this study focuses on those challenges by investigating the influence of organizational culture on a company's AI capability and its organizational performance. We conducted a quantitative study in Scandinavia and employed a questionnaire receiving 299 responses. The results reveal a strong positive relationship between organizational culture, AI capabilities, and organizational performance.

Keywords: Artificial intelligence capabilities · AI · Organizational culture · Organizational performance

1 Introduction

Society has been experiencing technological leaps for decades throughout the industrial revolution, computer age, internet, and social networks. Advances in technology and the abundance of data has prompted many industries to reposition themself to take advantage of the potential Artificial Intelligence (AI) technologies can provide them. This progress and change in technology lead to a change in how societies are organized, and how they are interacting with each other [1]. According to a recent survey the number of enterprises implementing AI grew 270% in the past four years [2]. And despite the impact of COVID-19, 47% of AI investments remained stable since the start of the pandemic, and 30% planned to increase their investments in AI [3].

© IFIP International Federation for Information Processing 2022
Published by Springer Nature Switzerland AG 2022
S. Papagiannidis et al. (Eds.): I3E 2022, LNCS 13454, pp. 13–24, 2022.
https://doi.org/10.1007/978-3-031-15342-6_2

While there is much interest about what potential AI technologies can provide to organizations, it is reported that the organizations adopting these technologies are facing challenges that prevent them from achieving the desired performance gains. According to MIT Sloan Management Review from 2019, seven out of ten companies report minimal to no impact by AI technologies [4]. Accordingly, the organizations that struggle to generate value from AI show up as having organizational challenges rather than technological. Whereas organizations that can capture value from their AI activities exhibit a distinct set of organizational behavior. Thus, while many organizations consider AI as a technological aspect, the organizations that consider AI from an organizational perspective are more likely to derive value from their AI investments [4].

Prior studies have been primary focusing on capabilities for adopting AI and Big Data Analytics, and less on the cultural perspective. A large proportion of empirical studies assume that there is a direct relationship between AI capability and performance, however there is a lack of research that investigates organizational culture as a primary influencing factor [5, 6]. Organizational culture impacts many different aspects of an organization and is viewed as a critical factor for why new technological initiatives fail [7]. Thus, we consider organizational culture as having a large (indirect) impact on the capability of an organization to apply AI; and thereby also indirectly on the performance of organizations. Therefore, the goal of this study is to understand the importance of organizational culture in the context of AI capabilities, and its implications on firm performance, which is generated by a successful implementation of AI technologies. By conducting a questionnaire-based quantitative empirical study in Scandinavia, we address the following research questions (RQ):

RQ1: What influence does organizational culture have on an organization's ability to adopt and use AI?
RQ2: How does an organization's AI capability influence its performance?

The remainder of the paper is structured as follows. The theoretical background provides an overview of the relevant concepts and explains the constructs for our survey. The Sect. 3 introduces the conceptual research approach and presents the hypotheses to be tested. Followed by the data analysis in Sect. 4 as well as the discussion of the results in Sect. 5. The paper is finalized by the research's implications and a conclusion in Sect. 6.

2 Theoretical Background and Constructs

To answer the proposed research questions, we initially conducted an extensive literature review regarding the concepts of interest. Based on our results we were able to narrow the field of investigation and retrieved the respective dimensions and indicators for the derivation of our measurement constructs.

2.1 Organizational Culture

Organizational culture describes the working environment and how it influences an employee's way of thinking, acting and experiencing work [8]. It can have a significant influence on performance, the way people engage, and their efforts and the organization's attraction towards new talent [9]. Organizational culture can be understood as a system of shared beliefs held by the members of an organization; those shared beliefs distinguish the organization from other organizations. Organizations do have common behavior patterns that are used by employees to achieve an objective and which are taught to new members and represent the tacit and intangible level of an organization [10]. Prior research suggests that organizational culture significantly influences financial performance and is more effective than organizational strategy and structure [11].

Although organizational culture is a well-researched area, it is complex and there is no consensus on a single definition. It is often defined as *"a collection of shared assumptions, values, and beliefs that is reflected in its practices and goals and further helps its members understand the organizational functions"* [12]. Organizational culture impacts the challenges that organizations are facing while adopting new technologies. Thus, the use of AI implies radical changes to the business- and organizational culture for the firms to achieve accurate decision-making and to improve innovation and performance [13]. To gain value from AI technologies organizations must create a work culture that values collaboration, working towards collective goals, and shared resources [5]. Thus, organizational culture might have a significant impact on the adoption of AI usage in an organization and can be critical for organizations that want to adopt AI into their organization. For the investigation of the RQs, we divided the construct of organizational culture into three dimensions with two to three indicators [14] (Table 1).

Table 1. Dimensions and indicators of organizational culture [14].

Artifacts	Values	Assumptions
Appreciation of employees	Risk-taking	Openness and flexibility
Inter-functional cooperation	Competence and professionalism	Internal communication
Success		Responsibility

The dimension of *artifacts* consists of three indicators. First, appreciation of employees addresses how an organization values their employees and rewards them for their accomplishments towards the organization's goals. It is measured by how an organization recognizes and rewards their individual employees and takes time to commemorate their work achievements. Inter-functional cooperation is about coordination and teamwork within the organization. It is measured by how organizations value cooperation, coordination and sharing information among different work teams. Success is to what extent an organization strives for the highest standards of performance by encouraging employees to excel and reach for challenging goals. Success is measured by how an organization values success and performance, and that they aspire to be the best firm in their market.

The dimension of *value* is divided into two indicators. Risk-taking is about how an organization values experimenting with new ideas and challenging the status in the organization. It is measured by how an organization values willingness to experiment with new ideas and challenge the status quo. Competence and professionalism refers to how organizations value knowledge and skills among their employees. They are measured by how much the organization values the professional knowledge and skills of its employees and whether advocacy for the highest level of professionalism is valued in the organization.

Lastly, the dimension of *assumptions* is represented by three indicators. Openness and flexibility refer to how much an organization values flexible approaches to problem solving and how open and receptive it is to new concepts. It is measured by how open an organization is to new ideas, how it responds to those ideas, and whether it places a high value on being flexible in solving problems. Internal communication is about having open communication that facilitates information flows within an organization. It is measured by whether an organization values open and high-quality internal communication. Responsibility refers to how organizations value their employees being proactive, taking initiative, and being responsible for their own work.

2.2 Artificial Intelligence

Due to the long history and the ongoing increase in research, it is challenging to identify a single and holistic definition for AI [15]. On a meta-level, McCarthy [16] define AI as being "*concerned with methods of achieving goals in situations in which the information available has a certain complex character. The methods that have to be used are related to the problem presented by the situation and are similar whether the problem solver is human, a Martian, or a computer program*". Whereas this definition describes the general potential for AI application, its instantiation in an organizational context can be defined by conducting functions like machine learning, robotics, natural language processing, expert systems, or speech recognition [15, 17]. However, for a company to implement and exploit the described functions, it needs to provide the respective capabilities to conduct AI (and its functions), rather than focusing on its technological features [18]. Thus, AI capabilities is the ability of a firm to select, orchestrate, and leverage its AI-specific resources. Based on the literature review, we were able to develop the construct of AI. According to Mikalef and Gupta [5], who define AI capabilities as "*the ability of a firm to select, orchestrate and leverage its AI-specific resources*", AI capabilities constructs can be conceptualized through three dimensions: *tangible resources, human resources*, and *intangible resources*. These dimensions are interdependent and can be summarized as consisting of several indicators (Table 2).

Table 2. Dimensions and indicators of artificial intelligence [5].

Tangible resources	Human resources	Intangible resources
Data	Technical skills	Data-driven culture
Technology	Business skills	Organizational learning
Basic resources		

Tangible resources are resources that can be sold or bought in a market, like physical or financial assets. Those resources are divided into data, technology, and basic resources.

Data is a key indicator for leveraging the potential of AI [19] and is measured by the organization's access to data and how it is managing the integration of data from multiple internal and external resources. Technology is required to be able to handle all forms of data. It is about how organizations need to have some type of database management systems to adopt AI in their business. This is measured by investigating how willing they are to explore or adapt to different computing approaches, visualization tools, services, software, and databases. Basic resources are referring to time and financial resources. They are measured by the strength of the organization's concepts and basic resources when investing in AI initiatives and giving the investments sufficient time to grow.

The dimension of *human resources* addresses the human capital of an organization. It addresses the employees and managers skills, knowledge, experience, leadership qualities, vision, communication and collaboration competencies, and problem-solving capabilities [5]. This dimension is divided into technical skills and business skills. These are the skills required to deal with implementation and realization of AI algorithms [5]. Measuring technical skills will provide an overview of an organization's ability to provide and own the skills to emphasize AI. Business skills are a necessary skill for managers in order to realize business value of AI investments. To manage such large-scale changes, leaders need to have a required understanding and commitment. It is important that leaders get familiar with AI technologies and its potential [5]. This is measured by how the AI managers understand and appreciate, ability to work, coordinate, and anticipate the needs of other functional managers, suppliers, and customers.

Intangible resources are those resources that are difficult for other companies to replicate and are regarded as of high importance in an uncertain market and which are difficult to identify [5]. Intangible resources are divided into the indicators of data-driven culture and intensity of organizational learning. Data-driven culture refers to the extent to which all managers and employees within an organization base their decisions on data. This is measured by the extent of data-based versus intuition-based decisions in an organization. In order to cope with an uncertain and changing market, organizations need to make efforts to exploit their existing knowledge and explore new knowledge. Firms with a high intensity of organizational learning are likely to have higher organizational knowledge [20]. This can be assumed to create a higher level of AI capabilities. Thus, the indicator of organizational learning is measures by an organization's ability to acquire new knowledge and how they exploit their existing one.

2.3 Organizational Performance

Based on our research approach, firm performance is divided into three dimensions: social performance, market performance and competitive performance. New technology gives many opportunities for increasing social performance, and previous research concludes that technology such as AI has a positive impact on **social performance** [21, 22]. The corporate social responsibility is represented by the contributions undertaken by organizations to society through its business activities and its social investment [23]. To create awareness of this issue, organizations have started to develop and share their responsibility report [24]. This construct is included to measure the social performance awareness in European based organizations and their focus on these issues. It refers to gender equality, workers and their family's health, poverty, and level of nutritional focus. **Market performance** is related to an organization's ability to attract and retain customers, and obtain market growth [11, 25]. The questions measure an organization's ability to satisfy their clients, the firm's ability to keep current and attract new clients, and their desire to grow their market share. **Competitive performance** refers to the consequences of an organization's strategic position, and to which extent the organization performs [26]. These activities generate a strategic advantage over its competitors that ensures them a large market share [26]. Early adopters of AI-driven technologies have shown an increase in profit margins in different sectors of the economy, which shows that they are more successful than their competitors [27]. The construct's questions measure strategic advantage, market share, success, earnings before interest and taxes (EBIT), return of investment (ROI), and return on sales (ROS). In the following the relations of the retrieved concepts are defined and the respective hypotheses explained.

3   Research Design and Hypotheses

The conceptual research model is based and developed on the previously derived constructs from the literature review. By developing measurement constructs from established research, we ensure quality and recognition to the field of IS. Further, we implemented our own empirical work to increase reliability and validity of the conceptual research model (Fig. 1).

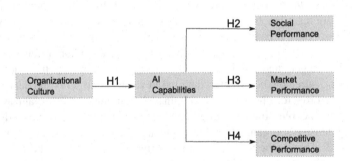

Fig. 1. Conceptual research model

Organizational culture refers to shared meanings and assumptions among the members of an organization. When incorporating AI, an organization will not be able to realize performance gains unless they change their existing way of doing business, even though all the other factors are in place [5]. To gain the best results from implementing AI, organizational culture should be carefully considered as many earlier technology acceptance studies recognize culture as an important influential factor [28]. AI implies radical changes for the organizational culture in businesses in order to achieve accurate decision-making and improved performance [13]. It uses large data sets in order to assist professionals with their tasks, is argued to facilitate better decision-making by providing a wider range of insight [29], and is seen as a crucial strategy for gaining a competitive advantage [30]. Thus, we formulated the first hypothesis:

H1: "Organizational culture has a positive effect on artificial intelligence capabilities".

Previous studies argue that AI technologies cannot provide a competitive advantage by themselves, as they are available for all firms in the market. However, an organization can achieve a competitive advantage by developing AI capabilities [5]. Furthermore, leveraging IT in order to build dynamic capabilities is a key component for gaining competitive advantage [5]. Building and seizing dynamic capabilities enables organizations to form a strategy, a business model, and organizational transformation that leads to increased performance [32]. Thus, developing AI capabilities – a combination of tangible, human and intangible resources – can result in performance gains for organizations [33]. We formulated the following hypotheses about the relation between AI capabilities and organizational performance:

H2: "AI capabilities have a positive effect on social performance"
H3: "AI capabilities have a positive effect on market performance"
H4: "AI capabilities have a positive effect on competitive performance".

4   Results

4.1   Measurements and Reliability

An online questionnaire was developed in order to answer the prosed research questions and to investigate the hypotheses. It consisted of 23 questions which used a seven-point Likert scale. Besides nine control questions, the construct of organizational culture was measured by eight indicators with 25 items, the construct of AI capabilities was measured by seven indicators with 32 items, and construct of firm performance was measured by three indicators using 14 items[1].

We primarily aimed at medium and large Scandinavian business and allowed some additions of small businesses, if they suited for the population criteria. The reason for mainly targeting medium and large businesses was the uncertainty of the population size and the challenge of identifying which organizations were actively using AI. Further, we used the social platform LinkedIn to reach out to the targeted population.

The selected population consisted of a wide range of organizations in different industries. Due to the use of the snowball method technique, the survey was initially distributed to an unknown number of organizations. We received a reply by 326 respondents, of which 299 of the questionnaires were complete.

Reliability and validity of the structural model is ensured by determining different statistical measures for the items and constructs. First, we determined Cronbach's alpha (CA) for the different constructs. All constructs exceed the recommended CA threshold of 0.7 and remain below 0.90, which is the maximum recommended value [34]. For the construct validity, the values of average variance extracted (AVE) should exceed the recommended AVE's threshold of 0.50, which is supported in our study. By using the Fornell-Larcker criterion we assured that the square root of the AVE of each construct is

---

[1] Due to space restrictions, we are not able to present the questionnaire in this paper. The reader is advised to contact the authors of the paper for access to the survey.

higher than any of the inter-factor correlations. Further, we identified the t-values of all formative items as a two tailed test and determined the p-values, that should be below 0.05. We also used SmartPLS to calculate the path coefficients (weights) of the latent variables. Lastly, we checked the VIF measurements to verify if they are below 10, which holds true. Thus, validity can be assumed for this model and the discriminant validity between the constructs is supported.

4.2 Hypotheses Testing

For testing the hypotheses, we calculated the weight of each single hypothesis as displayed in Table 3. The weight reveals, whether an investigated effect is negative or positive. All hypotheses show a positive effect which can be explained as an increase in the independent variable will affect the dependent variable with an increase as well. The significance of the relation is displayed as p-value. To be considered as having a significant influence, the p-value needs to be lower than 0.05.

Table 3. SEM analysis of the research model.

Hypotheses	Indep. variable	Dep. variable	Weight	T-value	P-value	Decision
H1	Org. Cul.	AI Cap.	0.619	15.601	p < 0.001	Supported
H2	AI Cap.	Soc. Per.	0.515	10.767	p < 0.001	Supported
H3	AI Cap.	Mar. Per.	0.472	9.423	p < 0.001	Supported
H4	AI Cap.	Comp. Per.	0.459	9.570	p < 0.001	Supported

Hypothesis 1 has a strong effect of 0.619. The hypothesis is supported with a T-value of 15.601, which is significantly above 99.9%, and a P-value below 0.001. The reliability and validity is acceptable, which confirms that hypothesis 1 is supported.

Hypothesis 2 has a strong effect of 0.515. The hypothesis is supported with a T-value of 10.767, which is significantly above 99.9%, and a P-value below 0.001. The reliability and validity is acceptable, which confirms that hypothesis 2 is supported.

Hypothesis 3 has a strong effect of 0.472. The hypothesis is supported with a T-value of 9.423, which is significantly above 99.9%, and a P-value below 0.001. The reliability and validity is acceptable, which confirms that hypothesis 3 is supported.

Hypothesis 4 has a strong effect of 0.459. The hypothesis is supported with a T-value of 9.570, which is significantly above 99.9%, and a P-value below 0.001. The reliability and validity is acceptable, which confirms that hypothesis 4 is supported.

5 Discussion

Our study is based on previous research and can therefore be viewed as confirmation on the measurements of AI capabilities, as well as the connection between AI capabilities and firm performance [5, 14]. Based on our literature review and our knowledge, the relationship between organizational culture and AI capabilities has not been empirically tested in the past. In addition, to our knowledge, there are no similar studies mainly focusing on Scandinavian organizations. We investigated four hypotheses to determine and evaluate the influence of organizational culture on AI capabilities and their influence on a firm's performance. Based on the questionnaires results we were able to confirm our anticipated relation between the three concepts.

First, we examined how the construct of organizational culture has an effect on the AI capability of a company; more specifically how it influences the ability of a company to introduce and use the potential of AI. Our results revealed a strong positive effect supporting the interdependence between organizational culture and AI and can be related to the challenges that organizations are facing when adopting AI in their organization. The use of AI implies radical changes to the business- and organizational culture within companies in order for them to achieve accurate decision-making to improve innovation and performance [13]. To gain value from AI technologies, organizations must create a work culture that values collaboration, working towards collective goals, and shared resources [5]. In a fast moving and rapidly changing business market due to the fast development of technology it is crucial for organizations to stay competitive. In order to achieve this goal, organizations are constantly adopting new technological tools such as AI. This finding can help organizations to understand what factors are important to utilize the value of AI, by showing that organizational culture has an important effect on AI capabilities. As it is unlikely that technical factors alone will increase performance, organizations also need to consider the organizational factors to increase their performance. Thus, organizational culture will have a significant impact on the adoption of AI usage in an organization and can therefore be regarded as critical for organizations that want to adopt AI into their organization.

As we were furthermore able to reveal the positive effect of AI capabilities on a company's performance in general, it is crucial for the organizations to deal with this competency and, thus, indirectly with their organizational culture to stay competitive. AI capabilities support organizations in keeping their clients satisfied and also in attracting new clients. Further, our findings reveal the important role of AI capabilities for market performance as well as their relevance for social performance. Additionally, in order to gain strategic advantages over competitors, this finding could help organizations to accept the important relation between AI capabilities and competitive performance.

To gain AI skills a data-driven business must ensure that business-analytics becomes a part of the organizational culture that is shared between all employees and especially between those who are responsible for the decision making. Data-driven decision-making skills cannot simply be gained through recruitment of data scientists [35]. As employees are likely to give up on using analytical systems if they do not understand how the systems work, or if it feels too time consuming [36], it requires a necessary AI orientation within the organization [38]. Thus, our results support the need for a culture of coordination, mutual understanding, and cooperation between the different departments within the organization [5, 32]. Further, our findings supports Ransbotham et al. [4], who state that organizations, that are looking at AI from an organizational perspective, rather than from a technological perspective, are more likely to derive value from AI. Our study also contributes to Pappas et al. [1], who revealed that developing a data-driven culture, fostering technical and managerial skills, and promoting organizational learning are critical factors in realizing value when going through a digital transformation.

6 Conclusions

The main goal of the study was to investigate the influence of organizational culture on AI capabilities and on firm performance. As we were able to confirm a positive influence between organizational culture and AI capabilities as well as between AI capabilities and firm performance, we were able to reveal an indirect positive effect of organizational culture on firm performance.

Previous research has often focused on the technical aspects of AI or the adoption of AI where organizational culture only is mentioned as one of several factors for success-ful AI implementation [15]. Less research has focused on how to achieve value from AI in the context of organizational culture. Thus, our research provides as a theoretical contribution a first attempt on addressing this research gap by providing a deeper under-standing of the relations between organizational culture as an important non-technical factor and performance relevant AI capabilities. Furthermore, as practical contribution, our results can help organizations to identify critical constructs of organizational culture and AI capabilities. An example of this could be an organization that has invested in tangible resources, but still has a lack considering the organizational culture. By using the constructs, a Chief Information Officer (CIO) could identify relevant weak resources and take necessary actions. These constructs could also be used to evaluate the culture and AI capabilities of an organization, and thereby evaluate if it has an organizational culture that is ready for AI technology adoption.

As in every research project there are limitations. Although our constructs are based on previous research, our research model could be extended. To achieve even more significant values, the performance, organizational culture, and AI constructs can be refined and extended. Further, the survey contained several questions with a technical context and terms that could have been difficult for participants with limited technical knowledge. Lastly, having chosen a quantitative approach can be regarded as a limitation of the study, as we were not able to ask the participants additional questions regarding their answers and thereby did not get further insights into their motives. However, this is subject to future research, as we would like to conduct qualitative interviews based on our current findings. Additionally, we intend to apply qualitative comparative analysis (QCA) to the data set in order to reveal necessary and/or sufficient combinations of orga-nizational culture conditions leading to successful AI capabilities [37, 38]. Thereby we will be able to compare and complement our SEM analysis results with QCA and provide further insights into the relation between organizational culture and AI capabilities.

References

1. Pappas, I.O., Mikalef, P., Giannakos, M.N., Krogstie, J., Lekakos, G.: Big data and business analytics ecosystems: paving the way towards digital transformation and sustainable societies. Inf. Syst. E-Bus. Manag. **16**(3), 479–491 (2018). https://doi.org/10.1007/s10257-018-0377-z

2. Howard, C., Rowsell-Jones, A.: 2019 CIO survey: CIOs have awoken to the importance of AI (2019)
3. Goasduff, L.: 2 Trends on the gartner hype cycle for artificial intelligence (2020). https://www.gartner.com/smarterwithgartner/2-megatrends-dominate-the-gartner-hype-cycle-for-artificial-intelligence-2020. Accessed 01 Apr 2022
4. Ransbotham, S., Khodabandeh, S., Fehling, R., LaFountain, B., Kiron, D.: Winning with AI - pioneers combine strategy, organizational behavior, and technology. MIT Sloan Management Review and Boston Consulting Group (2019)
5. Mikalef, P., Gupta, M.: Artificial intelligence capability: conceptualization, measurement calibration, and empirical study on its impact on organizational creativity and firm performance. Inf. Manage. **58**, 103434 (2021). https://doi.org/10.1016/j.im.2021.103434
6. Mikalef, P., Pappas, I.O., Krogstie, J., Giannakos, M.: Big data analytics capabilities: a systematic literature review and research agenda. Inf. Syst. E-Bus. Manag. **16**(3), 547–578 (2017). https://doi.org/10.1007/s10257-017-0362-y
7. Shamim, S., Zeng, J., Shariq, S.M., Khan, Z.: Role of big data management in enhancing big data decision-making capability and quality among Chinese firms: a dynamic capabilities view. Inf. Manage. **56**, 103135 (2019). https://doi.org/10.1016/j.im.2018.12.003
8. Warrick, D.D., Milliman, J.F., Ferguson, J.M.: Building high performance cultures. Organ. Dyn. **45**, 64–70 (2016). https://doi.org/10.1016/j.orgdyn.2015.12.008
9. Warrick, D.D.: What leaders need to know about organizational culture. Bus. Horiz. **60**, 395–404 (2017). https://doi.org/10.1016/j.bushor.2017.01.011
10. Atrian, N., Soltani, I., Rashidpour, A., Etebarian, A.: Presenting a comprehensive model of organizational culture change on the basis of Edgar Schein approach. Int. Bus. Manag. **10**, 1330–1336 (2016)
11. Hogan, S.J., Coote, L.V.: Organizational culture, innovation, and performance: a test of Schein's model. J. Bus. Res. **67**, 1609–1621 (2014)
12. Dubey, R., et al.: Big data analytics and organizational culture as complements to swift trust and collaborative performance in the humanitarian supply chain. Int. J. Prod. Econ. **210**, 120–136 (2019). https://doi.org/10.1016/j.ijpe.2019.01.023
13. Chatterjee, S., Chaudhuri, R., Vrontis, D.: Does data-driven culture impact innovation and performance of a firm? An empirical examination. Ann. Oper. Res. (2021)
14. Schein, E.H.: Organizational Culture and Leadership. Wiley, Hoboken (2017)
15. Collins, C., Dennehy, D., Conboy, K., Mikalef, P.: Artificial intelligence in information systems research: a systematic literature review and research agenda. Int. J. Inf. Manag. **60**, 102383 (2021). https://doi.org/10.1016/j.ijinfomgt.2021.102383
16. McCarthy, J.: Mathematical logic in artificial intelligence. Daedalus **117**, 297–311 (1988)
17. Dejoux, C., Léon, E.: Métamorphose des managers...: à l'ère du numérique et de l'intelligence artificielle. Pearson (2018)
18. Davenport, T., Ronanki, R.: Artificial intelligence for the real world (2018). https://hbr.org/2018/01/artificial-intelligence-for-the-real-world
19. Ransbotham, S., Gerbert, P., Reeves, M., Kiron, D., Spira, M.: Artificial intelligence in business gets real. MIT Sloan Manag. Rev. (2018)
20. Gupta, M., George, J.F.: Toward the development of a big data analytics capability. Inf. Manage. **53**, 1049–1064 (2016). https://doi.org/10.1016/j.im.2016.07.004
21. Bag, S., Gupta, S., Kumar, S., Sivarajah, U.: Role of technological dimensions of green supply chain management practices on firm performance. J. Enterp. Inf. Manag. **34**, 1–27 (2020). https://doi.org/10.1108/JEIM-10-2019-0324
22. Hong, Z., Zhang, H., Gong, Y., Yu, Y.: Towards a multi-party interaction framework: state-of-the-art review in sustainable operations management. Int. J. Prod. Res. 1–37 (2021)
23. Pothuraju, D.V.L., Alekhya, D.P.: Impact of corporate social responsibility on organization performance. Int. J. Adv. Sci. Technol. **29**, 2256–2261 (2020)

24. Jeble, S., Dubey, R., Childe, S.J., Papadopoulos, T., Roubaud, D., Prakash, A.: Impact of big data and predictive analytics capability on supply chain sustainability. Int. J. Logist. Manag. **29**, 513–538 (2018). https://doi.org/10.1108/IJLM-05-2017-0134

25. Ahmed, E.A.: Market sensing, innovation capability and market performance: the moderating role of internal information dissemination. Int. J. Adv. Appl. Sci. **4**, 56–67 (2017). https://doi.org/10.21833/ijaas.2017.08.009

26. Sambamurthy, V., Bharadwaj, A., Grover, V.: Shaping agility through digital options: reconceptualizing the role of information technology in contemporary firms. MIS Q. **27**, 237–263 (2003)

27. Kordon, A.: Applied artificial intelligence-based systems as competitive advantage. In: Proceedings of the 10th International Conference on Intelligent Systems (IS), pp. 6–18 (2020). https://doi.org/10.1109/IS48319.2020.9200097

28. Duan, Y., Edwards, J.S., Dwivedi, Y.K.: Artificial intelligence for decision making in the era of big data – evolution, challenges and research agenda. Int. J. Inf. Manag. **48**, 63–71 (2019). https://doi.org/10.1016/j.ijinfomgt.2019.01.021

29. Mazzone, M., Elgammal, A.: Art, creativity, and the potential of artificial intelligence. Arts. **8**, 26 (2019). https://doi.org/10.3390/arts8010026

30. Shi, G., Ma, Z., Feng, J., Zhu, F., Bai, X., Gui, B.: The impact of knowledge transfer performance on the artificial intelligence industry innovation network: an empirical study of Chinese firms. PLoS One **15**, e0232658 (2020). https://doi.org/10.1371/journal.pone.0232658

31. Mikalef, P., Pateli, A.: Information technology-enabled dynamic capabilities and their indirect effect on competitive performance: findings from PLS-SEM and fsQCA. J. Bus. Res. **70**, 1–16 (2017). https://doi.org/10.1016/j.jbusres.2016.09.004

32. Warner, K.S.R., Wäger, M.: Building dynamic capabilities for digital transformation: an ongoing process of strategic renewal. Long Range Plann. **52**, 326–349 (2019). https://doi.org/10.1016/j.lrp.2018.12.001

33. Mishra, A.N., Pani, A.K.: Business value appropriation roadmap for artificial intelligence. VINE J. Inf. Knowl. Manag. Syst. **51**, 353–368 (2021). https://doi.org/10.1108/VJIKMS-07-2019-0107

34. Tavakol, M., Dennick, R.: Making sense of Cronbach's alpha. Int. J. Med. Educ. **2**, 53–55 (2011). https://doi.org/10.5116/ijme.4dfb.8dfd

35. Carillo, K.D.A., Galy, N., Guthrie, C., Vanhems, A.: How to turn managers into data-driven decision makers: measuring attitudes towards business analytics. Bus. Process Manag. J. **25**, 553–578 (2019). https://doi.org/10.1108/BPMJ-11-2017-0331

36. Spano, A., Bellò, B.: Business intelligence in public sector organizations: a case study. In: Mancini, D., Dameri, R.P., Bonollo, E. (eds.) Strengthening Information and Control Systems. LNISO, vol. 14, pp. 133–143. Springer, Cham (2016). https://doi.org/10.1007/978-3-319-26488-2_10

37. Ragin, C.C.: Redesigning Social Inquiry. University of Chicago Press, Chicago (2008)

38. Vassilakopoulou, P., Haug, A., Salvesen, L. M., O. Pappas, I.: Developing human/AI interactions for chat-based customer services: lessons learned from the Norwegian government. Eur. J. Inf. Syst., 1–13 (2022, in press)

39. Pappas, I.O., Woodside, A.G.: Fuzzy-set qualitative comparative analysis (fsQCA): guidelines for research practice in information systems and marketing. Int. J. Inf. Manage. **58**, 102310 (2021)

Artificial Intelligence Ambidexterity, Adaptive Transformation Capability, and Their Impact on Performance Under Tumultuous Times

Rogier van de Wetering[1]([✉]), Patrick Mikalef[2], and Denis Dennehy[3]

[1] Faculty of Science, Open University, Heerlen, The Netherlands
rogier.vandewetering@ou.nl
[2] Department of Computer Science, Norwegian University of Science and Technology, Trondheim, Norway
[3] School of Management, Swansea University, Swansea, Wales

Abstract. Over the past two years, scholars have increasingly paid attention to firms' capability to adapt to their increasingly turbulent business ecosystem environments. This study embraces the dynamic capabilities theory, uses ideas from the accelerated corporate transformation, and posits that adaptive transformation capability, driven by ambidextrous artificial intelligence (AI) use, i.e., routine and innovative use in practice, serves as a mechanism for firms to gain superior organizational performance under COVID-19. Using a composite-based structural equation model (SEM) approach, we use survey data from 257 C-level practitioners with key decision-making roles and experience in AI and digital transformation initiatives. We used this data to analyze the theorized relationships. Outcomes show that the ambidextrous use of AI positively enhances a firm's adaptive transformation capability. This capability, in turn, fully mediates the impact of AI ambidexterity on competitive performance during COVID-19. These outcomes have important theoretical and practical implications.

Keywords: Artificial intelligence · Ambidexterity · Dynamic capability · Adaptive transformation capability · Competitive performance · COVID-19 · Composited-based SEM · PLS-SEM

1 Introduction

During the COVID-19 crisis, social, technological, demographic, political, and economic changes accelerated rapidly. Under these stressful conditions, contemporary firms should shape their adaptive capabilities to address customer behavior and market dynamics changes. Adaptive capabilities enable firms to evolve rapidly and serve as a foundation for organizational change and transformation [1, 2]. Incumbent firms use new innovative technologies to enhance their business operations and adapt. One of those technologies is artificial intelligence (AI), or "the next era of analytics", as Davenport denotes it [3].

The original version of this chapter was revised: A typing error in the name of the author Patrick Mikalef has been corrected. The correction to this chapter is available at
https://doi.org/10.1007/978-3-031-15342-6_38

AI is a broad term encompassing various advanced analyses, applications, and logic-based techniques that mimic human behavior, decision-making, and activities like learning and problem-solving [4]. AI in business is not new, as the field originated in the 50s of the last century [5]. However, AI solutions offer firms many opportunities to transform their business across various industries, typically part of the digital transformation [6]. For example, consider using AI-driven decision-making regarding loans, credit decisions, or sales forecasting [6]. Furthermore, AI can offer considerable advantages in automating previously manual processes [7] and enabling augmented processes where humans and AI interact mutually supportive [8].

According to a recent report from Gartner [9], senior executives regard analytics and AI as the key game changer to emerge stronger from the current pandemic. However, despite the excitement concerning the potential of AI, there is currently much scholarly debate about the adoption challenges and the competencies and capabilities needed for valuable results from AI [10–12]. Moreover, Forbes estimated that by 2023 34% of the employees expect their respective jobs to be replaced by AI solutions [13].

AI can bring substantial benefits to firms. However, when a major transformation is required, firms must articulate a compelling shared vision to adopt AI and enable a high impact that does not derail all the investments and effort [14–16]. Moreover, firms must leverage innovative and distinctive technologies like AI to develop adaptive transformation capabilities and sense and respond capabilities to drive innovation, improve service levels and customer experiences, and foster competitive performance [3, 17–19].

Thus, there is a clear need to unfold how AI is leveraged into the organizational fabric and how it aligns and drives business strategy. This objective becomes increasingly more complex when organizations face continuous shifts in their business environments and major disruptions due to unforeseen events, such as the COVID-19 pandemic.

The need for adaptive capabilities informs our approach to organizational change and transformation. We follow [20, 21] and define adaptive transformation capability as a firm's proficiency in identifying and capitalizing upon emerging market and technology opportunities and building organizational capabilities in parallel with implementing new strategic directions. In addition, this capability can be considered a dynamic capability, which can use and deploy organizational resources and competencies to achieve the desired result [22] and drive the firms' future entrepreneurial activities and business value opportunities [20]. However, currently, little is known about the equivocal capacity to routinely and innovatively use AI, i.e., AI ambidexterity, in firms and how this supports dynamic capabilities, especially how they collectively drive competitive performance under COVID-19 [16, 23, 24].

Therefore, this study addresses the following research question: *"to what extent does AI ambidexterity accelerate the development of an adaptive transformation capability to ensure the business can meet the needs of an increasingly complex environment under COVID-19?"*.

This research question builds on the growing use of AI to inform and adapt organizational operations. However, while today an increasing number of organizations are delving into such activities, there is little empirically supported evidence to guide them in the process. This study, therefore, attempts to understand how the ambidextrous use of AI can indirectly lead to competitive performance gains in turbulent conditions.

The remainder of this paper is structured as follows. First, the background to the theoretical context and proposition is discussed. Next, the research methodology and the developed model are presented.

2 Theoretical Context and Proposition

2.1 Artificial Intelligence and Its Ambidextrous Use

AI ambidexterity builds upon the foundation of the IT ambidexterity literature that concerns the equivocal capacity to innovate and explore IT resources and practices and, on the other hand, to routinize and exploit them [25, 26]. These practices are typically difficult-to-imitate as they are uniquely adopted, deployed, and used in a particular setting to create value [27, 28] and drive the formation of organizational capabilities [29, 30]. Routine use of AI describes how AI use is integrated as a normal part of the employees' work processes. This exploitation mode focuses on refining and extending current services and products, leading to incremental innovation [24, 31].

On the other hand, innovative use refers to embedding AI deeply and comprehensively in work processes and to "employees" discovering new ways to use AI to support their work [25]. This particular stance is sometimes called 'emergent use' [32] or "trying to innovate with IT" [33], or "creative IT use" [34].

The simultaneous use of these two AI modes, i.e., AI ambidexterity, allows firms to sense the business environment by analyzing real-time and high-volume data, identifying and capturing customer needs and trends, uncovering patterns, and extracting relevant information for decision-making processes [35, 36]. Specifically relevant for this study, the ambidextrous use of AI in firms will shape the firm's dynamic capabilities as AI is used to solve business issues and problems, identify creative solutions and ideas, contribute to the effectiveness of business operations integration and help accelerate change within the firm [14, 15, 37].

However, capturing the value from both opposing modes of operandi, i.e., routine vs. innovative use of AI, is not a straightforward process as different routines and capabilities and organizational routines. Instead, the literature argues that big data and.

AI should be deployed as a critical organizational resource to strengthen the firms' dynamic capabilities to use their full strategic potential [38–41]. Moreover, stakeholders should be involved to get fully engaged, and commitment from all employees for the new improvement initiatives and alignment with the strategic direction across the organization is crucial [42, 43]. Therefore, firms' simultaneous alignment of 'routinization' and 'innovation' will provide superior and sustained business benefits and strong adaptive capabilities [31, 44, 45].

2.2 Adaptive Transformation Capability and Competitive Performance Under COVID-19

Following Wang and Ahmed [1], we define dynamic capabilities as "...the firm's behavioral orientation constantly to integrate, reconfigure, renew and recreate its resources and capabilities and, most importantly, upgrade and reconstruct its core capabilities in response to the changing environment to attain and sustain competitive advantage". We consider adaptive transformation capability a dynamic capability that follows the philosophy of accelerated corporate transformations [46]. Hence, this capability can be regarded as an accelerator of rapid transformations that equips firms with the capacity to address possible transformation inhibitors by corresponding transformation accelerators [47].

Change initiatives provide opportunities to build a firm's ability to adapt and change. Therefore, change initiatives that facilitate and do not inhibit adaptive transformation capabilities are more likely to produce long-term results. However, unfortunately, various inhibitors become embedded in all organizations during transformation processes. Think, for instance, about disengaged employees, recalcitrant decision-makers, and business-as-usual processes [43].

Adaptive transformation capability addresses these inhibitors to overcome the transformation barriers and guides firms to orchestrate balanced transformation initiatives, engages the extended leadership team, and helps reshape the organization, its management, and resilience [48]. In addition, this capability drives healthy interfaces across organizational boundaries and collaborations within the firm that easily reconfigures and offers multiple paths for individual contribution. As such, adaptive transformation capability is crucial in enhancing competitive performance during tumultuous times, such as the COVID-19 pandemic [23].

In summary, as a strategic capability, adaptive transformation capability facilitates firms to anchor the transformation agenda and serves as the foundation to achieve high performance under tumultuous times. Driven by AI ambidexterity, this dynamic capability enables firms to rapidly orchestrate the launch of the next development phase and implement necessary changes [24]. In a high-engagement manner, firms ensure that sustainable changes drive competitive performance and achieve breakthrough results in turbulent times.

Based on the above, we define the following:

Proposition 1: *Firms' adaptive transformation capability mediates the relationship between AI ambidexterity and competitive firm performance under COVID-19.* (Fig. 1)

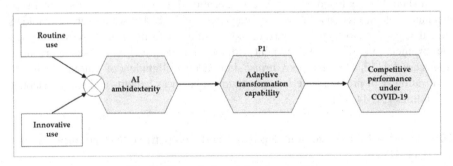

Fig. 1. Theoretical model and proposition.

3 Research Methodology and Dataset

3.1 Survey and Data Collection Procedure

The target population of this study was C-level practitioners (i.e., innovation and business managers, IT managers) with key decision-making roles and experience in AI and digital transformation initiatives within the organization.

An initial survey was developed and was iteratively pretested by three Ph.D. students, one scholar, and two senior business professionals. The final survey data were collected between October 2021 and November 2021 as the practitioners completed an executive education course. The survey was also sent to colleagues within their professional network using the 'snowball' technique. After removing incomplete ($N = 25$) or unreliable ($N = 21$) responses from our sample, a total of 257 responses were used for the final analyses. All firms are operating in the Netherlands. Furthermore, we controlled, using a survey question, if all the respondents could address all items given their knowledge and experience. Finally, survey items were operationalized based on previous empirically validated scales (Table 1). We used a 7-point Likert scale for all items (1. strongly disagree to 7. strongly agree).

Most respondents worked in the private sector (54%) or the public sector (37%). In addition, 4% worked in Private-Public Partnerships and 5% for a Non-Profit Organization.

3.2 Measures and Composite Operationalization

We used previously validated measures for the constructs of AI ambidexterity. Hence, we used three measures for routine and innovative AI use. Items were drawn from [49]. We used the item-interaction of the respective constructs to measure ambidexterity following [44] as routine and innovative use of AI are interdependent and nonsubstitutable. Nine (multiplicative) items were used as a (reflective) latent construct for the operationalization.

For adaptive transformation capability, we build upon theoretical and practical work by Miles [43, 46]. Adaptive transformation capability is operationalized following the accelerated corporate transformation process architecture that identifies five levers that collectively drive transformations successfully and ensure that the business can meet customer demands during tumultuous times. These levers include strategic assessments to create a limited set of balanced transformation initiatives, high engagement and alignment at all levels, and disciplined monitoring, assessment, and readjustment throughout the transformation process. This construct is operationalized as an emergent (formative) construct.

Finally, building upon work by [38, 50], we used five items to reflect organizational performance during COVID-19. Items include increased customer satisfaction, enhanced customer loyalty, and increased profit during the past one and a half years during the COVID-19 crisis relative to competitors operating in the same industry. The organizational performance also follows the operationalization logic of a latent reflective construct. All items can be found in Table 1.

Table 1. Constructs, items, sources, and reliability statistics

Construct	Survey item	Source	Reliability statistics
Nature of constructs: latent construct, reflective			
Routine use of AI	(RUA1) The use of AI has been incorporated into our regular work practices of the organization	[49]	CA:0.83 CR:0.90 AVE:0.75
	(RUA2) The use of AI is pretty much integrated as part of our normal work routines within the organization		
	(RUA3) The use of AI is now a normal part of our work		
Innovative use of AI	(IUA1) Our organization has discovered new uses of AI to enhance our work performance	[49]	CA:0.77 CR:0.87 AVE:0.69
	(IUA2) Our organization has used AI in novel ways to support our work practices		
	(IUA3) Our organization has developed new applications based on AI use to support work processes		
Nature of construct: emergent, formative			
Adaptive transformation capability	(ATC1) We concentrate on upfront strategic and organizational assessments to create a limited set of balanced transformation initiatives	[43, 46]	Weights are sign. ($P < 0.05$) $\text{VIF}_{Atc1\text{-}5} < 3.0$
	(ATC2) We have a high engagement planning process with the extended leadership team and high accountability and alignment across the organization		

(continued)

Table 1. (*continued*)

Construct	Survey item	Source	Reliability statistics
	(ATC3) We achieve agile alignment of individuals and departments with commitments from all employees		
	(ATC4) We established disciplined monitoring, assessment, and readjustment process throughout the transformation process		
	(ATC5) We provide an opportunity to build capabilities in parallel with implementing new strategic directions		

Nature of construct: latent construct, reflective

Construct	Survey item	Source	Reliability statistics
Performance	(P1) Increase market share	[38, 50]	CA:0.84 CR:0.89 AVE:0.61
	(P2) Increase customer satisfaction		
	(P3) Increase profit		
	(P4) Enhance business brand and image		
	(P5) Enhance customer loyalty		

4   Model Specification and Analyses

4.1   A Composite-Based SEM

As can be gleaned from the operationalization of the measures, we use composite-based SEM as the preferred approach to estimate our model and the study's central hypothesis [51]. The composite approach supports exploratory research contexts [52] and is most appropriate when using reflective and formative constructs in the research model [52]. Hence, we use latent and emergent constructs to operationalize our focal concepts.

We use SmartPLS for Windows version 3.3.6 [53] (http://www.smartpls.com) to run the analyses. When using a composite-based SEM approach, it is essential first to evaluate the reliability and validity of the measurement model, including both the latent and emergent constructs [52]. Hence, for the latent constructs, i.e., routine and innovative AI use and organizational performance under COVID-19, we assessed the psychometric properties of the theoretical model. Thus, we evaluated the latent constructs' internal consistency reliability through the use of Cronbach's alpha and the complementary composite reliability measure, convergent validity through the assessment of the AVE (average variance extracted), to identify the degree of variance captured by the latent construct), and discriminant validity [52].

After running the PLS-SEM algorithm, all latent constructs' outcomes showed reliable results (see Table 1). In addition, for the emergent construct, i.e., adaptive transformation capability, the variance inflation factor (VIF) values and the significance of the indicator (regression) weights were assessed. The VIF was used to check for possible collinearity of the formative measures. All obtained values were well below three as a threshold, and all items showed significant results [54].

4.2 Proposition Testing

This section examines whether firms' adaptive transformation capability mediates the relationship between AI ambidexterity and competitive firm performance under COVID-19, i.e., proposition 1.

Outcomes for overall model fit showed that the Standardized Root Mean Square Residual (SRMR) was 0.06 [55], and thus proposition can now be tested as well as the coefficient of determination (R^2) and associated predictive power values (Stone-Geisser values, Q^2). We used a non-parametric bootstrapping procedure for the analyses using 5000 replications in SmartPLS to get stable statistical estimates. Outcomes of the bootstrapping procedure show that AI ambidexterity positively influences adaptive transformation capability ($\beta = .54$; $t = 11.31$; $p < .0001$) that subsequently significantly influences organizational performance under COVID-19 ($\beta = .59$; $t = 11.52$; $p < .0001$).

Also, after following a systematic mediation procedure [56], results show that the impact of AI ambidexterity is fully mediated by adaptive transformation capability as the indirect effect (AI ambidexterity $\longrightarrow$ performance), among other affirmative results, was non-significant ($\beta = .03$; $t = .47$; $p = .64$). These outcomes confirm the main pro-position of this work. Finally, included control variables (size and industry) showed non-significant results, excluding confounding issues. Also, the model explains 29.6% ($R^2 = .30$) of the variance for adaptive transformation capability and 35% ($R^2 = .35$) for organizational performance under COVID-19.

Using SmartPLS's blindfolding procedure, we obtained Q^2 values to assess the model's predictive power. Hence, obtained Q^2 values were also well beyond 0, showing the model's predictive relevance.

5   Discussion and Implications

This study aimed to investigate the contribution of AI ambidexterity in firms and how this supports the organization's adaptive transformation capability and competitive performance under COVID-19. To test the central proposition of this work, we used data collected from 257 senior professionals from firms operating in various industries.

We found support for this proposition. Therefore, AI seems crucial in shaping a firm's adaptive transformation capability and thus its ability to accelerate rapid transformations and drive performance under COVID-19. However, while this claim has been argued in several practice-based studies and many editorial and opinion articles, there has been limited empirical support to document whether AI can produce business value in the organizational context and through what means. In this empirical investigation, we have documented the effect and the mechanisms of action through a large-scale quantitative study. Doing so opens up several important theoretical and practical which are discussed further.

5.1 Theoretical and Practical Implications

This study makes three vital theoretical contributions. *First*, this is the first empirical study that unfolds the crucial role of adaptive transformation capability, facilitated by AI, in achieving competitive results during tumultuous times. Therefore, this study extends numerous conceptual and empirical studies that highlight the crucial role of AI in developing capabilities, driving innovation, and obtaining business benefits [11, 15, 18, 35, 39]. This is important as scholars can now use these results to investigate transformation agendas and evaluate sustainable organizational changes.

Second, our current work also indicates that digital technologies such as AI can allow organizations to navigate demanding and changing business conditions by building digital capabilities that are hard to replicate from the competition. Thus, our work contributes to the extant literature and answers the call for more foundational research regarding AI in shaping dynamic capabilities [10, 14, 16, 23, 24]. In doing so, we highlight the role of AI as an agile enabler of business. This study outcome also goes against claims that AI is often monolithic and challenging to adapt to changing conditions due to its long life-cycle times. However, what is essential is that firms can leverage AI to facilitate rather than impede adaptive transformation [10, 23, 24, 36]. Our study constructs offer insights on how to achieve this.

Third, we also show how AI ambidexterity is a crucial enabler of adaptive transformation capability. The conceptualization of AI ambidexterity builds upon the foundations of IT ambidexterity, and we, therefore, extend this current knowledge base [25, 30, 41]. While there has been significant theoretical discussion about the role of AI in facilitating exploration and exploitation [24, 35, 36], there is limited empirical knowledge about whether being able to leverage AI in this manner impacts the adaptive transformation capability of firms. Findings such as this indicate that digital technologies can facilitate organizational fluidity and adaptability when leveraged under certain conditions.

This work has various practical implications addressing how firms can leverage these results. Based on the outcomes of this work, we argue that decision-makers should focus on an ongoing strategy and capability-building process enabled by AI. This means, for example, that decision-makers within the organization should emphasize seeing the AI phenomenon through a more holistic approach that considers technology a core component of competitive strategies. In doing so, firms should actively invest in routine, and innovative AI uses to develop and further shape dynamic capabilities to look forward, inform and optimize decision-making, and adapt to changing market conditions and demands. These steps will ensure that the firm refocusses on several strategic growth and performance improvement initiatives, keeps up with competitors, and achieves high levels of organizational performance.

Despite the study's contributions, several limitations should be acknowledged. First, we only surveyed respondents from the Netherlands. It would be a valuable research opportunity to execute this research in different countries in Europe or even on other Continents. Second, as we used a cross-sectional approach, we only measured at a single point in time. Thus, we could not follow the development of AI and its contributions to adaptive transformation capability over a more extended period. Nevertheless, this could be a valuable area for future work that several in-depth case studies can strengthen. Third, future work could also embrace a configurational perspective and unfold possible factors and conditions under which firms can realize high levels of organizational performance while capitalizing on their dynamic capabilities [57].

References

1. Wang, C.L., Ahmed, P.K.: Dynamic capabilities: a review and research agenda. Int. J. Manag. Rev. **9**(1), 31–51 (2007)
2. Zhou, K.Z., Li, C.B.: How strategic orientations influence the building of dynamic capability in emerging economies. J. Bus. Res. **63**(3), 224–231 (2010)
3. Davenport, T.H.: From analytics to artificial intelligence. J. Bus. Anal. **1**(2), 73–80 (2018)
4. Brynjolfsson, E., Mcafee, A.: Artificial intelligence, for real. Harvard Bus. Rev. **1**, 1–31 (2017)
5. Epstein, R., Roberts, G., Beber, G. (eds.): Parsing the turing test. Springer, Dordrecht (2009). https://doi.org/10.1007/978-1-4020-6710-5
6. Brock, J.K.-U., Von Wangenheim, F.: Demystifying AI: what digital transformation leaders can teach you about realistic artificial intelligence. Calif. Manage. Rev. **61**(4), 110–134 (2019)
7. Makowski, P.T., Kajikawa, Y.: Automation-driven innovation management? toward innovation-automation-strategy cycle. Technol. Forecast. Soc. Change **168**, 120723 (2021)
8. Jarrahi, M.H.: Artificial intelligence and the future of work: human-AI symbiosis in organizational decision making. Bus. Horiz. **61**(4), 577–586 (2018)
9. Barot, S., Agarwal, S., Antelmi, J.: Planning guide for analytics and artificial intelligence. In: Gartner. Gartner (2021)
10. Mikalef, P., Gupta, M.: Artificial intelligence capability: conceptualization, measurement calibration, and empirical study on its impact on organizational creativity and firm performance. Inform. Manage. **58**(3), 103434 (2021)
11. Davenport, T.H., Ronanki, R.: Artificial intelligence for the real world. Harv. Bus. Rev. **96**(1), 108–116 (2018)
12. Canhoto, A.I., Clear, F.: Artificial intelligence and machine learning as business tools: a framework for diagnosing value destruction potential. Bus. Horiz. **63**(2), 183–193 (2020)
13. Press, G.: AI stats news: 34% of employees expect their jobs to be automated in 3 years. In: Forbes (2020)
14. Wamba-Taguimdje, S.-L., Wamba, S.F., Kamdjoug, J.R.K., Wanko, C.E.T.: Impact of artificial intelligence on firm performance: exploring the mediating effect of process-oriented dynamic capabilities. In: Agrifoglio, R., Lamboglia, R., Mancini, D., Ricciardi, F. (eds.) Digital Business Transformation. LNISO, vol. 38, pp. 3–18. Springer, Cham (2020). https://doi.org/10.1007/978-3-030-47355-6_1
15. Haefner, N., Wincent, J., Parida, V., Gassmann, O.: Artificial intelligence and innovation management: a review, framework, and research agenda☆. Technol. Forecast. Soc. Change **162**, 120392 (2021)
16. Dwivedi, Y.K., et al.: Artificial Intelligence (AI): multidisciplinary perspectives on emerging challenges, opportunities, and agenda for research, practice and policy. Int. J. Inform. Manag. **57**, 101994 (2019)

17. Van de Wetering, R., Hendrickx, T., Brinkkemper, S., Kurnia, S.: The impact of EA-driven dynamic capabilities, innovativeness, and structure on organizational benefits: a variance and fsQCA perspective. Sustainability **13**(10), 5414 (2021)
18. Majhi, S.G., Mukherjee, A., Anand, A.: Business value of cognitive analytics technology: a dynamic capabilities perspective. VINE J. Inform. Knowl. Manag. Syst. (2021). https://doi.org/10.1108/VJIKMS-07-2021-0128
19. Wetering, R.: Achieving digital-driven patient agility in the era of big data. In: Dennehy, D., Griva, A., Pouloudi, N., Dwivedi, Y.K., Pappas, I., Mäntymäki, M. (eds.) I3E 2021. LNCS, vol. 12896, pp. 82–93. Springer, Cham (2021). https://doi.org/10.1007/978-3-030-85447-8_8
20. Eshima, Y., Anderson, B.S.: Firm growth, adaptive capability, and entrepreneurial orientation. Strateg. Manag. J. **38**(3), 770–779 (2017)
21. Akgün, A.E., Keskin, H., Byrne, J.: Antecedents and contingent effects of organizational adaptive capability on firm product innovativeness. J. Prod. Innov. Manag. **29**, 171–189 (2012)
22. Teece, D.J., Pisano, G., Shuen, A.: Dynamic capabilities and strategic management. Strateg. Manag. J. **18**(7), 509–533 (1997)
23. Wiwoho, G., Suroso, A., Wulandari, S.: Linking adaptive capability, product innovation and marketing performance: results from Indonesian SMEs. Manag. Sci. Lett. **10**(10), 2379–2384 (2020)
24. Van de Wetering, R.: The impact of artificial intelligence ambidexterity and strategic flexibility on operational ambidexterity. In: 2022 Proceedings of the Pacific Asia Conference on Information Systems (PACIS), Taipei/Sydney Virtual Conference (2022)
25. Lee, O.-K., Sambamurthy, V., Lim, K.H., Wei, K.K.: How does IT ambidexterity impact organizational agility? Inf. Syst. Res. **26**(2), 398–417 (2015)
26. Van de Wetering, R.: IT ambidexterity and patient agility: the mediating role of digital dynamic capability. In: Proceedings of the Twenty-Ninth European Conference on Information Systems (ECIS). AIS, Virtual Conference (2021)
27. Wang, N., Liang, H., Zhong, W., Xue, Y., Xiao, J.: Resource structuring or capability building? An empirical study of the business value of information technology. J. Manag. Inf. Syst. **29**(2), 325–367 (2012)
28. Seddon, P.B.: Implications for strategic IS research of the resource-based theory of the firm: a reflection. J. Strateg. Inf. Syst. **23**(4), 257–269 (2014)
29. Van de Wetering, R., Versendaal, J., Walraven, P.: Examining the relationship between a hospital's IT infrastructure capability and digital capabilities: a resource-based perspective. In: Proceedings of the Twenty-Fourth Americas Conference on Information Systems (AMCIS). AIS, New Orleans (2018)
30. Duhan, S.: A capabilities based toolkit for strategic information systems planning in SMEs. Int. J. Inf. Manage. **27**(5), 352–367 (2007)
31. Raisch, S., Birkinshaw, J., Probst, G., Tushman, M.L.: Organizational ambidexterity: balancing exploitation and exploration for sustained performance. Organ. Sci. **20**(4), 685–695 (2009)
32. Wang, W., Hsieh, J.: Beyond routine: symbolic adoption, extended use, and emergent use of complex information systems in the mandatory organizational context (2006)
33. Ahuja, M.K., Thatcher, J.B.: Moving beyond intentions and toward the theory of trying: effects of work environment and gender on post-adoption information technology use. MIS Q. **29**, 427–459 (2005)
34. Carter, M., Petter, S., Grover, V., Thatcher, J.B.: Information technology identity: a key determinant of IT feature and exploratory usage. MIS Q. **44**(3), 983–1021 (2020)
35. Huang, M.-H., Rust, R.T.: A strategic framework for artificial intelligence in marketing. J. Acad. Mark. Sci. **49**(1), 30–50 (2020). https://doi.org/10.1007/s11747-020-00749-9
36. Shrestha, Y.R., Ben-Menahem, S.M., Von Krogh, G.: Organizational decision-making structures in the age of artificial intelligence. Calif. Manage. Rev. **61**(4), 66–83 (2019)

37. Van de Wetering, R., Versendaal, J.: Information technology ambidexterity, digital dynamic capability, and knowledge processes as enablers of patient agility: empirical study. JMIRx Med 2(4), e32336 (2021). https://doi.org/10.2196/32336
38. Van de Wetering, R.: Enterprise architecture resources, dynamic capabilities, and their pathways to operational value. In: Proceedings of the Fortieth International Conference on Information Systems (ICIS). AIS (2019)
39. Braganza, A., Brooks, L., Nepelski, D., Ali, M., Moro, R.: Resource management in big data initiatives: processes and dynamic capabilities. J. Bus. Res. 70, 328–337 (2017)
40. Van de Wetering, R., Mikalef, P., Krogstie, J.: Strategic value creation through big data analytics capabilities: a configurational approach. In: 2019 IEEE 21st Conference on Business Informatics (CBI), vol. 1, pp. 268–275. IEEE (2019)
41. Van de Wetering, R., Bosua, R., Boersma, C., Dohmen, D.: Information technology ambidexterity-driven patient agility, patient service-and market performance: a variance and fsQCA approach. Sustainability 14(7), 4371 (2022)
42. Diaz-Fernandez, M., Pasamar-Reyes, S., Valle-Cabrera, R.: Human capital and human resource management to achieve ambidextrous learning: a structural perspective. BRQ Bus. Res. Q. 20(1), 63–77 (2017)
43. Miles, R.H., Kanazawa, M.T.: Big Ideas to big results: leading corporate transformation in a disruptive world. FT Press, New Jersey (2015)
44. Gibson, C.B., Birkinshaw, J.: The antecedents, consequences, and mediating role of organizational ambidexterity. Acad. Manag. J. 47(2), 209–226 (2004)
45. Jansen, J.J., Van Den Bosch, F.A., Volberda, H.W.: Exploratory innovation, exploitative innovation, and performance: effects of organizational antecedents and environmental moderators. Manage. Sci. 52(11), 1661–1674 (2006)
46. Miles, R.H.: Accelerating corporate transformations (don't lose your nerve!). Harv. Bus. Rev. HBR 88(1/2), 67–75 (2010)
47. Miles, R.H.: Beyond the age of Dilbert: accelerating corporate transformations by rapidly engaging all employees. Organ. Dyn. 29(4), 313 (2001)
48. Ali, Z., Sun, H., Ali, M.: The impact of managerial and adaptive capabilities to stimulate organizational innovation in SMEs: a complementary PLS–SEM approach. Sustainability 9(12), 2157 (2017)
49. Li, X., Hsieh, J.P.-A., Rai, A.: Motivational differences across post-acceptance information system usage behaviors: an investigation in the business intelligence systems context. Inf. Syst. Res. 24(3), 659–682 (2013)
50. Chen, J.-S., Tsou, H.-T.: Performance effects of IT capability, service process innovation, and the mediating role of customer service. J. Eng. Tech. Manage. 29(1), 71–94 (2012)
51. Henseler, J.: Composite-Based Structural Equation Modeling: analyzing latent and emergent variables. Guilford Publications, New York (2020)
52. Hair, J.F., Risher, J.J., Sarstedt, M., Ringle, C.M.: When to use and how to report the results of PLS-SEM. Eur. Bus. Rev. 31(1), 2–24 (2019)
53. Ringle, C.M., Wende, S., Becker, J.-M.: SmartPLS 3. Boenningstedt: SmartPLS (2015). https://www.smartpls.com
54. Petter, S., Straub, D., Rai, A.: Specifying formative constructs in information systems research. MIS Q. 31(4), 623–656 (2007)
55. Hu, L.T., Bentler, P.M.: Cutoff criteria for fit indexes in covariance structure analysis: conventional criteria versus new alternatives. Structural equation modelling. Multi. J. 6(1), 1–55 (1999)

56. Nitzl, C., Roldan, J.L., Cepeda, G.: Mediation analysis in partial least squares path modeling: helping researchers discuss more sophisticated models. Ind. Manag. Data Syst. **116**(9), 1849–1864 (2016)
57. Van de Wetering, R.: Understanding the impact of enterprise architecture driven dynamic capabilities on agility: a variance and fsQCA study. Pac. Asia J. Asso. Inf. Syst. **13**(4), 32–68 (2021)

AI Technologies for Delivering Government Services to Citizens: Benefits and Challenges

Ibrahim Mohamad[1,2], Laurie Hughes[1(✉)], Yogesh K. Dwivedi[1,3],
and Ali Abdallah Alalwan[4]

[1] Emerging Markets Research Centre (EMaRC), School of Management, Swansea University
Bay Campus, Swansea, UK
{i.m.k.mohamad.854977,d.l.hughes,y.k.dwivedi}@swansea.ac.uk
[2] Department of Business Administration, Faculty of Economics and Administrative Sciences,
The Hashemite University, Zarqa, Jordan
[3] Department of Management, Symbiosis Institute of Business Management, Symbiosis
International (Deemed University), Pune, Maharashtra, India
[4] Department of Management and Marketing, College of Business and Economics, Qatar
University, P.O. Box 2713, Doha, Qatar
aalalwan@qu.edu.qa

Abstract. This research presents a comprehensive understanding of AI in the
public sector based on a review of 78 studies. The literature review indicates that
an AI-analytical model and AI-based automation system are mostly used at the
organizational level whilst AI-recommender and chatbot applications are implemented within the citizens' services context. The results reveal that AI benefits
such as cost reduction and decision-making improvements are accrued by governments. Further, the benefits of personalization and positive user experiences
are directly useful to citizens. The review highlights that developing and adopting AI, presents two categories of challenges: AI obstacles at the organizational
level, such as employees' resistance, lack of managerial, and financial support,
and second - AI dilemmas linked to citizens such as AI ambiguity, bias, and privacy. Accordingly, this study provides recommendations for further research on
AI within the government and the public sector.

Keywords: Artificial intelligence (AI) · Public sector · AI technologies · AI
benefits · AI challenges

1 Introduction

Artificial Intelligence (AI) is described as the capacity of a machine or computer program
to complete tasks or undertake specific tasks and functions that simulate aspects of human
intelligence [92, 94]. Machines are now able to simulate human ability and behavior
within narrow applications and tasks [85]. Nowadays, the rapid development of AI
capabilities in process and service automation, has the potential to improve many aspects
of our lives, such as health [12, 13], transportation [47, 48], education [92], economics

© IFIP International Federation for Information Processing 2022
Published by Springer Nature Switzerland AG 2022
S. Papagiannidis et al. (Eds.): I3E 2022, LNCS 13454, pp. 38–57, 2022.
https://doi.org/10.1007/978-3-031-15342-6_4

[58], risk prediction and management [55, 58], and agriculture [59]. Researchers have indicated that AI-based automation will increase levels of productivity [49, 58], accuracy [47], efficiency [22, 83], and effectiveness [83].

In light of the above potential opportunities and benefits, there is an expectation of growth in global spending on AI technologies from $50.1 billion in 2020 to $110 billion by 2024, as reported by the International Data Corporation [41]. Likewise, the global AI technologies' market is expected to grow around 54% each year during the period from 2020 to 2025 [77]. This in turn, indicates that organizations within public and private sectors have realized the importance of the adoption and implementation of AI.

AI-based digital transformation initiatives are attracting many countries, including European Union countries [91], China, Japan, Canada, United States [74], India [19], and United Arab Emirates (UAE) [38] to develop national AI strategies. The recent study by Papadopoulos and Charalabidis [74] analyzed information from twelve AI national strategies around the world highlighting the race to adopt, develop and invest in AI technologies to boost their economy and improve citizens' services. Many researchers highlight the importance of governments' adoption of AI to add unique value to citizens' services [22, 61, 85, 89]. The technological advancement in AI will transform the way citizens interact with government [9, 52], will enhance service quality [85], personalization [21, 67], user experience [21, 98], transparency [1], and fairness [11].

Despite the importance of AI in our lives and the increasing interest of governments in investing and adopting AI solutions within the public sector to realize benefits, there exists a lack of a comprehensive academic understanding of AI from the public sector perspective. The existing literature also asserts that AI research in the public sector is still at an immature stage [76, 92, 94]. Noticeably, most review studies in this area (e.g., [27, 60, 86, 94]) focused on AI issues without organizing them according to the type of tasks or services, or target users within the public sector. Accordingly, this research realizes the need to conduct a comprehensive review and classify the AI aspects into the main categories in the public sector, namely organizational (government) and citizens' levels.

According to the above discussion, the main aim of the current research is to systematically review the related studies of AI in the public sector and synthesize and categorize them into two contexts: government and citizens. The results of the review literature will give direction for conducting further and specialized AI research according to organizational or citizens aspects. For instance, discovering AI benefits or challenges connected to citizens' services will help researchers interested in the citizens' domain. In addition, the findings will present practical contributions for practitioners (e.g., public services managers or policymakers) in line with their responsibilities.

This research comprehensively reviews and identifies the main AI technologies, benefits, and challenges associated with delivering government services to citizens via AI. The research is divided into seven sections. The next section presents a detailed overview of the literature search methodology. Section 3 will discuss AI technologies within the public sector. AI benefits for governments and citizens have been discussed in Sect. 4. The paper progresses to discuss the main AI challenges related to government and citizens in Sect. 5. This is followed by Sect. 6 which discusses research recommendations. The last Sect. 7 presents the conclusion.

2 Literature Search Methodology

The literature search process was carried out in five stages according to the guidelines by Snyder [80] on how to prepare a literature review. First, define the research topic direction - AI in the public sector or government. Second, identify relevant search terms (includes synonyms, abbreviations, and closely related keywords), as demonstrated in the following keyword structure: ("AI" OR "Artificial intelligence" OR "Machine learning" OR "ML" OR "intelligent application" OR "intelligent information system" OR "bots" OR "artificial agents" OR "intelligent system") AND ("Egovernment" OR "egov" OR "government" OR "digital government" OR "E-government" OR "Public sector" OR "mobile government" OR "m-government" OR "Electronic government"). Lastly, define a search strategy (article title, abstract, and keywords) via the Scopus database to identify all possible articles relevant to the research topic direction. This approach has been employed within many review papers (e.g., [27, 30, 94]). This stage of the analysis yielded 78 articles. The next stage entailed defining search inclusion criteria by limiting to journals and conferences to ensure the quality of studies. Define screening criteria, this research applied three inclusion criteria namely: 1. publication type is a journal article or conference proceeding to ensure academic quality; 2. the publication language is English; 3. studies that are directly related to AI in the public sector. Furthermore, the following exclusion criteria was used: (1) studies that are not peer-reviewed such as newspapers and dissertations; (2) studies where only an abstract is available; (3) studies not related explicitly to AI but technology in general; (4) studies related to AI, but are not explicitly related to AI in the public sector. The search and subsequent review resulted in 66 articles that were relevant to this research. The final element entailed the scanning of references within the selected articles [80, 94] and search within the Google Scholar database to check for any relevant studies not identified in previous searches. The final search and review yielded 78 separate articles.

In this research, the concept-driven systematic review approach [95] was utilized to identify and synthesize the key themes from the literature (technologies, benefits, and challenges). Furthermore, each of the themes were developed based on the frequency of the same concept in more than one study. The analysis and classification of concepts was centred on two categories: (1) AI issues related to governments, and (2) AI issues related to citizens. This high-level grouping was a natural separation of the key themes from the corpus of studies and aligned with the key topics, findings and conclusions. The review and subsequent analysis were undertaken by the first author under the direction of the co-authors. The subsequent drafting of the paper was primarily conducted by the first reviewer with the co-authors undertaking review and amendment of subsequent sections of the paper.

3 AI Technologies: An Overview

In general, AI technology involves the development of intelligent computer algorithms or models to complete simple and complex tasks in a unique way compared to other information technology applications [76, 94]. The development of AI technology is described in three levels [62, 71, 94]. First, Artificial Narrow Intelligence (ANI) which has simple capabilities to provide specific services without human intervention, such as answering citizens' enquiries utilizing chatbot technology [61]. Second, Artificial General Intelligence (AGI) which has the ability to learn from data and to analyze decision making similar to how the human mind would operate [96]. Finally, Artificial Super Intelligence (ASI) is a concept where the AI technology has superior capabilities that surpass human intelligence. Many studies highlight that the development of AGI and ASI has yet to emerge [15, 32, 37, 60].

In this context, some AI technologies implemented within the public sector have reached the level of ANI [61, 94]. For example, AI analytical and predictive modelling [48], and AI-based knowledge management [94]. Many technologies are considered under the umbrella of AI, which includes Machine Learning (ML), Deep Learning (DL), Artificial Neural Networks (ANN), Natural Language Processing (NLP), fuzzy logic, Multi-Agent System (MAS), semantic algorithm, and speech recognition [27, 85]. AI systems may incorporate more than one technology in the same AI application [25, 56]. For instance, AI-based self-service technology (SST) in the Administrative Approval Bureau (AAB) in China has integrated three technologies: natural language processing, face, speech recognition, and big data analytics [21].

The general aim of adopting AI technologies in the public sector is to perform automated tasks related to government functions or provide unique services to citizens. Accordingly, this literature review has identified two categories of AI technologies: AI technologies for government use and AI technologies for citizen interaction. These categories will be further discussed in the following sub-sections.

3.1 AI Technologies for Government

This paper has identified eight applications that are directly associated with government functions or tasks. The cases presented in Table 1 illustrate the key details of AI technologies and the unique benefits associated with each of them. Through the literature analysis, six studies have been identified within the AI-powered analytical topic [4, 26, 34, 48, 55, 56]. An AI-based analytical model has the capability to analyze a large set of data from governments or secondary sources (e.g., social media or Google) to provide statistical information. AI-powered advanced analytical models enable the automatic prediction of future events or outcomes with levels of accuracy depending on data quality [48, 55]. Accordingly, utilizing AI-based analytical models in the public sector will assist policymakers, managers, and public sector employees in a number of areas, namely budget management [34], public policy [55], public services planning [4, 26], and data security [56]. The technology used in these models may vary depending on the nature of the data and its sources, the area or sector, or the purpose of analysis. For example, Kouziokas [48] employed ANN to forecast high-risk transportation within urban areas. ANN can analyze data with a high degree of complexity derived from different sources. ANN collaborates with Geographic Information Systems (GPS) to utilize data location to contextualize the analysis. In contrast, the studies by Criado, Villodre [26], and Loukis et al. [55] used AI-based semantic analysis to analyze social media content to understand and assess languages based on meaning and human context.

In the study by Fernandez-Cortez et al. [34], ML was utilized to analyze numerical data related to the Mexican public budget. ML-based analytical models can deal with a large volume of numerical data and provide comprehensive classifications depending on patterns determined by researchers. The study by Loukis et al. [55] introduced AI analytical and predictive modelling to the Greek government to predict the economic crisis. This model is based on one of the ML algorithms, so-called, Feature selection algorithm (FS) that has a higher level of accuracy in analyzing and predictability when compared with traditional analytical techniques. A study by Luo [56], discussed an AI-based emergency management system to protect government data. The system was developed through collaboration between special ANN technology for network security that can understand events in case of attacks to help specialists to make the right decisions and prepare appropriate security policies for computer networks.

Two studies have concentrated on AI-based automation systems for managing citizens' requests in the transportation sector [47] and for managing citizens' complaints in the consumer protection sector [22]. These systems depend on the ML techniques that enable a computer program to conduct a task automatically like a human. Citizens' request and complaints systems will be able to automatically classify process requests and respond accordingly through ML techniques.

3.2 AI Technologies for Citizens

This research has identified two main types of AI applications for citizens, in the line with the nature of the service and target group of users: AI recommender systems and AI chatbots systems.

3.2.1 AI Recommender System

AI Recommender systems (RS) are computerized systems that provide advice, suggestions, and recommendations to citizens according to their interests, needs, and preferences [23]. Wirtz et al. [94] classified RS within AI applications as it provides recommendations autonomously. AI-based RS will increase the accuracy of personalized services for citizens by analyzing their data in a real-time or reasonable time. In addition, RS may analyze their previous behaviours or decisions in specific cases. For example, RS could analyze user behaviours over social media and then provide suggestions around services or products according to analysis results [97].

In the citizens' services context, Meza et al. [63] presented an AI-based RS to improve public tax payment in the municipality of Quito within Ecuador. The system aimed to present recommendations and advice to guide citizen payment behavior, providing information on taxes, discounts, and increasing financial flow to governments by encouraging citizens to pay taxes early. Terán and Meier [82] employed RS to improve electronic voting (e-voting) for citizens in Switzerland. The system analyzed the similarities among citizens' interests, tendencies, and candidates' information; then, provided suitable recommendations and information to citizens about qualified candidates.

3.2.2 AI Chatbots System

A chatbot is defined as a smart computer program designed to simulate human conversation with a single user or group of users [10] acting as a dialog system between a

Table 1. Summary of the key details of AI technologies within government

AI technology	Area/sector	Value add/benefits	Cited by
• Analytical model	Transportation	• Useful for developing risk management plan for transportation services • Assist public administration in identifying the factors that affect the level of transportation safety as well as reduce the number of crimes • Increase citizens comfort and reassure when traveling	[48]
• Analytical model	Budget management	• Evaluate the previous budget in terms of expenditures and revenues • Assist policymakers in planning upcoming budgets to maximize revenues and allocate expenditures • Provide useful information regarding the exploitation of investment opportunities and economic development	[34]
• Analytical model	Public policy	• Facilitate decision-making and preparing public policy • Present accurate information that helps decision-makers avoid risks of economic crises, such as economic recession • Exploit public and private sector data in strategic planning	[55]

(continued)

Table 1. (*continued*)

AI technology	Area/sector	Value add/benefits	Cited by
• Analytical model	Tourism sector	• Provide detailed information about tourists' interests in price, facilities, level of safety, and entertainment places • Assist the government in planning and improving tourism services according to citizens' perceptions. Consequently, it will increase their satisfaction • Present reliable feedback because the data were collected indirectly from citizens	[4]
• Analytical model	Public services planning	• Assist the government in planning and delivery of public services to citizens over social media platforms • Present information about the volume of citizens' interaction and engagement over Twitter • Provide comprehensive, accurate, and reliable information	[26]
• Analytical model	Data security	• Ensure data protection over e-government platforms during their sharing and exchange • Data and information verification and monitoring • Assist to make the right decision at the right time in case of errors or security matters	[56]

(*continued*)

Table 1. (*continued*)

AI technology	Area/sector	Value add/benefits	Cited by
• AI-based automation system	Transportation	• Increase the classification accuracy level and minimize classification errors • Reduce requests processing time and quick response	[47]
• AI-based automation system	Consumer protection sector	• Facilitate receiving and classifying data that are related to customers' complaints • Provide solutions to complaints in the shortest time	[22]

computer program and a human (user) [79]. Chatbots have been referenced within the literature as smart, digital, and intelligent agents [75, 94], virtual representatives, and Virtual Personal Assistants (VPA) [6, 69].

Modern chatbots depend primarily on Natural Language Processing (NLP) [10, 12] to develop AI techniques that enable computers to understand the natural language of humans (written or spoken) [2]. The chatbot system is based on the idea of interactions between a computer and a human to achieve a goal. Nimavat and Champaeria [72] classified chatbot applications into three categories depending on the purpose of their use: 1) informative - aims to provide information to users by searching algorithms within the stored databases like Answer and Question (AQ) chatbot, 2) chat-based conversational - talks to users interactively and aims to respond accurately to their sentences, as demonstrated in virtual doctor applications [12], 3) task based chatbot - focuses on providing a specific service or transaction such as public tax payments.

In line with the above categories, chatbots are developed to serve citizens in many ways: answering enquiries, filling out forms, searching for documents, guiding citizens to complete transactions, issuing governmental documents [61], and completing government transactions. As a result, chatbots can replace government employees to complete daily routine transactions and reduce workload [79], improve the level of service delivery to citizens, increase accessibility, improve flexibility, transparency, and interaction between government and citizens [52]. Some chatbot applications have significant and unique benefits according to the type of service. For instance, Medical Chatbot (Medbot) was implemented during the COVID 19 pandemic to aid citizens' access to health services from cities or rural areas. Medbot helps to improve, to triage medical consultations, and performs basic diagnosis of ailments and medical conditions [12].

The study by Sivčević et al. [79], highlighted the potential implementation of chatbots within the police service in Serbia to increase safety levels. The study highlighted the advantage of chatbot high availability (24/7) for citizens and potential to reduce human error in describing cases, crimes, or locations. An experimental study by Jones and Jones [44] aimed to investigate the impact of chatbots on BBC news productivity and distribution. The study was launched eight experimental chatbot applications from 2015 to 2017, four of them over social networking platforms such as Facebook and Twitter. The results found that chatbots could facilitate access, sharing content, and improvements to citizen engagement with BBC news. The research by Van Noordt and Misuraca [88] examined the effect chatbots have on government services by analyzing three case studies using chatbot applications within public administration. The main results indicated that chatbot applications accomplished citizen transactions and facilitated access to governmental services anywhere and anytime. Moreover, the application saved employees' effort and time in repetitive tasks.

4 Benefits of Using Artificial Intelligence

The existing studies have focused on two kinds of AI benefits. To further elaborate on these kinds, this section is broken down into two main sub-sections: the benefits of using AI for government and then the benefits for citizens.

4.1 Benefits of Using Artificial Intelligence for Government

AI technology is different from traditional information systems applications due to the automated aspects of task processing [42]. As a result, AI technologies have introduced a set of potential benefits to government, which are discussed below:

- **Cost reduction:** AI-based automation will reduce traditional costs, such as buildings, desks, and office administration. This is possible as AI-powered automation will reduce the number of visitors to public agencies, reduce manual operations, paperwork, and decrease the number of required government employees [24]. AI technology within infrastructure management systems can help governments save money and operate more efficiently [5]. For example, in the suburban town of Wellesley in the United States of America (USA), an AI smart system was implemented to manage energy and predict future consumption. This system enabled the local government to reduce energy consumption by 9% over three years, totaling savings of $132,000. Sivčević et al. [79] argue that AI solutions for accomplishing repetitive tasks will be cheaper than other information system applications and can subsequently be of long-term benefit to government and public sector authorities.
- **Performance improvement:** AI can improve public sector productivity [66, 67], especially daily and routine transactions. AI applications are operational 24/7, thereby reducing the workload of public employees to perform complex tasks [5, 6, 61], consequently increasing total productivity. According to Toll et al. [83], AI is described as an enabler for boosting the effectiveness and efficiency of governmental organizations and their performance and tasks. AI technologies have high accuracy in performing tasks [57, 76]. This is evidenced in the virtual chatbot application "Alex" that supports the Australian taxation office services. In the first test, Alex achieved an accuracy rate of 80% in fulfilling citizens' requests, surpassing the industry benchmark of 60–65% [5].

- **Management and Decision-making improvement:** The efficiency ability of some AI techniques will assist professional public administrators in performing their tasks [11]. For example, ML has the ability to predict or support decision-making based on analyzing managerial assumptions and values [7]. According to Bullock [16], AI will increase the flexibility of the decision-making process because the decision-making authority will be transferred to the AI application that is available electronically. Hence, it will be easily accessible by both employees and citizens. In addition, there is a possibility to reduce the centralization of decision-making.
- **Data and information processing:** AI technologies will help in exploiting, analyzing [7, 26, 93], and classifying [22] huge amounts of data with high interoperability [86], accuracy, processing speed, and effectiveness [7].
- **Government knowledge improvement:** AI technology increases the data that government holds and processes on their citizens, as demonstrated by AI-powered analytics tools. Here AI-powered analytics tools analyze citizens' interactions, perceptions, and opinions over websites or social media [4, 26, 46].

4.2 Benefits of Using Artificial Intelligence for Citizens

AI public services automation will bring substantial benefits to citizens. These benefits are discussed below:

Availability and Accessibility: AI-based automation services will support the 24/7 availability of service and ease of access over many platforms [83]. This is demonstrated in systems where chatbot applications provide direct and fast access to government services via e-government websites [24] or social networks [44]. This process can ultimately save citizens' time in browsing website pages to find services [24].

Personalization: Refers to the systems' ability to offer a better understanding of citizens' needs and attitudes and changes the content of the service or product accordingly [21, 83]. Many researchers highlight that AI applications will support and enhance the personalization level for citizens' services [21, 61, 67, 83, 85], as demonstrated in the recommender systems, see Sect. 3.2.1. Here the payment tax recommender system provides advice according to the attributes of each citizen [63]. AI processes enable virtual doctor applications to understand citizens' cases based on a set of questions and then present personalized health advice or prescriptions [12].

Ethical Principles: AI will reduce the intervention of government employees in the completion of transactions and provision of services [21, 99]. In some cases, AI systems make the decision and judgment automatically [36, 43]. AI machines and systems depend on computerized algorithms to perform their functions and processes [24, 92, 99]. AI can support employees integrity and engender citizen trust due to the potential for reduced levels of corruption within automated processes [29].

User experiences: Refers to the perceptions or impressions of users that result from systems use [51]. In the public sector context, some studies [21, 35, 98] have highlighted that AI attributes have a significant impact on facilitating and enhancing citizens' experience over time. Mainly AI attributes relate to personalization, design, smart aspects [21], and support transparency [98]. Citizens will directly interact with the AI system interface, as demonstrated in AI-based SST [21].

Citizens' satisfaction: AI applications are likely to optimize citizens' services in terms of reliability through reducing human errors [6], accuracy, effectiveness, efficiency, productivity [50], and quality [33, 73, 83]. These aspects may impact on increasing citizens' satisfaction toward governments [61].

5 Challenges of Using Artificial Intelligence

Despite all the benefits of AI technology, there are a number of challenges that hinder their adoption within the public sector. The overall analysis of the literature indicated that the challenges of developing and adopting AI technologies will be associated with government organizations and citizens. To further elaborate on these challenges, the section is broken down into two main sub-sections: challenges related to government, and challenges related to citizens.

5.1 Challenges Related to Government

- AI challenges that are related to government organization arise from several organizational and managerial issues, which are discussed below:
- Employees' exhibiting resistance to implementing new AI systems can believe that the system will reduce their authority and importance [64, 78]. AI could reduce the sense of managers and employees' responsibility toward work. This is due to the independent decision making of some AI systems and tasks [11, 94].
- Managerial and political challenges are those related to the lack of leadership and management support [17, 90], as well as the lack of managerial guidelines toward AI deployment [17, 39]. All these issues obstruct developing and adopting AI applications in the public sector since the decision to adopt AI needs to be supported by both managerial and political considerations [17, 28].
- Lack of financial support is related to insufficient financial support to develop and adopt AI applications [64, 94], especially in the initial phases of projects [74, 94]. This can result in some public organizations adopting cheap AI systems with limited functionality and specifications [11, 49].
- Data challenges are associated with the risk of using poor quality [83, 94], incomplete [31], unreliable, and biased data [28, 78]. AI systems depend primarily on data for analyzing, processing, learning, and solution implementation [31, 40]. Analyzing governmental data helps governments in the planning, decision making, and predictability of tasks [7]. Using poor or insufficient data with weak specifications will negatively affect performance and decisions making [43, 61]. The difficulty of assessing data and the shortage of data analytical specialists [31], may impact on the ability of organizations in presenting high data quality to ensure the success of AI systems within the public sector context [94]. There are also barriers related to the nature of governmental data. Many researchers described it as a huge amount of data that has a high degree of complexity in terms of volume, formats, and variety and can be unstructured [7, 40]. This is partly due to the nature of the public sector and its services compared with the private sector since the public sector involves many sub-sectors in different domains such as health, education, and finance [40, 54]. All these issues will affect gathering, classifying, and storing of data [40, 54, 94].

- AI skills and expertise. The greatest challenges that hinder the development and implementation of AI systems are lack of AI knowledge and talent [17] and shortage of AI specialists in general [8, 73] as global demand increases for skilled AI specialists [94]. Wirtz et al. [94] argue that AI experts' salaries and benefits are high compared with other IT specialists. This, in turn, indicates that organizations with limited budgets can find it difficult in recruiting and hiring AI experts.
- Legal and regulations challenges. With the widespread development and implementation of AI technologies, some governments have experienced challenges in presenting a solid legal and regulatory framework for using AI applications within the public sector context [45, 94]. Governments may find difficulties implementing adequate laws for AI systems due to the fact that these systems are associated with a range of issues [65], such as data protection and privacy [17, 65, 83, 94], AI ambiguity and level of transparency [29], responsibility and accountability [16, 17, 81, 94], human rights (either employees or citizens) [65, 83].

5.2 Challenges Related to Citizens

- AI challenges that are related to citizens arise from a number of issues that will be discussed below:
- Lack of citizen awareness and knowledge of AI systems has emerged as a key challenge because AI has been viewed as an emergent technology [61]. Even in some cases, citizens use and interact with AI applications without knowing that they are classified under the AI umbrella [5, 6].
- AI system ambiguity and lack of explainability is associated with many AI systems as they provide outcomes or make decisions without explaining the reasons as to how or why the process was carried out [29, 76]. For this reason, some researchers describe AI systems as a black box [29, 57]. AI ambiguity has negatively affected citizen acceptance in the public sector [29, 76]. This factor has also impact on trust and level of transparency toward AI systems [14, 29]. According to Chatterjee and Sreenivasulu [20] citizens are worried about sharing their data and information with the AI system because they do not know how the AI system will process or use the data.
- AI system bias occurs where the system creates outcomes or decisions, which may lead to negative results due to algorithmic bias potentially impacting citizens' gender, color, or cultural background [14, 29, 85]. The bias phenomenon may increase citizen concerns about transferring tasks or decision-making for AI [35, 86]. Bias within AI systems is not linked to all systems and in some cases, AI systems are utilized to avoid human bias and support citizen fairness [1, 92, 99]. AI-based virtual agents have been used for social insurance services in China. The agents aimed to ensure equality of citizens in obtaining public social insurance and increasing transparency levels [99].
- Privacy and security challenges arise from citizen's concerns about the privacy [7, 33, 68, 94] and protection [3, 65, 83] of their data and information when they interact with AI systems [35]. The degree of citizen's concerns are influenced by the type of data and the protection standards in place at the time [65, 87]. Also, citizen's concerns arise from unethical use of their data [33, 81], for example, the use of AI systems to monitor citizens [49]. Recently, many governments have implemented AI applications

for health purposes during the Covid19 pandemic [84]. Nevertheless, there are privacy anxieties stemming from some citizen's attitudes toward these technologies as they have the ability to monitor, store, and analyze personal data [70].

- Responsibility and accountability. AI accomplishes tasks and makes decisions without human (employee) intervention [53]. Many researchers highlight that citizens' concerns arise from who is responsible in the case of an error or misjudgment from the AI system and how their rights may be impacted [5, 18, 94].
- AI system performance challenges. This refers to AI applications that were unable to perform tasks adequately in comparison to employees within citizen services. Where a service context required extensive human interaction or emotion [10, 83]. Furthermore, prior studies indicated that some governments adopt cheap AI applications with limited functional specifications [11, 49]. As a result, it likely negatively impacts their performance in delivering public services to citizens.

6 Recommendations

This paper reviewed the existing literature on AI within the public sector. From this review, the study provides a set of recommendations for scholars interested in AI research. First, many existing studies indicated the importance of increasing the research effort that focused on conducting empirical studies to investigate the actual influence of AI benefits and challenges on organizational and individual levels within the public sector. Second, the majority of studies that have researched AI technologies for the government focused on technical aspects [4, 26, 34, 48, 55, 56]. The review has identified the lack of research in investigating the managerial aspects within this area. Accordingly, this research suggests increasing research interest in managerial issues such as AI technology adoption and risk management. Furthermore, this paper has explored the main challenges of AI implementation at the organizational and citizens' level. Therefore, future researchers' contributions must act on presenting theoretical solutions and frameworks to manage AI challenges accord to the nature of users (either citizens or employees). These contributions will support the successful adoption of these technologies and realize their benefits.

This research has discovered the unique benefits of AI technologies, such as improving personalization and user experiences. Future studies could utilize technology theories (e.g., TAM, UTUAT) to investigate the positive impact of AI benefits on citizens' adoption of AI technologies like chatbots and AI recommender applications. Furthermore, the literature review revealed the main AI technologies at the organizational and citizens' level. Therefore, future studies should pay more attention to assessing the success of AI technologies through a theoretical model (e.g., IS success model). This research identified the AI challenges connected to employees and citizens, such as bias, ambiguity, and technology resistance, this, in turn, could help establish a theoretical foundation for further research to examine their impact on AI acceptance and adoption within the different kinds of public sectors.

The literature review provides a set of recommendations for public services managers, policymakers, and practitioners who work in the e-government field. Governments should adopt clear and holistic plans and policies for developing AI technologies by presenting an adequate financial budget, providing accurate and reliable data, and preparing programs to attract or develop AI knowledge and expertise. Furthermore, it is essential to coordinate between governments' services managers and developers to earn the unique advantages of AI implementation at the organizational and citizens' services level. The review results identified several ethical issues related to AI in the areas of privacy, security, bias, responsibility, and accountability. Accordingly, this paper suggests that policymakers and managers should prepare a strict legal framework to govern these issues before integrating AI into citizens' services. Moreover, governments must utilize appropriate methods using relevant media channels to increase public awareness about AI and its benefits to citizens and institutions.

This research also recommends increasing the research effort that focuses on a particular sector because the public sector contains several sub-sectors (e.g., health, education), and each sector has unique attributes. For instance, the type of services, target users (patients or students), and type of data and procedures. The future contribution of specialized studies will support the literature on AI according to the sector type and provide practical recommendations in more detail to administrative or decision-makers for each sector.

7 Conclusion

In this paper, we have reviewed the available research on AI from the perspective of government and citizens to identify the main categories of AI technologies, benefits, and challenges. The overall analysis of the literature identified two types of applications that are specific to the organizational level, including AI-powered analytical models and AI-based automation systems. Furthermore, two applications directly use or interact with citizens to deliver public services, namely AI recommender systems and chatbots. This paper determines and classifies the main AI benefits found within the reviewed studies. AI will positively affect internal government functions through cost reduction, performance, management, decision-making improvement, data and information processing, and government knowledge improvement. Alike, AI will support and enhance citizens' services in five areas: availability, accessibility, personalization, support user experiences and satisfaction, and ethical principles.

In addition, the review of the existing studies explored two main groups of challenges. The first group relates to the organizational level involving five challenges: employees' resistance, managerial and political, data, AI skills and expertise, legal and regulations challenges, and lack of financial support. The second group attached firmly to citizens contains five challenges: lack of citizen awareness and knowledge of AI systems, AI system ambiguity, bias, privacy and security, performance, and responsibility and accountability. Although the current findings would be a valuable guide for researchers and practitioners interested to understand managerial issues related to the development and implementation of AI technologies across the public sector. There are some limitations that should be noted; the paper was limited to a set of keywords and academic databases in the literature search process. Therefore, future studies may consider other AI's public sector terms and databases. Moreover, the analysis of prior studies was focused only on three AI issues: technologies, benefits, and challenges. This gives an opportunity for researchers to investigate other AI themes, such as AI opportunities, adoption, and success factors.

References

1. Abdeldayem, M.M., Aldulaimi, S.H.: Trends and opportunities of artificial intelligence in human resource management: aspirations for public sector in Bahrain. Int. J. Sci. Technol. Res. 9(1), 3867–3871 (2020)
2. Adamopoulou, E., Moussiades, L.: An overview of chatbot technology. In: Maglogiannis, I., Iliadis, L., Pimenidis, E. (eds.) Artificial Intelligence Applications and Innovations, vol. 584, pp. 373–383. Springer, Cham (2020). https://doi.org/10.1007/978-3-030-49186-4_31
3. Agarwal, P.K.: Public administration challenges in the world of AI and bots. Public Adm. Rev. 78(6), 917–921 (2018)
4. Aggarwal, S., Gour, A.: Peeking inside the minds of tourists using a novel web analytics approach. J. Hosp. Tour. Manag. 45, 580–591 (2020)
5. Ahn, M.J., Chen, Y.C.: Artificial intelligence in government: potentials, challenges, and the future. In: The 21st Annual International Conference on Digital Government Research, pp. 243–252 (2020). https://doi.org/10.1145/3396956.3398260
6. Akkaya, C., Krcmar, H.: Potential use of digital assistants by governments for citizen services: the case of Germany. In: Proceedings of the 20th Annual International Conference on Digital Government Research, pp. 81–90 (2019). https://doi.org/10.1145/3325112.3325241
7. Alexopoulos, C., Lachana, Z., Androutsopoulou, A., Diamantopoulou, V., Charalabidis, Y., Loutsaris, M.A.: How machine learning is changing e-government. In: Proceedings of the 12th International Conference on Theory and Practice of Electronic Governance, pp. 354–363 (2019). https://doi.org/10.1145/3326365.3326412
8. Al-Mushayt, O.S.: Automating e-government services with artificial intelligence. IEEE Access 7, 146821–146829 (2019)
9. Androutsopoulou, A., Karacapilidis, N., Loukis, E., Charalabidis, Y.: Transforming the communication between citizens and government through AI-guided chatbots. Gov. Inf. Q. 36(2), 358–367 (2019)
10. Aoki, N.: An experimental study of public trust in AI chatbots in the public sector. Gov. Inf. Q. 37(4), 101490 (2020)
11. Barth, T.J., Arnold, E.: Artificial intelligence and administrative discretion: implications for public administration. Am. Rev. Public Adm. 29(4), 332–351 (1999)
12. Bharti, U., Bajaj, D., Batra, H., Lalit, S., Lalit, S., Gangwani, A.: Medbot: conversational artificial intelligence powered chatbot for delivering tele-health after covid-19. In: 2020 5th International Conference on Communication and Electronics Systems (ICCES), pp. 870–875. IEEE (2020). https://doi.org/10.1109/ICCES48766.2020.9137944
13. Bokefode, J.D., Komarasamy, G.: A remote patient monitoring system: need, trends, challenges and opportunities. Int. J. Sci. Technol. Res. 8(09), 830–835 (2019)
14. Boyd, M., Wilson, N.: Rapid developments in artificial intelligence: how might the New Zealand government respond? Policy Q. 13(4), 36–43 (2017)
15. Brennen, J.S., Howard, P.N., Nielsen, R.K.: What to expect when you're expecting robots: futures, expectations, and pseudo-artificial general intelligence in UK news. Journalism (2020). https://doi.org/10.1177/1464884920947535
16. Bullock, J.: Artificial intelligence, bureaucratic form, and discretion in public service. Inf. Polity Bus. Horiz. 25(4), 491–506 (2020)
17. Campion, A., Gasco-Hernandez, M., Jankin Mikhaylov, S., Esteve, M.: Overcoming the challenges of collaboratively adopting artificial intelligence in the public sector. Soc. Sci. Comput. Rev. 40(2), 1–16 (2020)

18. Cath, C.: Governing artificial intelligence: ethical, legal and technical opportunities and challenges. Philos. Trans. R. Soc. Lond. Ser. A **376**(2133), 1–8 (2018)
19. Chatterjee, S.: AI strategy of India: policy framework, adoption challenges and actions for government. Transform. Gov.: People Process Policy **14**(5), 757–775 (2020)
20. Chatterjee, S., Sreenivasulu, N.S.: Personal data sharing and legal issues of human rights in the era of artificial intelligence: moderating effect of government regulation. Int. J. Electron. Gov. Res. **15**(3), 21–36 (2019)
21. Chen, T., Guo, W., Gao, X., Liang, Z.: AI-based self-service technology in public service delivery: user experience and influencing factors. Gov. Inf. Q. **38**(4), 101520 (1–11) (2020)
22. Chen, Y., Wang, J., Cai, Z.: Study on the application of machine learning in government service: take consumer protection service as an example. In: 2018 15th International Conference on Service Systems and Service Management (ICSSSM), pp. 1–5. IEEE (2018). https://doi.org/10.1109/ICSSSM.2018.8465040
23. Cortés-Cediel, M.E., Cantador, I., Gil, O.: Recommender systems for e-governance in smart cities: state of the art and opportunities. In: Proceedings of the International Workshop on Recommender Systems for Citizens, pp. 1–6 (2017). https://doi.org/10.1145/3127325.312 8331
24. Corvalán, J.G.: Digital and intelligent public administration: transformations in the era of artificial intelligence. A&C-Revista de Direito Administrativo & Constitucional **18**(71), 55–87 (2018)
25. Criado, J.I., Gil-Garcia, J.R.: Creating public value through smart technologies and strategies: from digital services to artificial intelligence and beyond. Int. J. Public Sect. Manag. **32**(5), 438–450 (2019)
26. Criado, J.I., Villodre, J.: Delivering public services through social media in European local governments. An interpretative framework using semantic algorithms. Local Gov. Stud. **47**(2), 253–275 (2020)
27. De Sousa, W.G., de Melo, E.R.P., Bermejo, P.H.D.S., Farias, R.A.S., Gomes, A.O.: How and where is artificial intelligence in the public sector going? A literature review and research agenda. Gov. Inf. Q. **36**(4), 101392 (2019)
28. Desouza, K.C., Dawson, G.S., Chenok, D.: Designing, developing, and deploying artificial intelligence systems: lessons from and for the public sector. Bus. Horiz. **63**(2), 205–213 (2020)
29. Dwivedi, Y.K., et al.: Artificial Intelligence (AI): multidisciplinary perspectives on emerging challenges, opportunities, and agenda for research, practice and policy. Int. J. Inf. Manag. **57**, 101994 (2021)
30. Dwivedi, Y.K., Ismagilova, E., Rana, N.P., Raman, R.: Social media adoption, usage and impact in business-to-business (B2B) context: a state-of-the-art literature review. Inf. Syst. Front. 1–23 (2021). https://doi.org/10.1007/s10796-021-10106-y
31. Eisenberg, S.: Machine learning for the government: challenges and statistical difficulties. Fed. Data Sci. 29–40 (2018). https://doi.org/10.1016/B978-0-12-812443-7.00003-X
32. Everitt, T., Lea, G., Hutter, M.: AGI safety literature review. arXiv preprint arXiv:1805.01109 https://arxiv.org/pdf/1805.01109.pdf (2018). Accessed 10 Apr 2022
33. Fatima, S., Desouza, K.C., Dawson, G.S.: National strategic artificial intelligence plans: a multi-dimensional analysis. Econ. Anal. Policy **67**, 178–194 (2020)
34. Fernandez-Cortez, V., Valle-Cruz, D., Gil-Garcia, J.R.: Can artificial intelligence help optimize the public budgeting process? Lessons about smartness and public value from the Mexican federal government. In: 2020 Seventh International Conference on eDemocracy & eGovernment (ICEDEG), pp. 312–315. IEEE (2020). https://doi.org/10.1109/ICEDEG48599.2020.9096745
35. Floridi, L.: Artificial intelligence as a public service: learning from Amsterdam and Helsinki. Philos. Technol. **33**(4), 541–546 (2020). https://doi.org/10.1007/s13347-020-00434-3

36. Futó, I.: Machine learning or expert systems that is the question, which is to be used by a public administration. In: Kő, A., Francesconi, E., Kotsis, G., Tjoa, A.M., Khalil, I. (eds.) EGOVIS 2020. LNCS, vol. 12394, pp. 204–218. Springer, Cham (2020). https://doi.org/10.1007/978-3-030-58957-8_15

37. Gill, K.S.: Artificial super intelligence: beyond rhetoric. AI Soc. **31**(2), 137 (2016). https://doi.org/10.1007/s00146-016-0651-x

38. Halaweh, M.: Artificial intelligence government (Gov. 3.0): the UAE leading model. J. Artif. Intell. Res. **62**, 269–272 (2018)

39. Harrison, T.M., Luna-Reyes, L.F.: Cultivating trustworthy artificial intelligence in digital government. Soc. Sci. Comput. Rev. 1–18 (2020)

40. Harrison, T., Luna-Reyes, L.F., Pardo, T., De Paula, N., Najafabadi, M., Palmer, J.: The data firehose and AI in government: why data management is a key to value and ethics. In: Proceedings of the 20th Annual International Conference on Digital Government Research, pp. 171–176 (2019). https://doi.org/10.1145/3325112.3325245

41. International Data Corporation: Worldwide Spending on Artificial Intelligence. https://www.idc.com/getdoc.jsp?containerId=prUS46794720. Accessed 10 Apr 2021

42. Ivanov, S.H., Webster, C., Berezina, K.: Adoption of robots and service automation by tourism and hospitality companies. Revista Turismo & Desenvolvimento **27**(28), 1501–1517 (2017)

43. Janssen, M., Brous, P., Estevez, E., Barbosa, L.S., Janowski, T.: Data governance: organizing data for trustworthy Artificial Intelligence. Gov. Inf. Q. **37**(3), 101493 (2020)

44. Jones, B., Jones, R.: Public service chatbots: automating conversation with BBC News. Digit. Journal. **7**(8), 1032–1053 (2019)

45. Kaplan, A., Haenlein, M.: Rulers of the world, unite! The challenges and opportunities of artificial intelligence. Bus. Horiz. **63**(1), 37–50 (2020)

46. Kaya, T.: Artificial intelligence driven e-government: the engage model to improve e-decision making. In: ECDG 2019 19th European Conference on Digital Government, p. 43 (2019). https://doi.org/10.34190/ECDG.19.054

47. Kim, N., Hong, S.: Automatic classification of citizen requests for transportation using deep learning: case study from Boston city. Inf. Process. Manag. **58**(1), 102410 (2021)

48. Kouziokas, G.N.: The application of artificial intelligence in public administration for forecasting high crime risk transportation areas in urban environment. Transp. Res. Procedia **24**, 467–473 (2017)

49. Kshetri, N.: Artificial intelligence in developing countries. IEEE Ann. Hist. Comput. **22**(04), 63–68 (2020)

50. Kuziemski, M., Misuraca, G.: AI governance in the public sector: three tales from the frontiers of automated decision-making in democratic settings. Telecommun. Policy **44**(6), 101976 (2020)

51. Law, E.L.C., Roto, V., Hassenzahl, M., Vermeeren, A.P., Kort, J.: Understanding, scoping and defining user experience: a survey approach. In: Proceedings of the SIGCHI Conference on Human Factors in Computing Systems, pp. 719–728 (2009)

52. Lindgren, I., Madsen, C.Ø., Hofmann, S., Melin, U.: Close encounters of the digital kind: a research agenda for the digitalization of public services. Gov. Inf. Q. **36**(3), 427–436 (2019)

53. Lloyd, C., Payne, J.: Rethinking country effects: robotics, AI and work futures in Norway and the UK. N. Technol. Work. Employ. **34**(3), 208–225 (2019)

54. Lommatzsch, A.: A next generation chatbot-framework for the public administration. In: Hodoň, M., Eichler, G., Erfurth, C., Fahrnberger, G. (eds.) Innovations for Community Services, vol. 863, pp. 127–141. Springer, Cham (2018). https://doi.org/10.1007/978-3-319-93408-2_10

55. Loukis, E.N., Maragoudakis, M., Kyriakou, N.: Artificial intelligence-based public sector data analytics for economic crisis policymaking. Transform. Gov.: People Process Policy **14**(4), 639–662 (2020)

56. Luo, H.: An emergency management system for government data security based on artificial intelligence. Ingénierie des Systèmes d'Information **25**(2) (2020)
57. Gavighan, C., Knott, A., Maclaurin, J., Zerilli, J., Liddicoat, J.: Government use of artificial intelligence in New Zealand. The New Zealand Law Foundation (2019). https://www.otago.ac.nz/caipp/otago711816.pdf. Accessed 10 Apr 2022
58. Makridakis, S.: The forthcoming Artificial Intelligence (AI) revolution: its impact on society and firms. Futures **90**, 46–60 (2017)
59. Malhotra, C., Anand, R.: Accelerating public service delivery in India: application of internet of things and artificial intelligence in agriculture. In: Proceedings of the 13th International Conference on Theory and Practice of Electronic Governance, pp. 62–69 (2020). https://doi.org/10.1145/3428502.3428510
60. McLean, S., Read, G.J., Thompson, J., Baber, C., Stanton, N.A., Salmon, P.M.: The risks associated with artificial general intelligence: a systematic review. J. Exp. Theor. Artif. Intell. 1–17 (2021). https://doi.org/10.1080/0952813X.2021.1964003
61. Mehr, H., Ash, H., Fellow, D.: Artificial intelligence for citizen services and government. Ash Cent. Democr. Gov. Innov. Harvard Kennedy Sch. 1–12 (2017). https://ash.harvard.edu/files/ash/files/artificial_intelligence_for_citizen_services.pdf. Accessed 10 Apr 2022
62. Meskó, B., Hetényi, G., Gyorffy, Z.: Will artificial intelligence solve the human resource crisis in healthcare? BMC Health Serv. Res. **18**(1), 1–4 (2018)
63. Meza, J., Terán, L., Tomalá, M.: A fuzzy-based discounts recommender system for public tax payment. In: Meier, A., Portmann, E., Terán, L. (eds.) Applying Fuzzy Logic for the Digital Economy and Society, pp. 47–72. Springer, Cham (2019). https://doi.org/10.1007/978-3-030-03368-2_3
64. Mikalef, P., Fjørtoft, S.O., Torvatn, H.Y.: Artificial intelligence in the public sector: a study of challenges and opportunities for Norwegian municipalities. In: Pappas, I.O., Mikalef, P., Dwivedi, Y.K., Jaccheri, L., Krogstie, J., Mäntymäki, M. (eds.) Digital Transformation for a Sustainable Society in the 21st Century. LNCS, vol. 11701, pp. 267–277. Springer, Cham (2019). https://doi.org/10.1007/978-3-030-29374-1_22
65. Mikhail, B., Aleksei, M., Ekaterina, S.: On the way to legal framework for AI in public sector. In: Proceedings of the 11th International conference on Theory and Practice of Electronic Governance, pp. 682–684 (2018)
66. Misuraca, G., van Noordt, C., Boukli, A.: The use of AI in public services: results from a preliminary mapping across the EU. In: Proceedings of the 13th International Conference on Theory and Practice of Electronic Governance, pp. 90–99 (2020). https://doi.org/10.1145/3428502.3428513
67. Mohasses, M.: How AI-Chatbots can make Dubai smarter? In: 2019 Amity International Conference on Artificial Intelligence (AICAI), pp. 439–446. IEEE (2019)
68. Morkhat, P.M., Ponkin, I.V., Botnev, V.K., Turganbayev, A.O., Markhgeym, M.V.: Artificial intelligence versus public administration: limitations of application. Humanit. Soc. Sci. Rev. **7**(3), 516–520 (2019)
69. Mowbray, A., Chung, P., Greenleaf, G.: Utilising AI in the legal assistance sector—testing a role for legal information institutes. Comput. Law Secur. Rev. **38**, 105407 (2020)
70. Naudé, W.: Artificial intelligence vs COVID-19: limitations, constraints and pitfalls. AI Soc. **35**(3), 761–765 (2020). https://doi.org/10.1007/s00146-020-00978-0
71. Naudé, W., Dimitri, N.: The race for an artificial general intelligence: implications for public policy. AI Soc. **35**(2), 367–379 (2019). https://doi.org/10.1007/s00146-019-00887-x
72. Nimavat, K., Champaneria, T.: Chatbots: an overview types, architecture, tools and future possibilities. Int. J. Sci. Res. Dev **5**(7), 1019–1024 (2017)
73. Ojo, A., Mellouli, S., Ahmadi Zeleti, F.: A realist perspective on AI-era public management. In: Proceedings of the 20th Annual International Conference on Digital Government Research, pp. 159–170 (2019). https://doi.org/10.1145/3325112.3325261

74. Papadopoulos, T., Charalabidis, Y.: What do governments plan in the field of artificial intelligence? Analysing national AI strategies using NLP. In: Proceedings of the 13th International Conference on Theory and Practice of Electronic Governance, pp. 100–111 (2020). https://doi.org/10.1145/3428502.3428514

75. Pencheva, I., Esteve, M., Mikhaylov, S.J.: Big data and AI–A transformational shift for government: so, what next for research? Public Policy Adm. 35(1), 24–44 (2020)

76. Reis, J., Santo, P.E., Melão, N.: Impacts of artificial intelligence on public administration: a systematic literature review. In 2019 14th Iberian Conference on Information Systems and Technologies (CISTI), pp. 1–7. IEEE (2019)

77. Statista: worldwide-artificial-intelligence-market-growth. https://www.statista.com/statistics/607960/worldwide-artificial-intelligence-market-growth/. Accessed 10 Apr 2021

78. Shaw, J., Rudzicz, F., Jamieson, T., Goldfarb, A.: Artificial intelligence and the implementation challenge. J. Med. Internet Res. 21(7), e13659 (2019)

79. Sivčević, D., Košanin, I., Nedeljković, S., Nikolić, V., Kuk, K., Nogo, S.: Possibilities of used intelligence based agents in instant messaging on e-government services. In: 2020 19th International Symposium, Infoteh-Jahorina (Infoteh), pp. 1–5. IEEE (2020)

80. Snyder, H.: Literature review as a research methodology: an overview and guidelines. J. Bus. Res. 104, 333–339 (2019)

81. Sun, T.Q., Medaglia, R.: Mapping the challenges of Artificial Intelligence in the public sector: evidence from public healthcare. Gov. Inf. Q. 36(2), 368–383 (2019)

82. Terán, L., Meier, A.: A fuzzy recommender system for eElections. In: Andersen, K.N., Francesconi, E., Grönlund, Å., van Engers, T.M. (eds.) Electronic Government and the Information Systems Perspective, vol. 6267, pp. 62–76. Springer, Heidelberg (2020). https://doi.org/10.1007/978-3-642-15172-9_6

83. Toll, D., Lindgren, I., Melin, U., Madsen, C.Ø.: Values, benefits, considerations and risks of AI in government: a study of AI policy documents in Sweden . eJ. eDemocr. Open Gov. 12(1) (2020)

84. Vaishya, R., Javaid, M., Khan, I.H., Haleem, A.: Artificial Intelligence (AI) applications for COVID-19 pandemic. Diabetes Metab. Syndr. 14(4), 337–339 (2020)

85. Valle-Cruz, D., Sandoval-Almazan, R.: Towards an understanding of artificial intelligence in government. In: Proceedings of the 19th Annual International Conference on Digital Government Research: Governance in the Data Age, pp. 1–2 (2018). https://doi.org/10.1145/3209281.3209397

86. Valle-Cruz, D., Alejandro Ruvalcaba-Gomez, E., Sandoval-Almazan, R., Ignacio Criado, J.: A review of artificial intelligence in government and its potential from a public policy perspective. In: Proceedings of the 20th Annual International Conference on Digital Government Research, pp. 91–99 (2019). https://doi.org/10.1145/3325112.3325242

87. Vámos, T., Soós, I.: Data management and AI in e-government. In: Wimmer, M.A. (ed.) Knowledge Management in Electronic Government. LNCS, vol. 2645, pp. 230–238. Springer, Heidelberg (2003). https://doi.org/10.1007/3-540-44836-5_24

88. van Noordt, C., Misuraca, G.: New wine in old bottles: chatbots in government. In: Electronic Participation, pp. 49–59. Springer, Cham (2019). https://doi.org/10.1007/978-3-030-27397-2_5

89. van Noordt, C., Misuraca, G.: Evaluating the impact of artificial intelligence technologies in public services: towards an assessment framework. In: Proceedings of the 13th International Conference on Theory and Practice of Electronic Governance, pp. 8–16 (2020). https://doi.org/10.1145/3428502.3428504

90. van Noordt, C., Misuraca, G.: Exploratory insights on artificial intelligence for government in Europe. Soc. Sci. Comput. Rev. 40, 426–444 (2020)

91. Viscusi, G., Collins, A., Florin, M.V.: Governments' strategic stance toward artificial intelligence: an interpretive display on Europe. In: Proceedings of the 13th International Conference on Theory and Practice of Electronic Governance, pp. 44–53 (2020)

92. Wamba, S.F., Bawack, R.E., Guthrie, C., Queiroz, M.M., Carillo, K.D.A.: Are we preparing for a good AI society? A bibliometric review and research agenda. Technol. Forecast. Soc. Chang. **164**, 120482 (2020)

93. Wirtz, B.W., Müller, W.M.: An integrated artificial intelligence framework for public management. Public Manag. Rev. **21**(7), 1076–1100 (2019)

94. Wirtz, B.W., Weyerer, J.C., Geyer, C.: Artificial intelligence and the public sector—applications and challenges. Int. J. Public Adm. **42**(7), 596–615 (2019)

95. Webster, J., Watson, R.T.: Analyzing the past to prepare for the future: writing a literature review. MIS Q. xiii–xxiii (2002). http://www.jstor.org/stable/4132319. Accessed 10 Apr 2022

96. Yuan, X., Liebelt, M.J., Shi, P., Phillips, B.J.: Creating rule-based agents for artificial general intelligence using association rules mining. Int. J. Mach. Learn. Cybern. **12**(1), 223–230 (2020). https://doi.org/10.1007/s13042-020-01166-8

97. Zhang, Q., Lu, J., Jin, Y.: Artificial intelligence in recommender systems. Complex Intell. Syst. **7**(1), 439–457 (2020). https://doi.org/10.1007/s40747-020-00212-w

98. Zheng, Y., Yu, H., Cui, L., Miao, C., Leung, C., Yang, Q.: SmartHS: an AI platform for improving government service provision. In: Proceedings of the AAAI Conference on Artificial Intelligence, vol. 32, no. 1 (2018). https://www.aaai.org/ocs/index.php/AAAI/AAAI18/paper/viewPaper/16041. Accessed 10 Apr 2022

99. Zheng, Y., et al.: Addressing the challenges of government service provision with AI. AI Mag. **41**(1), 33–43 (2020)

From Responsible AI Governance to Competitive Performance: The Mediating Role of Knowledge Management Capabilities

Emmanouil Papagiannidis[1]([⊠]), Patrick Mikalef[1], John Krogstie[1], and Kieran Conboy[2]

[1] Norwegian University of Science and Technology, Trondheim, Norway
{emmanouil.papagiannidis,patrick.mikalef,john.krogstie}@ntnu.no
[2] National University of Ireland, Galway, Ireland
kieran.conboy@nuigalway.ie

Abstract. In a constantly changing environment, researchers and practitioners are concerned with the issue of whether responsible artificial intelligence (AI) governance can help build competitive advantage. Responsible AI governance should be viewed as a source of competitive edge rather than merely a quick fix for automating manual processes. Despite this, little empirical evidence is available to support this claim, and even less is understood about the dimensions and relationships that add business value. This paper develops a conceptual model to explain how responsible AI governance practices aligned with strategic goals lead to competitive performance gains. An investigation of 144 Nordic firms is conducted to verify our hypotheses using a PLS-SEM analysis. Findings reveal that deploying responsible AI governance will make a significant positive impact on an organizations' knowledge management capabilities directly and on competitive performance indirectly. These findings also suggest that implementing responsible AI governance improves firms' ability to acquire and distribute knowledge when there is strategic alignment with a firm's goals.

Keywords: Responsible AI governance · Knowledge management capabilities · Competitive performance · Strategic alignment

1 Introduction

Over the past few years, organizations are increasingly turning to AI to digitalize their activities. Schmidt, Zimmermann, Möhring and Keller [1] define AI as the endeavor to mimic cognitive and human capabilities on computers. AI contributes towards digital transformation by customizing solutions based on the available data [2]. Nevertheless, AI capabilities have not been used to their full advantage and companies like Google decided to govern AI in a responsible way to increase performance and limit negative consequences [3]. Another example is IBM who developed several tools to address fairness issues [4]. Responsible AI is the process of designing, developing, and deploying artificial intelligence with the purpose of enabling individuals and organizations

© IFIP International Federation for Information Processing 2022
Published by Springer Nature Switzerland AG 2022
S. Papagiannidis et al. (Eds.): I3E 2022, LNCS 13454, pp. 58–69, 2022.
https://doi.org/10.1007/978-3-031-15342-6_5

while also having a fair effect on customers and society, allowing businesses to create trust towards AI [5]. The relationship between responsible AI governance and a company's competitive performance is an important issue that has occupied information systems research for the last few years [6]. A growing body of research in Information Systems (IS) emphasizes the importance of developing responsible applications that transform competencies into differential economic value, with some studies attempting to determine the impact of responsible AI governance on a firm's competitive position [7]. Among other things, Knowledge Management Capabilities (KMC) are expected to enable firms to seek and disseminate updated knowledge in order to meet their needs, exploit innovation, and guide firms in responding quickly to external market changes to achieve high business performance [8, 9]. Furthermore, as competition has increased the need for dynamic capabilities in organizations, future research should focus on the conceptual development of dynamic KMCs incorporating new facets to resolve real-time problems and achieve better organizational outcomes [10]. Nevertheless, little empirical evidence is available to support this claim, and even less is understood about the dimensions and relationships that add business value.

To fill this gap, we developed a conceptual model, and developed an instrument of responsible AI governance based on the guidelines of MacKenzie, et al. [11] to explain how responsible AI governance practices aligned with digitalization goals lead to competitive performance gains. We collected data through a quantitative survey-based approach in which 144 Nordic businesses participated, and we examined our conceptual model and hypotheses using a partial least squares structural equation model (PLS-SEM) analysis. Therefore, the aim of this study is to determine whether responsible AI governance improves KMC, whether strategic alignment changes the strength between responsible AI governance and KMC, in other words, it has a moderating effect, and whether KMC provide any significant competitive performance advantages. The main point is that responsible AI governance will be useful only if it is used to support or enable critical KMC that are contributed by dynamic strategy alignment [12]. What is more, we contribute to the AI literature by demonstrating how responsible AI governance enhances a company's KMC, hence improving competitive performance. Using survey data from respondents with managerial responsibilities within their organization, we show empirical proof that these claims are correct. As a result, responsible AI governance reflects a company's ability to commercialize its knowledge skills. Consequently, this study seeks to answer the following two research questions: (1) *What is the relationship between responsible AI governance and competitive advantage gains? (2) What is the effect of strategic alignment on competitive performance gains?*

The rest of the paper is structured as follows. The subsequent section presents the background of this study and describes what responsible AI governance entails. Section 3 details our hypotheses, where we examine if a robust responsible AI governance can impact competitive performance. It is our theory that the indirect effect is mediated through the firm's capability to manage its knowledge, which is affected by the strategic alignment. As a result, these renewed operational capabilities provide a competitive advantage. Section 4 presents how our study analyzes factors associated with these associations using a survey-based design, and we describe the data collection methods and measures for each concept used. Afterwards, we present the results of our empirical analysis, followed by a discussion of their theoretical and practical implications as well as some significant limitations.

2 Background

Although there is no clear definition of responsible AI governance, there is a growing consensus about it. It can be defined as a function that describes the different ways AI can be governed ethically [5]. As an alternative, it can be defined as a process that spans all stages of AI projects' lifecycles by following the principles of responsible use [13]. Responsible AI governance is important to benchmark against competitive performance gains, particularly in examining what type of effect it has within organizations' capabilities to make continuous improvements and implement changes in business products, methods and services. For instance, Microsoft developed explainability tools to interpretate machine learning models which assist with decision making [4]. Hence, there is growing support for the claim that responsible AI governance not only has an impact on external entities' perception of organizations when using AI [14], but also on the internal capabilities related to managing organizational knowledge [8]. Consequently, responsible AI governance may influence KMC since it offers a framework for understanding the implications of the use of AI and propose which standards to follow so stakeholders will have confidence in the organization's use of AI. KMC is defined as an organizational mechanism to continually and intentionally create knowledge inside the organization [15].

Developing responsible artificial intelligence applications adds benefits not only from an ethical and moral standpoint but also can provide organizations with a medium to long-term competitive advantage [16]. By showcasing an organization's commitment to ethical practices, for example, it can gain an edge in recruiting technical professionals and also retain top talent, particularly when qualified developers are in short supply. According to the EIU report [17], ethically questionable practices discourage prospective employees from applying for jobs and undermine their faith in the industry, contributing to the so-called "techlash," a result of public disbelief and animosity towards large tech companies. Furthermore, responsible AI practices and processes enable the creation of documentation on how an organization addresses the challenges associated with artificial intelligence [16], allowing for a better understanding of potential operational issues or business opportunities that may arise [17]. As a result, responsible AI commences influencing performance because trustworthiness leads to increased retention, spending, and adoption of new services [18]. A well-crafted AI application can preserve and expand one's client base by adhering to ethical and responsible standards [16]. By developing inclusive products and services, businesses will be able to retain customers and increase their credibility by providing products and services that are effective for all types of customers, ensure safety, and are transparent. For instance, the acceptance of blockchain technologies in AI services for traceability and transparency can overcome trust issues from the side of customers [19]. Additionally, the development of a responsible AI governance is also essential from a compliance perspective. Authorities have begun monitoring AI applications and introducing regulations that include principles of standards and ethical considerations, such as auditing processes and algorithmic impact assessments. As a result, a number of privacy and data protection frameworks include privacy by design as an integral part of their frameworks.

Seven dimensions comprise the notion of responsible AI governance. These dimensions are accountability, environmental, societal well-being, transparency, fairness, robustness and safety, data governance, and human-centric AI [20]. A primary aim of responsible AI governance is to reduce the possibility that a modest change in the weight of an input can drastically alter the output of a machine learning model since it takes a lot of effort to create a responsible AI governance system. It is worth mentioning that this is a self-developed construct, where items and sub-dimensions have been validated through established methods [11]. Continuous examination is necessary to guarantee that an organization is dedicated to producing unbiased and reliable AI. Therefore, while creating and implementing an AI system, it is critical for a business to have a maturity model or standards to follow. The ability of an organization to effectively adapt information to future use and respond to changes in the environment is critical, as is the importance of knowledge in improving the organization's performance. KMC reflects an organization's ability to create, transfer, integrate and leverage knowledge within the organization [21]. The items used to measure the KMC of firms were adopted from the study of Mao, Liu, Zhang and Deng [22], where they also were empirically confirmed. The respondents were asked five questions about the degree to which they are able to manage knowledge within the organization.

Strategic alignment has been a top management priority since the inception of the information technology profession, and its favorable effects on business performance have been thoroughly documented in past research. The substance of plans and planning processes can be viewed as strategic alignment [23]. Tallon and Pinsonneault [24] supported the causal link between strategic alignment and performance by concentrating on the alignment of strategy, plans, operations, and processes. We measured strategic alignment based on an adapted scale used from the work of Preston and Karahanna [25] which comprised of three items. As for competitive performance, it refers to how well a company outperforms its key competitors [26]. Respondents were asked to rate how well they outperformed their primary competitors in a variety of areas such as market share, delivery cycle time, and customer satisfaction.

3 Research Model

The research model is presented (see Fig. 1), as are the hypotheses that surround it. We argue that responsible AI governance will affect a company's competitive performance. We also argue that strategic alignment between AI and business will amplify responsible AI governance's impact on KMC. Therefore, having a sensible AI governance model aligned with a company's strategic goals will enhance KMC, which will boost the company's competitive performance.

An organization that implements responsible AI governance should focus on assessing, monitoring, and evaluating the performance of an AI application, both before and after deployment [13]. It is also essential to have clear and concise ways to document both the data and AI aspects of AI governance, including how they relate to each other [3]. For instance, all steps from data collection to data use should be documented, including

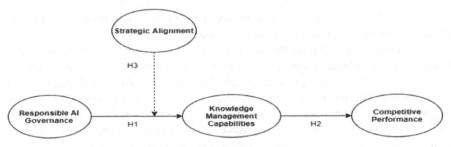

Fig. 1. Research model.

how the data was transformed [27]. Knowledge can flow within the organization more efficiently if the processes and mechanisms are well documented, therefore improving KMC. Documentation also decreases the dependence on one person's knowledge and abilities since documented processes are less likely to become obsolete. Furthermore, responsible AI governance places emphasis on designing based on inclusiveness and on enhancing human agency and autonomy. These are fundamental constituents for facilitating better use of human capital within organizations and, as a result, optimizing knowledge flows and interactions. Finally, responsible AI governance dictates that throughout the process of design, deployment and monitoring of AI applications, there is a strong focus on the safety and robustness of systems and entities that interact with AI agents. Establishing such privacy and safety policies facilitates easier cross-departmental access and knowledge sharing without the risk of critical knowledge being leaked or accessed by non-authorized employees [28]. Thus, we propose the following hypothesis: **H1:** *Responsible AI governance will have a positive effect on KMC.*

Several studies have indicated that KMC is related to organizational performance [21, 22, 29]. Information is regarded as one of a company's most valuable and critical resources, and businesses that can develop, apply, and manage the appropriate knowledge can reap a variety of benefits [29]. Having a strong KMC may aid in the improvement of product and service quality, as well as the development of new products and services. KMC helps businesses improve their processes, which is critical for competitive success. Several studies have been conducted to investigate the relationship between KMC and performance. Tanriverdi [21], for example, demonstrated that KMC has a positive effect on the corporate financial performance of multi-business firms. Thus, we propose the following hypothesis: **H2:** *KMC will have a positive effect on competitive performance.*

Strategic alignment of the information system has been linked to improved company performance (IS). It refers to the alignment of a company's business strategy with its information technology strategy. Other studies [30] investigated a wide range of factors that influence the alignment of business and IT strategies. Strategic alignment improves organizational outcomes, which indirectly increases competitive advantage. KM is also a strategy for developing new products, increasing value, and improving competitiveness by leveraging a company's intellectual assets and employee capabilities. In this scenario, if we view strategic alignment as the most important to the organization, and design a roadmap to accomplish its goals, then responsible AI governance could be the roadmap (framework) and KMC could be one of the organizational goals. That means strategic alignment could amplify the potential value that responsible AI governance has on KMC. Hence, to compete in today's highly competitive business environment, large corporations must integrate their IT with their KM policies and procedures. Thus, we propose the following hypothesis: **H3:** Strategic alignment *will have a positive moderating effect on the relationship between responsible AI governance and KMC.*

4 Methodology

A quantitative study was carried out to test the research paradigm proposed in this work. The survey approach was used as a strategy as a survey study collects the same type of data from a large number of key respondents such as managers, heads of departments and CEO, which can then be analyzed for trends that allow conclusions to be generalized. The study's population is Nordic enterprises because according to the Global Economic Forum's 2019 Global Competitiveness Report organizations in these countries have high levels of ICT adoption and the majority of individuals have strong digital skills, making them well equipped for digital transformation.

4.1 Data Collection

To put the study model to the test, Nordic businesses were sent an internet questionnaire-based survey. For each country, the percentage is 29.9% for Norway, 27.8% for Sweden, 27.7% for Finland and 14.6% for Denmark. According to the Global Economic Forum's 2019 Global Competitiveness Report, these countries are at the forefront of global competitiveness, ranking eighth, tenth, eleventh, and seventeenth, respectively [31]. The Nordic countries have a high rate of ICT adoption, and the majority of the population has advanced digital skills, putting them in a good position for digital transformation [32]. We utilized 58 questions to measure our items and we used a 7-point Likert scale, where a value of 1 means disagrees entirely, and 7 means agree entirely.

To ensure internal validity we used PLS' discriminant validity which establishes the distinctiveness of the constructs. In addition, we conducted a pre-study of 15 respondents to measure the statistical responses (respondent fatigue, quality of answers etc.) and we requested feedback from them to improve the survey. For external validity, we used purposive sampling as it is easier to generalize a sample of 144 respondents. Our sample is consistent since it exclusively covers Scandinavian nations, implying that they share comparable cultural traits, education level and IT infrastructure. The validity and reliability of the hierarchical research model were evaluated using a structural equation model (PLS-SEM). All analyses, in particular, were carried out using the software package SmartPLS 3. PLS-SEM is regarded as a suitable method for assessing multiple relationships between one or more dependent variables and one or more independent variables in this study because it allows for simultaneous estimation of multiple relationships [33]. As a variance-based method, PLS-SEM is adaptable and capable of evaluating both reflective and formative constructs and the ability to analyze complex models with smaller samples and theory building. PLS-SEM is widely used in data analysis for the estimation of complex relationships between constructs in a variety of subject areas, including business and management research [34].

5 Analysis

5.1 Measurement Model

We employed distinct assessment criteria to examine each of the reflective and formative constructs in the model because they are both reflective and formative. We tested reliability, convergent validity, and discriminant validity for the latent reflective components. The construct and item levels of reliability were tested. We looked at Composite Reliability (CR) and Cronbach Alpha (CA) values at the construct level and found that they were both over the 0.70 criterion. The construct-to-item loadings were checked to see if they were greater than 0.70, indicating indicator dependability. To see if AVE values were convergent, we looked at whether they were above the lower limit of 0.50, and the lowest observed value was 0.623, which is significantly higher than this threshold. To establish discriminant validity, two methods were used. The Fornell–Larcker criterion was used to ensure that the AVE square root of each construct was more significant than the highest correlation with any other construct. The second examined whether the outer loading of each indicator exceeded its cross-loadings with other constructs. The results (Table 1) show that the reflective measures are valid and that all items are good indicators for their respective constructs.

Table 1. Discriminant validity values.

	(1)	(2)	(3)	(4)	(5)	(6)	(7)	(8)	(9)	(10)
(1) Accountability	**0.78**									
(2) Data governance	0.63	**0.75**								
(3) Environmental and societal well-being	0.64	0.59	**0.81**							
(4) Fairness	0.62	0.55	0.60	**0.76**						
(5) Human-centric AI	0.58	0.73	0.63	0.52	**0.79**					
(6) Robustness and safety	0.69	0.73	0.62	0.58	0.75	**0.76**				
(7) Transparency	0.66	0.64	0.59	0.70	0.64	0.68	**0.69**			
(8) KMC	0.33	0.60	0.48	0.56	0.58	0.43	0.54	**0.82**		
(9) Strategic alignment	0.35	0.39	0.58	0.37	0.57	0.45	0.51	0.45	**0.91**	
(10) Competitive performance	0.47	0.68	0.59	0.55	0.62	0.48	0.58	0.75	0.54	**0.79**

5.2 Structural Model

Figure 2 summarizes the structural model from the PLS analysis by showing the explained variance of endogenous variables (R^2) and the standardized path coefficients (β). The structural model is validated using coefficients of determination (R^2). To determine the significance of estimates, a bootstrap approach with 10000 resamples is used (t-statistics).

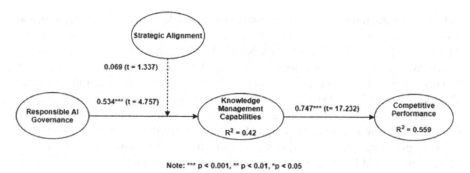

Note: *** p < 0.001, ** p < 0.01, *p < 0.05

Fig. 2. Structural model.

Figure 2 depicts support for two of the three hypotheses. The responsible AI governance of a company is found to influence KMC ($\beta = 0.534$, t = 4.757, p < 0.001). Strategic alignment, on the other hand, had no such significant effect on knowledge management competencies ($\beta = 0.069$, t = 1.337, p > 0.05). As predicted, knowledge management skills are positively associated with competitive performance ($\beta = 0.747$, t = 17.232, p < 0.001). The structural model explains 62.3% of the variation in competitive performance ($R^2 = 0.559$), 66.9% of the variation in KMC ($R^2 = 0.42$), and 82.7% of the variation in strategic alignment ($R^2 = 0.42$). These coefficients of determination suggest that the data have moderate to significant predictive power.

6 Discussion

There is a growing discussion around responsible AI governance, but still, literature lacks empirical evidence and thus, there is a gap that needs to be filled. Businesses should bridge this gap in order to gain the trust of their customers, employees, and other stakeholders. If they don't, their competitive performance might suffer, and their AI initiatives could fail to deliver the expected benefits and value. The outcomes of this research contribute to IS literature through key findings which raise several theoretical and managerial implications.

6.1 Implications for Research

This study contributes by developing a construct model for responsible AI governance and by examining how it affects KMC and through that competitive performance. We provide empirical evidence on the notion that responsible AI governance has an effect on KMC and has an indirect effect on competitive performance and we validate the concept through an empirical study that builds on a large sample from Scandinavian companies. Hence, policies and goals that define and orchestrate the business plan should consider how responsible AI governance can affect directly or not the performance outcomes of a firm.

In more specific terms, responsible AI governance appears to directly impact a firm's KMC by expanding both knowledge assets as well as knowledge operating capacities and providing them with greater opportunity in terms of their capacity, competence, and ability. Through this study, we add to the AI literature by illustrating how responsible AI governance improves a company's KMC, thereby enhancing competitive performance. We provide empirical evidence that these claims are true using survey data from 160 respondents with managerial responsibilities within their firm. According to Rana, Chatterjee, Dwivedi and Akter [35], the lack of understanding of how unintended consequences of an AI system could impact the overall competitive position of a firm is vital to the development and implementation of responsible AI government frameworks that add business value. Thus, exploring and investigating how responsible AI governance frameworks should function could give companies a competitive advantage over their competition.

Despite this, our empirical results did not support the assumption that strategic alignment impacts KMC. This may be because managers develop processes, policies, and practices from the top, and from there drill down to the bottom, while in practice, responsive AI is implemented from the bottom up based on the technical skills of the AI team. This entails pushing for changes in structures and processes may be antithetical to their goals and may conflict with what the organization currently supports [36]. Also, it is imperative that managers who wish to incorporate responsible AI concerns into their work first understand what it takes to achieve this, and then take the necessary steps to develop a responsible AI system. In the absence of an AI governance framework, it is a huge undertaking to redesign organizational structures, accommodate the responsible AI work, and finally carry out management changes to implement the new organizational practices.

6.2   Implications for Practice

The results of this study can be used by managers in key positions to benchmark results and identify areas for improvement. To accomplish this, a multitude of processes must be implemented, which requires top management commitment and a clear plan for firm-wide responsible AI integration. Since many companies are still at an early stage of adopting AI practices, it is important to do it in a responsible manner in order to gain value from the building of new capabilities which can boost performance. Since AI systems are complex and expensive, additional implementation considerations should be designed into the overall design, yet the benefits can quickly be realized on a managerial and economic level.

Aside from the fact that responsible AI governance practices enhance ethical and competitive value for the company, which is good for public perception, executives should also adopt them to improve the company's performance. Of course, there is the human factor to consider, as responsible AI is concerned with how human agents make data-driven decisions in order to maximize potential business performance [37]. At the same time, responsible AI governance has an impact on a company's overall strategy and development planning because features related to responsible AI necessitate time and effort. In contrast, the development team requires appropriate management and resources to create a trustworthy system.

Finally, due to the complexity of AI projects and the fact that most firms do not yet have an established AI development department, most projects are led by AI developers.

Management should clearly invest more resources and effort in AI capability development for two reasons. Firstly, AI is developed from the ground up, which means that new capabilities will emerge from the AI team itself, implying that capable AI development teams have the opportunity and power to change outcomes in a positive and profitable way by implementing AI-driven projects that adhere to a responsible AI framework. Second, in order to drive future business value, managers must plan and invest ahead of competitors in order to remain competitive. Keeping ahead of the competition, on the other hand, does not happen overnight. It necessitates a systematic approach in which all managerial efforts are contained within a framework that clearly guides the necessary steps to achieve representative AI practices.

6.3 Limitations and Future Research

There are several limitations to this study's methodology. First, companies taking part reside in Scandinavia, where countries are known to have high standards for responsible and ethical practices, so it will be interesting to see how countries in different geographical regions tackle the same problem, such as North America or southern Europe. Our survey is limited in another way by the fact that we only captured a snapshot of what these companies do. Because we are not familiar with how they develop their AI products or make them better over time, we cannot identify how their practices change and what mechanisms they apply. Finally, we do not measure various performance metrics, such as social responsibility, reputation, or trust, which can affect the position of a firm in the market, since such measures can capture the value that an organization can obtain in the medium or long term.

References

1. Schmidt, R., Zimmermann, A., Möhring, M., Keller, B.: Value creation in connectionist artificial intelligence–a research agenda. In: Value Creation in Connectionist Artificial Intelligence–A Research Agenda (Americas Conference on Information Systems: AMCIS/Association for 2020), pp. 1–10 (2020)
2. Rodrigues, A.R.D., Ferreira, F.A., Teixeira, F.J., Zopounidis, C.: Artificial intelligence, digital transformation and cybersecurity in the banking sector: a multi-stakeholder cognition-driven framework. Res. Int. Bus. Finan **60**, 101616 (2022)
3. (2021).   https://ai.google/static/documents/perspectives-on-issues-in-ai-governance.pdf. Accessed 16 Nov 2021
4. de Laat, P.B.: Companies committed to responsible AI: from principles towards implementation and regulation? Philos. Technol. **34**(4), 1135–1193 (2021). https://doi.org/10.1007/s13 347-021-00474-3
5. Singapore-Government: model artificial intelligence governance framework. In: Model Artificial Intelligence Governance Framework (2021)
6. Cihon, P., Schuett, J., Baum, S.D.: Corporate governance of artificial intelligence in the public interest. Information **12**(7), 275 (2021)
7. Enholm, I.M., Papagiannidis, E., Mikalef, P., Krogstie, J.: Artificial intelligence and business value: a literature review. Inf. Syst. Front. 1–26 (2021)
8. Sandhawalia, B.S., Dalcher, D.: Developing knowledge management capabilities: a structured approach. J. Knowl. Manage. **15**(2), 313–328 (2011)

9. Papagiannidis, E., Enholm, I.M., Dremel, C., Mikalef, P., Krogstie, J.: Toward AI governance: identifying best practices and potential barriers and outcomes. Inf. Syst. Front. 1–19 (2022). https://doi.org/10.1007/s10796-022-10251-y
10. Yang, X., Yu, X., Liu, X.: Obtaining a sustainable competitive advantage from patent information: a patent analysis of the graphene industry. Sustainability 10(12), 4800 (2018)
11. MacKenzie, S.B., Podsakoff, P.M., Podsakoff, N.P.: Construct measurement and validation procedures in MIS and behavioral research: integrating new and existing techniques. MIS Q. 35(2), 293–334 (2011)
12. Teece, D., Peteraf, M., Leih, S.: Dynamic capabilities and organizational agility: risk, uncertainty, and strategy in the innovation economy. Calif. Manage. Rev. 58(4), 13–35 (2016)
13. Amershi, S., et al.: Software engineering for machine learning: a case study. In: Software Engineering for Machine Learning: A Case Study, pp. 291–300. IEEE (2019)
14. Wang, Y., Xiong, M., Olya, H.: Toward an understanding of responsible artificial intelligence practices. In: Toward an Understanding of Responsible Artificial Intelligence Practices (Hawaii International Conference on System Sciences (HICSS)), pp. 4962–4971 (2020)
15. Von Krogh, G., Nonaka, I., Aben, M.: Making the most of your company's knowledge: a strategic framework. Long Range Plan. 34(4), 421–439 (2001)
16. Minkkinen, M., Zimmer, M.P., Mäntymäki, M.: Towards ecosystems for responsible AI. In: Dennehy, D., Griva, A., Pouloudi, N., Dwivedi, Y.K., Pappas, I., Mäntymäki, M. (eds.) I3E 2021. LNCS, vol. 12896, pp. 220–232. Springer, Cham (2021). https://doi.org/10.1007/978-3-030-85447-8_20
17. Adam Cutler, A.W., Paka, A.: Staying ahead of the curve: the business case for responsible AI. In: Staying Ahead of the Curve: The Business Case for Responsible AI (2020)
18. Mikalef, P., Gupta, M.: Artificial intelligence capability: conceptualization, measurement calibration, and empirical study on its impact on organizational creativity and firm performance. Inf. Manag. 58(3), 103434 (2021)
19. Sander, F., Semeijn, J., Mahr, D.: The acceptance of blockchain technology in meat traceability and transparency. Br. Food J. 120(9), 2066–2079 (2018)
20. Papagiannidis, E., Enholm, I.M., Dremel, C., Mikalef, P., Krogstie, J.: Deploying AI governance practices: a revelatory case study. In: Dennehy, D., Griva, A., Pouloudi, N., Dwivedi, Y.K., Pappas, I., Mäntymäki, M. (eds.) I3E 2021. LNCS, vol. 12896, pp. 208–219. Springer, Cham (2021). https://doi.org/10.1007/978-3-030-85447-8_19
21. Tanriverdi, H.: Information technology relatedness, knowledge management capability, and performance on multibusiness firms. MIS Q. 29(2), 311–334 (2005)
22. Mao, H., Liu, S., Zhang, J., Deng, Z.: Information technology resource, knowledge management capability, and competitive advantage: the moderating role of resource commitment. Int. J. Inf. Manage. 36(6), 1062–1074 (2016)
23. Wu, S.P.-J., Straub, D.W., Liang, T.-P.: How information technology governance mechanisms and strategic alignment influence organizational performance. MIS Q. 39(2), 497–518 (2015)
24. Tallon, P.P., Pinsonneault, A.: Competing perspectives on the link between strategic information technology alignment and organizational agility: insights from a mediation model. MIS Q. 35(2), 463–486 (2011)
25. Preston, D.S., Karahanna, E.: Antecedents of IS strategic alignment: a nomological network. Inf. Syst. Res. 20(2), 159–179 (2009)
26. Rai, A., Tang, X.: Leveraging IT capabilities and competitive process capabilities for the management of interorganizational relationship portfolios. Inf. Syst. Res. 21(3), 516–542 (2010)
27. Lwakatare, L.E., Raj, A., Bosch, J., Olsson, H.H., Crnkovic, I.: A taxonomy of software engineering challenges for machine learning systems: an empirical investigation. In: Kruchten, P., Fraser, S., Coallier, F. (eds.) XP 2019. Lecture Notes in Business Information Processing, vol. 355, pp. 227–243. Springer, Cham (2019). https://doi.org/10.1007/978-3-030-19034-7_14

28. Dignum, V.: Responsibility and artificial intelligence. Oxford Handb. Ethics AI **4698**, 215 (2020)
29. Tseng, S.-M., Lee, P.-S.: The effect of knowledge management capability and dynamic capability on organizational performance. J. Enterp. Inf. Manag. **27**(2), 158–179 (2014)
30. Avison, D., Jones, J., Powell, P., Wilson, D.: Using and validating the strategic alignment model. J. Strateg. Inf. Syst. **13**(3), 223–246 (2004)
31. Schwab, K.: The global competitiveness report 2019. In: World Economic Forum, vol. 9 (2019)
32. Schwab, K., Zahidi, S.: The global competitiveness report special edition 2020: how countries are performing on the road to recovery. In: World Economic Forum (2020)
33. Ringle, C.M., Wende, S., Becker, J.-M.: SmartPLS 3, Boenningstedt: SmartPLS GmbH (2015)
34. Ringle, C.M., Wende, S., Becker, J.-M.: SmartPLS 3. SmartPLS GmbH, Boenningstedt. J. Ser. Sci. Manag. **10**(3), 32–49 (2015)
35. Rana, N.P., Chatterjee, S., Dwivedi, Y.K., Akter, S.: Understanding dark side of artificial intelligence (AI) integrated business analytics: assessing firm's operational inefficiency and competitiveness. Eur. J. Inf. Syst. **31**(3), 1–24 (2021)
36. Rakova, B., Yang, J., Cramer, H., Chowdhury, R.: Where responsible AI meets reality: practitioner perspectives on enablers for shifting organizational practices. Proc. ACM Hum.-Comput. Interact. **5**(CSCW1), 1–23 (2021)
37. Duan, Y., Edwards, J.S., Dwivedi, Y.K.: Artificial intelligence for decision making in the era of big data–evolution, challenges and research agenda. Int. J. Inf. Manage. **48**, 63–71 (2019)

The "Other" Agent: Interaction with AI and Its Implications on Social Presence Perceptions of Online Customer Experience

Bianca Kronemann[1]([✉]), Hatice Kizgin[1,2,3], and Nripendra Rana[1,2,3]

[1] Faculty of Business, Law and Politics, University of Hull, Hull HU6 7RX, UK
bianca.kronemann@googlemail.com
[2] Faculty of Behavioural, Management and Social Sciences, University of Twente, 7500AE Enschede, The Netherlands
[3] College of Business and Economics, Qatar University, 2713 Doha, Qatar

Abstract. Advancements in Artificial Intelligence (AI) such as digital assistants and conversational agents are being adopted fast and wide across consumer industries such as e-commerce, where they act as frontline service agents and interact with customers in service encounters. It is suggested that technology is no longer only the mediator of communication between customers and a company but has potential to become the "other" with whom customers interact. Based on this idea, this research adopts Social Response Theory to measure the effects of anthropomorphism of AI, para-social interaction with AI and personalization on perceived social presence of the customer experience, customer loyalty and intentions to engage in eWOM. An online survey with a sample of online consumers, who have previously engaged with a form of AI-technology, is conducted. Quantitative analysis of the data through CFA and SEM shows that perceived social presence has a strong effect on both customer intentions to engage in eWOM and customer loyalty. Further, social presence serves as a mediator for the relationship between an anthropomorphism of AI and para-social interaction with AI on eWOM intentions and customer loyalty. A discussion of these findings and implications concludes this paper.

Keywords: Artificial Intelligence (AI) · Customer experience · Customer loyalty · Social presence · Social response theory

1 Introduction

The fourth industrial revolution witnesses a fast and widespread adoption of Artificial Intelligence (AI) as a disruptive technology that contributes to accelerating the shift towards a more algorithmic society (Huang and Rust 2018; Shankar 2018). Advancements in AI are being utilized across several consumer industries such as e-commerce and digital marketing. A popular application of AI in marketing are digital assistants also known as conversational agents (CAs), chatbots, virtual assistants, or dialogue systems (Rai 2020; Thomaz et al. 2020). These agents are designed to approximate human

© IFIP International Federation for Information Processing 2022
Published by Springer Nature Switzerland AG 2022
S. Papagiannidis et al. (Eds.): I3E 2022, LNCS 13454, pp. 70–81, 2022.
https://doi.org/10.1007/978-3-031-15342-6_6

speech and interact with people via a digital interface (Thomaz et al. 2020). They have the advantage of being highly scalable and the ability to deliver routine customer service to large numbers of people simultaneously (Davenport et al. 2020; Duan et al. 2019; Wilson and Daugherty 2018). Human-less transaction mediated by intelligent technology is growing in numbers and frequency (Hofacker and Corsaro 2020). However, research relating to the impact of AI and AI-enabled assistants, is still developing and relatively sparse (Davenport et al. 2020; Steinhoff et al. 2019).

Boden (2006) and Riskin (2007) state that from antiquity, humans have theorised about what it means to be human in contrast to artefacts made by humans. Key characteristics distinguishing human-made items from humans on an ontological dimension is the ability to communicate and experience emotion, yet, technology can now recreate communication in human-like ways, thus challenging existing paradigms (Edwards et al. 2019; Guzman 2020). Guzman (2020) argue that research into human-machine communication must re-examine interaction encounters and consider communicative technologies from a new perspective. Therefore, consistent with above discussion, this current study adapts Social Response Theory (SRT) to gain new insights of how people relate to AI because "communication is fundamental to both theory and practice of AI" (Gunkel 2012, p. 2). SRT posits that people relate to technologies as if they are people (Nass and Moon 2000; Reeves and Nass 1996). SRT is also known as Computers As Social Actors (CASA) paradigm because it states that humans mindlessly respond to computers in the same way as to humans if social cues are displayed. This research is anchored in SRT/CASA because this research is built on the assumptions that interaction with conversational agents is similar to human to human interaction and could approach relational nature. By adopting SRT/CASA as theoretical lens, this study contributes to the growing discussion in the marketing literature around consumers' interaction with AI-based digital assistants such as conversational agents, customer experience and customer loyalty. Literature relating to AI and related technologies is still in early stages (Grewal et al. 2020; Yadav and Pavlou 2020), thus, this study expands existing theory by investigating effects of AI on social presence perceptions of customer experience and customer loyalty. In contrast to previous research, which is mostly conceptual in nature, this study quantifies the impact of AI on customer experience and customer loyalty. In addition, the effects on electronic word of mouth (eWOM) are considered.

The remaining parts of this paper are structured into four sections: Firstly, a critical review of existing literature highlights the current state of knowledge in the areas of AI, customer experience and customer loyalty, which provides the background of this study and allows for the development of hypotheses. Following upon this, the research methods and methodology are outlined. Results are presented to confirm or reject the proposed hypotheses. A discussion of findings and implications follows and a brief summary concludes this paper.

2 Literature Review

2.1 AI-Based Agents

Interaction between AI-based service agents and consumers is becoming a central topic of discussion in the marketing and service literature. AI-based agents are addressed in academic literature under a variety of names such as conversational agents, chatbots, dialogue systems, (voice based) digital assistant and sometimes virtual assistants. These agents are natural language processing programs which are designed to approximate human speech and interact with humans via a digital interface (Rai 2020; Thomaz et al. 2020). Companies adopt these agents as new front-facing customer service that interact with consumers during service encounters (Thomaz et al. 2020; van Doorn et al. 2017; Wilson and Daugherty 2018). Ramaswamy and Ozcan (2018) as well as Haenlein and Kaplan (2019) suggest that AI will fundamentally change the nature of interaction between companies and their customers. Intelligent agents are adopted due to the underlying idea that they can enhance both the experience (Brandtzaeg and Følstad 2018; Hofacker and Corsaro 2020) as well as the outcome of consumer interaction with a company (Bleier et al. 2019; Thomaz et al. 2020). However, research relating to the impacts and outcomes of the integration of AI-based technology in the consumer context is sparse and still developing.

2.2 Anthropomorphism, Para-Social Interaction and Personalisation

A large body of marketing and consumer behaviour literature considers the topic of anthropomorphism (e.g. Aggarwal and McGill 2007; Epley et al. 2007; Kim and McGill 2018; Lu et al. 2019) because it represents an opportunity for marketers to affect consumption or affect consumer experience related to consumption (Epley 2018). Anthropomorphism refers to the level of an object's humanlike characteristics such as human appearance, self-consciousness and emotion (Kim and McGill 2018). Previous research argues that anthropomorphism is an important determinant of consumer behaviour (Epley 2018; Lu et al. 2019; van Doorn et al. 2017). Based on SRT, Nass and Moon (2000) showed that consumers treat computers like social actors if they display a minimum of social cues, such as asking questions or sharing information with the consumer. Anthropomorphism will impact consumers' evaluation of an entity because it encourages consumers to think about products as more human (Aggarwal and McGill 2007). Kim et al. (2019) state that anthropomorphism aims at influencing consumers to like them more, perceive them as more vivid and potentially treating them like sentient beings. The authors show how anthropomorphism of a consumer robot increases psychological warmth and positively affects consumers attitudes. Thus, it is proposed that anthropomorphism of AI will positively affect perceived social presence of the customer experience, which leads to:

H_1: Anthropomorphism of AI positively affects perceived social presence of the customer experience.

Interaction is important because it is expected that AI-enabled technology will reshape the ways in which firms try to communicate, interact, and connect with customers (Grewal et al. 2020; Haenlein and Kaplan 2019; Yadav and Pavlou 2020). It is argued that customer's perception of the interactions with the company has substantial influence on customer experience. AI can create new types of interactions. Reeves and Nass (1996) demonstrated how interactivity can reinforce social presence by investigating human encounters with computers. Building upon this notion, Keeling et al. (2010)

find that interactivity is a critical cue to the perception of social presence of an avatar due to its communication style. Taking these insights further into the context of AI, scholars (e.g. Saad and Abida 2016; Steinhoff et al. 2019; van Doorn et al. 2017) suggest that AI can change the nature of interaction with customers in marketing, and create new types of social interaction which can make the consumer feel accompanied by another social entity. Ramaswamy and Ozcan (2018) examine how new technologies co-create value with customers through continuous interaction. Further, Steinhoff et al. (2019) suggest that integrating AI into a company's online interaction with customers can enable companies to introduce a human touch, resembling interpersonal interactions. This is supported by Cherif and Lemoine (2019) who investigate the effect of voice of virtual assistants during interactions with consumers. The authors find that consumers who interact with a more human like virtual assistant have stronger impressions of social presence than consumers who do not interact through an assistant. Therefore, it is proposed that:

H_2: Parasocial interaction with AI positively affects perceived social presence of the customer experience

AI agents are being adopted by consumers because they enable individuals to access timely and useful information (Canbek and Mutlu 2016). These assistants meet customer demand for contextually relevant and highly personalised content that is delivered in real-time (Brill et al. 2018). It is argued that companies utilise AI to collect user details with the aim to improve the user experience and enhance lifetime value of customers (Shankar 2018; Wilson and Daugherty 2018). Due to the circumstance, that with AI, data about every individual consumer can be stored and analysed at unprecedented scale, marketers can now personalise their marketing mix for everyone. AI technology offers to improve and personalise interactions. Research by Gutierrez et al. (2019) finds that personalization of location-based advertising has significant impact on the acceptance of MLBA. Consequently, it is suggested that consumers react positively to personalization because of improved experience and perceptions of being better understood by a company. It is hypothesized that this understanding will lead to:

H_3: Personalisation positively affects perceived social presence of the customer experience.

2.3 Social Presence of the Customer Experience

Social presence captures the sociability and feeling of human context in a digital environment (Gefen et al. 2003) and describes the extent to which a website or technology allows users to experience others as psychologically present. It is argued that perceived social presence will be critical for advancements in frontline experiences in service encounters with technological advancements such as AI. Qiu and Benbasat (2009) demonstrate how social presence enhances behavioural intentions due to increased trust. Cherif and Lemoine (2019) find that perceived social presence of a virtual assistant influences behavioural intentions of consumers. Abrantes et al. (2013) find in their study on drivers of eWOM in the online environment that social interaction leads to increased sharing of eWOM. Therefore, it is proposed that perceived social presence of AI in the customer experience has a positive influence on intentions to engage in eWOM, which leads to:

H₄: Perceived social presence of the customer experience positively affects intentions to engage in eWOM

Choi et al. (2011) assessed the effect of social presence and social cues on engagement, reuse intentions and purchase behaviour. The authors find that webpages that convey social cues positively affect reuse intentions and engagement. Bleier et al. (2019) link social presence to purchase intentions in the online environment. The authors state that intelligent chat options, based on AI, can convey social presence, for instance through their linguistic style. Researchers (e.g. Bleier et al. 2019; Saad and Abida 2016; Steinhoff et al. 2019) suggest that AI can add a human touch to service in the online environment, which has the potential to influence consumer behaviour. Prentice and Nguyen (2020) examine how customers' service experience with human employees and AI influence customer engagement and loyalty. Their findings show that customer engagement and loyalty are driven by overall experience with both human and AI employees. It is proposed that:

H₅: Perceived social presence of the customer experience positively affects customer loyalty.

Finally, it is assumed that customer experience comprises a consumer's subjective, multidimensional, psychological response to a stimulus and then impacts consumer behaviour. Based on both studies by Bleier et al. (2019) and Holzwarth et al. (2006) it is argued that the perceived social presence of customer experience mediates the influence of the antecedents of anthropomorphism, interaction with AI, and personalisation of AI on intentions to engage in eWOM and customer loyalty, which leads to:

H₆: Perceived social presence of the customer experience mediates the effects of a) anthropomorphism of AI b) parasocial interaction with AI and c) personalisation on intentions to engage in eWOM and customer loyalty

Figure 1 summarizes the proposed relationships in a conceptual model:

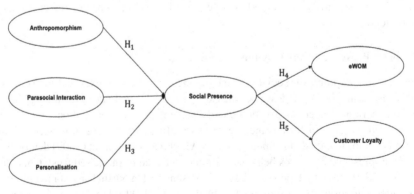

Fig. 1. Proposed research model and relationships based on Social Response Theory (Reeves and Nass 1996)

3 Methodology

3.1 Sample

An online survey was conducted with consumers who have previously encountered AI technology during an online service encounter. A screening question ensured that the sample requirement of a previous encounter with AI was met. The survey was distributed electronically through a convenience sampling approach on LinkedIn. Thus, respondents were recruited online, which is a common approach in online consumer behaviour research. In addition, answering a screening question in the affirmative regarding a previous encounter with AI, prospective respondents must be over 18.

3.2 Measures and Procedure

All measures and scales for this research were adopted from existing studies. 7-point Likert scales were utilized anchored from 1- Strongly disagree to 7-Strongly agree because Barnes et al. (2015) argue that a 7-point scale can improve reliability and validity of results. Anthropomorphism was measured on a scale with seven items adopted from Lu et al. (2019), who developed and validated a service robot integration willingness scale and found that anthropomorphism serves as a key determinant in consumers' willingness to integrate robots in their service transactions. Para-social Interaction was measured by five items adopted from Hartmann and Goldhoorn (2011). Personalisation measures through three items and social presence was measured with five items adopted from Qiu and Benbasat (2009). Customer loyalty was measured by eleven items taken and intentions to engage in eWOM through three items by Hennig-Thurau et al. (2004). The tool of a questionnaire to collect data was selected because it is an efficient means of data collection where respondents answer questions by completing the questionnaire themselves, which is a common approach in the social sciences (Bell et al. 2018). Self-completion questionnaires have the advantages that they are cheap and quick to administer, convenient for respondents because they can answer the questionnaire at a time and location of their choice, and lastly the questionnaire poses less risk of social desirability bias in respondents' answers in contrast to an interview because researcher and respondent are geographically distant and replying to the questionnaire is asynchronous (Bell et al. 2018; Saunders et al. 2019). The questionnaire was pilot tested in the summer 2021 and the main data collection took place in autumn of 2021. A total of 514 people answered the screening question, of which 489 answered "yes" and consequently provided full answers to all questions. Hence, the sample is n = 489. The sample has equal representation of gender (50.3% male, 49.3% female), and a good representation of age and income levels.

4 Analysis and Results

4.1 Measurement Model

Confirmatory Factor Analysis (CFA) was applied to examine the measurement model's fit and validity. The theoretical representation of the measurement model yields a χ^2 of 1284.688 (466 degrees of freedom), $\chi^2/df = 2.757$, a comparative fit index (CFI) of .955, Tucker-Lewis Index (TLI) of .949, Root Mean Square Error of Approximation (RMSEA) of .060 and Standardized Root Mean Residual (SRMR) of .0591 as an assessment of the data. Thus, the model achieves good fit based on criteria set out by Hair et al. (2007; 2010). Further, all path coefficients between indicators and their respective construct were significant and standardized regression weights all above .5. Further, the Average Variance Extracted (AVE) is above .5 for all constructs, indicating adequate convergent validity (Hair et al. 2010). Reliabilities are above .8 suggesting convergence or internal consistency. Discriminant validity was also confirmed through examination of AVE and Squared Inter-Construct Correlation.

4.2 Hypotheses Testing

Structural Equation Modelling (SEM) was conducted in AMOS to test the proposed hypotheses. The structural model yields a χ^2 of 1360.434 (473 degrees of freedom), $\chi^2/df = 2.876$, a comparative fit index (CFI) of .952, Tucker-Lewis Index (TLI) of .946, Root Mean Square Error of Approximation (RMSEA) of .062 and Standardized Root Mean Residual (SRMR) of .0734 as an assessment of the data. This means the structural model achieves good fit. The relationship paths and their strength are shown in Table 1.

Table 1. Direct path estimates

Proposed path	Path estimate	Significance
Anthropomorphism → Social presence	.455	***
Parasocial interaction → Social presence	.307	***
Personalization → Social presence	.183	***
Social presence → eWOM	.593	***
Social presence → Customer loyalty	.730	***

Mediation analysis was performed to test the proposed mediating role of perceived social presence of the customer experience. Table 2 shows the results of the analysis.

Table 2. Mediation path estimates

Mediation path	Estimate	P value
Anthropomorphism → Social presence → Customer loyalty	.384	.000
Anthropomorphism → Social presence → eWOM	.377	.000
Parasocial interaction → Social presence → Customer loyalty	.411	.000
Parasocial interaction → Social presence → eWOM	.404	.000
Personalization → Social presence → Customer loyalty	.146	.001
Personalization → Social presence → eWOM	.144	.001

5 Discussion and Conclusion

5.1 Discussion

The empirical assessment of the data shows statistical support for all five direct relationships, and also finds statistical support for the mediating effects of social presence. It is confirmed that anthropomorphism of AI has a strong effect ($\beta = .455$, $p = .000$) on the perceived social presence of the customer experience. This means that by imbuing humanlike characteristics on AI, perceptions of being accompanied by another human is increased. This finding extends insights gained Holzwarth et al. (2006), Kim et al. (2019) and Mende et al. (2019) suggested that anthropomorphism has positive effects on consumer evaluation of a technology and behavioural outcomes. Further, the finding gives an idea how the human-object relationship between AI and the customer can become more sociable and relatable, which answers a call by Schweitzer et al. (2019) to study these new types of relationships more closely. Findings indicate that human-likeness will results in a better experience. Adding to this, findings also support the hypothesised positive effect of para-social interaction on perceived social presence ($\beta = .307$, $p = .000$). This highlights the importance of examining para-social (human-like) interactions with technology because AI is changing the way in which companies engage with their customers (Grewal et al. 2020; Yadav and Pavlou 2020). Further, interaction is proved to become a source of value if it is able to affect customer experience, which shows the relevance of integrating AI into customer service where it can contribute to a positive customer experience. The results also show a positive effect of personalisation on perceived social presence ($\beta = .183$, $p = .000$). While not as strong as the effects of anthropomorphism and para-social interaction, the effect is still significant and important for marketing practitioners who integrate AI into their service offerings to collect, analyse and store customer data to provide higher levels of personalisation. The results show a clear link between higher personalisation and improved customer experience, thus providing reassurance for investment into AI for the purpose of improving the customer experience. Further, the findings reveal strong positive effects of perceived social presence on eWOM ($\beta = .593$, $p = .000$) as well as customer loyalty ($\beta = .730$, $p = .000$). Results from mediation analysis confirm all proposed paths and show that perceived social presence of the customer experience serves as mediator for the relationships between anthropomorphism of AI, para-social interaction with AI, and personalisation and both outcome variables (intentions to engage in eWOM and customer loyalty). This confirms and extends previous findings by Bleier et al. (2019) and provides clear evidence that AI is not only able to improve the customer experience but also outcomes of experience as suggested by Brandtzaeg and Følstad (2018).

5.2 Limitations

As with any research, this study is also subject to limitations that must be acknowledged and taken into consideration when interpreting its findings and conducting further research. One limitation of this research is that it has examined customer loyalty as outcome of company-customer interactions that are mediated by AI instead of measuring actual purchase behaviour. Operational or technical measurements relating to purchase behaviour or performance of the retailer who utilised the AI technology have not been included in this study. Another limitation related to the selected method of collecting data through a questionnaire with a non-probability sample. Non-probability samples cannot be automatically generalized beyond the context and scope of this study. However, the results provide a good indication of the effects of integrating AI as intelligent agents into customer service for the purpose of improving customer experience and customer loyalty.

5.3 Future Research

Future research should examine whether previous experience of interacting with AI technology has an influence on consumer evaluations and attitudes regarding their experience with AI agents during service encounters. This research required consumers to have engaged with AI prior to the study, however, no difference was made between the level of experience respondents had with AI technology. In addition, future research could examine the strategies by which humans try to distinguish AI and human employees and whether personal preference for AI or human service agents affects customer experience and loyalty. Schmitt (2020) argues that humans have a preference towards their own kind, which the author terms "speciesism". Future research should investigate the role of personal preference and speciesism and its implications to further strengthen our understanding of the effect of AI agents into service encounters.

5.4 Conclusion

Interactions between customers and AI-enabled technology are taking place every day in the online environment, where AI becomes "the other" with whom customers communicate during their shopping experience. This study advances our understanding of consumer experiences that are affected by AI technology and how AI affects customer loyalty and eWOM. The findings from this study confirm that AI affects perceived social presence of the customer experience, thus providing empirical evidence for marketers who invest heavily into efforts of making their AI technology more human-like. The study adopts SRT as theoretical lens and extends previous work by quantifying how AI is not only able to affect customer experience but also outcomes of experience, which contributes both to a better theoretical understanding of customer experience and customer loyalty in the online environment, but also a practical contribution due to the circumstance that findings clearly demonstrate how marketers can utilize AI as tool in their marketing strategies.

Acknowledgment. No acknowledgements.

Conflict of Interest. No potential conflict of interest is reported by the authors.

References

Abrantes, J., Seabra, C., Lages, C., Jayawardhena, C.: Drivers of in-group and out-of-group electronic word-of-mouth (eWOM). Eur. J. Mark. **47**(7), 1067–1088 (2013)

Aggarwal, P., McGill, A.: Is that car smiling at me? Schema congruity as a basis for evaluating anthropomorphized products. J. Consum. Res. **34**(4), 468–479 (2007)

Barnes, K., Coughlin, F., O'Leary, H., Bruck, N., Bazin, G., Kaufmann, W.: Anxiety-like behavior in Rett syndrome: characteristics and assessment by anxiety scales. J. Neurodev. Disord. **7**(1), 30–44 (2015)

Bell, E., Bryman, A., Harley, B.: Business Research Methods, 5th edn. Oxford University Press, Oxford (2018)

Bleier, A., Harmeling, C., Palmatier, R.: Creating effective online customer experiences. J. Mark. **83**(2), 98–119 (2019)

Boden, M.A.: Mind as Machine: a history of cognitive science, vol. 1. Oxford University Press, Oxford (2006)

Brandtzaeg, P., Følstad, A.: Chatbots: changing user needs and motivations. Interactions **25**(5), 38–43 (2018)

Brill, T., Munoz, L., Miller, R.: Siri, Alexa, and other digital assistants: a study of customer satisfaction with artificial intelligence applications. J. Mark. Manag. **35**(15–16), 1401–1436 (2019)

Canbek, N., Mutlu, M.: On the track of artificial intelligence: learning with intelligent personal assistants. Int. J. Hum. Sci. **13**(1), 592–601 (2016)

Cherif, E., Lemoine, J.: Anthropomorphic virtual assistants and the reactions of internet users: an experiment on the assistant's voice. Rech. Appl. Mark. **34**(1), 28–47 (2019)

Choi, J., Lee, H., Kim, Y.: The influence of social presence on customer intention to resuse online recommender systems: the roles of personalisation and product type. Int. J. Electron. Commer. **16**(1), 129–153 (2011)

Davenport, T., Guha, A., Grewal, D., Bressgott, T.: How artificial intelligence will change the future of marketing. J. Acad. Mark. Sci. **48**(1), 24–42 (2019). https://doi.org/10.1007/s11747-019-00696-0

Diederich, S., Brendel, A.B., Kolbe, L.M.: Designing anthropomorphic enterprise conversational agents. Bus. Inf. Syst. Eng. **62**(3), 193–209 (2020). https://doi.org/10.1007/s12599-020-006 39-y

Duan, Y., Edwards, J., Dwivedi, Y.: Artificial intelligence for decision making in the era of big data – evolution, challenges and research agenda. Int. J. Inf. Manage. **48**, 63–71 (2019)

Edwards, A., Edwards, C., Westerman, D., Spence, P.: Initial expectations, interactions and beyond with social robots. Comput. Hum. Behav. **90**, 308–314 (2019)

Epley, N.: A mind like mine: the exceptionally ordinary underpinnings of anthropomorphism. J. Assoc. Consum. Res. **3**(4), 591–598 (2018)

Epley, N., Waytz, A., Cacioppo, J.: On seeing human: a three factor theory of anthropomorphism. Psychol. Rev. **114**(4), 864–886 (2007)

Gefen, D., Karahanna, E., Straub, D.: Trust and TAM in online shopping: an integrated model. MIS Q. **27**(1), 51–90 (2003)

Grewal, D., Hulland, J., Kopalle, P., Karahanna, E.: The future of technology and marketing: a multidisciplinary perspective. J. Acad. Mark. Sci. **48**(1), 1–8 (2020)

Gunkel, D.: Communication and artificial intelligence: opportunities and challenges for the 21st century. Futures Commun. **1**(1), 1–25 (2012)

Gutierrez, A., O'Leary, S., Rana, N., Dwivedi, Y., Calle, T.: Using privacy calculus theory to explore entrepreneurial directions in mobile location-based advertising: identifying intrusiveness as the critical risk factor. Comput. Hum. Behav. **95**, 295–306 (2019)

Guzman, A.L.: Ontological boundaries between humans and computers and the implications for human-machine communication. Hum.-Mach. Commun. **1**, 37–54 (2020)

Haenlein, M., Kaplan, A.: A brief history of artificial intelligence: on the past, present, and future of artificial intelligence. Calif. Manag. Rev. **61**(4), 5–14 (2019)

Hair, J., Black, W., Babin, B., Anderson, R.: Multivariate data analysis. Pearson Prentice Hall, New Jersey (2010)

Hair, J., Money, A., Samouel, P., Page, M.: Research Methods for Business. Wiley. Hoboken (2007)

Hartmann, T., Goldhoorn, C.: Horton and Wohl revisited: exploring viewers' experience of parasocial interaction. J. Commun. **61**, 1104–1121 (2011)

Hennig-Thurau, T., Gwinner, K., Walsh, G., Gremler, D.: Electronic word-of-mouth via consumer-opinion platforms: what motivates consumers to articulate themselves on the internet? J. Interact. Mark. **18**, 38–52 (2004)

Hofacker, C., Corsaro, D.: Dystopia and utopia in digital services. J. Mark. Manag. **36**(5–6), 412–419 (2020)

Holzwarth, M., Janiszweski, C., Neumann, M.: The influence of avatars on online consumer shopping behavior. J. Mark. **70**(4), 19–36 (2006)

Huang, M., Rust, R.: Artificial intelligence in service. J. Serv. Res. **21**(2), 155–172 (2018)

Keeling, K., McGoldrick, P., Beatty, S.: Avatars as salespeople: communication style, trust, and intentions. J. Bus. Res. **63**, 793–800 (2010)

Kim, S., Schmitt, B., Thalmann, N.: Eliza in the uncanny valley: anthropomorphizing consumer robots increases their perceived warmth but decreases liking. Mark. Lett. **30**(1), 1–12 (2019)

Kim, H., McGill, A.: Minions for the rich? Financial status changes how consumers see products with anthropomorphic features. J. Consum. Res. **45**(2), 429–450 (2018)

Lu, L., Cai, R., Gursoy, D.: Developing and validating a service robot integration willingness scale. Int. J. Hosp. Manag. **80**, 36–51 (2019)

Mende, M., Scott, M., van Doorn, J., Grewal, D., Shanks, I.: Service robots rising: how humanoid robots influence service experiences and elicit compensatory consumer responses. J. Mark. Res. **56**(4), 535–656 (2019)

Nass, C., Moon, Y.: Machines and mindlessness: social responses to computers. J. Soc. Issues **56**(1), 81–103 (2000)

Prentice, C., Nguyen, M.: Engaging and retaining customers with AI and employee service. J. Retail. Consum. Serv. **56**, 102186 (2020)

Qiu, L., Benbasat, I.: Evaluating anthropomorphic product recommendation agents: a social relationship perspective to designing information systems. J. Manag. Inf. Syst. **25**(4), 145–182 (2009)

Rai, A.: Explainable AI: from black box to glass box. J. Acad. Mark. Sci. **48**(1), 137–141 (2020)

Ramaswamy, V., Ozcan, K.: Offerings as digitalised interactive platforms: a conceptual framework and implications. J. Mark. **82**(4), 19–31 (2018)

Reeves, B., Nass, C.: The Media Equation: how people treat computers, television, and new media like real people and places. CSLI Publications. Stanford **10**, 236605 (1996)

Riskin, J. (ed.): Genesis Redux: Essays in the History and Philosophy of Artificial Life. University of Chicago Press, Chicago (2007)

Saad, S., Abida, F.: Social interactivity and its impact on a user's approach behaviour in commercial websites: a study case of virtual agent presence. J. Mark. Manag. **4**(2), 63–80 (2016)

Saunders, M., Lewis, P., Thornhill, A.: Research Methods for Business Students, 8th edn. Pearson Education Limited, Boston (2019)

Schmitt, B.: Speciecism: an obstacle to AI and robot adoption. Mark. Lett. **31**(1), 3–6 (2020)

Schweitzer, F., Belk, R., Jordan, W., Ortner, M.: Servant, friend or master? The relationships users build with voice-controlled smart devices. J. Mark. Manag. **35**(7–8), 693–715 (2019)

Shankar, V.: How artificial intelligence (AI) is reshaping retailing. J. Retail. **94**(4), vi–xi (2018)

Steinhoff, L., Arli, D., Weaven, S., Kozlenkova, I.V.: Online relationship marketing. J. Acad. Mark. Sci. **47**(3), 369–393 (2018). https://doi.org/10.1007/s11747-018-0621-6

Thomaz, F., Salge, C., Karahanna, E., Hulland, J.: Learning from the dark web: leveraging conversational agents in the era of hyper-privacy to enhance marketing. J. Acad. Mark. Sci. **48**(1), 43–63 (2020)

Van Doorn, J., et al.: Domo arigato Mr. Roboto: emergence of automated social presence in organizational frontlines and customers' service experiences. J. Serv. Res. **20**(1), 43–58 (2017)

Wilson, H., Daugherty, P.: Collaborative intelligence: humans and AI are joining forces. Harv. Bus. Rev. **96**(4), 114–123 (2018)

Yadav, M., Pavlou, P.: Technology-enabled interaction in digital environments: a conceptual foundation for current and future research. J. Acad. Mark. Sci. **48**(1), 132–136 (2020)

Deriving Design Principles for AI-Adaptive Learning Systems: Findings from Interviews with Experts

Tumaini Kabudi[1]([⊠]) [iD], Ilias O. Pappas[1,2], and Dag H. Olsen[1]

[1] Department of Information Systems, University of Agder, Universitetsveien 25, 4630 Kristiansand, Norway
{tumaini.kabudi,ilias.pappas,dag.h.olsen}@uia.no
[2] Department of Computer Science, Norwegian University of Science and Technology, Sem Saelandsvei 9, 7491 Trondheim, Norway

Abstract. AI applications are increasing in the field of education, from laboratory set-ups to contemporary and complex learning systems. A great example of such systems is AI-enabled adaptive learning systems (AI-ALS) that promote adaptive learning. Despite its promised potential, there are challenges such as design issues, highly complex models, and lack of evidence-based guidelines and design principles that hinder the large-scale adoption and implementation of AI-ALS. The goal of this paper thus is to establish a set of empirically grounded design principles (DPs) of AI-ALS, that would serve well in a university context. 22 interviews were con-ducted with experts knowledgeable about the design and development of AI-ALS. Several rounds of coding and deep analysis of the expert interviews revealed features and functionalities of AI-ALS; purposes for designing and using AI-ALS; and recommended improvements for AI-ALS as requirements. These requirements were translated to 13 preliminary DPs. The findings of this study serve as a guide on how to better design AI-ALS, that will improve the learning experiences of students.

Keywords: AI · AIEd · Design principles · Adaptive learning systems · Adaptive learning

1 Introduction

The application of AI in Education (AIEd) has increased due to its promising potential to provide personalized and adaptive learning, provide instant and correct feedback, facilitate meaningful interactions, improve students' engagement and learning outcomes [1]. Thus, AI has been transforming the ways of teaching and learning in education and has contributed to maintaining high quality teaching learning during global crisis like the pandemic [2]. AI in the education field has evolved, from idealized laboratory set-ups to learning contexts with more complexity. These more complex and advanced learning systems are gaining traction in to be used in real learning settings. Examples of such systems include Adaptive Learning systems that are enabled by AI, intelligent tutoring systems, and recommender systems. AI enabled adaptive learning systems (AI-ALS) are platforms that adapt to the learning strategies of students, changing and modifying the order and the difficulty level of learning tasks, based on the abilities of students [3, 4].

The potential and importance of such systems is well established, however, AI enabled learning interventions and applications, especially AI-ALS remain largely at an experimental stage [5, 6]. A recent literature review in the area noted a critical gap between what AI-ALS could be and can do, and what the current systems do, that is how they are implemented in real educational environments [7]. Moreover, few studies in the AIEd field have addressed design issues and highly complex models of these contemporary learning systems [8–10]. In addition, there is still gap in the research of AIEd to provide evidence-based guidelines and support for AI-ALS, as AI technology advances rapidly [9]. Thus, lack of evidence-based guidelines and de-sign principles for AI-ALS applications affect its large-scale implementation and adoption [7, 11]. Most of these AI-ALS are still "restricted to research projects and a few commercial appli-cations" despite their known potential [12]. With AI evolving rapidly in the education field, issues such as the integration of AI-ALS systems within real education contexts need to be addressed.

To further advance AI-ALS in education, this article narrows the gap between exper-imental research and practice by establishing a set of empirically grounded design prin-ciples (DPs) of AI-ALS. These DPs are formulated based on the design, development, and implementation of AI-ALS, that would serve well in a university context. The main research question (RQ) that guided this empirical research is: *What fundamental design principles for developing and implementing an AI-ALS can be dis-tilled from practice?*

To address our RQ we conducted in-depth interviews with AIEd technological experts, who are knowledgeable with the design and development of AI-ALS. Our find-ings contribute to the ongoing research on the digitalisation of education and show how IS research can lead the way in designing the learning systems of the future. The paper will help the AI in Education (AIEd) community, including developers, designers, lecturers, researchers, and other stakeholders to build better understanding on AI-ALS research from different perspectives such as design, development, implementation, and evaluation.

2 Theoretical Background

With AI technology thriving in recent years, its applications in the form of AI-ALS have increased [1, 4]. AI-ALS generally are digital learning tools enabled by AI, that "adapts, as well as possible, to the learner, so that the learning process is optimized, and/or the stu-dent performance improve" [13]. Most recent AI-ALS include Smart Sparrow, Knewton, Fishtree, INSPIREus, ProSys, QuizBot, OPERA, LearnSmart, Connect ™, ACTIVE-MATH, and Student Diagnosis, Assistance, Evaluation System based on Artificial Intel-ligence (StuDiAsE) [7]. AI-ALS were developed to help address most challenges that occurred in technology enhanced learning environments. These included resource lim-itations, difficulty in students attaining and mastering their learning skills, variety in learning abilities of students, and diversity of students' backgrounds [9, 14]. AI-ALS motivates students to embark on their own learning journey through automated feedback cycles in these systems. The capability of AI-ALS to enable personalized learning of students sparks interest in the field of education, and thus marks its enthusiasm to be used [1]. This is mainly due to the promising potentials of the systems such to provide customized learning to students (adaptive learning), to offer fast feedback and dynamic assessments, and to facilitate meaningful group collaborations and engagements in learning settings [15].

The design of AI-ALS has been influenced by research on AI, learning analytics, educational data mining techniques, learning taxonomies and cognitive theories [10]. The essential and underlying design characteristics of these systems consist of user interface (that handles the interaction between the learning system and students); monitoring of the students' internal state (e.g., cognitive, behavioural, and emotional); observation of the external state of the learning environment; and adaptation [7, 16]. However, while numerous AI-ALS are modelled as above, the inherent and basic design principles that guide the design, development and even implementation of these systems are not clearly known. Most of these AI-ALS are still "restricted to research projects and a few commercial applications" despite their known potential [12]. Not only that, but design issues of these systems are also still mentioned in literature [7]. There are still several problems that have yet to be addressed by AI-ALS. These issues include difficulty in attaining learners' skills, issues related to students' backgrounds and profiles and personalization issues [3, 7]. Thus, this research aims to address the above-mentioned gaps by deriving fundamental and common user-centred DPs for AI-ALS.

3 Research Method

The authors accomplished the empirical examination of the DPs via expert inter-views and content analysis. Expert interviews, in a semi-structured format, were used to obtain, explore, and understand the perspectives of AI technological subjects in-volved on developing, designing, and implementing AI-ALS. Experts are defined as people who have the technical, process and interpretive knowledge in their areas of expertise [17, 18].We defined and categorized our experts in three major interview sub-jects: Developer & Designer and Researchers. Developer & Designer is an inter-view subject that discussed on the design and developing aspects of AI-ALS. The researchers group consisted of AI technological experts that are interested and re-search extensively on AI in education. The authors identified 143 experts, based on literature search and their Google Scholar profiles, and who appeared to be active in the AIEd community, based on their publications on AI-ALS. They were randomly selected using convenience sampling technique. The experts were then contacted via email. Data were collected until theoretical saturation was achieved on various aspects of participant experiences and perspectives regarding the development, design, and implementation of AI-ALS, which was the focus of this study. A total of 22 experts were interviewed. Table 1 shows the profile of our experts.

The interviews were conducted face-to-face, using videoconferencing tool. The interviews were conducted in English. The interviews were transcribed verbatim, focusing mainly on the spoken word. Qualitative content analysis was used to evaluate expert interviews. This method is the most comprehensive and exact way to analyse data collected

Table 1. Respondents profile

Expert ID	Category	Profession	Country
1	Designer & Developer	Professor	Australia
2	Designer & Developer	PhD Student	Switzerland
3	Researcher	Project Manager	France
4	Researcher	Lecturer	Tunisia
5	Researcher	Professor	Switzerland
6	Designer & Developer	Software Engineer	United Kingdom
7	Researcher	Professor	Germany
8	Researcher	Senior Lecturer	United Kingdom
9	Researcher	Assistant Professor	United States of America
10	Designer & Developer	PhD Student	United States of America
11	Designer & Developer	Head of Research Lab	Russia
12	Researcher	Professor	China
13	Researcher	Professor	United Kingdom
14	Designer & Developer	Professor	United States of America
15	Researcher	Professor	Brazil
16	Designer & Developer	Lecturer	Singapore
17	Designer & Developer	Professor	Morocco
18	Designer & Developer	PhD Student	South Korea
19	Researcher	Lecturer	Ukraine
20	Researcher	PhD Student	United States of America
21	Researcher	Professor	United Kingdom
22	Researcher	Professor	United States of America

qualitatively [19]. The data analysis involved transcribing the recorded conversation with interviewees. The interviews were recorded, both in video and audio formats, total approximately 22 h of conversation. This is a large amount of qualitative data, where each recording took 6 to 8 h of transcription work. Qualitative content analysis orders the obtained information according to certain theoretically and empirically reasonable points. In this study, the information obtained from experts, was analysed using codes. All transcriptions were entered into NVivo 12 software for qualitative analysis. An initial list of generated codes was created, based on identified and placed phrases, sentences, and paragraphs. Using an iterative approach, the patterns were revised, updated, and recategorized. In the next section provides the resultant first order categories, in form of requirements are provided.

4 Presentation of Results

This section presents the findings of our data collection. The findings reported in this paper are based on the analysed data collected from 22 interviewees. Of the 22 experts who were interviewed, 6 were female, and 16 were male. Majority came from USA (5) followed by UK (4) and Switzerland (2). Moreover, majority of these experts came from universities and research groups. Three types of results are provided be-fore discussing the findings of the study, as seen below.

4.1 Meaningful Features and Functionalities of AI-ALS

Based on the experts' answers, both functional and non-functional requirements for AI-ALS were gathered. The author derived and formed several categories. The first category, based on experts' answers on Part 2 questions, included identified meaningful features and functionalities of AI-ALS (features that worked well).

Experts identified Game-based learning component (F1) important and that worked well. Specifically, expert No.18 stated, *"Many of my students like to "play games"; gamifications seem nice to "catch" the student's attention"*. Moreover, experts identified Individualized/Personalized Feedback and Remediation as an important feature, and thus was coded as (F2). In particular, expert No.7 justified this by explaining that *"There are some students that really like that they get personalized feedback"."* Other themes that were coded as features and functionalities that worked well, are depicted in Table 2.

Table 2. Meaningful features and functionalities of AI-ALS

ID	Features and Functionalities of AI-ALS that worked well
F1.	Game based Learning Component
F2.	Individualized/Personalized Feedback and Remediation
F3.	Adaptation mechanisms - Adaptivity Methods
F4.	Effective Learning Analytics
F5.	Measurement Of Skills, And Thus Attainment of Mastery of Skills
F6.	Interactive visualized educational dashboard (e.g., LA dashboards)
F7.	AI & ML Techniques/Algorithms
F8.	Facial Affective Computing to Develop an Affective Interface
F9.	Application Of Learning Theories/Taxonomies
F10.	Affective Model (based on emotions)-Multimodal Analytics
F11.	Student Model -Knowledge Model
F12.	Learner Profiles
F13.	Teacher Writing their own Content for Assessment
F14.	Learning Early-Warning Model (based on Knowledge Points)
F15.	Well-scaffold activities and Interventions

4.2 Features and Functionalities of AI-ALS that Had Issues

The other category, based on experts' answers on Part 2 questions, included identified features and functionalities of AI-ALS that did not work well. Algorithm Not Recognizing the Level of Skill You need To Master was identified in this category, and thus was coded as (C1). Expert No.2 gave an example that highlights on this issue: *"If, if there's like a, you get like an augmentation, highlighting aggregation…and you think OK, you write a new argument, but the algorithm doesn't recognize it, and that's probably like the biggest flaw, right?"*.

Another feature that did not work well was coded as No Assessment of Open-Ended Questions as expected (C2). Expert No.1 gave an example of a scenario where such an issue occurred *"Another thing that we did not like is not to have any functionality that would assess an open-ended question"*. Lack of "Human in the Loop" Model was another functionality of AI-ALS that users complained on as an issue. More themes that were coded as features and functionalities of AI-ALS that did not work well, are identified in the Table 3.

Table 3. Meaningful features and functionalities of AI-ALS

ID	Features and Functionalities of AI-ALS that had issues
C1.	Algorithm Not Recognizing the Level of Skill You need To Master
C2.	No Assessment of Open-Ended Questions
C3.	Facial Affective Computing to Develop an Affective Interface is Missing
C4.	Not Enough Graduations of Difficulty for A student
C5.	Lack of "Human in the Loop" Model

4.3 Meaningful Features and Functionalities of AI-ALS

Purposes for developing and using AI-ALS was the type of results identified, based on the experts' answers on Part 2 questions. Our experts identified the reasons of developing and using AI-ALS in a learning environment. The main coded purpose stated by our experts was mainly to enhance Students' Cognitive & Learning Skills that need to be Mastered (i.e., Mastery Learning) (P1). Expert No. 20 highlighted the significance of enhancing students' skills: *"It's important to know when the students reach mastery…so that you can get them out of the current problem set ….and move them onto a new one….and keep them you know working efficiently….and not practicing problems that they don't need to practice."*

Another major identified and coded purpose was (P2) to provide (Adaptive, Individualized and Peer) feedback. Expert No.5 explained that such systems that provide peer feedback, or individualized feedback *"…try to inform your learning progress because it's important to reflect upon… like have I really understood this, am I really capable of applying this or something where you need?.......Something like feedback on right?"*.

To have AI techniques, ML, Adaptation mechanisms to provide recommendations and enhance adaptiveness was also coded as a theme (P3). Expert No.3 indicated that *"But in reality, an adaptive system is based really in some basic characteristic to adapt some aspects of the content..."*. Expert No.17 stated that *"The objective is to offer learners adaptive learning processes based on their style and knowledge. This will allow a personalized and efficient learning since the learner could use resources that he prefers and could advance on his own pace"*. Other coded themes that were mentioned by our experts as Purposes, and its frequency, are highlighted in the table below (Table 4).

Table 4. Purposes for developing and using AI-ALS

ID	Purposes for developing and using AI-ALS
P1.	Enhance Students' Cognitive & Learning Skills that need to be Mastered (i.e., Mastery Learning)
P2.	Provide (Adaptive, Individualized and Peer) Feedback
P3.	Have AI techniques, ML, Adaptation mechanisms to provide recommendations and enhance adaptiveness
P4.	To help students with boredom, frustrations, and emotion issues
P5.	Know Students' Personal Preferences and Skill Level
P6.	To detect Student's Progression
P7.	Provide Adaptive Assessment
P8.	To predict how the student is learning to determine what to do next
P9.	To be able to detect student inquiry
P10.	Enhance the Cognitive State and Abilities of Students
P11.	Provide Adaptive Support To students based on Learning Analytics Data

5 Discussion

As illustrated above in the Results Sections, 13 Features and Functionalities that worked well (F), 5 Features and Functionalities that had issues (C) and 11 Purposes of building AI-ALS (P) were identified. These Features, Functionalities and Purposes were identified as requirements for designing and developing AI-ALS. An interesting insight that is revealed from this study is the importance to enhance Students' Cognitive & Learning Skills that need to be Mastered (i.e., Mastery Learning). Moreover, provide (Adaptive, Individualized and Peer) Feedback is also identified as an important theme. These themes have been identified in accordance with the recommendations of [3, 7] for the design of AI-ALS to address issues such as difficulty obtaining learners' skills, background and profile issues, and personalization issues. Other relevant themes that were identified in this study included Learning Analytics and Automated Assessment. The functional requirements, that include the 13 Fs and 5 Cs emphasize on the features and functions AI-ALS should have and perform. The 11 Ps that comprises the non-functional requirements, emphasize more on the performance characteristics (i.e., what the system intends to do and help) of AI-ALS. Both these functional and non-functional requirements are used to build up the expected preliminary empirically DPs of an AI-ALS.

The importance of these features and functionalities were also identified during the expert interviews' session. Specifically, expert No. 22 stated that *"....to create mastery learning requires a complex interplay between the analytics, **the model design, the system activity design** and then how you deploy it in interventions"*. Furthermore, expert No. 19 also highlighted the essence of such models by stating *"if you don't use **the model of this student (student model) and the model of the of his knowledge**, you cannot automatically......Uh, consider the progress of the student"*. Thus, these functional and non-functional requirements are used to build up the expected preliminary empirically DPs of an AI-ALS. The requirements were analysed based on their similarities, differences, and dependencies, and then grouped to avoid differences.

It must be noted that the DPs are not organized in any prioritized order. Moreover, the author understands that these categorized and identified parts of the system are not separated but are so interconnected to form the complex connected AI-ALS environment. Expert No. 22 elaborated on these by stating *"In general, the design of these systems is a highly complex integrated process, and if you don't get all aspects of what you talked about ...for a certain kind of technology, the technology won't work."*. Thus, 13 preliminary DPs for an AI-ALS based on these results were formulated, and the number of experts that stated them are depicted below (Table 5).

Table 5. Preliminary DPs for an AI-ALS

Design principle	Requirements	Expert ID
Principle of Automated Assessment: AI-ALS should include more specialized AI-techniques and ML algorithms to detect and assess well the open-ended questions	F7. AI & ML Techniques/Algorithms	1, 7, 9, 11, 12, 13, 16, 17, 19, 20
	C1. Algorithm Not Recognizing the Level of Skill You need To Master	
	C2. No Assessment of Open-Ended Questions	
	P3. Have AI techniques, ML, Adaptation mechanisms to provide recommendations and enhance adaptiveness	

(continued)

Table 5. (*continued*)

Design principle	Requirements	Expert ID
	P8. To predict how the student is learning in order to determine what to do next	
	P9. To be able to detect student inquiry	
Principle of Human-in-the Loop (HITL): AI-ALS should incorporate Human in the Loop Model	C5. Lack of "Human in the Loop" Model	1, 16
Principle of Students' Skills Mastery: AI-ALS should have distinct Modules for Building and Measuring students' Cognitive & Learning Skills that need to be Mastered (i.e., Mastery Learning)	F5. Measurement Of Skills, And Thus Attainment of Mastery of Skills	2, 5, 7, 9, 10, 11, 13, 14, 15, 17, 18, 20, 21, 22
	P1. Enhance Students' Cognitive & Learning Skills that need to be Mastered (i.e., Mastery Learning)	
	P5. Know Students' Personal Preferences and Skill Level	
	P6. To detect Student's Progression	
	F11. Student Model-Knowledge Model	
	P10. Enhance the Cognitive State and Abilities of Students	
Principle of Early-Warning Model: AI-ALS should include an Early-Warning Model for Learning, based on Knowledge Points	F14. Learning Early-Warning Model (based on Knowledge Points	10, 11, 12, 19, 20, 22
Principle of Games-based learning: AI-ALS should include games resources and components for learning	F1. Game based Learning Component	10, 13, 14, 15
Principle of Learning Analytics (LA): AI-ALS should include an effective LA module	F4. Effective Learning Analytics	1, 2, 11, 12, 13, 14, 16, 19

(*continued*)

Table 5. (*continued*)

Design principle	Requirements	Expert ID
	P6. To detect Student's Progression	
	F6. Interactive visualized educational dashboard (e.g., LA dashboards)	
	P11. Provide Adaptive Support To students based on Learning Analytics Data	
Principle of Affecting Learning Model: AI-ALS should include an Affective Model (based on emotions), where Multimodal Analytics will be done. It should also include an Affective Interface	F10. Affective Model (based on emotions)-Multimodal Analytics	2, 6, 10, 13, 14, 16, 20, 21
	P4. To help students with boredom, frustrations, and emotion issues	
	F8. Facial Affective Computing to Develop an Affective Interface	
	C3. Facial Affective Computing to Develop an Affective Interface is Missing	
	P4. To help students with boredom, frustrations, and emotion issues	
Principle of Personalized and Adaptive Feedback: AI-ALS should provide Individualized/Personalized, Adaptive and Peer Feedback; and Remediation	F2. Individualized/Personalized Feedback and Remediation	2, 5, 7, 11, 12, 13, 16, 20, 22
	P2. Provide (Adaptive, Individualized and Peer) Feedback	
Principle of Sustainable Design: AI-ALS should be context-sensitive i.e., integrate environmental affordances and learning theories/taxonomies into the design	F9. Application Of Learning Theories/Taxonomies	1, 2, 5, 7, 11, 12

(*continued*)

Table 5. (*continued*)

Design principle	Requirements	Expert ID
Principle of Recommender and Adaptations Mechanisms: AI-ALS should include adaptation mechanisms, to provide recommendations, enhance adaptiveness and ensure graduations of difficulty	F3. Adaptation mechanisms - Adaptivity Methods	3, 4, 9, 10, 11, 12, 13, 15, 18, 22
	C4. Not Enough Graduations of Difficulty for A student	
	P7. Provide Adaptive Assessment	
	P3. Have AI techniques, ML, Adaptation mechanisms to provide recommendations and enhance adaptiveness	
Principle of Actionable information: AI-ALS should have "advanced/updated" learner profiles - classification of students based on their learning strategies	F12. Learner Profiles i.e., providing actionable information about learners and their learning, and give the right type of assessment tasks (whether to learn by text or videos)	11, 13, 17, 22
	F13. Well-scaffold activities and Interventions	
Principle of Teacher–AI Complementarity: Teachers should be included in the design and development of AI-ALS e.g. write and create their own content	F13. Teacher Writing their own Content for Assessment	2, 4, 10, 11, 14, 16, 20, 21, 22
Principle of Responsible AI: AI-ALS should be fair, transparent, explainable, and human-centric. Privacy and Security aspects should be considered	F14. Learning Early-Warning Model (based on Knowledge Points	12, 14, 20, 21
	C5. Lack of "Human in the Loop" Model	

6   Implications and Future Recommendations

The study contributes to the ongoing research on the digitalisation of education. We have identified a set of empirically grounded design principles (DPs) of AI-ALS that show how IS research can lead the way in designing the learning systems of the future. The findings presented above have both theoretical and practical implications. This study contributes to the field of AIEd, by identifying a set of empirically grounded design principles that can be used to develop, implement, and improve AI-ALS. This paper contributes to AIEd research by following the recent call for future work to build evidence-based guidelines and design principles for AI-ALS applications [7, 11]. Most of these design statements, support main findings in existing research such as of [4, 9, 10] and emphasize them. The findings of this study showed the essence analytics of learners' data, behaviour, and emotions, to support learning and teaching activities in education [10, 20]. This study also serves as a guide for developers and AIEd technological experts on how to better design AI-ALS, that will solve identified learning challenges and improve learning experiences of students. The study not only guide AI-ALS designers, developers, and technological experts, but also educators and researchers, who spearhead AI based learning interventions through research and practice.

The formulated DPs are not theoretically grounded only, but also empirically as they have been utilized to develop existing AI-ALS such as Smart Sparrow and ASSIST-MENTS. However, the extent of applicability of these DPs is not well known. Thus, our findings can help researchers and practitioners to better design the learning systems of the future and conduct studies on validating and examining the effectiveness of these DPs. In the long term, we aim to not only provide preliminary DPs, but also empirical evaluations of our DPs for AI-ALS. The preliminary empirically DPs serves as a snapshot of the current AIEd practice, which may stimulate more empirical studies in this field.

The study, especially with the methodology used, is not without limitations. The sample population chosen might hinder the transferability and generalizability of the study given that the author worked with a small sample within the context of AIEd field. Thus, given the small sample size of the study, further research should focus on incorporating more perspectives and opinions from other experts in AIEd community. Moreover, the provides perspectives from experts in a developed context (U.S and Europe) and little from the developing countries. This might lead a potential bias in our findings. Further research should include and compare from other countries, especially in the developing context.

References

1. Park, H., Kim, K., Robertson, C.: The impact of active learning with adaptive learning systems in general education information technology courses. In: SAIS 2018 Proceedings (2018)
2. Pappas, I.O., Giannakos, M.N.: Rethinking learning design in IT education during a pandemic. In: Frontiers in Education, vol. 6 (2021)
3. Xie, H., Chu, H.C., Hwang, G.J., Wang, C.C.: Trends and development in technology-enhanced adaptive/personalized learning: a systematic review of journal publications from 2007 to 2017. Comput. Educ. **140** (2019)

4. Nguyen, A., Gardner, L., Sheridan, D.: Data analytics in higher education: an integrated view. J. Inf. Syst. Educ. **31**(1), 61–71 (2020)

5. Verdú, E., et al.: Intelligent tutoring interface for technology enhanced learning in a course of computer network design. In: Proceedings - Frontiers in Education Conference, FIE 2015, vol. 2015-Febru, no. February (2015)

6. Baker, R.S.: Stupid tutoring systems, intelligent humans. Int. J. Artif. Intell. Educ. **26**(2), 600–614 (2016). https://doi.org/10.1007/s40593-016-0105-0

7. Kabudi, T., Pappas, I., Olsen, D.H.: AI-enabled adaptive learning systems: a systematic mapping of the literature. Comput. Educ. Artif. Intell. **2**, 100017 (2021)

8. Li, A.T., Liu, D., Xu, S.X.: Design challenge levels in e-learning? Insights from a large-scale field experiment. In: International Conference on Information Systems, ICIS 2020 - Making Digital Inclusive: Blending the Local and the Global (2020)

9. Wambsganss, T., Rietsche, R.: Towards designing an adaptive argumentation learning tool. In: 40th International Conference on Information Systems, ICIS 2019 (2019)

10. Nguyen, A., Tuunanen, T., Gardner, L., Sheridan, D.: Design principles for learning analytics information systems in higher education. Eur. J. Inf. Syst. **30**(5), 541–568 (2021)

11. Zhang, K., Aslan, A.B.: AI technologies for education: recent research & future directions. Comput. Educ. Artif. Intell. **2**, 100025 (2021)

12. Essa, A.: A possible future for next generation adaptive learning systems. Smart Learn. Environ. **3**(1), 1–24 (2016). https://doi.org/10.1186/s40561-016-0038-y

13. van der Vorst, T., Jelicic, N.: Artificial Intelligence in Education: Can AI bring the full potential of personalized learning to education? Calgary: International Telecommunications Society (ITS) (2019)

14. Kabudi, T., Pappas, I., Olsen, D.H.: Systematic literature mapping on AI-enabled contemporary learning systems. In: 26th Americas Conference on Information Systems, AMCIS 2020 (2020)

15. Addanki, K., Holdsworth, J., Hardy, D., Myers, T.: Academagogy for enhancing adult online learner engagement in higher education. In: Proceedings of the 2020 AIS SIGED International Conference on Information Systems Education and Research (2020)

16. Hou, M., Fidopiastis, C.: A generic framework of intelligent adaptive learning systems: from learning effectiveness to training transfer. Theor. Issues Ergon. Sci. **18**(2), 167–183 (2017)

17. Bogner, A., Littig, B., Menz, W.: Introduction: expert interviews—an introduction to a new methodological debate. In: Interviewing Experts, pp. 1–13. Palgrave Macmillan, London (2009)

18. Mergel, I., Edelmann, N., Haug, N.: Defining digital transformation: results from expert interviews. Gov. Inf. Q. (2019)

19. Creswell, J.W., Creswell, J.D.: Research Design: Qualitative, Quantitative, and Mixed Methods Approaches. SAGE Publications (2017)

20. Giannakos, M.N., Sharma, K., Pappas, I.O., Kostakos, V., Velloso, E.: Multimodal data as a means to understand the learning experience. Int. J. Inf. Manag. **48**, 108–119 (2019)

The Impact of Functional and Psychological Barriers on Algorithm Aversion – An IRT Perspective

Hasan Mahmud[1]([✉]) [ID], A. K. M. Najmul Islam[1] [ID], Ranjan Kumar Mitra[2] [ID], and Ahmed Rizvan Hasan[2] [ID]

[1] LUT University, 53850 Lappeenranta, Finland
{hasan.mahmud,najmul.islam}@lut.fi
[2] University of Dhaka, Dhaka 1000, Bangladesh
{ranjan.ais,rizvan}@du.ac.bd

Abstract. The application of artificial intelligence (AI) in decision-making is regarded as the most impactful disruption in an organization's digitalization. However, the benefits of the algorithmic decision can be leveraged only if the managers of an organization adopt this technology. Research found that despite the superior performance of algorithms, people discount algorithmic decisions either deliberately or unintentionally, a phenomenon known as algorithm aversion. In this regard, the current study seeks to investigate whether managers' innovation resistance, measured by different barriers, has any impact on algorithm aversion. Analyzing the survey data of 167 bank/financial managers, we found that while value barriers, tradition barriers, and image barriers are significantly associated with algorithm aversion, such relationships are absent in the case of usage barriers and risk barriers. The findings of this study have several theoretical and practical implications.

Keywords: Algorithm aversion · Innovation resistance theory · Decision making · Algorithmic decision-making · Artificial intelligence

1 Introduction

With the advent of the "Data Age," organizations are now inundated with a vast amount of information, which is also expected to grow at a faster pace [1]. Research demonstrated that organizations could grow by utilizing this information in decision-making [2]. To understand how an organization uses information in decision-making, understanding the individual's decision-making process is crucial [3]. Human, being "rational animal," [4] generally tends to make a rational decision through making an exhaustive search of available alternatives and selecting the best one [2]. Simon [5] suggested that an individual's rational choice is bounded because the number of alternatives he must identify is so enormous and the amount of information he must process is so big that even making a rational estimation is quite challenging. However, with the introduction

© IFIP International Federation for Information Processing 2022
Published by Springer Nature Switzerland AG 2022
S. Papagiannidis et al. (Eds.): I3E 2022, LNCS 13454, pp. 95–108, 2022.
https://doi.org/10.1007/978-3-031-15342-6_8

of computing technologies and artificial intelligence (AI), individuals' race towards optimal decision-making has been expedited to a great extent [6]. AI serves two basic functions of organizational decision-making: (i) provides suitable alternative courses of action and (ii) provides information processing power [7]. An AI-based system is capable of learning by itself and can reveal hidden insights thereon [8]. Such insight capability bestows AI to become more rational. Therefore, Lindebaum et al. [9] refer to AI decision algorithms as "supercarriers of formal rationality". Furthermore, the decision-making process and outcomes are highly replicable as they are based on transparent logic and mathematics [6]. Thus, given the calculation prowess, processing speed, ability to self-learn and adapt, and high level of rationality, AI algorithms can be seen as a boon in overcoming the bounded rationality of human and organizational decision-making [9].

The potential benefits of an algorithmic decision can be capitalized on if the managers of an organization adopt it. This study builds on innovation resistance theory (IRT) [10] in the managerial decision-making context to understand what prevents managers from adopting algorithms. There are two reasons why we are considering IRT in our study. First, Mahmud et al. [11] found that although there are some studies about the implications and adoption of algorithmic decision-making in the organizational context, there is no study investigating the impact of functional and psychological barriers perceived by the managers on algorithm aversion. An AI-based algorithmic decision is a relatively new addition to most organizations. Many managers even do not have any prior experience dealing with algorithmic decisions. They perceive several psychological and functional barriers while contemplating following the algorithmic decisions. Second, the algorithmic decision system is a complex technology, which is different from other digital technologies that are "easy-to-use and easy-to-deploy" [12]. Therefore, it is necessary to understand how IRT and algorithm aversion are related to each other. Such understanding will help to implement algorithmic decision systems in an organization.

We conducted a cross-sectional survey of 167 bank/financial managers who regularly make decisions about their businesses. Our study holds both theoretical and practical implications in algorithm aversion literature. In terms of theory, our study is among the first to examine IRT in the algorithmic decision. Further, we respond to the call of Mahmud et al. [11] by addressing the need for algorithm aversion research in real-world settings by developing a measurement scale for algorithm aversion. In terms of practice, our study highlights different barriers that affect the managers in adopting algorithmic decisions.

2   Background

2.1   AI Decision and Algorithm Aversion

Organizations are increasingly using AI algorithms in decision-making [9]. In the prior literature, although AI decision has been discussed to some extent, to the best of our knowledge, AI decision is defined nowhere. An AI decision can be better captured by putting together the definitions of both AI and algorithmic decisions. According to Mikalef and Gupta [13] "AI is the ability of a system to identify, interpret, make inferences, and learn from data to achieve predetermined organizational and societal goals". As follows, algorithmic decision-making or simply algorithm is "an automated process that provides decisions independently without the mediation of humans" [11]. Henceforth, AI-based algorithmic decision-making or AI decision can be defined as *an automated process that can identify, interpret, make inferences, and learn from data to suggest decisions or courses of action.*

Algorithm aversion occurs when people show reluctance to use algorithmic decisions either intentionally being familiar with the superior performance of algorithms [14] or unintentionally out of fundamental distrust towards algorithms [15]. Mahmud et al. [11] defined algorithm aversion as "a behavior of discounting algorithmic decisions with respect to one's own decisions or other's decisions, either consciously or unconsciously" [11]. Such aversion is viewed as a behavioral anomaly, which creates an obstacle to fully leveraging the benefits of algorithmic decision-making [16].

Various factors influence algorithm aversion. Based on a systematic literature review, Mahmud et al. [11] identified that factors related to the algorithm (design, delivery, and decision), task (complex vs. simple; subjective vs. objective), individual (personality, demography), and macro environment (uncertainty, cultural) are responsible for aversion. However, in their study, they did not find any study exhibiting the relationships between perceived functional and psychological barriers and algorithm aversion.

2.2 Innovation Resistance

Although some people are pro-innovation, many are resistant to innovation [10]. Their resistance can be attributed to their satisfactory status quo or conflicting belief structure [10]. Innovation resistance can be referred to as the resistance of an individual to innovation, resulting from a perceived belief of either potential changes in the status quo or potential conflicts with current beliefs [10, p. 6]. Several obstructors stymie the adoption of innovation, and scholars classified those into two groups: functional and psychological barriers [17]. Functional barriers consist of usage barriers, value barriers, and risk barriers and occur when an individual perceives a significant change due to the adoption of innovation. On the other hand, psychological barriers comprise traditional barriers and image barriers and arise when an individual perceives a conflict with his/her prior belief [18].

Existing innovation adoption research is primarily dominated by the investigation of motivators and drivers of adoption, thus the inhibitors that obstruct the adoption of innovations seem to be overlooked by the scholars [17]. Scholars imputed this trend to "pro-innovation bias," whereby it is assumed that "all innovations are good and should be adopted by all" [17]. On the contrary, it is found that the major cause of innovation failure is individuals' resistance to adoption [18]. Therefore, Arif et al. [18] suggest that instead of studying the reasons for adoption, researchers and practitioners should concentrate on what prevents adoption.

Innovation resistance theory has widely been used in understanding the adoption of new technology such as internet banking [18], mobile banking [19], mobile gaming [20], and e-tourism [21]. Kaur et al. [19] found that IRT is the most sought choice among researchers to investigate innovation resistance. It has a proven explanatory power of why individuals defy to adopt innovation [22]. It addresses all the major sources of barriers to adoption in the form of functional and psychological barriers [22]. This overarching nature of IRT has led us to borrow this theory in explaining why individuals are averse to an algorithmic decision.

3   Model and Hypothesis Development

To examine why individuals show algorithm aversion, we draw on IRT to investigate the relationship between different perceived barriers and algorithm aversion (Fig. 1).

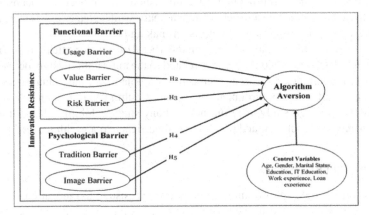

Fig. 1. Proposed research model

3.1   Usage Barrier

The usage barrier is functional and is regarded as the most common cause of innovation resistance [10]. Usage barrier arises when innovation is perceived to conflict with existing practices and requires a change in the status quo [10]. In the case of digital innovation, it is assumed that the usage barrier is related to the perceived complexity and ease of use of innovation [23]. In the context of the current study, being a disruptive innovation, algorithmic decision demands a radical change in existing practice. With the implementation of the algorithmic decisions, managers are expected to forgo their status quo. In addition, an algorithmic decision is complex technology. Therefore, managers need to spend sufficient time learning and getting familiar with the algorithmic decision. Earlier studies suggest that the usage barrier has a significant positive impact on the resistance to technology adoption [17, 21, 24]. Therefore, considering the above discussion and the evidence found in the extant literature, we hypothesize:

H1: Usage barrier is positively correlated with algorithm aversion.

3.2 Value Barrier

The value barrier represents the performance-to-price ratio compared to alternatives [25]. Such representation indicates that the value generated by the innovation should be greater than that of the existing one. Scholars have found a positive relationship between value barriers and innovation resistance in various contexts such as online learning [24], mobile banking [17], and e-tourism [21, 26]. However, the impact of the value barrier has never been studied in the context of algorithmic decision-making. Since using algorithmic decisions is a substantial monetary investment and there is a lack of perceived usefulness due to the black-box nature, we argue that the value barrier discourages managers from adopting algorithmic decisions. Thus, we define our next hypothesis:

H2: Value barrier is positively correlated with algorithm aversion.

3.3 Risk Barrier

The risk barrier represents the risks and uncertainties involved with an innovation [25]. The higher the risk an innovation entails, the slower the adoption of that innovation [10]. The risk barrier is regarded as the most cited barrier to digital innovation adoption [27]. In the context of algorithmic decision-making, managers may perceive various risks and uncertainties in using algorithms. For example, managers tend to work in a highly risky environment, in which they have to pursue decisions considering a lot of uncertainties. Again, many managers lack firsthand knowledge about the accuracy of algorithmic decisions at the pre-adoption stage. Therefore, they perceive uncertainty about the performance of the algorithms. Prior research demonstrates that people abandon even the best possible algorithms if the decision domain and environment are risky and volatile [15]. Extant literature confirmed the positive association between risk barriers and resistance behavior in mobile banking [17], online learning [24], and e-tourism [21]. Therefore, we also argue that the risk barrier obstructs managers to adopt algorithmic decisions. Thus, we propose our next hypothesis:

H3: Risk barrier is positively correlated with algorithm aversion.

3.4 Tradition Barrier

Individuals have their own established daily routines and tradition for their work. They are more comfortable with their habits [24]. Tradition barriers arise when innovation requires changes in this behavior or status quo [23]. John and Klein [28] stated that tradition is deeply ingrained in society and thereby any potential change results in strong repercussions in the form of negative word-of-mouth, boycotts, and even attacks on the change. Therefore, it is assumed that the tradition barrier has a strong negative effect on innovation adoption [29]. In the context of algorithmic decision-making, tradition barriers may arise if the managers are satisfied enough with their conventional way of decision-making and enjoy the discussion with their colleagues and seniors while making decisions. Prior studies found several instances when the tradition barrier is positively related to innovation resistance such as online learning [24], mobile banking [17], and e-tourism [21]. Therefore, bearing on these findings, we define our fourth hypothesis:

H4: Tradition barrier is positively correlated with algorithm aversion.

3.5 Image Barrier

Image is an impression that an entity imprints on the minds of others [30]. It serves as an important cue to evaluate an innovation [24]. If the perceived image is not favorable, then the image can produce a barrier to adoption. Image barriers can emerge from the perception of how difficult or easy to adopt the innovation [25]. In the context of algorithmic decision-making, it is found that negative perception is positively related to algorithm aversion [31]. People have a perception that an algorithm is good at performing objective tasks as it is deviant of subjective judgment capability [32]. Therefore, they trust less on algorithms. Again, people have a negative impression that algorithms may provide biased decisions and lead to some job losses in the future [33]. Prior literature has reported the positive relationship between image barriers and innovation resistance [21, 24]. According to the above discussion, we hypothesize:

H5: Image barrier is positively correlated with algorithm aversion.

4   Methodology

4.1   Measurement Development

Innovation resistance is measured by five constructs: usage barrier, value barrier, risk barrier, tradition barrier, and image barrier. The measurement items for these constructs are adapted from existing scales (see Table 1). For measurement of algorithm aversion, to the best of our knowledge, no previous study has developed scales. Therefore, we construct a five-item algorithm aversion construct following the procedures followed by Mäntymäki et al. [34]. In this regard, we interviewed nine senior bank managers who have experience working in both the information technology and credit department. Four of the interviewees were female and five were male, and their ages varied from 37 to 50 years. We asked them to describe their perceptions and experiences about what characterizes algorithm aversion and what behavior is observed when a user exhibits a reluctance to use algorithmic decision-making. Upon scrutinizing the information collected from interviewees, we identified a list of 7 candidate items measuring algorithm aversion. The items were reviewed by two managers, one Ph.D. student, and two senior academics. In the review process, one item was eliminated as it was deemed redundant by the reviewers. To maintain the quality of the developed items, we employed a card-sorting exercise with 11 managers, who were asked to evaluate the items according to the item's similarity [35]. Participants unanimously labeled five items homogenous and were divided into one item, which was dropped from the final measurement. Finally, five items were accepted to measure algorithm aversion. Consisting of all foregoing constructs and demographic items, a questionnaire was drafted and reviewed by two senior academics. The final survey instrument used in the measurement is presented in Table 1.

Table 1. Measurement items, items loadings, composite reliabilities, and AVEs

Construct	Item	Item loading	CR	AVE
Usage barrier [17, 23]	UB1: *AI Loan Decision Tool* will be difficult to use	0.82	0.89	0.68
	UB2: The use of *AI Loan Decision Tool* will be inconvenient to use	0.88		
	UB3: Usage of *AI Loan Decision Tool* will slow my task	0.84		
	UB4: The process of *AI Loan Decision Tool* is unclear	0.75		
Value barrier [17]	VB1: The use of *AI Loan Decision Tool* is uneconomical	0.72	0.91	0.66
	VB2: *AI Loan Decision Tool* will NOT offer any advantages compared to the current way of decision-making	0.82		
	VB3: The use of *AI Loan Decision Tool* will NOT increase my ability to control my loan decision tasks	0.87		
	VB4: *AI Loan Decision Tool* is NOT a good substitute for the current way of decision-making	0.87		
	VB5: *AI Loan Decision Tool* will NOT resolve the problems associated with the current way of decision-making	0.79		
Risk barrier [39, 40]	RB1: It is probable that *AI Loan Decision Tool* would frustrate me because of its poor performance	0.84	0.90	0.70
	RB2: Compared with the current way of decision making, using the *AI Loan Decision Tool* has more uncertainties	0.83		

(*continued*)

Table 1. (*continued*)

Construct	Item	Item loading	CR	AVE
	RB3: It is uncertain whether *AI Loan Decision Tool* would be as effective as I think. (Dropped)			
	RB4: *AI Loan Decision Tool* might not perform well and create problems	0.82		
	RB5: Overall, using *AI Loan Decision Tool* would be risky	0.85		
Tradition barrier [18, 19, 41, 42]	TB1: I am satisfied with my conventional way of loan decision-making	0.79	0.88	0.72
	TB2: I am so used to evaluating customers' creditworthiness by myself that I will find it difficult to switch to *AI Loan Decision Tool*	0.85		
	TB3: I think making a loan decision by myself will be more pleasant than following the decision provided by *AI Loan Decision Tool*	0.89		
	TB4: I enjoy the discussion with my colleagues and seniors about making loan decisions. (Dropped)			
Image barrier [17, 19, 41]	IB1: I have a very negative image of the *AI Loan Decision Tool*	0.90	0.89	0.73
	IB2: New technology is often too complicated to be useful	0.74		
	IB3: I have such an image that *AI Loan Decision Tool* is difficult to use	0.91		
Algorithm aversion (new scale)	AA1: In loan decisions, I will make the decision by myself rather than follow the decision given by *AI Loan Decision Tool*	0.78	0.89	0.62

(*continued*)

Table 1. (*continued*)

Construct	Item	Item loading	CR	AVE
	AA2: In loan decisions, I will follow the expert's decision rather than follow the decision given by *AI Loan Decision Tool*	0.79		
	AA3: In loan decisions, I will follow human decisions rather than follow decisions given by *AI Loan Decision Tool*	0.83		
	AA4: In loan decisions, I will follow human decisions even human does not provide consistently better decision than *AI Loan Decision Tool*	0.82		
	AA5: In loan decisions, I will NOT follow decisions given by *AI Loan Decision Tool* even it provides consistently better decisions than humans	0.72		

4.2 Data Collection and Analysis

The data were collected from the managers of the banking industry of Bangladesh. From a contextual standpoint, the bank is a forerunner in using algorithmic decisions for the core business process such as loan approval and risk analysis [36]. To collect data, an anonymous online survey link was distributed among the bank managers, selected through convenient sampling. At the beginning of the survey, a brief introduction of algorithmic decision-making and how it works were given to the respondents. Subsequently, an AI loan decision tool was demonstrated based on two loan scenarios. We received 193 responses, out of which 26 responses are discarded due to failing in answering attention check questions. Finally, 167 usable responses were considered for analysis. The age of the respondents ranged from 18 and 55 years, with a mean age of 41 years. Their average experience in working with loan approval is 5.40 years.

Collected data were analyzed using the partial least squares (PLS) approach using SmartPLS 3.0 software. To test the reliability and validity, we adhered to the limits recommended by Fornell and Larcker [37]. We maintained each item loading above 0.7, composite reliability (CR) above 0.8, and average variance extracted (AVE) above 0.5 to ensure the convergent validity (Table 1). To test the discriminant validity, we compare the inter-construct correlations and the square roots of the AVE values presented diagonally in Table 2. The lower off-diagonal correlation values against the square roots of the AVE values suggest a discriminant validity of the constructs. We also examined whether loadings are higher than the cross-loadings to ensure the discriminant validity on the item level and found satisfactory results [38].

Table 2. Square root of the AVEs and Inter-construct correlations

Item	Usage barrier	Value barrier	Risk barrier	Tradition barrier	Image barrier	Algorithm aversion
Usage barrier	**0.822**					
Value barrier	0.726	**0.814**				
Risk barrier	0.713	0.735	**0.834**			
Tradition barrier	0.517	0.523	0.631	**0.847**		
Image barrier	0.657	0.611	0.635	0.586	**0.853**	
Algorithm aversion	0.385	0.402	0.417	0.48	0.441	**0.787**

5 Results and Discussion

5.1 Hypothesis Test Results

To test our proposed hypotheses and examine the significance of the relationships between the dependent variable and the independent variables, we conducted a structural model test. As hypothesized, the results indicate that the value barrier ($\beta = 0.22$, $p < 0.05$), tradition barrier ($\beta = 0.20$, $p < 0.05$), and image barrier ($\beta = 0.22$, $p < 0.05$) have a significant positive effect on algorithm aversion. This result corroborates the findings of existing literature [17, 23]. However, the usage barrier ($\beta = -0.01$, ns) and risk barrier ($\beta = 0.04$, ns) have no significant impact on algorithm aversion. These findings bear a valuable insight for the practitioners and researchers. One explanation for this could be that since bank/financial managers are well-educated, knowledgeable, familiar with the use of technology to some extent, and are used to working in a risky environment, they are less concerned about usage barriers and risk barriers in adopting algorithms. Besides, we also examined the effect of control variables such as age, gender, marital status, education, IT education, work experience, and experience in loan decision-making on algorithm aversion and no such effect was found. The predictors explained 42.30 percent of the variance of algorithm aversion (Fig. 2).

5.2 Implications

Our study lends several contributions that could benefit researchers and practitioners. First, we contribute theoretically by investigating the IRT in the context of algorithm aversion. To the best of our knowledge, potential relationships between different barriers of IRT and algorithm aversion have not been examined in the extant literature. Although the IRT was developed to measure the extent to which different barriers thwart customers to accept technology-based products or services [10], we empirically show that it can be effectively applied in organizational settings to gain an understanding of different barriers to adopting and using technologies for decision making.

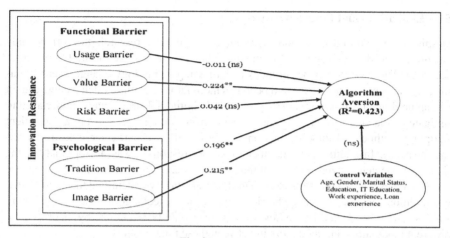

Fig. 2. PLS results

Second, developing a new measurement scale is viewed as a significant contribution to information system research [34]. In this study, we made an initial attempt to propose a new measurement scale for algorithm aversion which can be further validated across different contexts. As such, we contribute methodologically by responding to the call of Mahmud et al. [11], thus overcoming the limitation of algorithm aversion research in the real-world context. This construct will help future researchers to conduct algorithm aversion research with the subjects who are subjected to the use of algorithmic decision-making.

Third, our study reveals several important relationships. We found that managers' perceived psychological barriers and value barriers significantly impact algorithm aversion. Contrary to our hypotheses, we also found that usage barriers and risk barriers do not have any impact on algorithm aversion. This finding bears a valuable insight for the practitioners and researchers. One explanation for this could be that since bank/financial managers are well educated, knowledgeable, and familiar with technology use and working in a risky environment, they are less concerned about usage barriers and risk barriers in adopting algorithms. Rather they are skeptical about the potential benefits of using algorithmic decisions. The values of using algorithmic decisions are not evident to them. Furthermore, they might have developed a status quo and formed a negative image of the quality of AI-based decision algorithms.

Fourth, since organizations are gradually employing emerging technology to automate and streamline business operations, an understanding of different barriers to embracing technology will provide useful insights to the entrepreneurs or employers to decide about the appropriate technology-related strategy. In this regard, our study will guide managers while adopting or using algorithmic decision-making in their organizations.

5.3 Limitations and Future Research

Despite multiple implications and study rigor, like any other research, the current study has limitations that also open the avenue for future research. First, the study was cross-sectional. The perception and attitudes toward using technology change over time as the user gains more knowledge and becomes more familiar with it. Such change cannot be captured in a cross-sectional study. Thus, a longitudinal study can be undertaken to mitigate this lacuna. Second, the survey participants were selected using a convenient sampling method and they are predominantly based on a particular industry (banking/financial). In addition, the number of survey responses was not optimal for the findings to be generalized. Future studies can be undertaken by including an expansive set of samples to overcome this issue. Third, in our study, we identified that value barriers, tradition barriers, and image barriers significantly affect algorithm aversion. Future studies can be conducted to see how these barriers can be overcome by incorporating different moderators and mediators in between these relationships.

References

1. Splunk: The Data Age Is Here. Are You Ready? (2020)
2. Choo, C.W.: The knowing organization: how organizations use information to construct meaning, create knowledge and make decisions. Int. J. Inf. Manage. **16**, 329–340 (1996)
3. March, J.G., Simon, H.A.: Organizations. Blackwell, Oxford (1993)
4. Santos, L.R., Rosati, A.G.: The evolutionary roots of human decision making. Annu. Rev. Psychol. **66**, 321–347 (2015)
5. Simon, H.: Models of Man; Social and Rational (1957)
6. Shrestha, Y.R., Ben-Menahem, S.M., von Krogh, G.: Organizational decision-making structures in the age of artificial intelligence. California Manag. Rev. **61**, 66–83 (2019)
7. von Krogh, G.: Artificial intelligence in organizations: new opportunities for phenomenon-based theorizing. Acad. Manag. Discoveries **4**, 404–409 (2018)
8. Jovanovic, M., Sjödin, D., Parida, V.: Co-evolution of platform architecture, platform services, and platform governance: expanding the platform value of industrial digital platforms. Technovation 102218 (2021)
9. Lindebaum, D., Vesa, M., den Hond, F.: Insights from "the machine stops" to better understand rational assumptions in algorithmic decision making and its implications for organizations. Acad. Manag. Rev. **45**, 247–263 (2020)
10. Ram, S., Sheth, J.N.: Consumer resistance to innovations: the marketing problem and its solutions. J. Consum. Mark. **6**, 5 (1989)
11. Mahmud, H., Islam, A.K.M.N., Ahmed, S.I., Smolander, K.: What influences algorithmic decision-making? A systematic literature review on algorithm aversion. Technol. Forecast. Soc. Chang. **175**, 121390 (2022)
12. Lokuge, S., Sedera, D., Grover, V., Dongming, X.: Organizational readiness for digital innovation: development and empirical calibration of a construct. Inf. Manag. **56**, 445–461 (2019)
13. Mikalef, P., Gupta, M.: Artificial intelligence capability: conceptualization, measurement calibration, and empirical study on its impact on organizational creativity and firm performance. Inf. Manag. **58**, 103434 (2021)
14. Dietvorst, B.J., Simmons, J.P., Massey, C.: Algorithm aversion: people erroneously avoid algorithms after seeing them err. J. Exp. Psychol. Gen. **144**, 114–126 (2015). https://doi.org/10.1037/xge0000033

15. Kawaguchi, K.: When will workers follow an algorithm? A field experiment with a retail business. Manag. Sci. **67**, 1670–1695 (2021)
16. Filiz, I., René Judek, J., Lorenz, M., Spiwoks, M.: The Tragedy of Algorithm Aversion. Fakultät Wirtschaft (2021)
17. Leong, L.Y., Hew, T.S., Ooi, K.B., Wei, J.: Predicting mobile wallet resistance: a two-staged structural equation modeling-artificial neural network approach. Int. J. Inf. Manage. **51**, 102047 (2020)
18. Arif, I., Aslam, W., Hwang, Y.: Barriers in adoption of internet banking: a structural equation modeling - neural network approach. Technol. Soc. **61**, 101231 (2020)
19. Kaur, P., Dhir, A., Singh, N., Sahu, G., Almotairi, M.: An innovation resistance theory perspective on mobile payment solutions. J. Retail. Consum. Serv. **55**, 102059 (2020)
20. Oktavianus, J., Oviedo, H., Gonzalez, W., Putri, A.P., Lin, T.T.C.: Why do Taiwanese young adults not jump on the bandwagon of Pokémon Go? Exploring barriers of innovation resistance. J. Comput.-Mediated Commun. **13**, 827–855 (2017)
21. Jansukpum, K., Kettem, S.: Applying innovation resistance theory to understand consumer resistance of using online travel in Thailand. In: 4th International Symposium on Distributed Computing and Applications for Business Engineering and Science (DCABES), pp. 139–142. IEEE (2015)
22. Kushwah, S., Dhir, A., Sagar, M.: Understanding consumer resistance to the consumption of organic food. A study of ethical consumption, purchasing, and choice behaviour. Food Qual. Preference **77**, 1–14 (2019). https://doi.org/10.1016/j.foodqual.2019.04.003
23. Laukkanen, P., Sinkkonen, S., Laukkanen, T.: Consumer resistance to internet banking: postponers, opponents and rejectors. Int. J. Bank Mark. **26**, 440–455 (2008). https://doi.org/10.1108/02652320810902451
24. Ma, L., Lee, C.S.: Understanding the barriers to the use of MOOCs in a developing country: an innovation resistance perspective. J. Educ. Comput. Res. **57**(3), 571–590 (2018). https://doi.org/10.1177/0735633118757732
25. Laukkanen, T.: Consumer adoption versus rejection decisions in seemingly similar service innovations: the case of the Internet and mobile banking. J. Bus. Res. **69**, 2432–2439 (2016)
26. Talwar, S., Dhir, A., Kaur, P., Mäntymäki, M.: Barriers toward purchasing from online travel agencies. Int. J. Hospitality Manag. **89**, 102593 (2020). https://doi.org/10.1016/j.ijhm.2020.102593
27. Gerrard, P., Cunningham, J.B., Devlin, J.F.: Why consumers are not using internet banking: a qualitative study. J. Serv. Mark. **20**, 160–168 (2006)
28. John, A., Klein, J.: The Boycott puzzle: consumer motivations for purchase sacrifice. Manag. Sci. **49**, 1196–1209 (2003)
29. Antioco, M., Kleijnen, M.: Consumer adoption of technological innovations: effects of psychological and functional barriers in a lack of content versus a presence of content situation. Eur. J. Mark. **44**, 1700–1724 (2010)
30. Dichter, E.: What's In an image. J. Consum. Mark. **2**, 75 (1985)
31. Shaffer, V.A., Probst, C.A., Merkle, E.C., Arkes, H.R., Medow, M.A.: Why do patients derogate physicians who use a computer-based diagnostic support system? Med. Decis. Making **33**, 108–118 (2012)
32. Bigman, Y.E., Gray, K.: People are averse to machines making moral decisions. Cognition **181**, 21–34 (2018)
33. Davenport, T.H., Ronanki, R.: Artificial intelligence for the real world. Harv. Bus. Rev. **96**, 108–116 (2018)
34. Mäntymäki, M., Islam, A.K.M.N., Benbasat, I.: What drives subscribing to premium in freemium services? A consumer value-based view of differences between upgrading to and staying with premium. Inf. Syst. J. **30**, 295–333 (2020)

35. Moore, G.C., Benbasat, I.: Development of an instrument to measure the perceptions of adopting an information technology innovation. Inf. Syst. Res. **2**, 192–222 (1991)
36. Agarwal, A., Singhal, C., Thomas, R.: Global Banking & Securities. McKinsey & Company (2021)
37. Fornell, C., Larcker, D.F.: Evaluating structural equation models with unobservable variables and measurement error. J. Mark. Res. **18**, 39–50 (1981)
38. Gefen, D., Straub, D., Gefen, D., Straub, D.: A practical guide to factorial validity using PLS-Graph: tutorial and annotated example. Commun. Assoc. Inf. Syst. **16**, 91–109 (2005)
39. Featherman, M.S., Pavlou, P.A.: Predicting e-services adoption: a perceived risk facets perspective. Int. J. Hum. Comput. Stud. **59**, 451–474 (2003)
40. Im, I., Kim, Y., Han, H.J.: The effects of perceived risk and technology type on users' acceptance of technologies. Inf. Manag. **45**, 1–9 (2008)
41. Laukkanen, T., Sinkkonen, S., Kivijärvi, M., Laukkanen, P.: Innovation resistance among mature consumers. J. Consum. Mark. **24**, 419–427 (2007)
42. Sadiq, M., Adil, M., Paul, J.: An innovation resistance theory perspective on purchase of eco-friendly cosmetics. J. Retail. Consum. Serv. **59**, 102369 (2021)

Data and Analytics

Understanding Opportunities and Threats of Learning Analytics in Higher Education – A Students' Perspective

Alena Rodda(⊠)

Osnabrueck University, Katharinenstr., 49074 Osnabrueck, Germany
alena.rodda@uni-osnabrueck.de

Abstract. The Covid-19 pandemic has further fueled an increase of e-learning in higher education. The widespread use of online learning generates vast amounts of academic data. This data can be collected and analyzed with the help of Learning Analytics to improve teaching and learning. Although students are essential stakeholders of Learning Analytics, their views are underrepresented in current research. Therefore, this paper aims to give an overview of opportunities and threats regarding the use of Learning Analytics from students' perspective. For this purpose, a qualitative study with 136 students was conducted, and the answers were coded and classified by multiple researchers. The results show a generally positive attitude toward Learning Analytics. Noticeable in comparison with existing research were small-scaled answers of participants that focus primarily on the course level and students' everyday lives. The identified opportunities and risks provide a good foundation for further research.

Keywords: Learning Analytics · Higher education · Students' perspective

1 Motivation

The increase of e-learning in higher education in recent decades was further fueled by the Covid-19 pandemic. The majority of students worldwide were affected by measures such as lockdowns, social distancing, and university closures. Often face-to-face teaching was discontinued, and online teaching was offered instead [1]. The widespread use of online teaching creates vast amounts of academic data. The systematic evaluation of this data is called Learning Analytics (LA), generally defined as "the measurement, collection, analysis, and reporting of data about learners and their contexts, for purposes of understanding and optimizing learning and the environments in which it occurs" [2] (p. 32). Regarding teaching in times of the pandemic, LA offers, for example, the possibility of relieving students' sense of isolation by offering comparisons with peers. It can also provide teachers with guidance on how to adapt teaching materials to students' performance or interests without seeing them face-to-face. Nevertheless, before LA systems (LAS) are developed or refined, one should take a step back and consider what the educational stakeholders involved, namely students, teachers, and institutions [3],

S. Papagiannidis et al. (Eds.): I3E 2022, LNCS 13454, pp. 111–122, 2022.
https://doi.org/10.1007/978-3-031-15342-6_9

perceive as opportunities and threats. There has been an underrepresentation of student perspectives in research [4]. However, their inclusion is essential to the development and use of LAS and can increase satisfaction, motivation, and commitment [5]. This article aims to fill this gap by addressing the following research questions:

(1) *What are the opportunities and threats of LA from the students' perspective?*
(2) *How do students' views relate to those in current LA literature?*

To answer these questions, a qualitative survey with university students is conducted and groups of opportunities and threats are derived, which are then cross-referenced with findings from current literature. The paper contains six sections. Section two provides an overview of current LA research. Section three outlines the research design. Section four presents the study's results, identifying the opportunities and threats. Section five discusses the results in relation to findings in current literature and highlights further needs for research. Finally, section six presents the conclusion and limitations.

2 Theoretical Foundation

2.1 Learning Analytics

The increase in online learning and developments in the field of data analytics has led to a growing number of universities considering how the data generated in learning management systems (LMS), for instance, can be meaningfully analyzed and used. The usage of educational data can transform learning and teaching practices and serve as a foundation for educational research [6]. Higher Education Institutions (HEIs) use multiple interactive e-learning environments nowadays, collecting vast amounts of data that contain information about the users themselves (e.g., academic performance), their interaction with systems (e.g., log ins, user pathways, download activity), communication with other students or teachers (e.g., e-mails, forum posts), as well as information about courses with their underlying curriculum and learning objectives [3, 7]. Through descriptive and predictive models, such data is processed in real-time or a time-lagged manner to derive meaningful insights that can assist educational stakeholders in decision support and can help to improve learning and teaching contents and environments [8]. Predictions can involve an entire group of learners or individual students, looking at overarching issues like dropout or failure rates, and more small-scale matters like boredom and short-term learning [6], on a course-level or departmental-level [2].

Most LA research focuses on the learning process, "analyzing the relationship between learner, content, institution and educator" [2] (p. 36). The usability, effectiveness, and validity of LAS are often examined [7, 9]. There have also been studies about developing specific tools and underlying design principles for LAS [8]. The main stakeholders of LA are students, teachers, and institutions [3], however, there is surprisingly little research on students' perception of LA [7, 10]. Ferguson states that a focus on students' perspective is crucial to the development of LAS, concentrating on their demands rather than the institution's demands, to motivate and satisfy students to meet their career goals [5]. Although the remainder of this paper focuses solely on students' perspective, LA also poses many benefits and challenges to teachers and the institution [2, 11, 12].

2.2 Opportunities of Learning Analytics

There are typical issues in online teaching, some of which have intensified during the Covid-19 pandemic. For example, students may feel isolated due to a lack of contact with peers or lose track of the many online courses, materials, and assignments [13]. Some also struggle with technical problems and lose their motivation to study [13]. At the same time, teachers of online classes cannot rely on the visual cues of face-to-face classroom interaction anymore, which usually signals them if students feel satisfied, overwhelmed, or bored with the course content [14]. Again, the use of LA can provide valuable assistance here. With the help of LA, teachers can assess the learning behavior of their students, e.g., which topics were hardly worked on or which tasks were repeatedly solved incorrectly, to adapt course content or teaching methods [8]. The students benefit from customized assignments and courses, leading to an overall improvement of the academic program, enrichment of the student experience, and promotion of better learning [12]. LA offers students insights into their learning habits, enabling them to adjust their learning behavior accordingly [2]. Based on engagement data of previous cohorts, models for successful behavior can be developed to provide learners with automated guidance on how to achieve improvement [15]. Automated academic advising systems are also used, for example, to provide students with recommendations for course selection based on their learning style and performance [16].

Based on LA data, assessment analytics allow learners to evaluate their attainment across time, in relation to their personal goals or against their peers [2, 11]. The information about their place in the cohort, e.g., in terms of final grades or specific learning outcomes, provides students with a sense of belonging, reducing the feeling of isolation and encouraging them to work harder [2, 11]. By using data about weaknesses or common mistakes of former cohorts, learners can be provided pre-submission feedback before assignments, enhancing their approach to the same task [11]. Furthermore, LA is used to detect students whose performance in individual courses or their general studies is comparatively weak [9]. The at-risk students then benefit, for example, from automated alerts or early interventions by instructors, aiming to reduce dropout and failure rates and enabling as many students as possible to graduate successfully [5, 8].

2.3 Threats of Learning Analytics

The increasing amount of personal data collected about students and their activities also brings risks. Many ethical objections have been voiced [17]. Vast amounts of LA data can be analyzed with different objectives, possibly invading students' privacy [7]. Questions arise about student consent, data protection and security, the duration of data storage, and access to the data [5, 12]. In some cases, students are not offered an option to opt out of data collection, or the data is later used in a way that students did not actively agree to [18]. Security risks exist if student data is not stored in a secure location or if unauthorized individuals gain access to it [17, 19]. There are also country-specific differences as to whom the owner of personal data is, the individual or the collector [7], complicating, for example, students' chances to opt out at a later time. It is also problematic to base educational decisions or predictions exclusively on data, reducing students to a metric [19, 20] and putting them into categories by stereotyping and generalizing [21]. The collection and exploitation of LA data can add to one's overall sense of increasing surveillance in all areas of life [17, 22], interfering with students' privacy and their academic freedom [11]. Ellis states that, e.g., automated course recommendation systems infantilize students, pushing them to take classes that are most likely better for their GPA but do not necessarily fit students' interests or goals [11]. The same is described as a loss of autonomy or paternalism by other researchers. Students are supposed to choose an institutionally preferred action rather than acting out on their preferences [5, 20]. The underlying problem is that most predictive LA models are based on a behaviorist model, meaning that "individuals with approximately the same profile generally select and or prefer the same thing" [23] (p.191), compared to models used in other fields like the rational utility maximizer model or a habitual perspective of behavioral economics [20]. The misconception of students and teachers that LAS are value-neutral and provide objective aid is an opportunity threat should they decide to rely exclusively on the system [20].

LA also bears the threat of invalid predictions or false interpretations [24] due to inadequate or flawed data [17]. E-learning systems only capture a fraction of the learning, not providing a holistic view that considers all possible influences on students' failure or success, like personal problems or financial difficulties [19]. There is also the risk of mistaking correlation for causation. For example, students' engagement rates are often used to predict their success; however, one can argue that exceptional students need to engage less than weaker students to achieve good grades [17]. The use of LA can also demotivate students. Continual monitoring can cause conscious or unconscious behavior changes, making students feel pressured to constantly self-optimize, which leads to stress or non-participation [19]. Furthermore, classifying weaker students as at-risk students may influence their outlook on success and deflate their potential [21], leading to self-fulfilling prophecies [17]. Labeling of learners as, e.g., exceptional or at-risk, can also affect teacher's or faculty's perception, resulting in different or discriminative behavior [19]. Adjustments based on LA may focus on certain groups of students: For many institutions, the emphasis lies on minimizing student withdrawal or failure [5] or driving academic excellence [2]. Thus, at-risk and high achieving students get the biggest share of attention, ignoring others on the achievement spectrum [11].

3 Research Design

After section two has provided an overview of the opportunities and threats of LA for students in existing literature, the students' views will now be examined with the help of a qualitative survey. The aim is to get detailed insights of students' thoughts concerning the opportunities and threats of LA usage in HEIs. The study was designed as an online questionnaire and contained three open questions:

(Q1) Which opportunities do you see for Learning Analytics at universities?
(Q2) Which threats do you see for Learning Analytics at universities?
(Q3) Which outweighs the other for you personally, opportunities or threats?

The study was conducted in the participants' native language, and the results were translated afterwards. The study participants were undergraduate business administration and information systems students enrolled in a Business Intelligence course, having basic data modeling and applied analytics knowledge.

The answers to Q1 and Q2 were analyzed using the qualitative content analysis according to Mayring, a systematic approach to the qualitative analysis of texts [25]. Mayring promotes a step model for inductive category development, as part of his summative approach. For the evaluation of the questionnaire in this paper each step has been performed independently by two researchers. First, the participants answers were paraphrased and generalized to a level of suitable abstraction into core sentences. Then, in a first step of reduction, contents that did not answer the questions were cut out. In a second step of reduction, the core sentences were combined with similar ones and thus classified into categories. After working through 30% of the answers a revision of categories was carried out, combining similar categories and thus reducing the number of categories further. The participants' answers and the categories derived from them were checked for plausibility with a focus group of three other researchers. Finally, the results were interpreted, including quantitative steps like the calculation of frequencies.

4   Results

A total of 139 students participated in the study, with 136 questionnaires being valid. 64% of the participants were male and 36% female. Sections 4.1 and 4.2 provide an overview of the most commonly named opportunities, threats, and notable quotes. Regarding Q3, the result is as follows: 89% of the participants answered that the opportunities of LA outweigh the threats, 5% stated that the threats would outweigh the opportunities, and 6% said they consider opportunities and risks to be in balance.

4.1   Learning Analytics Opportunities from Students' Perspective

Table 1 summarizes the five identified categories of opportunities, containing 20 subcategories, each with the absolute and percentage numbers of mentions. The three most frequently mentioned opportunities are displayed with a gray background.

Category one refers to university-wide opportunities. Ten percent of participants envision new or adapted classes within the curriculum, according to the students' interests and popular classes, as shown by LA. Some (7%) also wish for an automated course recommender system that can help them navigate the many course offers and is based on their performance, following the curriculum, and presenting their interests. The **second category** focuses on LA opportunities for the course design. The adaption of contents and teaching materials was the second most named opportunity (36%). Teachers can identify students' strengths and weaknesses, as well as their likes and dislikes and modify courses accordingly. Also, 27% of the participants mentioned that this would motivate them to engage and study more. The most common answer (45%) was that the instructor could provide additional course work, explanations, or videos that solely focus on the most challenging topics of the class, as identified by LA. The **third category** contains opportunities that affect the individual learning behavior. One-fifth of participants would adapt their learning behavior based on LA, believing that it can help them study more effectively. Some participants (12%) express that LA supports more

Table 1. Learning analytics opportunities from students' perspective

Category	Subcategory	Frequency	
1. University-wide course offers	1.1 New or adapted courses	10	(7%)
	1.2 Automated recommender system for courses	7	(5%)
2. Adaption of teaching in courses	2.1 Adaption of teaching method	6	(4%)
	2.2 Adaption of the scope of coursework	8	(6%)
	2.3 Adaption of content and materials	49	(36%)
	2.4 Additional explanations for complex topics	61	(45%)
3. Improvement of individual learning behavior	3.1 Adaption of learning behavior	27	(20%)
	3.2 Overview of learning progress	40	(29%)
	3.3 Continuous automated feedback	7	(5%)
	3.4 Overview of weaknesses and mistakes	25	(18%)
	3.5 Better self-reflection	21	(15%)
	3.6 Comparison to peers	45	(33%)
	3.7 Early detection of shortcomings	13	(10%)
	3.8 More targeted exam preparation	16	(12%)
	3.9 Better time management	33	(24%)
4. Transparency	4.1 Overview of current and past grades; GPA	18	(13%)
	4.2 Comprehensibility of final course grades	36	(26%)
5. Communication with instructors	5.1 Tailored, efficient help for individual students	11	(8%)
	5.2 Interventions for at-risk students	10	(7%)
	5.3 Anonymous feedback through LA data	6	(4%)

targeted exam preparation. One participant wrote: *"One has a better overview of the learning success, especially compared to peers. The time still available until the exam can be better planned and used, considering other modules taken during the semester. It can have a positive impact on a student's time management."* The comparison to peers has been the most commonly named opportunity in this category (33%). Students can feel isolated or at loss of orientation in online classes. The constant knowledge of how they are doing (e.g., time-wise, knowledge-wise, grade-wise) compared to peers can be beneficial. One participant noted: *"Students are more motivated by this. The learning progress is considered during the semester, preventing students from postponing study-ing until the end of the semester. Through LA, it feels like a virtual classroom is formed, which is familiar to many students from high school. Thus, the learning situation at the university is not so strange for the students, and they gain more control. For some, the freedom (e.g., no compulsory attendance) at university is not a great thing."* The **fourth category** is about transparency. Easily accessible, clear overviews of grades and the current GPA have been outlined as a benefit by 13% of the participants. Even more (26%) view the traceability of final grades as an advantage, as they are often made up of individual components, e.g., assignments, participation, and midterms. Opportunities concerning the communication or interaction with instructors (**category 5**) have only been mentioned by a few participants. These include the possibility of tailored, more efficient help that an instructor can give individual students based on their performance, engagement, and time spent on particular course contents (8%). Interventions for at-risk students have been mentioned by 7%. The potential of automated, anonymous feedback to teachers about the course was described by 4%: "*Instructors can analyze whether the assignments are too complex or too easy. Often, students do not dare to ask questions or demand a further explanation in person*".

4.2 Learning Analytics Threats from Students' Perspective

Respectively to Table 1, Table 2 shows four categories and 21 subcategories of threats mentioned by participants. Again, the most common threats are highlighted in gray.

Table 2. Learning analytics threats from students' perspective

Category	Subcategory	Frequency	
1. Ethical concerns	1.1 Insufficient or poor data protection	59	(43%)
	1.2 Violation of privacy	36	(26%)
	1.3 Continual monitoring	22	(16%)
	1.4 Reduction of students to metrics	6	(4%)
2. Inadequate LA-systems	2.1 Technical difficulties	6	(4%)
	2.2 Collection of inadequate data	13	(10%)
	2.3 Collected data only refers to activity, not knowledge	11	(8%)
	2.4 Disregard of offline learning	17	(13%)
	2.5 Manipulation of the system by students	12	(9%)
3. Negative effects on student behavior	3.1 Increased pressure on students	35	(26%)
	3.2 Demotivation of students	21	(15%)
	3.3 Misinterpretation of data by students	21	(15%)
	3.4 Focus solely on data or learning objective	7	(5%)
4. Usage of LA by instructors	4.1 Lack of digital competencies and knowledge	8	(6%)
	4.2 Invalid interpretations and predictions	43	(32%)
	4.3 Discrimination of groups of learners	21	(15%)
	4.4 Discrimination of individual students	12	(9%)
	4.5 Less time for good quality teaching	14	(10%)
	4.6 Focus solely on course metrics	7	(5%)
	4.7 Less student-teacher-communication	11	(8%)
	4.8 Misuse of data	17	(13%)

Participants have most commonly voiced ethical concerns (**category 1**), especially the threat of insufficient data protection (43%). They fear that a LAS could be attacked and data leaked publicly or that unauthorized university personnel could access it for other purposes than they agreed on. Some participants believe that the collection of LA data violates their privacy (26%). However, they are less concerned about the academic data and more concerned about demographic data, e.g., gender, ethnicity, and income. A few participants worry (6%) that students will not be seen as individuals with their own preferences, feelings, personal challenges, and learning strategies anymore but rather be reduced to a metric defined by their academic success.

Regarding the threats of implementing a LAS (**category 2**), the risk of collecting inadequate data (10%) or that the system cannot represent offline learning (13%) are mentioned most commonly. One participant wrote: *"Teachers might rely too much on data. The data on how long someone reads a book borrowed from the library at home cannot be answered by learning analytics. If a professor then makes videos available online that are supposed to illustrate the material, but these are not viewed, the misconception could arise that the students are doing little for the module when in fact, they only have a different learning style than the one served by the professor."* Participants also voiced the concern that the LAS could be manipulated by students (9%), e.g., by creating data that makes instructors believe the topics are too complex or the scope of materials is too high so that the instructor feels pressured to make the course easier.

Findings of the survey show that the usage of LA could affect students' behavior in a negative way (**category 3**). Continuous monitoring, comparisons with peers, and the constant highlighting of own weaknesses can increase the pressure on students to self-optimize (26%). If they know that they are constantly performing worse than their peers, lower achieving students can feel demotivated by LA (15%). Students who prefer to study offline and do not feel represented by the LAS can also feel discouraged. One participant noted: *"For students, there is a risk of evaluating their learning success solely on the quantitative metrics of learning success (compared to fellow students). Thus, students might disregard relevant topics in which they initially achieved good test results but which require continuous and intensive study. Also, students' learning behaviors vary widely. Some will take advantage of and benefit from a time and place independent learning system. At the same time, other students lack the necessary self-discipline to work through the material. Also, computers are not suitable for everyone; e.g., some will experience greater fatigue due to screen time. I prefer to use pen and paper."* Students could also misinterpret the data (15%) or focus solely on fulfilling the given learning objective (5%) and not study voluntarily or do extracurricular activities.

Category four includes perceived threats associated with data analysis or interpretation by instructors. Some participants (6%) believe that teachers lack digital competencies and knowledge to properly evaluate LA data and results. Participants are most commonly concerned about invalid interpretations and predictions (32%), e.g., leading to the inadequate adaption of courses or teaching methods. The fear of discrimination against groups of learners (15%) or individual students (9%), e.g., based on bad academic performances, gender, or ethnicity, was also mentioned. Ten percent of the participants are concerned that teachers spend so much time becoming involved with LA and optimizing metrics that they have less time for core tasks, like good quality teaching and personal communication with students. Students fear that if teachers rely too much on data, they might think personal interaction and feedback from students is unnecessary (8%). Furthermore, the risk of misuse of LA data by instructors has been described by 13% of the participants. They are concerned that instructors may feel personally insulted if their videos are barely watched, or their assignments are not adequately completed. Teachers could then take "revenge" on students by focusing primarily on those topics in the exam that were little worked on or poorly understood.

5 Discussion

The participants of the study came up with numerous ideas, 449 opportunities that could be summarized in 20 categories, and 399 risks, categorized in 21 subcategories. Many of the opportunities and risks outlined by participants can also be found in current literature, albeit over- or underrepresented in some cases. On a promising note, most participants had a rather positive attitude toward LA. A positive stakeholder attitude provides a good foundation for the successful implementation of LA [7, 24].

The participants, who are students themselves, saw most of the benefits at the course level, especially in adapting course content and improving their learning behavior. University-wide effects of LA or faculty-student interaction played only a secondary role. The adaptation of course content based on LA data, which is supposed to improve teaching quality, is also commonly found in literature and illustrated in case studies, as is the comparison to fellow learners [10, 12, 17]. Especially online-only teaching, as it was common worldwide in times of the Covid-19 pandemic, can lead to a feeling of isolation [1]. Through comparisons with peers, learners develop a sense of belonging and can be motivated to get more involved [17]. Participants frequently mentioned this aspect, which is also often included in current research. There is a lot of literature concerned with automated course recommender systems [8, 16, 20] and interventions for at-risk students [11, 17, 21]. However, these opportunities have only been pointed out by five percent, respectively, seven percent, of the participants. A much higher percentage of participants viewed additional assignments and explanations for complex topics and the overview of the learning process as an opportunity of LA. One could argue that assignments and explanations are part of the adaption of course materials. However, most participants, 61 in total, pointed out that the focus on making content that is difficult to understand better comprehendible is one of the leading LA benefits. Therefore, it is presented individually in this study. This is sometimes mentioned in the literature but is usually not the focus of current research [12]. The same applies to the clear overview of the learning progress, often briefly referred to by researchers but not individually examined, e.g., by evaluating which visualization can provide the best overview using a LA dashboard [5, 9]. Four subcategories are interestingly hardly ever mentioned in LA research: The more targeted exam preparation, the better time management, transparency of the final course grade, and anonymous feedback through LA data. This might be because current literature views LA opportunities on a higher, more abstract level than the students who focus more on a micro-level, thinking about their everyday student life. This is partly because, as stated in the introduction of this article, there is very little research specifically addressing the demands of LAS students. When looking at the results concerning

LA threats, it can be stated that the majority of the study results have been examined in previous research. In particular, the ethical concerns indicated by many participants have already been investigated several times, and guidelines for handling, e.g., the collected data, have already been developed [17, 20–22]. Some participants worry that the data collected by the LAS do not adequately reflect their learning behavior and experiences. New approaches such as the use of multimodal data [26] or the use of artificial intelligence [27] can provide a solution in this regard. Nevertheless, some risks identified in this study hardly receive any attention in current research. For example, one concern is that students adapt their learning behavior to LA so that they solely focus on optimizing LA metrics and reaching the given learning objectives. Their own interests in the course material and the efforts that go beyond the required targets are pushed into the background. Another concern is that instructors spend so much time and effort on LA that the quality of teaching decreases. Also, participants worry that LA leads to less in-person student-teacher communication because teachers could rely solely on LA data to review their courses and on automated feedback to students. The last topic that does not receive attention in current research is the participants' fear that instructors take some metrics, like few video views, personally and then misuse the data to make assignments or exams harder. Thus, these aspects must be considered when introducing or adapting LAS and should be communicated.

The findings from this survey serve as a foundation for further research. To validate and extend the results, a larger group of students from different study programs and nations should be questioned. Results from interviews and focus groups can provide additional value. Potentially, the research could be expanded to the school context. To gain an overarching view, the perspectives of teachers and institutions should be included. The results could then be used to identify drivers and barriers of LA. Finally, for practitioners, an overview of stakeholder requirements for LAS can be derived.

6   Conclusion

The contribution of this paper is an in-depth view of students' perception of LA, which can help identify further needs for research and provide practitioners with guidance on what they should consider when implementing or adapting a LAS at university. Students are the most crucial stakeholder group, but their views are still underrepresented in current research. Ultimately, the more students are involved in the process of a LAS development, the higher the acceptance rate of the system can be. Therefore, a qualitative survey of 136 university students was conducted. Multiple researchers classified the responses, arranged them in tables, and enriched them with further explanations and quotes. The discussion then addressed how these results fit in with current literature and identified further research possibilities.

It can be inferred that the majority of participants felt generally positive toward LA. Many of the opportunities identified in the survey can also be found in academic literature, but the priorities are distributed differently in some areas. The benefits most frequently cited by participants were the customization of course materials using LA insights, additional explanations and assignments for complex content, and the comparison to other students. Very apparent is the small-scale and short-sighted nature of many answers, that focus mainly on the course-level, e.g., more targeted exam preparation or the comprehensibility of final grades. Only a few participants mentioned opportunities on a departmental or university-wide level. The three most commonly mentioned risks were insufficient data protection, privacy violation, and invalid predictions or interpretations based on LA data. In addition, many participants voiced their concern about predictions partly based on data that could be inadequate or not represent their offline learning efforts. Interestingly, students were also concerned that teachers could feel offended by specific LA data and then misuse LA to make exams harder to pass.

The results of our study are subject to some limitations, which mostly relate to the selection of participants for the survey. Firstly, it should be noted that the participants come from a specific European country and depending on the country, laws, and cultural background, the benefits and risks from the students' point of view may vary. Secondly, the participants were university students generally familiar with data analysis. Therefore, students' views from other disciplines or institutions should be considered in further investigations to enhance the foundation laid in this manuscript. In conclusion, digital teaching during the Covid19-pandemic has allowed students worldwide to continue studying despite lockdowns and closures. LA can improve online learning and motivate students through customized courses and comparisons with peers. Even after the pandemic, LA will continue to play an essential role in teaching and learning. However, universities should take the concerns of students seriously. The analytical processes should be transparent and accessible. Students' wishes and requirements must be considered so that LAS can develop their full potential.

References

1. Pokhrel, S., Chhetri, R.: A literature review on impact of COVID-19 pandemic on teaching and learning. High. Educ. Future **8**, 133–141 (2021)
2. Long, P., Siemens, G.: Penetrating the fog: analytics in learning and education. Educause Rev. **46**, 31–40 (2011)
3. Greller, W., Drachsler, H.: Translating learning into numbers: a generic framework for learning analytics. Educ. Technol. Soc. **15**, 42–57 (2012)
4. Ifenthaler, D.: Are higher education institutions prepared for learning analytics? TechTrends **61**(4), 366–371 (2016). https://doi.org/10.1007/s11528-016-0154-0
5. Ferguson, R.: Learning analytics: drivers, developments and challenges. Int. J. Technol. Enhanced Learn. **4**, 304–317 (2012)
6. Baker, R.S., Inventado, P.S.: Educational Data Mining and Learning Analytics. In: Larusson, J.A., White, B. (eds.) Learning Analytics, pp. 61–75. Springer, New York (2014). https://doi.org/10.1007/978-1-4614-3305-7_4
7. Ifenthaler, D., Schumacher, C.: Student perceptions of privacy principles for learning analytics. Educ. Tech. Res. Dev. **64**(5), 923–938 (2016). https://doi.org/10.1007/s11423-016-9477-y
8. Nguyen, A., Tuunanen, T., Gardner, L., Sheridan, D.: Design principles for learning analytics information systems in higher education. Eur. J. Inf. Syst. **30**, 541–568 (2021)
9. Gašević, D., Dawson, S., Siemens, G.: Let's not forget: learning analytics are about learning. TechTrends **59**(1), 64–71 (2014). https://doi.org/10.1007/s11528-014-0822-x
10. Droit, A., Rieger, B.: Learning analytics in the flipped classroom–learning dashboards from the students' perspective. In: Proceedings of the 53rd Hawaii International Conference on System Sciences, pp. 100–107 (2020)

11. Ellis, C.: Broadening the scope and increasing the usefulness of learning analytics: the case for assessment analytics. Br. J. Edu. Technol. **44**, 662–664 (2013)
12. Daniel, B.: Big Data and analytics in higher education: opportunities and challenges. Br. J. Edu. Technol. **46**, 904–920 (2015)
13. Mazza, R., Dimitrova, V.: Visualising student tracking data to support instructors in web-based distance education. In: 13th International World Wide Web Conference, pp. 154–161 (2004)
14. Dringus, L.P., Ellis, T.: Using data mining as a strategy for assessing asynchronous discussion forums. Comput. Educ. **45**, 141–160 (2005)
15. Nistor, N., Hernández-García, Á.: What types of data are used in learning analytics? an overview of six cases. Comput. Hum. Behav. **89**, 335–338 (2018)
16. Gavriushenko, M., Saarela, M., Kärkkäinen, T.: Towards evidence-based academic advising using learning analytics. In: Escudeiro, P., Costagliola, G., Zvacek, S., Uhomoibhi, J., McLaren, B.M. (eds.) CSEDU 2017. CCIS, vol. 865, pp. 44–65. Springer, Cham (2018). https://doi.org/10.1007/978-3-319-94640-5_3
17. Sclater, N.: Learning Analytics Explained. Routledge, New York (2017)
18. Prinsloo, P., Slade, S.: Student vulnerability, agency and learning analytics: an exploration. J. Learn. Analytics **3**, 159–182 (2016)
19. Campbell, J.P., DeBlois, P.B., Oblinger, D.G.: Academic analytics: a new tool for a New Era. Educause Rev. **42**, 40–57 (2007)
20. Johnson, J.A.: The ethics of big data in higher education. Int. Rev. Inf. Ethics **21**, 3–10 (2014)
21. Swenson, J.: Establishing an ethical literacy for learning analytics. In: Proceedings of the Fourth International Conference on Learning Analytics and Knowledge, pp. 246–250. ACM, New York (2014)
22. Pardo, A., Siemens, G.: Ethical and privacy principles for learning analytics. Br. J. Edu. Technol. **45**, 438–450 (2014)
23. Vialardi, C., Bravo, J., Shafti, L., Ortigosa, A.: Recommendation in higher education using data mining techniques. In: Barnes, T., Desmarais, M., Romero, C., Ventura, S. (eds.) Educational Data Mining 2009, pp. 190–199 (2009)
24. Siemens, G.: Learning analytics: envisioning a research discipline and a domain of practice. In: Dawson, S. (ed.) Proceedings of the 2nd International Conference on Learning Analytics and Knowledge, pp. 4–8. ACM, New York (2012)
25. Mayring, P.: Qualitative content analysis: theoretical foundation, basic procedures and software solution. SSOAR, Klagenfurt (2014)
26. Giannakos, M.N., Sharma, K., Pappas, I.O., Kostakos, V., Velloso, E.: Multimodal data as a means to understand the learning experience. Int. J. Inf. Manage. **48**, 108–119 (2019)
27. Kabudi, T., Pappas, I., Olsen, D.: AI-enabled adaptive learning systems: a systematic mapping of the literature. Comput. Educ. Artif. Intell. **2**, 100017 (2021)

Methods and Tools for Social Media Analytics to Support Citizen Relationship Management: A Dataset Analysis of Tweets from Germany and South Africa

Khulekani Yakobi[✉] [iD] and Brenda Scholtz[iD]

Nelson Mandela University, Gqeberha, South Africa
khulekaniy4@gmail.com, brenda.scholtz@mandela.ac.za

Abstract. Social Media Analytics (SMA) can provide methods and tools for government to monitor, analyse and visualise social media data, and assist with Citizen Relationship Management (CzRM) and decision making. However, social media presents an explosion of unstructured Big Data, leading to many challenges for government relating to the processes of SMA and CzRM. The purpose of this paper is to report on a Twitter Dataset Analysis conducted to evaluate SMA methods and tools and the extent to which they are useful for supporting CzRM. Twitter data from South Africa and Germany was used in the dataset. The findings revealed that the proposed SMA methods and three tools (NVivo, uClassify and PowerBI) were useful for collecting, analysing and visualising social media data. NVivo successfully collected Tweets from South Africa and Germany over a four-week period. These Tweets were analysed for negative and positive sentiments using uClassify and visualised for insights using PowerBI. The visualisations were useful for determining trends and insights into citizens' views and issues from their posts. The main contribution is the extended framework of SMA methods and techniques that was used to guide the dataset analysis. A practical contribution is the demonstration of the framework of SMA methods and techniques in terms of utility and usability in a real-world context.

Keywords: Social media analytics · Sentiment analysis · SMA tools · Citizen Relationship Management (CzRM)

1 Introduction

The rapid development of Internet and Information and Communication Technologies (ICTs) has coined some rapid advancements and changes in international government economies and citizen participation [1]. According to Shang and Zhang [2], the COVID-19 pandemic has presented both opportunities and challenges for ICT in many organisations. Some opportunities are being implemented by governments to aid with interventions for the COVID-19 crisis related to service delivery for citizens [3]. Citizen

© IFIP International Federation for Information Processing 2022
Published by Springer Nature Switzerland AG 2022
S. Papagiannidis et al. (Eds.): I3E 2022, LNCS 13454, pp. 123–135, 2022.
https://doi.org/10.1007/978-3-031-15342-6_10

Relationship Management (CzRM) has become an important concept as it can help governments to foster close relationships, create more efficient service delivery and increase e-participation through digital platforms [4]. The challenges revealed by Yang *et al.* [3] are the lack of reliable and accessible information for healthy public debate and meeting people's daily information needs. Other challenges are the spread of misinformation, disinformation and fake news, especially for organisations such as government. The advent of Social Media Analytics (SMA) as an ICT has presented some opportunities using methods and tools to monitor, analyse and visualise social media data [5].

Whilst there is some literature proposing SMA frameworks [6–9], only a few studies provide reports of empirical field studies of SMA tools for CzRM. The main problem addressed in this paper is the limited research on how SMA methods and tools can support CzRM in the context of government. The purpose of the paper is to report on a Twitter Dataset Analysis that was done through a demonstration and evaluation of SMA tools to determine the extent to which SMA can support CzRM in government, and to determine the potential usefulness of these tools. The paper is structured as follows: An overview of the literature review is presented in Sect. 2. The research methods and contributions are explained in Sect. 3. Section 4 provides the results while Sect. 5 discusses these. Several conclusions and recommendations are made in Sect. 6.

2   Literature Review

According to Singh and Verma [8], social media has evolved into presenting a widespread of opinion mining and sentiment analysis using a higher cognitive process, which motivates the need for real-time processing of social media data to generate insights. In the study conducted in [7], it is highlighted that there is a growing interest in using sentiment analysis methods and these methods should be considered when mining a large corpus of Tweets. There are suitable SMA methods and tools that organisations can use to monitor, analyse and visualise social media data [10]. However, challenges related to data privacy, data quality, skills, tools and budget to maximise SMA are still evident in these organisations such as governments [11, 12]. The lack of data management tools and techniques have resulted in a negative impact on the decision-making process of government [4].

Reka *et al.* [13] proposed a model that presents types of Big Data Analytics (BDA) including SMA. However, its shortcoming is that it does not consider specific SMA methods and tools to support CzRM. The framework of Singh and Verma [8] proposed a lightweight, efficient, SMA methodological framework to address SMA challenges and to handle the high-speed flow of social media posts. One limitation of the framework is that the support of tools, techniques, methods and architectures was not applied in the context of CzRM. While the literature review revealed several frameworks in the domain of SMA and BDA, these frameworks do not provide specific details for SMA that could be used by government to analyse citizens' Tweets. Those studies that mention tools propose complex customised algorithms and do not use commercial off-the-shelf (COTS) tools. In these studies, no investigation of the usefulness of SMA tools were conducted in the context of government or CzRM.

The SMA framework proposed in [9] was the most comprehensive one identified in a political context and was therefore considered the most relevant for government and CzRM. It provides an overview of different methodological approaches, methods, tools and techniques for SMA used in a political context. Figure 1 shows the Framework of SMA Methods and Techniques, which was extended from that of [9] to include the following three main types of COTS tools for SMA tasks:

- A social media monitoring tool (e.g. NVivo);
- A tool for performing SMA sentiment analysis (e.g. uClassify); and
- A visualisation tool (e.g. Microsoft PowerBI or PowerBI).

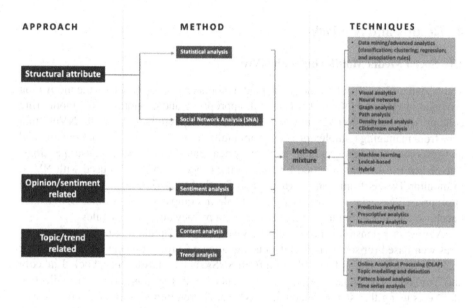

Fig. 1. Framework of SMA methods and techniques (extended from Stieglitz et al. [9]).

3 Research Method

The main research question to be answered in this paper is *"How useful are SMA methods and tools for supporting CzRM?"*.

The framework presented in Fig. 1 was used as the theoretical foundation for the study together with the theory of Technological, Organisational and Environmental (TOE) proposed in [14]. The TOE theory considers the three constructs of Technology, Organisation and Environment and how they influence the adoption of technology in an organisation. Since SMA is one such technology, it provides a relevant and appropriate model to use for assessing the potential adoption of SMA in government for CzRM. However, this paper reports on a sub-section of work done as part of a larger PhD study, which only focused on the technological construct of the TOE theory. The usefulness of technology is an attribute and measure of the technological construct and is determined by its utility (tasks) and usability. Usability is the extent to which a system, product or service can be used by a specified user to achieve certain goals effectively, efficiently and with a high level of satisfaction in the specified context of use [15]. TOE assisted with guiding the evaluation of the usefulness (utility and usability) of the SMA tools.

The research method used was a Dataset Analysis of Tweets from two countries, Germany and South Africa. The analysis was exploratory and consisted of informal evaluations by the primary researcher to investigate the potential adoption and aspects of usefulness of SMA methods and tools according to utility and usability. Formal usability evaluations were not conducted; these could form part of a further study.

4   Results and Analysis

4.1   Social Media Monitoring with NVivo

The NVivo tool was used for the social media monitoring tasks, based on the motivation provided in [16] and [10] that it is useful, appropriate and economical for monitoring content from Social Networking Sites (SNSs). The functionalities of the NVivo tool vary from managing complex projects from multiple sources to processing open-ended text responses with geographical and categorical data from fixed-response questions. The *Structural Attribute* method for monitoring proposed in [9] was used with NVivo to monitor Tweets from both Germany and South Africa. Twitter was selected as an appropriate SNS as it is more easily accessible in comparison with other SNSs since Facebook and Instagram have much stricter data privacy and security rules.

A browser extension is provided by NVivo called NCapture that monitors and captures web-based (or social media) data using Google Chrome that can then be used for analysis. It provides for data collection from SNSs such as Twitter, Facebook, LinkedIn and YouTube. The Dataset Analysis commenced with the monitoring and collection of Tweets using the NCapture addon of NVivo. A premium version was purchased to perform social media monitoring because the trial version is limited to collecting two weeks' worth of data. The NVivo tool was found to be useful for location detection from where users tweeted since there is a geotagging feature in Twitter's API that provides a more meaningful experience by contextualising Tweets, and this feature can be switched on by users to accompany a Tweet. Since most Twitter users opt out of tweeting with the location feature switched on, NVivo is also able to detect the home location provided by users on their public profiles. When monitoring Tweets, the data was filtered according to location using Twitter's advanced search functionality. The location of the user from his/her Twitter profile was also collected with the Tweet text.

During data collection, Tweets from all locations in Germany and South Africa were collected that contained one or more of the related keywords, for the following four keywords:

- For Germany - "Covid19De" and "Impfungen".
- For South Africa - "Covid19" and "VaccineRollOut".

The keyword could be either a hashtag e.g., *#Covid19de*, or a single standalone word anywhere in the Tweet text. Data collected was restricted to a four-week period from 23 August 2021 to 13 September 2021. The minimum target sample size was 500 Tweets per keyword per week. Once collected, the data was saved in the NVivo file format ". nvcx". The experiment considered only text and not emojis. After collection, the Tweets were cleaned and transformed; for example, duplicates and data containing the user's personal information were removed (except for location). A free web tool known as *"The Online Doc Translator"* was used for translating the German Tweets into English.

4.2 Performing SMA Sentiment Analysis with uClassify

The *Opinion/Sentiment Analysis* method of [9] was used to perform the SMA tasks [17], and the selected tool uClassify, was used since it has been argued [10] to be an appropriate tool for SMA. The uClassify sentiment analysis method uses a hybrid approach that combines machine learning and the lexicon-based method. Another motivation for using uClassify was because it offered a free machine learning web service that has proven to have trained classifiers for sentiment analysis [17]. uClassify presents benefits related to classifiers that are well suited for short and long texts (Tweets, Facebook statuses, blog posts, product reviews, etc.). It also has classifiers that can analyse sentiment, age, gender, text language and mood amongst a host of other classifiers.

The total number of Tweets collected over the four weeks was 103 308, and after data cleaning and removing duplicates there were 52 641 Tweets. Using uClassify, the dataset was analysed for sentiments that were either *"negative"* or *"positive"* and allocated a probability of accuracy for each sentiment. Unfortunately, *"neutral"* sentiments were

Table 1. Tweets with total sentiments for all keywords after cleaning

South Africa						
Week	Keyword	Sentiment		Keyword	Sentiment	
	Covid19SA	Pos	Neg	VaccineRollOutSA	Pos	Neg
1	2330	62%	38%	4931	57%	43%
2	3717	68%	32%	5917	37%	63%
3	2554	71%	29%	5672	47%	53%
4	592	62%	38%	3177	61%	39%
Germany						
Week	Keyword	Sentiment		Keyword	Sentiment	
	CovidDe	Pos	Neg	Impfungen	Pos	Neg
1	3476	47%	53%	6954	50%	50%
2	3073	42%	58%	3047	43%	57%
3	1704	49%	51%	3682	25%	75%
4	561	47%	53%	1254	81%	19%

not represented because uClassify does not provide an automatic feature for classifying *"neutral"* sentiments. This limitation could be addressed by classifying those sentiments with low accuracy (between e.g., 45% to 55%) in future research. Summaries of the dataset for the keywords and sentiments is provided in Table 1.

It is clear from the table that the sentiment of Tweets for the keyword *"Covid19SA"* did not have much variation in percentage from Week 1 to Week 4 and were positive (>50%) for each of the four weeks. The related *"CovidDe"* Tweets from German users also did not have much variation in the sentiment percentage, however, they were all neutral, tending towards negative (just under 50%) each week.

Overall, the *"VaccineRollOutSA"* keyword had a lower percentage of positive sentiments than the *"Covid19SA"* ones, with two weeks having a mean positive sentiment (>50%) and the other two weeks with more negative sentiments ($\leq$50%). There was a fairly significant drop of 20% in positive sentiments from Week 1 to Week 2 (or increase in negatives) for the *"VaccineRollOutSA"* Tweets. This tendency towards neutral or negative sentiments could indicate the negativity and possible frustration and fear of citizens towards vaccinations in South Africa.

For the German Tweets with the *"Impfungen"* keyword, all four weeks were neutral or negative. There was a large drop from Week 1 to Week 2 in positive sentiments for the *"Impfungen"* keyword, and then a larger drop from Week 2 to Week 3. There was a fairly large increase from Week 3 to Week 4 for positive Tweets for both *"VaccineRollOutSA"* (61%) and *"Impfungen"* (81%). This result could indicate a possible improvement in citizens' attitudes towards the vaccination, possibly due to awareness and education campaigns.

4.3 Visualisation in SMA

The first step in PowerBI was the transformation of data, specifically the Date and Location dimensions. The Tweet locations were grouped according to the German states or South African provinces in which they fell, using the *"Data groups"* functionality in PowerBI. South African provinces were also labelled as States to standardise labels. The next step was to design and develop the visualisations using PowerBI dashboards according to the following SMA methods in [9]:

- Social Network Analysis (SNA) and visual analytics; and
- Trend and topic analysis.

Social Network Analysis (SNA) and Visual Analytics. Visual analytics aims to identify patterns, trends and structures, and assists in gaining useful insights through the analysis of a vast amount of data collected from different SNSs [18]. The *Visual Analytics* method of SNA was used in PowerBI since with dashboards users can identify patterns by physically manipulating data displays. Computational methods were used for reducing the data and displaying correlations between selected options. PowerBI dashboards allow for multiple filters and use card visuals at the top of the dashboard to display statistical calculations that provide the user with indicators of the data. For example, Fig. 2 presents the visual analytics of a PowerBI dashboard that displays the totals (n = 52641) and percentages of positive (50,42%) and negative (49,58%) Tweets for all Tweets of all locations in Germany and South Africa for all four weeks. It also uses three types of visuals, namely the Bar Chart, the Word Cloud and a Treemap visual. A Treemap in PowerBI displays hierarchical data as a set of nested rectangles. Each level of the hierarchy is represented by a coloured rectangle known as a branch containing smaller rectangles known as leaves. As shown in Fig. 2 the Treemap in the bottom right corner of the dashboard represents a visual of the Tweet sentiments per state. Different colours are used for different states. It is clear from this visual that the Gauteng province has the most sentiments out of all the states. The Word Cloud visual in PowerBI illustrates the most common topics found in the Tweets, using topic modelling and detection methods with advanced statistics and machine learning. The themes discovered can be further explored using the navigational interfaces for drill down functionality. The Word Cloud visual was used on the hashtags column to identify themes and topics from the most frequent keywords/hashtags. An example in Fig. 2 of the Word Cloud is seen where the three most frequent keywords are Covid19, Covid19SA and Vaccinations.

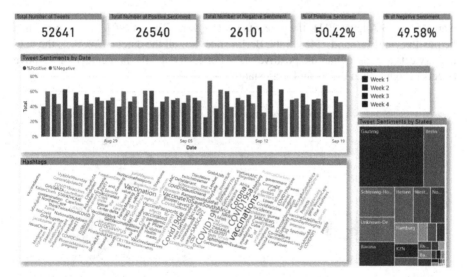

Fig. 2. Visual analytics of twitter dashboards (Germany and South Africa).

An example of filtering a dashboard can be seen where Fig. 3 illustrates the data from Fig. 2 filtered to only include Tweets with the South African keywords for all states (i.e., provinces) for Week 1 (n = 7261).

Figure 4 illustrates another example of filtering, where the data was filtered to only display data for the state of Berlin by hovering over the Berlin rectangle in the Treemap. Berlin was selected since it had many Tweets in Week 1. In the Bar Chart, green represents positive Tweets and red indicates negative Tweets. The light green/red-shaded bars represent the mean value and the dark-shaded bars represent the selected data. For

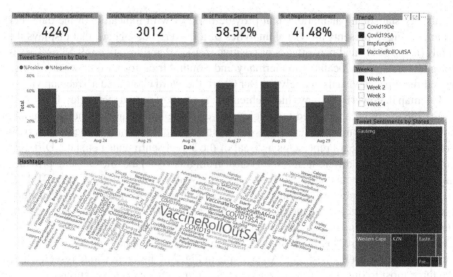

Fig. 3. Visual analytics example for the South African keywords (Week 1).

example, on 23 August 2021, the percentage of negative Tweets (90%) is far more than the positive ones (around 25%) in the Berlin state. For all the dates in Week 1, the negative Tweets are more than the positive ones. For each date, the percentage of negative Tweets is higher than the mean for all states.

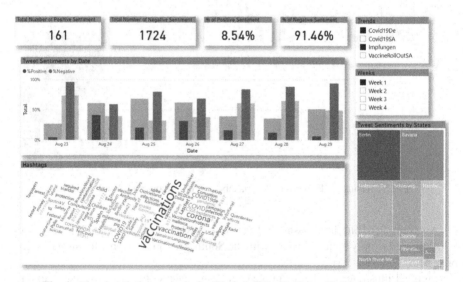

Fig. 4. Visual analytics example for Week 1 of Berlin State. (Color figure online)

Trend and Topic Analysis. Trend and topic analysis was evident when sentiments were visualised and insights were generated about topics and trends from sentiments. Fan and Gordon [19] believe that themes that are discovered can be used for other analytical tasks such as identifying users' interests, detecting emerging topics in social media postings or summarising parts. The Bar Chart in Fig. 5 visualises the percentage of positive to negative Tweets across various days (time periods) for the *"Covid19De"* and *"Impfungen"* keywords. Insights can be visualised in PowerBI by selecting the `Insights` icon followed by the `Trends` icon to show descriptions of top trends. In this case, the trend of *"Covid19De"* can be seen on the dashboard and the chart can be further drilled down into one of the four weeks. It can be seen from the dashboard's Treemap shown in Fig. 5 that the state with the most Tweets was the "Berlin State" (dark blue), closely followed by the "Schleswig-Holstein State".

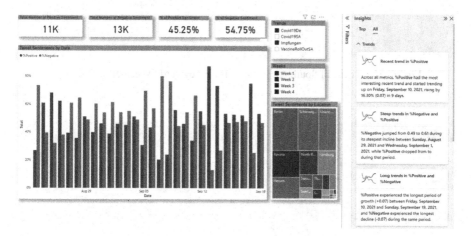

Fig. 5. Bar chart visual for the German case. (Color figure online)

The Map visual in PowerBI in Fig. 6 visualises the sentiment count across the various locations in South Africa and Germany. The keyword *"VaccineRollOutSA"* was used to filter and visualise the sentiment count for Tweets containing this keyword in South Africa. The size of the circle is representative of the number of Tweets. It can be seen that the area around Johannesburg had the most Tweets and a fairly even mix of positive and negative Tweets.

The Map visual in Fig. 7 indicates that the locations with the most Tweets were near Hamburg and north Germany. These areas also had more negative Tweets than positive. The significance of the colours, i.e., red and green, are again used for negative and positive Tweets respectively. A large percent of negative Tweets was also shown near Munich and Magdeburg. Near the Frankfurt and Berlin areas were Tweets that were mostly positive.

In Fig. 8a Pattern-based Analysis visualisation was used due to the richness of time series information and, because of the inadequacy of summary statistics to encapsulate structures and patterns. This visual is a type of Trend Technique, as it identifies data

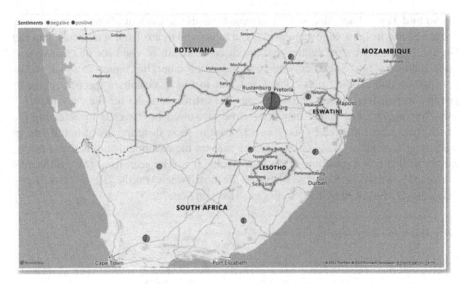

Fig. 6. Map visual of South African tweets for keyword "VaccineRollOutSA".

Fig. 7. Map visual of German tweets for keyword "CovidDe".

that repeats in a recognised way over a period of four weeks and shows the top 20 recognised keywords/hashtags with their associated sentiment counts for all the data from Germany for the *"Impfungen"* keyword. The top three keywords in this set of data were "Vaccinations" (*n = 3512*), *"Doctor safety report children vaccinations COVID"* (*n = 1602*), and *"Corona vaccinations"* (*n = 1023*).

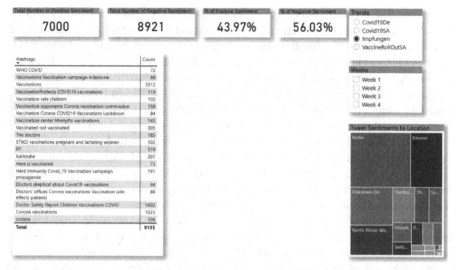

Fig. 8. Pattern-based analysis visual for keyword "Impfungen".

5 Discussion

The TOE theory proposed in [14] was used as the foundation and theoretical lens in the larger study to undergird the research by guiding the evaluation of the SMA tools in order to determine how useful they are or potentially can be for CzRM. The first characteristic of usefulness is the utility of the tools, which includes the tasks of SMA of monitoring data, analysing data and visualising data. These three tasks were achieved using the selected techniques from the framework in Fig. 1 which was extended from [9] to include COTS tools for SMA, for each of these tasks. The evaluation and demonstration of SMA tools in the Twitter Dataset Analysis revealed some interesting insights into citizens' views that may positively benefit government in supporting CzRM. The SMA tools used in this paper were effective and useful in collecting, analysing and visualising social media data. Locations that had the highest number of positive or negative Tweets could be identified, and the data could be drilled down into specific dates to determine trends and insights. For example, the user could visualise when sentiment become more negative. Other trends could be determined by identifying the most frequent keywords in the Pattern-based visual of PowerBI. The methods and tools used can therefore be useful to governments and assist managers conducting SMA projects and also assist with decision making and service delivery. PowerBI offered various dashboards and features that may support the government in extensive decision making to support CzRM.

6 Conclusion and Future Work

The practical contribution of the paper is the lessons learnt from the evaluations that can be used by SMA practitioners in government. The evaluations revealed that neither of the two evaluated tools, namely NVivo for social media monitoring and uClassify for performing SMA, could adequately visualise the collected Twitter dataset. Therefore, PowerBI was used in the evaluations as a possible suitable tool for the visualisation of the collected Tweets. The Twitter Dataset Analysis demonstrated and evaluated SMA methods and tools in terms of usefulness (utility and usability) as defined by TOE theory. The findings showed that the methods and tools used were useful for gaining insights into the Twitter data and can be used by government for SMA. The empirical experiments conducted using a real-world case and the lessons learnt provide a valuable contribution to other researchers and practitioners such as government managers involved in CzRM. One theoretical contribution is that TOE was used as a lens to guide the technological aspects to provide insights into future possible of adoption of SMA tools for CzRM. Another theoretical contribution is the Framework of SMA Methods and Techniques provided in Fig. 1 that was successfully used to guide the adoption of SMA for the cases of both the German and South African government departments.

The limitation of the paper is that the type of collected Tweets were limited to text and excluded emojis and pictures. The Dataset Analysis was conducted on only one SNS i.e. Twitter, since Facebook and Instagram have stricter privacy and security policies that made it more difficult to get access to citizens' posts. The collected Tweets from Twitter were only classified as "positive" and "negative" sentiments because uClassify is unable to classify "neutral" sentiments. The data collection history was limited to the last six months due to the restricted date range settings of Twitter. Another limitation was that the Twitter API settings were no longer providing the "near your area" feature. Therefore, the location was manually annotated using geo-coordinates from the user profile in Twitter. The geo-coordinates were used to detect the exact location of Tweets. Another limitation was the use of *"The Online Doc Translator"* for translating the German Tweets into English, which may have resulted in some unknown incorrect interpretations related to translating language structure, idioms, expressions, multiple meanings, sarcasm and missing names in translation. However, to overcome this a human German translator was used to verify the translation. Future research could include conducting usability evaluations of SMA tools, and possibly comparing the effectiveness of different SMA methods and tools. For practical recommendations for future research, government-related departments could adopt SMA methods and tools to monitor social media data to remain aware of trends and topics and be informed and insightful about citizens' needs.

References

1. Saleh, Y.: ICT, social media and COVID-19: evidence from informal home-based business community in Kuwait City. J. Enterp. Commun.: People Places Glob. Econ. **15**(3) 395–413 (2020). Emerald Publishing Limited. https://doi.org/10.1108/JEC-07-2020-0131
2. Shang, Y., Li, H., Zhang, R.: Effects of pandemic outbreak on economies: evidence from business history context. Front. Public Health **9**, 146 (2021)
3. Yang, S., Fichman, P., Zhu, X., Sanfilippo, M., Li, S., Fleischmann, K.R.: The use of ICT during COVID-19. In: Proceedings of the Association for Information Science and Technology, vol. 57, no. 1, p. e297 (2020)
4. Yakobi, K., Scholtz, B., vom Berg, B.: A conceptual model of the challenges of social media big data for citizen e-participation: a systematic review. In: Hattingh, M., Matthee, M., Smuts, H., Pappas, I., Dwivedi, Y.K., Mäntymäki, M. (eds.) I3E 2020. LNCS, vol. 12067, pp. 247–259. Springer, Cham (2020). https://doi.org/10.1007/978-3-030-45002-1_21

5. Ahmed, E., et al.: The role of big data analytics in internet of things. Comput. Netw. **129**, 459–471 (2017)
6. Oh, C., Sasser, S., Almahmoud, S.: Social media analytics framework: the case of Twitter and Super Bowl ads. J. Inf. Technol. Manag. **26**(1), 1–18 (2015)
7. He, W., Wu, H., Yan, G., Akula, V., Shen, J.: A novel social media competitive analytics framework with sentiment benchmarks. Inf. Manag. **52**(7), 801–812 (2015)
8. Singh, R.K., Verma, H.K.: Effective parallel processing social media analytics framework. J. King Saud Univ.-Comput. Inf. Sci. **34**(6), 2860-2870 (2020). https://doi.org/10.1016/j.jksuci.2020.04.019
9. Stieglitz, S., Mirbabaie, M., Ross, B., Neuberger, C.: Social media analytics – challenges in topic discovery, data collection, and data preparation. Int. J. Inf. Manage. **39**, 156–168 (2018)
10. Okuah, O.: A Social media method for eliciting Millennials' worldviews on the coastal and marine environment. Masters of Commerce Dissertation. Nelson Mandela University (2019)
11. Singh, P., Dwivedi, Y.K., Kahlon, K.S., Sawhney, R.S., Alalwan, A.A., Rana, N.P.: Smart monitoring and controlling of government policies using social media and cloud computing. Inf. Syst. Front. **22**(2), 315–337 (2020)
12. Moss, G., Kennedy, H., Moshonas, S., Birchall, C.: Knowing your publics: the use of social media analytics in local government. Inf. Polity **20**(4), 287–298 (2015)
13. Reka, R., Saraswathi, K., Sujatha, K.: A review on big data analytics. Asian J. Appl. Sci. Technol. (AJAST) **1**(1), 233–234 (2017)
14. Tornatzky, L.G., Fleischer, M.: The Processes of Technological Innovation. Lexington Books, Lexington (1990)
15. Jooste, C., Van Biljon, J., Mentz, J.: Usability evaluation for business intelligence applications: a user support perspective. South Afr. Comput. J. **53**(si-1), 32–44 (2014)
16. Jackson, K., Bazeley, P.: Qualitative Data Analysis with NVivo. 3rd edn. SAGE (2019)
17. Saqr, M., Alamro, A.: The role of social network analysis as a learning analytics tool in online problem-based learning. BMC Med. Educ. **19**(1), 1–11 (2019)
18. Wamba, S.F., Akter, S., Kang, H., Bhattacharya, M., Upal, M.: The primer of social media analytics. J. Organ. End User Comput. (JOEUC) **28**(2), 1–12 (2016)
19. Fan, W., Gordon, M.D.: The power of social media analytics. Commun. ACM **57**(6), 74–81 (2014)

The Impact of Machine Learning-Based Techniques on the Scouting and Screening Processes of Early-Stage Venture Capital Firms

Rocco Di Giannantonio, Matthias Murawski[✉], and Markus Bick

ESCP Business School, Berlin, Germany
rocco.di_giannantonio@edu.escp.eu, {mmurawski,mbick}@escp.eu

Abstract. Early-stage venture capital (VC) is a risky type of financing activity due to startups' extremely high failure rate and the many unknown variables related to a venture's future success. VCs' investment decisions are further challenged by a rise in competition, significant time constraints, and different cognitive biases. In recent years, Machine Learning (ML) models have been empirically studied and adopted in the industry as a solution to overcome the limits that VCs face in their investment decision-making process. Nevertheless, a qualitative assessment of such technology's impacts in early-stage VCs sourcing and screening processes lacks in the academic literature. In this regard, the findings of this paper highlight beneficial impacts on the quality of the deal flow from the adoption of ML-based tools. Concerning the screening process, the findings suggest limited impacts of such technologies mainly due to a lack of detecting crucial human capital components, investor strong reliance on their abilities and industry structural dynamics.

Keywords: Artificial Intelligence · Machine Learning · Early-stage venture capital · Qualitative research

1 Introduction

Venture capital (VC) is a medium-long term form of investment in unlisted companies with high growth potential. This form of private financing is mainly provided by firms or funds with the aim of obtaining a substantial capital gain from the sale of the acquired equity investment or by its listing in the stock exchange [1]. Since the establishment of the first actual VC firm in 1946 by MIT and Harvard Business School professors [2], VC played a fundamental role in the economy and in technological innovation. VC helped young companies, in their early stage, to develop their business, providing economic support, advice and non-monetary resources [3]. After the significant development in the United States from the '80s, this form of financing has been one of the main driving forces behind some of the most vibrant sectors of the world economy in recent decades [2]. In the high-technology sector, VC played a crucial role in allowing the tremendous

© IFIP International Federation for Information Processing 2022
Published by Springer Nature Switzerland AG 2022
S. Papagiannidis et al. (Eds.): I3E 2022, LNCS 13454, pp. 136–147, 2022.
https://doi.org/10.1007/978-3-031-15342-6_11

growth of companies such as Microsoft, Google, Facebook, WhatsApp and Alibaba in particular.

Access to capital is one of the main obstacles for the development of entrepreneurship [4]. As not all capital demand meets capital supply in the economy, there is always a *funding gap* for business development. This gap is even more relevant for start-ups that are looking for capital in their early stages of life and, as a result, they have limited access to traditional capital markets, bank loans or to other particular debt instruments. This phenomenon is widespread for those companies that operate on the frontier of emerging technologies, as these are mainly characterized by a high presence of non-tangible assets and projections of negative profits for several years [5].

Given the characteristics of the type of investments, VCs deal with a high degree of uncertainty. In fact, VCs investment activities are characterized by an extreme level of information asymmetry which results from adverse selection risks regarding hidden information of the business (i.e., VCs do not have the same level of information as entrepreneurs) and moral hazard risks (i.e., entrepreneurs are able to undertake actions that are not noticeable by the VCs). In this perspective, conventionally, VCs take on greater risks than most traditional types of investment funds, also considering that start-ups failure rate is exceptionally high [6]. For these reasons, after usually offering financing solutions and mentoring activities, VCs would expect to receive high returns out of their investments with a successful exit of their portfolio firms through acquisition or Initial Public Offering (IPO) [2].

Considering the high risks involved in the sector, it is crucial for VCs to possess good sourcing (i.e., find a pool of potential high-growth ventures) and screening abilities during the investment decision-making process [7]. Investors usually develop these abilities after many years of experiences which contribute to create a "gut feel" as criterion of their investment decision [8]. However, a large amount of research considers VCs decision-making process highly subjected to psychological biases such as over-confidence [6], local bias and loss aversion [9].

In this scenario, advanced analytical approaches to improve VCs investment decision-making are increasingly becoming an important field of research. Investment decisions are intrinsically complex as they require the analysis of a vast amount of data [10]. Machines proved to be highly efficient in weighting many different criteria and providing insights into human decision-making [11]. Considering the above, the idea of using Machine Learning (ML) to augment VC's ability to process and interpret information to improve the sourcing and screening processes is attractive both for entrepreneurs and investors. Particularly considering the benefits that the technology can bring in lowering risk, eliminating psychological biases, reducing time and costs, especially for early-stage investments [12].

Artificial Intelligence (AI) and ML are increasingly used to enhance decision making in a corporate context. Regarding the financial sector, AI has been adopted significantly for trading activities in the stock market and the hedge fund industry [12]. However, paradoxically most of the VC firms around the world that have been investing intensively in AI technology startups are not using such technology for the internal purposes of maximizing returns while lowering risks. Only recently, very few early-stage VCs started adopting such technologies to improve their scouting and screening abilities.

In the literature, for decades' researchers focused on empirically investigating the impact of certain variables on the future success of early-stage companies through statical methods. This vast field of research can be clustered according to the variables analyzed, such as human capital characteristics and business-related characteristics [7]. However, only in recent years few studies empirically assessed the impact of advanced ML algorithms predictions of success from a VC perspective.

Nevertheless, to the best of our knowledge, there are no studies available in the academic literature that provide a qualitative assessment on the impact of ML techniques in the scouting and screening processes of early-stage ventures. This gap is mainly attributed to the very recent application of such technologies in VC firms. Thus, the aim of this paper is to reduce the gap by answering the following research questions (RQ):

RQ1: What are the current main challenges for VC firms in the sourcing and screening processes of early-stage ventures?
RQ2: What advantages can the adoption of ML-based technologies bring to VCs in overcoming these challenges in these specific areas?

The remainder of the paper is structured as follow: Sect. 2 contains an overview about related work. Section 3 includes the methodology used in this study along with the data analysis conducted. Section 4 summarizes the findings of the study combined with a discussion, based on which a conclusion is provided in Sect. 5.

2 Related Work

The rise of available online data from several different sources has been the main driver that contributed to recent attention in the academic literature towards using advanced ML-based models to analyze and predict early-stage companies' success from a VC perspective [13]. As the volume and variety of data exploded in the last decade, various research methods in entrepreneurship did not have enough capacity to take full advantage of such an amount of information [13]. On the other hand, predicting future events by processing an almost infinitely large amount of data with computational methods has developed due to recent technological advancements in AI [13]. Also, the rise of commercial databases providing structured data related to companies aggregated from multiple sources such as CB-Insights, Dealroom, Pitchbook, Crunchbase and Preqin filled the gap of structured information needed both in entrepreneurial research and for practitioners in the industry [14]. Thus, driven by the increase in the availability of digital traces and the adoption of more sophisticated forms of ML applied, few empirical studies emerged recently in the literature on ML applied to VC.

Krishna et al. [15] investigated a method to forecast the outcome of startups considering variables such timing of the seed round, numbers and money raised in further funding rounds and severity factors such as the composition of capital structure, good management system, discipline, and determination and many more. The authors gathered data from several sources such as Crunchbase, Techcrunch and Forbes for more than 11.000 companies, including successful and failed ones. In the study, several ML techniques were used, such as Bayesian Networks and Random Forest. The authors found that their most successful models are able to predict startup success and failure with a precision accuracy between 73.3% and 96.3%.

Arroyo et al. [12] published a paper intending to investigate ML performances to support VC investment decisions. In particular, the paper focused on building an ML model to predict early-stage companies' success. Startup success is defined in several forms that can be useful for VC investors. Thus, the target variables include events such as company closes, new founding rounds, acquisition, and IPO. In the study [12], early-stage companies were defined as having less than four years at the time of investment, and it was considered that the company would not raise additional funds after three years from the time of investment. After applying these windows, the final sample from CrunchBase consisted of more than 120.00 companies, including information such as country age and sector, and more and 34.000 funding rounds events associated. The set of predictors consisted of company information such as location and business sectors, funding information such as the number of funding rounds and unique investors, founder information such as country of origin, gender, and type of degree. Several ML classifier algorithms were considered, such as Decision Trees, Random Forest and Gradient Tree Boosting (GTB). The study showed that GTB performed better than the other algorithms to determine the future success of an early-stage company with an accuracy of 82%. The authors concluded that their findings strongly suggest the importance of ML to help early-stage investors in their scouting and screening decisions.

Another relevant study is the one by Retterath [13], who benchmarked the screening performances between 111 VCs and a gradient boosted tree classification algorithm. He found that the algorithm performed 29% better that the average investor.

To sum up, the few articles available represent significant progress in the emergent field of study regarding the impact of ML techniques in the VCs investments decision making. We contribute to this increasing understanding with our empirical study which is introduced in the following section.

3   Research Design

The impact of AI in VC is still not a well-established topic in the academic literature. The implications of adopting ML-based techniques in the scouting and screening process of early-stage VC are still not fully understood. Thus, the underlying study uses an exploratory research design. Therefore, a qualitative method is considered the best strategy to answer the research questions. More detailed, we have conducted semi-structured interviews with a panel of expert professionals working within VC focusing on early-stage investments using and not using AI technologies within their firms. The selection of interview participants in our research is determined according to theoretical sampling. Under this method, the sample is not statistically defined before starting the interviews, but during the investigation itself, based on the representativeness of the sample concerning the issues that progressively emerged [16].

In order to form the basis for the data collection, a total of 54 VC professionals have been contacted between February and April 2021 through direct e-mail and the professional networking platform LinkedIn with a formal request to participate in the underlying study. Several sources such as magazines, articles, professional forums,

LinkedIn and company websites were used to identify potential participants. Especially, in the process of contacting potential interview participants, careful consideration was made regarding the years of experience of the professionals.

Table 1. Interview participants

IP	Company	Headquarter	Using AI?
1	Inria - former Index Ventures	Paris	x
2	InReachVentures	London	✓
3	P101	Milan	x
4	Luminous Ventures	London	x
5	Raized.Ai	Zurich	✓
6	LVenture	Rome	x
7	Mito Technology	Milan	x
8	Elaia	Paris	✓
9	United Ventures	Milan	x
10	Dealroom	Amsterdam	n/a
11	Balderton Capital	London	✓

The data collection process resulted in 11 semi-structured interviews (Table 1). The majority of the interview participants (IPs) have an extensive professional background in the field of VC. In particular, out of the 11 IPs, 4 professionals are currently working in firms adopting ML-techniques.

The interviews conducted lasted between 25 to 45 min. The data collection process was based on the interview guideline outlined in Fig. 1. The interview guideline contains a set of broad questions that are formulated based on the research questions of the underlying paper. The questions are formulated as open-ended to guarantee the IPs the possibility to introduce their points of view and introduce topics not initially foreseen. In this regard, careful attention was made in order to avoid "leading-the-witness questions" [17]. Thus, IPs were encouraged to share their personal experiences and opinions on the topic. The content of each interview, made on video-communication tools such as Google Meet and Zoom, was recorded and transcribed with Trint, an AI-driven audio transcription software.

The data analysis process has been conducted by following the so called *Gioia method*, which has been conceived as a practical inductive approach to analyse information with "qualitative rigor" [17]. The analysis has been started by reading through the data and inductively coding the content of the interview's transcripts, always keeping in mind the general focus of the research [16].

After conducting the first round of coding, many different words, concepts, and categories from the transcripts emerged. This is something expected within the Gioia method, as this first round of coding does not have to strictly focus on making sense of all the coded information, and it must stick to the informants' terms as much as possible [17].

The next step of the data analysis was to narrow down the vast number of codes by distilling the categories based on the focus of the research and finding similarities

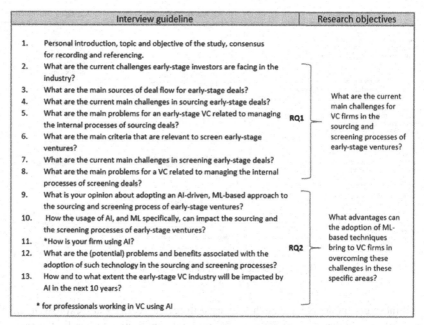

Fig. 1. Interview guideline

and relationships. Also, the number of codes was reduced to enable the emergence of the categories mentioned by the IPs more often. This process resulted in identifying 16 first-order concepts. Starting from the first-order concepts identified, the second step of the data analysis process focused on generating broader categories. In this second level of analysis, the target is to discover patterns and ideas that are helpful in explaining the topic investigated by grouping the first-order concepts into second-order themes [17]. The themes that emerged in the second step of the data analysis process are further investigated to create aggregate dimensions with a higher level of conceptualization [17]. These overarching dimensions are linked and embrace the second-order themes globally. Overall, out of the six second-order themes, three aggregate dimensions emerged (Fig. 2).

4 Findings and Discussion

4.1 ML Impacts in the Sourcing Phase

Regarding the deal flow generation, several themes emerged in the information collected during the interviews. Frequently, IPs highlighted that the current deal sourcing processes are significantly more inbound driven. Amongst other factors, the main reason behind this is that VCs value the sources from which they consider potential deals, and there is a general reliance on proposals coming from other VCs. The underlying idea is that the VC relies on the judgement of other VCs proposing and or signaling potential investments. Nevertheless, VCs' trustworthy sources are several and characterize the network-centric characteristic of this industry [18]. The inbound deal flow is further generated by the funding requests that come directly from the founders, especially for well-branded funds.

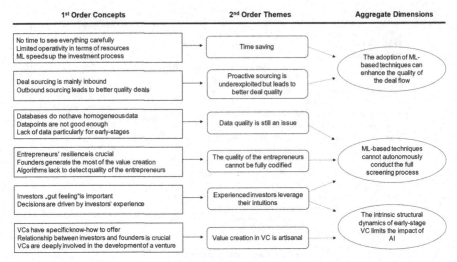

Fig. 2. Overview of Gioia procedure applied

All these components have been increased in recent years by an "explosion" of the number of potential deals, challenging VC internal capabilities to handle the increase in volume, making sure of not missing opportunities. Moreover, outbound deal flow generation activities are not fully exploited. In fact, in terms of volumes, most IPs refers that it counts to a less extent. The reasons regarding the underemployment of outbound sourcing are mainly due to a lack of human resources that can oversee such activities and the difficulty to find sources from which to proactively pull in deal flow, particularly for early-stage. Nevertheless, sourcing deals in a proactive manner tends to lead to deals that have more chances to successfully pass the screening phase, therefore having more quality characteristics. This is since with this sourcing approach, the investors scout directly according to the criteria that characterize their investment paper. Thus, they are already applying some specific filters enabling outbound-generated deals to have higher chances to pass the screening phase. It is in this context of potential development of outbound activities and of a lack of resources that AI can play a role. In fact, according to the IPs that are currently using such technologies, ML-based tools can help in sourcing out potential good deals that already match to different extent investors requirements and to filters out the "noise" in the deal flow generation.

The sourcing and filtering functionalities that ML-based tools use to scout potential early-stage deals were explained by the IPs adopting them as follow. The data are collected through many web crawlers that automatically scrap information from multiple sources that are both public (e.g., forums, pages, directories, seed investors and accelerators web pages) and private (e.g., Dealroom and Crunchbase) (IP2). The basic information about each company is then augmented with "signals" that are considered to be relevant in predicting its future success. This enrichment of the data is done by automatically associating to each venture data regarding variables such as founders' type of education or employee growth. These variables have similar characteristics as the one studied in empirical research [12, 13, 15].

During this process, the automatically collected data eventually may also include companies that are not in scope and irrelevant from an early-stage VC perspective, such as hotels or hairdresser (IP2). Then, an ML algorithm can distinguish "out of the noise", which are the potential deals that are relevant (e.g., between a hairdresser and a scalable startup). Thus, on top of the raw data, a "layer of intelligence" is applied to filter in terms of pertinence and in terms of what can be interesting for the VCs based on their investment paper.

Concerning the deals sourcing phase of the investment decision-making process, ML-based tools enable VC to automatically expand their outbound scouting capabilities and increasing the quality of the deal flow by providing a pre-filtered pool of potential investments to the investment team. By automatically apply the criteria embedded in the VC investment, the sourcing phase benefits not only from an increase in the quality of the deal flow but also from reducing the time-consuming scouting activities.

These benefits greatly impact the investment decision-making process because time, as it has been highlighted by most of the IPs, is the most worrying issue in all the investment activities, being VC "an activity marked by time" (IP3). In terms of internal management, having a time-reduction on the sourcing phase implies having the possibility to allocate resources more effectively for other value generation activities, thus increasing efficiencies (IP4). For this range of reasons, also IPs that did not yet adopt such tools within their firms showed a great interest in its application in the sourcing phase.

4.2 ML Impacts in the Screening Process

In the investment-decisions making process, also the screening phase is positively impacted by ML-based tools in different ways. First, having a pre-filtered pool of qualified potential investment opportunities results in investors making the most of their time appropriately screening more in-depth potential deals, avoid spending time to revise deals that are neither pertinent or interesting, thus increasing the quality of their work. The total amount of deals that are needed to be screened by funds in each year is enormous and there is little time to conduct such activities. Compared to the sourcing process, the screening phase has further considerations related to ML for a fully autonomous deals screen. Several concerns were raised during the interviews regarding the possibility of ML-based tools, after ranking the most interesting investment opportunities, to autonomously select the best potential deals and bring them forward in the investment decision-making process (e.g., due diligence, negotiations).

One of such reasons is related to the trust that investors have in conducting a full screen based on data that is not homogenous and can contains misleading information. Moreover, for early-stage ventures, the lack of historical information is an issue to generate sufficient insightful information by the ML tools to base an investment decision. According to IP10, who works in one of the largest data providers companies, there is a strong constant search by investors for gathering new and alternatives data points during the earliest phases of a venture.

ML tool's ability to entirely conducting the screening process is further challenged by the lack of such tools to detect entrepreneurs' human capital potential, a factor that is considered crucial for early-stage investors. The majority of the IPs highlighted the key role that entrepreneurs' characteristics play in the investment decision-making process, an aspect that is widely covered in academic literature [19, 20]. Although such tools are programmed to detect human capital with information such as founder's university, founder years of experiences or venture management team diversity of backgrounds, they are not able to provide a deeper level of analysis on the real entrepreneur's capabilities to manage a successful venture. In fact, many IPs stressed that such characteristics are not enough to provide a reliable assessment of the ventures' human capital components. One of the most crucial variables for VCs that emerged during the interviews is entrepreneur's resilience, understood as the capability of the managing team to face the unexpected challenges that will always happen during the life of a venture and to adapt accordingly:

Thus, IPs revealed a vital concern regarding ML-tools algorithms lacking the ability to recognize such crucial elements and establish the likelihood of a venture's future success. Their impact in the screening phase seems to be limited. Such tools are not able to provide a complete assessment on deal potential because many human capital aspects, especially in early-stage VC, cannot be codified.

The other main arguments that suggest potential limitation that emerged during the interviews are related to investors strong reliance on their intuitions while deciding on investment opportunities. Their intuition enables them to especially detect the crucial human components that they value to be determinant in predicting the likelihood of the venture's success.

Considering the above, the impacts of ML-based tools on the screening process is partial. This phase can benefit from the outcome of an automated algorithmic-driven outbound deal sourcing, i.e., receiving pre-filtered investment proposals within the scope of the investment paper. This creates efficiencies in the internal processes of reviewing deals due to human resources gaining time to assess the deals in a comprehensive manner. However, the findings suggest that the applications of such technologies are not yet able to autonomies the screening process. Also, the IPs that have adopted such technologies in their processes are not leveraging them for selecting deals but rather for providing recommendations and support in their processes. Thus, the "cherry-picking" activity is still human-based, even if supported by technology.

4.3   The Overall Impact of AI in Early-Stage VC

At the heart of early-stage VC value creation is the human relationship between the investors and the team of the backed venture. A relationship based on trust on both sides and the "chemistry" generated in their relationship (IP3). Furthermore, given the medium- to long-term time horizon of this investment activity, the personal dynamics involved in the process are even more important. In fact, this relationship was referred as something kind of a "marriage" (IP3, IP6, IP7, IP8).

The relevancy of the human component in early-stage VC, at least at the moment, is one of the primary limits of the impact of AI-driven technologies in the screening and even further phases of the VC investment decision-making process. Early-stage investments are risky and contain many unknown variables that are extremely difficult, if not impossible, to predict ex-ante (IP1). In this context, making a long-term investment in a venture that naturally will change dramatically over time, for better or worse, will entail several unknowns (IP3). Consequently, a solid relationship based on trust between the founder and the entrepreneurs is essential.

According to the findings, it is this relationship, this human component, that makes VC different from other types of investments categories. Investors' intuition is neither replicable, nor codifiable. In VC, these dynamic forces are the base for creating synergies that eventually will create value for all the parties involved in an investment decision. The relationship between these non-tangible elements lies at the core of this investment activity. These dynamics do not only govern the relationship between investors and the entrepreneurs but are also included within the structure of the investment firm.

Integrating ML-based tools and leveraging their superior ability to analyze a large volume of data and find "signals" of success have the potential to support the decision-making process in VC. However, at the moment that early-stage investors intuition is removed from the process along with the artisanal way of creating value for the companies, then this type of investment activity cannot be defined as venture capital anymore. Furthermore, creating investments screening processes entirely based on ML, would imply VC firms to change the composition of their investment teams, relying more on data scientist figures that would undoubtedly bring knowledge valuable for building and make functioning such machines. However, they may lack experience and specific knowledge needed to select promising ventures:

In the end, the findings highlighted a general skepticism towards a fully algorithm-based approach in the investment decision-making process for selecting deals. Despite the valuable contribution that this technology brings for scouting quality investment opportunities and the partial support it offers in the selection process, the overall ML-based tools impact is limited due to the intrinsic dynamics of early-stage VC investments, i.e., an artisanal, interpersonal, and intuitive-based approach that is essential to conduct this business.

5 Conclusion

The findings of this study highlight the main advantages and challenges of using ML tools during sourcing and screening in early-stage VC firms, and thereby provide answers to the two research questions that guided this research.

Recently, online media and industry-related research studies increasingly show arguments that direct towards a significant impact of AI-driven solutions in the way VC conduct investments. Gartner [21] claims that "75% of VCs will use AI to make investment decisions by 2025" and an increasing number of VC are declaring to be using AI in their processes. In this context, it should also be considered, as highlighted by IP11, that many funds that are promoting themselves as AI-driven, but very few are using such technology in its strict sense. Most of the time, they claim their investment decision to be AI-powered even though they are just improving the process with basic data analysis components.

Despite an increasing trend that is recently forming around the strong magnitude of the impacts that these technologies have on the decision-making processes in VCs, the results of this study underline serious cautions towards it. In early-stage investments, data can never be flawless, not all variables can be quantified, and it is extremely to determine ex-ante the success of something that would be affected by so many different variables. The impact of the collaboration between VC and investors, a crucial aspect for value generation, it is hard, if not impossible to be assessed a priori.

However, this exploratory research has several limitations. Despite the high level of experience of the professional who participated in the research, the number of interviews conducted is insufficient to generalize the findings to all the early-stage VCs. Also, the sample of participants has limitation in terms of diversity: all the participants are male European and work in firms headquartered in Europe, and a higher number of participants who are not currently adopting ML-techniques (7) were interviewed compared to professionals not using such tools (4). The research findings would have benefited from a more extensive and diversified pool of participants, particularly considering that the early-stage VC industry is particularly advanced in countries such as Israel, United States and China. Moreover, this research only focused on assessing the impact of ML-based tools on the sourcing and screening phases of the investment decision-making process of early-stage VC that, although they are widely considered extremely important, are only a portion of the overall VC value chain. Future research should therefore address further phases of the VC value chain towards a comprehensive understanding.

References

1. Da Rin, M., Hellmann, T.F., Puri, M.: A survey of venture capital research. SSRN Electron. J. (2011)
2. Gompers, P., Lerner, J.: The venture capital revolution. J. Econ. Perspect. 15, 145–168 (2001)
3. Dessí, R., Yin, N.: The Impact of Venture Capital on Innovation. The Oxford Handbook of Venture Capital. Oxford University Press, Oxford (2012)
4. Hamilton, R.T., Fox, M.A.: The financing preferences of small firm owners. Int. J. Entrep. Behav. Res. 4, 239–248 (1998)
5. Jeng, L.A., Wells, P.C.: The determinants of venture capital funding: evidence across countries. J. Corp. Finan. 6, 241–289 (2000)
6. Zacharakis, A.L., Shepherd, D.A.: The nature of information and overconfidence on venture capitalists' decision making. J. Bus. Ventur. 16, 311–332 (2001)
7. Corea, F.: An Introduction to Data Everything You Need to Know About AI. Big Data and Data Science. Springer, Cham (2019). https://doi.org/10.1007/978-3-030-04468-8
8. Huang, L., Pearce, J.L.: Managing the unknowable. Adm. Sci. Q. 60, 634–670 (2015)
9. Tversky, A., Kahneman, D.: Advances in prospect theory: cumulative representation of uncertainty. J. Risk Uncertain. 5, 297–323 (1992)
10. Fried, V.H., Hisrich, R.D.: Toward a model of venture capital investment decision making. Financ. Manag. 23, 28 (1994)
11. Dellermann, D., Calma, A.: Making AI ready for the wild: the hybrid intelligence unicorn hunter. SSRN Electron. J. (2018)
12. Arroyo, J., Corea, F., Jimenez-Diaz, G., Recio-Garcia, J.A.: Assessment of machine learning performance for decision support in venture capital investments. IEEE Access 7, 124233–124243 (2019)
13. Retterath, A.: Human versus computer: benchmarking venture capitalists and machine learning algorithms for investment screening. SSRN Electron. J. (2020)
14. Grover, V., Chiang, R.H., Liang, T.-P., Zhang, D.: Creating strategic business value from big data analytics: a research framework. J. Manag. Inf. Syst. 35, 388–423 (2018)

15. Krishna, A., Agrawal, A., Choudhary, A.: Predicting the outcome of startups: less failure, more success. In: Bonchi, F., Wu, X. (eds.) Proceedings of 16th IEEE International Conference on Data Mining Workshops, Barcelona, Catalonia, Spain, 12–15 December 2016, pp. 798–805. IEEE, Piscataway (2016)
16. Faggiolani, C.: Perceived identity: applying grounded theory in libraries. Ital. J. Libr. Arch. Inf. Sci. 2 (2011)
17. Gioia, D.A., Corley, K.G., Hamilton, A.L.: Seeking qualitative rigor in inductive research. Organ. Res. Methods 16, 15–31 (2013)
18. Gompers, P.A., Gornall, W., Kaplan, S.N., Strebulaev, I.A.: How do venture capitalists make decisions? J. Financ. Econ. 135, 169–190 (2020)
19. Cassar, G.: Industry and startup experience on entrepreneur forecast performance in new firms. J. Bus. Ventur. 29, 137–151 (2014)
20. Miloud, T., Aspelund, A., Cabrol, M.: Startup valuation by venture capitalists: an empirical study. Ventur. Cap. 14, 151–174 (2012)
21. Gartner Inc.: Gartner Says Tech Investors Will Prioritize Data Science and Artificial Intelligence Above "Gut Feel" for Investment Decisions By 2025. https://www.gartner.com/en/newsroom/press-releases/2021-03-10-gartner-says-tech-investors-will-prioritize-data-science-and-artificial-intelligence-above-gut-feel-for-investment-decisions-by-20250

Extended SESIM: A Tool to Support the Generation of Synthetic Datasets for Human Activity Recognition

Timothy Musharu[✉] and Dieter Vogts

Nelson Mandela University, Gqeberha 6001, South Africa
s217080421@mandela.ac.za

Abstract. The accessibility of datasets that capture the performance of Activities of Daily Living is limited by the difficulties in setting up test beds. The Covid-19 pandemic recently compounded such challenges. Smart Environments employed as test-beds consist of sensors and applications formulated to develop a comfortable and safe environment for their inhabitants. Despite the increase in quantities of Smart Environments, accessibility of these spaces for researchers has become even more challenging amidst a pandemic. Computing power has enabled researchers to generate virtual Smart Environments with fewer overheads and less complexity. This article proposes an Extended Smart Environment Simulator (ESESIM), with multiple inhabitants possibly utilised for dataset generation. The proposed simulation tool has a virtual space with multiple script-regulated inhabitants. While the various inhabitants probe the Smart Environment, sensor readings are recorded and stored in a dataset. The virtual space developed in this study generated synthetic datasets that can be employed for Human Activity recognition in machine learning. This study also evaluated two deep machine learning models and performance mechanisms in recognising four activities of daily living, namely personal hygiene, dressing, cooking and sleeping, on the SESIM dataset. Findings from this study indicate that simulation can be used as a tool for generating human activity datasets.

Keywords: Human activity recognition · Synthetic datasets · Machine learning · Deep learning

1 Introduction

Coronavirus 2019 (COVID-19) is a highly infectious disease afflicting humans and is associated with severe respiratory distress, with added mortality risk in specific vulnerable populations. Due to the negative impact of the 2020 COVID-19 outbreak, the World Health Organization (WHO) designated the situation as a Public Health Emergency of International Concern (PHEIC) on 30 January 2020 [1]. COVID-19 was classified as a pandemic disease due to its rapid spread of infection across large groups of individuals [2]. The epidemic was a gamechanger for society and organisational structures, affecting

© IFIP International Federation for Information Processing 2022
Published by Springer Nature Switzerland AG 2022
S. Papagiannidis et al. (Eds.): I3E 2022, LNCS 13454, pp. 148–163, 2022.
https://doi.org/10.1007/978-3-031-15342-6_12

how researchers in Human Activity and Smart healthcare work [3]. In a bid to combat the pandemic, healthcare systems primarily focused on implementing large-scale testing and effectively treating infected individuals. Additionally, to contain the infection and ensure the pandemic's sustainability, an alternative optimal solution on which governments agreed was to impose lockdowns within infected regions within individual nations. Test-beds that were easily accessible before the pandemic became challenging to access, resulting in reduced da- datasets being available for researchers to use for Human Activity Recognition activities. In addition, the requirement for social distancing within the sensor test-bed and minimising social contact has resulted in a reduction in the number of individuals that could occupy a test-bed simultaneously, consequently limiting the quantity and variety of out- put data. One example of a test-bed for HAR is a Smart Environment equipped with sensors and actuators.

Sensors and actuators in Smart Environments adapt to the inhabitant's demands. This is conducted to monitor, provide comfort and enhance living conditions [4]. The increase in Smart Environment research and the need for simulation environments or test-beds was sparked by the recent emergence of applications and systems being developed in this area [5, 6]. Human Activity Recognition (HAR) is a complex and dynamic area of research that has recently received significant attention [7].

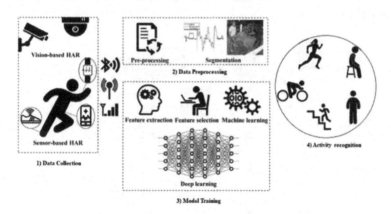

Fig. 1. Human Activity Recognition framework [8]

Although there are two types of HAR, video-based and sensor-based, the latter is more prevalent. HAR has grown in popularity as researchers attempt to overcome privacy concerns associated with image/video-based systems [8]. Figure 1 summarises the two classes of HAR and illustrates the HAR process framework [8]. This framework comprises (1) data collection for vision-based HAR (image-sensing technology) and sensor-based HAR (various types of sensors); (2) data pre-processing, which performs essential pre-processing steps for collected data; (3) training phase, which utilises machine learning (ML) or deep learning approaches to identify patterns from collected data, and (4) activities recognition.

Ambient Assisted Living (AAL) in smart homes is an example of how HAR is used in a wide range of applications [9, 10]. Other prominent interest domains include monitoring and detection [5, 11], computer engineering [12], physical science [13], health-related issues [14, 15], natural sciences, and industrial-academic areas [16]. Data collection is the main driver for all such research niches, forming the basis for Artificial Intelligence (AI) and machine learning (ML) in HAR. Without the availability of such data, the ML models cannot be adequately trained and evaluated.

The presence of dataset simulation tools mitigates the disadvantages/challenges associated with generating actual datasets. Technologies enable rapid dataset production and provide powerful ways for capturing sensor data. Additionally, they can give a solution, such as the ability to pause and fast-forward the simulation, allowing for increasingly precise activity labelling without violating COVID-19 safety rules. Activity labels are commonly referred to as annotations [17]. When researchers develop ML models to target specific activities, they rely on the availability of representative datasets. In the case of a real test-bed, if the results indicate the requirement to modify the experimental setting, this can be an expensive and impractical option, given that several sensors are fixed to the environment/non-portable. Consequently, the researcher could fine-tune model parameters post-evaluation, as illustrated in Fig. 2a. Conversely, with a simulated smart home, this can be easily accomplished, and the researcher can adjust the SE design, as shown in Fig. 2b.

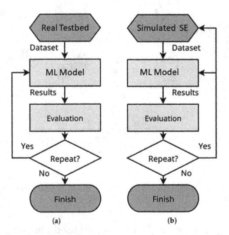

Fig. 2. The workflow of real and simulated smart environment test-beds. (a) real testbed; (b) simulated testbed [35].

This article presents the architecture and implementation of the Extended Smart Environment Simulator (ESESIM), an extension of the smart environment simulation (SESIM) tool created by [18]. This study's evaluation was extended to a six-room environment that supports multiple inhabitants and sensor data output in JavaScript Object Notation (JSON). This study further evaluates the performance of HAR on the SESIM dataset using differing deep ML models, namely, Long Short Term- Memory

(LSTM), together with Bi-Directional Long Short-Term Memory (Bi-LSTM). The following section reviews existing literature on HAR and smart home simulation tools compared to our proposed tool, Extended SESIM (ESESIM). Section 3 presents the proposed simulation tool SESIM and the implementation of ML models for HAR. Section 4 presents the results of ML models on the SESIM dataset. Section 5 closes and discusses recommended future work in simulation and HAR.

2   Related Works

The following section discusses related research and its relevance to the design, im-implementation and evaluation of the SESIM simulator, dataset, and application of ML models to support HAR. Additionally, this section discusses human activity and the difficulties associated with monitoring activity.

2.1   Smart Environments

Smart environments (SEs) respond to user actions and cater to individual needs. [19] defined a SE as "a small intelligent space where various devices continuously work to improve the inhabitants' lives." [26–29]. Such studies defined smartness and intelligence as the ability to acquire and apply knowledge autonomously within the environment. Based on that, they described a SE as a platform that can learn about the environment and use it to improve user experience [24]. [25] termed SE as intelligent or smart spaces. The study concluded that intelligent spaces enhance human functionality and experience through physical world data [26–29]. Sensors "perceive and understand what is happening within them" while actuators "enact a response". Intelligent buildings and spaces that gather data and respond autonomously have replaced single rooms or sections for testing [27]. For a physical environment to qualify as a SE sensing/actuation, control, communication, computation and intelligence are required [30].

Incorporation of computation sensing /actuation capabilities into a physical space should be performed to enhance the user experience within their environment. Recent research focused on improving the user experience in a SE, which requires large amounts of sensor data [19–21]. Providing new functionalities or enhancing current ones to support human activity without good sensor data remains challenging. Another critical challenge with SE is that they do not adequately cater for user requirements [22], which has been the key driver for research in this domain. Over and above this challenge, users view autonomous actions in a SE as patronising, which brings the need for SE to support means of allowing users to undertake independent steps [23]. However, SE remains aware of the human activity in this space.

2.2   SE and HAR: A Research Timeline

This niche has been extensive research, leading to several proposed simulators. [24] suggested a hybrid approach to the simulation, involving both a model-based and an interactive approach [24]. The model-based approach generated data by utilising pre-defined models of human activity [17, 24–26]. Each model specified the order of events, the probability of their occurrence and the duration of each activity [24]. The interactive approach relied on having an inhabitant that a researcher could control. The researcher then moves the inhabitant around the virtual SE. The dataset generated through this simulation is referred to as a synthetic dataset instead of a real dataset generated using an actual SE or test-bed with living inhabitants.

Within the study conducted by [27], a simulation tool was introduced, with a single inhabitant, four rooms and no wearable sensors. Within [28], the authors presented a context-driven approach to the Human Activity simulation. Context refers to the current setup of the HAR scenario. In this context-driven approach, the context was defined as a higher-level structure covering all SE state information such as space, sensors, objects, and virtual characters [28]. Previous research by [24] proposed the construction of simulation tools focused on dataset generation and HAR visualisation, forming the basis for this study. This study suggests using a simulator ESESIM, which provides an enhanced and comprehensive set of features, as established by [18] in Table 1.

2.3 Human Activities

Human activities can be grouped based on their complexity level and subdivided by type [29, 30]. Multiple studies defined what human activity means in the context of SE. However, no consensus was reached presently. Concerning this study, Human Activity refers to groups of actions, events and Activities of Daily Living (ADL) that a user performs within the SE.

ADLs
An individual's ability to function independently represents their quality of life. These are the six principal activities of day-to-day living that, if lacking, a person cannot be deemed as living healthily. Such ADL activities can be considered fundamental in the functioning of human life [31]. Recent studies have classified these activities as basic activities of daily living (BADLs), implying that such tasks are the most rudimentary of activities a human can perform, rendering them less complex for HAR.

Scarce research exists on activity grouping and recognition within the physical environment and simulators [18]. This focus area was previously studied using radio frequency identification (RFID) tags on many home objects to identify the activity performed. This was accomplished through detecting contacts with objects using a glove equipped with an RFID receiver [31, 32].

Daily routine activities such as housework, hygiene, washing and preparing a meal were selected due to the added requirement of various household objects. Individuals were monitored for 45 min, and overall, the results included 88% of detection accuracy for the differing activities using this dataset. Recent studies by [33] and [34] employed labelled data from wearables and smartphones to perform HAR upon ADLs such as sitting, standing and running.

Main ADLs are listed below:

a. Bathing: the ability to wash all or only one part of the body
b. Dressing: the ability to find clothes and self-dress
c. Toilet use: the ability to relieve oneself.

d. Transferring: the ability to move in and out of a bed or a chair.
e. Toileting: The ability to have complete control over bowels and bladder
f. Feeding: The ability to prepare or consume meals
g. Sleeping: the ability to go to bed and sleep

The above ADLs form the basis of human activity, recorded within various test-beds for application across differing domains, such as HAR. This study considered only four activities: cooking, dressing, toileting and sleeping. There is also a class of activities involving instruments, referred to as instrumented activities of daily living (IADL). Examples of these activities include the ability to communicate and study.

Challenges in ADL/IADL Monitoring
Since the manual assessment of individual ADLs is not feasible in real-life, automatic classification and monitoring of ADLs - using sensors deployed in households - is a crucial technology [35]. Across previous HAR studies, various types of sensors were deployed in experiments leading to differing architectures and overall system perfor-mance [36]. ADL monitoring yields several technical and non-technical issues that need to be addressed [17, 35, 37]. On the technical side, there is the 1) choice and setup of sensors, 2) optimal signal processing, and 3) ML algorithms to be considered for sensor-based HAR. On the non-technical side, there are issues of 1) privacy and 2) ease of use for such sensors and 3) managing inhabitants while preserving WHO guidelines for COVID-19. Figure 3 summarises challenges in ADL and IADL monitoring for HAR.

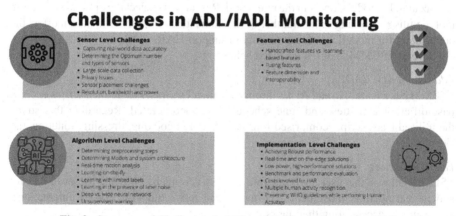

Fig. 3. Summary of Challenges in ADL and IADL monitoring for HAR

3 Proposed Approach

This study extends the SESIM tool by [18] to generate a synthetic dataset for HAR. The extension was performed to include multi-inhabitant support, extend the existing environment from a four-room space into a six-room space, and provide an additional wearable sensor. The following section discusses the Extended SESIM (ESESIM).

Below are several terms as used within this proposal.

1) Avatar: The inhabitant that is inside the virtual SE.
2) Smart Environment (SE): The virtual environment that consists of the house's sensors, actuators and components - these objects can communicate to provide data for the study dataset.
3) User: Refers to the system user, typically a researcher of smart technologies.
4) Bookmarks are text strings that label the activities performed within the SE.

3.1 Simulation

Simulators differ according to their scope and primary purpose [38]. Previous research work has established that researchers use them to demonstrate a virtual model of the actual subject to mitigate the difficulties that otherwise arise in implementing the project in reality [19]. Researchers continue to use simulators to decrease costs and time consumption for evaluation. ESESIM can be used as a substitution for a corresponding SE, and all the proposed appliances and sensors can be used for generating synthetic data [43, 44]. Table 1 compares features within several of the simulation tools by other studies. According to [24], SE simulators should 1)allow for human activity to be defined, 2) allow avatar management, manage addition or removal of home objects, 3) allow addition and removal of sensors,4) allow generation of datasets and 5) also provides the ability to design or redesign the SE. SESIM only satisfied a selection of these features. Hence, ESESIM's objective was to render the tool more comprehensive. With the help of key features, the simulation tools prove to be more relevant within several scenarios and can accurately model what is in the real world. Researchers select the optimal simulation tool to utilise according to the number of functions it can support. Simulation offers the opportunity for modelling human activity to support HAR.

Several ESESIM features are listed below:

Addition of ADL/IADL
ESESIM has a feature to add ADLs through the use of scripts. Pre-defined scripts encompass differing activities, and time schedules are incorporated. Regarding this study, the utilised (ran) scripts comprised four ADL/IADLs: cooking, dressing, toileting and sleeping.

Fast-Forwarding
ESESIM allows the user to accelerate task switching by moving the avatar faster and increasing time movement. The avatar can move quickly between interactions, consequently accelerating their tasks.

Sensor Format
ESESIM supports sensor reading output to a JSON format that can be used for HAR. This version extends the SESIM format, which already supports the SQLite database format. JSON was the selected format due to its flexibility and inter-operability with differing HAR architectures [40].

Multiple Level Environments
Previously, SESIM consisted of four rooms, namely, a kitchen, living room, bathroom and bedroom. ESESIM has an added study and bedroom, addinga level to the environment. Avatars move in the environment, triggering differing sensor readings.

Multiple Inhabitant Support

In reality, a SE has more than one inhabitant, typically leading to sensors being triggered differently according to human activity and individual behaviour performing such activity. ESESIM supports the presence of multiple inhabitants. There are three avatars within the environment, each with profiles that can be personalised for speed and variance of ADLs, aiming to provide the personality.

Figure 4a is a snapshot of the 3-dimensional space in ESESIM, while Figure 3b indicates the multiple avatars that constitute inhabitants of the virtual SE.

(a)   (b)

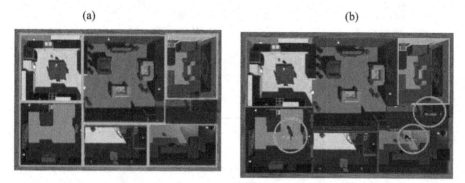

Fig. 4. (a) Floor-1 and (b) Floor-2 depicting the ESESIM environment.

3.2 ML for HAR

The following section analyses how ML models are applied to the SESIM dataset generated during the simulation. Figure 5 summarises the methodology used for this study, involving data collection/processing, model training and eventual analysis. Generating datasets covering a cross-section of different human activities within different contexts remains challenging. During data collection, data is collected from the sensors and stored for data processing. Data is cleaned during processing, and feature extraction is performed in exploratory data analysis. During model training, the dataset is split into training and test data, executed within the ML models for evaluation. This section probes the Recurrent Neural Networks (RNNs) used in the assessment within this study, namely LSTM and Bi-LSTM.

Recurrent Neural Networks (RNN)

The RNN is a deep model with cyclic connections that allows it to capture time-series data correlations. [41] used RNN successfully in handwriting and speech recognition applications. An RNN is a network with a loop that allows data to be retained. Data can be passed from one stage of the network to the next through RNN's iterative nature. RNNs are deemed as multiple replicas of the same network, with each network passing data onto the next. RNN is a very flexible and powerful network that works well to model short–term memory and does not require additional data labelling.

Table 1. Comparison of SE Simulators, based upon features.

Tools/ Authors	OS	ADL/IADL	PMS	PMS	FF	TS	EC	ESD	SDN	SF	MLE	MISS	3DE
Open SHS	☑				☑		☑	☑	☑				☑
Park et al					☑								☑
Persim 3D							☑	☑					☑
IE Sim					☑		☑	☑		☑			
Kormanyos et.al							☑		☑				
Adriana et.al			☑				☑				☑		
Fu et al							☑		☑				
Jahromi et.al			☑				☑	☑					
Buchmeyer et.al							☑	☑	☑				
SimCon							☑	☑	☑				☑
YAMAMOTO							☑			☑			☑
Simact 3D	☑		☑		☑								☑
SESIM			☑			☑	☑	☑	☑				☑
Extended SESIM	☑	☑	☑	☑	☑	☑	☑	☑	☑	☑	☑	☑	☑

Key:
OS - Open Source
ADL/IADL – Addition of ADL/IADL
PMS - Player/Avatar movement
Support FF - Fast Forwarding
TS - Time Scaling
EC - Environment creation
ESD - Extensible Sensor Design
SDN – Sensor dataset noise
SF - Sensor format
MLE - Multi-level environments
MISS - Multi-inhabitant support
3DE - 3 Dimensional Environment

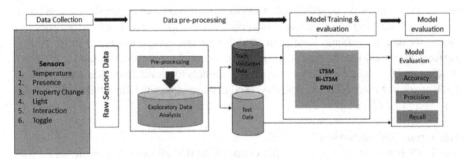

Fig. 5. ML pipeline design for HAR upon the SESIM dataset.

Consequently, it is an optimal candidate for modelling sequence learning or time–related problems, where one layer's output is used as an input for the next layer. The Long Short Term Memory (LSTM) and the Gated Recurrent Unit (GRU) are two types of RNNs. Such networks employ various gates and memory cells to store time-series sequences [42]. Across five public datasets, [43] used unidirectional, bidirectional, and cascaded deep RNNs. The group proposed three novel deep RNN architectures based on extracting discriminative features, employing deep layers and improving performance. [44] Proposed an RNN-based approach to improve recognition accuracy while simultaneously reducing recognition time.

Regarding this study, a version of the RNN, LSTM and bi-LSTM is applied to the SESIM dataset.

SESIM Dataset

The SESIM dataset employed in this study was collected following the extension of the SESIM simulator. The dataset comprises data collected from three inhabitants in a virtual SE, performing four differing ADL/ IADLs. Evaluation of the dataset is performed offline once the dataset has been previously recorded. The JSON dataset has 91,766 data tuples and seven columns with seven features. These features include a sensor name, label, time string, sensor value, area name, session ID for the reading, and sensor value. The dataset was gradually generated in ESESIM, built in Unity-3D® - a standard Windows/MAC graphical-based application. The dataset has five sensor types and four activities polled at 1 KHz.

4   Experimental Work and Results

This section describes the results of evaluations conducted to test the SESIM dataset against several deep learning models for HAR. These models are, namely, LSTM and Bi-LSTM. To experiment with such proposed models, these were constructed on Keras 2.8.0, Pandas 1.3.4, Tensor flow 2.8.0, Numpy 1.20.3 and Python 2.6.9. This was set up within anaconda 2.4.1, running a Jupyter® notebook 6.4.1 with 32 GB of RAM and a 256 Gb hard drive.

Data were split into 70% and 30% groups for training and test data, respectively, to ensure that the model could function on unseen data [18, 46]. According to [42, 46] and [47], the performance of a model that is trained using the split method is more reflective of the 'real world'. The primary metric used to evaluate such models is essentially accuracy, which can be computed as follows:

$$\text{Accuracy} = \frac{TP + TN}{TP + FP + TN + FN}$$

where TP is True Positive, FP is False Positive, TN is True Negative and FN is False Negative. Studies were carried out on four activities - sleeping, dressing, toileting and cooking. Other metrics considered are Precision, F-measure, recall rate and loss rate, as proposed by [42] in another study. F-Measure is regarded as a more suitable metric it caters for class imbalance within the dataset [17]. Table 2 summarises the parameters used for the LSTM and Bi-directional LSTM models. The bidirectional model had two Bi-LSTM layers, consisting of 64 and 32 neurons, respectively. Dense layers are added to the depth of model 1, which uses the Rectified Linear Unit (RELU) activation function as input and hidden layers [48].

Similarly, the LSTM model had two LSTM layers with one dense layer. The output function for both models was the softmax activation function. The models were run over 100 epochs with a validation split of 0.3. The results of the models' evaluation of the SESIM dataset are in the following section, which outlines their measured performance.

Table 2. Experimental parameters of Bi-Directional LSTM and LSTM models.

Bi-LSTM model		LSTM model	
Parameters	Value	Parameters	Value
Activation function	RELU	Activation function	RELU
Bi-LSTM layers	2	LTSM layers	2
Dense layers	1	Dense layers	1
Output function	Softmax	Output function	Softmax
Neurons	64,32	Neurons	64,32
Drop out	None	Drop out	None
Learning rate	0.001	Learning Rate	0.001
Batch size	128	Batch Size	128
Epoch	100	Epoch	100

4.1   Results

The accuracy of the Bi-LSTM model was 91%, while the LSTM model obtained 9 0% accuracy. Since these are the first deep learning models applied to the SESIM dataset as a proof-of-concept, this is an acceptable level of accuracy. Figure 6 depicts the confusion matrix for the Bi -LSTM, highlighting elevated confusion between the toileting and sleeping activities. This could be attributed to data noise or the presence of similar features within such activities. The least confusing activities are cooking and dressing.

Figure 7 shows the results of the confusion matrix generated by the LSTM model once applied for HAR. The models both indicate that activities (such as toileting and dressing) are being confused with sleeping - this suggests a requirement for additional training data [5]. As described in Table 3, the F-scores for toileting and dressing are closer to a value of 1 than cooking and sleeping, indicating that the Bi-LSTM model had enhanced performance at recognising those two activities. The LSTM model has reduced F-scores, indicating that the model was not performing as effectively for HAR. This variance can be attributed to the bi-directional flow of information within the Bi-LSTM network, allowing the preservation of past and future information [42].

Following the addition of a bi-directional flow of information within the LSTM, accuracy improved (from 90% to 93%), which indicates that further optimisation of the bi-LSTM model improve its accuracy.

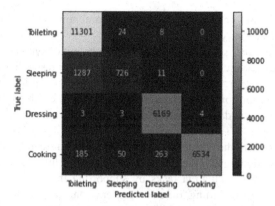

Fig. 6. Confusion matrix for Bi-LSTM.

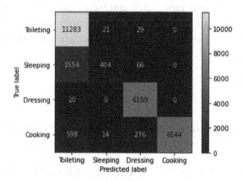

Fig. 7. Confusion Matrix for LSTM

Table 3. Precision, recall rate and F-score for differing ADLs.

Activity	Bi-LSTM model			LSTM model		
	Precision	Recall	F-Measure	Precision	Recall	F-Measure
Toileting	0.88	1.00	0.94	0.84	1.00	0.91
Sleeping	0.90	0.36	0.51	0.92	0.20	0.33
Dressing	0.96	1.00	0.98	0.94	1.00	0.97
Cooking	1.00	0.93	0.93	1.00	0.87	0.93

5   Conclusion and Future Work

Recently, it has become possible to have hybrid neural networks to improve the accuracy of a single model. Through the introduction of simulations to generate synthetic datasets, there is an opportunity to augment real datasets where specific contextual data might be missing or incomplete. RNN can work as a model for HAR. However, it will be required to address its weaknesses on sensor-based HAR by combining it with other deep learning models to improve accuracy.

This study argues that simulation and the development of synthetic datasets can be highly beneficial for researchers who be unable to reach their test individuals or test beds during a pandemic. With a stronger emphasis on model output optimisation, there is the possibility of further improving accuracy, recall, and F-scores. The results demonstrate that training on synthetic data makes it possible to predict human actions within a SE successfully.

This research adds to the current datasets for HAR that researchers can use to complete their duties. Additionally, the simulator proposed in this study provides a more comprehensive tool for simulation tasks by supporting the addition of ADL/IADL, avatar movement, fast-forwarding, time scaling, environment creation, extensible sensor design, dataset noise addition, multiple sensor formats, multi-level environments, multi-inhabitant support, and a three-dimensional virtual environment.

Future research can incorporate additional locations, such as factories, office buildings, and leisure spaces. Future research avenues could examine the addition of ADL, IADL and the merging of real and synthetic datasets to perform HAR for support user/activity tracking.

References

1. World Health Organization: Coronavirus (COVID-19) events as they happen (2020). https://www.who.int/emergencies/diseases/novel-coronavirus-2019/events-as-they-happen. Accessed 03 Apr 2022
2. Khan, H., Kushwah, K.K., Singh, S., Urkude, H., Maurya, M.R., Sadasivuni, K.K.: Smart technologies driven approaches to tackle COVID-19 pandemic: a review. 3 Biotech **11**(2), 1–22 (2021). https://doi.org/10.1007/s13205-020-02581-y
3. Ribeiro-Navarrete, S., Saura, J.R., Palacios-Marqués, D.: Towards a new era of mass data collection: assessing pandemic surveillance technologies to preserve user privacy. Technol. Forecast. Soc. Change **167** (2021). https://doi.org/10.1016/J.TECHFORE.2021.120681
4. Uelschen, M., Schaarschmidt, M.: Software design of energy-aware peripheral control for sustainable internet-of-things devices. In: Proceedings of the 55th Hawaii International Conference on System Sciences, vol. 7, pp. 7762–7771 (2022). https://doi.org/10.24251/hicss.2022.933
5. Shalaby, E., ElShennawy, N., Sarhan, A.: Utilizing deep learning models in CSI-based human activity recognition. Neural Comput. Appl. **34**(8), 5993–6010 (2021). https://doi.org/10.1007/s00521-021-06787-w
6. Cedillo, P., Sanchez, C., Campos, K., Bermeo, A.: A systematic literature review on devices and systems for ambient assisted living: solutions and trends from different user perspectives (2018). https://doi.org/10.1109/ICEDEG.2018.8372367
7. Zhang, S., et al.: Deep learning in human activity recognition with wearable sensors: a review on advances. Sensors **22**(4), 1476 (2022). https://doi.org/10.3390/s22041476
8. Dang, L.M., Min, K., Wang, H., Piran, M.J., Lee, C.H., Moon, H.: Sensor-based and vision-based human activity recognition: a comprehensive survey. Pattern Recogn. **108**, 107561 (2020). https://doi.org/10.1016/j.patcog.2020.107561
9. Chiridza, T.: A smart home environment to support saftey and risk monitoring for the elderly living independently. Nelson Mandela University (2017)

10. Kim, Y., An, J., Lee, M., Lee, Y.: An activity-embedding approach for next-activity prediction in a multi-user smart space (2017). https://doi.org/10.1109/SMARTCOMP.2017.7946985

11. Jalal, A., Mahmood, M., Hasan, A.S.: Multi-features descriptors for human activity tracking and recognition in indoor-outdoor environments. In: Proceedings of 2019 16th International Bhurban Conference on Applied Sciences and Technology (IBCAST) 2019, pp. 371–376 (2019). https://doi.org/10.1109/IBCAST.2019.8667145

12. Nafea, O., Abdul, W., Muhammad, G., Alsulaiman, M.: Sensor-based human activity recognition with spatio-temporal deep learning. Sensors 21(6), 1–20 (2021). https://doi.org/10.3390/s21062141

13. Awad, M.M.: Forest mapping: a comparison between hyperspectral and multispectral images and technologies. J. For. Res. 29(5), 1395–1405 (2017). https://doi.org/10.1007/s11676-017-0528-y

14. Gupta, S.: Deep learning based human activity recognition (HAR) using wearable sensor data. Int. J. Inf. Manag. Data Insights 1(2), 100046 (2021). https://doi.org/10.1016/j.jjimei.2021.100046

15. Cao, C., et al.: Deep learning and its applications in biomedicine. Genomics Proteomics Bioinf. 16(1), 17–32 (2018). https://doi.org/10.1016/j.gpb.2017.07.003

16. Lee, Y., Choi, T.J., Ahn, C.W.: Multi-objective evolutionary approach to select security solutions. CAAI Trans. Intell. Technol. 2(2), 64–67 (2017). https://doi.org/10.1049/trit.2017.0002

17. Irvine, N., Nugent, C., Zhang, S., Wang, H., Ng, W.W.Y.: Neural network ensembles for sensor-based human activity recognition within smart environments. Sensors (Switzerland) 20(1) (2020). https://doi.org/10.3390/s20010216

18. Ho, B., Vogts, D., Wesson, J.: A smart home simulation tool to support the recognition of activities of daily living. In: ACM International Conference Proceeding Series (2019). https://doi.org/10.1145/3351108.3351132

19. Nugent, C., et al.: Improving the quality of user generated data sets for activity recognition. In: García, C.R., Caballero-Gil, P., Burmester, M., Quesada-Arencibia, A. (eds.) UCAmI/IWAAL/AmIHEALTH 2016. LNCS, vol. 10070, pp. 104–110. Springer, Cham (2016). https://doi.org/10.1007/978-3-319-48799-1_13

20. Friday Nweke, H., Wah Teh, Y., Al-Garadi, M.A., Alo, R.: Deep learning algorithms for human activity recognition using mobile and wearable sensor networks: state of the art and research challenges. Expert Syst. Appl. 105, 233–261 (2018). https://doi.org/10.1016/j.eswa.2018.03.056

21. Fysarakis, K., Soultatos, O., Manifavas, C., Papaefstathiou, I., Askoxylakis, I.: XSACd—cross-domain resource sharing & access control for smart environments. Futur. Gener. Comput. Syst. 80, 572–582 (2018). https://doi.org/10.1016/j.future.2016.05.023

22. Dorri, A., Kanhere, S.S., Jurdak, R., Gauravaram, P.: Blockchain for IoT security and privacy: the case study of a smart home. In: 2017 IEEE International Conference on Pervasive Computing and Communications Workshops (PerCom Workshops), pp. 618–623 (2017) https://doi.org/10.1109/PERCOMW.2017.7917634

23. Nazari Shirehjini, A.A., Semsar, A.: Human interaction with IoT-based smart environments. Multimed. Tools Appl. 76(11), 13343–13365 (2016). https://doi.org/10.1007/s11042-016-3697-3

24. Alshammari, N., Alshammari, T., Sedky, M., Champion, J., Bauer, C.: OpenSHS: open smart home simulator. Sensors 17(5), 1003 (2017). https://doi.org/10.3390/s17051003

25. Lee, J.W., Helal, A., Sung, Y., Cho, K.: Context-driven control algorithms for scalable simulation of human activities in smart homes. In: Proceedings - IEEE 10th International Conference on Ubiquitous Intelligence and Computing, UIC 2013 and IEEE 10th International Conference on Autonomic and Trusted Computing, ATC 2013, pp. 285–292 (2013). https://doi.org/10.1109/UIC-ATC.2013.68

26. Wixom, B.H., Watson, H.J., Reynolds, A.M., Hoffer, J.A.: Continental airlines continues to soar with business intelligence (2015)
27. Ho, B., Vogts, D., Wesson, J.: SESim: a smart environment simulation tool to support human activity recognition (2018)
28. Lee, J.W., Cho, S., Liu, S., Cho, K., Helal, S.: Persim 3D: context-driven simulation and modelling of human activities in smart spaces. IEEE Trans. Autom. Sci. Eng. **12**, 1243–1256 (2015). https://doi.org/10.1109/TASE.2015.2467353
29. Forbes, G.: Employing multi-modal sensors for personalised smart home health monitoring (2019). www.rgu.ac.uk/dmstaff/forbes-glenn. Accessed 28 June 2020
30. Kormányos, B., Pataki, B.: Multi-level simulation of daily activities: why and how? In: Proceedings of the 2013 IEEE International Conference Computational Intelligence and Virtual Environments for Measurement Systems and Applications (CIVEMSA), pp. 1–6 (2013). https://doi.org/10.1109/CIVEMSA.2013.6617386
31. Oort, Q., Taphoorn, M.J.B., Sikkes, S.A.M., Uitdehaag, B.M.J., Reijneveld, J.C., Dirven, L.: Evaluation of the content coverage of questionnaires containing basic and instrumental activities of daily living (ADL) used in adult patients with brain tumors. J. Neurooncol. **143**(1), 1–13 (2019). https://doi.org/10.1007/s11060-019-03136-9
32. Spector, W.D., Katz, S., Murphy, J.B., Fulton, J.P.: The hierarchical relationship between activities of daily living and instrumental activities of daily living. J. Chronic Dis. (1987). https://doi.org/10.1016/0021-9681(87)90004-X
33. Qian, H., Pan, S.J., Da, B., Miao, C.: A novel distribution-embedded neural network for sensor-based activity recognition. In: IJCAI International Joint Conference on Artificial Intelligence, vol. 2019, pp. 5614–5620 (2019). https://doi.org/10.24963/ijcai.2019/779
34. Reyes-Ortiz, J.L., Oneto, L., Samà, A., Parra, X., Anguita, D.: Transition-aware human activity recognition using smartphones. Neurocomputing (2016). https://doi.org/10.1016/j.neucom.2015.07.085
35. Chiristian Debes, M.N., Sukhanov, S., Matheas, A., et al.: Monitoring activities of daily living in smart homes: understanding human behaviour. IEEE Signal Process. Mag. **33**(2), 81–94 (2016). https://doi.org/10.1109/MSP.2015.2503881
36. Roy, N., Misra, A., Cook, D.: Ambient and smartphone sensor assisted ADL recognition in multi-inhabitant smart environments. J. Ambient. Intell. Humaniz. Comput. **7**(1), 1–19 (2015). https://doi.org/10.1007/s12652-015-0294-7
37. Ferrari, A., Micucci, D., Mobilio, M., Napoletano, P.: Deep learning and model spersonalisation in sensor-based human activity recognition. J. Reliab. Intell. Environ. (2022). https://doi.org/10.1007/s40860-021-00167-w
38. Bradfield, K., Allen, C.: Advances in Informatics and Computing in Civil and Construction Engineering. Springer, Cham (2019)
39. Leodolter, M., Widhalm, P., Plant, C., Brandle, N.: Semi-supervised segmentation of accelerometer time series for transport mode classification (2017). https://doi.org/10.1109/MTITS.2017.8005596
40. ECMA-404: The JSON data interchange format. ECMA Int. (2013). https://doi.org/10.17487/rfc7158
41. Chauhan, N.K., Singh, K.: A review on conventional machine learning vs deep learning. In: 2018 International Conference on Computing, Power and Communication Technologies (GUCON), pp. 347–352 (2018). https://doi.org/10.1109/GUCON.2018.8675097
42. Wang, H., et al.: Wearable sensor-based human activity recognition using hybrid deep learning techniques. Secur. Commun. Netw. **2020**, 1–12 (2020). https://doi.org/10.1155/2020/2132138
43. Murad, A., Pyun, J.Y.: Deep recurrent neural networks for human activity recognition. Sensors (Switzerland) **17**(11), 2556 (2017). https://doi.org/10.3390/s17112556

44. Inoue, M., Inoue, S., Nishida, T.: Deep recurrent neural network for mobile human activity recognition with high throughput. Artif. Life Robot. **23**(2), 173–185 (2017). https://doi.org/10.1007/s10015-017-0422-x

45. Hamad, R.A., Kimura, M., Yang, L., Woo, W.L., Wei, B.: Dilated causal convolution with multi-head self attention for sensor human activity recognition. Neural Comput. Appl. **5** (2021). https://doi.org/10.1007/s00521-021-06007-5

46. Zebin, T., Sperrin, M., Peek, N., Casson, A.J.: Human activity recognition from inertial sensor time-series using batch snormalised deep LSTM recurrent networks. In: Proceedings of the Annual International Conference of the IEEE Engineering in Medicine and Biology Society, EMBS, vol. 2018-July, pp. 1–4 (2018). https://doi.org/10.1109/EMBC.2018.8513115

47. Kim, Y., Toomajian, B.: Hand gesture recognition using micro-doppler signatures with convolutional neural network. IEEE Access (2016). https://doi.org/10.1109/ACCESS.2016.2617282

48. Badura, M., Batog, P., Drzeniecka-Osiadacz, A., Modzel, P.: Evaluation of low-cost sensors for ambient PM2.5 monitoring. J. Sensors (2018). https://doi.org/10.1155/2018/5096540

Careers and ICT

Virtual Internships as Employer-Led Initiatives: Success Criteria and Reflections on the Diversification of Internships

Debora Jeske[(⊠)] [iD]

University College Cork, Cork T23 K208, Republic of Ireland
d.jeske@ucc.ie

Abstract. Many employers have trialed virtual internships over the past two years. Employer-led virtual internships (e-internships) have a long history that predates the Covid-19 pandemic. Previous research has already demonstrated the importance of how employers design their internships, and how they subsequently support, train and mentor interns for internship success. Fifty-one virtual interns completed a survey in 2020 about their virtual internships experience with employers in various countries. The survey examined predictors of internship satisfaction and usefulness. Multiple regression showed that information accuracy, perceived support (e.g., resources, access to help) and usefulness (in terms of knowledge advancement and consolidation) all significantly and positively predicted internship satisfaction. Social influence and perceived support also increased the ratings of perceived usefulness among virtual interns. The relationship between perceived support given by employers and internship satisfaction was partially mediated by perceived usefulness of the internship. This highlights the importance of employer-led provisions and the extent to the design of internships influence virtual interns' subsequent evaluations. The study concludes with a discussion of practical implications and reflections on the need to differentiate and study the various virtual internship types that have appeared to analyze which one will add value and which types might be less beneficial or even exploitative of talent wishing to gain more experience via virtual internships.

Keywords: Virtual internship · e-Internship · Expectation management · Perceived support · Mentoring · Training · Covid-19 · Diversification

1 Introduction

Virtual internships have been proposed, trialed, and examined for well over fifteen years. An early example here is the work by van Dorp (2008). This author was one of the first to propose the introduction of educationally focused virtual internships as a result of an educational research project. The European Social Fund has since funded several virtual internship projects over the last ten years. Numerous researchers, including the author of this paper, have studied the use of virtual internships over many years, numerous

S. Papagiannidis et al. (Eds.): I3E 2022, LNCS 13454, pp. 167–179, 2022.
https://doi.org/10.1007/978-3-031-15342-6_13

industries and countries – including the current author (Jeske and Axtell 2013, 2014, 2016, 2018a, b). Traditional internships are "temporary (non-permanent) work placements that reflect a period of transition from higher education to the world of work" (Bayerlein and Jeske 2018, pg. 29). E-internships are virtual internships that are entirely computer-mediated transitionary periods. These internships rely on numerous communication tools that support remote working (as these internships emerged alongside the remote working concept). In contrast to educational initiatives, most virtual internships run by employer are not focused primarily on supporting educational objectives such as placement requirements. However, these types of internships have hitherto been considered by both educators and many employers as less "real" and valuable, resulting in many virtual interns having their internship experience discredited in favor or more "traditional", on-site internships (Jeske and Axtell 2014).

The Covid-19 pandemic changed these beliefs to some degree. During the last two years (2020 to 2022), virtual internships have been rolled out by both educational and commercial organizations across the world. Yet, a significant research, theory and knowledge gap remains as to how virtual internships are run and what makes them effective. The lack of specific theoretical advancements can be attributed to the fact that these internships build on concepts from several different disciplines: From learning theory, to ICT, career development, and work-related concepts (such as the psychological contract). Part of this situation can also be attributed to the fact that we are still researching the fundamentals – such as how internships are defined and what their key characteristics are. The current paper thus wishes to contribute to clarifying fundamental basics regarding virtual internships and aims to answer the following research question: *What are the key benefits that virtual internships can provide to interns?* The current article outlines recent findings based on a study with 51 virtual interns and reiterates many of the key insights about the benefits of virtual internships when employers proactively consider the needs of their interns, their expectations and social environment. In addition, this conference paper identifies practical implications and outlines recent internship developments which speak to the diversification of virtual internships.

2   Success Factors for Employer-Run Virtual Internships

Many recent virtual internship initiatives have reportedly met with limited success (McKenzie 2021). While several other studies have confirmed the value of virtual internships run and organized by employers – if certain conditions are met (Jeske and Axtell 2016; AlGhamdi 2022). A short review of conditions will provide some insights – and also clarify why many recent initiatives failed. This includes the importance of having a meaningful and work-applied internship experiences (rather than focusing on educational imperatives which many universities pursue, see AlGhamdi 2022; Zehr and Korte 2020). For virtual internships to be effective, they need to be complemented by effective mentoring (Jeske and Axtell 2017) and networking. They need to foster a realistic, long-term employability perspective (e.g., by considering virtual interns as part of the potential recruitment pool, AlGhamdi 2022; Jeske and Axtell 2016; McKenzie 2021).

Recent findings about employer-led virtual internships (e-internships) validate what virtual internship researchers have known for a long time – that you can effectively onboard, teach, and develop interns if you put some effort and infrastructure in place (Jeske and Axtell 2016, 2017, 2018a, b; AlGhamdi 2022). In addition, when both the interns' predisposition for learning and the supervisors' willingness [or expectations] to support learning are high, both traditional and virtual interns are more likely to develop and grow effectively during their internship (Holyoak 2013; Maini et al. 2021; Zehr and Korte 2020). Virtual interns will benefit directly from these internships in their careers through the networking, references, and the experiences that they have gathered. Interns need to see the clear, practical benefits of their internship and role in their career success. A number of specific success factors are worth mentioning that will be relevant to both employers and interns alike. I outline some of these here in more detail.

2.1 Information Accuracy (Expectation Management)

A number of researchers have explored the effect of appropriate expectation setting (through expectation setting, correct information, goal clarity) and how these aspects can shape how interns ultimately evaluate their experiences (Jeske and Axtell 2017). This is also in line with traditional internship research that demonstrates the importance of perceived fit for interns when they select their internships (Stremersch and van Hoye 2020). If the initial information is flawed or inaccurate, interns will likely take more time to adjust to very different circumstances and feel less trusting of information that is shared by the employer, all of which may increase the likelihood that they report lower satisfaction as a result. The preparedness of both interns and employers is therefore critical to success (Maini et al. 2021; Zehr and Korte 2020). This makes information accuracy an important control variable in the analysis of internship reports. Based on these findings I propose the following:

H1: Information accuracy is a significant predictor of internship satisfaction, with less accurate information resulting in less satisfaction.

2.2 Social Influence (Role of Important and Significant Others)

Interns are often influenced by their social network in terms of how they rate new opportunities and the degree to which they are supported in their endeavors (Jeske and Axtell 2014). This is similarly the case when it comes to whether they feel supported when taking up internship offers. The preference towards traditional, on-site internships is deeply anchored in educational and experiential history: The parents of most college-age adults will not have been exposed to teleworking and virtual internships. Doubts about the validity and relevance of virtual internships remain a concern (McKenzie 2021). As a result, the social influence that important others can have on interns should not be underestimated. Accordingly, I propose that:

H2: Social influence has a significant effect on perceived usefulness ratings, with more support leading to more positive evaluations of internships.

2.3 Support and Assistance (Resources, Mentoring and Training)

The main goal of an internship is to enable the intern to gain relevant work experience with an employer while simultaneously learning more about their chosen or prospective profession, the employers, and industrial sector (Van Dorp et al. 2011). As a result, the training and support mechanisms in place for interns (e.g., in terms of a clear internship plan, access to help, software, tools, mentors, and training) are critical for the successful completion of the internship (e.g., AlGhamdi 2022; Jeske and Axtell 2016). Evidence in support of this comes from research that has shown that self-reported performance by interns is higher when interns feel valued, they are more satisfied, and they receive training (Jeske and Axtell 2017). Mentoring is very important for interns and their internship satisfaction (e.g., Jeske and Linehan 2020; Maini et al. 2021). These variables may further predict how virtual interns rate the usefulness of such internships for their skill development and knowledge acquisition (see AlGhamdi 2022; Boehm et al. 2021; Nghia and My Duyen 2018; Teng et al. 2022). This leads to the final set of hypotheses:

H3a/b: Perceived support and the training experience are significant positive predictors of internship satisfaction (H3a) and the perceived usefulness of the internship (H3b).

3 Methods

3.1 Data Collection Procedure

The study was approved by the Ethics Committee of the author's institution before data collection commenced. Participants were invited to complete the online survey using the author's network and social media connections (via LinkedIn). No limitations were placed on location of potential participants. The survey was only available in English and to those participants over 18 who had completed a virtual internship in 2020 or expected to complete one by 2021. The participants were further informed that their participation was voluntary and anonymous. IP addresses were not collected. Following an introduction to the survey, all participants were asked to first give their consent. They were subsequently presented with several subsections to assess how accurate the initial internship information had been, the impact of significant others in their life and the support during the internship (social influences, perceived support), their mentoring and training experience, and the perceived usefulness of their internship plus the satisfaction with the internship overall. At the end, demographic details were collected.

3.2 Participant Description

The survey was from July to December 2020 and received 118 hits. Participants who completed traditional/on-site internships and those that internships that involve simulated tasks/work environments (without contact to an actual internship provider) were excluded. Sixty-five participants gave consent and 51 completed the survey. The final sample included 26 women, 15 men, and 10 individuals who did not share their gender. The average age was 25 ($M = 24.73$, range 20–37). At the time of completion, 41 were still enrolled in education; 23 had already completed their virtual internship while another 26 indicated they were still completing the internship (2 missing cases), with 39 reporting that the internship was at least 90% remote/virtual, which reflects pre-Covid-19 reports for virtual internships (Jeske and Axtell 2018a, b). One participant had completed high school, 14 were in the process of completing their Bachelors, 22 were in the process of completing post-graduate education (e.g., MBAs), and three were pursuing PhDs at the time of the survey. On average, they had three years of work experience to date.

3.3 Measures

The following section outlines the number of items and origins of all scales. At the beginning of the survey, all participants were first asked to the location of the internship provider, the degree to which they worked remotely, in which sector, and type of organization. Please contact the author for a complete list of all items (d.jeske@ucc.ie).

Information Accuracy. All interns were asked "How accurate was the internship information you had before you started the internship?" and were presented with five response options from (1) 'not at all' to (5) 'to a very great extent' ($M = 3.32$, $SD = 1.17$, $n = 45$).

Social Influence. Social influence was measured using three modified items by Venkatesh et al. (2012), including "People who are important to me think that I should make the most of virtual internships." Response options included (1) 'strongly disagree' to (5) 'strongly disagree' ($\alpha = .81$, $M = 4.01$, $SD = 0.79$).

Perceived Support. Using four modified items from Venkatesh et al. (2012), participants were asked about access to support in their internship. One such example item was "I had the resources necessary to work remotely as a virtual/e-intern". Other items focused on access to help, software, platforms, and expertise. Response options ranged from (1) 'strongly disagree' to (5) 'strongly disagree' ($\alpha = .82$, $M = 4.15$, $SD = 0.73$).

Training Experience. This was assessed using three items based on questions posed by Geertshuis et al. (2002). Participants were asked to respond to items such as "The training was relevant for my work", "The training was pitched at the right level", and "Was there enough time to absorb/practice the new information". Response options included (1) 'not at all' to (5) 'to a very great extent' ($\alpha = .88$, $M = 3.59$, $SD = 1.03$).

Mentoring Experience. The mentoring experience was assessed using four items, including items from Ragins and McFarlin (1990). The original scale had seven response options, this was reduced to five ranging from (1) 'not at all' to (5) 'to a very great extent' ($\alpha = .87$, $M = 4.13$, $SD = 0.73$). In addition, we asked them if they had a mentor. The results of the analysis showed that $\approx 80\%$ (40/51) had a mentor at work.

Satisfaction with Feedback. This was assessed using one item: "Did you receive any performance feedback on the tasks you completed?". Participants had the option to say (1) 'Yes' and (2) 'No'. Followed up by "How satisfied are you were with the feedback you received about your work?" followed by five response options ranging from (1) 'very unsatisfied' and (4) 'very satisfied' ($M = 3.30$, $SD = 0.82$) and the option to select 'not applicable' ($n = 1$). This suggested that the large majority received some feedback, but it was of varying quality.

Satisfaction with the Internship. These four items were based on a satisfaction scale proposed by Brayfield and Rothe (1951) but modified to reflect internship satisfaction. An example item was "I felt satisfied with my virtual internship". The original response range was changed from six to five agreement responses from (1) 'strongly agree' and (5) 'strongly disagree' ($\alpha = .82$, $M = 3.65$, $SD = 0.80$).

Perceived Usefulness (Skills and Knowledge). Six items taken from Nghia and My Duyen (2018, pg. 76) were modified in reference to virtual internships. The first three items measured advancement and the second set of three items measured consolidation of professional skills and knowledge. An example item was "Completing a virtual/e-internship helped me to develop professional skills". Response options were changed to an agreement scale in line with other questions in the survey and ranged from (1) 'strongly agree' and (5) 'strongly disagree' ($\alpha = .87$, $M = 4.15$, $SD = 0.64$).

Demographics and Work Experience. All participants were asked to share their gender, age, location, highest level of qualification, and work experience.

4 Results

4.1 Description of the Internship Experience

A short overview provides more context to the internship experience of the current sample. Out of the 51 interns, 25 were paid by their employer. They completed internships in various sectors such as: education, healthcare, consulting, banking/insurance, IT, and telecommunications. Employers included 29 for-profit organizations, 3 non-profits, 4 governmental and 13 educational institutions. Over half of the participants worked for small organizations with up to 49 employees ($n = 18$) and medium-sized organizations with up to 199 employees ($n = 8$). The other half worked for employers that had up to 500 ($\underline{n} = 6$) and more than 500 employees ($n = 17$). Over half of the interns would have been unable to commute to the site where the employer was located ($n = 28$), which suggests that they would not have been able to take up a similar, on-site internship opportunity with the employer without relocating. Participants completed internships in one of eight locations: India, USA, Germany, Ireland, Australia, Mexico, the UK, and Finland (most frequently represented are listed first).

Internships lasted from six weeks up to 12 months. The average number of working hours each week was about 20 (this ranged from a minimum of 5 to 40 h) in teams. Team size ranged from two to 30 team members (average ranged about five or so team members). Thirty-eight reported that there were also other virtual interns working for the same employer at the same time. The average number of hours interns dedicated to their virtual internship was 633 h, the median was 422 (due to some outliers; hours reported by participants ranged from the minimum of 56 to 3600 h for a one-year virtual internship).

Twenty-eight received equipment and software from their employer to enable them to work effectively. The virtual internships had been located via university message boards and career services, through LinkedIn, personal and social networks, as well as special programs run by corporations (e.g., Google Summer of Code). Motivations to take up an e-internship varied. Twenty-four participants completed the internship for academic credit (e.g., because their programs required an internship/placement). Many switched from a traditional to an e-internship due to necessity (e.g., due to Covid-19). In addition, the interns wanted to gain more experience in specific industries/areas to improve their employability as well as chances to get accepted to graduate school).

4.2 Correlations and Group Comparisons

The measures correlated weakly to moderately, as expected; there was little evidence of multi-collinearity with correlations above .7 (except in the case of training experience, see Table 1). Some correlations are noteworthy. The correlation coefficients for mentoring and training experiences showed that both correlated positively and quite strongly ($p < .005$) with how accurate the information had been that employers had shared with their interns prior to them starting the internship. This speaks to the importance of setting appropriate expectations for interns from the get-go. The high correlation ($r = .727, p < .001$) between training experience and perceived support speaks to the interconnected nature of training and how interns access software, help, and other resources during their internship. Due to this multi-collinearity, all the following analyses were conducted with the perceived support variable alone (see Table 1).

To assess the influence of potential situational variables, I additionally checked if the internship status (having completed the internship vs. still completing it) had any significant effect on reports (using t-test). This was not the case for any of the variables listed in Table 1. Similar nonsignificant results were obtained when I compared the answers of paid vs. unpaid interns, and those who completed the internship for academic credits vs. those who did not (this also applied when I looked at payment/credit categories together). Further group comparison between female and all other participants (those who selected 'male' and opted out) did not reveal any group differences except one for mentoring ($t(49) = -2.030, p = .048$). The mentoring experience ratings from the female participants suggested they did not have as positive an experience ($M = 3.35, SD = 1.03, n = 26$) compared to participants who did not identify as female ($M = 3.84, SD = 0.63, n = 25$). Internship hours correlated significantly and positively with perceived usefulness ($r = .299, p = .048$), but not internship satisfaction.

4.3 Hypothesis Testing and Exploratory Analyses

To assess the effect of the control and independent variables (information accuracy, perceived support from the employer, social influence, mentoring experience, feedback satisfaction) on the dependent variables (satisfaction with the internship, perceived usefulness of the internship), a number of hierarchical regressions were computed. Control variables such as age and gender were not significant control variables and thus not included in the regression analyses.

Table 1. Correlation coefficients for all measures ($N = 51$)

Measures	1	2	3	4	5	6	7	8
1. Information accuracy	1							
2. Social influence	.245	1						
3. Perceived support	.544**	.419**	1					
4. Training experience	.543**	.368**	.727**	1				
5. Mentoring experience	.421**	.182	.343*	.396**	1			
6. Feedback satisfaction	.370*	.081	.236	.299*	.343*	1		
7. Perceived usefulness	.198	.571**	.540**	.421**	.275	.209	1	
8. Internship satisfaction	.441**	.292*	.629**	.620**	.345*	.450**	.570**	1

Note. *p < .05, **p < .01

Satisfaction with the Internship. Controlling for information accuracy ($\beta = .322, t = 3.219, p = .002$), regression analysis showed that the satisfaction with the internship overall was predicted by the perceived support interns received ($\beta = .358, t = 2.296, p = .027$) as well as the perceived usefulness of the internship ($\beta = .338, t = 2.530, p = .015$) in the way that it advanced and consolidated their professional experiences. These results lend support for the role of information accuracy (H1) and the role of perceived support (H3a) on internship satisfaction. The positive correlations between mentoring experience, training experience, feedback satisfaction and internship satisfaction further speak to the importance of interns receiving all three (mentoring, training, feedback) to increase their overall satisfaction (see Table 1).

Perceived Usefulness of Internship. Controlling for information accuracy ($\beta = .277, t = 1.846, p = .072$), regression analysis showed that the perceived usefulness of the internship was predicted by social influence as well ($\beta = .418, t = 3.024, p = .005$), even when we included perceived support ($\beta = .366, t = 2.228, p = .032$). This suggests that even when we consider the role of perceived support interns received during their internships, the influence of significant others in their social environment likewise had a positive effect on how useful they rated the internship (in support of H2 and H3b).

This suggests that the social and the employer-backed support interns receive will positively influence how they evaluate internships (e.g., they had the backing of those around them to complete the internship). It is noteworthy that in the case of perceived usefulness, only training appeared to be a positive correlate (but not mentoring and feedback satisfaction, see Table 1). This may be the case because training experience can be more readily transferable to new roles, while this might not be the case for mentoring and the feedback one received during the internship.

Exploratory Mediation Analysis. Given the earlier results, I wanted to examine whether perceived usefulness potentially mediated the relationship between perceived support during the internship and overall internship satisfaction. To test this exploratory hypothesis, I analyzed the mediation using the PROCESS macro (Hayes 2013), using the bootstrap procedure with 1000 samples (Model 4, vs. 2.16.1). As expected, perceived support was a significant and direct predictor of perceived usefulness ($\beta = .48$, $t = 4.49$, $p < .001$) but also internship satisfaction ($\beta = .50$, $t = 3.64$, $p < .001$). Usefulness in turn was a significant direct predictor of internship satisfaction ($\beta = .40$, $t = 2.61$, $p = .012$). The indirect effect of perceived social support on satisfaction via usefulness was likewise significant, suggesting partial mediation ($\beta = .19$, $z = 2.22$, $p = .027$). All variables explained 29.1% of the variance ($R = .64$, $R^2 = .29$, $F(1,49) = 20.15$, $p < .001$; Fig. 1).

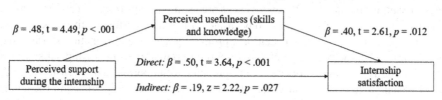

Fig. 1. Mediation analysis with perceived usefulness as mediator

5 Discussion and Conclusions

Given the Covid-19 pandemic, many traditional internships in 2020 and 2021 were quickly converted into virtual internships – with possibly very different degrees of success in terms of the learning that was facilitated in these newly designed internships (e.g., Maini et al. 2021; McKenzie 2021). The current study with 51 virtual interns from different countries focused specifically on e-internships which were run and hosted by employers for several weeks to months (Jeske and Axtell 2016; Jeske 2019). The results reflected the findings of several other recent research reports. I summarize the key findings here briefly.

Expectation management was argued to be an important precursor to satisfaction, specifically, information accuracy surrounding the role the intern was expecting to take (Jeske and Axtell 2017). As expected, more accurate information resulted in a more internship satisfaction (H1), potentially because interns were accurately prepared and briefed on what they would be doing. This matches other pre-pandemic findings on the importance of goal clarity (Jeske and Axtell 2017) and the importance of having clear internship deliverables planned out (AlGhamdi 2022). Interns were moreover influenced by the support and understanding others had shown to them, both in their personal environment and during the internship (Zehr and Korte 2020). This is in line with the relational investment that has shown to be critical for the psychological contract that virtual interns form with their employers (Jeske and Axtell 2018a, b).

And lastly, as expected, positive social support from important others (H2) and perceived support from the employer (in form of training, software, access to help) predicted both perceived usefulness of the internship (H3a) and internship satisfaction (H3a). This suggests that interns' evaluations will be in part independently influenced by how others in their personal environment view their internship, and how much support they are receiving during the internship from the employer (AlGhamdi 2022; Maini et al. 2021). This reflects pre-pandemic findings for such internships (Jeske and Axtell 2016, 2017; Teng et al. 2022). More positive training experiences also increased the sense of internships being useful (H3b), potentially because such experiences are transferable and increase skills as well as knowledge acquisition (Nghia and My Duyen 2018).

5.1 Practical Implications and Key Lessons

The current findings point to several areas where employers can be active. First and foremost, meaningful, and valuable experiences are as important to employees as to virtual interns. The same goes for obtaining buy-in and setting the stage for positive experiences. This means that addressing expectations, promoting accurate information sharing and goal clarity from the outset are clearly important predictors of internship satisfaction. Both interns as well as mentors need to be prepared to support virtual internships (Jeske and Linehan 2020; Maini et al. 2021). In addition, employers might need to recognize that how interns evaluate their experiences may also be shaped by actors outside their area of control, such as significant others. This speaks to the importance of sharing more information about the merits of their internship schemes online where this information might be accessible to important others such as educational advisors and parents. And lastly, the current findings suggest that investments in training experiences, appropriate mentoring (for all groups, particularly female interns), and feedback frequency appear to be as relevant for employees as for interns. Further practical guidance for employers can be accessed in several published resources (e.g., Jeske and Axtell 2016; Jeske 2019; Zehr and Korte 2020).

5.2 Limitations of Current Study

The current research was based on a small, self-selected, voluntary sample that provided self-reports. This may have introduced some other variables due to cultural or regional differences (e.g., acceptance of and access to internships). However, most virtual internship research is likely to incorporate these elements due to the often-global nature of these internships. More research based on programs run in specific locations may provide more detailed information for a comparative analysis of these findings.

5.3 Future Research Trajectories

Several research gaps continue to exist. The following two suggestions provide some suggestions for researchers interested in contributing further to our understanding of virtual internships.

Theoretical Development. The lack of theoretical exploration will require more work to provide a good foundation for future research. Future theoretical work in this domain may wish to explore areas and theories related to work environments (such as team and group dynamics), the role of personality (and how personality may determine success in remote work settings that are common to e-internships), usability and inclusiveness in computer-mediated environments (in terms of diversity and learning), and career developmental theories (that could help explain the career benefits and developmental growth of professionals as they are moving towards a specific career or changing their career trajectory).

Diversification of "Virtual" Internships. Over the last few years, virtual internships diversified. However, not all internship research has clearly differentiated these types nor realized the importance of who is leading the initiatives. There is some evidence emerging that educationally initiated and oriented internship programs may be less beneficial than those organized by employers themselves (see a critique by AlGhamdi 2022). In short, each of these types offer different learning options and limitations. The following section provides an overview here on these types and possible research gaps.

In this conference paper, I have focused on e-internships only – employer-led internships of significant duration, time investment (e.g., minimum of 240 h), focused on real-world tasks which featured interpersonal exchanges with team members, mentors, and the wider social environment. That said, several other "virtual" internship types exist that have very little in common with these e-internships. This circumstance is further complicated by how the research is often aggregated by researchers and journalists alike – without the necessary differentiation. Here are some other forms worthy of research.

Micro-internships have appeared over the last two years. While these are often called online or virtual internships, this type has more in common with gig work as they feature temporary (e.g., normally hourly assignments) that may involve no contact, feedback, or support from the actual organizations that put forward those experiences. As a result, several researchers criticized that these micro-internships are not meaningful learning experiences (e.g., McKenzie 2021; see details in Hora et al. 2021). While often pushed by educational initiatives to replace traditional internships that had been cancelled during the Covid-19 pandemic, these "experiences" have actually very little in common with e-internships. More work is required to fully understand at which point (hours and type of work) will generate the most benefits for the interns.

Other more recent types include "virtual experiences" where people can test their skills when completed real-world tasks set by companies, but again these are temporary and feature no real-world interaction as such with employers. These experiences share some similarities with a third category: gamified "internships". Both offer short-term skill development opportunities only. The gamified "internships" offer computer-simulated tasks and interactions that are often part of university programs (e.g., featuring real-world tasks, avatars). These internships feature no interactions with real individuals, have no long-term career potential, and are often very specific to enable students to train certain skills only. Given the focus on situation-based and task-specific learning, these "internships" carry some potential learning benefits like other simulated learning exercises (Bayerlein and Jeske 2018). In both cases, both "virtual experiences" and gamified "internships", there is a clear absence of actual involvement with an employer – in contrast to e-internships – which therefore limits the opportunities for virtual interns to apply, collaborate, and interact with others on real-world live projects that set the stage for meaningful and applied learning experiences to foster their employability.

Finally, there are virtual internships "for sale". The trend of more and more students opting for paid-for virtual internships is the unfortunate by-product of the lack of internships in several countries over the last ten years. Very little is known about these since they are not evaluated systematically, however, they appear to be more employer-led. In conclusion, more research in the pros and cons is urgently needed to better understand research findings and take account of how the diversification of internship leads to differential, positive and negative, effects for virtual interns. Stakeholder investment and involvement are also a worthwhile area to investigate in order to understand when interns' own goals or those of employers and/or educational objectives are being pursued and prioritized in internships (Zehr and Korte 2020).

In short, numerous areas of interest exist where more research and investigation efforts could generate insights and practical recommendations for employers and educators interested in running and supporting meaningful internships.

Acknowledgements. The author would like to thank the virtual interns who shared their experiences as well as all authors who made their recent research on virtual internships readily available.

References

AlGhamdi, R.: Virtual internship during COVID-19 pandemic: exploring IT students satisfaction. Educ. + Training **64**(3), 329–346 (2022)

Bayerlein, L., Jeske, D.: Student learning opportunities in traditional and computer-mediated internships. Educ + Training **60**(1), 27–38 (2018)

Boehm, R., Beyerlein, M., Potter, K., Moore, L., Lu, J.: A virtual internship experience. In: Conference Paper. American Society for Engineering Education (ASEE) Virtual Annual Conference, 26–29 July 2021 (2021)

Brayfield, A.H., Rothe, H.F.: An index of job satisfaction. J. Appl. Psychol. **35**(5), 307–311 (1951)

Geertshuis, S., Holmes, M., Geertshuis, H., Clancy, D., Bristol, A.: Evaluation of workplace learning. J. Work. Learn. **14**(1), 11–18 (2002)

Hayes, A.F.: Introduction to Mediation, Moderation and Conditional Process Analysis: A Regression-Based Approach. Guilford Press, Guildford (2013)

Holyoak, L.: Are all internships beneficial learning experiences? An exploratory study. Educ. + Training **55**(6), 573–583 (2013)

Hora, M.T., Lee, C., Chen, Z., Hernandez, A.: Exploring online internships amidst the COVID-19 pandemic in 2020: results from a mixed-methods study. Center for Research on College-Workforce Transitions (CCWT), University of Wisconsin-Madison, USA, May 2021. https://ccwt.wceruw.org/wp-content/uploads/2021/05/CCWT_report_Exploring-online-internships-amidst-the-COVID-19-pandemic-in-2020.pdf. Accessed 30 Mar 2022

Jeske, D.: Virtual internships: learning opportunities and recommendations. In: Shindell, R. (eds.) Total Internship Management - The Employer's Guide to Building and Sustaining the Ultimate Internship Program, 3rd edn., pp. 171–177. InternBridge, Inc., Cedar Park (2019)

Jeske, D., Axtell, C.M.: E-internship prevalence, characteristics, and research opportunities. In: Kommers, P., Isaias, P., Rodrigues, L. (eds.) Proceedings of the IADIS International Conference on e-Society, Lisbon, Portugal, 12–16 March, pp. 201–208 (2013)

Jeske, D., Axtell, C.M.: e-Internships: prevalence, characteristics and role of student perspectives. Internet Res. **24**(4), 457–473 (2014)

Jeske, D., Axtell, C.M.: Global in small steps: e-internships in SMEs. Organ. Dyn. **45**(1), 55–63 (2016)

Jeske, D., Axtell, C.M.: Effort and rewards effects: appreciation and self-rated performance in e-internships. Soc. Sci. **6**(4), 1–14, Article ID 154 (2017)

Jeske, D., Axtell, C.M.: The nature of relationships in e-internships: a matter of psychological contract, communication and relational investment. J. Work Organ. Psychol. **34**(2), 113–121 (2018a)

Jeske, D., Axtell, C.M.: Virtuality in e-internships: a descriptive account. In: Lazazzara, A., Nacamulli, R.C.D., Rossignoli, C., Za, S. (eds.) Organizing for Digital Innovation. LNISO, vol. 27, pp. 219–233. Springer, Cham (2018b). https://doi.org/10.1007/978-3-319-90500-6_17

Jeske, D., Linehan, C.: Mentoring and skill development in e-internships. J. Work-Appl. Manag. **12**(2), 245–258 (2020)

Maini, R., Sachdeva, S., Mann, G.K.: Unveiling business school interns' satisfaction toward online summer internship program amid COVID-19. Higher Educ. Skills Work-Based Learn. **11**(5), 1210–1223 (2021)

McKenzie, L.: Online Internships Fail to Meet Expectations, 19 May 2021. https://www.insidehighered.com/news/2021/05/19/research-paints-disappointing-picture-online-internships. Accessed 20 May 2021

Nghia, T.L.H., My Duyen, N.T.: Internship-related learning outcomes and their influential factors: the case of Vietnamese tourism and hospitality students. Educ. + Training **60**(1), 69–81 (2018)

Ragins, B.R., McFarlin, D.: Perception of mentor roles in cross-gender mentoring relationships. J. Vocat. Behav. **37**(3), 321–339 (1990)

Stremersch, J., Van Hoye, G.: Searching hard versus searching smart: the role of search process quality in an internship context. Int. J. Sel. Assess. **28**(1), 31–44 (2020)

Teng, C.W.C., Lim, R.B.T., Chow, D.W.S., Narayanasamy, S., Liow, C.H., Lee, J.J.-M.: Internships before and during COVID-19: experiences and perceptions of undergraduate interns and supervisors. High. Educ. Skills Work-Based Learn. **12**(3), 459–474 (2022)

van Dorp, K.-J.: A premier European platform for clearing e-internships. Br. J. Edu. Technol. **39**(1), 175–179 (2008)

Venkatesh, V., Thong, J.Y., Xu, X.: Consumer acceptance and use of informationtechnology: extending the unified theory of acceptance and use of technology. MIS Q. **36**(1), 157–178 (2012)

Zehr, S.M., Korte, R.: Student internship experiences: learning about the workplace. Educ. + Training **62**(3), 311–324 (2020)

van Dorp, C.A., Egaña, A.H., Monteros, E.D.: Virtual internship arrangements for development of professional skills and competences. Commun. Cognit. Monographies **44**(1), 33–52 (2011)

Teachers' Preparedness for Integrating Programming and Computational Thinking in Art and Crafts

Kristine Sevik[✉] and Cathrine E. Tømte

University of Agder, 4630 Kristiansand, Norway
{Kristine.Sevik,Cathrine.Tomte}@uia.no

Abstract. In recent years considerable emphasis has been placed on fostering students' computational thinking and programming skills through compulsory education. Norway is one of few countries where these skills are explicitly included in the curriculum for practical and aesthetical subjects. This paper concerns a qualitative study of potential barriers for teachers' adoption of programming in the subject A&C in Norwegian compulsory education. Preliminary findings suggest that a gap exists between the expectations from the curriculum concerning programming and CT in the subject art and crafts, and teachers' classroom practices.

Keywords: Programming · Computational thinking · Barriers · Art and crafts · Compulsory education

1 Introduction

Following several other European countries [1, 2], Norway made programming and computational thinking (CT) part of compulsory education with the introduction of a renewed national curriculum for primary and secondary schools in August 2020.

There are two main approaches to incorporating programming and CT into the curriculum for compulsory education; one is to teach these skills as part of a separate (technology) subject, and the other is to incorporate them into existing school subjects or as a cross-curricular theme [3]. Tannert & Lorenzen [4] refer to these two approaches as a "pure" and an "applied" perspective on integrating CT into the curricula, and the European countries have chosen different strategies for implementing these competences into compulsory education [3]. In the Norwegian curriculum, we find programming most prominently in mathematics and science, but also in for the subjects art and crafts (A&C), and music [5]. This makes Norway one of few countries that have chosen to integrate programming into practical and aesthetical subjects. These concepts are traditionally associated with computer science and are likely to be unfamiliar for many A&C teachers. In addition, the literature provides few examples on how programming and CT can be integrated into such subjects, especially in a Norwegian context. Kaufmann and Stenseth [6] write about a study of problem-solving using programming in mathematics in a Norwegian lower secondary school: "An interesting dilemma arises when working

S. Papagiannidis et al. (Eds.): I3E 2022, LNCS 13454, pp. 180–191, 2022.
https://doi.org/10.1007/978-3-031-15342-6_14

with problems of the type presented in this study: Have we designed a problem that utilizes programming to give a better understanding of mathematics, or are we using mathematics to improve the problem-solving skills in programming?" In other words, do the introduction of CT and programming support and enrich the existing subjects or is it teaching computer science in disguise?

The focus of this present paper is on what teachers view as barriers to integrate programming and CT into their teaching of A&C in Norwegian compulsory education. The theoretical foundation is based on Ertmer's (1999) work on barriers for technology integration in teaching. The research question addressed is: According to teachers, what are the external and internal barriers for integrating programming and CT in A&C?

1.1   Moving from Curriculum to Practice - New Demands on the Teachers?

The subject A&C has a long tradition in Norwegian compulsory education, in fact its roots can be traced back to three subjects introduced in the curriculum of 1889: Woodwork for boys, Textile for girls, and Drawing [7]. Many years and many curriculum reforms later, the subject A&C today is considered essential for students' development of practical skills and creativity, and at its core we find craft skills, art and design processes, visual communication, and cultural awareness [8]. A&C comprises about 8% of the total hours of teaching in the primary and lower secondary school.

Making programming and CT part of teaching a practical-aesthetical subject like A&C is likely to present some challenges for teachers. Programming and CT originates from the computer science domain, while A&C has its own long-standing traditions and knowledge domains. Although the subject A&C often involve the use of technologies, digital as well as non-digital, computer science concepts have not traditionally been part of the subject. Integrating programming and CT may represent a new form of digitalization of the subject in that it allows teachers and students to create digital products 'from scratch' through programming instead of using ready-made software, but also place new demands on what competences the teachers need. On the other hand, that something is in the curriculum does not necessarily lead to implementation. As Dexter et al. [9] states: "Teachers can choose, within these limits, the approach that works for them. This autonomy provides teachers with choices to adopt, adapt, or reject an instructional reform". That said, school leaders may encourage and facilitate professional development their teachers, in order to develop these new skills.

2   Background: Programming and CT in Compulsory Education

Programming can be defined as simply the process of creating computer programs. Programming in compulsory school subjects is often linked to the so-called STEM subjects [3], an acronym for the subjects Science, Technology, Engineering and Mathematics that became a popular term in the early 2000s discourse on education, focusing on the perceived future need for more students with skills in mathematics and science (e.g. [10]). This coincided with the focus on the so-called 21st century skills emphasizing 'softer' skills such as creativity, collaboration and problem solving [11, 12] leading to a call to 'move from STEM to STEAM', where the A represents the arts [13, 14]. This, in turn, coincided with the emerging maker movement, a grass-root culture of making and technological innovation that has made its way into education with many schools establishing their own makerspaces [15].

The term computational thinking was first introduced by Seymour Papert [16] related to his work with the programming language LOGO, but the more recent discourse concerning CT and initiatives to integrate CT into compulsory education are often linked to Jeanette Wing [17] who stated that CT "represents a universally applicable attitude and skill set everyone, not just computer scientists, would be eager to learn and use". CT in compulsory education lacks an agreed-upon definition, but most definitions describe an approach to problem solving that draws upon computer science concepts such as the use of algorithms, abstraction, decomposition, debugging and iteration (e.g. [18, 19]). Perhaps ironically, many definitions do not mention computation or computers explicitly at all but focus more on problem solving in general. Denning and Tendre [20] argue from a computer science point of view that the success of convincing policy makers, teachers, and curriculum designers to integrate CT into compulsory education may have contributed to an oversimplified view on what CT involves.

Exercising CT does not necessarily involve programming, but the process of programming involves drawing on CT concepts, and much of the literature about developing CT skills in compulsory education use learning to program as an example subject domain (e.g. [1, 21]). Tools for programming have become much more accessible for novices in the last decade, especially due to the development of visual programming environments that allows for program creation using graphical elements instead of writing code, so-called block-based programming. In addition, several programming tools and languages have been created specifically for the purpose of learning how to program within fields like visual arts and music. While this is likely to lower the threshold for programming in school subjects, some knowledge of the structures and logics of computer programs is still required.

3 Theoretical Foundation: Barriers for Technology Integration

Much research has been conducted on factors influencing teachers' adoption of technology in the classrooms over the years, and many models and frameworks concern barriers and how these may be overcome, both in information systems research and education research. Within education research, Ertmer's [22] framework describing first- and second-order barriers to technology integration in education is much cited by scholars and policymakers. First-order barriers are barriers that are extrinsic to the teachers, typically lack of resources such as equipment (hardware and software), time, training and support (both technical and administrative). Second-order barriers, on the other hand, are intrinsic to the teachers and are rooted in teachers' beliefs about teaching and learning, their confidence and perceived value of technology. While first order barriers can be overcome by providing more recourses, second-order barriers are harder to overcome [22]. Building on the works of Ertmer [22], Hew and Brush [23, 24] identified five core barriers to technology integration in compulsory education: resources, knowledge and skills, institution, attitudes and beliefs, and subject culture. Subject culture refers to the "general set of institutionalized practices and expectations which have grown up around a particular school subject" (Goodson & Mangan, 1995, as cited in [23]). Subject culture may be particularly relevant when researching a subject such as A&C because of its practical and aesthetical nature.

4 Research Design, Methods and Data

The present paper concerns a qualitative study focusing on teachers in Norwegian primary schools (year 1–7) and lower secondary schools (year 8–10). The empirical data sources comprise of interviews and participatory observations with teachers, conducted in two stages:

A pilot study was conducted by interviewing five teachers experienced in integrating programming into their teaching. These teachers were selected based on their experience with programming in school subjects in general, and not A&C specifically. Three out of the five teachers were mostly teaching STEM subjects. The main purpose of the pilot study was to identify what these experienced teachers considered to be potential affordances with introducing programming into the curriculum, as well as their perceptions of barriers for successful integration into subjects such as A&C. Findings from the pilot study was used in preparation of the main study.

The main study involved six A&C teachers enrolled in a professional development course (CPD) about using digital tools and resources in A&C. Programming and CT are one of several topics covered in the course. Data sources include individual interviews and participatory observations of teaching sessions during the CPD course and document analysis of products created by the participants related to programming (teachers' reflection notes and products of programming assignments, such as animations, 3D-design, cardboard robots and e-textiles). The course is still ongoing, and this paper is based on data from the first round of interviews conducted before the topic of programming and CT had been covered.

Seven out of the 11 teachers interviewed teach the subject A&C, and all but one of those have formal training to teach the subject. According to a survey from the government agency Statistics Norway conducted in 2018, only half the teachers in A&C had formal training (ECTS credits) in teaching the subject [25]. Table 1 summarizes all teachers included in the study.

4.1 Interviews

The interviews were semi-structured with open-ended questions and the interview guide was developed by looking to theories barriers for technology integration in education [22]. The interviews included questions concerning their background and experience for teaching A&C (where applicable), their prior experiences and opinions concerning teaching with digital tools in general and with programming in particular, their access to digital tools and resources, and the level of training and support they had received. The teachers were also asked to give their perspective on the recent curriculum change regarding programming and CT, as well as how prepared they felt to teach to it.

All interviews were recorded and has been transcribed by the (main) author, and the storing and use of the data follows the privacy guidelines recommended by the Norwegian Centre for Research Data (NSD).

Table 1. Overview of participants (all names have been pseudonymized), the level they teach, their formal background for teaching and whether they teach the subject A&C.

Respondent	Group 1 = pilot 2 = main	Teaching level (grades)	Formal training as	Teaches A&C?
Alex	1	Primary (5–7)	Teacher: math, science, and social science	N
David	1	Primary (5–7)	Teacher: math and music	N
Tuva	1	Primary (1–7)	Teacher including A&C	Y
Mia	1	Lower secondary (8–10)	Teacher: A&C, science	Y
Nora	1	Primary (grades 1–7)	Teacher: math and science	N
Heidi	2	Lower secondary (8–10)	Teacher: A&C, Norwegian, English, PE	Y
Kari	2	Primary and lower secondary school (grades: 1–10)	Teacher: math and bilingual students	N
Julia	2	Mostly primary, but also lower secondary (1–10)	General teacher with A&C	Y
Sarah	2	Primary (1–7)	No formal teacher training	Y
Berit	2	Lower secondary (8–10)	Art academy and art teacher	Y
Cecilie	2	Lower secondary (8–10)	A&C bachelor,	Y

4.2 Coding and Analysis of Data

Data was coded and analysed inspired by Tjora [26] where we initially applied inductive approach to data analysis starting from data generated in the empirical setting and moving towards developing a theory while constantly checking if the theory holds up when compared to the empirical data. In the first phase of the analysis, we coded the interviews with keywords close to the empirical data from the interviews, and for the next phase we reduced the number of codes by grouping them thematically [27], following the framing of first-order and second-order barriers, as suggested by the research literature.

Results from the coding demonstrated that one distinct first order barrier, 'training', and one distinct second order barrier, 'teacher competence/self-efficacy' were addressed by teachers from both the pilot study and the main study. The second order barriers that addressed 'beneficial affordances and pedagogical potential for learning with programming and CT' were mainly covered by the pilot study teachers. And the first order barriers 'access to technology appropriate for A&C, leader support' where highlighted by the main study teachers. These teachers were also addressing issues related to second order barriers that linked to 'subject culture'. We will elaborate on these findings in the following section, which is organised according to the first, and second order framing.

5 Findings

Most teachers highlighted several barriers, including both first- and second order barriers. In the following, we will elaborate more on these barriers, and we will organise our findings into the two overall categories known as first- and second-order barriers. First-order barriers are relatively easy to identify as they are both external to the teachers and often quantifiable (access to technology, time, training and support), while identifying second-order barriers require more consideration as teachers might be unaware of them or more unwilling to discuss questions concerning their own beliefs and confidence [22]. In the following, we will elaborate more on how we may understand the teachers coping with these extrinsic and intrinsic type of barriers.

5.1 First-Order Barriers

The following sections present findings related to first-order barriers such as access to technology, time, training and support. As will be demonstrated all these barriers are perceived as real for the teachers responsible for the subject A&C.

Access to Technology. All teachers in both studies reported that the students had their own device for use in schoolwork (PC, Chromebook or tablet), and none mentioned connectivity or similar issues as being a major source of problems. This is consistent with data from the Norwegian primary and lower secondary information system for pupils[1], indicating that close to 90% of students in Norwegian primary and secondary schools have access to their own digital device for school purposes. However, most of the A&C teachers from the main study reported that these devices were seldom used in the subject A&C except for the purpose of documentation and photo/video productions. Teachers also commented on a lack of appropriate digital learning resources for A&C, as this extract from the interview with teacher Cecilie (C) illustrates:

I: *But is there any software for your subject available?*
C: *No, we don't have that. Not directly for art and craft.*
I: *Would you have gotten it if you found something you wanted?*
C: *I don't think so because it is so… I mean, they would not have spent money on it. They don't even spend money on schoolbooks here. I used to have a private Photoshop that I was allowed to install on my work computer, but that is not possible after we changed to administrated PCs.*

---

[1] https://gsi.udir.no/ (in Norwegian).

While computers and tablets can be suitable for programming in school subjects and many tools for programming are web-based and thus only require a browser and internet access, to create physical products in practical subjects such as A&C, additional hardware may be required to utilise programming and CT (such as micro-controllers, electronics, sensors, LEDs etc.). All of the experienced teachers in the pilot study mentioned that they had access to the micro-controller *micro:bit*, and 4 out of 5 had already used it with their students. One teacher from the main study said that the school had a set of micro:bits, but she had never used them. After conducting the interview, one more teacher from the main study discovered that her school had in fact two sets of micro:bits that the math and science teachers were using. A key takeaway here is that while the teachers have access to overall digital resources, only few of them report admission to appropriate A&C digital resources.

Time and Training. A majority of the teachers from the main study report that they had not had the time to update themselves on programming and CT since the curriculum reform from 2020, and that they had not been afforded enough time to do this. They explain this by referring to the Covid-19 pandemic, which put professional development on hold. It might also be that the teachers responsible for the A&C subject are not being prioritised for professional development training, compared with teachers responsible for other subjects, as this quote from Julia illustrates:

No one would have come to offer me this (course). No, no, no. Math, Norwegian, English and Science have priority.

Our finding is consistent with a national survey that showed that in Norway 56% of the school owners that responded had taken measures to improve mathematics teachers' competence in programming, while only 19% had done the same for A&C teachers [28]. We may assume that programming in the A&C subject is not yet being considered as relevant for professional training for teachers, as it may be in the STEM subjects.

Support. Like training, the teachers in our study reported limited levels of support from their principals. In our main study, only one was encouraged by her principal to take the course, while the other five did it on their spare time. Moreover, when the teachers reflected on their support from principals, their statements can be interpreted as if their principals did not clearly understand that programming had become a distinct element in the new A&C curricula, and that they should support their teachers in gaining some training to become professionals in this. It might also be that the principals may need some guidance on what the appropriate type of support would be. For example, teacher Nora noted that:

This is my greatest concern. That we are not ready for it. (...) I asked my principal: "Can you say that everyone (in this school) works with programming the way they are supposed to?" He did not want to answer that question.

In Nora's quote, the principal refuse to discuss how to support Nora's colleagues in their professional teaching with programming. Kari reported that her leader warned her about getting too much professional training and thus becoming overeducated:

My participation (in the course) was not agreed with the principal, I just do it on my own like the other courses. Because I hold a full university degree, my principal said that I really have more than enough education. "So, if you want to change employment", he said, "they will consider if they have the means to employ you, so think carefully before you study more and become even more educated". Hence, I didn't ask for permission this time, I did it on my own.

It seems like Kari's principal did not fully understand her need to further educate herself and to feel prepared to teach in new ways. Even if teachers have the required formal background to work as teachers, technological developments and curriculum reforms may place new demands on teachers' competence. A key message here would be that the principals does not seem support teachers when they report need for further training in CT for the A&C subject. While our data does not provide any clear explanations to this, it may be worth to pursue in future studies.

5.2 Second-Order Barriers

Second order barriers are intrinsic to teachers and may be more difficult to grasp, for teachers themselves, and for us as researchers, as these refer to attitudes, beliefs about teaching and learning, and the confidence and perceived value of technology. In our study several sub-categories emerged when we looked into these overall categories. For example, we unpacked teachers' attitudes towards programming and CT in A&C, their perceptions of the subject culture in A&C, along with their perceptions of self-efficacy towards the use of digital resources and tools. In the following, we will elaborate more on these perspectives.

Attitudes Concerning Programming and CT in A&C. The participants of this study are either experienced in integrating programming into their teaching, though not necessarily in A&C, or have signed up for a CPD course focusing on digital tools. This suggests that they are likely to be more positive to the idea of integrating programming and CT into A&C than the general teacher population. Still, the teachers raised some critical perspectives towards this curriculum change. This excerpt from the interview with Julia illustrates both a feeling of insecurity and a positive attitude towards the curriculum change:

I: Do you have any feelings, positive or negative, about the inclusion of programming in your subject?

J: I think that is only positive. I don't think that is negative. Because it is... it is creative. It seems like you have to be creative, I imagine you have to use your creativity, even if I am unsure about what it really is.

We found that the teachers enrolled in the CPD course were curious and mostly positive about programming in A&C but also a bit hesitant, partly because they didn't feel that they know enough about it or how to utilise it in A&C. This is often referred to as teachers' ability beliefs (their subjective view on their ability to integrate technology into the classroom) and value beliefs (such as the perceived importance and usefulness of the technology) [29].

The term computational thinking was unfamiliar to all the teachers from the main study, while all the teachers from the pilot study knew of it and had thoughts about how CT could relate to the subject A&C. The teachers from the main study were asked to describe typical work processes in A&C prior to getting asked about CT, and both open-ended, creative work processes and more rigid step-by-step procedures were mentioned by most of the teachers as being integral parts of the subject. Most teachers said that they would often start with a more procedural approach, and gradually allow the students more freedom as they mastered the fundamental techniques. While they may not know the term CT, the teachers' description of typical work processes fits well with most definitions of CT in compulsory education [18, 19].

A key message here was that even teachers with an overall positive towards programming in A&C are concerned about how to integrate it into the subject.

Self-efficacy and Competence. Teachers' self-efficacy is key when it comes to using ICT as a tool for teaching (e.g. [30, 31]). Not surprisingly, teachers from the pilot study were less concerned with their own ability to integrate programming and CT into their teaching, but they expressed concerns on behalf of their colleagues as this excerpt with teacher David illustrates:

They probably have a lot of great ideas, but they might lack both a forum for and experience with how to get from an idea to a finished product where programming or other technologies are part of the process. They have too little experience with programming, and they don't see the possibilities.

The quote from David indicates that A&C teachers need more experience with programming in order to bridge the traditional subject with the possibilities offered by new technologies such as programming. In the main study, self-efficacy was a concern expressed by most teachers, moreover, they expressed this to be an important motivation for enrolling into the CPD course, as they were concerned with their own (lack of) abilities to integrate programming into the subject.

I: Do you have any thoughts about programming now becoming part of the A&C curriculum?

J: Yes, that... I am thinking that I can't picture what I am supposed to be doing. I haven't gotten that far in my thinking. I see that it is there, but I don't really understand what I am supposed to do about it. So maybe that's partly why I take part in this (CPD course)

Both teachers from the pilot study and the main study emphasized that there was a lack of examples for A&C teachers to model their teaching after when it came to programming in the subject. This is also apparent in the literature, where research on programming and CT in STEM subjects is dominating, while we find few examples related to subjects like A&C. The key message was that self-efficacy was dominant among the teachers from the main study, but that they wished to learn more about how they could integrate programming into A&C, both from formal training and from examples.

Subject Culture. The subject A&C consists of both an art part and a crafts part. The teachers with A&C background all stress the practical aspect of the subject, the importance of students making something physical, mastering techniques, work with their hands and express themselves. This seem to be at the core of the subject culture of A&C, as this quote from Cecilie illustrates:

> *What makes A&C special is that they work with their hands. They aren't simply producing a text or a calculation or a report. They create something tangible in 3D or something you can hang on a wall. It is more personal, they put their soul into it.*

Key message from teachers' perceptions of the A&C subject culture is that even if the integration of programming in the subject are welcomed by most teachers, this must not be done at the expense of the subjects' practical and creative core.

6   Summary and Implications for Further Work

Programming and CT in subjects such as A&C represent a new field for researchers. This study contributes to the research communities of education and information systems with insights about what teachers perceive to be barriers for integrating these concepts into their teaching. Identifying such barriers may in turn help to identify potential measures to overcome these barriers and contribute to narrowing an expectations-reality-gap between the curriculum goals and the teaching practice as described by the teachers in this study.

In this study, we used Ertmer's [22, 32] theory on barriers for technology integration in education as a lens to investigate what teachers of A&C consider barriers for integrating programming and CT into the subject. We found that while access to digital devices is generally good, A&C teachers lack access to digital technology specifically aimed at teaching the subject. They also report the need for training, and support from their school leaders. The most prevalent findings in our study relate to what Ertmer [22] refers to as second-order barriers. We found that self-efficacy and subject culture were perceived as being important barriers for integration of programming. The A&C teachers need feel competent to teach with programming and to see programming as affording something that benefits the subject and that aligns with the practical and aesthetical aspects that is at the core of the subject.

The theory of affordances [33] is relevant when researching barriers to technology integration, especially when looking at how to overcome these barriers. Since this study was conducted, the teachers enrolled in the CPD course participated in a two-day workshop on how to use programming in A&C where they got hands-on experiences with making and programming cardboard robots, e-textiles, 3D-printable models, and animations. It would be interesting to investigate whether this workshop changed the teachers' perceptions of barriers and possibilities with programming in A&C, and if they make any changes regarding their teaching practice in the upcoming school year. A follow-up study is planned for this fall where we plan to revisit these teachers and to investigate further how to the barriers identifies in this study may be overcome.

References

1. Bocconi, S., et al.: Developing computational thinking in compulsory education - implications for policy and practice (2016)
2. Bocconi, S., Chioccariello, A., Earp, J.: The nordic approach to introducing computational thinking and programming in compulsory education, 01 January 2018
3. Bocconi, S., et al.: Reviewing computational thinking in compulsory education. Publications Office of the European Union, Luxembourg (2022)
4. Tannert, M., Lorentzen, R.F., Berthelsen, U.D.: Computational Thinking as Subject Matter: As an Independent Subject or Integrated across Subjects? Routledge, New York and London (2021). https://www.routledge.com/Computational-Thinking-in-Education-A-Pedagogical-Perspective/Yadav-Berthelsen/p/book/9780367610357
5. Ministry of Education and Research. Læreplanverket for Kunnskapsløftet (2020). https://www.udir.no/laring-og-trivsel/lareplanverket/2019
6. Kaufmann, O.T., Stenseth, B.: Programming in mathematics education. Int. J. Math. Educ. Sci. Technol. **52**(7), 1–20 (2020)
7. Digranes, I.: The norwegian school subject art and crafts - tradition and contemporary debate. FormAkademisk - forskningstidsskrift for design og designdidaktikk **2**(2) (2009)
8. Ministry of Education and Research. Curriculum for Art and crafts (2019)
9. Dexter, S.L., Anderson, R.E., Becker, H.J.: Teachers' views of computers as catalysts for changes in their teaching practice. J. Res. Comput. Educ. **31**(3), 221–239 (1999)
10. Breiner, J.M., Harkness, S.S., Johnson, C.C., Koehler, C.M.: What is STEM? A discussion about conceptions of STEM in education and partnerships. Sch. Sci. Math. **112**(1), 3–11 (2012)
11. Binkley, M., et al.: Defining twenty-first century skills. In: Griffin, P., McGaw, B., Care, E. (eds.) Assessment and Teaching of 21st Century Skills, pp. 17–66. Springer, Dordrecht (2012). https://doi.org/10.1007/978-94-007-2324-5_2
12. Erstad, O.: The assessment and teaching of 21st century skills project. Nordic J. Digit. Lit. **4**(03–04), 204–211 (2010)
13. Land, M.H.: Full STEAM ahead: the benefits of integrating the arts into STEM. Proc. Comput. Sci. **20**, 547–552 (2013)
14. Perignat, E., Katz-Buonincontro, J.: STEAM in practice and research: an integrative literature review. Thinking Skills Creat. **31**, 31–43 (2019)
15. Papavlasopoulou, S., Giannakos, M.N., Jaccheri, L.: Empirical studies on the Maker Movement, a promising approach to learning: a literature review. Entertain. Comput. **18**, 57–78 (2017)
16. Mindstorms, P.S.: Children, Computers, and Powerful Ideas, viii, 230 p. Basic Books, New York (1980)
17. Wing, J.: Computational thinking. Commun. ACM **49**(3), 33–35 (2006)
18. Lye, S.Y., Koh, J.H.L.: Review on teaching and learning of computational thinking through programming: What is next for K-12? Comput. Hum. Behav. **41**, 51–61 (2014)
19. Brennan, K., Resnick, M. (eds.): New frameworks for studying and assessing the development of computational thinking. In: Proceedings of the 2012 Annual Meeting of the American Educational Research Association, Vancouver, Canada (2012)
20. Denning, P.J., Tedre, M.: Computational thinking: a disciplinary perspective. Inform. Educ. **20**, 361–390 (2021)
21. Shute, V.J., Sun, C., Asbell-Clarke, J.: Demystifying computational thinking. Educ. Res. Rev. **22**, 142–158 (2017)
22. Ertmer, P.A.: Addressing first- and second-order barriers to change: strategies for technology integration. Educ. Tech. Res. Dev. **47**(4), 47–61 (1999)

23. Hew, K.F., Brush, T.: Integrating technology into K-12 teaching and learning: current knowledge gaps and recommendations for future research. Educ. Tech. Res. Dev. **55**(3), 223–252 (2007)
24. Ertmer, P.A.: Teacher pedagogical beliefs: the final frontier in our quest for technology integration? Educ. Tech. Res. Dev. **53**(4), 25–39 (2005)
25. Perlic, B.: Lærerkompetanse i grunnskolen. Statistics Norway (2019)
26. Tjora, A.H.: Kvalitative forskningsmetoder i praksis. 4. utgave. Gyldendal, Oslo (2021)
27. Clarke, V., Braun, V., Hayfield, N.: Thematic analysis. Qual. Psychol.: Pract. Guide Res. Methods. **2015**(222), 248 (2015)
28. Rogde, K., et al.: Spørsmål til Skole-Norge: analyser og resultater fra Utdanningsdirektoratets spørreundersøkelse til skoler og skoleeiere våren 2020. The Nordic Institute for Studies in Innovation, Research and Education (NIFU) (2020)
29. Xie, K., Nelson, M.J., Cheng, S.-L., Jiang, Z.: Examining changes in teachers' perceptions of external and internal barriers in their integration of educational digital resources in K-12 classrooms. J. Res. Technol. Education. 1–26 (2021)
30. Ertmer, P.A., Ottenbreit-Leftwich, A.T.: Teacher technology change. J. Res. Technol. Educ. **42**(3), 255–284 (2010)
31. Hatlevik, O.E.: Examining the relationship between teachers' self-efficacy, their digital competence, strategies to evaluate information, and use of ICT at school. Scand. J. Educ. Res. **61**(5), 555–567 (2017)
32. Ertmer, P.A., Paul, A., Molly, L., Eva, R., Denise, W.: Examining teachers' beliefs about the role of technology in the elementary classroom. J. Res. Comput. Educ. **32**(1), 54–72 (1999)
33. Markus, M.L., Silver, M.S.: A foundation for the study of it effects: a new look at DeSanctis and Poole's concepts of structural features and spirit. J. Assoc. Inf. Syst. **9**(10), 5 (2008)

Factors Influencing Women's IT Career Choice in South Africa

Margaret Cullen[1] , Andre P. Calitz[2] , and Linda Motaung[1]

[1] Business School, Nelson Mandela University, Port Elizabeth, South Africa
Margaret.Cullen@Mandela.ac.za
[2] Department of Computing Sciences, Nelson Mandela University, Port Elizabeth, South Africa
Andre.Calitz@Mandela.ac.za

Abstract. The number of women professionals participating in the IT industry in South Africa is less than 20%. A number of factors influence women's IT career choices, such as previous programming exposure and the influence of parents, teachers and role models. Young women do not view the IT industry as a desirable career and those who are qualified and working in the IT industry, often leave the industry mid-career due to family commitments. This study followed a positivistic research philosophy and the approach was deductive. A quantitative study using a survey was conducted to test the conceptual model. The survey was conducted amongst women currently working in the IT industry in South Africa to establish the factors that have contributed to their participation in the IT industry and the factors that influence their longevity in the IT industry.

The main findings of the study indicate that women who choose a career in IT have high levels of intrinsic motivation and obtain the relevant IT qualifications. Women remain in an IT career if they are self-confident, maintain a work-life balance and have flexible working hours. Scholars, parents and teachers should be made aware of IT qualifications and careers. The lack of women in IT top-level management positions has resulted in less female role models. Women in IT face occupational challenges that can lead to females leaving the IT industry. The study identified factors that influenced women working in the IT industry selecting a career in IT and remaining in the IT industry.

Keywords: Women in IT · Women IT career choice · Women retention strategies

1 Introduction

Information technology (IT) has transformed all aspects of modern daily life. The United Nations Society Report of 2017 noted that modern society has been increasingly digitally engaged, with over 47% of the world's population or 3, 5 billion people having computer access, thus entrenching the use of technology within modern society [1]. Widespread computer-based technologies, such as mobile phones, Internet, wireless technologies and cloud-based applications have become commonplace with an increase in technology usage and reliance.

© IFIP International Federation for Information Processing 2022
Published by Springer Nature Switzerland AG 2022
S. Papagiannidis et al. (Eds.): I3E 2022, LNCS 13454, pp. 192–204, 2022.
https://doi.org/10.1007/978-3-031-15342-6_15

Businesses that invested in new technologies and used them as part of business operations have reaped benefits in the form of bigger market share and increased profits. IT is one of the main drivers of economic growth globally and more recently in Africa, Asia and the Middle East [2]. IT has given businesses the competitive edge by improving operational efficiencies, real time transaction processing and high availability of accurate information required for strategic decision making.

Worldwide, woman make up more than half of the global workforce [3], however in South Africa, less than 20% of IT professionals are women. Meehl, Huntoon and Kalyvaki [4] indicate that in many fields, such as IT, post-secondary school qualifications help women to decide on their career paths. However, the discipline of IT is largely male dominated and lacking in diversity [5]. Currently, an estimated 30% of the global IT workforce is female and an even lesser number is involved in IT leadership, academic and professional positions [6].

Examining the contrasts of the genders participating in IT leadership positions, Rogers [3] noted that the number of women professionals involved in high ranking professional IT jobs was significantly lower compared to their male counterparts. Less than 15% of females were noted to be in IT leadership positions [7]. Women's continued under-representation in the IT field is a matter of international concern [8], however the reasons for their low participation in South Africa have not been extensively investigated. The factors that influence a scholar's IT career choice include gender, culture, career perceptions, computer experience, advisors and awareness of IT jobs and careers [9].

Exposure to new technologies and programming concepts at school level creates IT career awareness and influences a scholar's career choice. IT graduates entering the IT industry were generally not familiar with IT career paths, IT job descriptions and career opportunities [10]. Women are approximately 2.5 times more likely to leave their career in IT than men. The factors that affect a woman IT professional remaining in the IT industry, called job embeddedness, include work-life balance, self-efficacy and the relationships women have with management and colleagues [11]. Women also prefer to have a flexible work schedule to manage both family and job responsibilities.

This paper will explore the various reasons for the low participation of women in the IT industry in South Africa. The study aims to identify the factors that have contributed to South African women's IT career choices and the factors that influence them to remain in the IT industry. The layout of the paper is as follows: in the literature, the intrinsic and extrinsic factors that influence women to choose an IT career are discussed in Sect. 2. The research problem, research question and the Women in IT survey are discussed in Sect. 3. The Women in IT survey results are presented in Sect. 4. Conclusions and recommendations, relevant to young women wanting to choose a career in IT and future work are presented in Sect. 5.

2 Literature Review

The IT industry is a broad professional field of study and is concerned with designing, developing, implementing and maintaining computer software and hardware [12]. The under-representation of women in the IT sector is a global challenge, which occurs in developed and developing nations [3, 8]. In the United States, the IT workforce is comprised of only 26% females as active participants [8], while in South Africa the number of woman professionals participating in IT is less than 20% [13]. Less than 15% of females are in leadership positions in the IT industry in South Africa [7].

IT is part of the universally significant STEM subjects (Science, Technology, Engineering and Mathematics) that are critical for modern society and have formally been largely male dominated. The previously male dominated fields such as the field of Medicine, Engineering and Science have been able to successfully change the demographics and increase the participation of females, due to their early career education, focused training methods and research strategies that are designed to attract female participants to the profession. However, this trend has not been similar in the IT industry [14].

A number of programmes now encourage girls and minorities to embrace technology at a young age and pursue a career in IT. However, qualified women in the IT industry are leaving the industry because they experience a "hostile" male culture, a sense of isolation and lack of a clear career path [15].

A number of specific factors influence a female scholar's career decisions. Numerous intrinsic and extrinsic factors affect a woman's career choice and the progression and retention within a field. A young person's intrinsic and extrinsic motivation, self-efficacy, culture, previous exposure to technology and specific programming, are all strongly correlated with the decision to pursue a career in IT [9]. The following intrinsic and extrinsic factors affect women's IT career choices and their decision to remain in the IT profession.

2.1 Intrinsic Factors

Personality Traits
Self-confidence plays an important part in women's participation in IT, affecting their entry and departure [16]. Career path choices are based on an individual's sense of self-confidence in the career subject and on the individual's perception of future success in the chosen field [16]. An individual's personality traits, specifically self-confidence are key qualities as they affect career choice and determine whether an individual succeeds at work [17].

Self-efficacy
Self-efficacy is considered to be the most important factor in career choice [18]. Perceived self-efficacy is defined by Bandura [19] as a person's beliefs about their capabilities to produce designated levels of performance, which exercise influence over events that affect their lives. A person's self-efficacy determines how they feel, think, motivate themselves and behave. Self-efficacy has had a greater influence on male students in deciding whether to choose IT majors than females [12].

Skills and Aptitudes
Career choices are made by young people during their early secondary school career [6]. IT is a field that requires problem solving, critical and analytical thinking, which

are key skills required to succeed [13]. These skills are not gender specific and hence the lack of confidence by females in technical ability is an incorrect perception.

Negative self-perception has made females less inclined to perceive themselves as excellent in the technical environment [12]. This is driven by their own internal personal limitations based on lack of confidence using computers and new technologies and additionally on societal perceptions. These are norms that everyone grows up with, which seek to channel females to people-oriented careers rather than the technical environment.

2.2 Extrinsic Factors

Environment During School Years

The choice of a future career, especially of the unusual career choices is achieved by rousing the interest of scholars, while they are in their early schooling years, between the ages of eleven and seventeen [20]. Teaching and training methods that capture the interest and inform of the content of the IT field can lead to increased positive perceptions from peers and scholars alike. In females, the interest is often captured in earlier classes, but the interest in IT reduces as the female scholars grow older [6].

Scholars make career choices during their early secondary school career [6]. The high school era is a critical time where students are guided by their family, teachers, career counsellors and those role models most influential to them to choose school subjects that later direct them to future fields of study and career [9]. Alshahrani, Ross and Wood [21] found that the impact of pre-university school education appeared to be of limited significance for females choosing to study IT. However, exposure to problem solving, programming, online self-learning and internships were important positive influences. Sources of information and the impact of relatives, teachers and IT role-models have been highlighted as important career choice influencers [13]. A young person's intrinsic and extrinsic motivation, self-efficacy, previous exposure to technology and specific programming are all strongly correlated with the decision to pursue a career in IT [9].

Post-school Environment

The gender gap amongst students choosing to study STEM subjects at university has received considerable attention in recent years and specifically females choosing a career in Computer Science [21]. In countries such as Scotland, females make up only 16% of students studying CS at university [21]. The perceptions of CS and IS graduates, post-graduates and Alumni and their opinion regarding the decision to work in industry or complete post-graduate studies were evaluated by Calitz et al. [22]. The results of the study indicated that 3rd year CS and IS students were generally advised to complete at least a 4-year IT degree or Honour's degree. The decision to start working in industry or to continue with a CS or IS Masters' degree or a MBA qualification, depended on the individual's career plan, to either stay in a technical environment, academia or to move into industry and possible managerial positions.

Family View of IT
Historically, some jobs have been linked to certain genders and technical jobs were reserved for males, while administrative jobs were reserved for women. Other professional fields of study, which were previously male dominated, such as the field of medicine, enjoy societal prestige. This has enabled them to receive favourable support from the general population and family structures, which culturally did not support female involvement in these careers [13]. Culture does play a significant role in IT career decisions for different ethnic groups in South Africa and research findings indicate that the factor culture plays an important role when women in South Africa, specifically African, Coloured and Indian women, make IT career choices as well as when they decide to remain in an IT career [13].

2.3 IT as a Career

While women live in modern times, the traditional family structure has not changed. Women continue to be the primary care givers of families. Pretorius and De Villiers [23] observed that women battle to balance a demanding IT job whilst still being heavily involved at home. Fifty percent of women prepare meals at home compared to 9% of males, 51% of women attend a sick child compared to 9% of males and house cleaning is done by 45% of women and 5% of men. These statistics reveal that women have demanding roles at home [23]. They thus have less free time than their male colleagues as they have demanding home activities to attend to while balancing work, family and social activities.

Family influence is the reason for the high volume of females participating in the IT field in Mauritius as the family and national culture encourage females to view IT as a potentially viable career [24]. Over 50% of Computer Science enrolments are women. This is a similar situation in the Indian society where the family structure supports the idea of women actively choosing the IT field as a career of choice.

Career Demands
Seventy-four percent of women working in IT, report that they "love the work", however 56% of women leave their science and technology jobs mid-career [8]. However, few women choose a career in IT in South Africa [10]. These low female participation statistics present a similar picture to the recorded numbers of global female participation in technology. Muro and Gabriel [7] noted that in 2012, women only accounted for 30% of operational technicians and 15% of managers in technical positions.

Family Demands
Women who actively participate by bringing their skills into the IT industry, find it necessary to take a break from the job environment during childbearing years. This natural passage causes a momentary pause in a woman's IT career, resulting in a disruption of career growth plans. As the industry moves at a fast pace, this pause ends up being the reason females leave the profession as they experience the stress of re-joining and

catching up when they resume the profession and often have to catch up and learn new systems [18].

Gender Bias

Gender bias is a preference or prejudice toward one gender over the other. The unconscious bias assumes that men are more closely associated with work and women are associated with family. The legality of gender bias is an area of huge contention with regard to pay equity between the sexes [25]. Historically in many countries, men make more money in a career than women, even if they hold the same job. While the disparity has dwindled since the mid-20th century, it still exists in most areas to some degree. The gender stereotypes of personal qualities and the blanket approach of norms for women as to 'what should' compared to 'what are' female behaviours, have resulted in individuals behaving in ways consistent to general gender perception and thus these set back the global advancement strides made by females in venturing into male dominated professions [14].

Male/Female Perceptions of Women in IT

As a male dominated field, the professional networks are skewed towards the needs of males. Networking is important for growth opportunities, skills sharing and building relationships, however the chances remain few for females to be involved in these networks as they are at times informal networks. The timing of these interactive sessions can be deterring as they are often after working time and thereby clash with other demanding family responsibilities for women [26]. Joining industry specific professional bodies assists women to have an equal footing in professional environment conversations and these associations bring a sense of belonging and connectedness to their male counterparts [26, 27].

2.4 Conceptual Model

Based on the literature discussed, an in-depth investigation was conducted to determine the factors that affect women's choice of an IT career and the reasons for women remaining in the IT industry. The identified independent factors included both intrinsic and extrinsic factors, as indicated in the proposed conceptual model (Fig. 1). The three dependent factors (DF) identified were:

1. Women choosing an IT career;
2. Women remaining in an IT career; and
3. Successful women in an IT career.

The three dependent factors were identified from previous research, specifically a study conducted by Rogers [3] where it was suggested that the recruitment, professional development and retention of women in the IT industry be investigated. The inclusion of the three dependent factors, specifically *Successful women in the IT industry* is based on previous research [8, 11]. The independent factors (IF) are intrinsic personality traits, skills and aptitude and management of an IT career. Extrinsic factors are environment during school years, the post-school environment, cultural and other societal attitudes regarding IT careers, cultural and societal attitudes regarding family, career demands, family demands, gender bias and male and female perceptions of women in IT.

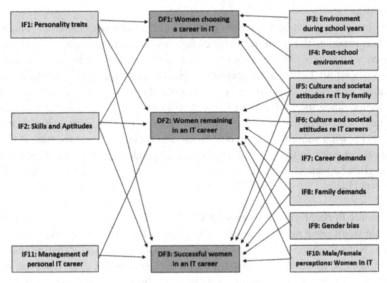

Fig. 1. Conceptual model

3   Research Design

The study followed a positivistic research philosophy and the approach was deductive, exploratory and quantitative. A systematic literature review was conducted and an initial questionnaire developed and evaluated in a pilot study. A main survey was then conducted amongst South African woman in the IT industry to assess the relations between eleven independent factors and three dependent factors. The woman participants were part of the membership database of the Institute of IT Professionals of South Africa (IITPSA), Department of Computing Sciences Alumni at the Nelson Mandela University and selected businesses employing women IT professionals. There were a total of 71 responses received after three calls for participation.

Data were collected using a questionnaire incorporating both closed and open-ended questions. The questionnaire was divided into two sections, consisting of demographic information including age, marital status and educational qualifications, while the second part of the questionnaire gathered data relating to items for each independent factor. A 5-point Likert scale was used, ranging from (1) Strongly disagree to (5) Strongly agree. A pilot study was conducted amongst female IT professionals and lecturers to validate the questionnaire. The online platform QuestionPro was used to collect the responses and the NMU statistical consultant performed the statistical analysis using the Statistica software. Descriptive statistics, ANOVA and Exploratory Factor Analysis (EFA) were conducted. Ethics approval was obtained from the university Business School Ethics Committee.

4 Women in IT – Results

Sixty percent (n = 42) of the respondents were from the Eastern Cape Province, followed by 29% (n = 20) from the Gauteng province (Table 1). A small number of respondents were from the other provinces in South Africa. The respondents were mainly married women (48%, n = 34) or single women (32%, n = 23). Forty-nine percent (n = 35) had between 1 to 2 children with 45% (n = 32) having no children and four respondents having 3–4 children. The age group of the respondents were 32% (n = 23) between the ages of 21 to 29 years, 32% (n = 23) between the ages of 30 to 39 and 35% (n = 25) between 40 to 59 years (Table 1).

The ethnicity of the respondents were 49% (n = 34) White women, 29% (n = 20) African women and a small number of Coloured and Indian women. The majority of the respondents had a degree or a post-graduate degree and 64% (n = 37) had a graduate or post-graduate IT degree (Table 1). The majority of the respondents had been working in the IT industry for five to 20 plus years (71%, n = 50) and 29% (n = 21) had up to 4 years work experience. The respondents' current work position were entry or operational level positions (23%, n = 16), followed by software developers (22%, n = 15) with only one respondent being self-employed and one in executive management.

Table 1. Demographic variables (n = 71)

Marital status		Number of children		Highest Qualification	
Divorced	10% (n=7)	None	45% (n=32)	Matric	8% (n=6)
Living together	8% (n=6)	1-2	49% (n=35)	Certificate	1% (n=1)
Married	48% (n=34)	3-4	6% (n=4)	Diploma	20% (n=14)
Single	32% (n=23)			Degree	23% (n=16)
Widowed	1% (n=1)			Honours	25% (n=18)
				Masters	23% (n=16)
Ethnicity		Age		Highest IT Qualification	
African	29% (n=20)	21-29	32% (n=23)	Certificate	15% (n=10)
Coloured	14% (n=10)	30-39	32% (n=32)	Diploma	21% (n=14)
Indian	6% (n=4)	40-49	21% (n=15)	Degree	27% (n=20)
White	49% (n=34)	50+	14% (n=10)	Honours	16% (n=12)
Other	3% (n=3)			Masters	21% (n=15)
Province		IT work experience		IT role models	
Eastern Cape	60% (n=42)	0-2 years	21% (n=15)	Yes	27% (n=19)
Gauteng	29% (n=20)	3-4 years	8% (n=6)	No	73% (n=52)
KwaZulu-Natal	1% (n=1)	5-9 years	28% (n=20)		
North West	2% (n=3)	10-19 years	20% (n=14)		
Western Cape	7% (n=5)	20 years +	23% (n=16)		

4.1 Measurement Items

In this study, for reporting purposes, the Likert scales were combined for "Strongly disagree" with "Disagree", and "Agree" with "Strongly agree". The factors after the EFA (Table 2), with mean scores the respondents strongly agreed with were Personality traits ($\mu = 4.12$, s.d. $= 0.68$), Confidence ($\mu = 4.67$, s.d. $= 0.41$), Conflict Management ($\mu = 4.22$, s.d. $= 0.61$), Family and Societal Encouragement ($\mu = 4.03$, s.d. $= 0.95$), Perceptions of female colleagues ($\mu = 4.08$, s.d. $= 0.64$) and Successful women in an IT career ($\mu = 4.39$, s.d. $= 0.55$).

4.2 Exploratory Factor Analysis

The factors identified in the literature (Fig. 1) and the factors identified by the EFA are presented in Table 2. The minimum factor loading deemed significant was 0,645 (n = 71). Table 2 illustrates the Eigenvalues and the percentage of each factor that can be explained by a single factor. The Cronbach's alpha values (Table 2) were all above 0.6 and 13 of the 21 factors recorded Excellent reliability and the remaining factors had Good or Acceptable reliability.

Table 2. Exploratory factor analysis (n = 71)

Factor	Conceptual model factors	Factors after EFA	n	Cronbach's alpha	Eigen values	Variance explained
IF1	Personality Traits	Personality Traits	71	0,81 (Excellent)	2,187	72,9%
IF2 A	Skills and Aptitudes	Confidence	70	0,88 (Excellent)	3,537	79,0%
IF2 B		Conflict Management	70	0,87 (Excellent)		
IF3 A	Environment during school years	Computer Access	70	0,84 (Excellent)	3,209	73,8%
IF3 B		Peer Perception	55	0,93 (Excellent)		
IF3 C		School Career Guidance	66	0,62 (Acceptable)		
IF4	Post-school environment	Tertiary Education	71	0,82 (Excellent)	2,616	65,4%
IF5 A	Cultural and societal attitudes re IT careers	Family and societal discouragement	65	0,79 (Good)	3,019	77,9%
IF5 B		Family and societal encouragement	63	0,86 (Excellent)		
IF6 A	Cultural and societal attitudes re family	Cultural understanding of career	70	0,88 (Excellent)	2,462	70,0%
IF6 B		Cultural expectations	71	0,61 (Acceptable)		
IF7 A	Career demands	Work-Life Balance	71	0,87 (Excellent)	3,145	77,7%
IF7 B		After-hour work	70	0,88 (Excellent)		
IF8	Family demands	Family Demands	70	0,89 (Excellent)	4,331	61,6%
IF9	Gender bias	Gender Bias	71	0,74 (Good)	2,591	51,8%
IF10 A	Male/Female perceptions of Women in IT	Perceptions of female colleagues	71	0,86 (Excellent)	3,722	63,3%
IF10 B		Perceptions of male colleagues	69	0,65 (Acceptable)		
IF11	Management of personal IT career	Management of IT Career	69	0,69 (Acceptable)	2,469	73,3%
DF1	Women choosing a career in IT	Successful Woman in IT - Personal	71	0,79 (Good)	2.229	74.3%
DF2	Women remaining in an IT career	Successful Woman in IT - In General	71	0,68 (Acceptable)	1,815	60,5%
DF3	Successful women in an IT career	IT as a Career	71	0,81 (Excellent)	3,360	56,0%

4.3 Pearson's Correlations

The correlations are statistically significant at 0.05 level for n ranging from 55 to 71 if |r| > = rcrit ranging from .234 to .266 and both statistically and practically significant if |r| > = .300 [28]. The factors Personality traits (r = 0.342), Confidence (r = 0.266) and Tertiary education (r = 0.352) correlated positively with the dependent factor, Women choosing an IT career (Table 3). The factors *Personality traits* (r = 0.342), *Cultural expectations* (r = 0.427), *Work-life balance* (r = 0.483), *Family demands* (r = 0.487), *Perceptions of female colleagues* (r = 0.385) and *Perceptions of male colleagues* (r = 0.525), correlated positively with the dependent factor, *Women remaining in an IT career* (Table 3). However, *Gender Bias* (r = −0.479) and *Management of Career* (r = −0.250) negatively correlated with the dependent factor, *Women remaining in an IT career.*

Table 3. Pearson's correlations (n = 71)

	Independent factors	DF1: Women choosing a career in IT	DF2: Women remaining in an IT career	DF3: Successful women in an IT career
IF1	Personality Traits	.342	.291	.153
IF2A	Confidence	.266	.048	.373
IF2B	Conflict Management	.113	.060	.069
IF3A	Computer Access	.114	-.151	-.047
IF3B	Peer Perception	.077	.191	-.032
IF3C	School Career Guidance	.158	.189	.109
IF4	Tertiary education	.352	.081	.286
IF5A	Family and societal discouragement	.036	.200	.348
IF5B	Family and societal encouragement	.145	-.088	.065
IF6A	Cultural understanding of career	.068	.202	.034
IF6B	Cultural expectations	.094	.427	-.076
IF7A	Work-Life Balance	.059	.483	.385
IF7B	After-hour work	.049	.041	.108
IF8	Family demands	.035	.487	.242
IF9	Gender Bias	-.237	-.479	-.142
IF10A	Perceptions of female colleagues	.207	.385	.299
IF10B	Perceptions of male colleagues	.042	.525	.035
IF11	Management of Career	.161	-.250	.331

The factors that correlated with the dependent factor, Successful women in an IT career were Confidence (r = 0.373), Tertiary Education (r = 0.286), Family and societal discouragement (r = 348), Work-Life balance (r = 0.385), Family demands (r = 242), Perceptions from female colleagues (r = 0.299) and Management of career (r = 0.299).

4.4 Key Findings and Recommendations

The findings of the study indicated the importance of a tertiary education (μ = 3.87, n = 71, t = 4.34, d.f. = 70, p < .0005) as it prepared women for the IT job environment. Over 69% believed that tertiary education prepared them for their career in IT and 82% believed that they had studied the correct qualification. These results indicate that tertiary education is a key tool to help women understand the IT environment and prepares women for the actual IT job environment.

The findings of the study indicate the importance of Personality traits ($\mu = 4.21$, $n = 71$, $t = 9.97$, d.f. $= 70$, $p < .0005$), high levels of confidence ($\mu = 4.67$, $n = 70$, $t = 26.07$, d.f. $= 69$, $p < .0005$) and conflict management skills ($\mu = 4.22$, $n = 70$, $t = 11.18$, d.f. $= 69$, $p < .0005$). Thus, nurturing confidence in young women from an early age can lead to more women opting for a career in IT as they will equally have the confidence in their abilities, which is a catalyst for women to opt for a career in IT.

The recommendations are aimed at improving the number of women who opt for and remain in an IT career. The following are the suggested recommendations from the study:

- Family members and teachers need to be made aware of IT careers and the benefits for women working in the IT industry. DuBow [8] further recommend creating awareness through educational materials;
- Access to new technologies and programming exposure at school level can assist with creating interest in females at a young age;
- The lack of knowledge of IT careers by students needs to be addressed at university level, specifically making use of educational materials [8];
- Traditional responsibilities of women have not changed. Women have dual roles at home and at work, which at times leads to career sacrifices and maintaining a work-life balance;
- Flexible work hours and remote work environments can assist with managing the demands of an IT career for women. This has specifically been observed during the COVID-19 pandemic period where people were required to work from home; and
- Lack of networking opportunities, role models and women in IT management positions result in one sided viewpoints and limited growth opportunities. Increasing the number of channels whereby women in IT can interact, introducing formal mentorship programmes and creating affirmative opportunities will increase the participation of women in IT [3; 11].

5   Conclusions and Future Research

Currently less than 20% of the 10000 + registered IITPSA members in the South African IT industry are female and only 15% of the females are in leadership positions [3, 13]. A number of factors influence young women's career decisions, including intrinsic and extrinsic motivation, previous exposure to technology and the impact of relatives, teachers and IT role-models [9]. The results from this study support the findings of Alshahrani et al. [21], who highlighted that the results of their study could be used to help present a more positive view of a CS education and an IT career to school children, their families and teachers.

The respondents in this study indicated that the factors influencing their IT career choice were self-efficacy, exposure to IT, sources of advice, financial expectations and the gender gap. The factors that influence women choosing an IT career included self-confidence, which relates to self-efficacy, obtaining a tertiary education and ignoring gender bias (r = −237). Work-life balance, managing family demands and ignoring gender bias (r = −0.479) were the factors affecting women to remain in the IT industry [8].

The findings of the study indicate that successful women in IT require an appropriate qualification (75%), they have work-life balance (61%), they overcome cultural prejudice (43%), they receive family support (54%) and they constantly keep ahead of change in the IT field and remain up to date with new technologies (90%). The EFA included items highlighting that women must consider a career in IT, that there are different career paths for women in IT, they have a rewarding career in IT and that their IT career makes a positive contribution [8]. The factors that correlated with Women remaining in an IT career were Personality Traits (r = 0.291), Cultural expectations (r = 0.427), Work-life balance (r = 0.483), Perceptions of female colleagues (r = 0.385) and Male colleagues (r = 0.525).

The lack of prominent female IT role models influences societal views on the profession. The contribution of the study is a model (Fig. 1) indicating the factors that affect women working in IT career choices and for them to remain in the IT industry. The EFA provided the factors and items to be included in a questionnaire that can be used for future research. The limitations of this study are that the study was conducted only in South Africa and with a small sample of IT professionals, thus future research can replicate the study with a larger sample.

References

1. UN information society report. Measuring the information society report. (2017). https://www.itu.int/en/ITU-D/Statistics/Documents/publications/misr2017/MISR2017_Volume1.pdf
2. Mustafa, M., Batool, A., Raza, A.A.: Designing ICT interventions for women in Pakistan. Commun. ACM **62**(11), 46–47 (2019). https://doi.org/10.1145/3355696
3. Rogers, V.: Women in IT: the endangered gender. In: Proceeding of the 2015 ACM Annual Conference on SIGUCCS, pp. 95–98 (2015)
4. Meehl, M., Huntoon, W., Kalyvaki, M.: Preparing women for leadership in IT–What wins is doing. In: PEARC '20: Practice and Experience in Advanced Research Computing, July 2020, pp. 481–483 (2020). https://doi.org/10.1145/3311790.3399626
5. Rankin, Y., Thomas, J.O.: The intersectional experiences of black women in computing. In: SIGCSE 2020: Proceedings of the 51st ACM Technical Symposium on Computer Science Education, February 2020, pp. 199–205 (2020). https://doi.org/10.1145/3328778.3366873
6. Njoki, M., Wabwoba, F., Micheni, E.: ICT definition implication on ICT career choice and exclusion among women. Inf. Technol. Comput. Sci. **5**, 62–71 (2016)
7. Muro, C., Gabriel, M.: Women engagement in ICT professions in Tanzania: exploring challenges and opportunities. Int. J. Comput. Inf. Technol. **5**(5), 443–447 (2016)
8. DuBow, W.: Attracting and retaining women in computing. IEEE Comput. Soc. **14**, 90–93 (2014)
9. Twani, M., Calitz, A.P., Cullen, M. Identifying relevant factors for an IT career choice model. In: SACLA 2020 Conference, 6-8 July 2020, South Africa
10. Esterhuyse, A., Calitz, A.P., Cullen, M.: Post-Graduate CS and IS students' career awareness. In: SACLA 2019, the 48th Annual Conference of the Southern African Computer Lecturers' Association conference, Alpine Heath Resort, Drakensberg, S.A, pp. 15–17, July 2019

11. Brown, M.L.: An examination of job embeddedness and intent to stay among women in information technology. Ph.D, Dissertation, Capella University (2020)
12. Govender, I., Khumalo, S.: Reasoned action analysis theory as a vehicle to explore female students intention to major in information systems. J. Commun. **5**(1), 35–44 (2014)
13. Calitz, A.P., Cullen, M., Fani, D.: The influence of culture on women's IT career choices. In: Hattingh, M., Matthee, M., Smuts, H., Pappas, I., Dwivedi, Y.K., Mäntymäki, M. (eds.) I3E 2020. LNCS, vol. 12067, pp. 345–357. Springer, Cham (2020). https://doi.org/10.1007/978-3-030-45002-1_30
14. Calitz, A. P., Greyling, J., Cullen, M.: South African scholar ICT career inclinations. In: SACLA 2018 Conference, Gordons Bay, South Africa, pp. 18–20, June 2018
15. Lien, T.: Why are women leaving the tech industry in droves? Los Angeles Times (2015). https://www.latimes.com/business/la-fi-women-tech-20150222-story.html#page=1
16. Cohoon, J., Wu, Z., Luo, L.: Will they stay or will they go. In: Proceedings of the 39th SIGSCE Technical Symposium in Computer Science Education, pp. 397–401 (2008)
17. Warren, J., Young, D., Williams, K.: Personality, gender and careers in information technology. In: Proceedings of the 2012 18th Americas Conference on Information Systems, pp. 1–9 (2012)
18. Alexander, T., Schoeman, M., Alexander, B., Piderit, R.: The influence of gender and age on choosing computing courses at South African universities. Commun. ACM **50**(10), 1–10 (2011)
19. Bandura, A.: Self-efficacy. In: Ramachaudran, V.S. (Ed.), Encyclopedia of Human Behavior, vol. 4, pp. 71–81, New York. Academic Press (1994)
20. Adya, M.: Work alienation among IT workers: a cross-cultural gender comparison. IN: Proceedings of the ACM SIGMIS Computer Personnel Research, pp. 66−69 (2008)
21. Alshahrani, A., Ross, I., Wood, M.I.: Using social cognitive career theory to understand why students choose to study computer science. In Proceedings of ACM ICER 2018 Conference, Espoo, Finland (2018). https://doi.org/10.1145/3230977.3230994
22. Calitz, A.P., Greyling, J.H., Cullen, M.: Industry versus Post-graduate studies: CS and IS alumni perceptions. In: Liebenberg, J., Gruner, S. (eds.) SACLA 2017. CCIS, vol. 730, pp. 192–205. Springer, Cham (2017). https://doi.org/10.1007/978-3-319-69670-6_13
23. Pretorius, H., De Villiers, C.: An analysis of the International discourse about women in information technology. In: Proceedings of the Annual Conference of the South African Institute of Computer Scientist and Information technologist, pp. 179–186 (2009)
24. Pretorius, H., De Villiers, C.: A South African perspective of the international discourse about women in information technology. ACM J. 265–274 (2010)
25. Rubery, J., Koukiadaki, A.: Closing the gender pay gap: a review of the issues, policy mechanisms and international evidence. International Labour Office, Geneva (2016)
26. Smith, L.: Working hard with gender: gender labour for woman in male dominated occupations of manual trades and Information technology (IT). Equality Divers. Incl. **30**(6), 592–603 (2013)
27. Thiele, L., Miller, K., Berg, K. Overcoming gender challenges in information and communications technology. AIM, pp. 1–10 (2013)
28. Gravetter, F.J., Wallnau, L.B.: Statistics for the Behavioral Sciences, 8th edn. Wadsworth, Belmont, CA (2009)

Digital Innovation and Transformation

Digital Transformation in the Public Sector: Investigating Success Factors in IRIDA System

Konstantinos Ioannou[1,2], Maria Kamariotou[1] (iD), and Fotis Kitsios[1,3](✉) (iD)

[1] Department of Applied Informatics, University of Macedonia, Thessaloniki, Greece
{k.ioannou,mkamariotou}@uom.edu.gr, kitsios@uom.gr
[2] Department of Cybersecurity, Ministry of Interior, 10183 Athens, Greece
[3] School of Social Science, Hellenic Open University, Parodos Aristotelous 18, 26335 Patras, Greece

Abstract. Recent advances in digital technologies have influenced the public sector but limited papers have been applied to assess the effectiveness of Information Systems (IS) in the public sector. Many e-government projects have been devalued because they were designed incorrectly, and effectively transfer existing bureaucracy to the digital world. Therefore, recognizing the efficacy of e-government systems, as well as the factors affecting the performance of employees in the public sector, clarifies an emergent field of inquiry to bridge the gaps in literature and tackle future study. The purpose of this article is to explore the factors affecting the IRIDA's success in e-government. Data was collected by 498 users in the Greek public sector. The findings show that the perceived ease of use and the perceived usefulness seem to be the factors with the most significant loadings. This paper is useful for professionals who design these systems to improve their effectiveness and to carefully consider these variables in the design and usage of IS in the public sector.

Keywords: Digital transformation · Strategy · Information systems success · IRIDA system

1 Introduction

Digital technology and Information Systems (IS) improvements have had a substantial impact on a variety of businesses and the public sector recently. Individuals, businesses, and all public agencies benefit from information technology (IT) and information systems (IS), which provide quick and secure access to all resources from a single point of access [11, 26]. Developing IS in government is part of a larger transformation cycle which helps the government be safer, more reliable, and more productive to people and businesses [4, 6, 15, 19–21].

Previous researchers have used existing IT/IS-related models to help businesses develop effective IS. A few of these models are the Technology Acceptance Model (TAM) [8], the Theory of Planned Behavior (TPB) [1], and the Unified Theory of Acceptance

S. Papagiannidis et al. (Eds.): I3E 2022, LNCS 13454, pp. 207–218, 2022.
https://doi.org/10.1007/978-3-031-15342-6_16

and Use of Technology (UTAUT) [31]. For IT/IS implementation to be a success, it is important to think about the factors that affect how people use IS and how they act. Evaluation models were made to look at what users need and how factors and aspects affect system growth in order to make people more satisfied and accept the system [14, 16–18]. DeLone and McLean's model of IS success (1992) [9] is one of the most commonly used models to explain how IS work. This model has been used in many studies in different countries [32]. Even though IS researchers have focused a great deal of attention on the IS success model, only a small number of papers have been applied to evaluate the effectiveness of IS in the public sector. E-government systems are effective, and factors that affect the productivity of public infrastructure workers are also important. This shows that there is a new field of study that can fill in gaps in the existing literature and help with future research.

Recent studies in the area of e-government have focused on public satisfaction as the end users. There have only been a few studies done about how internal users accept the new system. Furthermore, current IT success models place a strong emphasis on system-centric assessment as well as management structure and framework. Users'-centric assessments of IS in the public sector have not yet been addressed by academics. To develop a successful information system in e-government, it is necessary to accomplish a level of performance that mainly satisfies most internal users [24, 28]. People who study and work in e-government have taken note of the findings, which have led them to start looking into how digital technologies affect people and businesses in the public sector [23, 29]. Even though these topics have made a lot of progress in the literature on public management, there are still no studies that show how digital technologies affect public sector performance, and how IS affect staff's actions when they use e-government systems.

The effectiveness of e-government projects in Greece is hampered by a lack of know-how, reduced funding (especially in the decade of crisis), and a lack of sound policy initiatives and decisions [20, 30]. Many e-government projects were devalued in their infancy because they were misdesigned, effectively transferring the existing bureaucracy to the digital world. In addition, the cumbersome public sector in terms of organizational change has been a deterrent to any attempt to introduce innovation. Finally, the lack of political will and, primarily, financial and business interests "worked" for any digital venture to fail [12, 21]. Therefore, in recent years, highly costly investments were made in hardware and software. Every e-government project was not effective, implemented by the private sector for the state, without strategic planning, without the participation of specialized executives in the conception and implementation of the projects of the public, with only the big companies in the field of digital technologies winning, and finally losing the Greek society, which still had minimal and insufficient digital services. Simultaneously, the rest of Europe's citizens reaped the benefits of digital transformation in public administration [6, 27].

The above findings help us understand the magnitude of the frustration over what has not been done so far and indicate the need for immediate action to implement innovative projects, which will provide a comforting impression on the contact of citizens and businesses with the public sector. It is therefore critical that our country's public sector move even faster, but primarily more significantly, in the direction of the systematic use of digital technologies to reclaim the lost ground in the effort of digital transformation [15, 19].

This paper explores the factors that impact the IRIDA's success in e-government. IRIDA is a new, more efficient, faster, safer and more transparent electronic document management system which is used in the Ministry of Interior for the central management and handling of documents. Data was collected by 498 users in the Greek public sector.

That paper's structure is as follows. Section 2 includes the theoretical background on satisfaction in e-government. Section 3 explains the methodology, while Sect. 4 presents the findings. Section 5 discusses the outcomes and presents limitations and avenues for future researchers.

2 Theoretical Background

The introduction of IT and computer technology into public administration brought new administrative practices and led to what is now called e-government. E-government strengthens transparency, efficiency and public accessibility and is increasingly acknowledged as a central pillar to facilitating the transformation of public governance [24]. IT, moreover, has transformed government; it provides new opportunities for delivering better, more reliable and competitive services to people and businesses and its acceptance by employees and citizens is a top priority for governors. Therefore, the development of a theoretical model for the acceptance of digital technology in the public sector, such as that proposed by Sang et al. (2009) [25], is particularly useful for developing future political and strategic decisions to enhance the usage of such services.

Much of the literature focuses on users' satisfaction with the development of services in e-government, as the success of such initiatives depends largely on the percentage of their use [24]. User acceptance is expressed mainly through the TAM. It is applied to understand individuals' attitudes towards the use of technology, which can lead to further acceptance and adoption. That is to say, the attitude formed by TAM represents the attitude formed towards the use of technology. It is determined as one of the earliest and most commonly accepted research approaches; it is a dominant model in the field of technology and in the use of IS, along with the theory of IS success suggested by DeLone and McLean [9]. According to the TAM model, the important aspects that impact on the adoption and usage of digital technologies are perceived ease of use and perceived usefulness, with Davis (1989) [8] being its main exponent. According to Davis, the model can be used to investigate the frequency at which users use a specific technology, the characteristics of the system, and the reasons users ultimately accept or reject it. In conducting a research on users of two information systems in a Canadian company and evaluating the variables used in the initial research, Davis said that both perceived usefulness and ease of use are strongly associated with self-reported system indicators; and, therefore, the final degree of adoption and frequency of use of a system by its end users depends directly on what motivates each user.

Weerakkody et al. (2016) [33] attempt to fill a research gap by exploring the significance of users' trust in the efficiency of a system and its information in the UK, and to what extent cost affects satisfaction. The five dimensions highlighted in their paper have significantly affect users' satisfaction with services in the public sector. According to

Anwer et al. (2016) [5], a thorough evaluation of these services will help to highlight their strengths and weaknesses, identify their new guidelines and compare their organization locally, nationally and internationally. For this reason, they are proceeding with an analysis and assessment of the current state of Afghanistan's e-government services, through a combination of evaluation approaches. Sachan et al. (2018) [24] investigate users' satisfaction of e-government services and therefore suggest a model, incorporating the TAM into the process. This research can help app developers to gain an idea of the needs of users in order to enhance the design and implementation of these systems. According to Wirtz et al. (2016) [34], the key difficulty for local e-government portals is to define the most important dimensions affecting user satisfaction. For this reason, they develop a model to satisfy the users of such gates, using mixed methods. Also, the research of Danila et al. (2014) [7] explores user intentions and the usage of e-government services; it presents a model that combines the TAM, the designed behavior theory and the DeLone and McLean success model, to explore the dimensions affecting the purpose and the use of such services. Skordoulis et al. (2017) [27] study the TAXIS information system and examine the satisfaction of users with its use, using a multi-criteria methodology. Wang et al. (2008) [32] develop and validate a success model of e-government systems, based on the revised DeLone and McLean success model, that records the multidimensional and interdependent nature of these systems. The main aim of Horan et al. (2006)'s work [13] is to create a means for the success of e-government, as shown by the users of such e-services. Regardless of whether their model will be used in the future, they point out that as these services are more widespread, it is necessary to understand the manner in which they are perceived by the taxpayer. The research of Athmay et al. (2016) [2] was implemented to examine the dimensions affecting the acceptance of e-government services in the United Arab Emirates, considering the end-user. They are interested in knowing the significance of satisfied users and the effect they have on user intention for these services.

However, system developers are also considered employees, since they are primarily called upon to use the new applications either voluntarily or out of compulsion. Dukic et al. (2017) [10] examine the level of computer skills of staff in the public sector and the degree to which they uphold e-government. Using a questionnaire from Croatian central government officials, they concluded that the official felt they were very specialized and did not resist the change. It is considered that some improvements in e-services need to be made. Stefanovic et al. (2016) [28] also explore the success of such systems from the angle of employees. The findings verify the validity of the DeLone and McLean model in e-government. Floropoulos et al. (2010) [12] investigate the TAXIS system using employees in Public Financial Services. This is interesting since this system is applied in a country with a strong taxation system that is mandatory. Terpsiadou et al. (2009) [30], in their study, concluded that most users are generally satisfied with the features of the system. Al-Busaidy et al. (2009) [3] carried out a survey of civil servants from three e-government-related ministries. It is revealed in the survey that there is a strong link between the following factors: efficiency, accessibility, availability and trust.

Wang and Liao (2008) [32] using the DeLone's and McLean's (2003) [9] IS success model investigated the effect of the quality of information, the quality of service, the quality of system on users' satisfaction for e-government technologies. The results conclude that authorities in the public sector should develop IS which will execute accurate and useful information and a user-friendly system for users to accept. Additionally, the findings of their study highlighted that quality of information has a greater impact on user satisfaction and perceived net benefit than quality of service and system. Therefore, managers in the public sector will concentrate on executing up-to-date and accurate information. Many scholars explored the effect of the quality of information, the quality of the service, and the quality of the system on the employees' satisfaction who used municipal e-government systems [28, 29]. The findings of these studies concluded that the quality of service and the technical quality are increasing the satisfaction of staff. Employees have therefore the intention to use systems with a high degree of usability, user-friendliness, and ease of use. User satisfaction is a significant factor for the benefits of local government workers, such as increased efficiency, work performance and effectiveness [28, 29].

In e-government in particular, scholars have measured user satisfaction which adapt three factors: information quality, service quality and system quality. The first factor tests the content of IS containing variables such as precision, currency, timeliness of performance, reliability, completeness, mindfulness, ease of use and adequate amount of information. Level of service quality allows workers in the public sector to carry out their day-to-day work activities. Therefore, factors such as information production, the user-friendly interface, system compatibility and technical staff skills are essential to help users. The third aspect pertains to IS production efficiency. Quality of service involves variables such as information completeness, precision, format, currency, importance, timeliness, accuracy, validity, usability, and conciseness to calculate the user satisfaction impact on this aspect. IS users in the public sector indicated that the quality of system and service has a direct but not high and positive impact on users' satisfaction. Their expectations are focused on the quality of information, perceived ease of use and the interface of the system because the main goal is the improvement of their work. Users require timely information by accessing data in real-time; correct information, fewer incorrect data entries and more consistent data entry across users over time.

3 Methodology

To evaluate the IRIDA's success, a questionnaire was developed. The questionnaire was distributed to 3500 users of the system and 498 completed it. The proposed questionnaire is based on previous research and incorporates the two main research trends derived from the literature about technology acceptance [8, 9, 23, 24, 28] and specifically on both the DeLone and McLean success model for IS and Davis' TAM. Such a combination model helps to identify the degree to which a specific system fulfills its demands and proves its value, through the visual gaze of its immediate recipients, its users. Moreover, the use of variables in both models allows for a more comprehensive view of the application of such information systems, as it incorporates both objective and subjective elements of their definition. Applying the DeLone and McLean model, the key variables for evaluating an information system are system quality, information quality, and service quality. Respectively, the variables of perceived ease of use and perceived utility by the TAM are used. All of the above variables are key to evaluating technical success, semantic success, and application effectiveness and have a direct causal relationship with satisfaction [23, 24, 28]. A 5-point Likert-scale was used to measure these variables. Data analysis was implemented using Factor Analysis.

4   Results

The internal consistency, calculated via Cronbach's alpha, ranged from 0.959 to 0.970, exceeding the minimally required 0.70 level [22]. Factor analysis was used to analyze the detailed items of the questionnaire. Tables 1 and 2 present the principal component analysis using the Maximum Likelihood Estimate and the extraction of factors with Promax with Kaiser Normalization method. The factor loadings and cross loadings provide support for convergent and discriminant validity.

Table 1. Factor loadings.

Factors	Items	Loadings
Information quality	Accuracy of information (IQ1)	0.823
	Relevance of information (IQ2)	0.841
	Compliance with the information classification/indexing (IQ4)	0.874
	Update of the screens on time (IQ5)	0.819
	Transaction without reaching useless information (IQ6)	0.850
	Making the work easier of provided info (IQ7)	0.863
	Reliability of information (IQ8)	0.844
	Usefulness of information (IQ9)	0.822
	Accessibility information 7/24 (IQ10)	0.816
	Coherence of the words/statement in the system (IQ11)	0.837
	Appropriateness of information on the screens (IQ12)	0.789
System quality	Accessibility to the system (SYQ1)	0.756
	High speed access (SYQ2)	0.752
	User-friendly design (SYQ3)	0.717
	Accessibility to information (SYQ4)	0.703
	Availability of the system (SYQ5)	0.796
	Interoperability of the system (SYQ6)	0.733
Service quality	The technical staff provided services quickly (SEQ1)	0.620

(*continued*)

Table 1. (*continued*)

Factors	Items	Loadings
	The call centers responded quickly (SEQ2)	0.634
	Fast service of online support center (SEQ3)	0.618
	Willingness of technical staff (SEQ4)	0.653
	Capabilities of technical staff (SEQ5)	0.662
	Secure transactions with the system (SEQ6)	0.687
Perceived ease of use	Ease of learning (PEoU1)	0.912
	Competence of system's making work easier (PEoU2)	0.945
	Ease of interaction with the system (PEoU3)	0.936
	Capabilities needed to use the system (PEoU4)	0.977
Perceived usefulness	Increment of work efficiency (PU1)	0.985
	Perception of using system useful for users' job (PU2)	0.924
	The use of the system helps users complete their tasks faster (PU3)	0.919
	The use of the system increases users' productivity at work (PU4)	0.966
	Perception of using system useful for themselves (PU5)	0.991
Satisfaction	Satisfaction with information quality (SA1)	0.822
	Satisfaction with system quality (SA2)	0.751
	Satisfaction with service quality (SA3)	0.618
	Satisfaction with perceived ease of use (SA4)	0.989
	Satisfaction with perceived usefulness (SA5)	0.971

Table 2. Pattern matrix.

	Factors					
	Information quality	System quality	Service quality	Perceived ease of use	Perceived usefulness	Satisfaction
IQ1	0.823					
IQ2	0.841					
IQ3	0.836					
IQ4	0.874					
IQ5	0.819					

(*continued*)

Table 2. (*continued*)

	Factors					
	Information quality	System quality	Service quality	Perceived ease of use	Perceived usefulness	Satisfaction
IQ6	0.850					
IQ7	0.863					
IQ8	0.844					
IQ9	0.822					
IQ10	0.816					
IQ11	0.837					
IQ12	0.789					
SYQ1		0.756				
SYQ2		0.752				
SYQ3		0.717				
SYQ4		0.703				
SYQ5		0.796				
SYQ6		0.733				
SEQ1			0.620			
SEQ2			0.634			
SEQ3			0.618			
SEQ4			0.653			
SEQ5			0.662			
SEQ6			0.687			
PEoU1				0.912		
PEoU2				0.945		
PEoU3				0.936		
PEoU4				0.977		
PU1					0.985	
PU2					0.924	
PU3					0.919	
PU4					0.966	
PU5					0.991	
SA1						0.822

(*continued*)

Table 2. (*continued*)

	Factors					
	Information quality	System quality	Service quality	Perceived ease of use	Perceived usefulness	Satisfaction
SA2						0.751
SA3						0.618
SA4						0.989
SA5						0.971

5 Discussion

This article explored the factors affecting the IRIDA's success in e--government. The transition of the state and its structures to the digital age is a goal for public administration. We know that digital technologies, applied in government structures, offer a digital environment that creates acceleration in decision-making and execution processes, relieving staff and citizens from trivial and time-consuming processes of signing, handling, and searching for documents, thus saving time and money, reducing their energy footprint and ultimately providing high quality services to citizens.

The findings show that the perceived ease of use and the perceived usefulness seem to be the factors with the most significant loadings. Confirmation of the significant effect of the above factors can be easily explained when it comes to the users of the system. This is because they are the ones who mainly enter the data in this electronic document management system and therefore are particularly interested in having a system with that will ultimately make it functional and useful for the exercise of their duties.

When comparing the findings of the current study with those of the authors of the articles included in the literature review, it is important to note that the majority of their findings are coincidental. Internal system users are more satisfied with their work if all three factors of quality are good, but which one has a bigger impact on total satisfaction depends on the research being looked at [23, 28, 29]. While surveys vary in their results, most indicate that users believe that the system can assist them in performing their jobs more effectively. Most surveys show that people are more likely to use and like IS if they are easy to use and if they think they are useful [23, 24].

The use of the system essentially completely eliminates the printing of documents, their printed circulation, their handwritten assignment and signature, and their time-consuming archival and retrieval. A series of unnecessary and time-consuming procedures are eliminated from the employee's workload, increasing his effectiveness, transparency in procedures, hierarchical control, and pivotal collaboration with public services, and thus his overall administrative ability to respond with the pace, precision, and versatility required to meet the operational requirements of a modern organizational environment while realizing significant savings.

6 Conclusion

There was a restriction on the number of people who have participated in the survey. However, because the survey was only conducted at the Ministry of the Interior, the sample size was small compared to most empirical studies that used the questionnaire method. It has also not been possible to evaluate system performance at a more comprehensive level because there hasn't been a more detailed analysis. More research is needed to look at these factors in a representative sample of users across the country, and any generalization of results should be done with care.

Future researchers could use behavioral IS usage models to better understand how people use IS in a variety of settings (such as at the operational, tactical, and strategic levels) where IS usage can be measured by the amount of time spent on the system. The findings of the study show that people who use IS and suppliers of applications for public IS pay a lot of attention to improving the efficiency and performance of these systems. They also think about these things when they design and use IS. This paper is also good for professionals because it helps them make those systems more effective and think carefully about these things when they make and use IS. Due to the increasing use of IT for the delivery of public services, a better understanding of such constructs is required to enhance their acceptance.

References

1. Ajzen, I.: The theory of planned behavior. Organ. Behav. Hum. Decis. Process. **50**(2), 179–211 (1991)
2. Athmay, A.A.A.A., Fantazy, K., Kumar, V.: E-government adoption and user's satisfaction: an empirical investigation. EuroMed J. Bus. **11**, 57–83 (2016)
3. Al-Busaidy, M., Weerakkody, V., Dwivedi, Y.K.: Factors influencing eGovernment progress in Oman: an employee's perspective. In: Proceedings of the 15th Americas Conference on Information Systems (AMCIS), San Francisco, California, USA (2009)
4. Angelopoulos, S., Kitsios, F., Babulac, E.: From e to u: towards an innovative digital era. In: Symonds, J. (ed.) Ubiquitous and Pervasive Computing: Concepts, Methodologies, Tools, and Applications, chap. 103, pp. 1669–1687. IGI Global Publishing (2010)
5. Anwer, A.M., Esichaikul, V., Rehman, M., Anjum, M.: E-government services evaluation from citizen satisfaction perspective: a case of Afghanistan. Transform. Gov. People Process Policy **10**, 139–167 (2016)
6. Charalabidis, Y., Loukis, E., Lachana, Z., Alexopoulos, C.: Future research directions on the science base and the evolution of the digital governance domain. In: Proceedings of the International Conference on Information Systems (ICIS 2019), Munich, Germany (2019)
7. Danila, R., Abdullah, A.: User's satisfaction on E-government services: an integrated model. Procedia. Soc. Behav. Sci. **164**, 575–582 (2014)
8. Davis, F.D.: Perceived usefulness, perceived ease of use, and user acceptance of information technology. MIS Q. **13**, 319–340 (1989)
9. Delone, W.H., McLean, E.R.: The DeLone and McLean model of information systems success: a ten-year update. J. Manag. Inf. Syst. **19**(4), 9–30 (2003)
10. Dukić, D., Dukić, G., Bertović, N.: Public administration employees' readiness and acceptance of e-government: findings from a Croatian survey. Inf. Dev. **33**(5), 525–539 (2017)
11. Faro, B., Abedin, B., Cetindamar, D.: Hybrid organizational forms in public sector's digital transformation: a technology enactment approach. J. Enterp. Inf. Manag. (2021). (in press)

12. Floropoulos, J., Spathis, C., Halvatzis, D., Tsipouridou, M.: Measuring the success of the Greek taxation information system. Int. J. Inf. Manag. **30**(1), 47–56 (2010)
13. Horan, T.A., Abhichandani, T., Rayalu, R.: Assessing user satisfaction of e-government services: development and testing of quality-in-use satisfaction with advanced traveler information systems (ATIS). In: Proceedings of the 39th Hawaii International Conference on System Sciences (HICSS 2006), Kauia, HI, USA (2006)
14. Kitsios, F., Kamariotou, M.: Information systems strategy and strategy-as-practice: planning evaluation in SMEs. In: Proceedings of the 25th Americas Conference on Information Systems (AMCIS), Cancun, Mexico (2019)
15. Kamariotou, M., Kitsios, F.: Critical factors of strategic information systems planning phases in SMEs. In: Themistocleous, M., Rupino da Cunha, P. (eds.) EMCIS 2018. LNBIP, vol. 341, pp. 503–517. Springer, Cham (2019). https://doi.org/10.1007/978-3-030-11395-7_39
16. Kitsios, F., Kamariotou, M.: Strategizing information systems: an empirical analysis of IT alignment and success in SMEs. Computers **8**(4), 1–14 (2019)
17. Kitsios, F., Kamariotou, M.: Decision support systems and strategic information systems planning for strategy implementation. In: Kavoura, A., Sakas, D.P., Tomaras, P. (eds.) Strategic Innovative Marketing. SPBE, pp. 327–332. Springer, Cham (2017). https://doi.org/10.1007/978-3-319-56288-9_43
18. Kitsios, F., Kamariotou, M.: Strategic IT alignment: business performance during financial crisis. In: Tsounis, N., Vlachvei, A. (eds.) Advances in Applied Economic Research. SPBE, pp. 503–525. Springer, Cham (2017). https://doi.org/10.1007/978-3-319-48454-9_33
19. Kamariotou, M., Kitsios, F.: Information systems phases and firm performance: a conceptual framework. In: Kavoura, A., Sakas, D.P., Tomaras, P. (eds.) Strategic Innovative Marketing. SPBE, pp. 553–560. Springer, Cham (2017). https://doi.org/10.1007/978-3-319-33865-1_67
20. Loukis, E., Charalabidis, Y.: Why do eGovernment projects fail? Risk factors of large information systems projects in the Greek public sector: an international comparison. Int. J. Electron. Gov. Res. (IJEGR) **7**(2), 59–77 (2011)
21. Loukis, E.N., Tsouma, N.: Critical issues of information systems management in the Greek public sector. Inf. Polity **7**(1), 65–83 (2002)
22. Newkirk, H.E., Lederer, A.L., Srinivasan, C.: Strategic information systems planning: too little or too much? J. Strat. Inf. Syst. **12**(3), 201–228 (2002)
23. Rai, A., Lang, S.S., Welker, R.B.: Assessing the validity of IS success models: an empirical test and theoretical analysis. Inf. Syst. Res. **13**(1), 50–69 (2002)
24. Sachan, A., Kumar, R., Kumar, R.: Examining the impact of e-government service process on user satisfaction. J. Global Oper. Strateg. Sourcing **11**, 321–336 (2018)
25. Sang, S., Lee, J.-D.: A conceptual model of e-Government acceptance in public sector. In: Proceedings of the 3rd International Conference on Digital Society (ICDS 2009), Cancun, Mexico (2009)
26. Simmonds, H., Gazley, A., Kaartemo, V., Renton, M., Hooper, V.: Mechanisms of service ecosystem emergence: exploring the case of public sector digital transformation. J. Bus. Res. **137**, 100–115 (2021)
27. Skordoulis, M., Alasonas, P., Pekka-Economou, V.: E-government services quality and citizens' satisfaction: a multi-criteria satisfaction analysis of TAXISnet information system in Greece. Int. J. Prod. Qual. Manag. **22**(1), 82–100 (2017)
28. Stefanovic, D., Marjanovic, U., Delić, M., Culibrk, D., Lalic, B.: Assessing the success of e-government systems: an employee perspective. Inf. Manag. **53**(6), 717–726 (2016)
29. Stefanovic, D., Mirkovic, M., Anderla, A., Drapsin, M., Drid, P., Radjo, I.: Investigating ERP systems success from the end user perspective. Technics Technol. Educ. Manag. **6**(4), 1089–1099 (2011)
30. Terpsiadou, M.H., Economides, A.A.: The use of information systems in the Greek public financial services: the case of TAXIS. Gov. Inf. Q. **26**(3), 468–476 (2009)

31. Venkatesh, V., Morris, M.G., Davis, G.B., Davis, F.D.: User acceptance of information technology: toward a unified view. MIS Q. **27**(3), 425–478 (2003)
32. Wang, Y.S., Liao, Y.W.: Assessing eGovernment systems success: a validation of the DeLone and McLean model of information systems success. Gov. Inf. Q. **25**(4), 717–733 (2008)
33. Weerakkody, V., Irani, Z., Lee, H., Hindi, N., Osman, I.: Are U.K. Citizens satisfied with e-Government services? Identifying and testing antecedents of satisfaction. Inf. Syst. Manag. **33**(4), 331–343 (2016)
34. Wirtz, B.W., Kurtz, O.T.: Local e-government and user satisfaction with city portals – the citizens' service preference perspective. Int. Rev. Public Nonprofit Mark. **13**(3), 265–287 (2016). https://doi.org/10.1007/s12208-015-0149-0
35. Angelopoulos, S., Kitsios, F., Papadopoulos, T.: New service development in e-government: identifying critical success factors. Transform. Gov. People Process Policy **4**(1), 95–119 (2010)

The Role of Digital Transformation in Fostering Transparency: An e-Court System Case Study

Rozha K. Ahmed[1,4]([⊠]) (iD), Omer Ahmed[2], Ingrid Pappel[3](iD),
Aleksander Reitsakas[4], and Dirk Draheim[1](iD)

[1] Tallinn University of Technology, Information Systems Group, Tallinn, Estonia
{rozha.ahmed,dirk.draheim}@taltech.ee
[2] Judicial Council of the Kurdistan Region of Iraq, Sulaymaniyah, Iraq
omer.ahmad@sulicourt.com
[3] Tallinn University of Technology, Next Gen Research Group, Tallinn, Estonia
ingrid.pappel@taltech.ee
[4] Aktors Company, Tallinn, Estonia
{rozha.ahmed,aleksander.reitsakas}@aktors.ee

Abstract. Transparency is a crucial element in the judiciary to promote citizen confidence in courts and ensure fair case administration by court staff. Therefore, digital transformation of courts is becoming a mandatory step to increase transparency by providing a new opportunity for court data to be open, visible, and accessible to the citizen. Digital transformation of courts is initiated through digitizing court processes and implementing e-court systems to enhance transparency, efficiency, and effectiveness of court processes. The objective of this research is to explore the role of e-court systems in fostering transparency in justice administration by delving into the e-court system of the Sulaymaniyah Appellate Court in the Kurdistan Region of Iraq (KRI) as a case study. The analysis was based on the mixed method of both quantitative and qualitative approaches, with a triangulation of multiple data sources including surveys, expert interviews, observations, and document analysis. The results show that implementing an e-court system enhances transparency in the court processes and results in a more efficient and effective court system with improved justice delivery to the public.

Keywords: e-Court · Digital transformation · ICT · Transparency · Kurdistan Region · Iraq

1 Introduction

The concept of transparency is considered one of the key foundations for building citizens' trust in governments [5,9,10,16]. Transparency is referred to as the availability of public data to citizens and engaging them in the decision-making processes to promote democracy and good governance [16]. "Transparency is experienced when citizens' desire for such knowledge is met easily on their terms

S. Papagiannidis et al. (Eds.): I3E 2022, LNCS 13454, pp. 219–230, 2022.
https://doi.org/10.1007/978-3-031-15342-6_17

in respect to format, time, location, and level of aggregation, and at an affordable cost" [16], and this transparency can be achieved through the digital transformation of governments. Globally [9, 10], governments are increasingly integrating information and communication technologies (ICT) into their processes and shifting towards the implementation of e-government [11, 23], aiming to enhance the transparency of government processes. ICT tools tend to positively affect government service delivery processes in terms of increasing transparency in public sector management, and the reduction of the level of corruption [5], as "the digital platform establishes a high benchmark for transparency and accountability" [14]. In the same vein, they increase trust in ICT as a means to solve governmental tasks and trust in the government as a reliable party. As part of the e-government realm, Judiciaries are also engaged in the flow of digital transformation to deliver better justice services to the citizen. Transparency in courts is essential to show the public how court proceedings apply the law and ensure fair justice administration [13, 19].

Relevant literature showed that the justice sector is investing in the implantation of e-court systems to ensure transparency and enhance efficiency and effectiveness of court processes [6, 8, 15, 17–19, 22, 24–26, 28, 29, 32, 37]. However, all the available research showed a marginal study. The concrete focus with a systematic study on the impact of e-court systems on increasing transparency remains a research gap to be filled. Therefore, this research aims to identify the impact of justice digital transformation on fostering transparency through delving into the implementation of the e-court system in the Kurdistan Region of Iraq (KRI) as a case study, as no previous studies have been conducted in this area before.

The analysis is based on a mixed-method of both qualitative and quantitative approaches. Results of this research aims to extend the body of knowledge and literature for judiciaries and practitioners concerning the digital transformation in the justice sector, academic researchers, and serve the decision-makers in the Kurdistan regional government towards expanding the project to all other courts in the KRI.

Section 2 presents literature views on the impact of digital transformation on enhancing transparency. Section 3 provides an overview of the case of the e-court system in the Sulaymaniyah Appellate Court in the KRI. Section 4 includes detailed information on the research design, data collection, and analysis phase. Then, Sect. 5 presents the result of the analysis and discusses them. Finally, Sect. 6 delivers concluding remarks with research limitations and future direction.

2   Relevant Studies

The United Nations survey of 2018 emphasizes the importance of trust between government and citizens that can be achieved through principles of "transparency, inclusion, and collaboration" [9]. Transparency is considered a critical key to gaining citizens' trust in government [16]. Recent studies show that transparency can be achieved in government processes by utilizing technological tools in the government service delivery processes and adopting e-government [9,10,16].

Delivering government services in electronic format offers a new way for citizens to access data and processes easily and transparently. Hence, it positively affects their trust in government and makes "government more trustworthy and making the "right to know" a salient democratic value" [16]. The United Nations survey of 2018 also considered ICT as important tool to enhance transparency by providing a new opportunity for the citizen to access government data and decisions and assess the quality of the processes, which provides an additional resource for the government to engage citizens in policy-making. Moreover, the survey also showed a noticeable shift of governments globally towards Open Government Data (OGD) to increase transparency and referred to as "government information proactively disclosed and made available online for all to access, without restriction" [9]. A further survey of the United Nations of 2020 showed a vital role of ICT during the COVID-19 crisis that allowed keeping societies connected while collecting and sharing health and safety information served governments in making better and faster decisions depending on the analysis of real-time data. Additionally, The survey revised 193 government portals that have used different platforms to share health statuses and reports at a very high level of transparency [10]. Additionally, this latest survey of 2020 outlined the importance of (OGD) and a citizen-oriented approach to ensure greater transparency in the e-government and increases citizen trust by engaging them in the decision-making processes [10]. In broad terms, ICT and technological tools "can be used for the creation of applications and software that increase transparency, reduce corruption, streamline e-procurement, and improve overall governance while minimizing the potential risks" [10].

Hence, within the same flow, judiciaries are integrating ICT tools in court processes through the implementation of e-court systems to increase transparency, ensure better justice delivery and allow the public to access data and contents [19]. Lopucki outlined several benefits of transparency for the justice sector, including "exposing and reducing corruption and impropriety, enhancing legislative control over the courts, apprising the public of the real rules by which they are governed, enabling lawyers and parties to predict the outcomes of their cases, providing a substantial new source of general knowledge, reducing legal malpractice and increasing court-system efficiency" [19]. Furthermore, the Transparency International report explicitly stated that "transparency in the judiciary leads to increased efficiency and effectiveness and promotes confidence in the judicial system and the fair administration of justice" [13]. Also, [28] added that "transparency is assisting individuals in obtaining fair redress in the courts."

Concerning the importance of transparency for judiciaries, relevant studies ensured that digitization of court processes gives possibility to increase transparency and delivers better justice services to the citizen [28,33]. In the study of assessing e-justice smartness and evaluation of public values for the justice domain, Lupo referred to transparency as a "fundamental value of justice" and defined it as the accessibility to information and procedures in the digital justice systems that can be achieved through the implementation of e-court systems [20]. Relevant studies have a common understanding that digital justice transformation leads to increased transparency in processing court cases. [21] introduced an electronic notification system to increase the transparency in the notification process of the court cases. Moreover, [6] explored a technology integration with court systems and implementation of the new visualization tool to enhance the transparency of court docket and processes. [22] considered an ICT integration to courts as an innovation in managing court cases that tends to increase transparency in the whole process. [32] viewed ICT as a significant key to improving transparency and assisting courts in providing better services. [8] also considered ICT adoption as a potential tool towards openness in government data and justice systems and enhancing transparency in the processes. [24] implemented a remote monitoring system for judges to follow cases emphasized the transparency improvement through the system, and they considered that lack of transparency is a key for late case dispensation. [25] noted that technology integration into court processes increases the transparency of court processes which is essential for courts and the public. [15] outlined the transparency enhancement after implementing the electronic filing system. [26] considered that transparent justice is a key to democracy, as transparent court information systems allow accessibility of citizens to their data. In turn, this transparency in data and processes increases their trust in government and justice systems. [18] added that ICT has a critical role in improving transparency in the judicial institutions to provide an opportunity for data accessibility of legal information. [17], stated that through online court systems, data would be available to litigants, which can increase transparency. [29] also appointed that the implementation of electronic court systems improves the transparency of court processes. [37] considered that transparency is one of the notable benefits of the implementation of decision support systems in the court systems, in addition to providing transparent algorithms in the decision-making processes. And finally, [28] noted that implementation of e-court systems increases transparency and fairness in resolving public disputes.

Relevant studies presented marginal studies on the ICT integration with court processes and transparency enhancement, while the current study presents the role of the e-court system in increasing transparency of the court's daily processes with a systematic and in-depth study through the case of the e-court system in the Sulaymaniyah Appellate Court in the KRI. There is no previous studies have been conducted in this area before.

3   The Case of e-Court System in the KRI

Studies appointed that the initiatives of digital transformation in the KRI started in 2014 with the implementation of the e-court system as a pilot project for the Sulaymaniyah Appellate Court in the Sulaymaniyah city [1–4]. This project was implemented in 2014 in six stages (planning, system analysis/master plan, prototyping, building infrastructure, piloting, and implementation) and launched in 2016.

The system comprises integrated subsystems to provide smooth and efficient communication and secure data exchange between different parties. The system manages both civil and criminal cases. All the case management processes are digitized through a central database with various functionalities to assist users in performing all daily tasks. In addition to the courthouse users, the prosecution office and police stations use the system for collaborative activities. At the same time, citizens, lawyers, and outside agencies can also access it through a public portal. Figure 1 shows the e-court system of the Sulaymaniyah Appellate Court.

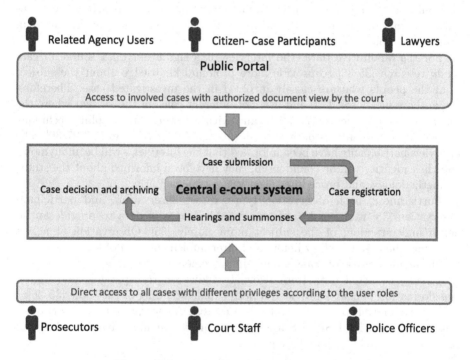

Fig. 1. Sulaymaniyah appellate court system

4   Research Methodology

This study aims to investigate the role of implementing an e-court system in fostering transparency in the court's daily operations. This is through answering the following research question:

Does the implementation of the e-court system foster transparency in court processes?

To answer the research question authors employed an exploratory case study strategy with a mixed method of both qualitative and quantitative approaches [35]. Combinations of qualitative and quantitative methods provide a "richer and stronger array of evidence" [36].

The authors used a triangulation of multiple data sources such as surveys, expert interviews, personal observations, and document analysis to strengthen the result and get a more comprehensive picture of the context by providing various perspectives on the subject.

For the quantitative survey, a questionnaire was designed for the system users, and 66 responses were collected from different roles such as judge, clerk, lawyer, prosecutor, judicial investigator, police officer, and typist who are actively using the system daily. The authors considered this sample valid and generalizable as the total population number of active users is 875; while calculating the margin of error % 12 and the confidence level of % 95 valid minimum sample size would be N = 63.

For the qualitative data, the interview is a significant data source in case study research [35,36] to provide more profound knowledge about the subject from the people who are closely involved in the investigated case. Therefore, the authors interviewed 30 end-users of different roles in the system where the saturation is approached [7,27,31], and with a purposeful sampling technique to focus on the quality of data and information-rich participants [7,27,30]. The interview participants have been informed that the interviews will be anonymous, and their identity will be confidential, they have been informed about the study, its methodology, and procedures clearly and transparently.

Furthermore, both observation types, direct observation, and participant observation [35] were conducted as a reliable source of data to provide an in-depth understanding of the subject more closely [35]. Observation aimed at observing the case workflow before and after implementation of the e-court system to monitor areas of transparency improvements.

Finally, collected data from relevant studies on transparency and digital transformation of courts provided a better understanding of the topic [35,36].

For the analysis phase, the authors used RQDA software for analyzing qualitative data and IBM SPSS Statistics software for quantitative data. Figure 2 shows the research methodology process.

5   Results and Discussion

Transparency is considered a core aspect of justice to ensure gaining citizen trust in court processes and decisions [20,26]. In this regard, respondents assured the importance of transparency for courts through various statements from Judges in different courts, saying: *"Transparency will prevent corruption in judiciaries"*. and *"Transparency in courts and judicial systems is not only important, but it is also obliged by the law"*. Furthermore added by judges from civil courts with stating:

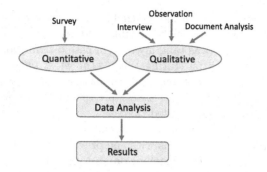

Fig. 2. Research methodology

"*Transparency is very important in courts, specifically in civil courts hearings are obliged to be held publicly and transparently, while for the criminal court there are some situations which investigation process should be kept secret*". and "*Transparency is one of the key points in justice systems.*" Several respondents confirm the same point of view from criminal courts by saying: "*Transparency is important in every field, yet, is more important in courts.*" and "*Speaking broadly, as transparency is increased, in turn, citizen trust is increased, and suspicions are decreased side by side.*"

As a consequence, judiciaries are approaching new technologies to achieve transparency in courts through integrating different technological tools into court processes and implementing e-court systems to ensure delivering better justice services to the citizens [6, 8, 22, 28, 28, 29, 32, 33]. The role of implementing e-court systems in fostering transparency also confirmed by interviewees with number of statements such as: "*With the e-court system, we eliminate corruption and foster transparency.*" and "*Transparency which is achieved through digitizing court processes is very important*". Next response added: "*Transparency can be clearly seen in the e-court system. I can say that all system users can notice this improvement in compression to the old conventional system.*" And further confirmation with another statement saying: "*e-Court is more transparent and fair, it provides better services to the public and finally, presents a justice without corruption*".

Transparency is seen by many studies as openness of court data and providing a new opportunity for case data, documents, and legal information to be visible and accessible by participants [17, 18, 20, 34]. The current e-court system allows case details and documents to be visible by authorized related users who are case participants to track the case statuses.

Interviewees outlined that the accessibility of case data in the current e-court system has enhanced the court processes' transparency by stating: "*In our system, all necessary data will be visible to participants according to their role equally.*" A further respondent said: "*e-Court has improved transparency in a way that case participants are allowed to access their cases from the public portal and track the progress of their cases.*"

Furthermore, analysis of data showed that transparency in the current e-court system is not only achieved through visibility and accessibility of data but also transparency enhancement was tangibly seen in case distribution processes that interviewees clearly outline by stating that: *"The most important property in the e-court system is systematic and transparent case distribution."* and *"In the system, transparency is implemented well, more specifically in case distribution"*. And the court president finally added that:

"The case distribution in all courts is now more transparent, systematic and fair." While there were many claims with the previous paper-based system case allocation process due to unfair distribution and manual distribution processes could leave room for lawyers to select the desired judge. The importance of transparency in case distribution over judges is highlighted by [12]. This study also confirms the significance of a transparent case allocation system in the e-court system, which is already achieved in the implemented system. Now judge selection is made automatically, systematically, and visible by lawyers and case participants during the case registration process.

In general, increasing transparency by the current system is visible to all court users, which is also confirmed by a statement from an interviewee by saying: *"Now, transparency is implemented by 95%"*

Moreover, the results of quantitative data analysis of 66 responses of court users showed that the system is now more transparent than a paper-based system. One of the survey questions sought to know the participant's opinions to what extent they agree with the transparency enhancement with the current e-court system. As shown in Fig. 3, the majority of the responses agreed that transparency of court processes is now increased with the current e-court system. In contrast, 21 responses strongly agreed that transparency is now clearly noticeable in the system. Further, 11 participants from 66 stayed neutral and preferred not to show their views on this aspect. However, only three disagreed, and six strongly disagreed with the system's transparency enhancement.

Another question in the survey was about rating the transparency in the current e-court system by the participants. As can be seen from Fig. 4, major responses of 22 participants rated the transparency of the processes in the system as good, while further 19 considered it as very good. Another 17 participants thought that the system's transparency was acceptable, and only 4 participants from 66 responses considered it a poor level, and the last 4 rated it as very poor.

Analysis of quantitative data supported the results from the qualitative data and confirmed that the current e-court system had increased the transparency of court processes. Notably, open question answers showed that almost all participants agreed on the visible transparency enhancement in the case distribution and case data visibility. At the same time, some other responses also added that case statics is now more transparent and robust.

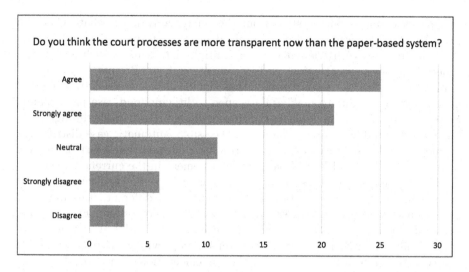

Fig. 3. Participants view on transparency enhancement through the e-court system

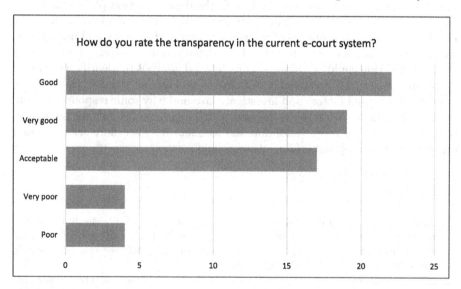

Fig. 4. Participants rate on transparency enhancement through the e-court system

6   Conclusion

Transparency is considered one of the valuable aspects of the justice domain; therefore, judiciaries are using technological tools to deliver more transparent services to the citizen through the digitization of court processes and implementation of the e-court system. This study explored the role of the e-court system in fostering transparency in the court case management processes through the case study of an e-court system from the Sulaymaniyah Appellate Court in the KRI. Analysis was based on the mixed method of qualitative and quantitative approaches with triangulation of multiple data sources such as surveys, expert interviews, observation, and document analysis. Results revealed that implementation of the e-court system has significantly increased transparency in court processes due to making data open to litigants and case participants. More particularly, transparency in the current system is noticeable through making case data and documents visible and accessible, automatic case distribution on judges, and case statistics. Further results confirmed that court users were satisfied with the notable transparency enhancement in the current system.

The findings of if this research aims to practically serve the decision-makers in the KRI to expand the solution in other courts from different cities and other practitioners who are on the way to implement e-court system. Furthermore, the study aims to theoretically expand the body of knowledge and literature for academic researchers in the justice domain to provide a better overview of justice digital transformation and how the implementation of the e-court systems fosters transparency in courts.

This study's limitations were mainly in the data collection phase due to the lack of available literature on transparency for the justice domain in the KRI. Furthermore, the late response of the participants to the survey and unavailability of interviewees for the interviews have delayed data analysis phase. Future research direction could be towards more detailed analysis to identify more areas of the processes that transparency is increased and further study of the negative views to understand factors and investigate how and why some respondents were not mainly satisfied with the transparency in the system. A further interest of the authors includes more validation and assessments with more scenarios and targeting a wider population for interview and survey.

References

1. Ahmed, R.K., Muhammed, K.H., Pappel, I., Draheim, D.: Challenges in the digital transformation of courts: a case study from the Kurdistan Region of Iraq. In: Proceedings of ICEDEG 2020 - the 7th International Conference on eDemocracy and eGovernment, pp. 74–79. IEEE (2020)
2. Ahmed, R.K., et al.: A legal framework for digital transformation: a proposal based on a comparative case study. In: Kö, A., Francesconi, E., Kotsis, G., Tjoa, A.M., Khalil, I. (eds.) EGOVIS 2021. LNCS, vol. 12926, pp. 115–128. Springer, Cham (2021). https://doi.org/10.1007/978-3-030-86611-2_9
3. Ahmed, R.K., Muhammed, K.H., Reitsakas, A., Pappel, I., Draheim, D.: Improving court efficiency through ICT integration: identifying essential areas of improvement. In: Fong, S., Dey, N., Joshi, A. (eds.) ICT Analysis and Applications. LNNS, vol. 93, pp. 449–461. Springer, Singapore (2020). https://doi.org/10.1007/978-981-15-0630-7_44
4. Ahmed, R.K., Muhammed, K.H., Pappel, I., Draheim, D.: Impact of e-court systems implementation: a case study. Transforming Gov. People Process Policy 15(1) (2021)

5. Bhattacherjee, A., Shrivastava, U.: The effects of ICT use and ICT laws on corruption: A general deterrence theory perspective. Gov. Inf. Q. **35**(4), 703–712 (2018)
6. Chada, D.M., Silva, F.A.: Visualizing Brazilian justice: the supreme court 2.0 project. In: Proceedings of ICAIL 2015 - the 15th International Conference on Artificial Intelligence and Law, pp. 176–180. ACM (2015)
7. Coyne, I.T.: Sampling in qualitative research. Purposeful and theoretical sampling; merging or clear boundaries? J. Adv. Nurs. **26**(3), 623–630 (1997)
8. Deligiannis, A.P., Anagnostopoulos, D.: Towards open justice: ICT acceptance in the Greek justice system: the case of the integrated court management system for penal and civil procedures (OSDDY/PP). In: Proceedings of CeDEM 2017 - the 2nd Conference for E-Democracy and Open Government, pp. 82–91. IEEE (2017)
9. Department of economic and social affairs: E-Government survey 2018 - Gearing E-Government to support transformation towards sustainable and resilient societies. United Nations (2018)
10. Department of economic and social affairs: E-Government survey 2020 - digital government in the decade of action for sustainable development. United Nations (2020)
11. Draheim, D., Krimmer, R., Tammet, T.: On state-level architecture of digital government ecosystems: from ICT-driven to data-centric. Trans. Large-Scale Data-Know.-Centered Syst. **48**, 165–195 (2021)
12. European commission for the efficiency of justice: European judicial systems - efficiency and quality of justice, CEPEJ STUDIES No. 24. Council of Europe (2016)
13. France, G., Costantino, F.: Transparency of court proceedings. Transparency Int. (2019). https://www.jstor.org/stable/resrep20468
14. Goede, M.: E-Estonia: The e-government cases of Estonia, Singapore, and Curaçao. Arch. Bus. Res. (2), 216–227 (2019)
15. Gorham, U.: State courts, e-filing, and diffusion of innovation: a proposed framework of analysis. In: Proceedings of dg.o 2012 - the 13th Annual International Conference on Digital Government Research, pp. 232–239. ACM (2012)
16. Halachmi, A., Greiling, D.: Transparency, e-government, and accountability. Public Perform. Manag. Rev. **36**(4), 572–584 (2013)
17. Hou, Y., Lampe, C., Bulinski, M., Prescott, J.J.: Factors in fairness and emotion in online case resolution systems. In: Proceedings of the 2017 CHI Conference on Human Factors in Computing Systems, pp. 2511–2522. ACM (2017)
18. Kurtz, L.P., Santos, P.M., Rover, A.J.: Access to information on websites of Brazilian superior courts of justice. In: Proceedings of dgo 2018 - the 19th Annual International Conference on Digital Government Research Governance in the Data Age, pp. 1–5. ACM (2018)
19. Lopucki, L.M.: Court-system transparency. Iowa Law Rev. **94**(2), 481–538 (2009)
20. Lupo, G.: Assessing e-justice smartness: a new framework for e-Justice evaluation through public values. In: Rodriguez Bolivar, M.P. (ed.) Setting Foundations for the Creation of Public Value in Smart Cities. PAIT, vol. 35, pp. 77–113. Springer, Cham (2019). https://doi.org/10.1007/978-3-319-98953-2_4
21. Luzuriaga, J.M., Cechich, A.: Electronic notification of court documents: a case study. In: Proceedings ICEGOV 2011 - the 5th International Conference on Theory and Practice of Electronic Governance, pp. 45–50. ACM (2011)
22. Machado, M., Sousa, M., Rocha, V., Isidro, A.: Innovation in judicial services: a study of innovation models in labor courts. Innovation Manag. Rev. **15**(2), 155–173 (2018)

23. Pappel, I., Tsap, V., Draheim, D.: The e-LocGov model for introducing e-governance into local governments - an Estonian case study. IEEE Trans. Emerg. Top. Comput. **9**(2), 597–611 (2013)

24. Rahman, A., Nawaz, H., Naeem, O., Zaffar, F., Naseer, F., Zaffar, A.: Finding needle in the case-stack: effective remote monitoring of courts. In: Proceedings of HICCS 2014 - the 47th Hawaii International Conference on System Sciences, pp. 1906–1915 (2014)

25. Reiling, D.: Technology in courts in Europe: opinions, practices and innovations. Int. J. Court Adm. **4**, 11–20 (2012)

26. Rosa, J., Teixeira, C., Sousa Pinto, J.: Risk factors in e-justice information systems. Gov. Inf. Q. **30**(3), 241–256 (2013)

27. Sandelowski, M.: Sample size in qualitative research. Res. Nurs. Health **18**(2), 179–183 (1995)

28. Schmitz, A.J.: Expanding access to remedies through e-court initiatives. Buff. L. Rev. **67**(1), 89 (2019)

29. Singh, M., Sahu, G.P., Dwivedi, Y.K., Rana, N.P.: Success factors for e-Court implementation at Allahabad High-Court. In: Proceedings of PACIS 2018 - the 22th Pacific Asia Conference on Information Systems. AIS (2018)

30. Taherdoost, H.: Sampling methods in research methodology; how to choose a sampling technique for research. Int. J. Acad. Res. Manag. **2**, 18–27 (2018)

31. Vasileiou, K., Barnett, J., Thorpe, S., Young, T.: Characterising and justifying sample size sufficiency in interview-based studies: systematic analysis of qualitative health research over a 15-year period. BMC Med. Res. Methodol. **18**(1), 1–18 (2018)

32. Velicogna, M.: Justice systems and ICT: what can be learned from Europe? Utrecht Law Rev. **3**(1), 129–147 (2007)

33. Watson, A.C., Rukundakuvaga, R., Matevosyan, K.: Integrated justice: an information systems approach to justice sector case management and information sharing. Int. J. Court Adm. **8**(3), 1–9 (2017)

34. Xu, A.L.: Chinese judicial justice on the cloud: a future call or a Pandora's box? an analysis of the 'intelligent court system' of China. Inf. Commun. Technol. Law **26**(1), 59–71 (2017)

35. Yin, R.K.: Case Study Research: Design and Methods. SAGE (2014)

36. Yin, R.K.: Case Study Research and Applications: Design and Methods. SAGE (2018)

37. Zolbanin, H.M., Delen, D., Crosby, D., Wright, D.: A predictive analytics-based decision support system for drug courts. Inf. Syst. Front. **22**, 1–20 (2019). https://doi.org/10.1007/s10796-019-09934-w

How Can Hackathons Facilitate Employee-Driven Digital Innovation in Public Organizations?

Leif Erik Opland[1([⊠])] and Ilias O. Pappas[1,2]

[1] Norwegian University of Science and Technology (NTNU), Trondheim, Norway
leif.e.opland@ntnu.no
[2] University of Agder, Kristiansand, Norway

Abstract. New approaches to innovation have emerged creating needs for new explanatory models for discussing, understanding and implementing innovation, among these employee-driven innovation. Employee-driven innovation appears as a direction within innovation where the focus is on ordinary employees and how these can contribute to innovation within already existing private and public organizations. This form of innovation has especially been seen as appropriate in relation to companies engaged in digital innovation, also formulated as employee-driven digital innovation. Innovation in public organizations has recently received more attention, but still appears to be under-researched in many contexts compared to private organizations. Not only have we received new approaches to innovation, but we have also seen the emergence of new ways of organizing and managing innovation. Hackathons have over time emerged and gained a role as a way to facilitate innovation in many organizations, especially organizations related to IT. Hackathons can therefore be perceived to have contributed to a movement towards more open innovation processes, both internally, but also in relation to the organizations' stakeholders externally. In this conceptual paper we will present and discuss how hackathons can act as a facilitator to spur employee-driven digital innovation in public organizations, and how we want to use hackathons as an artifact in a design science research approach to study employee-driven digital innovation in a public organization.

Keywords: Employee-driven innovation · Digital innovation · Hackathon · Public sector

1 Introduction

In a global society facing extensive and radical changes as a result of, among other things, technological development and increased focus on sustainability, innovation is increasingly being highlighted as the answer to the questions. Innovation is emphasized by many, and in particular digital innovation, as a necessity in the pursuit of digital transformation [1]. This increasing focus on innovation itself has not only influenced the

© IFIP International Federation for Information Processing 2022
Published by Springer Nature Switzerland AG 2022
S. Papagiannidis et al. (Eds.): I3E 2022, LNCS 13454, pp. 231–237, 2022.
https://doi.org/10.1007/978-3-031-15342-6_18

organizations' focus and priorities, but also paved the way for discussions related to how to organize, facilitate, and manage innovation processes. For decades organizations have relied heavily on closed approaches to innovation such as senior experts and research and development units. The introduction of more open approaches to innovation in recent times has led academics and practitioners to re-think how innovation is best organized and facilitated [2]. The way that organizations choose to organize for innovation might affect the outcomes achieved. There has been a movement towards more open approaches like open innovation [3], user-driven innovation [4] and employee-driven innovation [5]. These new approaches have been mainly studied and applied in private organizations, raising the question if they can be applied in public organizations. While innovation is gaining increased focus in public organizations [6] the challenge remains on how to support practitioners and managers to organize and facilitate innovation in the public sector.

Hackathons, since their introduction in the early 1990s, have been seen as a design process for working with idea development and innovation especially in software development companies [7]. Through a strong focus on problem solving and prototyping [7], hackathons have emerged as a solution that can bring out creativity and idea creation through collaboration within and across organizations. In this way, hackathons have also contributed to the movement towards more open innovation [8]. While the main focus has been on running hackathons in private organizations, recently, hackathons in the public sector have also received increased focus through the emergence of open innovation approaches [9].

Based on this premise, we seek to examine how the process perspective, and the structured approach to innovation that hackathons can bring to organizations, can be compatible with the autonomous and non-structured approach that employee-driven digital innovation is resting on. Our goal in this short paper is to discuss how hackathons can act as a facilitator of employee-driven digital innovation, and what considerations must be done before conducting it. If hackathons can be used to facilitate employee-driven digital innovation, practitioners will have a completely new tool in their toolbox when trying to facilitate and manage employee-driven digital innovation in public, and private, organizations. Therefore, we propose the following research questions (RQ's).

RQ1: How hackathons act as a facilitator of employee-driven digital innovation in public organizations and which benefits we gain from it?
RQ2: Which preconditions must be taken for hackathons to be a facilitator for employee-driven digital innovation in public organizations?

This paper is structured in the following way, Sect. 2 presents related work to the research field, Sect. 3 describes the proposed research method for the study and Sect. 4 briefly discusses expected results from the study.

2 Background

Employee-driven innovation emerged as a research stream in the 2000's and put emphasis on how organizations can utilize the creative practices in and around ordinary employees

[5]. In this approach, there is a recognition that innovation can arise at the intersection where knowledge of the organization's products, services, processes and business models and customers' needs meet. It is also a recognition that precisely this knowledge in many contexts is possessed by ordinary employees. Employee-driven innovation as an approach to innovation is a reaction to previous strong belief on top-down approaches to innovation and the one-sided focus on organizing innovation through R&D's [10]. Instead, employee-driven innovation has brought with it a bottom-up approach [5], where the creativity and initiative of ordinary employees are main elements, and where deep insight into customers' needs has been central in the creation of innovation.

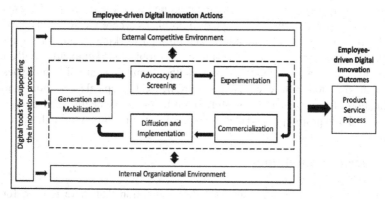

Fig. 1. Employee-driven digital innovation [13].

We draw on a recent systematic literature review [13] that developed a conceptual model for structuring employee-driven digital innovation (Fig. 1). Employee-driven digital innovation describes a merge of innovation perspectives and characteristics stemming from employee-driven innovation [5] and digital innovation [14]. Much of the research in employee-driven digital innovation stems from information systems field and has focused on how digital tools can be used to support and facilitate different parts of the innovation processes, such as [11]. This has led to an excessive focus on solutions for the fuzzy front end of the innovation process, and tools for ideation, such as [12]. To a lesser extent, research has focused on how the context in which employee-driven digital innovation takes place affects the outcomes of the innovation processes.

The concept of employee-driven digital innovation (Fig. 1) is defined as the process of idea creation and realization related to digital products, services, processes or business models by ordinary employees. The specific characteristics of digital information create these opportunities, through that information easily can be stored, changed, transmitted and tracked [14]. The conceptual model from [13] describes five activities that form the core of employee-driven digital innovation. Generation and mobilization, where motivation to create solutions and idea generation takes place; Advocacy and Screening, where the ideas are evaluated and selected based on the organization's context; Experimentation, where experiment with possible digital solutions and technologies to enable solutions take place; Commercialization, where the digital solutions are tried out on actual customers or users and finally; Diffusion and Implementation, where finished digital products, services or processes are implemented or made available in the organization. This process is influenced and made possible by both internal factors in the organization and external factors around the organization [13].

Hackathons has received a lot of attention as an accelerated design process used to promote innovative thinking within a limited period of time [7]. From being a format that has traditionally only been focused on software development, it has now moved towards being a format that is also used by government institutions, non-profit organizations and education [7]. The scope of hackathons has undoubtedly also extended to non-digital arenas, as a technique or way of working related to problem solving. In its implementation, it has also adopted an approach from agile development where it is used hypothetically driven with development around issues iteratively [15]. This is an approach that is particularly well adapted to problems where the solutions may lie in the application of the digital. The aim is that through working in smaller groups with ideating, developing, and presenting a solution to a problem [15] innovation will emerge. However, there is no agreed definition of hackathons, and there are different types, e.g., related to the duration of the event [15]. According to [15] typical hackathons start with a presentation of the goals and team formation before work begins. During the event teams ideate, build prototypes and at the end presents their solution through a pitch [15].

3   Research Methodology

Information Systems research rests upon the assumption that there is need for both theoretical contributions and solving the current and anticipated problems addressed by practitioners [16, 17]. In [18] the use of action design research (ADR) methodology is described to study employee-driven digital innovation in public organizations. Among other studies this has led to studies identifying innovation drivers and barriers related to employee-driven digital innovation in public organizations [19]. The study of drivers and barriers [19] showed that in a public organization one of the most important drivers for employee-driven digital innovation are innovation champions. In other words, employees with a particularly strong engagement towards innovation. On the other side this study also identified lack of innovation culture as one of the most important barriers [19]. It is therefore obvious to ask how public organizations can facilitate activities so that more of the innovation potential can be utilized, cf. RQ1 and RQ2.

Our aim with the study described in this paper is to propose hackathons as an artifact in an ADR project that will be designed and evaluated through interventions within a public organization. We seek to examine if this design process can better facilitate employee-driven digital innovation in public organizations to increase the interest and engagement associated with innovation. We claim that the use of hackathons as a design structuring process can increase creativity and focus on innovation in public organizations. We see from studies, though focusing on hacking from virtually, that hackathons both provide individual and organizational benefits, as well as participants acquiring new skills and competences [20]. The ADR research method can be broken down into four different stages [21], (1) problem formulation, (2) building, intervention, and evaluation, (3) reflection and learning and (4) formalization of learning which are described in the following sections.

3.1 Problem Formulation

ADR emphasizes the problem formulation as the starting point [21] and we claim that the identification of drivers and barriers in [19] underlines the challenges faced by public organizations when trying to utilize the innovating potential possessed by ordinary employees. These identified challenges show that there is a need to think differently when it comes to finding ways to implement and manage employee-driven digital innovation. This relates to how to approach the processes [13] described in Fig. 1. The problem formulation as such is therefore rooted in [13, 19].

3.2 Building, Intervention, and Evaluation

Originating from the problem formulation in 3.1, we will use hackathon as an artifact to intervene in the process of and to facilitate employee-driven digital innovation. According to [21] the phase of building, intervening, and evaluating is dependent on the framing and theoretical perspectives from the problem formulation.

As described by [15] hackathons can be designed and implemented in a myriad of different ways. This originates from that hackathon has been used in various domains as well as for a variety of goals [22]. In planning a hackathon, 12 key decisions can be used to customize the organization of the event [22]. We will use these 12 key decisions when establishing the artifact to be used in the intervention. The 12 key decisions [22] are goal, themes, competition/cooperation, stakeholder involvement, participant recruitment, specialized preparation, duration/breaks, ideation, team formation, agenda, mentoring and continuity planning. The goal refers to the intended outcome of the event, while the theme refers to the topic selected as a focus point. The competition/cooperation refers to whether the event will be run as a competition or not, while stakeholder involvement refers to how involved stakeholders will be in the event. Participation recruitment is one of the most crucial elements in the design of a hackathon [22] and refers to who will participate in the event, while specialized preparation refers to if there is a need for preparation like training before the event. Duration/breaks refers to when the event starts and ends, while ideation refers to how idea generation is planned in the event. Team formation refers to how the teams in the event will be put together, while agenda refers to which activities will be arranged during the event. Mentoring refers to if teams during the event will get feedback on the progress, while continuity planning refers to how to follow up on the outcomes from the hackathon. These 12 key decisions are in line with and relate to the employee-driven digital innovation process, as presented in Fig. 1.

Based on the 12 key decisions, choices must be made towards the specific organization when designing a hackathon. There are also opportunities at this stage to try hackathons in several iterations to optimize the method and its use, cf. [18].

3.3 Reflection and Learning

We believe that by conducting hackathon as a facilitator of employee-driven digital innovation in public organizations, we will be able to gain insight into the extent to which this method can actually be suitable. This must be done through studying the design process as a whole, the outcomes of the experiments, as well as interviews with participants to uncover how they experienced the process and participation in the event.

3.4 Formalization of Learning

Our ambition with this study is to gain knowledge and practical experience in phase 3.3 with how to facilitate employee-driven digital innovation in public organizations. We aim to use this knowledge and experiences to create and provide some general solution concepts for how to use hackathons as a method to increase the use of employee-driven digital innovation in public organizations as part of the formalized learning by using ADR method [21].

4   Expected Results

In this research-in-progress paper propose how the 12 key decisions [22] can be used to customize hackathons when designing and conducting hackathons in a public organization with the ambition to use hackathons to facilitate employee-driven digital innovation. This is also in accordance with [18] that describes how creating an artifact can increase the adoption of employee-driven digital innovation in public organizations in accordance with the ADR method.

If the experiences with the use of hackathon as a facilitator for employee-driven digital innovation are positive in public organizations, this can help to give managers and practitioners a methodology for approaching this form of innovation in their own organization or unit. Through the 12 key decisions [22], there is flexibility for organizations to make active choices in the design process of the hackathon to adjust the artifact to the context of the individual organization and unit. We see this as a crucial factor for the success of the use of hackathon in public organizations, as many of their characteristics (e.g. goals, size and composition) varies.

References

1. Vial, G.: Understanding digital transformation: a review and a research agenda. J. Strat. Inf. Syst. **28**(2), 118–144 (2019)
2. Flores, M., et al.: How can hackathons accelerate corporate innovation? In: Moon, I., Lee, G.M., Park, J., Kiritsis, D., von Cieminski, G. (eds.) APMS 2018. IAICT, vol. 535, pp. 167–175. Springer, Cham (2018). https://doi.org/10.1007/978-3-319-99704-9_21
3. Bogers, M., et al.: The open innovation research landscape: established perspectives and emerging themes across different levels of analysis. J. Ind. Innov. **24**(1), 8–40 (2017)
4. von Hippel, E.: The Sources of Innovation. The MIT Press, Cambridge (1988)
5. Høyrup, S.: Employee-driven innovation and workplace learning: basic concepts, approaches and themes. Transfer **16**(2), 143–154 (2010)
6. Demircioglu, M.A., Audretch, D.: Conditions for innovation in public sector organizations. Res. Policy **46**, 1681–1691 (2017)
7. Olesen, J.F., Halskov, K.: 10 years of research with and on hackathons. In: Proceedings from DIS 2020 (2020)

8. Choi, M.: Organizing open digital innovation: evidence from hackathons. In: Proceedings from ICIS 2016 (2016)
9. Yuan, Q., Gasco-Hernandez, M.: Open innovation in the public sector: creating public value through civic hackathons. Public Manag. Rev. **23**(4), 523–544 (2019)
10. Haapasaari, A., Engeström, Y., Kerosuo, H.: From initiatives to employee-driven innovations. Eur. J. Innov. Manag. **21**(2), 206–226 (2018)
11. Ciriello, R.F., Richter, A., Schwabe, G.: Designing an idea screening framework for employee-driven innovation. In: Proceedings of the 49th Hawaii International Conference on System Sciences (2016)
12. Zimmerling, E., Höflinger, P.J., Sandner, P., Welpe, I.M.: Increasing the creative output at the fuzzy front end of innovation – a concept for a gamified internal entreprise ideation platform. In: Proceedings of the 49th Hawaii International Conference on System Sciences (2016)
13. Opland, L.E., Pappas, I.O., Engesmo, J., Jaccheri, L.: Employee-driven digital innovation: A systematic review and a research agenda. J. Bus. Res. **143**, 255–271 (2022)
14. Ciriello, R.F., Richter, A., Schwabe, G.: Digital innovation. J. Bus. Inf. Syst. Eng. **60**(6), 563–569 (2018)
15. Flus, M., Hurst, A.: Design at hackathons: new opportunities for design research. Des. Sci. **7**(4), 1–24 (2020)
16. Rosemann, M., Vessey, I.: Toward improving the relevance of information systems research to practice: the role of applicability checks. MIS Q. **32**(1), 1–22 (2008)
17. Cole. R., Purao, S., Rossi, M. Sein, M.: Being proactive: where action research meets design research. In: Proceedings International Conference on Information Systems (ICIS) (2005)
18. Opland, L.E., Jaccheri, L., Engesmo, J., Pappas, I.O.: Toward employee-driven digital innovation in public organizations through the use of action design research. In: Hattingh, M., Matthee, M., Smuts, H., Pappas, I., Dwivedi, Y.K., Mäntymäki, M. (eds.) I3E 2020. LNCS, vol. 12067, pp. 39–45. Springer, Cham (2020). https://doi.org/10.1007/978-3-030-45002-1_4
19. Opland, L.E., Pappas, I.O., Engesmo, J., Jaccheri, L.: Employee-driven digital innovation in public organizations – a case study. In: Proceedings of the 25th Pacific Asia Conference on Information Systems (PACIS, 2021) (2021)
20. Ulfsnes, R., Stray, V., Moe, N.B., Šmite, D.: Innovation in large-scale agile - benefits and challenges of hackathons when hacking from home. In: Gregory, P., Kruchten, P. (eds.) XP 2021. LNBIP, vol. 426, pp. 23–32. Springer, Cham (2021). https://doi.org/10.1007/978-3-030-88583-0_3
21. Sein, M.K., Henfridsson, O., Purao, S., Rossi, M., Lindgren, R.: Action design research. MIS Q. **35**(1), 37–56 (2011)
22. Nolte, A., et al.: How to organize a hackathon – a planning kit. (2020). https://hackathon-planning-kit.org

Agility as a Driver of Digital Transformation - a Literature Review

Inga F. Schlömer[(✉)] [iD]

IU International University of Applied Sciences, Juri-Gagarin-Ring 152, 99084 Erfurt, Germany
inga.schloemer@iu.org

Abstract. Agility has become increasingly relevant in research and practice in recent years. Originating from software development, it is now progressively applied beyond this field. This agile scaling enables companies to harness the benefits of a flexible and rapid response to change. Widespread digitalisation, increasing complexity and dynamic competitive conditions require companies to demonstrate flexibility and speed of response to drive a digital transformation (DT) towards a digital business. In the wake of the COVID-19 pandemic, many companies have been confronted with DT. Against this background, this paper aims to derive from previous research how companies can benefit from agile project management and agile scaling in DT. For this purpose, a structured literature review was conducted on four scholarly databases, 225 articles were found and reduced to 28 relevant articles through a methodical approach. The review revealed that agility is defined as a driver of DT. Starting from agile digitalisation projects, agility can be carried into the organization and thus support DT. Nevertheless, while the connections between pandemic and DT and between agility and DT are already the subject of research, the two fields have not been linked in the analysed articles. The findings synthesize the current state of knowledge and suggest first agile approaches to framing DT in the context of the pandemic. Future research efforts are needed to provide companies with measures for dealing with the "new normal".

Keywords: Digital transformation · Agility · Scaling agile · COVID-19

1 Introduction

Digitalisation is no longer a new phenomenon. Both research and practice have been dealing with digitalisation for decades. The result of increasing digitalisation can be seen in all areas of life – the resulting changes are defined as DT [1, 2]. For companies, DT leads to structural changes, new forms of customer interaction, value creation and proposition, and thus decisively changes a company's business model [3, 4].

In the course of the global COVID-19 pandemic, digitalisation is accelerated in many organisations. Digital solutions can help companies respond to the identified threats and opportunities that surfaced as a result of the COVID-19 pandemic. Central digitalisation

S. Papagiannidis et al. (Eds.): I3E 2022, LNCS 13454, pp. 238–253, 2022.
https://doi.org/10.1007/978-3-031-15342-6_19

effects of the pandemic are a shift to remote working, which drives the use of digital platforms for collaboration and video conferencing [5]. But it is also accelerating the development towards paperless work. In addition, business trips are being greatly reduced, lowering the company's environmental footprint. As a consequence of social contact restrictions, digital channels are becoming relevant, especially for traditional sales. Thus, the pandemic is forcing companies, even those without digital experience, to make quick digitalisation decisions. The COVID-19 pandemic has accelerated the DT of companies and entire industries [6]. Business leaders need to define and implement strategies that address the impact of DT and improve the business performance – even more urgently in the "new normal". DT is often also organized in the form of projects [7] or is driven by individual digitalisation projects [8, 9]. Thus, project management continues to gain central importance in DT. Since the often disruptive nature of transformation is associated with uncertainty and difficulty for many decision-makers [10], agile project management and agile scaling approaches are becoming prevalent. Agility addresses the challenges of an unpredictable environment and emphasises the value that skilled people and their relationships contribute to digitalisation [11].

The origins of agility lie in the management of small IT development projects. Due to the high number of IT projects, agile project management has already become established in this area. Accordingly, there are highly educated and qualified employees in the field of agile IT project management [9]. Through a diverse team structure and self-organisation, these agile teams develop user-centric products based on an iterative and incremental approach. The main aspects of agility are the (1) "autonomy" of the team, which can work and make decisions in a self-organised way; the (2) "equality", so that all team members work together as equals; and the (3) "iterative" process, along which the project goal and the realisation of it evolve based on customer feedback [12]. These benefits of agile project management are progressively being explored beyond the field of IT. This agile scaling can take different forms depending on the context: the application of agile approaches in a large organisation, in a large development effort in a large organisation, and finally the use of agility throughout the company so that the entire organisation is agile [13]. This introduction of agile practices throughout the organization, i.e. beyond the team level and IT, is defined as 'agile transformation' [14]. In this way, agile approaches are being used as a valid means of dealing with the all-embracing digitalisation. Agility is therefore often regarded as the driver of an organisation's DT [15–17]. Still, introducing agile methods in new areas, beyond IT, poses challenges [18]. Also, responses to the COVID-19 pandemic show that companies tend to innovate more incrementally and develop new capabilities and routines that are close to existing knowledge [5]. Due to the pandemic, agile project management skills have already become more established to be more flexible and quick to respond [19]. However, agility is often limited to the management of individual projects. For example, in the pandemic, individual teams were able to organise themselves to work remotely in an agile way, but the companies' infrastructures could not support this because agile working was not yet anticipated here [20]. However, companies can respond better to highly disruptive situations, such as those caused by COVID-19, if they have invested in agile capabilities in advance [21]. To help in the transformation process, the relevant agile practices and methods, as well as agile scaling frameworks, are to be identified. This becomes particularly relevant in the context of COVID-19 to provide guidance to decision-makers on how agility can drive the DT of their business. Against this background, this paper aims to answer the following research question:

How can companies benefit from agility in DT?

There is already a broad knowledge base on agility, especially agile project management and agile transformation, as well as on DT. Based on this knowledge, it is intended to identify how agility can support the DT of companies in times of sudden changes in environmental conditions. Accordingly, a literature review is conducted, based on [22]. This work builds on the extensive knowledge of existing research and attempts to grasp the inherent interconnection between agility and DT. The contribution of this literature review is twofold: First, it highlights the mutual influences of digitalisation and agility identified in previous research. Likewise, the relevant agile practices and methods as well as frameworks for agile scaling in the context of DT are identified. This contributes to the discourse on agility and DT by providing a synthesis of previous research and motivating new research approaches.

The remainder of this paper is organized as follows: First, the methodology used to select and analyse the articles for this review is described. Then, the results are presented. The implications of these findings for promising directions of future research are discussed, especially considering the COVID-19 pandemic. A conclusion summarizes the results and outlines limitations.

2 Methodology

A systematic literature review was conducted in December 2021, guided by the following phases: definition of review scope, the conceptualisation of topic, and literature analysis and synthesis, which finally resulted in proposals for a research agenda [22]. The review scope was defined as a summary of previous research activities and their underlying theories on agility and DT [23]. For this purpose, the literature review was conceptually structured, and oriented towards the research question raised in the introduction. A concept matrix was developed for the literature analysis (see Appendix).

The literature review was organized in four iterations. Figure 1 gives an overview of the selection process and the resulting number of articles. In the first step, the databases Science Direct, IEEE, Springer and EBSCO were searched for the keywords "digital transformation" AND (agility OR agile) AND "project management". In the next step, the abstracts of the articles were read and, according to the criteria listed below (see Table 1), articles were included or excluded.

Table 1. Inclusion and exclusion criteria for the literature analysis

Criterion	Description
Inclusion	Focus on DT
	Agility is a central component of the article (Agile project management and its scaling)
	Focus on the business domain
	Completed research projects
Exclusion	No access to the full article
	Language non-English
	DT is not a central aspect of the article
	Agility is not a central component of the article (Agile project management and its scaling)

Subsequently, the included articles were read in full and based on the defined criteria, further articles were excluded. In addition, backward and forward searches were performed. The final selection of articles was analysed in full text. The analysis of the literature identified as relevant was done using a concept matrix as proposed by [24], which was formed based on the following concepts (see Appendix):

- Classification of articles
- Agility and DT
- Agility comprehension
- Agile scaling
- Agile practices and methods
- Agility characteristic

Identified concepts within the literature could thus be discussed and synthesized. The first concept 'Classification of article' aims to present general aspects of the selected articles and includes the following deductive categories: 'Publication type' and 'Year of publication'. 'Publication type' distinguishes between 'Journal' and 'Conference' publications. The second concept, 'Agility and DT', focuses on understanding how researchers define the connection between agility and DT. A distinction is made between the following two categories: 'Agility as a driver of digitalisation' and 'Digitalisation as a driver of agility'. The 'Agility comprehension' concept aims to identify how the idea of agility is understood in literature: Either as 'Agile project management' or 'Agile transformation'. The concept of agile scaling serves to identify predominant scaling frameworks discussed in the literature. To complement this, further 'Agile practices and methods' will be highlighted. Finally, the 'Agility characteristics', which are emphasized in the literature will be examined. The synthesis of the literature then yields a research agenda that poses questions for further research. Based on the research agenda, under-researched areas are pointed out so that the state of research can be further developed [22].

3   Analysis and Results

The literature search followed the four steps explained above (see Fig. 1): (1) Database search for the keywords "digital transformation" AND (agility OR agile) AND "project management" yielded an initial set of 225 articles. (2) Reading the article abstracts and excluding articles according to the criteria in Table 1 reduced the articles to 99. (3) Full reading of the previously selected articles and exclusion of additional articles based on the defined criteria reduced the number to 24. (4) Backward and forward search resulted in a final number of 28 articles to be analysed.

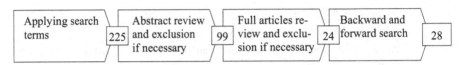

| Applying search terms | 225 | Abstract review and exclusion if necessary | 99 | Full articles review and exclusion if necessary | 24 | Backward and forward search | 28 |

Fig. 1. Literature selection process

The classification of the articles shows that the publication timeframe of the relevant articles spans from 2016 to the year of the literature review (2021) (see Fig. 2). A peak in the number of publications is seen in 2020 with eleven articles. This may be related to the increased relevance of DT in the wake of the pandemic. In any case, a trend towards increasing relevance of the topics of agility and DT is emerging. The distribution between conference and journal articles shows a clear focus on conference papers, with 75% of the articles analysed. The individual concepts are discussed in the following sections. A summary of the results can be found in the concept matrix in the appendix.

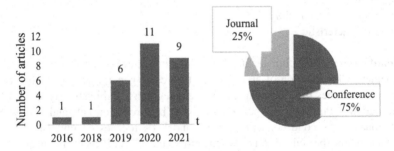

Fig. 2. Distribution of articles by publication year and outlet

3.1   Connections Between Agility and Digital Transformation

In seven publications, a direct connection is made between digital and agile transformation [25–31]. Agile transformation here, according to [13], refers to the entire organization. Operational productivity, quality, and greater flexibility in responding to change in customer behaviour and market conditions are cited reasons for an agile transformation.

This form of agile scaling is described as particularly relevant for large companies [25]. However, the framework conditions and requirements of the DT are rarely addressed.

Against the backdrop of failing projects caused by the increasing complexity of the digital era, [30] define individual mindfulness and stewardship climate as significant positive influences of project management conducts. In addition, ambidextrous projects, meaning that both exploratory and exploitative aspects are pursued, and hybrid project management methods, combining plan-driven and agile approaches, are recommended [30]. Other success factors for an agile transformation mentioned by [28] are agile coaches. For these coaches, the following skills are identified as essential: leadership qualities, project management skills, technical skills, and expertise in agile methods.

In public administration, the need for a structured approach to agile transformation is emphasized to support projects in the development of user-centric products [27]. As a measure for this, the authors propose the analysis of the degree of agility at team level, based on the following six dimensions: communicative, change-affine, iterative, self-organized, product-driven, and improvement-oriented.

Also [29] take a structured classification of companies and their degree of agility. As a result of their study four profiles of agile organisations are defined: "laggards", "execution specialists", "experimenters", and "leaders". The authors further identify project management, delivery and software development, processes, and product development as organisational dimensions that are primarily affected by an agile transformation. According to the authors, with increasing organizational agility, leaders pay less attention to the project level and more to the processes and product management. The authors argue that attempts to achieve greater organisational agility are linked to building more agile business processes rather than focusing on project work. In addition, the study by [29] reveals that among the "leaders", culture, values and goal-setting approaches are also increasingly affected by the agile transformation.

Overall, in the literature the connection between agility and DT is presented in an ambivalent manner: In many articles, the focus is on digitalisation, with less attention being paid to transformation. This will be discussed further in Sect. 4. On the one hand, agility is considered a driver of digitalisation, and, on the other hand, digitalisation is considered a driver of agility.

Agility as a Driver of Digitalisation. As already outlined above, the majority of the articles analysed consider agility to be a driver of digitalisation and DT [25–46] (see Fig. 3). Agility is described as "a driving force for mastering digital innovation and transformation" [41]. Especially in the context of increasing digitalisation, agility is described as necessary to cope with the current complexity [35, 36, 38]. This complexity is caused by new technological challenges, such as cloud solutions, smart technologies, IoT and 5G [40]. Thus, agility becomes a necessary enabler of a successful DT [43]. However, how agility can be achieved is not the subject of the articles analysed.

Fig. 3. Agility and digital transformation

Digitalisation as a Driver of Agility. By contrast, digitalisation is seen as a driver of agility in eight articles [43, 44, 47–52]. Especially articles with a more technical orientation, place digitalisation in the foreground. Several technologies are suggested to promote agility. In particular, AI, cloud, Internet of Things, Big Data, DevOps, API programming, Service-Oriented Architectures, Microservice Architecture, Digital Twin of an Organization, Robotic Process Automation (RPA) and Blockchain Technology are cited [43, 44, 47–50]. The authors describe that these technologies force companies to adapt their IT and business strategy and emphasize the importance of agility [47]. So this demonstrates how digitalisation becomes a driver of agility when these new technologies are intorduced: According to [51], the application of these technologies makes developers more agile and thus fosters agile project management. It is even considered to have an impact on the entire organization, which [52] describes as being able to respond more quickly to business needs and shorten the time to value, thereby promoting DT. In the articles by [43] and [44] both perspectives are addressed.

3.2 Agility Comprehension

The majority of the articles analysed deal with agile transformation and the scaling of agility [25–29, 31–33, 35, 37, 38, 41–43, 47–49]. The remaining articles focus on agile project management [30, 34, 36, 39, 40, 44–46, 50–52] (see Fig. 4).

Fig. 4. Agility comprehension

Agile project management is considered the basis of an agile organisation. From here, the scaling of agility is further advanced. Agile project management is considered in different areas: In the context of product and service development [34], in software development [40], in service innovation [45] and project procurement [50]. For product and service development the authors identify Integrated Design Engineering and Design Thinking as approaches to promote agility [34]. The use of DevOps is considered in the context of software development projects [40]. Also, in the context of agile project management, the benefits of standards are emphasised [39]. According to [44], agile methods become necessary when RPA is introduced. RPA in turn increases the agility of the company, which indicates a scaling of agility. Likewise, in the context of DT, competencies in agile project and program management become relevant [53].

Even if the focus is on agile scaling, either practices and methods at the team and project level or no further definition of scaling are specified. The articles reviewed do not address the concrete implementation of scaling frameworks. Overall, there is a lack of detailed explanations on definitions, understanding and application of agile scaling.

3.3   Relevant Agile Practices, Methods, and Scaling Frameworks

Most articles deal with general agile methods and practices that can be assigned to agile project management (see Fig. 5). Scrum, as the most widespread framework [54], is mentioned most frequently in the articles analysed [29, 31, 32, 34, 45–47, 50]. In addition, lean methods form a large part of the agile approaches discussed [25, 29, 37, 41, 45, 47]. In third place Design Thinking [32, 34, 36, 45, 46] and DevOps [25, 28, 29, 40, 47] are addressed as promising agile methods.

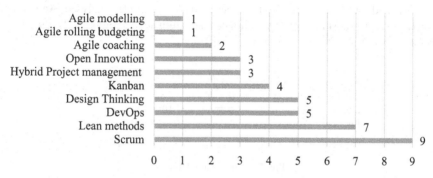

Fig. 5. Agile practices and methods

The literature review reveals that only a small number of articles explicitly discuss scaling frameworks. Where scaling frameworks are mentioned, the following established ones are referred to most often (see Fig. 6): Scaled Agile Framework (SAFe) [25, 29, 31], Large Scale Scrum (LeSS) [25, 29, 31], Scrum of Scrums [29, 31], Spotify model [25] or Disciplined Agile Delivery (DAD) [25, 29].

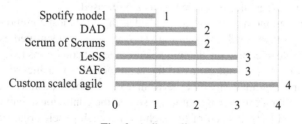

Fig. 6. Agile scaling

In the study by [25], SAFe is identified as the most common scaling framework among the 116 companies surveyed, followed by individual internal approaches. In

[29], companies with the highest level of organisational agility, primarily adopt Scrum of Scrums, followed by internally developed methods in second place, and SAFe in third place. However, frameworks such as Scrum of Scrums, LeSS, SAFe and DAD are described as complex and fraught with many risks in implementation [31, 45]. According to the authors, these approaches are particularly suitable for large companies. Therefore, scaling frameworks are recommended that are customised to the respective company, its culture and limitations, the market and the technology [31]. Overall, therefore most frequently cited approaches for agile scaling are individual customizations, followed by LEss and SAFe (see Fig. 6).

3.4 Agility Characteristics

The perception of agility is diverse. The articles analysed also differ in their definitions and focus. In accordance with the definition by [12] above, the aspects 'iterative', 'equality' and 'autonomy' are also the main focus of the articles analysed. An iterative approach was the most frequently mentioned characteristic of agility [25, 27, 29, 31–37, 40–42, 45–47, 50].

Fig. 7. Agile characteristics

The authors define iterations as particularly relevant to managing uncertainty and minimising risks [35, 45]. According to [37], it is only possible to react quickly to changes by continuously reviewing market requirements. They recommend the use of early and continuous customer and user feedback as well as the use of prototypes and Minimum Viable Products (MVPs), which enable continuous improvement through learning processes [37]. It is precisely here that agile differs from traditional project work: detailed planning in advance is replaced by continuous iterative planning [29]. This increases the frequency at which results are released.

Equality and autonomy were evenly ranked as the third most common characteristic of agility in the articles analysed (see Fig. 7). Autonomy is identified as an important factor in being able to cope with changing environmental conditions [27, 31, 34, 36, 41, 42, 47]. According to [36] autonomy of the team members is achieved by transferring responsibility and accountability for tasks from leaders to the team and individuals. Decisions are made without managing authority so that the continuous planning mentioned above can succeed [27]. Instead of hierarchical leadership, self-organization and personal responsibility become important components of agility [34]. This entails "speed, adaptability, flexibility, dynamism, connection and trust" [47]. Accordingly, [47] considers agility a guiding concept based on a modern idea of humanity and in line with the exponential progress of the technology-driven world.

This also connects to the aspect of equality, which was also addressed in seven articles [29, 31, 32, 34, 35, 45, 47]. In this context, [47] and [45] emphasize that teams must be cross-functional to be able to handle all sorts of different tasks that arise. This cross-functional collaboration is underlined as another critical differentiator of agile organisations from non-agile organisations [29]. This makes it possible for teams to be composed fluidly according to the current requirements. According to the authors, equal teams work across different locations and also across company boundaries [29, 31]. This enables network thinking that integrates different perspectives [34].

However, agile mindset and agile values were mentioned even more frequently than autonomy and equality, ranking second to the iterative approach [27–31, 34, 36, 38, 46, 47]. The agile mindset is seen as the foundation of agility, which for example laggards should introduce first [29]. By applying agile values and agile practices, the agile mindset can guide agile work [27, 32]. According to [29], culture and values determine management style, behaviour and cooperation within the company and with external partners. The successful introduction of agile values requires a continuous improvement process based on feedback [27]. For this purpose, the authors suggest measurements that can be used to map the development of agile values. Linked to this, [29] defines the attitude toward risk-taking as a key differentiator between agile and non-agile organisations. In this context, companies with a high degree of organizational agility view failure as an essential part of learning and take calculated risks [29].

4 Discussion

The literature review findings will be discussed in light of the new requirements posed to many companies in the wake of the COVID-19 pandemic. In the selected articles, only two publications address the COVID-19 pandemic. One just in reflecting on the general situation [51], and the other evaluates project management methodologies used for an AI transformation caused by the COVID-19 pandemic [55]. These articles discuss Scrum and agile methods, so agility is considered here as agile project management. Overall, the literature review revealed that the pandemic and DT have not yet been linked, although both areas are already the subject of research. The low mention of COVID-19 may be due to the study period of this article. Some research projects may not yet be completed. There are certainly more findings in the meantime and there will be in the future. Future research efforts are needed to provide companies with measures for dealing with the "new normal". Because, in the context of the COVID-19 pandemic, many companies have been challenged to reconfigure their business model and sustain and drive it through digital technologies [6]. Hence, in many cases, a distinct DT can be identified. Companies whose previous focus or core competencies were not related to digital technologies need guidance in DT [42]. From the literature review, it can be concluded that for a successful DT, greater attention should be paid to agility. Section 3 summarises the main concepts which were identified in the dataset. Agility allows for flexible and timely reactions to changing market conditions and customer behaviour, the distribution of responsibility, more operational productivity, and better mitigation of risks. The prerequisites for harnessing this potential, however, are agile values and an agile mindset. Far-sighted management should take into account this evolutionary approach, building on agile values and then extending agility further [36]. The authors suggest that corresponding structures should be built up step by step within the organization and in this way agile principles should be integrated. In doing so, companies should pay particular attention to the aspects of an iterative approach, equality, and autonomy. Although a pandemic requires a quick response, neither an agile nor a digital transformation can be implemented abruptly. Thus, roles, practices, tools, behaviours, mindsets and responsibilities need to be continuously transformed [28]. It is therefore also important to proceed iteratively in the transformation itself and increase the degree of agility through successive steps. While agility may initially be established as agile project management in individual isolated digitalisation projects or departments, it should find further application in the company from here to support DT. The focus of these first agile projects is often on the introduction of digital technologies, such as AI, cloud, Internet of Things, Big Data, DevOps, API programming, Service-Oriented Architectures, Microservice Architecture, Digital Twin of an Organization, RPA and Blockchain Technology. These can be good starting points to take advantage of agility, especially in the COVID-19 pandemic, which calls for rapid integration of digital technologies. First experiences made with agility in these digital projects should then be transferred further into the organisation. Here, it is important to consider the transformational component, and not to mistakenly consider individual completed digitalisation projects as a successful DT. As organizational agility increases, i.e., beyond agile project management, the focus then shifts to process and product management rather than projects. Approaches to this can be found, for example, in [29]. Here, a five-step process is proposed, based on an assessment of organisational agility. Starting from the current level of agility, appropriate goals should be set and a roadmap for achieving them should be defined. To assess organisational agility, the authors suggest to continuously monitor progress in achieving set goals and to follow an iterative approach. From the authors' perspective agile scaling frameworks should only be used at a higher degree of agility. Thus, the entire value chain is finally considered, which is a prerequisite for successful digitalisation of the company. This finally enables the DT of the organization.

Moreover, the literature review revealed that agile scaling frameworks are described as complex and risky. Therefore, the literature also considers the individual composition of agile practices and methods to be useful for scaling. It became apparent that there is no conceptual clarity in agile scaling. There is little precise description of the context, as proposed, for example, in the classification according to [13], which subdivides agile scaling into agility for large organisation, for large development efforts, or for the entire organisation. In addition, the postulated complexity of agile scaling frameworks is not presented conclusively. In many places, agile frameworks, such as Scrum, which is designed for small teams, are used for scaling. Here, too, there is a need to clarify the concept of agile scaling in more detail. This indicates an obvious need for further research on the use of scaling frameworks in practice, especially in the context of the COVID-19 pandemic. There still is a gap in literature on how researchers and practitioners have addressed agile scaling in case studies, clearly explaining definitions as well as understanding and application of agile scaling. The general applicability, drivers as well as challenges should be researched more closely to support companies to adopt established frameworks and to make informed decisions on the selection of suitable components. For this, clear definitions of agile scaling should be used to precisely name the context of the application of agility.

In addition, it became evident that DT and the specific challenges it poses for companies were not defined in detail. It seems common that any project that involves digital technologies is called a DT. However, the framework conditions and requirements of DT are rarely addressed. Although the use of individual digital technologies represents an innovation and also a change for many companies, the transformational dimension is disregarded. Yet it is precisely the transformation of value creation through digital technologies that is the central characteristic of DT. But the terms digitisation, digitalisation and DT are not used with sufficient distinction. Research should offer a more precise definition here in the future. Only then it can be more clearly derived which aspects of agility are favourable for the requirements of DT. Establishing a common understanding of concepts between researchers and practitioners is important to progress research in this area.

5 Conclusion and Limitations

Agility is crucial for companies to successfully manage DT. In this context, agile scaling is a critical factor for companies to align the entire organisation to DT. In the current challenge of the COVID-19 pandemic, which has accelerated digitalisation and DT in many organisations, the question arises how agility can support DT. This research question is addressed by a literature review of 28 relevant papers, identified by a structured literature search on four databases. The structured review provided insights to the connection of agility and DT. Agility in general is considered as a driver of DT. Relevant practices, methods, and scaling frameworks, based on previous research, were identified. A continuous scaling of agility, starting at the project level to organization-wide agility is proposed. Since little research has been done on the COVID-19 pandemic in the context of agility and DT, this paper synthesized the current state of knowledge and suggest first agile approaches for framing DT in the context of the pandemic. The review showed that the concepts of DT and agile scaling, especially in the context of the COVID-19 pandemic, need further theorization.

However, there are also limiting aspects regarding the results. Additional databases might have led to more selected publications. More journal articles may be considered for further investigation in this research topic. But also, additional practitioner literature could enrich future research in this topic. Furthermore, the possibility of inaccuracies in data collection and analysis is inherent to literature reviews. Other researchers might have created different concepts and combinations from the findings. Additionally, in the wake of the COVID-19 pandemic, additional findings have certainly been published in the meantime and will be in the future, which should be taken up in follow-up research projects.

Appendix

Category	Paper / Concept	32	25	33	26	27	28	29	30	31	34	47	35	48	36	37	38	39	40	41	42	52	43	51	49	44	45	50	46	Σ
Agility and DT	Agility as a driver of digitalisation	x	x	x	x	x	x	x	x	x	x		x		x	x	x	x	x	x	x		x			x	x		x	22
	Digitalisation as a driver of agility										x			x								x	x	x	x	x			x	8
Agility comprehension	Agile project management						x				x				x		x	x		x			x			x	x	x	x	11
	Agile transformation	x	x	x	x	x	x	x			x				x	x	x		x	x			x	x	x	x				17
Agile scaling	SAFe		x								x			x																3
	Scrum of Scrums										x			x																2
	Large Scale Scrum (LeSS)		x								x			x																3
	Spotify model		x																											1
	Disciplined Agile Dellivery (DAD)		x													x														2
	Custom scaled agile		x								x			x												x				4
Agile practices and methods	Scrum	x									x			x	x	x	x									x	x	x		9
	Hybrid Project management						x																			x	x			3
	Kanban		x			x										x	x													4
	Design Thinking	x														x		x								x	x			5
	Lean methods		x			x	x									x		x		x						x				7
	Open Innovation																x				x						x			3
	DevOps		x			x	x									x				x										5
	Agile rolling budgeting		x																											1
	Agile modelling		x																											1
	Agile coaching							x																		x				2
Agility characteristics	Mindset, values				x	x	x	x	x	x	x					x		x											x	10
	Iterative	x	x	x	x		x				x	x	x	x		x	x		x	x		x				x	x	x		17
	Equality	x			x						x	x	x	x												x				7
	Autonomy							x			x	x	x			x			x	x										7

References

1. Hess, T.: Digitale transformation strategisch steuern. Vom Zufallstreffer zum systematischen Vorgehen. Springer Gabler, Wiesbaden (2019)
2. Piccinini, E., Gregory, R.W., Kolbe, L.M.: Changes in the producer-consumer relationship - towards digital transformation. Changes **3**, 1634–1648 (2015)
3. Hess, T., Matt, C., Benlian, A., Wiesböck, F.: Options for formulating a digital transformation strategy. MIS Q. Exec. **15**, 123–139 (2016)
4. Pousttchi, K., Gleiss, A., Buzzi, B., Kohlhagen, M.: Technology impact types for digital transformation. In: 2019 IEEE 21st Conference on Business Informatics (CBI), pp. 487–494. IEEE (2019). https://doi.org/10.1109/CBI.2019.00063

5. Amankwah-Amoah, J., Khan, Z., Wood, G., Knight, G.: COVID-19 and digitalization: the great acceleration. J. Bus. Res. **136**, 602–611 (2021). https://doi.org/10.1016/j.jbusres.2021. 08.011

6. Soto-Acosta, P.: COVID-19 pandemic: shifting digital transformation to a high-speed gear. Inf. Syst. Manag. **37**, 260–266 (2020). https://doi.org/10.1080/10580530.2020.1814461

7. World Economic Forum: World Economic Forum White Paper Digital Transformation of Industries: In Collaboration with Accenture. Digital Enterprise (2016)

8. Ngereja, B., Hussein, B., Hafseld, K.H.J., Wolff, C.: A retrospective analysis of the role of soft factors in digitalization projects: based on a case study in a public health organization in Trondheim-Norway. In: 2020 IEEE European Technology and Engineering Management Summit (E-TEMS). IEEE (2020)

9. Kiselev, C., Winter, R., Rohner, P.: Project success requires context-aware governance. MIS Q. Exec. **19**, 199–211 (2020). https://doi.org/10.17705/2msqe.00033

10. Klötzer, C., Pflaum, A.: Toward the development of a maturity model for digitalization within the manufacturing industry's supply chain (2017)

11. Nerur, S., Balijepally, V.: Theoretical reflections on agile development methodologies. Commun. ACM **50**, 79–83 (2007)

12. Koch, J., Schermuly, C.C.: Who is attracted and why? how agile project management influences employee's attraction and commitment. Int. J. Manag. Proj. Bus. **14**, 699–720 (2020). https://doi.org/10.1108/IJMPB-02-2020-0063

13. Dingsøyr, T., Moe, N.: Towards principles of large-scale agile development. In: Dingsøyr, Torgeir, Moe, Nils Brede, Tonelli, Roberto, Counsell, Steve, Gencel, Cigdem, Petersen, Kai (eds.) XP 2014. LNBIP, vol. 199, pp. 1–8. Springer, Cham (2014). https://doi.org/10.1007/ 978-3-319-14358-3_1

14. Barroca, L., Dingsøyr, T., Mikalsen, M.: Agile transformation: a summary and research agenda from the first international workshop. In: Hoda, R. (ed.) XP 2019. LNBIP, vol. 364, pp. 3–9. Springer, Cham (2019). https://doi.org/10.1007/978-3-030-30126-2_1

15. Mikalsen, M., Moe, N.B., Stray, V., Nyrud, H.: Agile digital transformation: a case study of interdependencies. In: ICIS (2018)

16. Thrassou, A., Vrontis, D., Bresciani, S.: The Agile innovation pendulum: a strategic marketing multicultural model for family businesses. Int. Stud. Manag. Organ. **48**, 105–120 (2018). https://doi.org/10.1080/00208825.2018.1407178

17. Mikalsen, M., Stray, V., Moe, N.B., Backer, I.: Shifting conceptualization of control in agile transformations. In: Paasivaara, M., Kruchten, P. (eds.) XP 2020. LNBIP, vol. 396, pp. 173–181. Springer, Cham (2020). https://doi.org/10.1007/978-3-030-58858-8_18

18. Dyba, T., Dingsoyr, T.: What do we know about agile software development? IEEE Softw. **26**, 6–9 (2009)

19. Kudyba, S.: COVID-19 and the acceleration of digital transformation and the future of work. Inf. Syst. Manag. **37**, 284–287 (2020). https://doi.org/10.1080/10580530.2020.1818903

20. Sonjit, P., Dacre, N., Baxter, D.: Homeworking project management and agility as the new normal in a COVID-19 world. Adv. Proc. Manag. **21** (2021)

21. Batra, D.: The impact of the COVID-19 on organizational and information systems agility. Inf. Syst. Manag. **37**, 361–365 (2020). https://doi.org/10.1080/10580530.2020.1821843

22. vom Brocke, J., Simons, A., Niehaves, B., Niehaves, B., Reimer, K., Plattfaut, R., Cleven, A.: Reconstructing the giant: On the importance of rigour in documenting the literature search process. In: 17th European Conference on Information Systems, ECIS 2009 (2009)

23. Cooper, H.M.: Organizing knowledge syntheses: a taxonomy of literature reviews. Knowl. Soc. **1**, 104–126 (1988)

24. Webster, J., Watson, R.T.: Analyzing the past to prepare for the future: writing a literature review. MIS Q. **26**, xiii–xxiii (2002)

25. Kettunen, P., Laanti, M., Fagerholm, F., Mikkonen, T.: Agile in the Era of digitalization: a finnish survey study. In: Franch, X., Männistö, T., Martínez-Fernández, S. (eds.) PROFES 2019. LNCS, vol. 11915, pp. 383–398. Springer, Cham (2019). https://doi.org/10.1007/978-3-030-35333-9_28

26. Limaj, E., Bernroider, E.W.N.: A systematic analysis and synthesis of case study based agile scaling research in the context of digital transformations. In: Doucek, P., Basl, J., Tjoa, A.M., Raffai, M., Pavlicek, A., Detter, K. (eds.) CONFENIS 2019. LNBIP, vol. 375, pp. 74–84. Springer, Cham (2019). https://doi.org/10.1007/978-3-030-37632-1_7

27. Looks, H., Fangmann, J., Thomaschewski, J., Escalona, M.-J., Schön, E.-M.: Towards a standardized questionnaire for measuring agility at team level. In: Gregory, P., Lassenius, C., Wang, X., Kruchten, P. (eds.) XP 2021. LNBIP, vol. 419, pp. 71–85. Springer, Cham (2021). https://doi.org/10.1007/978-3-030-78098-2_5

28. Stray, V., Memon, B., Paruch, L.: A systematic literature review on agile coaching and the role of the agile coach. In: Morisio, M., Torchiano, M., Jedlitschka, A. (eds.) PROFES 2020. LNCS, vol. 12562, pp. 3–19. Springer, Cham (2020). https://doi.org/10.1007/978-3-030-641 48-1_1

29. Kovynyov, I., Buerck, A., Mikut, R.: Design of transformation initiatives implementing organisational agility: an empirical study. SN Bus. Econ. 1(6), 1–28 (2021). https://doi.org/10.1007/ s43546-021-00073-6

30. Dehnert, M., Santelmann, B.: Are individual mindfulness and stewardship climate success factors for digital transformation projects? In: 2021 IEEE 23rd Conference on Business Informatics (CBI), pp. 21–30. IEEE (2021). https://doi.org/10.1109/CBI52690.2021.00013

31. Ebert, C., Kirschke-Biller, F.: Agile systems engineering for critical systems. In: Bargende, M., Reuss, HC., Wagner, A. (eds) 20. Internationales Stuttgarter Symposium. Proceedings. Springer Vieweg, Wiesbaden (2020).https://doi.org/10.1007/978-3-658-30995-4_49

32. Gurusamy, K., Srinivasaraghavan, N., Adikari, S.: An integrated framework for design thinking and agile methods for digital transformation. In: Marcus, A. (ed.) DUXU 2016. LNCS, vol. 9746, pp. 34–42. Springer, Cham (2016). https://doi.org/10.1007/978-3-319-40409-7_4

33. Kirchmer, M., Franz, P.: Process reference models: accelerator for digital transformation. In: Shishkov, B. (ed.) BMSD 2020. LNBIP, vol. 391, pp. 20–37. Springer, Cham (2020). https:// doi.org/10.1007/978-3-030-52306-0_2

34. Burchardt, C., Maisch, B.: Advanced agile approaches to improve engineering activities. Procedia Manufact. 25, 202–212 (2018). https://doi.org/10.1016/j.promfg.2018.06.075

35. Sjödin, D., Parida, V., Kohtamäki, M., Wincent, J.: An agile co-creation process for digital servitization: a micro-service innovation approach. J Bus Res 112, 478–491 (2020). https:// doi.org/10.1016/j.jbusres.2020.01.009

36. Burchardt, C., Maisch, B.: Digitalization needs a cultural change – examples of applying agility and open Innovation to drive the digital transformation. Procedia CIRP 84, 112–117 (2019). https://doi.org/10.1016/j.procir.2019.05.009

37. Jesemann, I., Beichter, T., Constantinescu, C., Herburger, K., Rüger, M.: Investigation of the "lean startup" approach in large manufacturing companies towards customer driven product innovation in SMEs. Procedia CIRP 99, 711–716 (2021). https://doi.org/10.1016/j.procir. 2021.03.095

38. Maran, T.K., Liegl, S., Davila, A., Moder, S., Kraus, S., Mahto, R.V.: Who fits into the digital workplace? Mapping digital self-efficacy and agility onto psychological traits. Technol. Forecast. Soc. Chang. 175, 121352 (2021). https://doi.org/10.1016/j.techfore.2021.121352

39. Al-Mahrezi, J., Bakar, N.A.A., Sjarif, N.N.A.: Digital government competency for omani public sector managers: a conceptual framework. In: Saeed, F., Mohammed, F., Al-Nahari, A. (eds.) IRICT 2020. LNDECT, vol. 72, pp. 1009–1020. Springer, Cham (2021). https://doi. org/10.1007/978-3-030-70713-2_90

40. Bordeleau, F., Cabot, J., Dingel, J., Rabil, B.S., Renaud, P.: Towards modeling framework for DevOps: requirements derived from industry use case. In: Bruel, J.-M., Mazzara, M., Meyer, B. (eds.) DEVOPS 2019. LNCS, vol. 12055, pp. 139–151. Springer, Cham (2020). https://doi.org/10.1007/978-3-030-39306-9_10

41. Imgrund, F., Janiesch, C.: Understanding the need for new perspectives on BPM in the digital age: an empirical analysis. In: Di Francescomarino, C., Dijkman, R., Zdun, U. (eds.) BPM 2019. LNBIP, vol. 362, pp. 288–300. Springer, Cham (2019). https://doi.org/10.1007/978-3-030-37453-2_24

42. Kiefer, D., van Dinther, C., Spitzmüller, J.: Digital innovation culture: a systematic literature review. In: Ahlemann, F., Schütte, R., Stieglitz, S. (eds.) WI 2021. LNISO, vol. 48, pp. 305–320. Springer, Cham (2021). https://doi.org/10.1007/978-3-030-86800-0_22

43. Riss, U.V., Maus, H., Javaid, S., Jilek, C.: Digital twins of an organization for enterprise modeling. In: Grabis, J., Bork, D. (eds.) PoEM 2020. LNBIP, vol. 400, pp. 25–40. Springer, Cham (2020). https://doi.org/10.1007/978-3-030-63479-7_3

44. Hofmann, P., Samp, C., Urbach, N.: Robotic process automation. Electron. Mark. **30**(1), 99–106 (2019). https://doi.org/10.1007/s12525-019-00365-8

45. Poeppelbuss, J., Ebel, M., Anke, J.: Iterative uncertainty reduction in multi-actor smart service innovation. Electron Markets (2021).https://doi.org/10.1007/s12525-021-00500-4

46. Barbosa, A.M.C., Pego Saisse, M.C.: Hybrid project management for sociotechnical digital transformation context. BJO&PM, **16**, 316–332 (2019).https://doi.org/10.14488/BJOPM.2019.v16.n2.a12

47. Jesse, N.: Agility eats legacy - the long good-bye. IFAC-PapersOnLine **52**, 154–158 (2019). https://doi.org/10.1016/j.ifacol.2019.12.464

48. Hustad, E., Olsen, D.H.: Creating a sustainable digital infrastructure: the role of service-oriented architecture. Procedia Comput. Sci. **181**, 597–604 (2021). https://doi.org/10.1016/j.procs.2021.01.210

49. Williams, O., Olajide, F., Al-Hadhrami, T., Lotfi, A.: Exploring process of information systems and information technology for enterprise agility. In: Saeed, F., Mohammed, F., Gazem, N. (eds.) IRICT 2019. AISC, vol. 1073, pp. 1042–1051. Springer, Cham (2020). https://doi.org/10.1007/978-3-030-33582-3_98

50. Rane, S.B., Narvel, Y.A.M.: Leveraging the industry 4.0 technologies for improving agility of project procurement management processes. Int. J. Syst. Assur. Eng. Manag. **12**(6), 1146–1172 (2021). https://doi.org/10.1007/s13198-021-01331-4

51. Tyagi, A.K., Fernandez, T.F., Mishra, S., Kumari, S.: Intelligent automation systems at the core of industry 4.0. In: Abraham, A., Piuri, V., Gandhi, N., Siarry, P., Kaklauskas, A., Madureira, A. (eds.) ISDA 2020. AISC, vol. 1351, pp. 1–18. Springer, Cham (2021). https://doi.org/10.1007/978-3-030-71187-0_1

52. Phalake, V.S., Joshi, S.D.: Low code development platform for digital transformation. In: Kaiser, M.S., Xie, J., Rathore, V.S. (eds.) Information and Communication Technology for Competitive Strategies (ICTCS 2020). LNNS, vol. 190, pp. 689–697. Springer, Singapore (2021). https://doi.org/10.1007/978-981-16-0882-7_61

53. Hayretci, H.E., Aydemir, F.B.: A multi case study on legacy system migration in the banking industry. In: La Rosa, M., Sadiq, S., Teniente, E. (eds.) CAiSE 2021. LNCS, vol. 12751, pp. 536–550. Springer, Cham (2021). https://doi.org/10.1007/978-3-030-79382-1_32

54. Komus, A., Kuberg, M.: Status quo (scaled) agile 2019/20. In: 4th International Survey Benefits and Challenges of (Scaled) Agile Approaches (2020). https://www.process-and-project.net/studien/studienunterseiten/status-quo-scaled-agile-2020-en/

55. Najdawi, A., Shaheen, A.: Which project management methodology is better for AI-transformation and innovation projects? In: 2021 International Conference on Innovative Practices in Technology and Management (ICIPTM), pp. 205–210. IEEE (2021). https://doi.org/10.1109/ICIPTM52218.2021.9388357

Clustering Design Science Research Based on the Nature of the Designed Artifact

Joakim Laine[1], Markus Philipp Zimmer[1,2] (ID), Matti Minkkinen[1](✉) (ID),
Hannu Salmela[1] (ID), and Matti Mäntymäki[1] (ID)

[1] University of Turku, 20014 Turku, Finland
matti.minkkinen@utu.fi
[2] Leuphana University Lüneburg, Universitätsallee 1, 21335 Lüneburg, Germany

Abstract. During the past two decades, Design Science Research (DSR) has become a central research paradigm in information systems (IS) science. It provides a possibility for researchers to contribute to their field's existing knowledge base by abstracting knowledge from constructing and using design artifacts. DSR scholars have classified their research paradigm by its potential knowledge contributions looking into dimensions such as researcher role, research activity, and knowledge type. Despite the central role of design artifacts in DSR, we know little about the role of these artifacts for DSR's knowledge contribution. We therefore extend the discussion on DSR knowledge contributions to the nature of design artifacts, asking how the nature of design artifacts clusters DSR research and its potential knowledge contributions. To answer this research question, we conducted a literature review of DSR research and selected a sample of 20 papers published during the years 2017–2021 in four major IS journals. We found that the nature of the design artifact forms clusters of knowledge contribution and research activity. Our study suggests a relationship between design artifacts, abstractions of knowledge from these artifacts and the conducted research activities. We acknowledge that this relationship stems from a relatively small sample of DSR studies and propose that further research is needed to confirm our findings.

Keywords: Design Science Research · Design artifact · Classification · Methodology · Literature review

1 Introduction

Design science research (DSR) is a central research paradigm within information systems (IS) science [6, 12, 20]. One core tenet of DSR is constructing contributions via design artifacts [12]. These artifacts can be instantiations, constructs, models, and methods within and for the software development process [12]. That is, design artifacts are at the core of DSR and tie the research paradigm strongly to IS and its endeavor to solve wicked problems by leveraging technology. However, the potential contributions of DSR extend beyond producing design artifacts that solve practical problems.

© IFIP International Federation for Information Processing 2022
Published by Springer Nature Switzerland AG 2022
S. Papagiannidis et al. (Eds.): I3E 2022, LNCS 13454, pp. 254–266, 2022.
https://doi.org/10.1007/978-3-031-15342-6_20

IS scholars have outlined process models and guidelines for DSR to produce not only design artifacts but knowledge contributions [12, 15, 24]. These process models provide blueprints for bridging the rigor and relevance cycles of DSR [12]. They provide guidance on iterating between the existing knowledge base that can inform the design artifact and abstracting knowledge contributions from constructing and using the design artifacts [15, 24]. We can also find guidelines on design principles [8], design theories [10], and classifications of DSR knowledge contributions [6, 9, 19]. Thus, the DSR community has focused on crafting blueprints that underpin the DSR research paradigm illustrating that it contributes knowledge beyond the design artifact [6, 9, 14].

Multiple frameworks classifying the knowledge contribution of DSR emerged. Gregor and Hevner [9] classify DSR studies' knowledge contribution by maturity of the solution and its application domain maturity. Similarly, Baskerville et al. [6] suggest a continuum from novel artifacts to routine design. Maedche et al. [19], classifying DSR activities, differentiate between researcher role and knowledge contribution. These frameworks share a focus on the potential knowledge contributions of DSR but they are silent on how the nature of the design artifact underlies these contributions.

Science is about producing knowledge beyond the efficacy of design artifacts [12]. Thus, DSR, to differentiate itself from mere design, cannot solely rely on the contribution that stems from the design artifact [9, 12]. This view is reflected in the frameworks for classifying potential DSR knowledge contributions. However, since March and Smith's [20] classification of different design artifacts, the debate has lost view of one centerpiece of DSR – the design artifact – and how it relates to the knowledge contributions that emerged over the course of instilling rigor in DSR. Therefore, we aim to extend the discussion on DSR knowledge contributions to the nature of design artifacts, positing the research question of *how the nature of design artifacts clusters combinations of the potential knowledge contributions and research activities of DSR.*

To answer this question, we conducted a literature review of DSR published in major IS journals. Taking a random sample, we classify DSR studies' knowledge contributions and activities leveraging Gregor and Hevner's [9] and Maedche et al.'s [19] frameworks. In addition, we classify the design artifacts using March and Smith's [20] classification. Then, we identify clusters of knowledge contributions and research activities per nature of the design artifact. We argue that these clusters contribute to DSR scholars' debate on the potential knowledge contribution and the role of the design artifact. Our study suggests that different design artifacts tend to underlie certain types of knowledge contributions and research activities. This implies that different guidelines are applicable depending on the artifacts' nature and that different design artifacts can produce different abstractions of knowledge contribution.

2   Design Science Research: Classifying the Design Artifacts, Knowledge Contributions, and Research Activities

DSR is a problem-solving paradigm with roots in engineering and the sciences of the artificial [12, 20]. DSR scholars create artifacts that help accomplish analysis, design, implementation, and use of IS effectively via ideas, practices, technical capabilities, and products [6]. The DSR relevance for IS research is related to its applicability in design as researchers apply technological artifacts to new areas. DSR provides intellectual and computational tools that were not previously believed to be possible [12].

Constructing artifacts to solve wicked problems, DSR appears similar to what practitioners do: solving problems by developing technological solutions. This comparison inspired debate in the DSR community on what differentiates DSR from practicing design [9]. Researchers contributed to this debate by suggesting process models [15, 24], guidelines for conducting and publishing DSR [9, 12], guidelines for developing design theories [10], and frameworks on the knowledge contribution of DSR [6, 9, 19]. These efforts share the ideas that DSR differs from practicing design in being rigorous, drawing on the existing knowledge base, following certain guidelines, and abstracting knowledge from constructing the design artifact. This means that the design artifact takes center stage in the knowledge production through DSR [12].

Design artifacts can be decision support systems, modeling tools, governance strategies, methods for IS evaluation, and IS change interventions [9]. Given the importance of the design artifact, scholars have proposed guidelines for good artifacts, how to present artifacts, and how artifacts differ. March and Smith [20] differentiate between research outputs and research activities (see Table 1). *Research outputs* comprise constructs, models, methods, and instantiations. These can be vocabulary and symbols (constructs), abstractions and representations (models), algorithms and practices (methods), and implemented or prototype systems (instantiations). *Research activities* include build, evaluate, theorize, and justify. Build refers to constructing the design artifact. Evaluation captures the development of design and performance criteria and assessing the design artifact's performance. Theorize describes how and why the artifact accomplishes the criteria. Justify refers to providing a theory that informed the design. According to March and Smith [20], these activities form the iterative DSR process.

Table 1. March and Smith's [20] framework of research outputs and research activities

		Research activities			
		Build	**Evaluate**	**Theorize**	**Justify**
Research outputs	**Constructs**				
	Model				
	Method				
	Instantiation				

Hevner et al. [12] build on the research outputs and research activities presented in March and Smith [20]. They draw on the research outputs to define design artifacts and refer to the research activities as the "build-and-evaluate loop." However, they put forth that theorizing and justifying present the distinct value of DSR, not the research outputs. This argument entailed a discussion of the knowledge contribution of DSR. While the design artifact presents a contribution, this falls short of what we expect in science: a contribution to knowledge [9]. This argument entailed that DSR scholars engaged in developing frameworks that classify DSR's potential knowledge contributions. We will present two of these frameworks: Gregor and Hevner [9] and Maedche et al. [19].

Gregor and Hevner [9] created a framework of two dimensions: solution maturity and application domain maturity. Solution maturity captures whether existing artifacts have the development status to tackle the problem. Application domain maturity refers to the degree of understanding of the problem for which, or within which, the artifact will be used. Conceptualizing the resulting four quadrants, the authors differentiate between routine design, improvement, exaptation, and invention (see Table 2).

Table 2. DSR knowledge contribution framework (Gregor and Hevner 2013)

Solution maturity	Low	**Improvement** New solutions for known problems	**Invention** New solutions for new problems
	High	**Routine design** Known solutions for known problems	**Exaptation** Known solutions to new problems
		High	Low
		Application domain maturity	

Maedche et al. [19] present a framework for classifying design research activities based on researcher role and knowledge contribution (Table 3). Accordingly, researchers can create or observe, and the knowledge contribution can be descriptive or prescriptive statements. Creating means that researchers develop artifacts or their variants while observing means that researchers examine the application of artifacts. Descriptive knowledge focuses on understanding IT's nature (what-is), while prescriptive knowledge focuses on improving IT's performance (how-to). These two dimensions form four quadrants: deployment, elucidation, construction, and manipulation.

Table 3. Design research activities classification framework [19]

Researcher role	Observation	**Deployment**	**Elucidation**
	Creation	**Construction**	**Manipulation**
		Prescriptive	Descriptive
		Knowledge contribution	

The frameworks indicate three complementary ways of classifying DSR: the nature of the design artifact [20], the knowledge contribution [9], and research activities [19]. However, these frameworks remain silent on the relation between these classifications. Therefore, we aim to identify clusters of DSR by the nature of the design artifact.

3 Methodology

We conducted a literature review to classify DSR studies employing the presented frameworks. Afterward, we analyzed the published papers for patterns, i.e., whether the nature of the design artifact suggests combinations of knowledge contribution and research activities. For the literature review, we undertook a systematic mapping of DSR published in four major IS journals, MIS Quarterly (MISQ), Information Systems Research (ISR), Journal of Management Information Systems (JMIS), and Journal of the Association for Information Systems (JAIS), between 2017 and 2021. This scope and period were selected as a starting point which future studies can broaden. To identify the DSR studies, we screened the titles, abstracts, and keywords of all articles published in these journals. We marked articles as DSR if they contained an explicit statement on using DSR or created an artifact based on the definition of March and Smith [20].

We found 303 DSR studies. Of these, 67 were published in the JAIS, 93 in the MISQ, 67 in the JMIS, and 77 in ISR. Considering this breadth and our deductive approach to cross-tabulating existing frameworks, we decided to take a random sample. We selected one article per year from each journal. This resulted in a subsample of 20 studies (Table 4). Analyzing the selected articles, we classified them using the three frameworks presented in Sect. 2: the nature of the artifact, the knowledge contribution, and DSR activities. This cross-tabulation revealed that knowledge contribution and DSR activity form combinations in relation to the nature of the artifact.

Table 4. Random sample of the identified DSR studies in the four IS journals

Author	Title	Source	Design artifact
Lin et al. 2017	Healthcare predictive analytics for risk profiling in chronic care: A Bayesian multitask learning approach	MISQ	Bayesian multitask learning (BMTL)
Abbasi et al. 2018	Text Analytics to Support Sense-Making in Social Media: A Language-Action Perspective	MISQ	The language-action perspective (LAP)
Li et al. 2019	Modeling Multi-Channel Advertising Attribution Across Competitors	MISQ	An integrated individual-level choice model
Haki et al. 2020	The Evolution of Information Systems Architecture: An Agent-Based Simulation Model	MISQ	Theory-informed simulation model

(*continued*)

Table 4. (*continued*)

Author	Title	Source	Design artifact
Baird and Maruping 2021	The Next Generation of Research on IS Use: A Theoretical Framework of Delegation to and from Agentic IS Artifacts	MISQ	IS delegation theoretical framework
Piel et al. 2017	Promoting the System Integration of Renewable Energies: Toward a Decision Support System for Incentivizing Spatially Diversified Deployment	JMIS	A model for the quantification of location-based investment
Lehrer et al. 2018	How Big Data Analytics Enables Service Innovation: Materiality, Affordance, and the Individualization of Service	JMIS	Theoretical model of BDA-enabled service innovation
Maruping et al. 2019	A Risk Mitigation Framework for Information Technology Projects: A Cultural Contingency Perspective	JMIS	A holistic nomological network that integrates consideration of people, process, and technology
Silic and Lowry 2020	Using Design-Science Based Gamification to Improve Organizational Security Training and Compliance	JMIS	A gamified security training system
Xie et al. 2021	Unveiling the Hidden Truth of Drug Addiction: A Social Media Approach Using Similarity Network-Based Deep Learning	JMIS	SImilarity Network-based DEep Learning (SINDEL)
Wu et al. 2017	Understanding User Adaptation toward a New IT System in Organizations: A Social Network Perspective	JAIS	A cognitive-affective-behavioral classification

(*continued*)

Table 4. (*continued*)

Author	Title	Source	Design artifact
Akhlaghpour and Lapointe 2018	From Placebo to Panacea: Studying the Diffusion of IT Management Techniques with Ambiguous Efficiencies: The Case of Capability Maturity Model	JAIS	A multi-perspective framework
Miah et al. 2019	A Metadesign Theory for Tailorable Decision Support	JAIS	A metadesign theory for tailorable DSS
Mingers and Standing 2020	A Framework for Validating IS Research Based on a Pluralist Account of Truth and Correctness	JAIS	An overall framework of truth and correctness
Velichety and Ram 2021	Finding a Needle in the Haystack: Recommending Online Communities on Social Media Platforms Using Network and Design Science	JAIS	The nominal process model
Ho et al. 2017	Disconfirmation Effect on Online Rating Behavior: A Structural Model	ISR	Conceptual Framework of the Online Rating Behavior
Barua and Mani 2018	Reexamining the Market Value of Information Technology Events	ISR	An exploratory framework involving the maturity and scope of an IT event
Bouayad et al. 2019	Audit Policies Under the Sentinel Effect: DeterrenceDriven Algorithms	ISR	The Diffusion-Deterrence Model / deterrence-based audit algorithm under network effects
Ye et al. 2020	Developing and Testing a Theoretical Path Model of Web Page Impression Formation and Its Consequence	ISR	A theoretical model of web page impression formation
Abbasi et al. 2021	The Phishing Funnel Model: A Design Artifact to Predict User Susceptibility to Phishing Websites	ISR	The phishing funnel model (PFM)

4 Findings

In this section, we present the results of our cross-tabulation of the randomly selected DSR studies using the existing DSR frameworks. Table 5 presents the findings of our analysis sorted by the nature of the design artifact. Across the random sample, models were the most prominent artifact (10 papers), followed by methods (4 papers), instantiations, and constructs (3 papers each). We found no deployment, invention, or routine design studies. After the table, we present the combinations of potential knowledge contribution and DSR activities clustered by the nature of the design artifact.

Table 5. Classifying the random sample by the nature of the design artifact

Paper	Knowledge contribution [9]	Design research activities [19]
Constructs		
Baird and Maruping 2021	Exaptation	Elucidation
Wu et al. 2017	Exaptation	Manipulation
Mingers and Standing 2020	Improvement	Elucidation
Models		
Li et al. 2019	Improvement	Construction
Haki et al. 2020	Improvement	Elucidation
Piel et al. 2017	Improvement	Construction
Maruping et al. 2019	Exaptation	Manipulation
Xie et al. 2021	Improvement	Construction
Lehrer et al. 2018	Exaptation	Construction
Ye et al. 2020	Exaptation	Construction
Ho et al. 2017	Improvement	Manipulation
Barua and Mani 2018	Improvement	Manipulation
Abbasi et al. 2021	Improvement	Construction
Methods		
Lin et al. 2017	Improvement	Construction
Abbasi et al. 2018	Improvement	Construction
Miah et al. 2019	Improvement	Elucidation
Velichety and Ram 2021	Improvement	Construction
Instantiations		
Silic and Lowry 2020	Improvement	Manipulation
Akhlaghpour and Lapointe 2018	Improvement	Elucidation
Bouayad et al. 2019	Improvement	Construction

4.1 Design Science Studies Presenting Constructs

Three studies in our sample provided a construct as design artifact. Two constructs had exaptation as the knowledge contribution. The theoretical framework developed by Wu et al. [28] focuses on post-adoption IT use. It integrates coping theory with the social network literature, classifies different types of post-adoption coping strategies, and focuses on the effects of post-adoption responses in new IT systems. The researcher role was to create a framework to address new problems, therefore, it goes into the manipulation category. Baird and Maruping [4], the only study in the exaptation and elucidation category, aimed to understand IS artifacts by developing a delegation theoretical framework and exploring the relationship between humans and IS. Mingers and Standing [23] developed a framework that encompasses multiple methods. It was considered an observation study as they examined existing artifacts and considered how problems and solutions are defined. It was marked as an improvement as their focus was on developing solutions for known problems.

4.2 Design Science Studies Presenting Models

For models, there was significant variation in the researcher role and knowledge contribution. Of the eight improvement studies, four of the DSR activities were marked as construction, three as manipulation, and one as elucidation. Construction methods, such as Li et al. [17], aimed to develop a solution by developing a new cross-channel attribution model that expands the literature's single-seller scope across multiple sellers, while Abbasi et al. [1] created a phishing funnel model (PFM) which represented solutions that predicts user susceptibility to phishing websites. Piel et al. [25] aimed to improve the distribution of wind energy deployment by proposing an IT artifact that integrates resource models, an economic viability model, and a spatial distribution model. Xie et al. [29] presented a novel IT system, Similarity Network-based Deep Learning (SINDEL), that aims to design analytics solutions to problems with societal impact.

The improvement–manipulation subset included two models. A framework developed by Barua and Mani [5] involved the maturity and scope of an IT event as they surveyed the suitability of short- versus long-term abnormal returns. Ho et al. [13] modeled individual perceptions of a review system to study how disconfirmation affects online consumer rating behavior. Haki et al. [11] (improvement–elucidation), in turn, developed a theory-informed simulation model that explores how IS architecture emerges under various levels of pressures and how their dynamic changes over time.

The models that contributed to exaptation were the construction models by Lehrer et al. [16] and Ye et al. [30] and the manipulation model by Maruping et al. [21]. Ye et al. [30] formulated a theoretical model that demonstrates the visual aesthetics of web page impressions, while Lehrer et al. [16] developed a model that explains how big data analytics technologies provide features of sourcing, storage, event recognition and prediction, behavior recognition and prediction, rule-based actions, and visualization. The holistic nomological network of technical risk mitigation processes developed by Maruping et al. [21] aimed to extend current IT project risk frameworks.

4.3 Design Science Studies Presenting Methods

The method cluster included four studies. All method studies were marked as improvement. In three of them, the researcher role was to create artifacts (construction). Lin et al. [18] presented a Bayesian multitask learning (BMTL) artifact, Abbasi et al. [2] proposed the language-action perspective (LAP)-based text analytics framework, and Velichety and Ram [27] proposed a combination of a method and a process. The BMTL approach [18] allows healthcare actors to simultaneously model a random number of events and outcomes, improving clinical decision-making and facilitating preventive and personalized care. The LAP approach [2], in turn, improves the design of IS that consider communicative context and actions and emphasizes the interplay between conversations, communication interactions between users and messages, and the speech act composition of messages. Velichety and Ram [27] surveyed the relationships among online communities and types of social media users and what features guide them.

The only method study which did not appear in the construction cluster was marked as an elucidation. Miah et al. [22] developed a decision support system design environment for both client context and tailored technologies. They focused specifically on DSR methods as a solution for practical decision-making issues. They observed meta-design theory for the general solution concept and design principles and illustrated innovation in tailorable technology, focusing specifically on DSR studies that use design science methods as a solution to articulated practical decision-making issues.

4.4 Design Science Studies Presenting Instantiations

Instantiations show that constructs, models, or methods can be implemented in a system. We found three improvement studies, one being construction, one manipulation, and one elucidation. Silic and Lowry [26] presented a DSR approach for a gamified security training system. Bouayad et al. [7] presented an algorithm that provided a new approach for auditing in healthcare, showing the value of deterrence-based auditing algorithms. Akhlaghpour and Lapointe [3] developed a multi-perspective framework for IT management techniques.

5   Discussion and Conclusion

We examined how artifacts, knowledge contributions, and activities can cluster DSR. While IS scholars have classified DSR's knowledge contributions and research activities, they remained silent on how the nature of artifacts underlies them. This observation warrants examination since contributing the artifact is a core tenet of DSR [6, 12]. Therefore, we analyzed DSR in major IS journals to identify clusters of knowledge contributions and activities based on the nature of the designed artifact.

The clusters suggest that certain design artifacts underlie specific knowledge contributions [9] and DSR activities [19] (Table 6). For example, models have not been deployed (observation and prescriptive statements) but present DSR knowledge contributions of improvement (high solution maturity and low application domain maturity) and exaptation (low solution maturity and high application domain maturity). This suggests that models fit certain DSR activities and knowledge contributions. Models are cognitive representations of reality. While they can take tangible form, agency in solving the problem rests with human actors taking action based on the model. The nature of the artifact thus has implications for the knowledge contribution and design of DSR.

Table 6. Clustering combinations of DSR knowledge contributions and research activities by the nature of the design artifact

Nature of the designed artifact	Knowledge contribution and research activity types
Construct	Exaptation–Elucidation Exaptation–Manipulation Improvement–Elucidation
Model	Improvement–Construction Improvement–Elucidation Exaptation–Manipulation Improvement–Manipulation
Method	Improvement–Construction Improvement–Elucidation
Instantiation	Improvement–Manipulation Improvement–Elucidation Improvement–Construction

These findings suggest two implications for DSR. First, the nature of the design artifacts supports certain knowledge contributions and DSR activities. The random sample suggests that if scholars construct a model, they are unlikely to contribute an invention. Similar relations can be drawn for other design artifacts. Hence, if we confine DSR to specific types of knowledge contribution and DSR activities, we exclude artifacts that cannot make these contributions or cannot be investigated through these activities. This implies that in future DSR, we should consider knowledge claims not only against the research process but also against the nature of the artifact and whether the combination of artifact and activity can support these knowledge claims.

Second, the nature of the design artifact requires aligned DSR guidelines. While we can construct models to offer prescriptive statements, we cannot observe and prescribe models. This means that the nature of the design artifact affects the DSR process and thus the applicable guidelines. If we applied the same guidelines regardless of the nature of the design artifact, we would limit DSR to design artifacts that emerge from design activities conducive to these guidelines. However, these activities may not support the construction of a model, method, or other artifacts. Thus, the guidelines can have a constraining effect on the breadth of the artifacts that DSR produces. If we consider that different problems require different solutions, limiting the artifacts entails limiting the problem space that DSR can address. Hence, our findings imply that the nature of the artifact produced in a DSR has implications for the applicable DSR guidelines.

Deciding to analyze a random sample, we acknowledge the risk that extending the analysis to the entire sample might falsify some conclusions. However, if we evaluate our findings against their plausibility, we can deduce that this random sample provides credible contributions by drawing on existing classifications of DSR. Nonetheless, we suggest that future research should extend our analysis to the entire sample.

References

1. Abbasi, A., Dobolyi, D., Vance, A., Zahedi, F.M.: The phishing funnel model: a design artifact to predict user susceptibility to phishing websites. Inf. Syst. Res. **32**(2), 410–436 (2021). https://doi.org/10.1287/isre.2020.0973
2. Abbasi, A., Zhou, Y., Deng, S., Zhang, P.: Text analytics to support sense-making in social media: a language-action perspective. MIS Q. **42**(2), 427–464 (2018). https://doi.org/10.25300/MISQ/2018/13239
3. Akhlaghpour, S., Lapointe, L.: From placebo to panacea: studying the diffusion of IT management techniques with ambiguous efficiencies: the case of capability maturity model. J. Assoc. Inf. Syst. **19**(06), 441–502 (2018). https://doi.org/10.17705/1jais.00498
4. Baird, A., Maruping, L.M.: The next generation of research on IS use: a theoretical framework of delegation to and from agentic IS artifacts. MIS Q. **45**(1), 315–341 (2021). https://doi.org/10.25300/MISQ/2021/15882
5. Barua, A., Mani, D.: Reexamining the market value of information technology events. Inf. Syst. Res. **29**(1), 225–240 (2018). https://doi.org/10.1287/isre.2017.0718
6. Baskerville, R., Baiyere, A., Gergor, S., Hevner, A., Rossi, M.: Design science research contributions: finding a balance between artifact and theory. J. Assoc. Inf. Syst. **19**(5), 358–376 (2018). https://doi.org/10.17705/1jais.00495
7. Bouayad, L., Padmanabhan, B., Chari, K.: Audit policies under the sentinel effect: deterrence-driven algorithms. Inf. Syst. Res. **30**(2), 466–485 (2019). https://doi.org/10.1287/isre.2019.0841
8. Gregor, S., Kruse, L.C., Seidel, S.: The anatomy of a design principle. J. Assoc. Inf. Syst. (2020). https://doi.org/10.17705/1jais.00129
9. Gregor, S., Hevner, A.R.: Positioning and presenting design science research for maximum impact. MIS Q. **37**(2), 337–355 (2013). https://doi.org/10.25300/MISQ/2013/37.2.01
10. Gregor, S., Jones, D.: The anatomy of a design theory. J. Assoc. Inf. Syst. **8**(5), 312–335 (2007). https://doi.org/10.17705/1jais.00129
11. Haki, K., Beese, J., Aier, S., Winter, R.: The evolution of information systems architecture: an agent-based simulation model. MIS Q. **44**(1), 155–184 (2020). https://doi.org/10.25300/MISQ/2020/14494
12. Hevner, A.R., March, S.T., Park, J., Ram, S.: Design science in information systems research. MIS Q. **28**(1), 75–106 (2004)
13. Ho, Y.-C., Wu, J., Tan, Y.: Disconfirmation effect on online rating behavior: a structural model. Inf. Syst. Res. **28**(3), 626–642 (2017). https://doi.org/10.1287/isre.2017.0694
14. Iivari, J.: Editorial: a critical look at theories in design science research. J. Assoc. Inf. Syst. **21**(3), 502–519 (2020). https://doi.org/10.17705/1jais.00610
15. Kuechler, B., Vaishnavi, V.: On theory development in design science research: anatomy of a research project. Eur. J. Inf. Syst. **17**(5), 489–504 (2008). https://doi.org/10.1057/ejis.2008.40
16. Lehrer, C., Wieneke, A., vom Brocke, J., Jung, R., Seidel, S.: How big data analytics enables service innovation: materiality, affordance, and the individualization of service. J. Manag. Inf. Syst. **35**(2), 424–460 (2018). https://doi.org/10.1080/07421222.2018.1451953
17. Li, Y., Xie, Y., Zeng, Z.: Modeling multichannel advertising attribution across competitors. MIS Q. **43**(1), 287–312 (2019). https://doi.org/10.25300/MISQ/2019/14257

18. Lin, Y.-K., Chen, H., Brown, R. A., Li, S.-H., Yang, H.-J.: Healthcare predictive analytics for risk profiling in chronic care: a Bayesian multitask learning approach. MIS Q. **41**(2), 473–495 (2017). https://doi.org/10.25300/MISQ/2017/41.2.07
19. Maedche, A., Gregor, S., Parsons, J.: Mapping design contributions in information systems research: the design research activity framework. Commun. Assoc. Inf. Syst. **49**(1), 355–378 (2021). https://doi.org/10.17705/1CAIS.04914
20. March, S.T., Smith, G.F.: Design and natural science research on information technology. Decis. Support Syst. **15**(4), 251–266 (1995). https://doi.org/10.1016/0167-9236(94)00041-2
21. Maruping, L.M., Venkatesh, V., Thong, J.Y.L., Zhang, X.: A risk mitigation framework for information technology projects: a cultural contingency perspective. J. Manag. Inf. Syst. **36**(1), 120–157 (2019). https://doi.org/10.1080/07421222.2018.1550555
22. Miah, S.J., Gammack, J.G., McKay, J.: A Metadesign theory for tailorable decision support. J. Assoc. Inf. Syst. 570–603 (2019). https://doi.org/10.17705/1jais.00544
23. Mingers, J., Standing, C.: A framework for validating information systems research based on a pluralist account of truth and correctness. J. Assoc. Inf. Syst. 117–151 (2020). https://doi.org/10.17705/1jais.00594
24. Peffers, K., Tuunanen, T., Rothenberger, M.A., Chatterjee, S.: A design science research methodology for information systems research. J. Manag. Inf. Syst. **24**(3), 45–77 (2007). https://doi.org/10.2753/MIS0742-1222240302
25. Piel, J.-H., Hamann, J.F.H., Koukal, A., Breitner, M.H.: Promoting the system integration of renewable energies: toward a decision support system for incentivizing spatially diversified deployment. J. Manag. Inf. Syst. **34**(4), 994–1022 (2017). https://doi.org/10.1080/07421222.2017.1394044
26. Silic, M., Lowry, P.B.: Using design-science based gamification to improve organizational security training and compliance. J. Manag. Inf. Syst. **37**(1), 129–161 (2020). https://doi.org/10.1080/07421222.2019.1705512
27. Velichety, S, Ram, S.: Finding a needle in the haystack: recommending online communities on social media platforms using network and design science. J. Assoc. Inf. Syst. **22**(5), 1285–1310 (2020). https://doi.org/10.17705/1jais.00694
28. Wu, Y., Choi, B., Guo, X., Chang, K.: Understanding user adaptation toward a new IT system in organizations: a social network perspective. J. Assoc. Inf. Syst. **18**(11), 787–813 (2017). https://doi.org/10.17705/1jais.00473
29. Xie, J., Zhang, Z., Liu, X., Zeng, D.: Unveiling the hidden truth of drug addiction: a social media approach using similarity network-based deep learning. J. Manag. Inf. Syst. **38**(1), 166–195 (2021). https://doi.org/10.1080/07421222.2021.1870388
30. Ye, X., Peng, X., Wang, X., Teo, H.-H.: Developing and testing a theoretical path model of web page impression formation and its consequence. Inf. Syst. Res. **31**(3), 929–949 (2020). https://doi.org/10.1287/isre.2020.0924

Information Systems Strategy: A Multiple Criteria Decision Analysis Perspective for Business Performance in SMEs

Maria Kamariotou and Fotis Kitsios(✉)

Department of Applied Informatics, University of Macedonia, Thessaloniki, Greece
mkamariotou@uom.edu.gr, kitsios@uom.gr

Abstract. Small-Medium Enterprises (SMEs) face many difficulties to make investments in effective Information Technology (IT) projects that will increase business performance because they ignore the importance of Information Systems (IS) strategy. This article explores the satisfaction of IT managers using the IS strategic planning process to develop IS. Data was collected from 294 IS managers in Greek SMEs The MUSA method which is a Multiple Criteria Decision Analysis (MCDA) approach was used to analyze data. As the results of this survey indicate, SMEs cannot improve firm profitability without strategic planning. IT managers should be knowledgeable about IT issues because this can be an obstacle for the organization and will prevent them achieving their planning goals and increasing the value of the business.

Keywords: Information Systems · Digital strategy · MCDA · SMEs · Business performance

1 Introduction

Executives must contend with both environmental disclosure and the complexity of developing Information Systems (IS) in order to enhance the performance of their companies [1, 11]. Meanwhile, as a result of the development of world trade, new competitive obstacles and challenges have been initiated. This is an actuality that forces businesses to evaluate their internal business environments in order to enhance their efficiency and obtain the preferred competitive advantage. However, it is possible to believe that only if the IT strategy is aligned with organizational strategy will it be able to increase sustainable competitive advantage. The fact that many organizations have invested their money in achieving this goal can be explained by the fact that they have examined their internal processes [9]. For all businesses, but especially Small-Medium Enterprises (SMEs), such a barrier is necessary.

In this new environment businesses face financial challenges, due to a lack of technical, organizational, and human resources. Therefore, these challenges can reduce their ability to face the same financial crisis [21, 22]. Managers could use structured processes

© IFIP International Federation for Information Processing 2022
Published by Springer Nature Switzerland AG 2022
S. Papagiannidis et al. (Eds.): I3E 2022, LNCS 13454, pp. 267–276, 2022.
https://doi.org/10.1007/978-3-031-15342-6_21

in terms of both strategic planning and information handling to improve business performance in SMEs. Information Technology (IT) investment affects business value, while also supports managers to align organizational strategy with firm performance. Investment in IT is a significant challenge for IT executives. Therefore, businesses should develop structured processes in dynamic environments based on formal rules and procedures to in order to increase environmental sustainability and competitive advantage [15, 23].

Traditionally, the field of alignment has always been determined as the level to which the IS strategy corresponds to that of the business. Many studies have shown that the relationship between alignment and success is positive [26]. Nevertheless, with regard to this relationship, scholars conclude that SMEs can use various means to achieve a high degree of alignment, depending on their strengths and market position. Therefore, alignment is a decision-making process where decision makers have to identify alternative scenarios [16].

Regrettably, IS strategy is a research area that has been examined as a homogenous research topic. What SMEs reflects, however, is a different type of companies in which both business size and resource constraints significantly affect both alignment and performance [20]. Existing studies conclude that developments in IT increase the extent of IS adoption in SMEs. As a result, practitioners should be aware of the impact of the aligning the business strategy with the IT strategy on firm performance [10]. For all the aforementioned reasons, this article explores the satisfaction of IT managers who use the IS strategic planning process to develop IS. The main research questions is the following: "How satisfied are IS executives with IS performance?". All data were obtained form 294 IS managers in Greek Small-Medium Enterprises (SMEs) and analyzed using the MUSA method, a Multiple Criteria Decision Analysis (MCDA) approach.

The outcomes of this paper can support executives to understand the IS strategic planning process. It is crucial to be aware of this process and do not ignore its tasks. IT managers will pay attention to organizational goals and realize the significance of the IS strategic planning process for their businesses if they understand the IS strategic planning process and its importance. Otherwise, there will be challenges in aligning business strategy with IT strategy. The outcomes of this paper can support practitioners to realize how IT strategy help the development of IS projects that provide new opportunities for businesses to enhance business value, innovation and sustainability.

Another contribution of this papers the implementation of MCDA, a decision making method to evaluate firm performance. Previous researchers have not used MCDA methods to examine the relationship between business and IT alignment. MCDA can be used to solve decision-making problems that are characterized by the multidisciplinary or multi-criteria nature of the factors that need to be examined and evaluate alternatives for a specific problem. IS strategic planning is a process which involves multiple conflicting objectives. Thus, implementing MCDA methods decision makers can define alternatives and select the most suitable for their case during the implementation of the process.

The article is structured as follows. Sect. 2 includes the theoretical background on IS strategy and firm performance. Sect. 3 explains the methodology and Sect. 4 presents the findings. The final section provides suggestions for future research.

2 Theoretical Background

SMEs develop ineffective IS projects due to the lack of strategic planning, alignment between organizational goals and IT goals, and formal processes. Existing studies have explored the relationship between organizational strategy alignment and IS strategy or the relationship between organizational goals and IS goals [2, 17, 20]. IS executives try to achieve a high level of alignment between IT and organizational structure in order to develop services that support business goals and increase business value [14]. Managers should be knowledgeable about the structure of the company and IT to achieve strategic IT alignment which is unique to each company. Therefore, the alignment of IT with strategy has to be unique so that each firm can achieve its objectives [4, 7].

Strategic alignment allows firms to effectively realize the position of IT effectively, a significant factor that can increase business value. Moreover by strengthening the relationship between market aspects and technology, alignment as a mechanism supports firms to expand their market share and infrastructure. Scholars concluded that the current alignment models are more business-driven than IT-driven, which means that managers concentrate more on IT. IT executives should be aware of business strategy to support it with the development of IS projects [20].

It is interesting to explore the challenges that hinder many businesses from aligning IT with organizational strategy. First of all, often IT decisions are taken by IT executives who are ignorant of it, which inevitably leads to a misalignment of the organization. If IT managers are not knowledgeable about organizational goals, they cannot understand the organizational strategy. IT managers have conflicts among them and may not to trust each other, a fact which negatively influence not only the IS strategic planning process but also their firm's competence [29, 31].

What has been indicated by surveys analyzing the impact of IS strategic planning process on effectiveness have shown that IS executives have focused on strategic conception. Combined with opportunity analysis and evaluation, the strategy's conception could offer more realistic alternatives. Understanding IS objectives can enable the company to define future IS and business goals, as well as better options and choices can be defined to achieve better outcomes. The frequently encountered challenges that emerged during the implementation of the IS strategic planning process were the lack of top management engagement and the inability to develop effective action strategies to develop IS projects. If executives do not support the development of IS projects team members will not focus on the plans and will have difficulties in the implementation of the IT strategy. Thus, it is preferable for managers to define priorities that could support their IT strategy to be better executed and achieve their objectives. Previous researchers indicate that IT managers tend to focus on IS strategy implementation because they consider the execution of the strategy as a complex process [8, 28].

Findings also indicate that there are managers who are overworked with respect to the IS strategic planning process whilst others who are doing too little. Such two approaches may prove ineffective. In the first case, the process could be misunderstood, postponed or stopped from being enforced, while in the second approach the implementation plans could be unsuccessful, meaning that their objectives could not be accomplished. The evaluation of the process is obviously of great importance if managers wish to minimize these unsatisfactory outcomes. Researchers have indicated that IT managers pay attention at strategy conception and strategy implementation, ignoring the significance of strategic awareness and situation analysis. As a consequence, the IT strategy which is being developed is not efficient and effective and it does not meet IT goals [25, 33]. Furthermore, IT executives focus on reducing the time and cost of the implemented project. Executives pay attention at process implementation and this fact has negative results. Nevertheless, it reduces the time of the IS strategic planning process implementation, but the organization's strategic goals are not aligned with IT objectives [3, 5, 6].

As the usage of IT enhances the firm's competitive advantage by using scarce resources and acting as a modulation factor against change, the effectiveness of internal processes is improved. Knowledge is important because it highlights the limitation of the cost coordination, improves internal control, increases the productivity of internal methods, and reduces both the costs of functions and of data handling. In addition, the adoption of IT helps organizations improve their relationship with customers because they have the opportunity to learn more about their demands and supports companies to reduce uncertainty, because it enables them to pay attention to rapidly changing consumer needs while reducing response times. Finally, it enables organizations to develop innovative products that meet the demands of the customers and provide more effective services while offering their existing products. This fact increases customer satisfaction, which in effect leads to improved firm performance [21].

3 Methodology

3.1 Data Collection

A field survey was used for the IS executives. A five-point Likert-scale ordinal satisfaction scale was used to evaluate business performance. The instrument was based on the existing literature that examined business performance [9, 18, 19, 24]. These items were used in order to evaluate the level of IS executives' satisfaction with IS performance. Figure 1 presents the criteria used based on the existing literature to evaluate IS executives' satisfaction with IS performance.

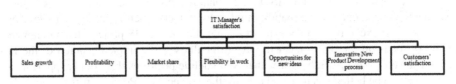

Fig. 1. IT managers' satisfaction criteria.

Four managers participated in a pilot survey to provide feedback regarding the content, of the questionnaire. The survey sample consisted of IT managers in Greek SMEs that are included in the Icap list [27–29]. The survey sample was chosen from the SMEs who provided contact information. The questionnaire was assigned to 1246 IT executives and 294 responses received.

3.2 The MUSA Method

The MUSA method was implemented to evaluate IS managers' satisfaction. MUSA calculates the satisfaction indicators of each criterion and the weights that IS executives evaluate for each criterion. Furthermore, MUSA was implemented because it develops the action and improvement diagrams that are significant for IT executives to be knowledgeable about the weak and strong dimensions of satisfaction. These diagrams help executives understand the actions that they have to do in order to improve firm performance [12, 13].

MUSA has several advantages. First, data represents the satisfaction of IS managers and can be readily acquired through a questionnaire. Second, results are not only presented at a descriptive analysis of IS managers' satisfaction as the method's outcomes. Moreover, findings support the assessment of an integrated benchmarking system. Third, the outcomes do not expect significant assumptions regarding IS managers' satisfaction or IS managers' behavior in general [12, 13]. More details about the method can be found in [13].

4 Results

One of the most significant outcomes of MUSA is the calculation of weights of the criteria. The criteria weights present the relative importance based on a set of criteria or subcriteria that IT managers assign to the satisfaction dimensions. The most important criteria for IT managers' satisfaction are the flexibility in work (weight = 17.143) and customers' satisfaction (weight = 15.676). On the other hand, the following criteria present lower levels of importance; market share (weight = 11. 524) and sales growth (weight = 12.229).

Another outcome of MUSA is the calculation of the average satisfaction indicators. These indicators are ranged between [0, 1] and represent the extent of customer global or criteria satisfaction. These indicators can be used to determine the firm's significant average performance indicators (globally or by criteria). High levels of satisfaction are noticed in criteria such as flexibility in work and customers' satisfaction. Nevertheless, lower levels of satisfaction are noticed in criteria such as market share and profitability.

Combing these outcomes we can identify the strong and weak dimensions of firm performance, highlighting which satisfaction dimensions should be improved (Fig. 2). Criteria such as opportunities for new ideas and innovative new product development are defined by high performance and importance. When IT executives implement the IS strategic planning process, they develop new ideas and innovative products that enhance company's performance. These dimensions contribute to IT managers' satisfaction since they are distinguished by high performance and importance.

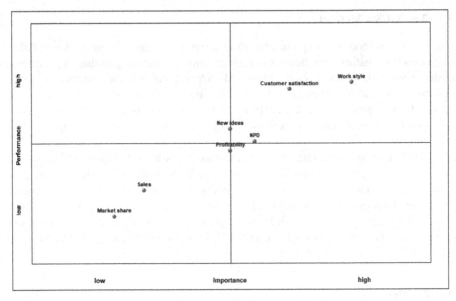

Fig. 2. Action diagram.

5 Discussion

According to the outcomes that are presented in Fig. 2 dimensions such as opportunities for new ideas and innovative new product development are described by high performance and high importance. Based on the analysis of action diagrams, these dimensions belong to the leverage opportunity quadrant. This quadrant involves dimensions that can be described as competitive advantage. The transfer resources quadrant at that point is defined by high performance and low importance. These assets might be better utilized somewhere else. Therefore, when managers implement IS planning, they develop new ideas and innovative products that increase firms' competitive advantage. As these dimensions are described by high performance and high importance, they contribute to IS executives' satisfaction. The criteria such as opportunities for new ideas and innovative new product development could be linked with organizations' interest in supporting employee-driven digital innovation and its outcomes [34].

The important dimensions of IT managers' satisfaction about firm performance are related to the flexibility of work and customers' satisfaction. These dimensions have been defined important by IS managers, despite the fact that they may be of greater importance. Especially, the COVID-19 pandemic has increased the need for flexibility of work. In such unprecedented times companies have to respond with unprecedented measures that had a similarly unprecedented impact.IS play a vital role and executives have to decide which existing digital services will be extended and new ones will be rolled out in order to increase customers' satisfaction. To preserve business continuity, IT executives had to react quickly to a rapidly increasing crisis and devise inventive solutions.

This is a crucial finding which influences the decision of IS executives regarding the acceptance of the IT strategy as well as the future actions that should be guided by the goal of maintaining a sustainable competitive edge. Market share is the most crucial dimension which does not add to IS managers' satisfaction. Sales growth is another important factor which leads to dissatisfaction. Park et al. (2017) [30] noticed that existing scholars have failed to develop an important relationship between strategic IT alignment and business performance because IS projects are not characterized by improved effectiveness, market share, and sales growth. Therefore, it is recommended for IS managers to align organizational strategy and IS strategy.

The decisions taken by IT managers do not pay attention at organizational goals, a fact which can impede both business performance and competitive advantage. Thus, a culture of innovation which can support IT projects is needed if the advantages of SMEs can be enhanced through the IS strategic planning process. Accordingly, Canhoto et al. (2021) [7] and Park et al. (2017) [30] concluded that executives' perception of the significance of the IS strategic planning process may affect the importance given to the alignment between organizational strategy and IS strategy.

The results of this paper has theoretical contribution for IS managers. The IS strategic planning process is fundamental to businesses because it supports the efficient development and implementation of IS projects. Furthermore, it helps organizations improve their market share. The execution of the IS strategic planning process is a difficult challenge. Executives should be knowledgeable about business goals and strategies because organizations have several planning aspects to encounter multiple issues. If managers understand the significance of the IS strategic planning process they will be aware of business goals as well as the significance of the IS strategic planning process to organizational strategy. Contrarily, it will be difficult to reach both and increase the company's performance. Likewise, Tan and Gallupe (2006) [33] noticed that organizations with clear strategic goals and IS projects can increase business value because managers support the investment of IS to develop qualitative products and services. Therefore, the degree of customers' satisfaction is increased and firm's profitability will be increased.

This paper has practical contribution for IS managers. The results of this article support decision makers in SMEs in order to analyze how the IT mangers evaluate the business performance and which dimensions of satisfaction must be improved. The implementation of MUSA highlighted the strong and weak points of IS executives' satisfaction. Executives can make decisions to increase the effectiveness of the IS strategic planning process. The evaluation of IS managers' perceptions help them recognize the dimensions that have to be improved and as a result increase their satisfaction regarding their business performance. Moreover, the findings of this paper help managers recognize which factors do not affect IT executives' satisfaction and pay attention at specific actions to improve the efficiency of the IS strategic planning process.

A significant factor for IS managers is the transformation of new ideas into opportunities for sustainable development for organizations that implement the IS strategic planning process. When executives recognize the significance of the IS strategic planning process, its value is improved, the challenges during the execution of the process are reduced, and IS managers are aware of organizational goals.

6 Conclusion

This article explored the satisfaction of IT managers who implement the IS strategic planning process to develop IS. Data was analyzed using MCDA to provide significant insights to executives in SMEs and help them recognize which dimensions of firm performance should be improved. The results show that IT investment assists executives to set business strategy focusing on the improvement of organizational market share, flexibility in work and generation of opportunities for new product development. In this way, what SMEs should do is identify and communicate a culture of innovation and alignment with business strategy and IT goals in order to increase flexibility in work and opportunities for new product development. IS managers should be aware knowledgeable about organizational issues because this can be a challenge for them to achieve the planning goals and improve the market share of the business [5, 32].

A limitation of this paper is the fact that the survey was done only in Greek SMEs. Future scholars can expand the results of this article and compare them with outcomes of other companies operating in several nations. To compare the differences in IS strategic planning process implementation between businesses from different industries, data can be analyzed using cluster analysis by future researchers. It would be interesting to discuss how the findings could be completed in a future study by employing fsQCA [35]. Furthermore, future researchers could implement semi-structured follow-up interviews with IT managers in several types of firms to provide some helpful insights about the implementation of the IS strategic planning process in several contexts. Specifically, semi-structured interviews, in particular, allow respondents to have an open debate about the effect of IS and organizational strategy on firm performance.

References

1. Al-Ammary, J.H., Al-Doseri, S., Al-Blushi, Z., Al-Blushi, N., Aman, M.: Strategic information systems planning in kingdom of bahrain: factors and impact of adoption. Int. J. Bus. Inf. Syst. **30**(4), 387–410 (2019)
2. Andersen, T.J.: Information technology, strategic decision making approaches and organizational performance in different industrial settings. J. Strateg. Inf. Syst. **10**(2), 101–119 (2001)
3. Arvidsson, V., Holmström, J., Lyytinen, K.: Information systems use as strategy practice: a multi-dimensional view of strategic information system implementation and use. J. Strateg. Inf. Syst. **23**(1), 45–61 (2014)
4. Balhareth, H.: The relationship between business-IT alignment and organisational performance: an empirical investigation from multilevel view. Int. J. Bus. Inf. Syst. **29**(4), 421–435 (2018)
5. Brown, I.: Strategic information systems planning: comparing espoused beliefs with practice. In: Proceedings of 18th European Conference on Information Systems (ECIS), Pretoria, South Africa (2010)
6. Brown, I.T.: Testing and extending theory in strategic information systems planning through literature analysis. Inf. Resour. Manag. J. (IRMJ) **17**(4), 20–48 (2004)
7. Canhoto, A.I., Quinton, S., Pera, R., Molinillo, S., Simkin, L.: Digital strategy aligning in SMEs: a dynamic capabilities perspective. J. Strateg. Inf. Syst. **30**(3), 1–17 (2021)

8. Chan, Y.E., Sabherwal, R., Thatcher, J.B.: Antecedents and outcomes of strategic IS alignment: an empirical investigation. IEEE Trans. Eng. Manag. **53**(1), 27–47 (2006)

9. Chatzoglou, P.D., Diamantidis, A.D., Vraimaki, E., Vranakis, S.K., Kourtidis, D.A.: Aligning IT, strategic orientation and organizational structure. Bus. Process. Manag. J. **17**(4), 663–687 (2011)

10. Drechsler, A., Weißschädel, S.: An IT strategy development framework for small and medium enterprises. IseB **16**(1), 93–124 (2017). https://doi.org/10.1007/s10257-017-0342-2

11. Gable, G.: Strategic information systems research: an archival analysis. J. Strateg. Inf. Syst. **19**(1), 3–16 (2010)

12. Grigoroudis, E., Siskos, Y.: MUSA: multicriteria satisfaction analysis. In: Customer Satisfaction Evaluation; Methods for Measuring and Implementing Service Quality. Springer International Publishing, New York (2010). https://doi.org/10.1007/978-1-4419-1640-2_4

13. Grigoroudis, E., Siskos, Y.: Preference disaggregation for measuring and analysing customer satisfaction: the MUSA method. Eur. J. Oper. Res. **143**(1), 148–170 (2002)

14. Ilmudeen, A., Bao, Y., Alharbi, I.M.: How does business-IT strategic alignment dimension impact on organizational performance measures. J. Enterp. Inf. Manag. **32**(3), 457–476 (2019)

15. Johnson, A.M., Lederer, A.L.: IS strategy and IS contribution: CEO and CIO perspectives. Inf. Syst. Manag. **30**(4), 306–318 (2013)

16. Kappelman, L., Johnson, V., Torres, R., Maurer, C., McLean, E.: A study of information systems issues, practices, and leadership in Europe. Eur. J. Inf. Syst. **28**(1), 26–42 (2019)

17. Kamariotou, M., Kitsios, F.: Critical factors of strategic information systems planning phases in SMEs. In: Themistocleous, M., Rupino da Cunha, P. (eds.) EMCIS 2018. LNBIP, vol. 341, pp. 503–517. Springer, Cham (2019). https://doi.org/10.1007/978-3-030-11395-7_39

18. Kitsios, F., Grigoroudis, E.: Evaluating service innovation and business performance in tourism: a multicriteria decision analysis approach. Manag. Decis. **58**(11), 2429–2453 (2020)

19. Kitsios, F., Grigoroudis, E., Giannikopoulos, K., Doumpos, M., Zopounidis, C.: Strategic decision making using multicriteria analysis: new service development in Greek hotels. Int. J. Data Anal. Tech. Strat. **7**(2), 187–202 (2015)

20. Kitsios, F., Kamariotou, M.: Information systems strategy and strategy-as-practice: planning evaluation in SMEs. In: Proceedings of Americas Conference on Information Systems (AMCIS), Cancun, Mexico (2019)

21. Kitsios, F., Kamariotou, M.: Strategizing information systems: an empirical analysis of IT alignment and success in SMEs. Computers **8**(4), 1–14 (2019)

22. Kitsios, F., Kamariotou, M.: Decision support systems and strategic information systems planning for strategy implementation. In: Kavoura, A., Sakas, D.P., Tomaras, P. (eds.) Strategic Innovative Marketing. SPBE, pp. 327–332. Springer, Cham (2017). https://doi.org/10.1007/978-3-319-56288-9_43

23. Lee, J.J.Y., Randall, T., Hu, P.J.H., Wu, A.: Examining complementary effects of IT investment on firm profitability: are complementarities the missing link? Inf. Syst. Manag. **31**(4), 340–352 (2014)

24. Luftman, J., Lyytinen, K., Zvi, T.B.: Enhancing the measurement of information technology (IT) business alignment and its influence on company performance. J. Inf. Technol. **32**(1), 26–46 (2017)

25. McCardle, J.G., Rousseau, M.B., Krumwiede, D.: The effects of strategic alignment and competitive priorities on operational performance: the role of cultural context. Oper. Manag. Res. **12**(1–2), 4–18 (2019). https://doi.org/10.1007/s12063-019-00139-7

26. Merali, Y., Papadopoulos, T., Nadkarni, T.: Information systems strategy: past, present, future? J. Strateg. Inf. Syst. **21**(2), 125–153 (2012)

27. Mirchandani, D.A., Lederer, A.L.: "Less is more:" information systems planning in an uncertain environment. Inf. Syst. Manag. **29**(1), 13–25 (2012)

28. Newkirk, H.E., Lederer, A.L., Srinivasan, C.: Strategic information systems planning: too little or too much? J. Strateg. Inf. Syst. **12**(3), 201–228 (2003)
29. Newkirk, H.E., Lederer, A.L.: The effectiveness of strategic information systems planning under environmental uncertainty. Inf. Manag. **43**(4), 481–501 (2006)
30. Park, J., Lee, J.N., Lee, O.K.D., Koo, Y.: Alignment between internal and external IT governance and its effects on distinctive firm performance: an extended resource-based view. IEEE Trans. Eng. Manag. **64**(3), 351–364 (2017)
31. Peppard, J., Ward, J.: Beyond strategic information systems: towards an IS capability. J. Strateg. Inf. Syst. **13**(2), 167–194 (2004)
32. Piccoli, G., Ives, B.: IT-dependent strategic initiatives and sustained competitive advantage: a review and synthesis of the literature. MIS Q. **29**, 747–776 (2005)
33. Tan, F.B., Gallupe, R.B.: Aligning business and information systems thinking: a cognitive approach. IEEE Trans. Eng. Manag. **53**(2), 223–237 (2006)
34. Opland, L.E., Pappas, I.O., Engesmo, J., Jaccheri, L.: Employee-driven digital innovation: a systematic review and a research agenda. J. Bus. Res. **143**, 255–271 (2022)
35. Pappas, I.O., Woodside, A.G.: Fuzzy-set qualitative comparative analysis (fsQCA): guidelines for research practice in information systems and marketing. Int. J. Inf. Manag. **58**, 102310 (2021)

Electronic Services

The Role of Quality, Trust, and Empowerment in Explaining Satisfaction and Use of Chatbots in e-government

Ingvild Tisland[1]([✉]), Marthe Løvsland Sodefjed[1], Polyxeni Vassilakopoulou[1] [iD], and Ilias O. Pappas[1,2] [iD]

[1] Department of Information Systems, University of Agder, Universitetsveien 25, 4630 Kristiansand, Norway
`{ingvit18,martlo17}@student.uia.no`, `{polyxenv, ilias.pappas}@uia.no`
[2] Department of Computer Science, Norwegian University of Science and Technology, Sem Sælandsvei 9, 7491 Trondheim, Norway

Abstract. With technology advancements within the field of AI there has been an increased interest in chatbots used for e-government services. Despite this increased interest, there is a knowledge gap in terms of what contributes to the satisfaction with e-government chatbots. To fill this gap, this study investigates factors affecting the satisfaction and use of chatbots from a citizen perspective. To this end, this study builds on the Information Systems success model, by examining the role of key critical antecedents (i.e., information quality, system quality, service quality) and extends it by considering the role citizens' trusting beliefs and perceived empowerment when using e-government chatbots, in order to explain citizens' satisfaction and intention to use chatbots. A model that captures the multidimensional and interdependent nature of chatbot success is suggested and tested on data collected from 105 users of e-government chatbots in Norway. The findings indicate that information and service quality positively influence the degree of trusting beliefs by the citizens while all three quality dimensions positively influence empowerment perceived by citizens. The degree of trusting beliefs and empowerment positively affect satisfaction, while satisfaction positively affects intention to use. This study identifies the impact of quality dimensions on trusting beliefs and empowerment and is the first study to investigate both empowerment and trusting beliefs in the context of e-government chatbots.

Keywords: Empowerment · Trust · E-government · Chatbot · IS Success Model

1 Introduction

The rapid evolution of information technology contributes to improving the delivery of services for both private and public organizations worldwide [1]. In Norway, novel e-government services are increasingly changing the way citizens interact with the government. Venkatesh et al. [1] define e-government as "the use of the Internet by government

S. Papagiannidis et al. (Eds.): I3E 2022, LNCS 13454, pp. 279–291, 2022.
https://doi.org/10.1007/978-3-031-15342-6_22

agencies to provide informational and transactional services to citizens" (p. 87). One of the latest additions to e-government services is artificial intelligence (AI) technology. AI technology enables performing tasks that traditionally were dependent on human intelligence [2]. We use the definition by Thierer et al. [2] to define AI as: "the exhibition of intelligence by a machine. An AI system can undertake high-level operations; AI can perform near, at, or beyond the abilities of a human." (p. 8). The benefits of introducing AI into e-governmental services are many and include increasing efficiency and cost savings and reducing administrative burdens and waiting time [3]. There are several use cases for AI in public organizations, and within these, there is an increasing trend related to virtual agents, also known as conversational agents or chatbots [4]. Chatbots are virtual service robots that are used for human-computer interactions in conversational mode [5]. Several Norwegian public organizations including the Tax Authorities, the Welfare Services Organization and several municipalities have implemented such service robots, hereafter chatbots, for service delivery.

Chatbots are an important emerging technology with potential to empower citizens [6]. The use of chatbots in e-government is not only viewed as a way of achieving efficiency improvements but also as a way of improving information access and enhancing citizens´ control over servicing options (for instance by offering extended service hours). Citizen empowerment is strongly emphasized and is a key aspect for e-government initiatives. Citizen empowerment entails more than providing basic access to information and services; it is about transforming citizens from general users into empowered individuals through digital services [7]. UNESCO sees citizen empowerment as one of the three main objectives of e-governance, namely: to engage, enable and empower the citizen [8], while OECD sees citizen empowerment as a necessary condition for enhancing the quality of service delivery [9]. However, the empowerment of citizens in the context of e-government has not been clearly understood or systematically studied [10]. Empowerment can come out of users´ competence, self-determination and also, meaningful and impactful chatbot use [11, 12]. Interestingly, although there is a growing body of research on chatbots in the context of public service delivery [3, 4, 13], the relationship between chatbot users´ satisfaction and empowerment has not been previously investigated.

Overall, there is limited prior research about the full potential of using AI in e-governmental services and on how AI in e-governmental services affects citizens [4]. As public organizations have been investing and implementing chatbots into their e-governmental services already for some years, it is now possible to perform empirical studies exploring citizens actual experiences and perspectives. This paper suggests a comprehensive model for citizens´ satisfaction from chatbot use that brings together empowerment, quality and trust. The model is developed by extending Delone & Mclean´s IS Success Model [14, 15] which foregrounds the role of information, system and service quality by including empowerment and trust. Trust is included because prior research has shown that a key factor for achieving e-government success is building trust [16]. Specifically, Teo and colleagues [16] found that trust in e-government is positively associated with the quality and satisfaction of e-government websites [16]. Furthermore, McKnight and colleagues [17] found that users´ perceived quality of web-based services is correlated with trusting beliefs. Hence, a model that includes quality, trust and empowerment brings together key dimensions of user experience affecting satisfaction. The study provides insights that can be used by government agencies that aim to achieve higher citizen satisfaction with e-government chatbots and build stronger citizen government relationships.

The remainder of the paper is organized as follows, the background and related work is presented first, followed by hypotheses and a conceptual model. Next the methodology is presented, followed by the presentation and discussion of the results. The study concludes by elaborating on limitations and discussing implications for theory and practice.

2 Background and Related Work

2.1 Information, System, and Service Quality

The updated IS Success Model by Delone & Mclean [14] provides an integrated multidimensional view on IS success. The model suggests that information quality, system quality and service quality influence satisfaction and intention to use, which in turn influence and are influenced by net benefits. The goal of our study is to understand and explain citizens' satisfaction and their intention to use chatbots in e-government. To this end, we adopt information quality, system quality, service quality, user satisfaction, and intention to use. Information quality is the extent of how accurate, relevant, precise and complete the information provided by the system is and how it fits the users needs [5, 14]. In the context of this study, information quality relates to how well e-government chatbots provide information. System quality is the extent of how consistent, easy to use and fitting to user needs an IS is [5, 14]. In the context of this study, system quality relates to chatbots´ consistency and ease of use. Service quality is the extent of the reliability, responsiveness, assurance and empathy of an IS [5]. In the e-government chatbots context, service quality relates to how reliable, responsive, assuring and empathic chatbots are. User satisfaction is the degree of satisfaction felt by the user towards the system and how well it satisfies the user´s needs [14]. In the context of e-government chatbots, user satisfaction is how satisfied citizens are with the chatbots. Intention to use is the degree of intention a user has to use a system and has in IS research been found to be a strong predictor of actual system usage [18, 19]. In the context of our study this is about citizens' intention to use e-government chatbots.

2.2 Human Empowerment

Empowerment revolves around increasing power in social interactions [20]. Li & Gregor [10] argue that empowering citizens through e-government is important, as the more empowered the citizens, the more likely they are to value government agencies and build a healthier relationship with government. Feeling powerful comprises a range of mechanisms which humans utilize to increase their influence. Increasing a person's power leads to a greater influence in social relations - including interactions with other humans, systems and machines [20]. A successful empowerment process is described by by Cattaneo & Chapman [20] as "a personally meaningful increase in power that a person obtains through his or her own efforts" (p. 647). Four dimensions are central for a human to feel empowered: Competence, Impact, Meaning and Self-determination [11]. Kim & Gupta [12] operationalized these four dimensions into the context of work Information Systems: Competence of user, Meaning of system usage, Self-determination of user and Impact of system use [12]. We adopt the same four dimensions of empowerment into the context of citizens using e-government chatbots.

2.3 Trusting Beliefs

A key factor for achieving success with e-government websites is building trust [16]. Trust is a complex concept consisting of multiple interrelated dimensions that has been defined in multiple ways in previous literature [21]. Trusting beliefs is a dimension of trust that has been put forward as an antecedent to consumers' internet behavior in previous research [22]. Trusting beliefs is by Mcknight et al. [17] defined as "the confident truster perception that the trustee has attributes that are beneficial to the truster" (p. 337). Mcknight et al. [17] found that perceived website quality is greatly correlated with trusting beliefs and intentions [17]. In this study we introduce trusting beliefs as a potential factor affecting satisfaction with e-government chatbots.

3 Hypotheses and Conceptual Model

3.1 Quality and Empowerment

Li & Gregor [10] argue that the government agency has to increase the service delivery mechanism and improve the quality of the information or service being delivered in the context of advisory services in the public sector [10]. To test if this applies to the context of e-government chatbots, we developed the following hypotheses with quality elements based on the IS Success Model [14].

H_1 = Information quality of chatbots provided by public organizations is positively associated with the citizens' feeling of empowerment
H_2 = System quality of chatbots provided by public organizations is positively associated with the citizens' feeling of empowerment
H_3 = Service quality of chatbots provided by public organizations is positively associated with the citizens' feeling of empowerment

3.2 Quality and Trusting Beliefs

Mcknight et al. [17] found that a high-quality website builds consumers trusting beliefs that the vendor is competent, honest and benevolent [17]. To test if this applies to the context of e-government chatbots, we developed the following hypotheses on quality and trusting beliefs using quality elements based on the IS Success Model [14].

H_4 = Information quality is positively associated with Citizens' trusting beliefs in chatbots provided by public organizations
H_5 = System quality is positively associated with Citizens' trusting beliefs in chatbots provided by public organizations
H_6 = Service quality is positively associated with Citizens' trusting beliefs in chatbots provided by public organizations

3.3   Empowerment, Trust, Satisfaction and Intention to Use

In our study, we apply trust and personal satisfaction to the context of citizen empowerment of e-government chatbots. As website quality has been found to build trusting beliefs of the users [17], we test if trusting beliefs can be a potential key factor that affects the intention to use and satisfaction citizens have with e-government chatbots. Furthermore, several studies have found a correlation between satisfaction with IS and intention to use [14, 15].This indicates that satisfaction with e-government chatbots may affect the citizens' intention to use them. We have therefore formulated the following hypotheses:

H_7 = Citizens' trusting beliefs are positively associated with the satisfaction by chatbots provided by public organizations
H_8 = Citizens' empowerment is positively associated with the satisfaction by chatbots provided by public organizations
H_9 = Citizens' satisfaction is positively associated with the intention to use chatbots provided by public organizations

Figure 1 presents the comprehensive model developed. Empowerment is modeled as a second-order reflective construct with four first order sub-constructs based on the four dimensions of empowerment by Kim & Gupta [12]: user competence, impact of system use, meaning of system use, and user self-determination.

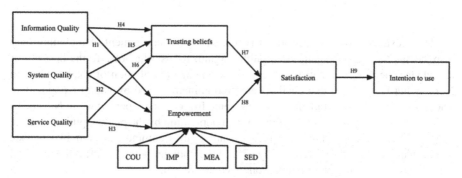

Fig. 1. Research model.

4   Method

4.1   Data Collection

To test our conceptual model and hypotheses we conducted a survey among users of chatbots provided by public organizations in Norway. Using a survey allowed us to collect information from a broad number of respondents in a standardized and quantifiable manner [8]. We constructed a questionnaire using a 7-point Likert scale. The questionnaire was distributed by sharing posts with a public link to the questionnaire through social media following a snowball sampling method. We also distributed the link via personal messages to acquaintances we saw fit and encouraged family members and friends to share it in their networks. The target respondents were adults that have used e-government chatbots in Norway. To control for respondents' experience with chatbots we asked them about their prior use of chatbots. The survey was performed in February 2022 and yielded 105 fully filled-in questionnaires by individuals that are experienced with e-government chatbots, thus comprising the sample for this study. Table 1 provides an overview of the survey respondents.

Table 1. Descriptives statistics of survey respondents

Demographic variable		Frequency	Percentage
Gender	Female	57	54.2
	Male	46	43.8
	Prefer not to say	2	1.9
Age	18–25	41	39
	26–35	38	36.1
	35–45	12	11.4
	46–55	9	8.5
	56–65	5	4.7

The prevalence of younger adults is related to the requirement of including only respondents that have actually used public organizations´ chatbots. To the best of our knowledge there are no statistics available on the age distribution of chatbot users in Norway but it is known that chatbots are predominantly used by younger population. The most recent related statistics available come from a survey performed in November 2020 on a representative sample of the French population by the public opinion institute (IFOP). This survey [23] showed that a chatbot (in a commercial or public service context) has been used at least once by 62% of the younger population (aged 35 or less) but only by 39% of the older population (aged above 35).

4.2 Measures

For the different constructs included in the research model, we leveraged previous research. An overview of all constructs and their sources is included in Table 2.

Table 2. Constructs

Construct	Description	Source
Empowerment (EMP)	"a personally meaningful increase in power that a person obtains through his or her own efforts" (p. 647)	[20]
Competence of user (COU)	"an individual's belief in his or her capability to use the system in tasks with relevant knowledge, skills and confidence" (p. 658)	[12]
Impact of system usage (IMP)	"the degree to which an individual can influence task outcomes based on the use of the system" (p. 658)	[12]
Meaning of system usage (MEA)	"the importance an individual attaches to system usage in relation to his or her own ideals or standards" (p. 658)	[12]
Self- determination (SED)	"an individual's sense of having choices (i.e., authority to make his or her own decisions) about system usage" (p. 658)	[12]
Intention to use (USE)	The degree of intention a user has to use a system	[24]
Information Quality (IQ)	The extent of how accurate, relevant, precise and complete the information provided by the IS is and how it fits the users needs	[5, 14]
System Quality (SQ)	The extent of how consistent, easy to use and responsive a IS is, and to what degree it fits the users needs	[5, 16]
Service Quality (SVQ)	The extent of the reliability, responsiveness, assurance and empathy of an IS	[5, 16]
Trusting beliefs (TRB)	The confident truster perception that the trustee—in this context, a specific e-government chatbot—has attributes that are beneficial to the truster	[22]
Satisfaction (SAT)	The degree of satisfaction felt by the user towards the system and how well it satisfies the users needs	[14, 16]

4.3 Data Analysis

Structural equation modeling (SEM) was performed using SmartPLS version 3.3.7. The analysis included the development of a measurement model and structural model and a confirmatory factor analysis was performed. The measurement theory was tested before testing the hypothesis with the structural model. Kim & Gupta [12] propose using empowerment as a second-order construct, thus empowerment was computed into a second-order latent construct by combining the latent variables from its four dimensions (COU, IMP, MEA, SED) forming the empowerment construct.

5 Findings

As a first step, we evaluated the measurement theory, performing evaluations of the reliability. This was done by assessing the indicator loadings and composite reliability, with values over 0.8 for all constructs, showing acceptable indices of internal consistency. The validity of the first-order constructs was evaluated with the average variance extracted (AVE) and the Fornell-Larcker Criterion (FLC), shown in Table 3. Establishing validity requires that average variance extracted (AVE) is greater than 0.50, that the correlation between the different variables in the confirmatory models does not exceed 0.8 points, as this suggests low discrimination, and that the square root of each factor's AVE is larger than its correlations with other factors [25]. After confirmations of the measurement model, the hypotheses were tested by assessing the path coefficients and significance in the structural model (Fig. 2).

Table 3. Discriminant validity and construct descriptive statistics.

Discriminant validity (FLC)							Construct				
	EMP	IQ	USE	SAT	SVQ	SQ	TRB		Mean	SD	CR	AVE
EMP	1.00							EMP				
IQ	0.58	**0.84**						IQ	3.54	1.39	0.87	0.70
USE	0.66	0.61	**0.92**					USE	3.43	1.48	0.94	0.84
SAT	0.76	0.68	0.70	**0.95**				SAT	3.12	1.58	0.96	0.90
SVQ	0.63	0.61	0.67	0.70	**0.84**			SVQ	3.87	1.42	0.88	0.71
SQ	0.60	0.50	0.61	0.64	0.65	**0.87**		SQ	3.76	1.59	0.90	0.76
TRB	0.69	0.70	0.70	0.85	0.79	0.64	**0.91**	TRB	3.67	1.49	0.95	0.82

Diagonal values (in bold) are the square root of the average variance extracted (AVE).
Off-diagonal elements are the correlations between constructs.

To test the hypotheses, the structural model was analyzed by assessing the path coefficients and their significance. Figure 2 presents the results of the analysis. All the three quality dimensions were found to have significant positive influence on empowerment, supporting H1, H2 and H3. The analysis shows that there is a significant positive influence of information and service quality on trusting beliefs, supporting H4 and H6. The effect of system quality on trusting beliefs was not found significant and H5 is therefore dismissed. By looking at the path coefficients, the strength of the relationships differs. Out of the three quality dimensions, service quality has the strongest influence on trusting beliefs with 0.504, while the influence the quality dimensions have on empowerment is more similar, with service quality as the strongest relationship of 0.332. There is a significant positive effect of trusting beliefs and empowerment on satisfaction, supporting H7 and H8. Lastly, the analysis also shows that satisfaction has a positive significant influence on intention to use, supporting H9.

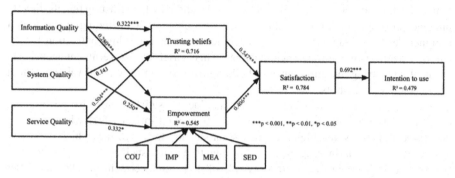

Fig. 2. Research model with hypotheses testing results.

6   Discussion and Conclusion

In this study we investigate citizens' satisfaction and intention to use chatbots in e-government. To this end, we focus on the role of information, system, and service quality in forming citizens' empowerment and trusting beliefs, which in turn may explain citizens' satisfaction and intention to use chatbots. The results of this study indicate that information and service quality have a significant effect on the citizens' trusting beliefs when using e-governmental chatbots, with service quality as the strongest influence. This indicates that citizens' builds trusting beliefs based on how citizens perceive the information and service quality of the e-government chatbots. This finding is consistent with the findings by Mcknight et al. [17] on website quality and trusting beliefs [17] and the findings of Nicolaou & Mcknight [26] on information quality and trusting beliefs in data exchanges [26]. Our study adds to their findings by adding information and service quality as significant factors affecting citizens' trusting beliefs when using e-governmental chatbots. This indicates that increased quality of e-government chatbots will help build more solid trusting beliefs to such services among citizens. This study adds to the increasing discussion on the role of chatbots in public organizations for AI/human augmentation [27, 28] and can contribute to research on AI and autonomous agents, as part of big data analytics ecosystems for successful digital transformation [29].

All the three quality dimensions had a significant influence on citizens' perceived empowerment when using e-government chatbots. The higher degree of information, system and service quality, the more citizens' feel empowered to use such chatbots. Our findings add new insights to theory by adding empowerment as a factor that is affected by the information, system and service quality of e-government chatbots. This finding is a valuable insight of the importance of prioritizing quality in e-government chatbots to empower citizens and enable citizens to use and value e-government services as Li &

Gregor [10] argues in their review. Our findings further support the that in service design we should consider the totality of interactions that going beyond digital automation [27, 30].

Previous studies have addressed the relationship of quality and multiple dimensions of trust [16]. We complement previous findings by showing how trusting beliefs directly influence citizens' satisfaction with e-government chatbots. Our findings indicate that a higher degree of satisfaction is an outcome when there are higher trusting beliefs among citizens using e-government chatbots. This is useful for government agencies in terms of addressing the importance of building trust to achieve the full value potential of e-government chatbots.

Further, we find that citizen empowerment influences satisfaction with e-government chatbots. This finding show that the more empowered citizens feel when using e-government chatbots, the higher degree of satisfaction they will feel which our study also shows will result in a higher degree of intention to use such chatbots. The findings support previous arguments on the key role of user empowerment in relation to user behavior (i.e., using the system to its full potential in an extended, integrative, and emergent way) in the IS usage context [12]. Citizen empowerment goes beyond providing basic access to information and services, towards transforming citizens from general users into empowered individuals through digital services [12]. These findings give valuable knowledge of addressing the dimensions of empowerment when developing, managing, and maintaining e-government chatbots.

To summarize, this study is one of the very first that address both empowerment and trusting beliefs in the context of e-governmental chatbots. To fill this research gap, our research model sufficiently explains how quality, trusting beliefs, empowerment, satisfaction, and intention to use relate to each other. Our findings show the importance of quality affecting citizens trusting beliefs and empowerment and how these factors influence citizen satisfaction. Future studies should investigate these factors and relationships more thoroughly and include several research methods such as observations and logs of citizens' interaction with e-governmental chatbots.

There are limitations to this study that provide significant ground for further research. Five of the constructs from the IS Success Model were adapted, excluding net benefits as the main objective of this study was to investigate satisfaction and usage rather than the success of e-government chatbots. Future studies can extend this work also investigating the overall success of e-government chatbots. Another limitation is that most of the sample analyzed in this study is within a young age group. Thus, it is expected that most of the respondents is familiar with the use of technology and can easily adapt to developments within e-governmental services and chatbots. Future studies should investigate how e-government chatbots empower or disempower the general population including more responses from the elderly. Additionally, the sample was collected with convenience sampling, thus the respondents that chose to participate might not represent the general capabilities of the population or might have had particularly negative experiences with e-governmental chatbots etc. Finally, the questionnaires were in Norwegian, with items adapted and translated from English. This may have affected how the items were interpreted and some may have been misunderstood from its original meaning by the respondents.

Appendix

Const.	Item	Load.	Mean	SD
Information quality				
In my experience information provided by such chatbots...				
IQ1	...meets my needs	0.87	2.98	1.7
IQ2	...is accurate	0.84	3.55	1.7
IQ3	...is up-to-date	0.82	4.19	1.6
Satisfaction				
SAT1	I feel that chatbots adequately meet my needs for interaction with the government	0.96	3.09	1.6
SAT2	Chatbots are effectively fulfilling my needs for interaction with the government	0.95	3.14	1.6
SAT3	Overall, I am satisfied with chatbots	0.94	3.15	1.7
System quality				
In my experience, such chatbots...				
SQ1	...are easy to use	0.93	3.95	1.9
SQ2	...are user-friendly	0.94	3.51	1.7
SQ3	...require a lot of effort to use	0.72	3.79	1.7
Service quality				
In my opinion, such chatbots...				
SVQ1	...provide dependable services	0.89	3.54	1.5
SVQ2	...give prompt service to citizens	0.85	4.50	1.7
SVQ4	...are designed with citizen's best interests at heart	0.82	3.54	1.8
Trusting beliefs				
I believe that such chatbots are...				
TRB1	...are competent and effective in providing governmental information	0.88	3.91	1.6
TRB2	...perform their role of giving governmental information very well	0.93	3.51	1.7
TRB3	...are capable and proficient governmental information providers	0.91	3.69	1.6
TRB4	In general, such chatbots are very knowledgeable about governmental services	0.91	3.70	1.6
Intention to use				
USE1	I would use chatbots for getting government information	0.92	3.94	1.8
USE2	I would use government services provided by chatbots	0.93	3.73	1.7
USE3	Interacting with the government using chatbots is something that I would do	0.93	3.67	1.7
Empowerment				

(*continued*)

(*continued*)

Const.	Item	Load.	Mean	SD
COU1	I have the skills necessary to use chatbots	0.93	6.39	1.1
COU2	I am self-assured about my capabilities of using chatbots	0.96	6.13	1.1
COU3	I am confident about my ability to use chatbots	0.97	6.18	1.1
IMP1	Based on using chatbots, I feel that I'm in control of the task I want to accomplish	0.87	4.18	1.8
IMP2	Based on using chatbots, I have significant influence over what happens in the interaction	0.90	3.73	1.7
IMP3	Based on using chatbots, I have a great deal of control over what happens in the interaction	0.92	3.70	1.7
MEA1	Using chatbots for public services is very important to me	0.93	2.86	1.7
MEA2	Using chatbots for public services is meaningful to me	0.93	3.02	1.7
MEA3	My chatbot activity are personally meaningful to me	0.90	2.48	1.6
SED1	I have significant autonomy in determining how I use the chatbot	0.93	3.99	1.6
SED2	I have considerable opportunity for independence and freedom in how I use the chatbot	0.89	3.60	1.6
SED3	I can decide on my own how to go about using the chatbot	0.88	3.82	1.8

References

1. Venkatesh, V., Thong, J., Chan, F., Hu, P.: Managing citizens' uncertainty in e-government services: the mediating and moderating roles of transparency and trust. Inf. Syst. Res. **27**, 87–111 (2016)
2. Thierer, A., Sullivan, A., Russell, R.: Artificial intelligence and public policy. Mercatus Research (2017)
3. Wirtz, B., Weyerer, J.: Artificial intelligence in the public sector. Global Encyclopedia of Public Administration, Public Policy, and Governance (2019)
4. Androutsopoulou, A., Karacapilidis, N., Loukis, E., Charalabidis, Y.: Transforming the communication between citizens and government through AI-guided chatbots. Gov. Inf. Q. **36**(2), 358–367 (2018)
5. Chen, J., Jubilado, R., Capistrano, E.P., Yen, D.: Factors affecting online tax filing – an application of the IS success model and trust theory. Comput. Hum. Behav. **43**, 251–262 (2015)
6. Følstad, A., et al.: Chatbot research and design. In: Third International Workshop, CONVERSATIONS 2019, Amsterdam, The Netherlands, 19–20 November 2019
7. Sharma, S., Kar, A.K., Gupta, M.P., Dwivedi, Y.K., Janssen, M.: Digital citizen empowerment: a systematic literature review of theories and development models. Inf. Technol. Dev. 1–28 (2022)
8. Palvia, S., Sharma, S.: E-government and E-governance: definitions/domain framework and status around the world (2022)
9. OECD. OECD Annual Report 2001 (2001)

10. Li, M., Gregor, S.: IT empowerment or exclusion? The dilemma of online government advisory services. In: ACIS 2010 Proceedings of the 21st Australasian Conference on Information Systems (2010)
11. Gsenger, R., Human, S., Neumann, G.: End-user empowerment: an interdisciplinary perspective. In: HICSS (2020)
12. Kim, H.-W., Gupta, S.: A user empowerment approach to information systems infusion. Eng. Manag. IEEE Trans. **61**, 656–668 (2014)
13. Scutella, M., Plewa, C., Reaiche, C.: Virtual agents in the public service: examining citizens' value-in-use, Public Manag. Rev. pp. 1–16 (2022)
14. Delone, W., McLean, E.: The delone and mclean model of information systems success: a ten-year update. J. Manag. Inf. Syst. **19**, 9–30 (2003)
15. Delone, W., McLean, E.: Measuring e-commerce success: applying the delone & mclean information systems success model. Int. J. Electron. Commer. **9**, 31–47 (2004)
16. Teo, T., Srivastava, S., Jiang, L.: Trust and electronic government success: an empirical study. J Manag. Inf. Syst. **25**, 99–132 (2009)
17. McKnight, D., Choudhury, V., Kacmar, C.: Developing and validating trust measures for e-commerce: an integrative typology. Inf. Syst. Res. **13**, 334–359 (2002)
18. Chau, P., Hu, P.: Information technology acceptance by individual professionals: a model comparison approach. Decis. Sci. **32**, 699–719 (2001)
19. Venkatesh, V., Morris, M., Davis, G., Davis, F.: User acceptance of information technology: toward a unified view. MIS Q. **27**, 425–478 (2003)
20. Cattaneo, L., Chapman, A.: The process of empowerment a model for use in research and practice. Am. Psychol. **65**, 646–659 (2010)
21. Gefen, D., Karahanna, E., Straub, D.: Trust and TAM in online shopping: an integrated model. MIS Q. **27**, 51–90 (2003)
22. Mcknight, D., Chervany, N.: What trust means in e-commerce customer relationships: an interdisciplinary conceptual typology. Int. J. Electron. Commer. **6**, 35–59 (2002)
23. Notoriété et image de l'Intelligence Artificielle auprès des Français et des salaries. IFOP (2020). https://www.ifop.com/wp-content/uploads/2021/01/Rapport-IFOP-pour-Impact-AI-Decembre-2020.pdf
24. Belanger, F., Carter, L.: Trust and risk in e-government adoption. J. Strateg. Inf. Syst. **17**, 165–176 (2008)
25. Fornell, C., Larcker, D.F.: Evaluating structural equation models with unobservable variables and measurement error. J. Mark. Res. **18**(1), 39–50 (1981)
26. Nicolaou, A., Mcknight, D.: Perceived information quality in data exchanges: effects on risk, trust, and intention to use. Inf. Syst. Res. **17**, 332–351 (2006)
27. Vassilakopoulou, P., Haug, A., Salvesen, L.M., Pappas, I.O.: Developing Human/AI interactions for chat-based customer services: lessons learned from the Norwegian Government. Eur. J. Inf. Syst. **3** (2022). https://doi.org/10.1080/0960085X.2022.2096490
28. Vassilakopoulou, P., Pappas, I.O.: AI/Human augmentation: a study on chatbot – human agent handovers. In: International Working Conference on Transfer and Diffusion of IT (2022)
29. Pappas, I.O., Mikalef, P., Giannakos, M.N., Krogstie, J., Lekakos, G.: Big data and business analytics ecosystems: paving the way towards digital transformation and sustainable societies. IseB **16**(3), 479–491 (2018). https://doi.org/10.1007/s10257-018-0377-z
30. Vassilakopoulou, P., Grisot, M., Aanestad, M.: Enabling electronic interactions between patients and healthcare providers: a service design perspective. Scand. J. Inf. Syst. **28**, 71–90 (2016)

The Experiential View of Regressive Discontinuance

Mohina Gandhi$^{(\boxtimes)}$ ⓘ, Arpan Kumar Kar ⓘ, and P. Vigneswara Ilavarasan ⓘ

Bharti School of Telecommunication Technology and Management, IIT, Delhi 110016, India
mohina.gandhi@gmail.com

Abstract. Social media has become an essential forum for young adults to engage with each other by exchanging informative, engaging, and entertaining content. Some mobile social media applications are consistently popular among individuals, while some get abandoned after the initial usage. The behavior of early discontinuance is formerly known as regressive discontinuance. This qualitative study explores the experiences of social media users behind the regressive discontinuance of a mobile social media application. We have utilized the grounded theory approach in this exploratory study which has led us to explain the short-term usage experience of an individual using stimulus, organism, and response theory. This qualitative study proposes the conceptual model and tentative hypotheses to be tested in future work. The findings of this study can be of great importance while creating or maintaining a mobile social media application. If not paid heed to, the criticism of such applications can eventually lead to the abrupt discontinuation of the application.

Keywords: Regressive discontinuance · Post adoption research · Generation Z

1 Introduction

The internet has become the defining trait of the current society. The same effect is visible in the shift of social interests [1]. It is especially true for Generation Z, including children born between 1993 and 2005. These children have been reared in the first truly mobile era and therefore possess a special relationship with technology. The rise of affordable internet and smartphones has strengthened this relationship [2]. Social media has become an important forum to engage with each other and exchange content [3]. However, not every mobile social media application is used by all. Many of these applications are used by consumers for a short time and get discontinued. The application marketers strategize their campaign for massive adoption. Although, the success of mobile social applications does not come from downloading the application. The number of active users defines the success of a mobile application. Today, when the application design and making it available on the play store is not strenuous. But the challenge lies in keeping the consumer active on the mobile application. Not many studies have addressed this challenge, which led us to perform an exploratory study to identify the potential reasons

S. Papagiannidis et al. (Eds.): I3E 2022, LNCS 13454, pp. 292–304, 2022.
https://doi.org/10.1007/978-3-031-15342-6_23

behind the discontinuation of a mobile social media application after initial usage among Generation Z users. The unique relationship of Generation Z with mobile social media applications might bring exciting insights that can help practitioners design practical applications. This phenomenon was introduced in IS literature by [4] as an "acceptance discontinuance anomaly." The studies have found that the expectation (dis)confirmation theory is the most suitable explanation of this behavior [5]. However, we propose that there can be many other experiential factors that the social media users might have experienced during their initial use, leading them to discontinue after the initial use of the application.

To some extent, social media solves many problems; it is also a root cause of many issues such as FOMO, self-absorption, anxiety, etc. Usage of mobile social applications is a high engagement activity for mobile users. The unique relationship of social media applications with generation Z makes understanding the cause behind their regressive discontinuance behaviour interesting. In this qualitative study, we use the grounded theory approach to acquire knowledge about the individuals' experiences of short usage and their decision to discontinue the mobile application after a short duration. We have considered TikTok and Instagram as sample cases while interviewing young adults. Both platforms are visual content-based and significantly popular mobile applications among young adults. In January 2022, TikTok had almost 1 billion users, and Instagram had approximately 1.5 billion users worldwide [6]. These platforms give easy access to the users for designing, developing, and sharing videos that can be playful, entertaining, or informative. Despite being the most popular application among young adults globally, it invites criticism from a section of youth. This exploratory study focuses on understanding the primary causes of disillusionment with these platforms and eventual discontinuation by Generation Z users after a short first-hand experience of these applications. The following research questions are the pivot point of this exploratory study:

RQ1. How does the initial experience of mobile social media applications influence intentions of discontinuation among Generation Z users?

The contribution of our study lies in exploring an underemphasized area of research in the information systems literature, that is, the regressive discontinuation behaviour of individuals. The exponential rise in mobile social media applications makes it salient to understand this action. Our study proposes a conceptual model that exhibits the significant factors that influence the regressive discontinuance behaviour of individuals. The remaining part of the paper is organized as follows: First, the theoretical background in the context of IS discontinuation, followed by the research methodology, findings, and model development section. Later, the discussion section is followed by the limitations and conclusion section, which summarizes this study, our plans for the study, its limits, and recommendations for social media practitioners.

2   Theoretical Background

2.1   IS Discontinuance

Initially, the researchers believed that the continuation and discontinuation are opposite, i.e., the presence of certain factors motivates an individual to continue using IS, and the absence of these factors will lead to discontinuation of IS [4]. This belief did not sustain for long as the prior research in other domains suggested that there could be different factors associated with the behaviour of continuation and discontinuation [7]. The termination phase starts with the intention of the user to leave the IS. These intentions can be due to social media addiction leading to guilt and self-efficacy for discontinuing a social media platform. [8] has identified that the self-realization of overuse and addiction to social media platforms can affect someone's behaviour and experiences of an individual. This self-regulation can influence an individual's intentions for discontinuation. Although a study performed by [9] has modified work on social media platform discontinuation by integrating the theory of planned behaviour with self-determination theory. This study has found that excessive use of social media platforms can influence unpleasant experiences for individuals, affecting the intentions of discontinuation usage behaviour. Various other studies have also suggested consequences of excessive use of social media platforms, such as information overload, communication overload, system feature overload, and social overload, which are the influential factors that cause mental health disorders [9, 10]. The termination phase is presumed to be complete when the user leaves the social media platform and abandons it. The above studies explain the quitting and temporary discontinuance forms of discontinuance. This discontinuance occurs after an individual has been through the exploring, adoption, and continued use phase.

2.2 Regressive Discontinuance and Expectation Confirmation Theory

In IS literature, there are five forms of discontinuance: rejection, regressive discontinuance, quitting, temporary discontinuance, and replacement [5]. The above discussion represents the exploration of quitting and temporary discontinuance in depth. However, we suggest that it is time that we make efforts to understand the phenomenon where after initial adoption, the user decides to discontinue the usage of mobile social media applications. A limited number of studies have been conducted in regressive discontinuance [5]. However, most have utilized expectation (dis)confirmation theory to explain the early discontinuation. This theory was introduced in IS from consumer behaviour literature to understand an individual's choice to continue using IS [4]. The post-adoption model of IS continuance is inspired by expectation (dis)confirmation theory and is based upon confirmation, perceived usefulness, and satisfaction. The study has shown that the confirmation of pre-adoption expectations can positively influence post-adoption satisfaction and perceived usefulness. In the post-adoption phase, the perceived usefulness and satisfaction impact the IS continuation intention. However, the high differences in confirmations and perceived usefulness negatively impact satisfaction that might turn into IS discontinuation. Examples can be a lack of user's capabilities, misunderstanding about characteristics, expectation gaps, or performance mismatch [11, 12]. Generally, new products are designed to fulfil some unmet needs of individuals. It also applies to the mobile social media applications; that is, they are being designed to meet some expectations of individuals, such as new connections, chat, multimedia support, less response time, and respective features. However, there can be bad experiences of individuals that can be experienced after the initial usage of the application, such as non-productive and repetitive content on the platform. Our study proposes that there can be other experiential factors that a mobile social media user might experience during the initial phase of usage. These factors might not have been expected before adoption and plays their role in deciding discontinuation. This study is an initial exploration of consumers' experiences that have led them to discontinue application usage after short use.

3 Research Methodology

3.1 Associated Interviews

To explore and explain the reasons behind the regressive discontinuance of a mobile social media application, a commonly used approach of grounded theory study has been adopted due to the limited availability of relevant literature [13]. The theoretical framework for the regressive discontinuation of mobile social media applications has been developed with the help of an inductive approach. TikTok and Instagram were the short video-based platforms that were taken as sample cases to explore the framework. On the one hand, these platforms were massively adopted among users, and on the other hand, discontent was also observed among users about these applications. We conducted 34 in-depth semi-structured interviews in the year 2021. The saturation in the participants' responses stopped us from further conducting the interviews. Purposive sampling was used for the selection of the sample population. We approached 133 people, out of which the interviews were conducted with those mobile social media users who have used TikTok or Instagram for a few days and discontinued it later. The respondents were between 15 to 26, i.e., young adults who are the prime users of mobile social media applications. The anonymity of participants was ensured to the adults and the parents of teenagers. The demographics of the interview respondents are shown in Table 1.

Table 1. Demographics of the interview respondents.

Gender	Women	50.0
(In percentage)	Men	50.0
Application discontinuers (In percentage)	Instagram TikTok	44.0 56.0
Age	15–18	36.7
(In percentage)	19–22	26.6
	23–26	36.7

3.2 Data Analysis

The interview questions were open-ended, which were followed by probing questions. This approach helped us to gather relevant evidence in depth. After compiling all the interviews, each of us skimmed through interview scripts and came up with broad themes visible in the interviews. Two researchers were given the emergent themes and asked to code all the interviews separately to control the effect of forceful fitting of data. After the successful coding of the interviews, the coding was cross-checked by another researcher for validation [14]. In tandem, the emerged constructs are introduced to the literature-based constructs. Each construct and the relevant user response are indicated in the following section. With an increase in their scope as per the collected data, this study's constructs have emerged and are presented in Table 2.

4   Findings and Model Development

The following section summarize the findings by discussing the constructs identified through the grounded theory approach.

4.1   Dissatisfaction

Individuals might have sole motives for adopting social media applications such as monetary benefits, fame, knowledge gathering about recent trends/ events and broadcasting of their opinions to the mass, etcetera. The expectation confirmation theory can be applied here to understand user satisfaction after adopting a social media platform. While using the platform, a user experiences the platform's performance and compares it with his expectations. If the expectations are higher than the perceived performance of the platform, then the disconfirmation is negative, decreasing post-adoption satisfaction. The dissatisfaction with the platform increases discontinuation intentions [4, 15]. Our study found that after initial usage of social media applications, users might experience dissatisfaction due to unmet expectations. Such experiences have also led the users to decide on early discontinuation.

Indicative Code: "I am a singer. I joined Tik-Tok few months ago for getting popular and earn some money by performing. It did not work for me due to which I lost my interest in Tik-Tok and uninstalled it".

> "I didn't find IG as informational application, there was no knowledgeable discussions happening over platform rather just complementing each other on their personal photos or videos… not my type."

4.2   System Concerns

The User Interface of each social media application has some unique features and flow experiences that enable the customer to use it seamlessly [16, 17]. In this manuscript, the concerns related to system features refer to the complexities and shortcomings of the platform that cause difficulty in use, such as prolonged process, complex features, lack of privacy and security controls, etc. A user can experience these difficulties after the initial use of the application. The interviewees have mentioned their experiences related to the friendly interface design and the difficulty in finding simple buttons due to the background design of the application. Users also said that the availability of too many features was creating distractions. They also expect the use of complex algorithms at the backend, giving them greater control over the content as per their interests.

Indicative Code: "The availability of so many options for filters, sounds, and other effects increased the time and efforts that were required to create a simple video. It irritates me a lot."

"The photo editing was a tedious task. It took 15–20 min for editing and later all the changes just vanished. I faced lots of glitches and crashes in photo editing."

4.3 Information Concerns

In general, the individual opens a social media application to get distracted from their day-to-day life and know the exciting stuff. That is, the users might feel excited about the information provided by the platform. It can happen if the content available on the platform is innovative, original, entertaining, or knowledgeable for users [18]. Issues like content quality, content adequacy, information of interest, copyright issues, overload of information, etc., were found during the interviews. In this manuscript, we have grouped them as Information concerns. We observed that these issues potentially created feelings of disinterest, boredom, confusion, and embarrassment among users. The users mentioned age-inappropriate posts, fake posts or comments by bots, and no clarity on copyrights. Users prominently discussed the issues of irresponsibility and incomplete information by the platform. Another example was viral posts of influencers who market any product for monetary benefits without paying attention to the quality standards. Although social media platforms have content that users create, the discussed concerns were potentially creating trust issues among users for the platform and its quality [19, 20].

Indicative Code: "Most of the content on IG is cringe-worthy, over dramatized, and unreal".

"The content on Tik-Tok gets vulgar and unpleasant sometimes. It is not meant for people of different age and of different interest"

4.4 Social Network Concerns

Social media is adopted by individuals to be in touch with their friends and families, to form virtual interest groups, and for many more social needs. The formation of a strong network was the key reason behind the popularity of social media applications. However, we observed in interviews that this network could also create feelings of discomfort in self-expression for individuals. Studies have also found that the users might have depicted different personalities on social media platforms [21]. The observation during interviews was that using these entertainment-based social media applications like TikTok, and Instagram might have been inducing the experiences of social anxiety, comparison, or body image concerns. The realization of these symptoms in the initial phase motivated the individuals to discontinue the usage of these applications. Relevant studies have shown the mental health concerns raised among individuals due to these applications [9, 10, 22].

Indicative Code: "I was focusing on my career and felt that posting content on TikTok might affect my impression on the hiring firms. People were quite judgy about using TikTok."

"I was comparing myself with my friends' selfies and felt bad about my body weight and shape. I was using different filters to hide my real body shape."

4.5 Communication Concerns

Communication on social media includes creating, sharing, and reading posts, commenting on posts, forwarding posts to others, sending, and receiving messages in personal chats, etc. These features encourage users to post content frequently and keep them indulged in the social media application. However, we found that some female users received inappropriate messages from unknown people, which bittered their experience with social media applications. The unconfined rules and regulations on these platforms have been observed severely affect the communication quality on these social media applications. Cyberbullying is a commonly discussed issue related to social media usage [23]. On the other hand, users also discussed how the frequent notifications as an active communication thread between the platform and the user had affected their experience using these applications. We also learned from the interviews that the users of these mobile social media applications have expectations from each other to like/ comment on their content. The frequent occurrence of these incidents created feelings of fatigue and invasion. It increases the intention to discontinue the use of social media. Providing features like the customized control on notifications can help a user not to get burdened because of communication concerns.

Indicative Code: "As females, we are prone to receiving inappropriate messages on the platform. It created undesired situation and made me angry".

"I was communicating over Instagram quite often. It was like I am supposed to respond to all the posts which was consuming lot of my time and energy. Sometimes, I felt like others' posts about bad experiences was reflecting stress in my life too. Whole day I am thinking how he will overcome his breakup and all"

4.6 Individual Specific Concerns

The individual users might have different traits that differentiate them from one another. Such as skills, demographics, self-efficacy, innovativeness, and many more [24]. It was observed from the interviews that individuals expressed feelings of guilt for excessive usage or unproductive usage of these social media applications. The hedonic use of social media applications is known to all, but wrong practices can have consequences for using these applications [8]. Some social media users with different goals expressed that their usage of these applications created terrible feelings about themselves. To overcome such a tug of war from within, they discontinued using this application after a while. The fear of missing out is also a phenomenon that has been observed among social media users. Our participants also expressed that they frequently accessed the application and were immersed in the content. However, the different intrinsic or extrinsic motivations graciously helped them stop the bad behaviour and abruptly discontinued the usage of the application.

Indicative Code: "I installed TikTok for a few days. I used to watch lot of videos on TikTok, I couldn't resist myself. I wasted lot of time there which affected my daily life. One day, I decided that before it ruins my personal life and health further, I should uninstall it from my phone."

> "I felt like an urge to open Instagram again and again, check if someone has posted something new. I didn't want to miss any post. I was checking my phone after every 4–5 min."

4.7 Emotions

The SOR theory suggests that external factors affect the feelings of individuals, that is, organisms. Our context is a cognitive assessment state of mobile social media use based on their individual experiences. It acts as a medium to understand the resulting response, that is, the regressive discontinuance behaviour of individuals. In literature, the consumption emotion is about the experiential response of individuals while using the product/ mobile social media application. The perceived enjoyment is an essential emotional response discussed in information systems literature for continued usage intentions [25]. The study suggests that individuals repeat their actions based on their emotional experiences. These experiences can include joy, love, excitement, fear, hate, anxiety, and many more [26]. In our study, participants reflected that their emotional response was not good when using these mobile social media applications. This emotional response acted as a motivation to decide on early discontinuation.

Indictive Code: In the above-mentioned interview statements, it can be observed that users have mentioned the experience of "boredom, fatigue, stress, guilt, disinterest, and unpleasant" while using these mobile social media applications.

4.8 Regressive Discontinuation

A mobile social media application user might decide to discontinue the usage of these applications after a short period, formally known as regressive discontinuation [5]. The limited exploration of this behaviour of discontinuation has motivated us to investigate it further [27]. In our study, we utilized the grounded theory approach to explore the potential factors that can be the reason behind this discontinuation behaviour. The iterative process followed in our research has helped us compare and analyze the data appropriately. The users shared their experiences and the feelings that they experienced while using these applications. The grounded approach has helped us explore the relevant factors and relationships that influence the decision of regressive discontinuance. Still, none of these can be said to be dominant over others due to the limitation of this approach. The proposed model for discontinuation behaviour of individuals toward mobile social media applications is shown in Fig. 1.

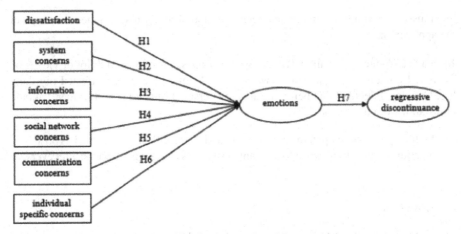

Fig. 1. Proposed model

5 Discussion

5.1 Theoretical Implications

The aim of this exploratory study is to answer how the initial experience of mobile social media applications influences an individual's intentions of discontinuation? The limited exploration of this question has encouraged us to utilize the grounded theory approach, a qualitative exploratory research methodology. The appropriate use of this approach brought rigor to this methodology [13]. It also helped us answer this research question by identifying the triggering factors (dissatisfaction, system concerns, information concerns, social network concerns, communication concerns, and individual-specific concerns). The earlier studies on regressive discontinuance have found that expectation disconfirmation is the reason behind the discontinuation behaviour of individuals, which has also been found as one of the influential factors for such behaviour among users [5]. This study has also indicated that system concerns can be a potential reason for discontinuation. The participant mentioned the experience of unpleasant feelings due to the glitches in mobile social media applications. The earlier studies on website designing have also identified that these features can influence the users' emotions [28]. We have also found that information, communication, and social concerns can create unpleasant user experiences, which is partially supported by the earlier studies conducted to understand the quitting and temporary discontinuance [9, 10]. Although, our findings also suggest that individual-specific concerns can be potential triggering factors for individuals. Everyone has different cognitive abilities or biases that can affect their decision-making, and the theory of planned behaviour explains such behavioural actions of individuals [26]. Using grounded theory has encouraged us to reach the proposed model inductively. However, we can observe partial support for our findings is present in the literature. Table 2. depicts the resulting tentative hypotheses yet to be tested statistically. The theoretical contribution of our study lies in developing an experiential model to explain the regressive discontinuation behaviour of individuals. The underlying constructs have been discussed in this study, and the proposed relationship between them.

Table 2. Broad categories, descriptions, labels, and tentative hypotheses

Broad categories	Description	Labels	Resulting tentative hypotheses
Dissatisfaction	Expression of dis-confirmation and unsatisfaction	Dissatisfaction	H1: The higher dissatisfaction of an individual from a mobile social media application positively influences the experience of negative emotions
Platform specific technical issues	Flow experience, privacy and security features, unwanted changes to the platform, no unique features	System Concerns	H2: The higher system concerns of an individual from a mobile social media application positively influence the experience of negative emotions
Information related issues	Information Overloading, information quality, content related issues (type, authenticity, copyrights)	Information Concerns	H3: The higher information concerns of an individual from a mobile social media application positively influence the experience of negative emotions
Social network and community	Social Overloading, Social dynamics related	Social Network Concerns	H4: The higher social network concerns of an individual from a mobile social media application positively influence the experience of negative emotions
Communication on platform	Communication Overloading, Self-disclosure	Communication Concerns	H5: The higher communication concerns of an individual from a mobile social media application positively influence the experience of negative emotions

(continued)

Table 2. (*continued*)

Broad categories	Description	Labels	Resulting tentative hypotheses
Individual's differences	Perceived un-usefulness, Culture, Environmental, Life cycle related, Addiction of the platform, Guilt, Regret	Individual Specific Concerns	H6: The higher individual specific concerns of an individual from a mobile social media application positively influence the experience of negative emotions
Experience and feelings	Expression of negative emotions like boredom, tiredness, Anger, Frustration, Irritation	Emotions	H7: The increase in negative emotions experienced by an individual from a mobile social media application positively influence the regressive discontinuance

5.2 Practical Implications

This study has been designed to capture the experiential details of Generation Z users, especially for their regressive discontinuance behaviour. The popularity of Instagram and TikTok is evident among teenagers and young adults. Our study has proposed a conceptual model to extend the current knowledge present in IS literature to take a leap from expectations to users' experiences. A recent study indicates a significant difference in the usage of social media platforms by generation Z than others which also makes our study relevant for current times [29]. The application developers can do multiple practices to overcome the identified issues in using these mobile social media applications. Taking control of individual inputs can also be one of the initiatives to make the users comfortable for more extended usage of the applications. With the current advancements in artificial intelligence and machine learning algorithms, it might be possible to overcome the identified factors. For example, disclosure of availability, default privacy settings, personalized content, and similar steps might prevent regressive discontinuance behaviour of users.

6   Conclusion, Limitations, and Future Research

In conclusion, this study proposes a conceptual model of regressive discontinuance based upon the experiential consumption of mobile social media applications. This study is one of the initial attempts to address this issue. The utilization of grounded theory has supported this exploratory study and given us direction to propose the tentative hypotheses. This study is a work in progress. We will conduct a survey study soon to validate the results of this study while also suggesting the comparative difference between the effects of the triggering factors over the discontinuance behaviour. This research provides academics and the business community a wealth of knowledge about the fall of any mobile social media application by looking at the regressive discontinuance behaviour of individuals. The valuation of any social media platform relies on its active number of subscribers. Our findings might help the business pioneered social media platforms to take preventive measures about the identified significant concerns of individuals and, therefore, retain its active user base for as long as possible. A few recommendations for practitioners are to keep in mind while introducing mobile social media applications. The use of artificial intelligence and machine learning algorithm to curate customized content for each user, special measures for information security and privacy, dedicated efforts towards building a positive and encouraging environment on the social media platform, and features to control notifications and the reaction of others on an individual's content can be some valuable practices. The study also has a few limitations that can also be overcome in the future, such as a comparative study between the generations of social media users to study the similarities and differences between their trigger factors for regressive discontinuance. Another limitation lies in taking participants from only two mobile social media platforms, which can be further extended to a broader range of social media platforms.

References

1. Tamilmani, K., Rana, N.P., Alryalat, M.A.A., Al-Khowaiter, W.A.A., Dwivedi, Y.K.: Social media research in the context of emerging markets: an analysis of extant literature from information systems perspective. J. Adv. Manag. Res. **15**(2), 115–129 (2018)
2. Salehan, M., Negahban, A.: Social networking on smartphones: When mobile phones become addictive. Comput. Hum. Behav. **29**(6), 2632–2639 (2013)
3. Sarin, P., Kar, A.K., Ilavarasan, V.P.: Exploring engagement among mobile app developers – Insights from mining big data in user generated content. J. Adv. Manag. Res. **18**(4), 585–608 (2021)
4. Bhattacherjee, A.: Understanding information systems continuance: an expectation-confirmation model. MIS Q. Manag. Inf. Syst. **25**(3), 351–370 (2001)
5. Soliman, W., Rinta-Kahila, T.: Toward a refined conceptualization of IS discontinuance: reflection on the past and a way forward. Inf. Manag. **57**(2), 103167 (2020)
6. Statista research department. Global social networks ranked by number of users 2022. https://www.statista.com/statistics/272014/global-social-networks-ranked-by-number-of-users/. Accessed 12 May 2022
7. Pollard, C.: Exploring continued and discontinued use of IT: a case study of OptionFinder, a group support system. Explor. Contin. Discontin. USE IT Gr. Decis. Negot. **12**, 171–193 (2003)
8. Turel, O.: Quitting the use of a habituated hedonic information system: a theoretical model and empirical examination of Facebook users. Eur. J. Inf. Syst. **24**(4), 431–446 (2015)
9. Luqman, A., Cao, X., Ali, A., Masood, A., Yu, L.: Empirical investigation of Facebook discontinues usage intentions based on SOR paradigm. Comput. Hum. Behav. **70**, 544–555 (2017)
10. Maier, C., Laumer, S., Eckhardt, A., Weitzel, T.: Giving too much social support: Social overload on social networking sites. Eur. J. Inf. Syst. **24**, 447–464 (2015)

11. De Graaf, M., Ben Allouch, S., Van Dijk, J.: Why do they refuse to use my robot? Reasons for non-use derived from a long-term home study. In: ACM/IEEE International Conference on Human-Robot Interaction, vol. F1271, pp. 224–233 (2017)

12. Aggarwal, R., Kryscynski, D., Midha, V., Singh, H.: Early to adopt and early to discontinue: the impact of self-perceived and actual IT knowledge on technology use behaviors of end users, **26**(1), 127–144 (2015)

13. Corbin, J., Strauss, A.: Basics of Qualitative Research, 3rd (edn.) Sage publications (2012)

14. Miles, M.B, Huberman, A.M.: Qualitative Data Analysis: A Methods Sourcebook. Sage publications (1994)

15. Kar, A.K.: What affects usage satisfaction in mobile payments? modelling user generated content to develop the "digital service usage satisfaction model." Inf. Syst. Front. **23**(5), 1341–1361 (2020). https://doi.org/10.1007/s10796-020-10045-0

16. Chhonker, M.S., Verma, D., Kar, A.K., Grover, P.: M-commerce technology adoption: thematic and citation analysis of scholarly research during (2008–2017). Bottom Line **31**(3–4), 208–233 (2018)

17. Ross, G.M.: I use a COVID-19 contact-tracing app. Do you? Regulatory focus and the intention to engage with contact-tracing technology. Int. J. Inf. Manag. Data Insights **1**(2), 100045 (2021)

18. Gkikas, D.C., Tzafilkou, K., Theodoridis, P.K., Garmpis, A., Gkikas, M.C.: How do text characteristics impact user engagement in social media posts: modeling content readability, length, and hashtags number in Facebook. Int. J. Inf. Manag. Data Insights **2**(1), 100067 (2022)

19. Kitsios, F., Mitsopoulou, E., Moustaka, E., Kamariotou, M.: User-generated content behavior and digital tourism services: a SEM-neural network model for information trust in social networking sites. Int. J. Inf. Manag. Data Insights **2**(1), 100056 (2022)

20. Jadil, Y., Rana, N.P., Dwivedi, Y.K.: Understanding the drivers of online trust and intention to buy on a website: an emerging market perspective. Int. J. Inf. Manag. Data Insights **2**(1), 100065 (2022)

21. Devito, M.A., Birnholtz, J., Hancock, J.T.: Platforms, people, and perception: using affordances to understand self-presentation on social media. ACM Conf. Comput. Support Coop Work Soc. Comput. (2017)

22. Koch, J., Plattfaut, R., Kregel, I.: Looking for talent in times of crisis – the impact of the Covid-19 pandemic on public sector job openings. Int. J. Inf. Manag. Data Insights **1**(2), 100014 (2021)

23. Van Hee, C., Jacobs, G., Emmery, C., et al.: Automatic detection of cyberbullying in social media text. PLoS ONE **13**(10), e0203794 (2018)

24. Agarwal, N., Chauhan, S., Kar, A.K., Goyal, S.: Role of human behaviour attributes in mobile crowd sensing: a systematic literature review. Digit Policy, Regul Gov. **19**(2), 56–73 (2017)

25. Thong, J.Y.L., Hong, S.J., Tam, K.Y.: The effects of post-adoption beliefs on the expectation-confirmation model for information technology continuance. Int. J. Hum. Comput. Stud. **64**(9), 799–810 (2006)

26. Holbrook, M.B., Hirschman, E.C.: The experiential aspects of consumption: consumer fantasies, feelings, and fun. J. Consum. Res. **9**(2), 132 (1982)

27. Glaser, B.G.: The Basics of Qualitative Research: Emergence vs Forcing. Sociology Press, Mill Valley (1992)

28. Tuch, A.N., Bargas-Avila, J.A., Opwis, K., Wilhelm, F.H.: Visual complexity of websites: effects on users' experience, physiology, performance, and memory. Int. J. Hum. Comput. Stud. **67**(9), 703–715 (2009)

29. Lu, J.D. (Evelyn), Lin, J.S. (Elaine).: Exploring uses and gratifications and psychological outcomes of engagement with Instagram stories. Comput. Hum. Behav. Rep. **6**, 100198 (2022)

Acceptance of Common Service Centers versus Self-service e-Government Portal: An Uncertainty Reduction Perspective

Sujeet Kumar Sharma[✉] and Jang Bahadur Singh

Information Systems and Analytics Area, Indian Institute of Management Tiruchirappalli, Sooriyur, India
{sujeet,jbs}@iimtrichy.ac.in

1 Introduction

Developments in the information and communication technologies (ICT) in the past two decades have enabled organizations to deliver services with greater transparency and lower cost. In the government sector, ICT tools are being employed to deliver public services to citizens (Dwivedi, Weerakkody and Janssen 2012). In fact, there is a clear shift towards electronic mode of public service delivery. A number of developed and developing countries are allocating significant resources to e-government services to ensure the effective and time-bound public service delivery (UNPAN 2014; Nishant, Srivastava and Teo 2019). Many researchers (Evans and Yen 2006; Shareef, Archer, Kumar and Kumar 2010; Venkatesh, Thong, Chan and Hu 2016; Kumar, Sachan and Mukharjee 2017; Nishant, Srivastava and Teo 2019) have attempted to define *e-government* in multiple ways but have converged at a unique and generic objective- efficient delivery of government services using ICT tools to citizens. E-government has become a two-way channel where government communicates directly with citizens and vice-versa.

Despite a large number of potential benefits like quick communication, 24×7 availability of government information, reduction in corruption, low level of utilization of e-government services is still a challenge. The problem of under-utilization of e-government resources hinders achieving the full potential of e-government in terms of efficiency and saving of public money (Venkatesh et al. 2016). Some of the possible reasons for under-utilizations are lack of information technology infrastructure and low level of digital literacy in developing countries (Dwivedi et al. 2016). As per the UN e-Government survey 2016, the Internet access to population in developed countries is 82% whereas this figure is just 35% in developing countries (United Nations 2016).

In such scenario, citizens cannot be dependent only on websites for accessing e-government services and they need an alternate channel to access public services. In many countries, governments are providing public access outlets where an intermediary provides necessary support to citizens to complete e-governance transactions (Sharma and Mishra 2017). This may not be the most efficient solution to public service delivery as financial sustainability of such outlets is unclear (reference). There is a need to understand

© IFIP International Federation for Information Processing 2022
Published by Springer Nature Switzerland AG 2022
S. Papagiannidis et al. (Eds.): I3E 2022, LNCS 13454, pp. 305–314, 2022.
https://doi.org/10.1007/978-3-031-15342-6_24

the citizen's usage of self-service portals vis a vis intermediated use of e-governance and develop a strategy to improve the usage of self-service portal by the citizens.

Governments in developing countries have been investing heavily on developing digital infrastructure in particular on Internet. Though the usage of Internet is increasing for social media and other entertainment purposes. As per Statista in Jan 2020, there were 687 million Internet active users in India whereas this figure was just 239 million in 2014. These figure are indicators of the heavy investment by the private industry in the digital infrastructure and a sharp focus of State and Union Governments on building these infrastructures. In case of Tamil Nadu, a developed state in India where this study is being conducted, about 83% citizens[1] are using intermediary mediated common service centers in comparison to 17% citizen using self-service e-government portals for availing e-public service delivery. Given the fact that the state government's ambitious program of providing laptops to 12th grade students has been a success (approximately 6 Million laptops given so far), every 4th household in Tamil Nadu has a laptop. This coupled with the fact that Tamil Nadu has second highest rural internet usage in the country (Lok Sabha reply[2]) makes Tamil Nadu a digital leader in the country. Yet it is surprising that the usage of online self-service portal is relatively low. Could it be that the IT systems available with citizens are being used mostly for shopping or entertainment? What are the barriers for people trying to use self-service online portals? What kind of facilitation from government would make these barriers vanish?

In this context, our objective is to explore and investigate the mechanism governments can use to support citizens in mitigating the various uncertainties faced while using self-service portals for e-services. Venkatesh et al. (2016) examined how citizen's' uncertainties can be managed in accessing e-services but did not deal with the specific uncertainties and its sources rather posits that trust and transparency reduces uncertainty and thus influencing the adoption e-services. The contexts of developing countries like India is unique as both self-service government portal and intermediary mediated common service centers (see Fig. 1) are simultaneously available for citizens. Therefore, this study uses the uncertainty reduction theory to understand the sources of uncertainty and citizen's strategies to mitigate the uncertainty in the context of e-public service delivery.

The organization of this article is as follows. The next section presents the brief overview of the previous research on e-government services and description and justification of the theoretical lenses used in this study to achieve its objectives. We then described the adopted research methodology, research context, and preliminary findings including potential to promising contributions. Finally, we conclude this article with the future research plans.

---

[1] Authors collected data from Tamil Nadu e-governance agency.

[2] https://timesofindia.indiatimes.com/city/chennai/tn-second-in-rural-smartphone-use/articl eshow/67291628.cms.

2 Literature Review

2.1 Previous Research on e-Government Services

Previous researches on e-government have mainly focused on the technology adoption of e-government services using popular theoretical models namely technology acceptance model (Davis 1989) and the unified theory of acceptance and use of technology (UTAUT; Venkatesh et al. 2003). For instance, the aforementioned models have been used to understand the factors of various e-government services such as e-voting technologies (Yao and Murphy 2007; Choi and Kim 2012), predictors of e-government (Alomari, Woods and Sandhu 2012), e-government services (Sharma 2015; Lalmahomed et al. 2017), mobile government services in China (Wang, Teo and Liu 2020). Furthermore, other theoretical models were used to study e-government websites are Rational Choice Theory (Nishant et al. 2019) and role of trust and risk in e-government adoption (Belanger and Carter 2008). These models have provided theoretical basis for understanding citizen's perception towards public service delivery using government websites. In addition, researchers have also studied alternative models such as common service centers where intermediaries such as data entry operator help citizens to access the delivery of public services electronically (Meng, Samah, and Omar 2013; Sharma and Mishra 2017). The aforementioned research studies have focused on factors influencing citizen's decision to adopt e-government services in general. Therefore, there is a need to explore other theoretical lenses to develop sustainable electronic public service deliver model in developing countries with no intermediaries to achieve the macro level objective of government to deliver public services to citizens directly. To the best of author's knowledge, there is only one article on uncertainty reduction in e-government services (Venkatesh et al. 2016). We are attempting to investigate deeper the role of uncertainty in the context of e-government services, details are given in the following section.

2.2 Theoretical Background

Nature and Dimension of e-Government User Uncertainties in Developing Country
Uncertainty refers to the inability of users, in decision making situation, to accurately predict or understand the future due to lack of information (Knight 1921) and hence difficulty in anticipating the outcome of the prospective transactions (Akerlof 1970). Uncertainty is different from the risk as former deals with the subjective probabilities of loss rather than calculable probabilities of loss (Knight 1921). In the context of Internet based self-service portals, user's evaluation of the negative consequence is essentially subjective (Pavlou et al. 2007), hence we focus here uncertainty rather than risk. Recent studies in IS research have utilized the concept uncertainty in explaining the adoption of e-government services and virtual world for collaboration (Venkatesh et al. 2016; Srivastava and Chandra 2018). Venkatesh et al. (2016) study examines how citizen's' uncertainties can be managed in the context of e-government services. However, the study does not deal with the specific uncertainties and its sources rather posit that trust and transparency in the e-government context reduces uncertainty and thus influencing the adoption. In many developing nations like India, Malaysia, Bangladesh, Pakistan

and African countries citizens do not only access e-public services using self-service government portals but also intermediary mediated common service centers (Fig. 1).

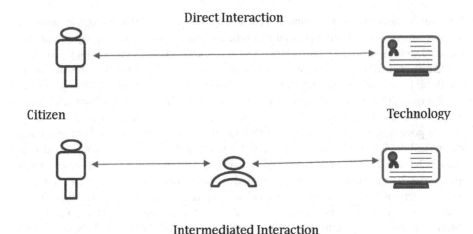

Fig. 1. Direct and intermediated access of e-government services

Venkatesh et al. (2016) suggest three dimensions of uncertainty in the new technology environment: task uncertainty, workflow uncertainty and environment uncertainty. Task uncertainty is the difference in the information possessed and required to perform the task by the user. In this context, this uncertainty may arise due to incorrect input, not knowing the user instruction and supporting documents required to perform the task. Workflow uncertainty may arise from lack of information about when and how citizen initiate, pause, save or resume the application during the usage (Wieler et al. 2019). Larsen (2003) defines environment uncertainty as "the extent to which critical information about organizations, activities, and events is unknown. It also pertains to lacking clarity about cause-and-effect relationships among environmental elements" (p-188). Citizen needs to be sure that service delivery through e-government channel i.e. citizen portal's availability and accountability related to the service performance (Venkatesh et al. 2016). Channel use behaviour of users are primarily driven by their "pre-factual thinking" that is assessment of potential benefits and losses (Kemp et al. 2012) so if uncertainty is not resolved with respect to a channel then it may lead to the hesitation in using that channel. To understand that how uncertainty influence the use of self-service citizen portal, it is important to understand that how citizen mitigate these uncertainties and how it influences channel selection behaviour.

Mitigating Uncertainties-Intermediated Technology Use
Uncertainty reduction theory, URT (Berger and Clabarese 1975) suggest that in initial interaction individuals try to reduce uncertainty to make outcomes of the interaction more predictable. One of the ways to reduce uncertainty is to try to seek information during their initial interaction, so URT suggest three primary information seeking strategies i.e. passive, active and interactive strategies. Passive strategies involve observing

the target individuals' environment in a non-intrusive way and collecting information to make prediction and draw conclusions about it. Active strategies involve getting the information about the target from the third party without directly contacting the target individual, for example, asking information from the acquaintances. Through interactive strategies individuals connect and directly communicate with target person for the information. Overall, uncertainty reduction strategies involve gathering information about other party's behaviour to reduce uncertainty and increase predictability which in turn decreases the one's perceived risk of interaction (Venkatesh et al. 2016).

URT was originally developed in the face-to-face communication context, however its application in IS research has been in computer mediated communication (Gibbs et al. 2010), online markets (Dimoka et al. 2012) and e-government satisfaction (Venkatesh et al. 2016). URT is particularly suitable for the context of this research as e-government system is after all "technology" of the state and kiosk operator (intermediary user) is the closest contact point for the citizen (De and Singh 2011). As these two channels (Fig. 1) are the only mechanism available for the public service delivery and self-service portals are relatively new in the developing countries, first time users of such portals are common in this setting. We conceptualize here that citizen would use three main strategies to acquire information to mitigate uncertainty encountered during the interaction with "technology" of the state. We further posit that intermediary user and service centre provide an appropriate setting and act as communication strategy facilitator for citizen in their pre-interaction information gathering process. Kiosk setting provides the space and resources for the active and passive strategy information acquisition and citizen directly can connect and communicate with the intermediary user to acquire information to access the services. In general, we postulate that intermediary use setting act as the communication strategy facilitator and in turn reduces the uncertainty of citizen and consequently influencing channel selection behaviour. Our research framework is presented in Fig. 2.

Fig. 2. Research framework: intermediated use as facilitation of uncertainty reduction

3   Research Methodology: A Mixed Method Approach

In this research, we are planning to combine qualitative as well as quantitative research methods, also known as mixed method approach. Mixed methods approach is not a new phenomenon in the IS research. In fact, mixed method approach provides researchers new ways to collect and analyze data as well as foster theory building. It is also important to note that mixed method does not mean the joining two distinct methods rather a continuum of two methods. This research study is a part of a major project undertaken by authors in Tamil Nadu, a southern state of India. This research study is planned to complete in three phases.

3.1   Research Context

Common Service Centers in Tamil Nadu (India): An Overview

The government of Tamil Nadu formed Tamil Nadu e-Governance Agency (TNeGA) in 2007 as a nodal agency to support and drive all e-governance initiatives throughout the state. As per Government of India guidelines it was initially decided that 1 Common Service Centre (CSC) will be established for 6 Village Panchayats. In accordance with this it was expected that 2770 CSCs will be established by the Government of Tamil Nadu. However, the Government of Tamil Nadu, taking various aspects into account, has proposed to roll out 5440 CSCs throughout the State in the ratio of 1 CSC for every 3 Village Panchayats in a Public Private Partnership (PPP) model as envisaged by Government of India. In line with this, Common Service Centers (CSCs) centers, also known as e-SEVAI centers, were created to make IT enabled Government Services accessible to the citizens of the state through efficient, transparent, reliable and affordable means. e-SEVAI centers act as One stop solution in availing various government services across departments with minimum efforts. Community Certificates, Income Certificates, First Graduate Certificates, Legal heir certificates are some of the extensively availed and most popular services offered by e-SEVAI centers.

Enablement and consolidation of online services under a single technology platform, thereby making the service delivery at CSCs accountable, transparent, efficient and traceable, with a technology-driven relationship between all stakeholders, providing a centralized technological platform for delivery of various services in a transparent manner to the citizens, increasing sustainability of Village Level Entrepreneurs (VLEs), non-discriminatory access to e-Services for rural citizens, expansion of self-sustaining CSC network, empowering District e-Governance Society (DeGS) under the district administration for implementation, creating and strengthening the institutional framework for rollout and project management are some of the visions and objectives of eSEVAI system.

At present there are more than 12000 e-SEVAI working centers across 37 districts of the state with its key stakeholders being the citizens, operators, businesses, TNeGA, eDMs, service center agencies, Departments at backend responsible for services. The e-SEVAI centers are maintained by state PSUs and other non-state organizations under Public Private Partnership model envisaged by the Government of India. In partnership with various agencies across Tamil Nadu, 12798 centers[3] are currently providing 2071 government services. It has already served 8558987 people1 since the start of 2020 and has served 10399662 people1 in the year 2019. eSEVAI centers have improved

---

[3] As of 18th Apr 2020., according to the official website of TNeGA.

the citizens' perception on governmental activities by changing the conventional mode of relationship between the government and its users. It has led the government to attain significant transformation by reducing corruption, increasing transparency, cost reduction, overall revenue growth, expanding convenience and ease of access.

3.2 Data Collection

Phase 1: Qualitative Interviewing and Exploratory Survey
In this phase, we conducted exploratory survey of 350 citizens who visited various common service centers in 10 districts of Tamil Nadu (India). On the basis of preliminary findings in the exploratory survey, the research team conducted in-depth interviews with 10 users ranging from 30 to 45 min who visited intermediary mediated common service centers to avail public service delivery. A sample of questions asked by research team in exploratory and in-depth interviews is given below.

1. Do you use Internet at home? If yes, which of the following facility you use?

    - Online cash transactions
    - Online non cash transactions
    - General purpose use like social media or entertainment

2. Do you know that you can avail these services using e-government self-service portal?
3. Have you ever used self-service portal?

    The findings of the phase one are revealing some nuances related to the working of common service centers.

Phase 2: Quantitative Survey
On the basis of findings in phase one, we are planning to develop a research model to manage the migration of citizens from intermediary mediated common service centers to self-service e-government portals.

Phase 3: Qualitative Interviews of Users Availing Services from Self-service Portals
In addition to the development and testing of the proposed model, we will conduct in-depth interviews of citizens who are using self-service e-government portals and on the basis of thematic analysis, we will suggest recommendations to decision makers to develop effective strategies to smooth transition of citizens from CSCs to self-service e-government portals.

4 Preliminary Findings

To achieve the objectives of the research article, research team collected data from 350 citizens who visit common service centers to avail e-government services in Tamil Nadu.

In the preliminary findings, it has been observed that 64% of citizens use Internet for online cash as well non-cash transactions whereas remaining 36% do not use Internet for online transactions. Furthermore, 71% citizens were aware about the services that can be availed using self-service portals but never used and 29% user who were aware as well as used self-service portals (see Fig. 3). These findings provide evidences to support the puzzle we proposed in the introduction section that majority of the citizens are using Internet for online transactions but low percentage of citizen are using self-service portals for availing e-government services. The findings in exploratory survey show that the low percentage (29%) of citizens is using self-service centers that are consistent with the data (17%) obtained by authors from state government agency.

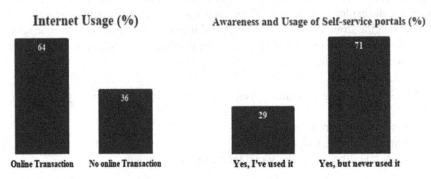

Fig. 3. Descriptive statistics charts

Phase 2 qualitative interviews (currently 10 in total) and observation notes have been transcribed. The authors spent over 20 man-hours in interpretive dialogue for data analysis and derived the preliminary findings. In our interim analysis, which is currently an ongoing process, we have chosen thematic analysis to collectively evaluate the interview data. Emerging themes are being matched with the theory grounded uncertainty themes and how citizen resolve these uncertainties. For example, one of the themes that are emerging is "incorrect use" (task uncertainty), to overcome they rely on the intermediary user's expertise on performing the task. Another theme that is emerging is that of "fear of accountability" (environmental uncertainty) which citizen believes that intermediary user would take the responsibility if something goes wrong. These are some themes, which are emerging form our ongoing iterative analysis.

In this study, we attempt to understand the possible reason of underutilization of self-service e-government portals in the context of developing countries. In spite of having reasonable digital literacy and consequently greater use of Internet for social media and other entertainment purposes, the usage of self-service e-government portal is relatively low. The findings of this study have potential to contribute to the literature by explaining uncertainty about citizen's initial interaction and mitigation strategies. Furthermore, our findings will provide insights to decision makers in the government settings to mitigate the concerns of citizens related to uncertainties in the self-service e-government portals by incorporating necessary design changes and consequently smooth migration of citizens from intermediary mediated CSCs to a sustainable self-service e-government portals for electronic public service delivery.

5 Future Research

The preliminary research findings are providing promising insights and further investigations are on. We will continue qualitative interviews and data collection. Further, we will develop a novel research model using uncertainty reduction theory as a part of findings in the phase one and empirically test the same. In addition, we will conduct in-depth interviews of citizens who are availing electronic public services using self-service portals. The final study will provide a comprehensive model with theoretical and managerial implications to all stakeholders who are managing CSCs across developing countries in particular India.

References

Ackelof, G.: The market for lemons: qualitative uncertainty and the market mechanism. Quart. J. Econ. **84**, 488–500 (1970)

Alomari, M., Woods, P., Sandhu, K.: Predictors for e-government adoption in Jordan. Inf. Technol. People **25**(2), 207–234 (2012)

Bélanger, F., Carter, L.: Trust and risk in e-government adoption. J. Strateg. Inf. Syst. **17**(2), 165–176 (2008)

Berger, C.R., Calabrese, R.: Some explorations in initial interactions and beyond: toward a developmental theory of interpersonal communication. Hum. Commun. Res. **1**, 99–112 (1975)

Choi, S.O., Kim, B.C.: Voter intention to use e-voting technologies: security, technology acceptance, election type, and political ideology. J. Inform. Tech. Polit. **9**(4), 433–452 (2012)

De', R., Singh, J.B.: Scarcity, exit, voice and violence: the state seen through eGovernment. In: Janssen, M., Scholl, H.J., Wimmer, M.A., Tan, Y.-H. (eds.) EGOV 2011. LNCS, vol. 6846, pp. 273–284. Springer, Heidelberg (2011). https://doi.org/10.1007/978-3-642-22878-0_23

Dimoka, A., Hong, Y., Pavlou, P.A.: On product uncertainty in online markets: theory and evidence. MIS Q. **36**(2), 395–426 (2012)

Venkatesh, V., Morris, M.G., Davis, G.B., Davis, F.D.: User acceptance of information technology: toward a unified view. MIS Quart., 425–478 (2003)

Sharma, R., Mishra, R.: Investigating the role of intermediaries in adoption of public access outlets for delivery of e-Government services in developing countries: an empirical study. Gov. Inf. Quart., **34**(4), 658–679 (2017)

Dwivedi, Y.K., Sahu, G.P., Rana, N.P., Singh, M., Chandwani, R.K.: Common Services Centres (CSCs) as an approach to bridge the digital divide: reflecting on challenges and obstacles. Transforming Gov.: People, Process Policy, **10**(4), 511–525 (2016)

Dwivedi, Y.K., Weerakkody, V., Janssen, M.: Moving towards maturity: challenges to successful e-government implementation and diffusion. ACM SIGMIS Database Database Adv. Inf. Syst. **42**(4), 11–22 (2012)

Evans, D., Yen, D.C.: e-Government: evolving relationship of citizens and government, domestic, and international development. Gov. Inf. Q. **23**(2), 207–235 (2006)

Gibbs, J.L., Ellison, N.B., Lai, C.H.: First comes love, then comes Google: an investigation of uncertainty reduction strategies and self-disclosure in online dating. Commun. Res. **38**(1), 70–100 (2010)

Kemp, E., Bui, M., Chapa, S.: The role of advertising in consumer emotion management. Int. J. Advert. **31**(2), 339–353 (2012)

Knight, F.H.: (1921) Risk, Uncertainty and Profit. LSE, London (1946)

Kumar, R., Sachan, A., Mukherjee, A.: Qualitative approach to determine user experience of e-Government services. Comput. Hum. Behav. **71**, 299–306 (2017)

Lallmahomed, M.Z., Lallmahomed, N., Lallmahomed, G.M.: Factors influencing the adoption of e-Government services in Mauritius. Telematics Inform. **34**(4), 57–72 (2017)

Larsen, K.R.: A taxonomy of antecedents of information systems success: variable analysis studies. J. Manag. Inf. Syst. **20**(2), 169–246 (2003)

Meng, C.C., Samah, B.A., Omar, S.Z.: A review paper: critical factors affecting the development of ICT projects in Malaysia. Asian Soc. Sci. **9**(4), 42–50 (2013)

Nishant, R., Srivastava, S.C., Teo, T.S.: Using polynomial modeling to understand service quality in e-Government websites. MIS Q. **43**(3), 807–826 (2019)

Weiler, S., Matt, C., Hess, T.: Understanding user uncertainty during the implementation of self-service business intelligence: a thematic analysis. In: Proceedings of the 52nd Hawaii International Conference on System Sciences, January 2019

Pavlou, P.A., Liang, H., Xue, Y.: Understanding and mitigating uncertainty in online exchange relationships: a principal-agent perspective. MIS Q. **31**(1), 105–136 (2007)

Shareef, M.A., Archer, N., Kumar, V., Kumar, U.: Developing fundamental capabilities for successful e-government implementation. Int. J. Public Policy **6**(3–4), 318–335 (2010)

United Nations Department of Social and Economic Affairs (2016). http://workspace.unpan.org/sites/Internet/Documents/UNPAN96407.pdf

Srivastava, S.C., Chandra, S.: Social presence in virtual world collaboration: an uncertainty reduction perspective using a mixed methods approach. MIS Q. **42**(3), 779–804 (2018)

Venkatesh, V., Thong, J.Y., Chan, F.K., Hu, P.J.: Managing citizens' uncertainty in e-Government services: The mediating and moderating roles of transparency and trust. Inf. Syst. Res. **27**(1), 87–111 (2016)

Wang, C., Teo, T.S., Liu, L.: Perceived value and continuance intention in mobile government service in China. Telematics Inform. **48**, 101348 (2020)

Sharma, S.K.: Adoption of e-government services. Trans. Gov. People Process Policy **9**(2), 2017–2222 (2015)

Yao, Y., Murphy, L.: Remote electronic voting systems: an exploration of voters' perceptions and intention to use. Eur. J. Inf. Syst. **16**(2), 106–120 (2007)

UNPAN, N.U.: United Nations E-government Survey 2014: E-government (2014). https://public administration.un.org/egovkb/en-us/#.VsqE7OYbPz0

United Nations E-Government Survey 2016 (2016)

Factors Affecting Adoption of eWOM Communications: A Synthesis of Research Using Meta-analysis

Elvira Ismagilova[1](✉), Yogesh K. Dwivedi[2,4], Nripendra Rana[3],
and Ramakrishnan Raman[4]

[1] Faculty of Management, Law and Social Sciences, University of Bradford, Bradford, UK
e.ismagilova@bradford.ac.uk

[2] Emerging Markets Research Centre, School of Management, Swansea University, Swansea, UK
y.k.dwivedi@swansea.ac.uk

[3] College of Business and Economics, Qatar University, Doha, Qatar
nrana@qu.edu.qa

[4] Symbiosis Institute of Business Management, Pune and Symbiosis International (Deemed University), Pune, India
director@sibmpune.edu.in

Abstract. Information plays an important role in consumer's decision-making process. Adoption of electronic word of mouth (eWOM) communications can change consumers' attitudes, and, as a result, have an impact on their purchase decisions. Researchers have investigated factors affecting credibility and usefulness of eWOM, which can help to predict eWOM adoption. However, findings are contradictory causing confusion among researchers and practitioners. Hence, this research aims to synthesise results from existing work on adoption of eWOM communications by using meta-analysis. The findings can help e-commerce companies to design more effective online review platforms. Additionally, this research will enhance the understanding of information processing by individuals.

Keywords: Electronic word of mouth (eWOM) · Information adoption · Usefulness · Credibility · Meta-analysis

1 Introduction

Nowadays, consumers face challenges in making online purchase decisions due to limited and incomplete information about the product/service provided by sellers [1–4]. As a result, ever more consumers are consulting electronic word of mouth (eWOM) communications to reduce the uncertainty of their purchase decision [5]. While more consumers seek eWOM, more consumers also contribute eWOM. Nowadays, it is common for products listed on e-commerce websites to have thousands of reviews; for instance, an average ranked book on Amazon.com can have several hundred reviews,

© IFIP International Federation for Information Processing 2022
Published by Springer Nature Switzerland AG 2022
S. Papagiannidis et al. (Eds.): I3E 2022, LNCS 13454, pp. 315–326, 2022.
https://doi.org/10.1007/978-3-031-15342-6_25

while popular technology products can have thousands of reviews [6]. However, the volume and variety of reviews can lead to information overload, potentially hindering rather than facilitating the decision-making process [7]. Thus, it is important for websites to display reviews which could aid consumers in their decision-making process and to avoid information overload.

Information adoption refers to the degree to which consumers accept and use eWOM communications in their decision-making process [8]. Adoption of eWOM can lead to the changes in consumers' attitudes towards products/services and influence their buying decisions [9]. Previous studies have discovered that information adoption is influenced by credibility and usefulness of eWOM communications [10–15]. Researchers investigated factors affecting credibility and usefulness of eWOM, which can help to predict eWOM adoption [13]. Nevertheless, studies have contradictory findings. For instance, Rabjohn et al. [16] claimed that information relevance affects perceived usefulness of eWOM, but Cheung [17] found that it does not. Mixed findings on the factors affecting credibility/usefulness of eWOM and information adoption can result in confusion among researchers and practitioners [18].

Mixed research results in the area of social and behavioral sciences are common and can be caused by the research context [18]. Meta-analysis is often used to synthesise existing findings by previous research [19] and find "a common truth behind all conceptually similar studies" [18]. An increasing number of research outputs in eWOM field apply a meta-analysis [18, 20]. However, the existing meta-analysis studies fail to explain which factors affect consumers' adoption of eWOM communications. Hence, it is important to undertake meta-analysis of results relating to factors affecting adoption of eWOM communications, as it can directly affect sales. Therefore, the aim of this research is to use meta-analytic approach to synthesise findings from existing research on eWOM adoption. It will help to reconcile and understand the mixed findings related to the factors related to adoption of eWOM. The findings can potentially aid marketing practitioners to design more effective online review platforms. Additionally, this research will enhance the understanding of information processing by individuals.

The remaining of the paper is organised as follows. First, the literature review and hypotheses development section are presented in Sect. 2. Next, in Sect. 3 the research methodology is presented focusing on the collection of studies and meta-analysis procedures. After, the results of meta-analysis are presented, followed by the discussion. In the final section, contributions and limitations of the study are discussed and directions for future research are outlined.

2 Literature Review

Previous studies on eWOM communications found that eWOM adoption results in changes in attitude and purchase intention, which in turn will influence the level of sales [21]. Thus, it can be seen that information adoption is an important determinant of consumer decision making journey and behaviour [9]. Scholars have examined how eWOM affects information adoption behaviour. Some studies found that eWOM credibility plays a significant role in information adoption [8]. Other scholars discovered that helpfulness of eWOM significantly affects eWOM adoption [11, 22, 23]. Thus, in order to know which factors affect eWOM adoption, it is important to consider factors which affect eWOM credibility and usefulness. According to Elaboration Likelihood Model (ELM), variables affecting the persuasiveness of eWOM can be based on central (e.g. comprehensiveness) or peripheral (e.g. information consistency, volume rating) cues [24].

Relevance. The relevance of the message plays an important role in the consumer decision process as they are conscious of their time. It was found by Madu and Madu [25] that internet users usually scan pages in order to find the relevant information rather than reading in detail. Users want to find information, which helps them to make a decision quickly and with less effort [26]. Thus, it is important to provide users with only relevant information, as it is an important element in the decision-making process. Thus, the following is proposed:

H1: Relevance of the message is positively related to eWOM usefulness.

Timeliness. Timeliness of eWOM communications refers to the extent to which the message is current and up-to-date. A study conducted by Madu and Madu [25] found that if the website is not updated regularly, users cannot use it as the source to deliver expected performance and provides no value to the users. The more timely the messages are the higher the perceived usefulness of eWOM communications. Several studies have investigated the relationship between timeliness of the message and eWOM usefulness [17]. Thus, the following is proposed:

H2: Timeliness of the message is positively related to eWOM usefulness.

Accuracy. Accuracy of the message refers to the user's perception that the information provided in the message is correct. According to media richness theory accuracy of the information exchange is important across a medium. Some studies investigated the link between accuracy of the message and eWOM usefulness [16, 22, 27].

H3: Accuracy of the message is positively related to eWOM usefulness.

Comprehensiveness. The comprehensiveness of eWOM communications is associated with its completeness. It is argued that the more detailed the information in the message the more users will use it in their decision making [22]. A number of studies investigated the relationship between comprehensiveness of the message and eWOM usefulness [16, 22, 27]. Based on the above discussion it is proposed that:

H4: Comprehensiveness of the message is positively related to eWOM usefulness.

Argument quality. The quality of information refers to the content of the message that is judged to provide objective and supporting information for the consumer's purchase decision [17]. Qualitative research conducted by Schindler and Bickart [28] found that, as most online reviews are unfamiliar, people will not accept the information unless it provides sufficient information on the arguments used when making claims about products or services. As a result, it is proposed:

H5: Argument quality is positively related to eWOM usefulness.

Previous studies argue that valid and persuasive arguments will lead consumers to have a positive attitude towards the received information and consider it to be credible

[29]. High quality eWOM communications offer consumers more potentially problem-solving evidence, which can improve their ability to make an intelligent assessment of the credibility of information they read [30]. Thus, it is proposed that:

H6: Argument quality is positively related to eWOM credibility.

Volume. In eWOM communications, a high volume of reviews can lead to a higher probability that users will find information useful for them. Thus, it is argued by researchers that a high number of reviews are more helpful for familiarising with a product or service and better understanding its performance and quality in comparison with a small number of reviews [11]. A study conducted by Filieri [11] found that information quantity significantly affects eWOM usefulness. Based on the above discussion the following hypothesis is proposed:

H7: Volume of eWOM communications is positively related to eWOM usefulness.

Rating. Rating is a common feature on e-commerce pages and connected to an information cue with the degree of how all other reviewers assessed one product. Such information is an aggregated crowd's opinion and it helps to classify products or service according to the overall evaluation of reviewers [11]. Studies on eWOM found that the aggregated ranking influences consumer behaviour and evaluation of the information. For example, a study conducted by Luo et al. [31] found that aggregated rating also affects information credibility. Thus, it is proposed that:

H8: Overall product rating is positively related to eWOM credibility.

H9: Overall product rating is positively related to eWOM usefulness.

Consistency. Information consistency refers to the extent to which the information included in the message is in line with the previous information provided by other reviewers. On eWOM forums, discussion boards, and online reviews a reader can check previous eWOM communications and compare consistency [29]. It was found by other studies on eWOM communications that information that is consistent with other same target information will be perceived as credible by the consumer [32].

H10: Information consistency is positively related to eWOM credibility.

Sidedness. The content of eWOM communications can vary. Some messages only contain positive or negative information (one-sided information), while others contain both positive and negative information (two-sided information). For consumers, each product can have positive and negative features and, as a result, two-sided eWOM communications are generally considered as more reliable in comparison with one-sided [33], as readers might consider them as unbiased [29]. This, it is proposed that:

H11: Sidedness is positively related to eWOM credibility.

Source expertise. Individuals use a variety of ways to determine the expertise of the source, such as number of reviews posted, content of posts, and duration of membership on the platform. Previous research investigated relationships between source expertise and eWOM usefulness and information credibility [7, 34]. It is claimed by previous research that reviewers' comments are perceived as more helpful when they are provided by an expert source [34]. By using data from 570 online surveys in the context of accommodation and restaurants, Filieri, Hofacker and Alguezaui [7] found that source expertise positively influences information usefulness. Thus, it is hypothesised that:

H12: Source expertise is positively related to eWOM usefulness.

Previous research found that the perceived expertise of the information source could influence information credibility [8, 10]. According to the source-credibility model, the perceived expertise of the sender significantly determines credibility. Individuals seek information from a person who is perceived as knowledgeable and experienced.

H13: Source expertise is positively related to eWOM credibility.

Trustworthiness. The trustworthiness of the sender is another determinant of source credibility. Information is considered as trustworthy when it is judged as valid, honest and to the point. When the source is perceived as trustworthy the credibility of information is doubted less by a receiver [35]. Thus, it is proposed that:

H14: Source trustworthiness is positively related to eWOM usefulness.

By using the source-credibility model, Lis [8] found that a reviewer's trustworthiness can affect the perceived credibility of eWOM communications. A reviewer who is perceived as trustworthy is considered more credible as they show a high degree of objectivity and sincerity. Thus, the following is hypothesised:

H15: Source trustworthiness is positively related to eWOM credibility.

Homophily. Homophily refers to the degree to which two or more individuals who interact are similar in certain attributes (e.g. demographic characteristics, perceived attributes) [8]. Although when communicating online consumers do not have face-to-face interactions, it is still possible to make inferences about the similarity with information providers by appraising review content and looking at profile information. It can help individuals to learn more about a sender's personality, values, preferences, and experience [7]. Thus, the following hypothesis is proposed:

H16: Homophily between an information source and receiver is positively related to eWOM credibility.

eWOM usefulness. Based on technology acceptance theories, previous researchers argued that if the consumer perceives eWOM communications as useful for familiarising with a product or service, and to indicate quality and performance, then they will be more likely to consider these recommendations in their decision making [11].

H17: eWOM usefulness is positively related to eWOM adoption.

eWOM credibility. The success of the eWOM communications process is determined by the extent of adoption of the information. Information adoption is defined by Sussman and Siegal (2003) as the acceptance of the recommendation. Studies found that credibility plays an important role in the eWOM adoption process (Lis, 2013; Fan & Miao, 2012). A consumer will adoption eWOM communications which are perceived as credible more readily in comparison with those perceived as unreliable (Bansal & Voyer, 2000). Based on the above discussion the following is proposed:

H18: eWOM credibility is positively related to eWOM adoption.

3 Research Method

3.1 Selection of Studies

To identify relevant studies for this research, the following steps were taken, similar to other studies which applied meta-analysis techniques [18]. First, a multi-channel literature search was performed in numerous databases (EBSCO, Web of Science, Scopus) in order to avoid publication bias. Keywords such as "Electronic word-of-mouth" OR "Electronic word of mouth" OR "eWOM" OR "Internet word-of-mouth" OR "Internet word of mouth" OR "iWOM" OR "Online word-of-mouth" OR "Online word of mouth" OR "Virtual word-of-mouth" OR "vWOM" OR "Virtual word of mouth" were used to perform the search. Second, in line with the research goal, the following selection criteria were used to choose relevant studies from the above-mentioned pool: 1) empirical research on eWOM adoption, eWOM credibility and eWOM usefulness 2) report relevant statistics (sample size, Pearson correlation, and significance of the relationships). As a result, the final dataset included 45 studies that fulfilled the above requirements. It has also been suggested that a meta-analysis should include a minimum of fifteen studies [18]; the final dataset also satisfied this condition.

3.2 Meta-analysis Procedure

In order to perform a meta-analysis, effect sizes from previous studies were extracted. To measure the effect size of eWOM communication on information adoption, this research used correlations, as per other meta-analysis studies [18]. It was decided to apply correlations to calculate effect size rather than elasticities as it is independent of the measurement scale and as a result enables a more informative and objective comparison [36]. The meta-analysis includes the following steps: 1) calculating the Fishers' Z and combined effect sizes; and 2) testing the significance of the combined effect size (p-value).

A trial version of Comprehensive Meta-Analysis software was used, which is successfully applied by previous studies in meta-analytic reviews [18]. Comprehensive Meta-Analysis software generates a cumulative correlation coefficient, effect size (p-value), Z-value and 95% confidence interval by using the correlation coefficient between each pair of dependent and independent variables and sample size.

4 Meta-analysis

Table 1 contains the results of meta-analysis of the 18 investigated relationships. Correlation coefficients between dependent and independent variables were employed to calculate the cumulative correlation coefficient (Avg (r)), significance of the combined effect (P(ES)), and 95% lower and upper confident interval levels. The results of meta-analysis demonstrate that 17 out of 18 investigated relationships are significant.

Table 1. Meta-analysis results

Types of factors	IV	DV	Total number of studies	Avg (r)	95% L(r)	95% H(r)	Z-value	p(ES)
eWOM message	Relevance	eWOM usefulness	3	0.631	0.559	0.694	12.919	0.000
	Timeliness		3	0.400	0.301	0.49	7.362	0.000
	Accuracy		3	0.630	0.557	0.693	12.884	0.000
	Comprehensiveness		3	0.760	0.708	0.804	17.32	0.000
	Argument quality		3	0.688	0.623	0.744	14.441	0.000
	Volume		3	0.660	0.162	0.809	2.47	0.014
	Rating		3	0.247	-0.506	0.786	0.61	0.542
Source of eWOM	Expertise		3	0.459	0.228	0.641	3.689	0.000
	Trustworthiness		7	0.521	0.353	0.656	5.442	0.000
eWOM message	Argument quality	eWOM credibility	6	0.645	0.615	0.673	29.981	0.000
	Rating		5	0.541	0.502	0.578	22.069	0.000
	Consistency		4	0.528	0.431	0.612	9.15	0.000
	Recommendation sidedness		3	0.269	0.201	0.335	7.472	0.000
Source of eWOM	Expertise		5	0.448	0.352	0.534	8.254	0.000
	Trustworthiness		3	0.539	0.21	0.758	3.036	0.002
	Homophily		4	0.494	0.233	0.532	4.586	0.000
Persuasiveness	eWOM usefulness	eWOM adoption	5	0.650	0.612	0.685	24.033	0.000
	eWOM credibility		5	0.584	0.412	0.716	5.683	0.000

Note: Avg Average, DV Dependent variable, ES Effect size, IV Independent variable, H(r), Higher correlation, L(r) Lower correlation

5 Discussion

Considering the increasing volume of research outputs on eWOM adoption it becomes vital to analyse and discuss their combined findings. The meta-analysis of 18 factors relating to eWOM usefulness and credibility, which in turn relate to eWOM adoption provided the cumulative correlation coefficients and significance of the combined effect. The results of meta-analysis supported seventeen hypotheses our of eighteen (H8 was not supported).

Relevance was found to positively related to eWOM usefulness (H1 supported). Literature demonstrates that internet users value information relevance [25] as it makes the decision-making process quick and easy [26]. Relevance refers to the central cue in ELM. The findings are consistent with previous research on eWOM [16, 22, 27].

Three factors affecting eWOM usefulness - timeliness, accuracy, and comprehensiveness - were found to be significant based on the results of meta-analysis supporting hypotheses H2, H3, and H4. These cues are considered as central according to ELM. People perceive more recent reviews to be more useful in their decision making, in comparison with old and outdated reviews. The findings are in line with Cheung [17]. Also, consumers perceive accurate reviews to be more useful in comparison with the ones which do not provide any precise and accurate information. Usually when people search for products/services they have some background knowledge about them. When reading reviews people check if part of the message has some information that they already know. If the information is in line with their prior acquired knowledge they would consider a review to be accurate [27]. Comprehensiveness plays an important part in eWOM helpfulness. It is argued that greater amount of information comprehensiveness is essential for individuals to make a purchase decision [16, 22].

Another factor, argument quality was found to positively related to eWOM usefulness confirming H5. Argument quality refers to the central cue in ELM [29]. It was found that argument quality is also positively related to eWOM credibility (H6 supported). Argument quality is referred to as a central cue in ELM. Individuals' judgment about a review is mainly based on its content. The higher the quality of content, the higher the perceived credibility. The findings are in line with previous studies on eWOM [10, 30].

Based on the result of meta-analysis, volume was also found to be positively related to eWOM usefulness (H7 supported). Volume is a peripheral cue, which helps consumers to evaluate helpfulness of eWOM communications. The more opinions consumers access about a product/service online, the more eWOM has an influence on their decision-making [37]. The findings are supported by studies that found a positive relationship between volume and eWOM usefulness [24, 37].

Surprisingly, rating showed non-significant results in the meta-analysis in relation to eWOM usefulness (H8 not supported). The findings can be justified by the fact that ratings do not provide detailed information regarding features. For identical performance of a product, different consumers can give different overall ratings, as individuals have different product evaluation criteria. Thus, it will not be considered useful in the decision-making process. However, based on the result of meta-analysis it was found that rating is significantly and positively related to credibility of eWOM (H9 supported). In this case, looking at the overall rating, and also its distribution, can provide consumers with clues about eWOM credibility. Rating is considered as a peripheral cue in ELM. The results on the relation of rating to eWOM credibility are in line with previous research [8, 31].

It was found that consistency, being a peripheral cue in ELM, is positively related to eWOM credibility (H10 supported). If a similar experience is repeatedly reported by various users, the information receiver is more likely to believe in this experience, increasing confidence in the review. The findings are in line with the previous studies [31, 32].

Meta-analysis showed that recommendation sidedness is positively related to eWOM credibility, which is in line with Luo, Wu, Shi and Xu [32] (H11 supported). When a review consists of both positive and negative points about a product/service the reader will perceive it more credible in comparison with the ones which just have positive or negative information. An extremely positive or negative review could be considered as fake eWOM communications [38].

It was found that expertise is positively related to eWOM usefulness (H12 supported). Being a peripheral cue of eWOM persuasiveness has a significant effect on its evaluation. Based on the results it means that if the reader perceives the source as having a high level of expertise about a discussed product/service, the reader will perceive the review as more useful in the decision-making process. The findings are similar to some studies on eWOM [7, 27].

Expertise of eWOM source was also found to be positively related to eWOM credibility (H13 supported). Expertise refers to peripheral route in ELM. An individual will consider information credible only if it came from a knowledgeable and experienced source [39]. The findings are in line with previous research [8, 10].

It was found that source trustworthiness is positively related to eWOM usefulness (H14 supported), which is also considered a peripheral cue in judging eWOM usefulness. It means that if the reader of eWOM communications perceives the source as trustworthy they will perceive it as useful for the decision-making process. The findings are in line with López and Sicilia [37]. Trustworthiness was also found to be positively related to eWOM credibility, supporting H15. A receiver considers information provided by a trustworthy source as credible as it shows a high degree of objectivity and sincerity. The findings are similar to Lis [8].

Additionally, based on the results of meta-analysis it was found that source homophily is positively related to eWOM credibility (H16 supported). A greater homophily between sender and receiver of the information has a positive impact on the sender's influence. People have a tendency to trust information coming from people who have similar views. According to ELM, homophily is considered as a peripheral cue. The findings are supported by previous literature [8].

eWOM usefulness and eWOM credibility have significant meta-analysis results confirming the relationships. It was found that eWOM usefulness is positively related to consumers' decision to adopt eWOM (H17 supported). The findings are supported by previous research [23, 27]. When the information receiver feels that eWOM is unable to help to learn and evaluate the product they will likely discount this information and reject the recommendation. It was also found that credibility positively related to eWOM adoption (H18 supported), confirming previous research findings [8, 10, 11, 21]. The higher the level of perceived eWOM credibility, the greater its influence on consumers' decision-making [11].

6 Conclusion

This study aimed to conduct meta-analysis of existing empirical findings in eWOM research. In order to achieve the above aim, data from 45 studies focusing on factors affecting adoption of eWOM communications were collected and analysed. The study focused on eWOM message characteristics and source characteristics as factors affecting eWOM helpfulness and eWOM credibility, which in turn affect eWOM adoption. The study provided a consolidated view of factors affecting eWOM adoption, which advances current knowledge on information processing of eWOM communications.

The outputs from this study provide valuable recommendations for marketing practitioners. The research illustrates that useful and credible communications affect adoption of eWOM information. As a result, marketers should encourage and help individuals to provide information, which will be perceived as useful and credible.

Nowadays, many websites use voting systems (e.g. "was this review useful for you?") to determine useful reviews and display them prominently. However, the helpfulness vote might not solve all the problems. Firstly, very few reviews receive helpfulness votes and without them, the helpfulness mechanism does not work efficiently. Secondly, newer reviews will have had less time to accumulate helpfulness votes, and as a result, may not be ranked as helpful in a search. There is also a possibility that helpful reviews will get lost among less helpful ones due to the speed with which new reviews are added. Online reviews with fewer helpfulness votes - regardless of whether this truly reflects the helpfulness of the review - are generally ignored by consumers, while reviews with more helpfulness votes become more visible [6]. Companies can use the proposed factors which affect eWOM usefulness and apply them for machine learning algorithms, which can analyse the reviews and display the most helpful ones on top.

This study has some limitations, which provide directions for future research. First, the current study tested the proposed hypotheses for the research model separately. Future studies should test them together by applying regression based meta-analysis structural equation modelling technique. Second, this study did not investigate the impact of moderating variables on the proposed relationships due to an insufficient number of studies of moderating effects suitable for meta-analysis. Thus, future research could investigate the moderating effect of involvement, age, personality traits, platform, and product type on information adoption as sufficient studies emerge. Finally, studies which are included for this research were collected from EBSCO, Web of Science, and Scopus, which could result in missing some studies eligible for inclusion in this meta-analysis. Thus, future research could search a wider range of databases.

References

1. Dimoka, A., Hong, Y., Pavlou, P.A.: On product uncertainty in online markets: theory and evidence. MIS Q. **36**(2), 395–426 (2012)
2. Ismagilova, E., Dwivedi, Y.K., Rana, N.: The use of elaboration likelihood model in eWOM research: literature review and weight-analysis. In: Dennehy, D., Griva, A., Pouloudi, N., Dwivedi, Y.K., Pappas, I., Mäntymäki, M. (eds.) I3E 2021. LNCS, vol. 12896, pp. 495–505. Springer, Cham (2021). https://doi.org/10.1007/978-3-030-85447-8_41
3. Dwivedi, Y.K., et al.: Setting the future of digital and social media marketing research: perspectives and research propositions. Int. J. Inf. Manage. **59**, 102168 (2021)
4. Krishen, A.S., Dwivedi, Y.K., Bindu, N., Kumar, K.S.: A broad overview of interactive digital marketing: a bibliometric network analysis. J. Bus. Res. **131**, 183–195 (2021)
5. Erkan, I., Evans, C.: The influence of eWOM in social media on consumers' purchase intentions: an extended approach to information adoption. Comput. Hum. Behav. **61**, 47–55 (2016)
6. Singh, J.P., Irani, S., Rana, N.P., Dwivedi, Y.K., Saumya, S., Roy, P.K.: Predicting the "helpfulness" of online consumer reviews. J. Bus. Res. **70**, 346–355 (2017)
7. Filieri, R., Hofacker, C.F., Alguezaui, S.: What makes information in online consumer reviews diagnostic over time? the role of review relevancy, factuality, currency, source credibility and ranking score. Comput. Hum. Behav. **80**, 122–131 (2018)
8. Lis, B.: In eWOM we trust. Wirtschaftsinformatik **55**, 121–134 (2013). https://doi.org/10.1007/s11576-013-0360-8
9. Fan, Y.-W., Miao, Y.-F., Fang, Y.-H., Lin, R.-Y.: Establishing the adoption of electronic word-of-mouth through consumers' perceived credibility. Int. Bus. Res. **6**, 58 (2013)

10. Fang, Y.-H.: Beyond the credibility of electronic word of mouth: exploring eWOM adoption on social networking sites from affective and curiosity perspectives. Int. J. Electron. Commer. **18**, 67–102 (2014)
11. Filieri, R.: What makes online reviews helpful? a diagnosticity-adoption framework to explain informational and normative influences in e-WOM. J. Bus. Res. **68**, 1261–1270 (2015)
12. Hsu, L.-C., Chih, W.-H., Liou, D.-K.: Investigating community members' eWOM effects in Facebook fan page. Ind. Manag. Data Syst. **116**, 978–1004 (2016)
13. Hussain, S., Ahmed, W., Jafar, R.M.S., Rabnawaz, A., Jianzhou, Y.: eWOM source credibility, perceived risk and food product customer's information adoption. Comput. Hum. Behav. **66**, 96–102 (2017)
14. Teng, S., Khong, K.W., Goh, W.W.: Conceptualizing persuasive messages using ELM in social media. J. Internet Commer. **13**, 65–87 (2014)
15. Wang, T., Yeh, R.K.-J., Yen, D.C.: Influence of customer identification on online usage and purchasing behaviors in social commerce. Int. J. Hum.-Comput. Interact. **31**, 805–814 (2015)
16. Rabjohn, N., Cheung, C.M., Lee, M.K.: Examining the perceived credibility of online opinions: information adoption in the online environment. In: Proceedings of the 41st Annual Hawaii International Conference on System Sciences (HICSS 2008), p. 286. IEEE (2008)
17. Cheung, R.: The influence of electronic word-of-mouth on information adoption in online customer communities. Glob. Econ. Rev. **43**, 42–57 (2014)
18. Hong, H., Xu, D., Wang, G.A., Fan, W.: Understanding the determinants of online review helpfulness: a meta-analytic investigation. Decis. Support Syst. **102**, 1–11 (2017)
19. Dwivedi, Y.K., Rana, N.P., Jeyaraj, A., Clement, M., Williams, M.D.: Re-examining the unified theory of acceptance and use of technology (UTAUT): towards a revised theoretical model. Inf. Syst. Front. **21**, 719–734 (2019). https://doi.org/10.1007/s10796-017-9774-y
20. Ismagilova, E., Rana, N.P., Slade, E.L., Dwivedi, Y.K.: A meta-analysis of the factors affecting eWOM providing behaviour. Eur. J. Mark. **55**(4), 1067–1102 (2021)
21. Fan, Y.-W., Miao, Y.-F.: Effect of electronic word-of-mouth on consumer purchase intention: the perspective of gender differences. Int. J. Electron. Bus. Manag. **10**, 175–181 (2012)
22. Cheung, C.M., Lee, M.K., Rabjohn, N.: The impact of electronic word-of-mouth: the adoption of online opinions in online customer communities. Internet Res. **18**(3), 229–247 (2008)
23. Wang, P.: Exploring the influence of electronic word-of-mouth on tourists' visit intention: a dual process approach. J. Syst. Inf. Technol. **17**(4), 381–395 (2015)
24. Yan, Q., Wu, S., Wang, L., Wu, P., Chen, H., Wei, G.: E-WOM from e-commerce websites and social media: which will consumers adopt? Electron. Commer. Res. Appl. **17**, 62–73 (2016)
25. Madu, C.N., Madu, A.A.: Dimensions of e-quality. Int. J. Qual. Reliab. Manag. **19**(3), 246–258 (2002)
26. Nah, F.F.-H., Davis, S.: HCI research issues in e-commerce. J. Electron. Commer. Res. **3**, 98–113 (2002)
27. Ahmed, J.R., Farid, H.S.A.: Consumer's reliance on word of mouse: influence on consumer's decision in an online information. J. Bus. c/conomics (2013)
28. Schindler, R.M., Bickart, B.: Published word of mouth: referable, consumer-generated information on the Internet. In: Online Consumer Psychology: Understanding and Influencing Consumer Behavior in the Virtual World, vol. 32, pp. 35−61 (2005)
29. Cheung, C.M.-Y., Sia, C.-L., Kuan, K.K.: Is this review believable? a study of factors affecting the credibility of online consumer reviews from an ELM perspective. J. Assoc. Inf. Syst. **13**, 2 (2012)
30. Tsao, W.-C., Hsieh, M.-T.: eWOM persuasiveness: do eWOM platforms and product type matter? Electron. Commer. Res. **15**(4), 509–541 (2015). https://doi.org/10.1007/s10660-015-9198-z
31. Luo, C., Luo, X.R., Xu, Y., Warkentin, M., Sia, C.L.: Examining the moderating role of sense of membership in online review evaluations. Inf. Manag. **52**, 305–316 (2015)

32. Luo, C., Wu, J., Shi, Y., Xu, Y.: The effects of individualism–collectivism cultural orientation on eWOM information. Int. J. Inf. Manag. **34**, 446–456 (2014)
33. Mauri, A.G., Minazzi, R.: Web reviews influence on expectations and purchasing intentions of hotel potential customers. Int. J. Hosp. Manag. **34**, 99–107 (2013)
34. González-Rodríguez, M.R., Martínez-Torres, R., Toral, S.: Post-visit and pre-visit tourist destination image through eWOM sentiment analysis and perceived helpfulness. Int. J. Contemp. Hosp. Manag. **28**(11), 2609–2627 (2016)
35. Sparkman, R.M., Jr., Locander, W.B.: Attribution theory and advertising effectiveness. J. Consum. Res. **7**, 219–224 (1980)
36. Babić Rosario, A., Sotgiu, F., De Valck, K., Bijmolt, T.H.: The effect of electronic word of mouth on sales: a meta-analytic review of platform, product, and metric factors. J. Mark. Res. **53**, 297–318 (2016)
37. López, M., Sicilia, M.: Determinants of E-WOM influence: the role of consumers' internet experience. J. Theor. Appl. Electron. Commer. Res. **9**, 28–43 (2014)
38. Huang, J.H., Chen, Y.F.: Herding in online product choice. Psychol. Mark. **23**, 413–428 (2006)
39. Bansal, H.S., Voyer, P.A.: Word-of-mouth processes within a services purchase decision context. J. Serv. Res. **3**, 166–177 (2000)

The Use of Structuration Theory in Empirical Information Systems Research: A Systematic Literature Review

Khando Khando$^{(\boxtimes)}$ (D), M. Sirajul Islam (D), and Shang Gao (D)

Department of Informatics, Örebro University School of Business, Örebro, Sweden
{khando.khando,sirajul.islam,shang.gao}@oru.se

Abstract. Structuration Theory (ST) is increasingly used in the field of Information Systems (IS) and has been widely cited by IS researchers. However, despite the widespread use of ST in IS research, there is a lack of systematic literature reviews on the application of ST in the IS research domain. The purpose of this study is, therefore, to review how ST has been applied in IS research focusing more on the core ST concepts applied in the studies. A systematic review of 33 empirical IS papers published in the last seven years (2015–2021) informs that ST has been used as a theoretical lens by applying general and selective structural concepts. It is also found that a good number of studies have applied ST in combination with other theories to complement as well as to extend the theoretical perspectives. Most studies empirically applied the IS specific version of ST, the Adaptive Structuration Theory (AST), to analyse the IS phenomena. This review also presents the six most used core ST concepts in the reviewed papers. Overall, the paper contributes to offering a better understanding about the application of ST in the IS as a social practice and provides the state-of-the-art insights on the structural concepts used in the empirical IS research.

Keywords: Structuration theory · Information system · Empirical research · Systematic literature review · Structural concepts

1 Introduction

The research in the Information Systems (IS) field has drawn on several different social theories to gain insights of IS as a social practice [23]. The Structuration Theory (ST) proposed by contemporary sociologist Anthony Giddens has been widely used and cited by IS researchers [5]. This is mainly because ST is relevant and appropriate to study mainstream IS phenomena. For example, one of the core concepts of ST is the 'duality of structure' and the non-dualistic account of the structure and agency relationship offers the possibility of going beyond the deterministic conceptualization of IT artefacts and provides a new perspective of technology. Moreover, the dynamic conceptualization of structure as being continuously produced and reproduced through situate practice makes it conducive to study change [39]. Furthermore, the use of ST in IS research provides

© IFIP International Federation for Information Processing 2022
Published by Springer Nature Switzerland AG 2022
S. Papagiannidis et al. (Eds.): I3E 2022, LNCS 13454, pp. 327–339, 2022.
https://doi.org/10.1007/978-3-031-15342-6_26

a theoretical lens that helps in enhancing our understanding of the interaction between users and information technology, the implications of these interactions, and the way to control their consequences [24].

However, despite the widespread use of ST in IS research, there is a lack of systematic literature reviews on the use of ST in the IS domain particularly on the application of ST concepts in empirical IS research. Previous studies have conducted similar literature reviews; however, they are limited and lack the focus on the use of core concepts. For example, Kort and Gharbi [24] conducted a review on the use of ST in the IS field that focused on the criticisms of ST. Similarly, Pozzebon and Pinsonneault [40] also reviewed the application of ST in the IS domain concentrating on the assessment of research strategies. Although both studies reviewed the use of ST in IS research, they differ from the current review in terms of focus. The former review [24] focused on criticising ST features while the latter [40] focused on the methodological strategies adopted by IS researchers using ST. In contrast, the current review focuses on identifying the application of key ST concepts in empirical research. There are also some systematic reviews on the application of ST which particularly focused on the use of core ST concepts. However, they are not related to the field of IS. For example, Englund and Gerdin [10] reviewed the use of ST concepts in accounting and Turner [49] in the field of human resource development.

A related work by Jones and Karsten [23] presented a critical review on the work of Giddens and its applications in the IS field. They reviewed 331 IS articles published between 1983 and 2004 that drew on Gidden's work and analysed their use of ST. However, their study focuses on Gidden's overall work as a whole and its implication for IS research and did not focus specifically on the application of ST in empirical IS research. Thus, the purpose of this study is to systematically review IS studies published within the last seven years, to provide a state-of-the-art insight of the use of ST in empirical IS research, focusing on the application of its core concepts. The review aims to address two overarching research questions: RQ1 - *How has ST been used within empirical IS research?* and RQ2 - *What are the ST concepts used in empirical IS research?*

2   Overview of the Structuration Theory

One of the core concepts of Gidden's ST is the 'duality of structure' which Gidden's argues that just as an individual's autonomy is influenced by structure, structures are maintained and adapted through the exercise of agency. According to the theory, a 'structure' is a macro-sociological perspective, which is conceptualized in terms of 'Rules & Resources'. 'Rules' are the generalized procedures which guide the actions of individuals whereas 'resources' are the facilities that provide capacity to perform various tasks. The individual internalizes rules and resources during the process of socialization and becomes part of the stock of knowledge. On the other hand, 'agency' is a micro-sociological perspective referring to the individuals' ability to make choices in society, which aren't guided by anything but by their own desires, needs, and fulfilments. This is rather a concept of 'free will'. The prominence of structure resolves that the behaviour of individuals is largely determined by their socialization into the structure such as conforming to a society's expectations with respect to gender or social classes [23]. When individuals engage in action, they draw on from this stock of knowledge to construct their lines of action. This internalization of rules and resources ensures similarity of action and thereby the reproduction of structure. Thus, the enactment of structure in terms of rules and resources reproduces the objective structure [23]. Giddens identified three dimensions of structure for analytical purposes. These are, i) Signification - where meaning is coded in the practice of language and discourse, that is how an event should be interpreted, ii) Domination - concerned with how power is applied, particularly in the control of resources, that is what means should be used to accomplish goals, and iii) Legitimation - consisting of the normative perspectives embedded as societal norms and values, that is what should happen in a given situation [15]. Structuration theory takes the position that social action cannot be fully explained by the structure or agency theories alone. Instead, it recognizes that actors operate within the context of rules produced by social structures, and these structures are reinforced only by acting in a compliant manner [23].

One of the important features of Gidden's ST is 'Agent's Knowledgeability' which means that "every member of a society must know a great deal about the workings of that society by virtue of his or her participation in it" [13:250]. Knowledgeability basically means a person's awareness of his/her own behaviour. It can occur at three levels, such as discursive, practical consciousness, and unconsciousness knowledgeability. 'Discursive consciousness' refers to all those things that actors can say, put into words, about the conditions of their action [14] - they are able to discuss why they do what they do. 'Practical consciousness' refers to what actors know, but cannot necessarily put into words, about how to go on in the multiplicity of contexts of social life. 'Unconsciousness knowledgeability' is an action where actors respond to the environment, but they can't explain why they are doing what they do [13]. Another key concept of ST is the concept of 'unintended consequences' where the knowledgeability of human agents is bounded on the one hand by the unconscious and on the other by the unacknowledged conditions and unintended consequences of action [15]. The production and reproduction of structure by action may not occur exactly as expected, as there may be both unacknowledged conditions and unintended consequences of intentional actions. Thus, we must understand that social actors' understanding of their practices is necessarily limited.

3 Method

A systematic literature review was carried out to address the proposed two research questions. The review followed an eight-step systematic guide to conducting a review of IS research by Okoli and Schabram [36] and the concept centric guidelines of Webster and Watson [50] for synthesizing the literature. These two guidelines are specifically relevant to the field of IS research. A brief about those steps is provided as follows.

Step 1: Purpose of the review - Defining the purpose of the review is the first step of conducting a literature review [36]. The goal of this review is to synthesize the results of prior empirical IS research to understand the application of ST and its core concepts.
Step 2: Protocol - The delimitation protocols were set up prior to searching the literature. Only journal articles and conference proceedings published during the past seven years (2015–2021) were selected, to focus our review on contemporary literature. The articles written in English; papers written in other languages were excluded.
Step 3: Searching the literature - The search process was conducted using Elsevier's database (i.e., Scopus). Scopus database offers a wider range of peer-reviewed journals and conference papers compared to other databases [11]. For the purpose of accuracy and reach and to get only the relevant articles that focus on the use of Structuration Theory in IS, the keywords were combined using the search string AND/OR operators and wild card "*" was used to include possible segments after the phrase which produced the following search strings: *(TITLE-ABS-KEY ("Structuration Theory") AND TITLE-ABS-KEY ("Information System*") OR TITLE-ABS-KEY ("Information System* Research"))*. These keywords were searched in the title, abstract and keywords for the wider coverage and quest for accuracy in the search results. A total of 293 articles were retrieved through the initial search process. The delimitation criteria were then applied on these 293 articles which resulted in 65 articles for the review on April 25, 2022 (see Table 1).

Table 1. Search process with delimitation criteria used and hits obtained.

Keywords	Database	Delimitation criteria	Hits
Structuration theory, Information systems, Information systems research	Scopus		293
		Language: English **Document Type:** Conference and Journal Articles **Publication Year:** from 2015 to 2021 **Publication stage:** Limited to Final Publication	65

Step 4: Practical Screening - Sixty-five articles found through the searching process were screened for inclusion by reading the title and abstract to determine the relevance for the review. Here, the articles were screened based on 2 criteria, i) the articles having information system focus and, ii) the papers with a substantial use of Giddens' ST. The papers with marginal use of ST and papers with only a marginal information systems focus were screened out. With the practical screening, 15 articles were weeded out which resulted in a set of 50 papers.
Step 5: Quality Screening – Fifty articles selected through practical screens were examined closely to assess their quality. The quality appraisal is conducted after reading each articles' content focusing mainly on the methodology and findings. The quality screening excludes the articles that did not meet the standard or scoring of the methodological

quality. For example, the articles were screened out based on the judgement of the article's data collection methodology [12]. Only empirical papers with relevance and rigour in terms of methods used as well as providing clear and valid practical and theoretical contributions based on primary data were selected. For example, the conceptual and literature review papers using secondary data were excluded. Altogether, 17 articles were screened out through the quality screening and 33 articles were selected for the review (see Table 2).

Step 6: Data Extraction - The practical screening and quality appraisal resulted in a final set of 33 papers for this review study (see Table 2). The data were extracted into an excel sheet which included notes on various aspects related to the research question such as the recording of general and specific key concepts used in each individual study, other versions of ST and theories used in combination with ST, methodology, references, key findings etc.

Step 7: Data Synthesis - The concept-centric approach was used in synthesizing the data [50]. Based on the initial extracted data of each paper, we examined the similarities and differences among each paper which resulted in several themes for the review. Within these themes, we created classification related to the application of ST and categorized the themes under four different applications which helped to synthesize the studies (see Table 3). Furthermore, the core ST concepts used in each individual paper were identified and six commonly applied structural concepts have been analysed for the review (see Table 4).

Step 8: Writing the review - After completion of all the seven systematic steps of review, the final step of the review was about writing the review which includes mainly reporting the findings. The findings on the use of Gidden's ST are presented below in Sect. 4.

4 Results and Discussions

As stated above, the review covers 33 IS empirical papers which applied Structuration Theory. The review findings are organized into three parts. Firstly, the overview of the literature chosen for the review is presented. Secondly, the emerging themes are categorized to answer *RQ1 - How has ST been used within empirical IS research?* And lastly, the commonly used structural concepts are presented to answer *RQ2 - What are the ST concepts used in empirical IS research?*

4.1 Overview of the Selected Structuration-Oriented Empirical IS Literature

Table 2 shows an overview of the literature. All selected 33 papers are empirical IS research papers published in the past seven years, between 2015 and 2021, to focus the study on contemporary research and the latest trends in the usage of ST in IS research.

Table 2. Overview of selected structuration-oriented empirical IS research papers

Authors	Year	Method used	Published in
Nguyen, Chen & Nguyen	2021	Questionaire Survey	Information & Management Journal
Carraher-Wolverton & Burleson	2021	Field Study & Survey	Information Systems
Matilal	2021	Longitudinal case study	ICIS Conference Proceedings
Ilie & Turel	2020	Survey	Information & management Journal
Shaanika & Iyamu	2020	Case study	EJISDC
Mutudi & Iyamu	2020	Qualitative - interviews	EJISDC
Slaughter, Smith & Hajek	2019	Case study	European Association for Computer Assisted Language Learning
Price, Green & Suhomlinova	2019	Longitudinal case study	Journal of the American Medical Informatics Association
Wherton, Greenhalgh, Procter, Shaw & Shaw	2019	Case study	Qualitative Health Research Journal
Laux & Kranz	2019	Multiple case study	International Conference on Information Systems
Miķelsone, Volkova & Lielā	2019	Content Analysis	12th International Scientific and Practical Conference
Gonzalez, Vargas, Malaver & Ortiz	2019	Case study	Journal of Cases on Information Technology
Köse, Semenov & Tuunanen	2018	Case stduy	Hawaii International Conference on System Sciences
Bernardi	2017	Case study	Journal of the Association for Information Systems
Sergeeva, Huysman, Soekijad, Van Den Hooff	2017	Ethnographic study	MIS Quarterly
Spierings, Kerr & Houghton	2017	Case study	Information Systems Journal
Larkotey, Effah & Boateng	2017	Interpretive Case study	Pacific Asia Conference on Information Systems
Cochran & Gupta	2017	Qualitative case study	Association for Information System Conference
Bresciani & Comi	2017	Experiment	Cross Cultural & Strategic Management (CCSM) Journal
Alsharari & Abougamos	2017	Case study	Asian Review of Accounting Journal
Lee & Zo	2017	Survey	Information Development Journal
Schmitz, Teng & Webb	2016	Survey	MIS Quarterly
Omar, Weerakkody & Millard	2016	Case study	ICEGOV
Janson, Ernst & Matthias	2016	Survey	European Conference on Information Systems (ECIS)
Al Rawahi, Coombs & Doherty	2016	Mixed Method	International Conference on Information Systems
Shahid & Elbanna	2016	Case study	Scandinavian Conference on Information Systems (SCIS)
Grgecic, Holten & Rosenkranz	2015	Survey	Journal of the Association for Information Systems
Janson, Söllner & Leimeister	2015	Mixed Method	International Conference on Information Systems
Hage & Noseleit	2015	Survey	ECIS 2015 Proceedings
Mokosch, Klesel & Niehaves	2015	Multiple case study	Americas Conference on Information Systems
Liang, Peng, Xue, Guo & Wang	2015	Survey	Journal of Management Information Systems
Pozzebon, Rozas & Delgado	2015	case study	RAE Revista de Administracao de Empresas Journal
Kung, Ho, Hung & Wu	2015	Case study	Industrial Marketing Management Journal

The table above shows that the great majority of the ST papers are published in peer-reviewed journals. Out of 33 papers reviewed, 20 papers are published in journals and 13 papers in conference proceedings. In particular, four journals dominate - MIS Quarterly (3), Information Systems Journal (3), Information & Management Journal (2) and the Electronic Journal of Information Systems in Developing Countries (EJISDC) (2). In terms of conference papers, 3 conference venues have more papers than the rest, namely, ICIS (4 papers) and ECIS (2) and AMCIS (2).

In terms of methodologies used, case study approach dominates as shown in Table 2 above. The studies are mostly designed as longitudinal cases studies e.g., [31, 42], other studies involve single or multiple case organization e.g., [3, 28]. The case study methods are also used in specific digital platforms such as twitter and e-portals e.g., [25, 27]. The data collection strategies and analysis of individual case study also varies largely depending on the nature of the case. Another frequently used method is 'survey', mostly used by quantitative IS studies. A couple of them also used mixed method involving both qualitative interviews and quantitative surveys e.g., [1, 22].

4.2   Use of Structuration Theory in Empirical IS Research

To address RQ1 on how ST has been used in empirical IS research, four application themes are categorized through the data synthesis process. As shown in Table 3 below, the first category demonstrates the general application of core ST concepts which enhances our understanding of the IS as a social practice and contributes to offering insights in ST-oriented IS phenomena [23]. For example, Bernardi [3] used the theoretical perspective of ST to analyse a case-study of health information systems in.

Table 3. Emerging themes in the use of structuration theory in empirical IS research

Application	Description	References
General application of core ST concepts	Use of core ST ideas in order to better understand IS as a social practice	3, 16, 17, 27, 42, 44–48, 51
Selective ST concepts	Analysis of the studies focus on a specific structural concept	31, 33, 34
Adaptive Structuration Theory (AST)	Use of AST as an IS-specific version of ST in the empirical IS research	4, 6, 7, 18, 19, 28, 29, 32, 35, 43
Theory combination	Combines ST with other theories to complement and extend theoretical perspectives	1, 2, 9, 20–22, 25, 26, 30, 37, 41

Kenya and raised the understanding of accountability and the role of IT materiality in the process of structuration. The papers under this category adopt Gidden's ST ideas and uncritically reflect upon and apply the core ST concepts such as social structures, duality of structure, social systems, knowledgeable agent, unintended consequences etc. For instance, Sergeeva [44] drew upon the concept of unintended consequences to study how onlookers shape the use of technology at work. The onlooker effect provides a more in-depth explanation for unexpected patterns of technology use emerging in the workplace [44]. Out of 33 studies reviewed, 11 applied general structural concepts in their research. Similarly, the second category of papers under 'selective application of core ST concepts' also extensively draw upon ST concepts to provide insights on IS phenomena. However, this second category of papers are more selective and use only a specific ST concepts in the study. For example, Matilal [31] in the longitudinal case study, specifically used the ST concept of "duality of structure and agency' to study time practices of women who have returned to work after maternity leave in the Indian software services sector. Matilal [31] argued that it is not merely access to information but agency over the scheduling of working time in practice that enables participation of women in the workforce [31]. Similarly, Mutudi and Iyamu [34] adopted the same ST perspective 'duality of structure' to analyse their qualitative data collected on improving the issuance of identity documents in the Republic of Angola. The analysis resulted in development of a framework which enhanced the quality of data and improved the accuracy of issued IDs.

The third category of papers used Adaptive Structuration Theory (AST), a modified version of Gidden's structuration theory to address the mutual influence of technology and social processes [8, 23]. AST was proposed by DeSanctis and Poole [8] as a viable approach for studying the role of advanced information technologies in organizational change. Thus, AST is considered as an IS specific version of ST, and because of its functional approach, AST has an important influence on structurational IS research [23]. Several papers applied AST, particularly in the Group Decision Support System (GDSS) where the studies empirically examine factors affecting GDSS and the mediating effect of structural appropriation in technology-organization-environment e.g., [29], and technology-mediated learning, including examining team structures and roles of teams e.g., [28]. The studies in this category also adapted and extended AST through introduction of new theoretical perspectives for analysing data. For example, a theoretical perspective of adaptation behaviours to the level of individuals e.g., [43] and expansion of its original concept of change process as a single step appropriation process [7]. Out of 33 papers reviewed, 9 applied AST in their research (Table 3).

The fourth theme and last category of papers broaden the perspective of ST by combining ST with other theories. The ST is combined with other theoretical approaches mainly to complement and expand the theoretical perspectives. For example, Köse [25] combined ST and Service Dominant Logic as lenses to study different uses of IS and Ilie and Turel [20] integrated the theory of interpersonal influence and leadership with AST to develop a comprehensive theoretical model anchored in social influence. The combined theoretical model was used to examine how influence tactics can be used to manipulate user resistance and subsequent usage behaviours in the context of large-scale, newly implemented IS. The IS studies have also applied a combination of ST with other theories such as Institutional Theory as a new theoretical lens. The triangulation is used in data collection, including interviews and observations to achieve further progress in institutional theory to tackle issues, and provide a more holistic understanding of institutional changes e.g., [2]. The concepts of these two theories are also used to examine digital-enabled service transformation in the public sector e.g., [38]. Other empirical studies developed and evaluated a theoretical model capturing the cultural effects in the context of technology-mediated learning appropriation based on the combination of AST with other constructs such as espoused cultural values e.g., [21]. Overall, the studies show that the application of a combination of ST with other theories complement each other although each theory has a separate realm of applicability.

4.3 Structuration Theory Concepts used in Empirical IS Research

This section addresses *RQ2 What are the ST concepts used in empirical IS research?* The review has identified six commonly used core ST concepts in the IS research. Table 4 illustrates the core ST concepts used by each individual study. As observed in the table, the empirical IS studies have given most attention to the two core ST concepts of 'social structure' and 'social system'. Social structure is a macro-sociological perspective which resolves that the behaviour of individuals is largely determined by their socialization into the structure. And with use of Gidden's social system concept, the studies acknowledge the distinction between social structure and reproduced actions organized recursively. Almost all the 33 empirical IS papers reviewed have used ST's notion of 'social structure' and 'social system' in their study.

Table 4. Structuration theory concepts used by each individual paper

Authors	Year	Social Structure	Duality of Structure	Social System	Knowledgeable agent	Rules & Resources	Unintended Consequences
Nguyen, Chen & Nguyen	2021	✓			✓	✓	✓
Carraher-Wolverton & Burleson	2021	✓		✓	✓	✓	
Matilal	2021	✓	✓	✓	✓		
Ilie & Turel	2020	✓	✓	✓	✓	✓	✓
Shaanika & Iyamu	2020	✓	✓	✓	✓	✓	✓
Mutudi & Iyamu	2020	✓	✓	✓		✓	✓
Slaughter, Smith & Hajek	2019	✓		✓	✓		✓
Price, Green & Suhomlinova	2019	✓		✓	✓		
Wherton, Greenhalgh, Procter, Shaw & Shaw	2019	✓		✓	✓	✓	✓
Laux & Kranz	2019	✓		✓		✓	
Miķelsone, Volkova & Lielā	2019	✓	✓	✓	✓	✓	✓
Gonzalez, Vargas, Malaver & Ortiz	2019	✓	✓	✓	✓	✓	
Köse, Semenov & Tuunanen	2018	✓	✓	✓	✓	✓	
Bernardi	2017	✓	✓	✓	✓	✓	✓
Sergeeva, Huysman, Soekijad, Van Den Hooff	2017	✓		✓	✓	✓	✓
Spierings, Kerr & Houghton	2017	✓	✓	✓	✓	✓	✓
Larkotey, Effah & Boateng	2017	✓	✓	✓	✓	✓	
Cochran & Gupta	2017	✓		✓	✓	✓	
Bresciani & Comi	2017	✓		✓		✓	✓
Alsharari & Abougamos	2017	✓	✓	✓			
Lee & Zo	2017	✓		✓		✓	
Schmitz, Teng & Webb	2016	✓	✓	✓	✓	✓	✓
Omar, Weerakkody & Millard	2016	✓	✓	✓	✓	✓	✓
Janson, Ernst & Matthias	2016	✓		✓		✓	
Al Rawahi, Coombs & Doherty	2016	✓	✓	✓	✓	✓	
Shahid & Elbanna	2016	✓		✓	✓	✓	✓
Grgecic, Holten & Rosenkranz	2015	✓	✓	✓		✓	
Janson, Söllner & Leimeister	2015	✓		✓		✓	
Hage & Noseleit	2015	✓	✓	✓		✓	
Mokosch, Klesel & Niehaves	2015	✓	✓	✓		✓	✓
Liang, Peng, Xue, Guo & Wang	2015	✓		✓	✓		
Pozzebon, Rozas & Delgado	2015	✓		✓	✓	✓	✓
Kung, Ho, Hung & Wu	2015	✓		✓	✓	✓	

The idea of 'knowledgeable agent' has also been frequently used in the IS studies. This is one of the key features of ST considering that all human beings are knowledgeable i.e. human agents are purposive and know much about the grounds for their actions and also have a capability to reflexively monitor their own and others' actions [23]. The researchers consider social actors as being highly knowledgeable about what they do. More attention is also given to Gidden's concept of 'rules and resources'. In ST, structure is conceptualized in terms of rules and resources where rules refer to generalized procedures which guide the actions of individuals, and the resources are the facilities that provide capacity to perform various tasks. In comparison, the ST concepts of 'duality of structure' and 'unintended consequences' have been sparsely used in the literature. This could be because the idea of 'duality of structure' has been selectively applied in the empirical IS studies e.g., [31, 34]. The notion of 'unintended consequences' is less used because some researchers may not have considered their accounts as offering only a partial explanation of their actions, which needs to be supplemented by other evidences [23].

4.4 A Short Discussion on the Findings

This paper reviews the contemporary empirical IS papers to determine how ST is empirically applied in the IS research. Thus, during the paper selection process, we closely examined the methodologies applied in the studies. As presented in the overview under Sect. 4.1, the 'case study' research strategies dominate the overall research design - more than 50% of the studies used case studies with variations in data collection strategies such as qualitative interviews and quantitative surveys. By and large, we have come to an understanding that Gidden's ST have been used in different ways in the field of IS. The categorization of ST application into four different themes clearly and concisely depicts how ST has been used in empirical IS research. The first category of 'application of general structural concepts' and second category of 'selective application' both uncritically apply ST concepts to contribute to the existing structuration-oriented IS literature. The papers in these two categories passively adopt core ST concepts without being critical about the limitations of the ST ideas or expanding original perspectives. The third and fourth category of papers have reflected more on the use of ST in the IS domain. The application of AST addresses Gidden's lack of attention to IS research [8] and having been developed as an IS specific version of ST, about a third of the papers used AST demonstrating its influence in the structural IS research. It is also found that the application of ST under the category of 'combine theory' is extensively used in the IS literature. More than 30% of the papers are in this category. The ST is combined with other theories mainly to form new theoretical perspectives which also indicates that ST has not only contributed as a standalone theory but also applied in extending into other theoretical lenses.

Our review of IS papers shows that the core ST concepts are empirically applied in the research. Each individual paper cited at least three to four concepts in the studies. Out of the 6 commonly used structural concepts identified in the literature, the most attention has been given to the concept of 'social structure' and 'social system'. The other notions such as 'knowledgeable agent' and 'rules & resources' are also frequently cited. The concept of 'duality of structure' and 'unintended consequences' are less cited comparatively.

We are also aware of some limitations of this study. Firstly, the literature search was conducted with only one database (i.e., Scopus). Additional searches through other databases might provide some additional relevant papers. Secondly, we only analysed the contemporary empirical IS research from the last seven years in this study.

5 Conclusion

This study explores the ways in which IS researchers have used Gidden's ST, focusing on the structural concepts frequently drawn upon in their research. Overall, ST has been used as a theoretical lens in analysing the IS phenomena by applying general and selective core ST concepts. Several studies have also applied Adaptive Structuration Theory which is a modified version of ST specifically developed for the IS field while others combined ST with other theories to extend the theoretical perspectives. The core structural concepts of social structure, duality of structure, social system, knowledgeable agent, rules & resources, and unintended consequences are identified as the most used concepts in the literature. We extend previous research by categorizing the application of ST in the IS domain and identifying the core ST concepts found in the reviewed studies. Additionally, the study also provides a collection of methodologies applied in the empirically oriented IS literature. Thus, the paper contributes to offering a better understanding on how technologies interact with organizations through the application of ST and provides a state-of-the-art insight on the structural concepts used in contemporary IS research.

References

1. Al Rawahi, K., Coombs, C., Doherty, N.F.: The realization of public value through e-government: a structuration perspective. In: The proceedings of 2016 International Conference on Information Systems, (ICIS 2016), AIS (2016)
2. Alsharari, N.M., Abougamos, H.: The processes of accounting changes as emerging from public and fiscal reforms an interpretive study. Asian Rev. Acc. **25**(1), 2–33 (2017)
3. Bernardi, R.: Health information systems and accountability in Kenya: a structuration theory perspective. J. Assoc. Inf. Syst. **18**(12), 931–958 (2018)
4. Bresciani, S., Comi, A.: Facilitating culturally diverse groups with visual templates in collaborative systems: increasing structuration to improve precision. Cross Cult. Strateg. Manag. (CCSM) **24**(1), 78–98 (2017)
5. Bryant, C.A., Jary, D.: The Contemporary Giddens: Social Theory in a Globalizing Age. Palgrave, Basingstoke (2001)
6. Carraher-Wolverton, C., Burleson, J.: Toward an understanding of how post-deployment user-developer interactions influence system utilization. ACM SIGMIS Database DATABASE Adv. Inf. Syst. **52**(4), 45–64 (2021)
7. Cochran, J.D., Gupta, S.: Business-driven information systems change: establishing an alternate lens for understanding the change process. In: The Proceedings of Americas Conference on Information Systems 2017 (AMCIS 2017), AIS (2017)
8. DeSanctis, G., Poole, M.S.: Capturing the complexity in advanced technology use: adaptive structuration theory. Organ. Sci. **5**(2), 121–147 (1994)
9. Engelbert, R., Graeml, A.: Beyond IT acceptance. In: The Proceedings of 21st Americas Conference on Information Systems (AMCIS (2015), AIS (2015)
10. Englund, H., Gerdin, J.: Structuration theory in accounting research: applications and applicability. Crit. Perspect. Account. **25**(2), 162–180 (2014)
11. Falagas, M.E., Pitsouni, E.I., Malietzis, G.A., Pappas, G.: Comparison of PubMed, Scopus, web of science, and Google scholar: strengths and weaknesses. FASEB J. **22**(2), 338–342 (2008)
12. Fink, A.: Conducting Research Lit Reviews: From the Internet to Paper. SAGE, California (2019)
13. Giddens, A.: Central Problems in Social Theory. Macmillan, Basingstoke (1979)
14. Giddens, A.: Comments on the theory of structuration. J. Theory Soc. Behav. **13**(1), 75–80 (1983)
15. Giddens, A.: The Constitution of Society. Polity Press, Cambridge (1984)

16. Gonzalez, R.A., Vargas, M., Malaver, F., Ortiz, E.: Structuration and learning in a software firm: a technology-based entrepreneurship case study. J. Cases Inf. Technol. **21**(1), 1–18 (2019)
17. Grgecic, D., Holten, R., Rosenkranz, C.: The impact of functional affordances and symbolic expressions on the formation of beliefs. J. Assoc. Inf. Syst. **16**(7), 580–607 (2015)
18. Fuchs, C., Hess, T.: Adapting agile methods to develop solutions for the industrial internet of things. In: the proceeding of 2017 European Conference on Information Systems (ECIS 2017), Association for Information Systems (2017)
19. Hage, E., Noseleit, F.: Changes and variations in online and offline communications patterns: including peer effects. In: The Proceedings of the 23rd European Conference on Information Systems (ECIS 2015), Association for Information Systems (2015)
20. Ilie, V., Turel, O.: Manipulating user resistance to large-scale information systems through influence tactics. Inf. Manag. **57**(3), 103178 (2020)
21. Janson, A., Ernst, S.-J., Matthias, S.: How cultural values influence the appropriation of technology-mediated learning research. In: The Proceedings of the 24th European Conference on Information Systems (ECIs2016), AIS (2016)
22. Janson, A., Söllner, M., Leimeister, J.M.: Towards a holistic understanding of technology-mediated learning appropriation. In: The Proceedings of 2015 International Conference on Information Systems (ICIS2015), Association for Information Systems (2015)
23. Jones, M.R., Karsten, H.: Giddens's structuration theory and information systems research. MIS Q. **32**(1), 127–157 (2008)
24. Kort, W., Gharbi, J.E.: Structuration theory amid negative and positive criticism. Int. J. Bus. Soc. Res. **3**(5), 92–104 (2013)
25. Köse, D. B., Semenov, A., Tuunanen, T.: Utilitarian use of social media services: a study on twitter. In: Bui T.X. (ed.) The Proceeding of 2018 Hawaii International Conference on System Sciences (HICSS 2018), IEEE Computer Society (2018)
26. Kung, K.-H., Ho, C.-F., Hung, W.-H., Wu, C.-C.: Organizational adaptation for using PLM systems: group dynamism and management involvement. Ind. Mark. Manag. J. **44**, 83–97 (2015)
27. Larkotey, W.O., Effah, J., Boateng, R.: Development of e-passport application portal: a developing country case study. In: The Proceedings of the 21st Pacific Asia Conference on Information Systems (PACIS 2017), Association for Information Systems (2017)
28. Laux, I., Kranz, J.: Coexisting plan-driven and agile methods: how tensions emerge and are resolved. In: The Proceedings of the 40th International Conference on Information Systems (ICIS2019), Association for Information Systems (2019)
29. Lee, H.-K., Zo, H.: Assimilation of military group decision support systems in Korea: the mediating role of structural appropriation. Inf. Dev. **33**(1), 14–28 (2017)
30. Liang, H., Peng, Z., Xue, Y., Guo, X., Wang, N.: Employees' exploration of complex systems: an integrative view. JMIS **32**(1), 322–357 (2015)
31. Matilal, O.: "Time" to be more inclusive? flexi-time and retention in the information system workforce. In: The Proceedings of 2020 International Conference on Information Systems (ICIS 2020), Association for Information Systems (2020)
32. Miķelsone, E., Volkova, T., Lielā, E.: Potential benefits of web-based idea management system based on practical evidence. In: the Proceeding of 12th International Scientific and Practical Conference on Environment Technology Resources (2019)
33. Mokosch, G., Klesel, M., Niehaves, B.: Putting flesh on the duality of structure: the case of IT consumerization. In: the Proceeding of the 21st Americas Conference on Information Systems (AMCIS2015), Association for Information Systems (2015)
34. Mutudi, M., Iyamu, T.: An information systems framework to improve the issuance of identity documents through enhanced data quality in the Republic of Angola. Electron. J. Inf. Syst. Developing Countries **86**(1), e12111 (2020)

35. Nguyen, T., Chen, J.V., Nguyen, T.P.H.: Appropriation of accounting information system use under the new IFRS: impacts on accounting process performance. Inf. Manag. **58**(8), 103534 (2021)
36. Okoli, C., Schabram, K.: A guide to conducting a systematic literature review of information systems research. Working Papers on SSRN (2010)
37. Omar, A., Elhaddadeh, R.: Structuring institutionalization of digitally-enabled service transformation in public sector: does actor or structure matters? In: the Proceeding of the 22nd Americas Conference on Information Systems (AMCIS2016), AIS (2016)
38. Omar, A., Weerakkody, V., Millard, J.: Digital-enabled service transformation in public sector: Institutionalization as a product of interplay between actors and structures during organisational change. In: The Proceedings of ICEGOV - International Conference on Theory and Practice of Electronic Governance, ACM (2016)
39. Orlikowski, W.J.: Using technology and constituting structures: a practice lens for studying technology in organizations. Organ. Sci. **11**(4), 404–428 (2000)
40. Pozzebon, M., Pinsonneault, A.: Structuration theory in the IS field: an assessment of research strategies. In: The Proceeding of the 9th European Conference on Information Systems Bled, Slovenia, 27–29 June (2001)
41. Pozzebon, M., Rozas, S.T., Delgado, N.A.: Use and consequences of participatory GIS in a Mexican municipality: applying a multilevel framework. RAE Revista de Administracao de Empresas J. **55**, 290–303 (2015)
42. Price, C., Green, W., Suhomlinova, O.: Twenty-five years of national health IT: Exploring strategy, structure, and systems in the English NHS. J. Am. Med. Inf. Assoc. **26**(3), 188–197 (2019)
43. Schmitz, K.W., Teng, J.T.C., Webb, K.J.: Capturing the complexity of malleable IT use: adaptive structuration theory for individuals. MIS Q. **40**(3), 663–686 (2016)
44. Sergeeva, A., Huysman, M., Soekijad, M., Van Den Hooff, B.: Through the eyes of others: how onlookers shape the use of technology at work. MIS Q. **41**(4), 1153–1178 (2017)
45. Shaanika, I., Iyamu, T.: The use of mobile systems to access health care big data in the Namibian environment. Electron. J. Inf. Syst. Developing Countries **86**(2), e12120 (2020)
46. Shahid, A.R., Elbanna, A.: Who is in control in crowdsourcing initiatives? an examination of the case of crowdmapping. In: Lundh Snis, U. (ed.) SCIS 2016. LNBIP, vol. 259, pp. 135–148. Springer, Cham (2016). https://doi.org/10.1007/978-3-319-43597-8_10
47. Slaughter, Y., Smith, W., Hajek, J.: Videoconferencing and the networked provision of language programs in regional and rural schools. J. Eur. Assoc. Comput. Assist. Lang. Learn. **31**(2), 204–217 (2019)
48. Spierings, A., Kerr, D., Houghton, L.: Issues that support the creation of ICT workarounds: towards a theoretical understanding of feral IS. ISJ **27**(6), 775–794 (2017)
49. Turner, J.R., Morris, M., Atamenwan, I.: A theoretical literature review on adaptive structuration theory as its relevance to human resource development. Adv. Dev. Hum. Resour. **21**(3), 289–302 (2019)
50. Webster, J., Watson, R.T.: Analyzing the past to prepare for the future: writing a literature review. MIS Q. **26**(2), 13–23 (2002)
51. Wherton, J., Greenhalgh, T., Procter, R., Shaw, S., Shaw, J.: Wandering as a sociomaterial practice: extending the theorization of GPS tracking in cognitive impairment. Qual. Health Res. J. **29**(3), 328–344 (2019)

Health and Wellbeing

Affordances of Sleep-Tracking: Insights from Smart Ring Users

Shan Feng⬤, Matti Mäntymäki(⊠) ⬤, and Hannu Salmela⬤

Turku School of Economics, University of Turku, 20014 Turku, Finland
matti.mantymaki@utu.fi

Abstract. This study explores the usage and the respective affordances of sleep-tracking with a smart ring and the associated app. Sleep-tracking is a growing area of self-tracking. While the use and influences of self-tracking have drawn considerable scholarly attention, the specific affordances of sleep-tracking are not well understood. Hence, this study aims to explore what affordances can be attributed to using a sleep-tracking device and the correspondence between affordances and features. We used the Gioia method to analyze and theorize on interview data from 14 Oura ring users. We identified four affordances of sleep-tracking executed through a smart ring, namely, dynamic goal setting, self-quantification, learning, and nudging. Drawing on the affordances, we further corresponded affordances with device features. The findings extend the body of knowledge on the affordances of self-tracking.

Keywords: Sleep-tracking · Usage · Affordance · Features · Smart ring

1 Introduction

Getting enough restorative sleep is crucial for the health and well-being [1, 2]. Conversely, a vast body of research has documented that problems with sleep lead to many negative health consequences [3, 4]. In 2019, the size of the sleep technology market was $15 billion, accounting for 3.48% of the so-called global sleep economy 2019 [5]. The demand for sleep technology is enormous, and the supply of dedicated sleep-tracking devices is growing. Compared with fitness and diet, sleep is an unconscious and passive behavior that cannot be manually tracked [6]. Sleep-tracking devices have the potential to overcome this limitation.

Self-tracking "involves practices in which people knowingly and purposely collect information about themselves, which they then review and consider applying to the conduct of their lives" [7]. According to the self-tracking definition, sleep-tracking refers to collecting and reflecting on data about an individual's sleep through various digital technologies, such as devices, applications, and platforms. Sleep-tracking represents a new area of self-tracking. The dedicated sleep-tracking devices provide details of sleep data, like sleep stages, sleep efficiency, time in bed, and resting heart rate. It also offers bedtime window notifications, sleep analysis reports, sleep recommendations,

© IFIP International Federation for Information Processing 2022
Published by Springer Nature Switzerland AG 2022
S. Papagiannidis et al. (Eds.): I3E 2022, LNCS 13454, pp. 343–355, 2022.
https://doi.org/10.1007/978-3-031-15342-6_27

and meditation for calming down. Furthermore, compared with general self-tracking devices, dedicated sleep-tracking devices connect all relevant data with sleep data to help establish healthy sleep habits. All features of sleep-tracking devices give a basis for affordances of sleep-tracking devices.

While there is a body of literature that employs the affordance lens to explore self-tracking device usage [8–12], the relationship between features and affordances of self-tracking devices [13–15], and the framework of affordances of self-tracking devices [10, 12], there is a paucity of research that focusing particularly on sleep-tracking [16]. Moreover, the previous research has indicated a need for further research on how people perceive, are influenced by, and act on the information produced by self-tracking devices [17–20].

To fill in this theoretical and empirical void, this study aims to explore the affordances of sleep-tracking executed through a smart ring. In doing so, we address the following research question: *what affordances do users attribute to a sleep-tracking focused smart ring?* We have conducted 14 in-depth interviews among users of a leading smart ring, Oura, that is designed particularly for sleep-tracking. We used the Gioia method [21] in coding, analyzing, and theorizing on our empirical data. Finally, this research came up with four sleep-tracking affordances executed through a smart ring and corresponded to technology features. The results enriched the self-tracking affordances and helped users understand their potential behaviors with sleep-tracking devices.

The remainder of this paper is structured as follows. The second section reviews prior research on affordance theory and self-tracking affordances. Thereafter, we present the research method, followed by the data analysis. In the fourth section, we report the research findings, followed by their discussion in the fifth section.

2 Background

The concept of affordance was introduced by the ecological psychologist James J. Gibson [22]. According to Gibson [22], the affordances of the environment are "what it offers the animal, what it provides or furnishes, either for good or ill" (p. 127). Norman [23] applied the affordance lens in human-computer interaction and defined affordances to describe the perceived properties as "the perceived and actual properties of the thing, primarily those fundamental properties that determine just how the thing could possibly be used" [23].

Recent IS research tends to follow the Gibson-based definition of affordance [10, 24, 25]. Building on Gibson's conception, Volkoff and Strong [25] conceptualized affordances to refer to "what is offered, provided, or furnished to someone or something by an object" [25]. The potential for behavior arises from the relationship between the object and someone or something [26]. In other words, the affordance concept denotes that objects offer the possibility for people to do something, which in turn is determined by the features of the technical object and the actors' characteristics [24].

In the context of self-tracking, some research tried to clarify the affordance categories of self-tracking devices. In prior research, based on the devices' properties, affordances of self-tracking devices can be classified into informational and motivational affordances [11]. In terms of motivational affordance, it can be divided into master and performance motivational affordance [27], or self-monitoring, rewards, and social comparison affordance [28]. Furthermore, the affordances of self-tracking devices can be grouped into learning and behavior-focused affordance based on how these functions were used [13]. Oriented by functions, affordances of self-tracking devices contain self-monitoring, performance analysis, exercise guidance, rewards, social comparison, watching others, social recognition, and self-presentation [15]. Multiple affordances of self-tracking devices can also help users achieve their activity goals, like activity improvement, planning, and monitoring [10].

Overall, affordance theory is a new way of thinking about the relationship between technology and users from a socio-technical perspective [29]. Applying affordance to sleep-tracking devices, this study aims to explore sleep-tracking affordances executed through a smart ring and correspondence between affordances and technology features.

3 Method

3.1 Research Context

We chose the Oura ring as the focal device to investigate the affordances of sleep-tracking devices. The ring is made of titanium and has a battery life up to 4–7 days. Since Oura is a ring, it does not have a display, but all information is provided through the smartphone app and the Oura cloud, including short-term and long-term trends. The Oura app synthesizes the data collected by the sensors of the ring into three scores: sleep, activity, and readiness. It also provides dynamic daily activity goals and recommendations based on the users' activity and sleep data. According to Oura, the ring operates with 92% accuracy for body temperature tracking [30] and 98% for heart rate variability (HRV) [31]. During the Covid-19 pandemic, body temperature tracking has helped early detect the disease [32].

Compared with activity tracking devices, a dedicated sleep-tracking device like Oura has been designed to collect, analyze, and synthesize several types of sleep-related data. Compared with other sleep-tracking devices, like smart mattresses, the Oura provides daytime data to enrich the sleep-related data and improve sleep-related recommendations. To sum up, the Oura ring is a representative sleep-tracking device.

3.2 Data Collection

The data was collected with semi-structured interviews among users of Oura ring. The interviews aimed to obtain in-depth insights into users' usage patterns and explore the affordances of sleep-tracking executed with a smart ring. The interviews were conducted in English from March to April 2021 in Finland. Because of the Covid-19 pandemic, Zoom was used to conduct the interviews. The interviews were video recorded with the consent of the informants. The interview questions include users' personal backgrounds (gender, age, education background, and occupation), general use habits (reasons for using, expectations, use duration, frequency of use), and user experience (data tracking, functions, best/worst thing, well-being management).

We used a snowball sampling approach to recruit informants. Interviews began with authors' personal networks and asked them to nominate potential informants who meet the requirements for more interviews. According to Oura, the ring needs to accumulate data for ca. two weeks to be able to make inferences regarding the user. So, informants in this research must be at least 18 years old and have used Oura for at least two weeks. In total, 14 Oura ring users, of which 8 were males and 6 females, were interviewed. Table 1 provides the background information about the informants. All informants had either a master's or a Ph.D. degree.

The interviews lasted from 23 to 58 min, totaling up to 498 min of interview videos and 52,486 words of interview transcripts. After 14 interviews, the interviews no longer generated new insights [33]. Thus, we concluded that the point of saturation was reached.

Table 1. Background of the informants

Informants	Age range	Gender	Usage time (months)	Informants	Age range	Gender	Usage time (months)
1	45–65	Female	8	8	25–44	Female	48
2	45–65	Male	8	9	25–44	Male	24
3	45–65	Female	24	10	25–44	Male	12
4	25–44	Male	3	11	45–65	Female	24
5	65 +	Male	10	12	25–44	Male	1
6	45–65	Female	41	13	25–44	Male	16
7	45–65	Female	41	14	25–44	Male	20

In addition to the primary data collected through interviews, the two first authors have been using the ring and following discussions in the Oura groups on Facebook to obtain an in-depth first-hand understanding of the phenomenon of interest.

3.3 Data Analysis

The interviews were transcribed from video recordings and imported to NVivo 12.6.0 software. We applied the Gioia method [21] to guide the data analysis.

The Gioia method can be seen as an adaptation grounded theory [21] with a specific emphasis on capturing people's retrospective and real-time statements through, e.g., interviews and observation [21, 34]. Gioia et al. [21] further suggest practices to enhance the rigor in qualitative research, for example, organizing the data into a more structured form. The analysis process includes identifying first-order codes from the data, combining them into second-order themes, and finally establishing theory-informed aggregate dimensions. These three stages form a basis for building a data structure [21, 34]. As typical inductive research, our analytical process was iterative and overlapped with data collection.

We started with open coding to break data apart and use phrases to stand for original data [35]. When identifying the first-order codes, the researcher reads the materials from beginning to end and names instances of text with codes that reflect the raw data [36].

We used the research question to guide the creation of first-order codes. We focused on identifying the possible behaviors that users can do with the sleep rings as the affordance of the ring.

In the second stage of the analysis (Gioia et al., 2013), we further summarized the first-order codes into more general concepts. Annotations in NVivo and brief notes help to record and develop the analysis processes. Finally, in the third stage of the analysis, we scrutinized the categories through the mapped affordances. Figure 1 presents the data structure that summarizes the data analysis process and its results.

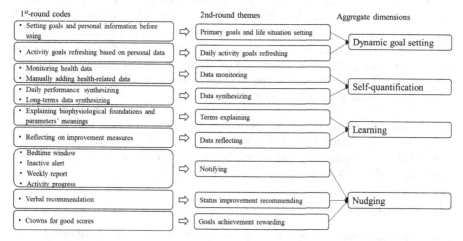

Fig. 1. The three stages of the analysis process of affordances

4 Affordances of Sleep-Tracking with a Smart Ring

Four aggregate dimensions described the affordances of sleep-tracking with a smart ring as a result of inductive research. These four affordances describe the potential behaviors that arise from the relationship between users and the rings, including dynamic goal setting, self-quantification, learning, and nudging.

4.1 Dynamic Goal Setting

The first aggregate dimension of affordance is dynamic goal setting affordance, which refers to the ring that enables users to set or adjust their primary goals and daily goals through recommendations, default, or personalized settings [11, 14]. In Oura, the dynamic goal setting can be divided into the primary goal, life situation setting, and dynamic activity goal refreshing.

The primary goal and life situation setting provide an opportunity for users set primary goals and refine their basic information. After having the installed the Oura app, the user needs to provide a set of background information (such as gender, age, height, and weight), his/her primary goal (e.g., reduce stress, increase physical activity, etc.), and answers questions regarding the life situation, such as my current goals, current sleep habits, and factors affecting sleep. The Oura app will provide the user updates and reminders.

> *"There are many options like you can choose if you have some goals for your Oura ring usage, like, if you want to increase your fitness, then there is something. What I have set for Oura is that I want to improve my sleep. And I want to reduce my stress". (P09)*

Dynamic activity goal refreshing provides an opportunity for users to have automatic refreshing daily activity goals based on their personal data. The Oura app will provide flexible daily activity goals based on users' activity level in the past day and the quality and amount of user's sleep in the last night. Thus, after a stressful day and badly slept night, the activity goal will be lower than usual, or the app will recommend taking a rest for a day. This flexible goal setting was frequently praised by our informants and considered the main advantage of the ring.

> *"The goals of Oura ring are always activity-based, so it has flexible goals.... During the day, I tried to check that, like the activity goals, so I try to balance my workouts.... In the evening, I also look if I have reached the activity goal or not, because it does change in Oura". (P3)*

4.2 Self-quantification

The second aggregate dimension of affordance is self-quantification affordance. It refers to how the ring enables users to observe and document their personal information [10, 28], process the data collected by the sensor of the ring, and present the insights through the app's dashboard in various visualized formats [9, 10]. The self-quantification affordance includes two sub-categories, namely data monitoring and data synthesizing.

Data monitoring provides an opportunity for users to observe and document their personal information [10, 28]. The fundamental function of a sleep-tracking ring is sleep data monitoring. Other self-monitoring features, such as activity and readiness, can support getting better sleep. Furthermore, The Oura ring provides several sleep-related parameters, such as HRV, sleep stage, respiratory rate, and body temperature. In addition, the informants described how they focus on certain specific parameters, depending on their goals and life situation. In addition, the user can manually add a workout, breathing exercise, meditation, and tags about the activities. Oura provides several guided and unguided audio sessions to boost energy or improve sleep and focus.

> *"Do mostly using it for tracking my quality of sleep in general, and then also my activity". (P14)*

> *"And also, the Oura ring measures the skin temperature. The Wrist [Apple watch] doesn't.... When you go to home [Oura app home], you can use the plus here and add a workout [record exercise manually]. I do my yoga. It takes about 20 min. And I record that through the application. It's important to do it with the Oura ring" (P5)*

Another part of self-quantification affordance is data synthesizing. The Oura ring combines measured parameters and uses three simple scores to show the users' performance. The interviews generally indicated that the three key scores provided by the ring, namely sleep, activity, and readiness, were regarded as the most important indicators. As a result of synthesizing the data, long-term data is aggregated for users to check long-term trends related to sleep, readiness, and physical activity.

"The way I figure it out is if I fulfill the activity goals, then I sleep better. My readiness score goes up. And if I sleep better. My readiness goal is up, and then I can do the activities much easier. So it's a kind of a fulfilling circle". (P05)

"Usually I like looking at the weekly trend, like how the week has been and how many times have I achieved my goals as in the activity, and so I like to look at the trends as well". (P06)

4.3 Learning

The third aggregate dimension of affordance is learning, which refers to users being better able to listen to themselves by increasing users' knowledge of the biophysiological foundations, parameters' meanings, and improvement measures [13]. Learning affordance includes term explaining and data reflecting.

Terms explaining provides information about the biophysiological foundations of each measured parameter and thus help the user learn and understand the meaning of each parameter. In addition, the app provides information about the typical range of the parameters and guidance on how to interpret different trends with respect to these parameters. In order to get a better understanding of terms and guide their workouts, some informants like to dig into and study the scientific backgrounds.

"I will probably look more into the different data they are providing. Because there are a lot of articles about how to use the HRV, for example, you know, better designing your exercises, and so on". (P05)

"So, I have studied quite a bit of what does heart rate variability mean and what's the science in the background of the stuff". (P13)

Data reflecting provides improvement measures to teach users how to improve their health status. The mobile app affords the user a better understanding of the scientific basis underlying sleep and sleep quality. Informants announced that they would think after receiving the scores and consider what affected their scores. And then, they can follow the improvement measures and find more targeted ways to improve their sleep.

"It easy that I can afterward work from the Oura data. Okay, now this is the situation, and then I can sort of access what I did the previous day and what has maybe impacted my sleep. So that's how I have learned what I should do to sleep better". (P03)

4.4 Nudging

The fourth aggregate dimension of affordance is nudging, which refers to guiding a user in a certain direction. In Oura, three sub-categories make up nudging affordance: notifying, status improvement recommending, and goal achievement rewarding.

The notifying reminds users to raise their attention to something. As exemplified by the quotation, the Oura app has notification functions that provide users with reminders, such as bedtime windows, inactive alerts, weekly reports, and activity progress. Depending on personal data, Oura provides users a bedtime window and reminds them to start relaxing before this window. As for activity, when users are sedentary for a long time, Oura will remind them to stretch their legs a bit. Oura also reminds users of the activity progress to encourage them to reach the goal. Moreover, Oura pays much attention to data trends and pushes out the weekly report on Sunday. Users can review the overall data in this report.

> *"There might be some notifications during the day. For example, it's time to take a break, or I'm close to achieving the activity score, or I've achieved it". (P07)*

> *"I can see from the weekly report. Oh, it was that night I took some whiskey, that was the result". (P12)*

Status improvement recommending provides verbal recommendations to nudge users based on collected data. In the Oura app, users can get short verbal recommendations on the app's home. The verbal recommendations are adjusted based on prior data and users' rhythm. For example, if users do not sleep well, Oura will recommend them to take it easy and pay attention; if users get good scores, Oura will suggest them take on a creative challenge or do what they like. In addition, the Oura app provides audio and video materials before sleep to start winding down in the evening and go to bed in an optimal time window.

> *"And I do feel that it's easier to obey the signals from the Oura in a way. Because if I feel sick. I'm like, maybe still trying to do too much, but the Oura in the sense that tells me to slow it down, then I can tell my supervisor: Okay, Oura is telling that". (P03)*

Goal achievement rewarding provides crowns for users who perform well. In Oura, there is a calendar view of your crowns and dots each day. The three dots reflect sleep, readiness, and activity, respectively. When scores above 85, they may receive a crown. The three scores will be reflected in the dots below each crown icon. The crown encourages users to get enough scores to earn rewards.

> *"This is the month screen where dots are there. You can see how many dots in the goal... I won't look at that screen too much, but sometimes I notice that I'm a bit frustrated, because there are no crowns". (P07)*

5 Discussion and Conclusion

5.1 The Affordance-Features for Sleep-Tracking

This study set out to explore the affordances of sleep-tracking devices. Based on our analysis of the empirical data, we identified four sleep-tracking affordances executed through a smart ring: dynamic goal setting, self-quantification, learning, and nudging. In order to reveal the support of sleep-tracking features for affordances, this study extracted the features mentioned by the informants corresponding to affordances. Table 2 shows the results of correspondence between affordances and features.

First, goal-related and personal background collection features support the dynamic goal setting affordance, which helps users prepare well and provide a personalized set of baselines for the subsequent tracking. Furthermore, flexible daily activity goals enable users to adjust their activity based on collected data. The dynamic goal setting affordance is unique for Oura compared to prior self-tracking affordances, like preparation affordance [14] and motivational affordance [11].

Second, self-quantification is the chief affordance. It encompasses affordances explored in prior research such self-monitoring [15, 28], tracking [9], and visualizing [8–10]. Affordances related to self-quantification can be found in almost all available health and fitness tracking applications [37] since self-tracking technologies generally enable users to automatically and manually track their health information, analyze performance, and visualize data.

Third, learning affordance offers the possibility for users to go deep insight into the parameters. The Oura provides much information to support learning affordance, like biophysiological foundation, typical ranges, and detriment causes of measured parameters. This affordance is aligned with the prior learning affordances in self-tracking [12, 13, 27].

Fourth, the Oura app has notifications, short verbal recommendations, and rewards for supporting nudging affordance. Prior research illustrated similar affordance in self-tracking, for example, activity alerts [10] and rewards [10, 15, 28]. However, nudge affordance gives a comprehensive way to describe those affordances that guide users in a certain direction. In addition, prior self-tracking research has also pointed out that digital technologies can nudge people into behavioral changes [38]. Nudging is an important affordance to help users change their behaviors to improve their sleep.

5.2 Implications

This study explores sleep-tracking affordances executed through a smart ring and corresponds affordance with technology features. From the research implications, first, our study contributes to the self-tracking and quantified self literature by adding to the thus far scant research on the affordances of sleep-tracking. Considering that the current research on self-tracking affordances which focused on comprehensive or activity-focused smart-watches or smart bands [10–13], this study focused on sleep-tracking with a smart ring. We outlined four affordances to present the potential actions enabled by the smart ring, namely dynamic goal setting, self-quantification, learning, and nudging.

Table 2. Affordance-features for sleep-tracking

	Dynamic goal setting	Self-quantification	Learning	Nudging
Conceptualization	The ring enable users to set or adjust their primary goals and daily goals through recommendations, default or personalized settings [11, 14]	How the ring enables users to observe and document their personal information [10, 28], process the data collected by the sensor of the ring, and present the insights through the app's dashboard in various visualized formats [9, 10]	Users being better able to listen to themselves by increasing users' knowledge of the biophysiological foundations, parameters' meanings, and improvement measures [13]	Guiding a user in a certain direction
Technology features	1. Primary goal 2. Life situation survey 3. Personal background information 4. Flexible daily activity goals	1. Monitoring personal data 2. Add a workout, breathing and meditation 3. Add tags to the activities 4. Performance analysis 5. Data visualization	1. Biophysiological foundation of each parameter 2. Information about the typical range of the parameters 3. Information about detriment causes of sleep	1. Notifications 2. Short verbal recommendations 3. Rewards

Second, In prior research, most self-tracking studies have examined the relationship between affordances and features [13–15]. This research corresponded sleep-tracking affordances with features, comparing the similarity and differences between sleep-tracking and self-tracking affordances. As a result, this research emphasized the unique affordance (dynamic goal setting affordance) and the core affordance in sleep-tracking usage (self-quantification affordance). At the same time, this research also highlighted the direct affordances (nudging) for users changing their behavior.

From the practical implications, first, this research summarized four affordances of sleep-tracking executed through a smart ring. Our observations highlight the value of unique dynamic goal setting and gentle and encouraging nudging as particular affordances of sleep-tracking executed through a smart ring. The informants stated that the flexible goals and nudging affordance influenced their behavior to some extent. However, the main effect of using a smart ring is an increased focus on sleep as an element of health and well-being. Thus, the system designed could find ways to provide features supporting unobtrusive and encouraging nudging and flexible personalization.

Second, our results corresponded affordances with technology features. Prior research concluded that potential behavior is determined by users' characteristics and features of the technical object [26, 39]. Clarifying the relationship between affordances and technology features can help understand the potential affordances and affordance perceptions. Revealing the relationship can help users make better use of sleep-tracking devices.

5.3 Limitations and Future Research

Our results and the respective findings are bound to the context in which the research was conducted and limited to the data available. First, the exploratory and qualitative nature of the study has to be kept in mind when evaluating the generalizability of the findings. Hence, future research could expand upon the current study with a larger number and a broader spectrum of informants.

Second, the sleep-tracking affordances identified in the current study are unlikely an exhaustive presentation of all potential affordances. This study focused on the affordances of the Oura ring. The results cannot be directly generalized to other sleep-tracking devices. Hence, future research could examine other sleep-tracking devices to identify common affordances across sleep-focused self-tracking devices and technologies. Moreover, to keep up with the development of new sleep-tracking, future research is needed to explore potential additional affordances [24].

Third, as people increasingly use multiple self-tracking technologies in their daily lives, future research could adopt a personal media repertoire perspective to better understand people's overall use of self-tracking and the roles of different tools in this personal self-tracking repertoire [40–42]. For example, future research could examine how people integrate data collected with different devices to form insights [43].

References

1. Paige, S.R., et al.: Examining the relationship between online social capital and eHealth literacy: implications for instagram use for chronic disease prevention among college students. Am. J. Heal. Educ. **48**(4), 264–277 (2017)
2. Matricciani, L., Paquet, C., Galland, B., Short, M., Olds, T.: Children's sleep and health: a meta-review. Sleep Med. Rev. **46**, 136–150 (2019)
3. Grandner, M.A.: Sleep, Health, and Society. Sleep Med. Clin. **12**, 1–22 (2017)
4. Taheri, S., Lin, L., Austin, D., Young, T., Mignot, E.: Short sleep duration is associated with reduced leptin, elevated ghrelin, and increased body mass index. PLoS Med. **1**(3), 210–217 (2004)
5. Casper. Size of the sleep economy worldwide in 2019, by product category. https://www.statista.com/statistics/1119487/size-of-the-sleep-economy-worldwide-by-product-category/. Accessed 19 May 2021
6. Ravichandran, R., Sien, S.-W., Patel, S.N., Kientz, J.A., Pina, L.R.: Making sense of sleep sensors: how sleep sensing technologies support and undermine sleep health. In: Conference on Human Factors in Computing Systems, pp. 6864–6875 (2017)
7. Lupton, D.: The Quantified Self. Wiley, Hoboken (2016)
8. Elmholdt, K.T., Elmholdt, C., Haahr, L.: Counting sleep: ambiguity, aspirational control and the politics of digital self-tracking at work. Organization **28**(1), 164–185 (2021)

9. Suh, A.: Sustaining the use of quantified-self technology: a theoretical extension and empirical test. Asia Pacific J. Inf. Syst. **28**(2), 114–132 (2018)
10. Abouzahra, M., Ghasemaghaei, M.: Effective use of information technologies by seniors: the case of wearable device use. Eur. J. Inf. Syst. **31**(2), 1–15 (2021)
11. Jarrahi, M.H., Gafinowitz, N., Shin, G.: Activity trackers, prior motivation, and perceived informational and motivational affordances. Pers. Ubiquit. Comput. **22**(2), 433–448 (2017). https://doi.org/10.1007/s00779-017-1099-9
12. Benbunan-Fich, R.: An affordance lens for wearable information systems. Eur. J. Inf. Syst. **28**(3), 256–271 (2019)
13. Rieder, A., Lehrer, C., Jung, R.: Affordances and behavioral outcomes of wearable activity trackers. In: ECIS (2020)
14. Jiang, J., Cameron, A.F.: IT-enabled self-monitoring for chronic disease self-management: an interdisciplinary review. MIS Q. Manag. Inf. Syst. **44**(1), 451–508 (2020)
15. Rockmann, R., Gewald, H.: Activity tracking affordances: identification and instrument development. In: PACIS (2018)
16. Feng, S., Mäntymäki, M., Dhir, A., Salmela, H.: How self-tracking and the quantified self promote health and well-being : systematic review. J. Med. Internet Res. **23**, e25171 (2021)
17. Gordon, M.L., Althoff, T., Leskovec, J.: Goal-setting and achievement in activity tracking apps: a case study of myfitnesspal. In: The World Wide Web Conference, pp. 571−582 (2019)
18. Rockmann, R., Salou, T., Gewald, H.: If you are happy and don't know IT: continuance? analyzing emotion carry-over effects in activity tracking continuance decisions. In: PACIS (2018)
19. Zhou, Y., Kankanhalli, A., Huang, K.W.: Effects of fitness applications with SNS: how do they influence physical activity. In: ICIS, pp. 1−11 (2016)
20. Spotswood, F., Shankar, A., Piwek, L.: Changing emotional engagement with running through communal self-tracking: the implications of 'teleoaffective shaping' for public health. Sociol. Heal. Illn. **42**(2), 772−788 (2020)
21. Gioia, D.A., Corley, K.G., Hamilton, A.L.: Seeking qualitative rigor in inductive research: notes on the Gioia methodology. Organ. Res. Methods. **16**(1), 15–31 (2013)
22. Gibson, J.J.: The theory of affordances. In: The Ecological Approach to Visual Perception, pp. 127−137. Houghton Mifflin, Boston (1979)
23. Norman, D.A.: The Design of Everyday Things. Basic Books Reprint edition, New York (2002)
24. Markus, M.L., Silver, M.: A foundation for the study of IT effects: a new look at DeSanctis and poole's concepts of structural features and spirit. J. Assoc. Inf. Syst. **9**(10), 609–632 (2008)
25. Volkoff, O., Strong, D.M.: Critical realism and affordances: theorizing it-associated organizational change processes. MIS Q. **37**(3), 819–834 (2013)
26. Strong, D.M., et al.: A theory of organization-EHR affordance actualization. J. Assoc. Inf. **15**(2), 53–85 (2014)
27. Zhang, J., Lowry, P.B.: Designing quantified-self 2.0 running platform to ensure physical activity maintenance: the role of achievement goals and achievement motivational affordance. In: PACIS (2016)
28. Rockmann, R., Maier, C.: On the fit in fitness apps: studying the interaction of motivational affordances and users' goal orientations in affecting the benefits gained. In: Wirtschaftsinformatik, pp. 1017−1031 (2019)
29. Volkoff, O., Strong, D.M.: Affordance theory and how to use it in IS research. In: The Routledge Companion to Management Information Systems, pp. 232−246. Routledge (2017)
30. OuraTeam: How Accurate Is My Oura Temperature Data? https://ouraring.com/blog/temperature-validated-accurate/. Accessed 12 May 2021

31. OuraTeam: How Accurate Are Oura's Heart Rate & HRV Measurements? https://ouraring. com/blog/how-accurate-is-oura/. Accessed 12 May 2021
32. OuraTeam: How Oura Ring Data Could Help Identify Early COVID-19 Symptoms. https:// ouraring.com/blog/early-covid-symptoms/. Accessed 19 May 2021
33. Charmaz, K.: Constructing grounded theory: a practical guide through qualitative analysis. Sage (2006)
34. Langley, A., Abdallah, C.: Templates and turns in qualitative studies of strategy and management. Routledge (2015)
35. Corbin, J., Strauss, A.: Elaborating the Analysis. In: Basics of Qualitative Research, 3rd ed. Techniques and Procedures for Developing Grounded Theory, pp. 195–228. SAGE Publications, Inc., Thousand Oaks (2012)
36. Corbin, J., Strauss, A.: Analyzing data for context. In: Basics of Qualitative Research: Techniques and Procedures for Developing Grounded Theory, pp. 229−246. SAGE Publications, Inc., Thousand Oaks (2012)
37. Lister, C., West, J.H., Cannon, B., Sax, T., Brodegard, D.: Just a fad? gamification in health and fitness apps. JMIR Serious Games 2(2), 1–12 (2014)
38. Lupton, D.: Self-tracking modes: reflexive self-monitoring and data practices. In: Imminent Citizenships: Personhood and Identity Politics in the Informatic Age' workshop, pp. 1−19 (2014)
39. Bernhard, E., Recker, J., Burton-jones, A.: Understanding the actualization of affordances: a study in the process modeling context. In: ICIS (2013)
40. Watson-Manheim, M.B., Bélanger, F.: Communication media repertoires: dealing with the multiplicity of media choices. MIS Q. 31(2), 267–293 (2007)
41. Kim, S.J.: A repertoire approach to cross-platform media use behavior. New Media Soc. 18, 353–372 (2016)
42. Huang, S.L., Chang, C.Y.: Understanding how people select social networking services: media trait, social influences and situational factors. Inf. Manag. 57(6), 103323 (2020)
43. Li, I., Dey, A., Forlizzi, J.: A stage-based model of personal informatics systems. In: CHI, pp. 557−566 (2010)

Understanding the Patients' Usage of Contactless Healthcare Services: Evidence from the Post-COVID-19 Era

Abeer F. Alkhwaldi$^{(\boxtimes)}$ (iD)

Department of Management Information Systems, College of Business, Mutah University, Al Karak, Jordan
AbeerKh@mutah.edu.jo

Abstract. This study aims to investigate patients' behavioral intention toward the adoption of contactless healthcare applications in the post- COVID-19 pandemic era. Therefore, the study model extends the unified theory of acceptance and use of technology (UTAUT) with the task technology fit (TTF) model, personal innovativeness, and avoidance of personal interaction to determine patients' intention to adopt contactless healthcare applications for medical purposes. A research questionnaire was conducted on Jordanian citizens in a voluntary environment. In response, 383 valid questionnaires were retrieved. The study model is empirically analyzed with structural equation modeling (SEM). Findings of the structural model imply that was jointly predicted by UTAUT constructs, TTF, and API and explained substantial variance R^2 78.4% in user behavior to adopt contactless healthcare applications. The current research contributes to theory by extending the UTAUT with the TTF model, API, and PI and enriching information systems literature in the context of users' intention to adopt e-health technology. Practically, this research suggests that healthcare services providers should focus on IT fitness including internet-enabled devices and the number of facilities to operate the healthcare applications which in turn boost individual confidence towards the adoption of contactless healthcare technology. This research develops a unique model that examines user behavior towards the adoption of contactless healthcare technology to improve the healthcare industry. The findings of this research provide an answer on how to recover from COVID-19 repercussions on the healthcare sector while using such applications. Moreover, this study provides guidelines for clinical management through a virtual setting and guides health consultants, applications developers, and designers to design user-friendly applications for e-healthcare purposes.

Keywords: e-health · UTAUT · TTF · Contactless services · Jordan · COVID-19

1 Introduction

Recently, the trend of fatal diseases (e.g., AIDS, influenza, Swine Flu, and now COVID-19 pandemic) is swiftly growing. These diseases have generated significant challenges

© IFIP International Federation for Information Processing 2022
Published by Springer Nature Switzerland AG 2022
S. Papagiannidis et al. (Eds.): I3E 2022, LNCS 13454, pp. 356–373, 2022.
https://doi.org/10.1007/978-3-031-15342-6_28

for health institutions that how to save people's lives through delivering rapid healthcare services. A potential way is to exploit information and communication technologies (ICTs) in the healthcare sector to offer awareness among the public regarding pandemics [1]. The majority of the healthcare professionals are approved that the telemedicine/contactless healthcare applications using ICTs help in saving time, and money and improve productivity in healthcare delivery systems [2]. The term contactless healthcare application is defined as "an application that is used to transfer medical information which is established by medical experts or patient from one location to another using information communication technologies (ICT) as a mode of communication" [3]. Contactless healthcare services describe a process that integrates different software and hardware in order to design virtual medical interfaces for patients and healthcare professionals using smartphones, tablets, desktop/personal computers, and any internet-enabled devices [4].

Contactless healthcare applications might be utilized as an alternative healthcare delivery system during and post the COVID-19 era. Coronavirus is fatal and infectious and thus precautionary measures can save people's life. During the COVID-19 outbreak, it is noted that healthy citizens are getting infected by visiting hospitals. A recent report indicated that doctors and the paramedical workforce are suffering from Coronavirus due to the spreadable nature of the virus [5]. Therefore, this research draws researchers' attention towards the use of contactless healthcare applications for e-health services. E-health applications have been revealed effective in delivering and tracking patients' healthcare services to control fatal diseases [6]. In addition to that, the World Health Organization (WHO) has agreed that the use of e-health applications (mobile-health) is functional and cost-effective for healthcare surveillance [7]. Previous research had discussed the success of smart hospital systems using innovative technologies (e.g., IoT) [6, 8]. The IoT applications have indicated the perceived usefulness of this technology in tracking patients' records, real-time surveillance, correct drug patient association, etc. [8, 9]. Despite several advantages, the adoption of contactless healthcare services/applications (e-Health) is revealed less successful [2, 10]. Scholars stated that insufficient financial support, vague e-health services, visions, and missions are the key challenges to the successful implementation of contactless healthcare applications [11]. Also, others suggested that healthcare professionals have inadequate knowledge and skills about e-health applications in developing countries compared to developed countries. Consequently, investigating factors that influence patient behavior to adopt contactless healthcare services/applications is needed, particularly during and the post-COVID-19 pandemic [2].

Since the beginning of IoT applications, patients are reluctant to adopt e-health applications [9]. A possible explanation could be a lack of awareness about innovative technology in the shape of contactless healthcare applications [2]. Literature on e-healthcare systems had revealed that the e-health projects failure rate is 0.75 around the world [12]. Although e-health contributes to the healthcare industry, its implementation is still a significant challenge [8, 10]. For health surveillance and wellbeing, the usage of a contactless healthcare application is a cost-effective choice [2]. Therefore, the current research fills the knowledge gap by investigating factors that affect patient behavior to adopt contactless healthcare applications to monitor Jordanian patients' health and deliver healthcare services in the post-COVID-19 era. The study model includes factors underpinning the unified theory of acceptance and use of technology (UTAUT), task technology fit (TTF), personal innovativeness (PI), and avoidance of personal interaction (API) in order to investigate patient behavior towards the adoption of contactless healthcare applications. This study is significant as it offers unique guidelines and helps to develop strategies and policies for physicians, healthcare advisors, and applications developers and designers in designing compatible healthcare applications that raise patients' confidence and motivate them to adopt contactless healthcare applications.

2 Literature Review and Hypotheses Development

2.1 Theoretical Background

Existing literature has developed many theories and models to understand UT/IS acceptance, e.g., the Theory of Planned Behavior (TPB) [13], Technology Acceptance Model (TAM) [14], and UTAUT [15]. UTAUT has been acknowledged as the most comprehensive one [16–18]. It integrates constructs across eight previous theoretical models and demonstrates stronger predictive power than any of the eight models [15]. UTAUT postulates that performance expectancy (PE), effort expectancy (EE), social influence (SI), and facilitating conditions (FC) have an impact on both behavioral intentions (BI) and actual usage (AU) behavior [15]. UTAUT has been consistently confirmed to be able to demonstrate a large amount of variance in IT/IS usage and acceptance behavior across different contexts, such as mobile banking [19–21], distance learning [22], and health informatics [9, 23].

The academic literature across the disciplines of technology, sociology, and psychology argues that the BI of human beings to refrain from performing or perform a specified behavior could be considered the best predictor to carry out a particular action [14, 15, 24]. This presumption has been widely confirmed in IT/IS research [25, 26]. Drawing on consistent findings of the earlier research work that BI is a determinant of actual human behavior, the literature has examined factors that could influence the BI to use, rather than actual usage. Thus, this study investigates the Jordanian patients' BI toward accepting contactless healthcare services.

The TTF model has been utilized to explain how task-technology fit affects users' acceptance of IT/T, such as innovative technologies [27], healthcare technologies [28], and learning technologies [29]. In the TTF model, task and technology characteristics are two predictors of task technology fit [30, 31]. The model suggests that if the task is out of the capabilities of information technology, or the technology is poorly designed and owns inadequate functions to accomplish the task, the task-technology fit would become less. In this study, the authors did not integrate utilization, an additional construct in TTF [31], as it has been accounted for by acceptance in IT/IS acceptance research [20, 29].

In summary, while the UTAUT has been extensively validated and extended in different contexts, its application to the modeling of contactless healthcare services acceptance after the crisis times has been limited [32]. There is a concurrent need to obtain empirical evidence for the support of such a model within contactless healthcare services during the post-COVID-19 era and examine users' acceptance to facilitate the development and implementation of such services. In addition, some have suggested that the model needs to be extended with other related theories to improve model explanation and prediction power, particularly given the fact that the UTAUT model is not particularly formulated for the context of healthcare services [33, 48]. In fact, the investigation of further explanatory factors drawn from related theories and models is a common and widely accepted practice in IT/IS research [20, 29]. Given that UTAUT highlights users' perceptions of IT/IS, and TTF contributes to the understanding of users' acceptance from the perspective of task-technology fit, the authors developed a unified model by integrating the two theories, in addition to PI, and API to generate a comprehensive understanding of individuals' acceptance of contactless healthcare services after the crisis time. Figure 1 illustrates the proposed study model. In the remainder of this section, the authors described the rationale of constructs in the model and developed hypotheses among them.

2.2 Hypotheses Development

The proposed model included ten constructs drawn from UTAUT, TTF, and two additional constructs which were contextualized in scenarios related to contactless healthcare services. The author used behavioral intention to measure user acceptance as it is a widely used predictor of actual behavior (e.g., using a technology) [15, 34]. The following sections discuss the model constructs and hypotheses among them:

2.2.1 UTAUT Constructs

- **PE**

   PE refers to "the degree to which an individual believes that using the system will help him or her to attain gains in job performance." [15]. In the context of mobile health services (m-health), authors like Barua Z. and Barua A. (2021) have investigated m-health users' behavior towards the adoption of m-health applications amid the COVID-19 pandemic and revealed that PE significantly affects users' behavioral intention to adopt telemedicine services [23]. Similarly, Rahi et al. (2021) have confirmed the relationship between PE and the adoption of telemedicine services [35]. Previous literature has confirmed the significant linkage between PE and users' intention to adopt information systems in general and e-health systems in particular [36–39]. In the context of contactless healthcare, when users believe such services enable them to increase healthcare effectiveness, they are more likely to accept and use the technology. Therefore, PE is hypothesized as:

H1. *PE has a positive impact on the patient's intention to use contactless healthcare services.*

- **EE:**

   EE can be defined as "the degree of ease associated with the use of the system" [15]. Therefore, in healthcare applications context refers to the extent to which users perceived ease during the use of healthcare applications [28, 38]. The degree of ease to use IT is revealed an influential factor in to use of IoT in the e-health context [9]. Authors like Wang et al. (2020) had found that EE significantly impacts users' behavioral intention to adopt healthcare wearable devices. This indicates that thee-health devices or applications that comprehend with easy features had more chance to influence user behavior to adopt health care applications. This indicates that different healthcare services and devices that comprehend with "ease to use" feature were more likely to affect users' behavior toward adopting e-healthcare services. According to Gu et al. (2021), the e-health technologies having ease characteristics benefit users in developing countries and bring positive change in their behavior intention towards adoption of such IT [32]. Earlier studies have confirmed significant impact of EE on user adoption of healthcare applications and other technologies [22, 28, 32, 38]. When users believe that using contactless healthcare services is easy and effortless, they would be more likely to accept and use these services. Therefore, EE is proposed as:

H2. *EE has a positive impact on the patient's intention to use contactless healthcare services.*

- **SI:**

The term social influence is identified as "the degree to which an individual perceives that important others believe he or she should use the new system" [15]. In the e-health application settings, SI is the extent to wherein a person believes that important others' recommendations to use e-health for healthcare purposes [32]. A recent study conducted by Rahi et al. (2021) found that SI significantly affects user intention to adopt telemedicine health services. SI also reflects a trend that is created by successful and educated individuals while sharing experiences and pleasure. In later stages, that trend becomes a kind of inspiration for neighbors, colleagues, friends, and family. This current study postulates that SI boosts people's confidence to use contactless healthcare services and enriches their e-health experience. Previous studies have found that SI strongly affects individuals' behavior to adopt e-health applications and services [23, 38]. In this study, users are more likely willing to accept contactless healthcare technology if important others approve of the use of this technology. Following the above-mentioned argument and consistent with IT/IS literature [40–42], SI is proposed as:

H3. SI has a positive impact on the patient's intention to use contactless healthcare services

- **FC:**

FC is defined as "the degree to which an individual believes that an organizational and technical infrastructure exists to support the use of the system" [15]. Therefore, FC in contactless healthcare services is explained as the degree to which users believe that contactless healthcare service providers will offer technical infrastructure to use e-health applications. In a more detailed fashion and in accordance with the current research context, FC is an environmental factor that indicates the users' awareness and perceptions of the existence of both the technology itself (e.g., contactless healthcare services) and the relevant essential level of resources such as knowledge, training, technical infrastructure, and services required to deliver the desired support for implementing contactless healthcare systems successfully, productively and effortlessly. Availability of sufficient technical infrastructure develops users' IT skills to use software applications [43], and skilled users have revealed more incline towards acceptance and use of IT [26]. Hence, it is postulated that the availability of IT infrastructure offers technical skills and knowledge to users that how to use contactless healthcare services in order to avail of e-health. According to Hossain et al. (2019), IT resources, required knowledge, and system compatibility significantly affects users' behavior to adopt electronic health record (EHR) in healthcare system [44]. Thus, the current study assumes that FC aid individual to adopt contactless healthcare applications. Therefore, FC is proposed as:

H4. FC has a positive impact on the patient's intention to use contactless healthcare services.

2.2.2 TTF Constructs

The TTF model suggests that people will adopt IT based on the fit between the technical characteristics and task requirements [30, 31]. In addition, the TTF is defined as "the degree to which technology assists an individual in performing the respective tasks"[31]. The TTF has been developed to check if IT offers adequate support for task achievement in the acceptance of new IT. The task technology fit model integrates three main variables namely "technology characteristics TechC, task characteristics TaskC, and task technology fit" [30]. In this study, context TechC is defined as the contactless healthcare applications that are used to perform an e-healthcare task. TechC in the context of contactless healthcare services could also indicate the functionality and interface design of the application [28]. While TaskC refers to individuals' actions that are implemented while using contactless healthcare applications. TaskC could also indicate the complexity and requirements for individuals to manage their e-health services [28]. Previous studies have validated the important role of the TTF model in the adoption of information systems [19, 27, 45]. A study conducted by Zhou et al. (2010) supported a positive relationship between TechC and task-technology fit, and a negative relationship between TaskC and task-technology fit [20]. Therefore, and backed up by extant literature in the field, the following hypotheses are suggested:

H5. TechC has a positive impact on task technology fit.

H6. TaskC has a negative impact on task technology fit.

2.2.3 Relationships Among the Constructs of TTF and UTAUT

Based on the TTF model, users will not adopt an IT if the task-technology fit is not satisfied [30, 31]. Likewise, if contactless healthcare applications cannot meet the requirements of e-health management tasks, users are more likely will not use such applications/services. Previous literature has stated a positive relationship between task-technology fit and individuals' acceptance of IT/IS [20, 27, 32]. Thus, the authors hypothesized the following:

H7. Task-technology fit has a positive impact on the patient's intention to use contactless healthcare services.

Moreover, previous research has reported that task-technology fit has a positive effect on PE [20, 21, 27, 29]. In the context of contactless healthcare services, only when individuals perceive a satisfying match between functions of contactless healthcare services and e-health management tasks, they will believe that using such services could improve their e-healthcare management performance. In addition, it is likely that contactless healthcare services' characteristics (e.g., high-speed data collection, transmission, and processing) enable individuals to monitor and perform their health-related services swiftly and thus reduce their cost of effort [20]. Based on the abovementioned arguments, the following hypotheses are proposed:

H8. *Task-technology fit has a positive impact on PE.*

H9. *"Technology characteristics" has a positive impact on EE.*

2.2.4 Personal Innovativeness

Personal innovativeness (PI) is referred to "the degree of the speed of an individual to adopt new ideas in relation to other members of the social system" [46, 47]. Furthermore, Agarwal and Prasad (1998) (p. 206) describe PI in the field of IT as "the willingness of an individual to try out any new information technology" [48]. Previous studies in IT/IS acceptance and adoption demonstrate how PI construct, has a direct (e.g., [49–51]) and indirect (e.g., [52, 53]), effect the users' intentions to use different technologies. For instance, Alalwan et al. (2018) were successfully able to confirm the significant effect of PI on the Saudi individuals' intentions to use mobile internet. Likewise, Slade et al. (2015) reveal that PI has a significant role in determining behavioral intentions to use mobile payment services in the United Kingdom [54]. Hossain et al. (2019), found that PI has a positive effect on the user's intention to use the new eHealth services [44]. In this study context, as contactless healthcare services introduce a new healthcare technology that is technologically different compared to other healthcare legacy systems, it is expected that a "personal innovativeness" construct will play a significant role in patients' intentions toward such services. As this relationship is promising in the current research context, the following is hypothesized:

H10. *Personal innovativeness has a positive impact on the patient's intention to use contactless healthcare services.*

2.2.5 Avoidance of Personal Interaction

Avoidance of personal interaction (API) can be described as the degree to which IT/IS allows users to access and use web-based services without the prerequisite for physical interactions with any individual (Chan et al. 2010; Molina, Moreno, & Moreno, 2013). Contactless healthcare services facilitate self-services—i.e., an operation by which web-based services are initiated and conducted by end-users themselves without the prerequisite to physical interaction with the services providers, such as remote consultation through real-time audio call or audio-video calls via smartphones, tablets, or computers, and patients' data can be stored on particular platforms [35, 55]. These benefits are vital to the perceived effectiveness of web based services and have significant implications for individuals' usage intentions. Due to the repercussions of COVID-19 pandemic, governments in many countries have encouraged their citizens to use online services (e.g., online e-healthcare services) and help healthcare sector keep functioning through various technologies [56]. E-healthcare services have emerged as an efficient healthcare delivery scheme during the COVID-19 pandemic and this trend is expected to accelerate in the post the pandemic era [57].In the context of information systems, Al Amin et al. (2021) applied the social distance (SD) concept referring to API construct which could be defined as "the impartial physical segregation of human beings from others or living alone geologically and temporally or a condition for which people maintain a complete or near-complete lack of communication due to emergencies (e.g., COVID-19 outbreaks)". The SD was revealed to have a positive influence on the behavioral intention to use mobile applications (Al Amin et al. 2021). Also, social isolation/social distance was revealed to have a positive and significant relationship with behavioral intention to use learning management systems (LMS) (Raza et al. 2021). Ohme et al. (2020) illustrate that mobile applications are a key instrument that assists citizens to cope with the COVID-19 crisis, especially during the social isolation periods. In the same regard, it has been argued that innovative technologies are significant as they can mitigate the effects of social distancing during and after the crisis times [58]. Therefore, the current study postulated that the "avoidance of personal interaction" situation could influence patients' behavioral intentions to use contactless healthcare applications as these applications are favorable for hygiene maintenance to complete e-healthcare services during and post the COVID-19 era, which will make such IT a proper practice even post-pandemic. Thus, the researchers suggest the following hypotheses:

H11. *Avoidance of personal interaction has a positive impact on the patient's intention to use contactless healthcare services.*

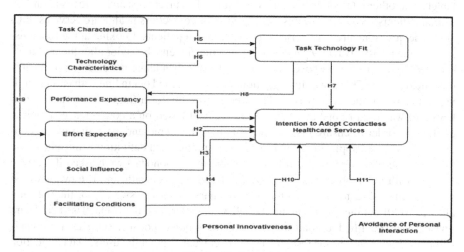

Fig. 1. Study model

3 Research Methodology

3.1 Questionnaire Development

Based on a quantitative research approach this research evaluates the proposed model with scale items. Information systems literature was used for scale devolvement. All questionnaire items were adapted from earlier studies into a contactless healthcare services study. There was a total of ten variables that measure patient intention to adopt contactless healthcare applications. Instrument items used to measure TechC, TaskC, and task technology fit were adapted from [20, 28, 30, 31]. Instrument items for API were adapted from [59]. Next to this, PI questionnaire items were adapted from [10]. While items for EE, PE, FC, SI, and behavioral intention to adopt contactless healthcare services were adapted from Venkatesh et al. (2003); Alkhwaldi & Absulmuhsin, (2021); Wang, et al. (2020); and Alam et al. (2020). The questionnaire items were measured on a 7-point Likert scale where 1: "strongly disagree" and 7: "strongly agree" as suggested by [60]. These variables were further analyzed using the "measurement model" and confirmed the reliability and validity of the proposed items. The details of the measurement model analysis are presented in the section "measurement model assessment".

3.2 Instrument Design, Participants, and Data Collection

This research is based on the positivist paradigm and collects data using a questionnaire. The questionnaire consists of the model constructs' items and demographic information of the study sample. The study model is tested using empirical data collected from participants who were familiar with contactless healthcare applications, smart mobile phones, tablets, and other internet-enabled devices. Since the current research is focused on Jordanian patients' behavior towards the adoption of contactless healthcare services, thus an online questionnaire was carried out on Jordanian patients. Looking at the repercussions of the post-COVID-19 pandemic era and the citizens' behavior after the protocols executed by the Jordanian government to control the pandemic it was difficult to carry out a field survey. Thus, an online questionnaire was carried out in line with earlier studies conducted in the same period. The web survey platform (https://www.surveymon key.com) was used to operate the study instrument based on a convenience sampling method. In order to ensure that respondents have the same understanding of the contactless healthcare applications and services, a summarized definition is introduced on the first page of the online questionnaire. Then, the respondents were asked if they are familiar with the applications and services of contactless healthcare. If they answered yes, they are asked to complete the questionnaire. If they answered no, they are not allowed to fill out the questionnaire. People who understand the contactless healthcare services were qualified respondents. Since the development of such services in Jordan is still in the initial phases, the respondents were current or potential users. Data collection was carried out between January-March 2022; in the end, 383 valid questionnaires were received.

4 Data Analysis

SPSS and AMOS software was used to analyze the collected data and conduct structural equation modeling (SEM). For SEM researchers have applied a two-stage approach: (1) measurement model and (2) structural model. SEM researchers have applied a two-stage approach: (1) measurement model and (2) structural model [60]. The measurement model was applied to evaluate the reliability and validity of the model constructs. Therefore, the structural model was applied to assess the causal path (relationships) between suggested hypotheses. In the following section, the measurement model and structural model are deliberated in detail.

4.1 Measurement Model

The measurement model estimates the convergent and discriminant validity of the model constructs. Construct reliability was attained with Cronbach alpha (α), composite reliability (CR), and factor loadings. To satisfy construct reliability researchers have followed the guidelines that the values of CR and α must be >0.7, which indicates adequate construct reliability [60, 61]. In addition to that factor, loading should be >0.6 showing the construct is valid. Consequently, the convergent validity of the construct was attained with average variance extracted (AVE) following guidelines that AVE values must be > 0.50, which indicates acceptable convergent validity of the model constructs. Findings of the measurement model showed acceptable reliability and convergent validity. The values of α, CR, AVE, and factor loadings are described in Table 1.

Discriminant validity was assessed based on the squared correlations between model constructs and their AVE. An acceptable level of discriminant validity is assumed to be attained if the square root of AVE for each construct (which is across the diagonal cells) is higher than the squared correlation between that construct and all other constructs [60].

Table 1. Measurement model

Constructs	(α)	CR	AVE	Factor loadings
PE	0.887	0.917	0.745	0.753–0.935
EE	0.917	0.941	0.803	0.825–0.943
FC	0.850	0.908	0.773	0.834–0.903
SI	0.772	0.850	0.591	0.681–0.843
TaskC	0.896	0.923	0.759	0.794–0.948
TechC	0.799	0.898	0.625	0.761–0.809
TTF	0.965	0.976	0.938	0.955–0.973
PI	0.878	0.923	0.805	0.864–0.926
API	0.863	0.902	0.758	0.808–0.935
BI	0.853	0.908	0.772	0.861–0.889

According to the correlation analysis listed in Table 2, the AVE values for the reflective constructs are higher than the off-diagonal squared correlations, indicating acceptable discriminant validity for the study samples (Table 2).

Table 2. Discriminant validity

	PE	EE	FC	SI	TaskC	TechC	TTF	PI	API	BI
PE	**.86**									
EE	.251	**.90**								
FC	.324	.349	**.88**							
SI	.104	.105	.083	**.77**						
TaskC	.416	.364	.564	.080	**.87**					
TechC	.221	.145	.297	.077	.289	**.79**				
TTF	.296	.286	.520	.027	.547	.349	**.97**			
PI	.046	.050	.140	.054	.092	.096	.067	**.90**		
API	.272	.180	.404	.002	.268	.219	.320	.103	**.87**	
BI	.464	.434	.704	.146	.643	.432	.778	.166	.454	**.88**

4.2 Structural Model (Hypotheses Testing)

The study model of the current research includes variables underpinning UTAUT theory, TTF model, PI, and API to determine patient intention to adopt contactless healthcare services for e-health purposes. Results indicate that PE had a significant impact on patients' intention to adopt contactless healthcare services (H1). EE had shown a significant impact on patients' intention to adopt contactless healthcare services and is statistically supported by (H2). Similarly, SI and FC had revealed a significant impact on patients' intention, thus, approving (H3 and H4). Concerning TTF antecedents, the analysis showed that TaskC and TechC had exhibited a significant impact on patients' intention, thus, confirming (H5 and H6).

The study model was further extended to TTF and UTATU constructs. TTF had revealed to have a positive influence on PE and therefore H8 was accepted. Next to this TechC had revealed to have a significant influence on EE and was statistically confirmed by H9. Moreover, the relationship between TTF and behavioral intention to adopt contactless healthcare services was also revealed significantly and supported by H7. The PI factor has shown an insignificant impact on patients' behavioral intention (H10). Likewise, the relationship between API and patients' behavioral intention was confirmed significant and statistically accepted by H11. Results of the structural model (see Table 3) indicates that patients' intentions to adopt contactless healthcare services are jointly measured by PE, EE, FC, SI, TTF, and API and explained substantial variance R^2 78.4% in individuals' intention. These results confirmed the theoretical and statistical validity of the study model to investigate patients' intention to adopt contactless healthcare services.

Table 3. Hypotheses testing

Hypothesis	Constructs' relationship	Path coefficient (β)	Results
H1	PE > BI	0.147^{***}	Validated
H2	EE > BI	0.116^{***}	Validated
H3	SI > BI	0.074^{**}	Validated
H4	FC > BI	0.291^{***}	Validated
H5	TaskC > TTF	0.487^{***}	Validated
H6	TechC > TTF	0.207^{***}	Validated
H7	TTF > BI	0.506^{***}	Validated
H8	TTF > PE	0.297^{***}	Validated
H9	TechC > EE	0.287^{***}	Validated
H10	PI > BI	-0.061	Rejected
H11	API > BI	0.102^{**}	Validated

$\mathbf{R^2}$ **(BI)** $= 0.784$

*p < 0.05, **p < 0.01, ***p < 0.001

5 Discussion

The adoption of contactless healthcare applications and services is considered challenging in developing countries, Jordan for example, due to behavioral and environmental barriers [37, 38]. Hence, examining the role of UTAUT and TTF in the adoption of contactless healthcare technology is considered appropriate. Conclusions of the structural model showed that patient intention to adopt contactless healthcare applications has jointly predicted by PE, EE, SI, FC, API, TechC, TaskC, and TTF and explained substantial variance R^2 78.54% in individual adoption of contactless healthcare by Jordanian users in the post-COVID-19 era. Results of SEM confirmed that PE is a significant impact on patient intention to adopt contactless healthcare services and is consistent with previous studies literature by Rahi et al. (2021) and Alam et al. (2020). This implies that if patients feel that the adoption of contactless healthcare applications will improve and support their task performance they will adopt such applications. Similarly, the EE has shown a significant impact on patient intention to adopt contactless healthcare applications and confirms earlier scholars' conclusions Gu et al. (2021), Wang et al. (2020). SI and FC had shown a significant impact on patients' intention to adopt contactless healthcare applications and in line with earlier IS literature Moudud-Ul-Huq et al. (2021) and Alkhwaldi & Absulmuhsin (2021). These results indicate that patients have concerns about ease of use, help from service providers and society/friends pressure and consequently prefer to utilize contactless healthcare applications.

The TTF model has shown a significant impact in predicting individual intention to adopt contactless healthcare applications for e-health services. Findings showed that TaskC and TechC had a significant impact on individual intention to adopt contactless healthcare applications and therefore in line with prior literature of Faqih & Jaradat, (2021) and Zhou et al. (2010). Similarly, the TTF and TechC have shown significant influence on PE and EE respectively. These results are consistent with Faqih & Jaradat, (2021), Wang et al. (2020); and Zhou et al. (2010). This indicates that IT fitness matters more in increasing individual performance expectations and also IT characteristics affect users' perceptions regarding expected efforts during the use of contactless healthcare services.

The current research adds two factors: API and PI to investigate individual intention to adopt contactless healthcare applications. Unexpectedly, unlike what has been hypothesized in this research, the results showed that PI does not have a significant influence on patients' behavioral intention toward using contactless healthcare services during and after the COVID-19 pandemic. What has been revealed in this research context is inconsistent with the results of other researchers such as Kasilingam, (2020); and Van Droogenbroeck & Van Hove, (2021), who confirmed the direct impact of PI on the intentions to adopt state-of-the-art technologies. The possible explanation for such insignificance impact of PI would be the education level of the targeted sample. Therefore, it is likely that IT acceptance and adoption is a reasonable decision based on the available information, skills, and knowledge rather than individuals' intuition [62]. Accordingly, IT adoption does not happen because of human curiosity; unless the criteria of such a decision are met. Few studies rejected the significance of the PI factor on an individual's intention towards adopting new IT/IS (e.g., Jameel et al. 2021). Finally, the findings confirm the prediction of Hypothesis (H11), which assumes the influence of API on patients' intentions to use contactless healthcare services during and after the COVID-19 era. It is assumed that by avoiding personal interactions, the individuals can confirm proper hygiene maintenance for their well-being, health, and safety during and post the crisis period. This is consistent with the conclusions of previous research in the context of IT/IS [63, 64].

6 Theoretical and Practical Implications

From a theoretical perspective, the current research has different contributions to theory in the context of contactless healthcare services and applications. First, this study has validated the extension of UTAUT with the TTF model, and API to determine individuals' intention to adopt contactless healthcare services. Second, the study model has indicated a substantial variance R^2 78.4% in predicting patient behavior towards the adoption of contactless healthcare applications and therefore supporting the validity of the study model. Third, in this research, the TTF factors showed interesting results. It is revealed that the TTF significantly influences PE and TechC significantly influences EE. Additionally, the influence of TTF was found as a significant factor in determining individual intention to adopt contactless healthcare applications. Therefore, this research contributes to IT/IS literature by developing strong causal relationships among constructs underpinned by UTAUT and TTF. Likewise, this research confirmed the significant role of the API construct in understanding behavioral intention in the post-COVID-19 crisis. Finally, the current research revealed although SI significantly affects individuals' behavioral intention to accept and use contactless healthcare services, the effect size of SI is found small. This indicates social pressures are less important for the usage intentions of contactless healthcare technology in line with Venkatesh and Davis [65].

From a practical perspective, the findings of the current research shed light on individual behavior towards the adoption of contactless healthcare services for e-health purposes that have not been addressed by earlier studies. First, the current study found that although variables underpinned UTAUT had a significant influence on individual intention to adopt healthcare applications for e-health consultations, for example. FC was revealed as one of the influential factors that need to be considered effectively to improve the adoption of contactless healthcare technology. This finding indicates that the services providers (e.g., health consultants) should focus on strategies that offer facilities to a patient during the use of contactless healthcare applications. For healthcare service providers also, it is essential that they need to know that individuals have the required IT resources, skills, and knowledge to utilize contactless healthcare services. In addition to healthcare services' providers should pay attention to the compatibility of contactless healthcare applications with other technologies and systems in order to achieve maximum benefits.

Second, the current research suggests that TTF has a significant impact in predicting individual intention to adopt contactless healthcare services. This implies that accurate healthcare information with user-friendly IT might assist individuals to adopt contactless healthcare services for reliable and trustworthy e-health services. Third, based on this study's findings, developing strategies to attain user IT fitness ease of use and sufficient facilities will boost users' confidence to adopt contactless healthcare services for telemedicine and e-healthcare. During the COVID-19 time, the citizens' typical behaviors swiftly changed around the world, which substantially influenced the healthcare industry. Since the COVID-19 outbreaks have generated a long-term impact on this industry, most healthcare institutions continued to deliver their services within limited circumstances. However, some of these institutions have encountered different challenges to deal with this exceptional setting. Thus, the authorities should enhance different supports, such as IT infrastructure, IT training, affordable internet broadband, and cyber security guarantees, to their citizens to overcome such situations. With the restricted physical movements during crisis time, healthcare institutions encounter recovery challenges. Yet, contactless healthcare apps can be considered a promising effective alternative that can benefit different parties by sustaining a safe social distancing (avoiding personal interaction) during and after this pandemic.

7 Limitations and Future Work

This study has few limitations and hence attention should be paid when generalizing the findings. First, the results of this research are based on a single country i.e. Jordan therefore, results could differ when applying the proposed model to other countries. Consequently, future studies may use this study model in other developing countries to further the generalization of this research findings. In addition, the effects of culture should be taken into account in future studies since various studies have shown that user acceptance of novel and modern technology is directly tied to their specific characteristics (e.g., [66]). Second, the current study is cross-sectional and examined phenomena at a single point in time. Consequently, testing the proposed study model in a longitudinal context may lead to interesting results. Third, the questionnaire was carried out online and participants included in this research were selected via a non-random convenience sampling method. Consequently, the generalizability of the study model could be improved if the study model is verified with a random sampling approach. Finally, the study model considers only the direct influence between exogenous and endogenous constructs. Consequently, future researchers could suggest mediating and moderating causal relationships among TTF and the UTAUT constructs in order to investigate individuals' intentions to adopt contactless healthcare services.

References

1. Pai, R.R., Alathur, S.: Assessing awareness and use of mobile phone technology for health and wellness: insights from India. Health Policy Technol. **8**(3), 221–227 (2019)
2. Albarrak, A.I., et al.: Assessment of physician's knowledge, perception and willingness of telemedicine in Riyadh region, Saudi Arabia. J. Infect. Public Health **14**(1), 97–102 (2021)
3. Hsu, W.-Y.: A customer-oriented skin detection and care system in telemedicine applications. The Electronic Library (2019)
4. Abo-Zahhad, M., Ahmed, S.M., Elnahas, O.: A wireless emergency telemedicine system for patients monitoring and diagnosis. Int. J. Telemed. Appl. **2014** (2014)
5. Healthline. Here's What Could Happen If Doctors Get COVID-19 (2020). https://www.healthline.com/health-news/what-happens-if-nurses-and-doctors-get-covid-19. Accessed 27 Mar 2022
6. Kayyali, R., et al.: Awareness and use of mHealth apps: a study from England. Pharmacy **5**(2), 33 (2017)
7. Ryu, S.: Telemedicine: opportunities and developments in member states: report on the second global survey on eHealth 2009 (global observatory for eHealth series, volume 2). Healthcare Inform. Res. **18**(2), 153–155 (2012)
8. Kashyap, R.: Applications of Wireless Sensor Networks in Healthcare, in IoT and WSN Applications for Modern Agricultural Advancements: Emerging Research and Opportunities, pp. 8–40. IGI Global, Hershey (2020)
9. Arfi, W.B., et al.: The role of trust in intention to use the IoT in eHealth: application of the modified UTAUT in a consumer context. Technol. Forecast. Soc. Chang. **167**, 120688 (2021)
10. Alalwan, A., et al.: Examining the factors affecting behavioural intention to adopt mobile health in Jordan. In: Challenges and Opportunities in the Digital Era, vol. 11195, pp. 459–467. Springer, Cham (2018). https://doi.org/10.1007/978-3-030-02131-3_41
11. Alaboudi, A., et al.: Barriers and challenges in adopting Saudi telemedicine network: the perceptions of decision makers of healthcare facilities in Saudi Arabia. J. Infect. Public Health **9**(6), 725–733 (2016)
12. Van Dyk, L., Schutte, C.S.L.: The telemedicine service maturity model: a framework for the measurement and improvement of telemedicine services. Telemedicine 217–238 (2013)
13. Ajzen, I.: The theory of planned behavior. Organ. Behav. Hum. Decis. Process. **50**(2), 179–211 (1991)
14. Davis, F.D.: Perceived usefulness, perceived ease of use, and user acceptance of information technology. MIS Q. 319–340 (1989)
15. Venkatesh, V., et al.: User acceptance of information technology: toward a unified view. MIS Q. 425–478 (2003)
16. Al-Okaily, M., et al.: The determinants of digital payment systems' acceptance under cultural orientation differences: the case of uncertainty avoidance. Technol. Soc. **63**, 101367 (2020)

17. Alkhwaldi, A., Kamala, M.: Why do users accept innovative technologies? A critical review of technology acceptance models and theories. J. Multidiscip. Eng. Sci. Technol. (JMEST) 4(8), 7962–7971 (2017)
18. Al-Okaily, M., Alalwan, A.A., Al-Fraihat, D., Alkhwaldi, A.F., Rehman, S.U., Al-Okaily, A.: Investigating antecedents of mobile payment systems' decision-making: a mediated model. Global Knowl. Mem. Commun. (2022)
19. Wang, S.: A study of Chinese mobile banking users' behavioural intention to try new functions with the integrated model of UTAUT, TTF and customer service. Int. J. Transitions Innov. Syst. 6(4), 311–340 (2021)
20. Zhou, T., Lu, Y., Wang, B.: Integrating TTF and UTAUT to explain mobile banking user adoption. Comput. Hum. Behav. 26(4), 760–767 (2010)
21. Oliveira, T., et al.: Extending the understanding of mobile banking adoption: when UTAUT meets TTF and ITM. Int. J. Inf. Manag. 34(5), 689–703 (2014)
22. Alkhwaldi, A.F., Absulmuhsin, A.A.: Crisis-centric distance learning model in Jordanian higher education sector: factors influencing the continuous use of distance learning platforms during COVID-19 pandemic. J. Int. Educ. Bus. (2021)
23. Barua, Z., Barua, A.: Acceptance and usage of mHealth technologies amid COVID-19 pandemic in a developing country: the UTAUT combined with situational constraint and health consciousness. J. Enabling Technol. (2021)
24. Ajzen, I., Fishbein, M.: Understanding attitudes and predicting social behaviour (1980)
25. Taylor, S., Todd, P.: Decomposition and crossover effects in the theory of planned behavior: a study of consumer adoption intentions. Int. J. Res. Mark. 12(2), 137–155 (1995)
26. Venkatesh, V., Thong, J.Y.L., Xu, X.: Consumer acceptance and use of information technology: extending the unified theory of acceptance and use of technology. MIS Q. 36(1), 157–178 (2012)
27. Faqih, K.M.S., Jaradat, M.-I.R.M.: Integrating TTF and UTAUT2 theories to investigate the adoption of augmented reality technology in education: perspective from a developing country. Technol. Soc. 67, 101787 (2021)
28. Wang, H., et al.: Understanding consumer acceptance of healthcare wearable devices: an integrated model of UTAUT and TTF. Int. J. Med. Inform. 139, 104156 (2020)
29. Wu, B., Chen, X.: Continuance intention to use MOOCs: integrating the technology acceptance model (TAM) and task technology fit (TTF) model. Comput. Hum. Behav. 67, 221–232 (2017)
30. Goodhue, D.L.: Understanding user evaluations of information systems. Manag. Sci. 41(12), 1827–1844 (1995)
31. Goodhue, D.L., Thompson, R.L.: Task-technology fit and individual performance. MIS Q. 213–236 (1995)
32. Gu, D., et al.: Assessing the adoption of e-health technology in a developing country: an extension of the UTAUT model. SAGE Open 11(3), 1–16 (2021)
33. Holden, R.J., Karsh, B.-T.: The technology acceptance model: its past and its future in health care. J. Biomed. Inform. 43(1), 159–172 (2010)
34. Davis, F.D., Bagozzi, R.P., Warshaw, P.R.: User acceptance of computer technology: a comparison of two theoretical models. Manag. Sci. 35(8), 982–1003 (1989)
35. Rahi, S., Khan, M.M., Alghizzawi, M.: Factors influencing the adoption of telemedicine health services during COVID-19 pandemic crisis: an integrative research model. Enterp. Inf. Syst. 15(6), 769–793 (2021)
36. Alkhwaldi, A.F.A.H.: Jordanian Citizen-Centric Cloud Services Acceptance Model in an e-Government Context: Security Antecedents for Using Cloud Services (2019)
37. Hoque, M.R., Bao, Y., Sorwar, G.: Investigating factors influencing the adoption of e-Health in developing countries: a patient's perspective. Inform. Health Soc. Care 42(1), 1–17 (2017)

38. Alam, M.Z., et al.: Factors influencing the adoption of mHealth services in a developing country: a patient-centric study. Int. J. Inf. Manag. **50**, 128–143 (2020)
39. Taamneh, A., et al.: University lecturers acceptance of moodle platform in the context of the COVID-19 pandemic. Global Knowl. Mem. Commun. (2022)
40. Lian, J.-W.: Critical factors for cloud based e-invoice service adoption in Taiwan: an empirical study. Int. J. Inf. Manag. **35**(1), 98–109 (2015)
41. Alkhwaldi, A.F., Al-Ajaleen, R.T.: Toward a conceptual model for citizens' adoption of smart mobile government services during the COVID-19 pandemic in Jordan. Inf. Sci. Lett.**11**(2), 573–579 (2022)
42. Dwivedi, Y.K., et al.: A meta-analysis based modified unified theory of acceptance and use of technology (Meta-UTAUT): a review of emerging literature. Curr. Opin. Psychol. **36**, 13–18 (2020)
43. Moudud-Ul-Huq, S., Swarna, R.S., Sultana, M.: Elderly and middle-aged intention to use m-health services: an empirical evidence from a developing country. J. Enabling Technol. **15**, 23–39 (2021)
44. Hossain, A., Quaresma, R., Rahman, H.: Investigating factors influencing the physicians' adoption of electronic health record (EHR) in healthcare system of Bangladesh: an empirical study. Int. J. Inf. Manag. **44**, 76–87 (2019)
45. Aljarboa, S., Miah, S.J.: An integration of UTAUT and task-technology fit frameworks for assessing the acceptance of clinical decision support systems in the context of a developing country. In: Yang, XS., Sherratt, S., Dey, N., Joshi, A. (eds.) Proceedings of Sixth International Congress on Information and Communication Technology, vol. 236, pp. 127–137. Springer, Singapore (2022). https://doi.org/10.1007/978-981-16-2380-6_11
46. Rogers, E.M.: Diffusion of Innovations, p. 551. Free Press, New York (2003)
47. Rogers, E.M., Singhal, A., Quinlan, M.M.: Diffusion of Innovation. Routledge, Milton Park (2014)
48. Agarwal, R., Prasad, J.: A conceptual and operational definition of personal innovativeness in the domain of information technology. Inf. Syst. Res. **9**(2), 204–215 (1998)
49. Alalwan, A.A., et al.: Examining adoption of mobile internet in Saudi Arabia: extending TAM with perceived enjoyment, innovativeness and trust. Technol. Soc. **55**, 100–110 (2018)
50. Kasilingam, D.L.: Understanding the attitude and intention to use smartphone chatbots for shopping. Technol. Soc. **62**, 101280 (2020)
51. Van Droogenbroeck, E., Van Hove, L.: Adoption and usage of E-grocery shopping: a context-specific UTAUT2 model. Sustainability **13**(8), 4144 (2021)
52. Li, H., et al.: Examining individuals' adoption of healthcare wearable devices: an empirical study from privacy calculus perspective. Int. J. Med. Inform. **88**, 8–17 (2016)
53. Patil, P., et al.: Understanding consumer adoption of mobile payment in India: extending meta-UTAUT model with personal innovativeness, anxiety, trust, and grievance redressal. Int. J. Inf. Manag. **54**, 102144 (2020)
54. Slade, E.L., et al.: Modeling consumers' adoption intentions of remote mobile payments in the United Kingdom: extending UTAUT with innovativeness, risk, and trust. Psychol. Mark. **32**(8), 860–873 (2015)
55. Bestsennyy, O., et al.: Telehealth: a quarter-trillion-dollar post-COVID-19 reality? (2021). https://www.mckinsey.com/industries/healthcare-systems-and-services/our-insights/telehealth-a-quarter-trillion-dollar-post-covid-19-reality
56. MOH. Government platforms to deal with the COVID-19 crisis (2021). https://corona.moh.gov.jo/
57. Global Market Insights, Telemedicine Market Share Report (2021)
58. Al-Okaily, M., et al.: Examining the critical factors of computer-assisted audit tools and techniques adoption in the post-COVID-19 period: internal auditors perspective. VINE J. Inf. Knowl. Manag. Syst. (2022)

59. Chan, F.K.Y., et al.: Modeling citizen satisfaction with mandatory adoption of an e-government technology. J. Assoc. Inf. Syst. **11**(10), 519–549 (2010)
60. Hair, J.F., et al.: Multivariate Data Analysis: Pearson New International Edition, Always Learning. Pearson, Harlow (2014)
61. Sekaran, U., Bougie, R.: Research Methods for Business: A Skill-Building Approach, 7th edn. Wiley, Chichester (2016)
62. Jameel, A.S., Karem, M.A., Ahmad, A.R.: Behavioral intention to use e-learning among academic staff during COVID-19 pandemic based on UTAUT model. In: Al-Emran, M., Al-Sharafi, M.A., Al-Kabi, M.N., Shaalan, K. (eds.) Proceedings of International Conference on Emerging Technologies and Intelligent Systems, vol. 299, pp.187–196. Springer, Cham (2021). https://doi.org/10.1007/978-3-030-82616-1_17
63. Al Amin, M., et al.: Understanding the predictors of rural customers' continuance intention toward mobile banking services applications during the COVID-19 pandemic. J. Global Mark. 1–24 (2021)
64. Al Amin, M., et al.: Evaluating the determinants of customers' mobile grocery shopping application (MGSA) adoption during COVID-19 pandemic. J. Global Mark. 1–20 (2021)
65. Venkatesh, V., Davis, F.D.: A theoretical extension of the technology acceptance model: four longitudinal field studies. Manag. Sci. **46**(2), 186–204 (2000)
66. Al-Okaily, M., et al.: The effect of digital accounting systems on the decision-making quality in the banking industry sector: a mediated-moderated model. Global Knowl. Mem. Commun. (2022)

Motivations and Challenges Related to the Use of Fitness Self-tracking Technology

Jenna Jones⏺, Pitso Tsibolane⁽⊠⁾⏺, and Jean-Paul van Belle⏺

University of Cape Town, Cape Town, South Africa
JNSJEN015@myuct.ac.za, {pitso.tsibolane,
jean-paul.vanbelle}@uct.ac.za

Abstract. Self-tracking technologies have the potential to increase users' motivation to engage in healthy behaviours. However, the Theory of Self-Determination (SDT) shows that motivation lies on a spectrum. The ways behaviours are initiated and sustained have a significant impact on a person's physical and emotional wellbeing. Research suggests that self-tracking technology can have a positive effect on user wellbeing. However, conflicting studies suggest that the use of this technology can lead to anxiety, guilt and other negative consequences. The objective of this study was to determine the impact of fitness self-tracking on users' wellbeing. This was achieved by a) analysing the impact of achievement and social related elements on the satisfaction of the three basic psychological needs b) analysing the effect that the fulfilment of these needs have on autonomous and controlled motivation and lastly c) determining if the type of motivation experienced by users impacts their levels of wellbeing. Data was collected from 411 users of fitness self-tracking technology in South Africa through an online survey based on models of SDT in health contexts and gamification in sports apps. It was analysed using partial least squares structural equation analysis (PLS-SEM). The results show that the achievement and social elements inherent in self-tracking technology contribute to the satisfaction of the needs for competence and relatedness. The fulfilment of these needs results in increased levels of autonomous motivation and improved user wellbeing. These insights can be applied in the design of new fitness self-tracking technology, with the aim of increasing users' levels of autonomous motivation and wellbeing.

Keywords: Self-tracking · Wearable fitness tracker · Mobile fitness application · Self-determination theory

1 Introduction

Self-tracking or self-quantification refers to the use of modern technologies with embedded sensors to automatically track and collect personal information, with minimal effort from the user [1]. This is not a new phenomenon. People have been recording personal details for centuries, as a way to assist self-reflection and self-optimisation. However,

S. Papagiannidis et al. (Eds.): I3E 2022, LNCS 13454, pp. 374–387, 2022.
https://doi.org/10.1007/978-3-031-15342-6_29

the advancement in wearable technologies that support the collection, storage, computation and display of personal data has enabled the pervasive, real-time monitoring of everyday life [2]. A range of wearable technologies and activity- tracking apps have been effectively utilised in fields such as fitness, health and medicine, to track and analyse the physical functioning of human bodies. However, apart from benefits, there is a "dark side" to activity trackers, claiming that they "lead to obsessive tendencies, rumination, and anxiety in users who worry about checking their data or meeting their daily goals" [3:2].

Despite the extensive application of self-tracking in fitness contexts, little research has been conducted to understand the motivations and challenges faced by users, particularly the effects on users' wellbeing [3]. In addition, the majority of related studies have treated motivation as a unilateral concept. Studies have revealed that different kinds of motivation (e.g., intrinsic and extrinsic motivation), as described in the Theory of Self-Determination, can have significantly different effects on one's wellbeing [1]. As the demand for these technologies grow in South Africa, it is vital that the unintended consequences and the potential negative effects on users are considered.

One of the selling points of self-tracking technology is the promise to increase a user's motivation to engage in healthy behaviours. However, as the Theory of Self-Determination has shown, the way behaviours are initiated and sustained will significantly influence a person's physical and emotional well-being. This study aims to determine the impact of fitness self-tracking on users' wellbeing by analysing the satisfaction of psychological needs and predominant types of motivation experienced.

With this purpose in mind, three research questions were established. The primary question for this research is: "What is the impact of fitness self-tracking on users' wellbeing?" The two secondary questions are "What is the impact of the achievement and social elements inherent in fitness self-tracking technology on the fulfilment of the three basic psychological needs of competence, autonomy and relatedness?"; and "What are the predominant motivations for using fitness self-tracking technology?" We focussed on discovering the motivations and challenges experienced by users of fitness self-tracking technology in South Africa. Fitness self-tracking technology includes mobile applications and wearable electronic devices with the main purpose of recording physical activity [1].

2 Literature Review

2.1 Self-tracking

In recent years, the phenomenon of recording and analysing details of everyday life has become increasingly pervasive. From exercising, eating and sleeping, to recording daily moods, productivity levels and vital signs, people have more information available to them than ever before [2]. Self-tracking refers to "the practice of gathering data about oneself on a regular basis and then recording and analysing the data to produce statistics and other data (such as images) relating to regular habits, behaviours and feelings" [4:77]. Fitness self-tracking technology includes mobile applications (e.g., Strava, Nike+) and electronic devices that are worn or attached to one's body (e.g., Garmin and Fitbit) with the main purpose of recording physical functions [1]. Through recording workouts, individuals can monitor calories burned, heart rate, VO2 Max, training load, fitness progress and a range of other variables. In addition to the ability to record and display the history of physical activity, many fitness trackers include gamification features to increase motivation and support positive behavioural change [5]. Examples include achievement related elements e.g. "badges, points, leader boards, virtual currencies, progress bars and different difficulty levels" [6:368] and social-related elements (competition with other users, opportunity to join teams and the ability to share exercise records on social media) [6].

2.2 Motivations for Self-tracking

The Theory of Self-Determination describes people's tendency to pursue personal growth and outlines the conditions that nurture this development [7]. It has been extensively applied in the study of sport [8], health [9] and exercise [1, 5, 10, 11].

The following is a brief review of the applications of the Self-Determination Theory (SDT) in the health and fitness context. [12] investigated whether wearable fitness devices influenced adolescents' motivation to participate in physical activity. Qualitative evidence suggested that participants experienced a short-term increase in motivation due to competition, guilt and internal pressure. [13] did a systematic review on the relationship between "key SDT-based constructs and exercise and physical activity behavioural outcomes" (p. 1). They concluded that SDT provides a good framework to understand exercise behaviour. [14] analysed the impact of a one-year weight management intervention programme, based on SDT on physical activity levels, weight and body composition. Their results showed that SDT based interventions, aimed at increasing autonomous motivation are effective in weight reduction and enable exercise adherence. [8] did a questionnaire-based study, directed at dragon boaters, testing the "hypothesis that self-determined motivation would mediate the relationship between psychological need and affective and behaviour outcomes" (p. 645) [5] surveyed the motivational effects of activity trackers on 210 users. The outcome indicated that users' experienced decreased motivation to exercise when the devices were unavailable. In addition, the study showed that users with "high extrinsic motivation for physical activity and tracker usage, high need for cognitive closure, and a low hope of success" [5:211] experienced the dependency effect most significantly. The aim of [11] was to discover if the gamification features of fitness trackers motivate users to increase their physical activity. A mixed method approach was taken to explore the intrinsic and extrinsic motivations experienced by users. [15] explored the "impact of novelty effect on activity tracker adoption and the motivation for sustained use" (p. 62) using a mixed methods approach. [10] applied the SDT framework to demonstrate that gamification features and the design of fitness trackers significantly affect user motivation and self-efficacy. [9] performed a meta-analysis of 184 studies to evaluate the relationship between medical practitioner support and patients' psychological need satisfaction, and the effects on the patient's mental and physical well-being. Results suggest that SDT can be applied as a conceptual framework to study the motivations for health-related behaviour.

Self-determination theory proposes that individuals can experience six types of motivation on a spectrum, ranging from lower to higher levels of self-determination or autonomy. These can be divided further into three categories: autonomous motivation, controlled motivation and amotivation. Autonomous motivation includes intrinsic motivation (for inherent enjoyment), integrated regulation (to achieve a personal goal) and identified regulation (valuing the outcomes of a certain behaviour e.g., health benefits). On the other hand, controlled motivation includes introjected regulation (e.g., to avoid guilt and anxiety) and external regulation (e.g., to earn a reward or avoid punishment). Lastly, amotivation refers to the state where individuals have no intention to act [12].

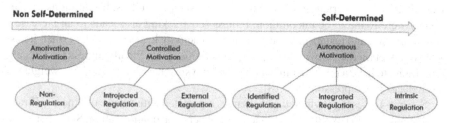

Fig. 1. Self-determination continuum showing types of motivation. Adapted from [7].

The two main categories of human motivation are "intrinsic motivation, which refers to doing something because it is inherently interesting or enjoyable and extrinsic motivation, which refers to doing something because it leads to a separable outcome" [7:56]. Individuals experience higher levels of physical and emotional wellbeing when their actions are more self-determined, or intrinsically motivated, as opposed to extrinsically motivated [12].

The theory also outlines three core psychological needs, namely autonomy, competence and relatedness, which when satisfied increase autonomous motivation and improve well-being. On the other hand, when these needs are not met, individuals experience low motivation and decreased well-being [7]. External motivators (e.g. rewards, competition and positive performance feedback) inherent in fitness tracking technology can promote the three psychological needs, to the degree that they are internalized [6]. However, these external motivations may undermine self-determined (autonomous) motivation through the reduction in need satisfaction [12].

2.3   Outcomes of Self-Tracking

[1] identified four main outcomes of fitness tracking, namely task motivation, physical activity, task experiences and well-being/health. Fitness tracking has been shown to increase users' motivation and has a positive impact on user' physical activity level, specifically relating to an increase in moderate-to-vigorous exercise [16, 17]. The effect of fitness tracking technologies on user's task-experience remains unclear. Studies suggest that fitness trackers increase users' level of enjoyment whilst exercising [10]. However, other studies have found that fitness tracking has the opposite effect, due to the undermining effects on intrinsic motivation [17].

Researchers found that fitness trackers positively affect physical health (e.g. aid weight loss, reduce blood pressure) and well-being (e.g. improved emotional state, increased feeling of satisfaction) [3, 16, 18]. However, other research has identified negative impacts of the continued use of this technology on users' subjective well-being [1]. For example, failing to meet one's goals may lead to feelings of frustration and guilt, resulting in the abandonment of one's fitness tracking device. Other challenges may include significant decreases in psychological need satisfaction, increased internal pressure, competition and negative feelings of self [12].

Several studies highlight the benefits of fitness self-tracking. [17] found that using these devices had positive effects on users' wellbeing (empowerment, motivation and accountability). Experiences of negative effects such as guilt, self-consciousness and anxiety were found to be uncommon. Fitness self-tracking also leads to an increase in user motivation and results in increased physical activity levels [16, 17]. Further, it has a positive effect on the enjoyment of physical activities [10]. Finally, fitness trackers also were found to have a positive impact on users' physical health e.g., supports weight loss and reduces blood pressure [16, 18].

Several studies highlighted the challenges associated with the use of fitness selftracking technology. [17] explored the hidden cost of personal quantification. Six experiments demonstrated that while self-tracking increases activity levels, it has the potential to reduce user enjoyment, due to the undermining effects on intrinsic motivation. [19] used an international survey to examine users' experiences and perceptions of self-tracking practices and data sharing. This study highlights the benefits and risks of self-tracking and critically reflects on these practices. [12] explored qualitatively whether wearable activity trackers affected adolescents' motivation for physical activity. Findings showed a significant decrease in psychological need satisfaction and a reduction in autonomous motivation. Short-term increases in motivation were due to competition among peers, guilt and internal pressure. However, there was a significant increase in amotivation after eight weeks of wearing the devices. Finally, in circumstances where activity trackers are unavailable, e.g., the device ran out of battery, users' motivations to exercise decrease significantly [5]

2.4 Theoretical Background

The theoretical model (Fig. 1) was adapted from [6]'s proposed model studying the users of gamified sports applications and [9]'s self-determination theory model. It provides a framework to look at how the interaction with achievement and social related elements in fitness self-tracking technology affects the fulfilment of the three psychological needs. In addition, it provides a framework to test the relationship between the fulfilment of these needs and autonomous and controlled motivation. Lastly, it provides a basis to determine if the type of motivation a user experiences positively or negatively affects their wellbeing. Each of the indicated arrows represents a hypothesised relationship.

3   Research Methodology

A positivist research philosophy was adopted. The purpose of the research is explanatory with the aim of establishing the relationship between fitness self-tracking features, the satisfaction of the three psychological needs (autonomy, competence, and relatedness), types of motivation and user well-being. A deductive approach was taken as the Theory

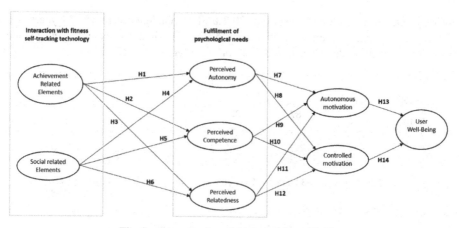

Fig. 2. Conceptual model adapted from [6, 9].

of Self-Determination was used to formulate hypotheses on the relationships between fitness self-tracking features, the satisfaction of the three psychological needs, types of motivation and user well-being. This study followed the survey strategy. The target population are people over the age of 18, using fitness self-tracking technology, located in South Africa. The sampling frame for this study was UCT students and members of South African exercise related Facebook groups, using fitness self-tracking technology.

This study made use of questionnaires to gather primary data from participants [20]. The questionnaire was based on the conceptual model (Figure 2) and was be used to test the research hypotheses outlined in Table 2. The questions based on achievement and social related elements were adapted from a study by [6]. The questions based on the three physiological needs were adapted from [21]. Responses were measured using five-point Likert scales. The research design and study instruments were approved by the Research Committee. Participants were required to give informed consent prior to participating in the online questionnaire.

4   Data Analysis and Findings

Simple random probability sampling was adopted with a sample frame of the host university students and members of South African fitness related Facebook groups. The online survey was conducted over three weeks and responses were recorded in Qualtrics. In total, 482 responses were received. All respondents confirmed they were over the age of 18 and gave consent to participate in the study. However, 71 responses were incomplete leaving 411 usable responses.

4.1   Demographic Analysis

The sample was distributed quite evenly across age groups, bearing in mind that South Africa has a relatively young population. Most respondents (27%) were between the ages of 18−24 years old. 21.2% of respondents were 25−34 years old, equally, 21.2%

of respondents were 35−44 years old. 20.2% of respondents were 45−54 years old. 10.5% of respondents were over 55 years old (Fig. 3). Most respondents were female (56%); 43% were male; 1% selected other or preferred not to say.

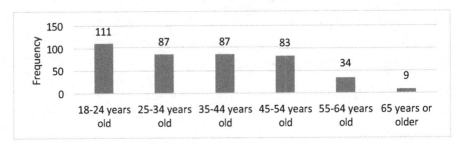

Fig. 3. Respondents' age distribution.

The majority (36.7%) of respondents claim to be regular exercisers i.e. for 3−6 h per week. 26% of respondents exercise for 1 to 3 h, whilst 22.1 % exercise for 6−9 h per week. Only 5.3% exercise for less than an hour and 9.7% exercise for more than 9 hours per week (Fig. 4).

Out of the 132 respondents that made use of mobile applications, the majority (39%) use Strava and 16% use Garmin Connect. Most respondents (52%) have been using their apps for two years or longer and 62% use their apps for less than three hours per week. By contrast, out of the 368 respondents that make use of wearable devices, the majority (53%) use a Garmin, 17% use Apple and 12% use Fitbit. 57% have been using their device for more than 2 years and 60% use their device for more than 9 hours per week. It is important to note here that respondents who make use of wearable devices interact with their tracker for significantly more hours per day than those using mobile applications.

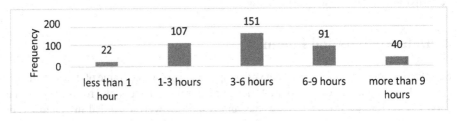

Fig. 4. Hours of exercise per week distribution

4.2 Measurement Model, Structural Model and Hypothesis Testing

Creating the Revised Structural Model

Partial Least Squares Structural Equation Modelling (PLS-SEM) was used for the evaluation of the measurement model, evaluation of the structural model and hypothesis testing. After running the initial PLS model on SmartPLS v3.3.3 using the variables instrument, the indicator reliability was assessed. According to [22], indicator loadings in reflective measurement models should be higher than 0.70. After assessing the outer loadings, the following indicators were dropped: Aut1, Com1_r, Com2_r, ExtR1, ExtR2, ExtR3, IntroR1, Well3_r, Well4_r and Well5_r. A revised model was then formed and assessed (Fig. 5). Dropping the indictors resulted in a reduced R^2. Originally, 42% of the variance in well-being was explained by the model, but now only 30.3 % of the variance is explained.

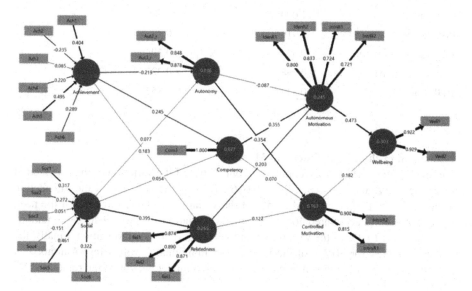

Fig. 5. Revised research model

Internal Consistency Reliability and Convergent Validity

The composite reliability for the model (Table 1) shows that all constructs pass the composite reliability check with values above the 0.7 thresholds [22]. Convergent validity was tested using average variance extracted. Convergent validity is "the extent to which a construct converges in its indicators by explaining the items' variance" [23:17]. The average variance extracted (AVE) should exceed 0.50 [22]. The AVE extracted for the model (Table 1), shows all constructs above the 0.50 threshold [23].

A Heterotrait-Monotrait Ratio (HTMT) test was run to check the discriminant validity - that two measures that are not supposed to be related are in fact, unrelated. The acceptable threshold values for HTMT are <0.90 [23]. All values were, in fact, far less than 0.9 (the highest value was 0.640 between Wellbeing and Autonomous Motivation) and the model thus passes the discriminate validity test.

The formative measurement model was assessed by evaluating indicators' outer weights and loadings. Bootstrapping was used to assess their significance. Most indicators had low and/or non-significant outer weights. All but one (Ach2) have loadings above 0.50, indicating that they can be retained in the model [23]. Collinearity was assessed based on the variance inflation factor (VIF) values. The VIFs range from 1.80 to 2.72, all lower than 5, suggesting that multicollinearity is not an issue [22].

Table 1. Composite reliability and average variance extracted.

Construct	Composite reliability	Average variance extracted
Autonomy	0.854	0.745
Competency	1.000	1.000
Relatedness	0.910	0.772
Autonomous motivation	0.854	0.594
Controlled motivation	0.848	0.737
Wellbeing	0.923	0.857

Assessment of the Final Structural Model

The revised model (Fig. 5), accounted for only 3.6% of the variation of the satisfaction for the need for autonomy (i.e., $R^2 = 0.036$), 7.7% of the variation of the satisfaction of the need for competency and 26.5% of the variation of the satisfaction of the need for relatedness. It accounted for 24.5% of the variation in individuals' autonomous motivation and 16.3% of the variation in individuals' controlled motivation. Finally, the model accounted for 30.3% of the variation in individuals' well-being. Autonomous motivation and well-being values can be considered moderate, whilst the remaining R^2 values are fairly weak.

Table 2 shows the results of the structural model assessment. Paths that are not significant or have a sign contrary to the hypothesized direction (indicated with *No**) do not support a prior hypothesis [23:147].

4.3 Findings

Effect of Achievement on the Satisfaction of the Three Psychological Needs

The interaction with achievement elements in fitness self-trackers were found to promote the satisfaction of the needs for competence ($\beta = 0.245$; $t = 3.454$) and relatedness ($\beta = 0.183$; $t = 2.950$), which supports H2 and H3. The effect of achievement related elements on autonomy was also significant, however, the path coefficient is negative, contrary to the hypothesised direction ($\beta -0.219$; $t = 2.735$). As a result, H1 is rejected.

Effect of Social Related Elements on the Satisfaction of the Psychological Needs

The results indicate that the interaction with social related elements in fitness self-trackers promoted the satisfaction of the need for relatedness ($\beta = 0.395$; $t = 6.720$), which supports H6. However, no significant effect of social related elements were found

Table 2. Path coefficients of the structural model and significance testing results.

Hyp	Path	β Path coeff	t-value	p- value	Sig level	Supported
H1	Achievement => Autonomy	−0.219	2.735	0.006	1%	No*
H2	Achievement => Competency	0.245	3.454	0.001	1%	Yes
H3	Achievement => Relatedness	0.183	2.950	0.003	1%	Yes
H4	Social => Autonomy	0.077	0.976	0.329	–	No
H5	Social => Competency	0.054	0.860	0.390	–	No
H6	Social => Relatedness	0.395	6.720	0.000	1%	Yes
H7	Autonomy => Autonomous motivation	−0.087	2.036	0.042	5%	No*
H8	Competency => Autonomous motivation	0.355	6.714	0.000	1%	Yes
H9	Relatedness => Autonomous motivation	0.203	4.746	0.000	1%	Yes
H10	Autonomy => Controlled motivation	−0.354	8.379	0.000	1%	Yes
H11	Competency => Controlled motivation	0.070	1.354	0.176	–	No
H12	Relatedness => Controlled motivation	0.122	2.402	0.016	5%	No*
H13	Autonomous motivation => Wellbeing	0.473	9.901	0.000	1%	Yes
H14	Controlled motivation => Wellbeing	0.182	4.145	0.000	1%	No*

on the satisfaction for the need of autonomy ($\beta = 0.077$; $t = 0.976$) or competence ($\beta = 0.054$; $t = 0.860$). As a result, H4 and H5 are rejected.

Effect of the Satisfaction of the Psychological Needs on Autonomous Motivation
The results demonstrated that the satisfaction of the needs for competence ($\beta = 0.355$; $t = 6.714$) and relatedness ($\beta = 0.203$; $t = 4.746$) when using fitness self-trackers has a significant positive influence on autonomous motivation, supporting H8 and H9. The satisfaction of the need for autonomy also has a significant effect on autonomous motivation ($\beta = -0.087$; $t = 2.036$). However, the path coefficient is negative, contrary to the hypothesised direction, resulting in the rejection of H7.

Effect of the Satisfaction of the Psychological Needs on Controlled Motivation
The results demonstrated that the satisfaction of the need for autonomy ($\beta = -0.354$; $t = 8.379$) has a significant negative influence on controlled motivation, which supports H10. The satisfaction of the need for competence ($\beta = 0.070$; $t = 1.354$) has an insignificant effect on controlled motivation, resulting in the rejection of H11. Lastly, the satisfaction

of the need for relatedness has a significant effect on controlled motivation ($\beta = 0.122$; t = 2.402). However, the path coefficient is positive, contrary to the hypothesised direction, resulting in the rejection of H12.

Effect of Autonomous Motivation and Controlled Motivation on User Wellbeing
Autonomous motivation was positively related to user wellbeing ($\beta = 0.473$; t = 9.901), which supports H13. Controlled motivation is also shown to have a significant effect on user wellbeing ($\beta = 0.182$; t = 4.145), however, the path coefficient is positive, contrary to the hypothesised direction, resulting in the rejection of H14.

5   Discussion

This study aimed to determine the impact of fitness self-tracking on users' wellbeing. This was achieved by a) analysing the impact of achievement and social related elements on the satisfaction of the three basic psychological needs, their effect on autonomous and controlled motivation and determining if this impacts their levels of well-being. The results show that interacting with achievement related elements in self-tracking technology fulfils the need for competence and relatedness. For example, receiving a badge may make a user feel that they have the necessary skills to achieve a fitness goal, contributing to the feeling of competence. A user may feel more connected to the fitness community when they view themselves on a leader board, contributing to the feeling of relatedness with other self-trackers. These results are similar to those observed by [6]. However, achievement related elements contribute negatively to the satisfaction of the need for autonomy. This is concerning as it suggests that keeping track of progress bars, points and badges may make a user feel less in control of their own behaviour and goals.

The interaction with social related elements in fitness self-trackers only promoted the satisfaction of the needs for relatedness, not autonomy or competence. These results are in line with the study conducted by [6]. Virtually competing with other users, joining exercise groups and sharing exercise records on social media could make users feel more connected, cared for and understood by others.

The satisfaction of the needs for competence and relatedness when using fitness self-trackers has a significant positive influence on autonomous motivation. This aligns with self-determination theory: users who feel confident in their abilities and connected to others are more autonomously motivated-driven by enjoyment and personal goals. However, the satisfaction of the need for autonomy had a significant, but weak, negative effect on autonomous motivation, contrary to self-determination theory. The satisfaction of the need for autonomy showed a significant negative influence on controlled motivation, in line with the theory of self-determination. As users begin to feel more competent i.e., in control of their behaviour and goals, they experience higher levels of autonomous motivation [7].

Finally, autonomous motivation is positively related to user wellbeing. This supports findings that intrinsic motivation, a form of autonomous motivation, is positively related to psychological health and improvements in wellbeing [13]. However, controlled motivation had only a significant, but weak, positive effect on user wellbeing. This is contrary findings that suggests that a relationship exists between introjected regulation (a form of controlled motivation) and negative psychological outcomes e.g., anxiety, dissatisfaction and depression [9].

A number of considerations can be incorporated into the improved design of fitness self-tracking technology. Designers should include more achievement and social related elements that promote the satisfaction of the needs for competence and relatedness. This study confirmed that the satisfaction of these two needs has significant positive influences on autonomous motivation, which in turn, has a significant positive effect on user wellbeing. In addition, the study could not confirm that achievement related elements promote the satisfaction of the need for autonomy. It is suggested that developers include more customisation features where users can feel free to set their own goals and challenges, enhancing the satisfaction of the need for autonomy [6].

6 Conclusion

The use of modern technology to record and analyse details of everyday life has become increasingly pervasive [2]. Self-tracking technology has the potential to increase a user's motivation to engage in healthy behaviours, however as the Theory of Self-Determination has shown, motivation is not unilateral. The way behaviours are initiated and sustained can have a significant influence on a person's well-being [1]. As the demand for these technologies grow in South Africa, it is vital that the unintended consequences and the potential negative effects of fitness self-tracking are considered.

This study used the Theory of Self-determination to demonstrate that the elements inherent in self-tracking technology contribute to the satisfaction of the needs for competence and relatedness. The fulfilment of these needs results in increased levels of autonomous motivation and improved user wellbeing. These valuable insights can be applied to the design of new fitness self-tracking technology, with the aim of increasing users' levels of autonomous motivation.

Future research could follow a longitudinal approach where the changes in the satisfaction of the three psychological needs and user wellbeing could be assessed over an extended period. In addition, further research can be conducted to assess whether gender, age or duration of device use has an impact the effect of self-tracking technology on user wellbeing. This study focused on the effects of fitness self-tracking technology on psychological factors namely, the satisfaction of the three psychological needs, types of motivation experienced and the effects on user wellbeing. Future studies could explore the impact of achievement and social related elements on levels of physical activity, not only motivation and well-being. In addition, this study grouped all social related elements together and all achievement related elements together. Future research could differentiate between each element and examine their individual impact on the fulfilment of the three psychological needs.

References

1. Jin, D., Halvari, H., Maehle, N., Olafsen, A.H.: Self-tracking behaviour in physical activity: a systematic review of drivers and outcomes of fitness tracking. Behav. Inf. Technol. **41**(2), 1–20 (2020). https://doi.org/10.1080/0144929X.2020.1801840

2. Lupton, D.: Understanding the human machine. IEEE Technol. Soc. Mag. **32**(4), 25–30 (2013). https://doi.org/10.1109/MTS.2013.2286431

3. Edney, S., Maher, C., Ryan, J.: Anxious or empowered? a cross-sectional study exploring how wearable activity trackers make their owners feel. BMC Psychol. **7**(1), 1–8 (2019). https://doi.org/10.1186/s40359-019-0315-y

4. Lupton, D.: Self-tracking cultures: towards a sociology of personal informatics. In: Paper Presented at the 26th Australian Computer-Human Interaction Conference, pp. 77–86 (2014)

5. Attig, C., Franke, T.: I track, therefore I walk – exploring the motivational costs of wearing activity trackers in actual users. Int. J. Hum Comput Stud. **127**, 211–224 (2019). https://doi.org/10.1016/j.ijhcs.2018.04.007

6. Bitrián, P., Buil, I., Catalán, S.: Gamification in sport apps: the determinants of users' motivation. Eur. J. Manag. Bus. Econ. **29**(3), 365–381 (2020)

7. Ryan, R.M., Deci, E.L.: Self-determination theory and the facilitation of intrinsic motivation, social development, and well-being. Am. Psychol. **55**(1), 68–78 (2000)

8. McDonough, M.H., Crocker, P.R.: Testing self-determined motivation as a mediator of the relationship between psychological needs and affective and behavioral outcomes. J. Sport Exerc. Psychol. **29**(5), 645–663 (2007)

9. Ng, J.Y., et al.: Self-determination theory applied to health contexts: a meta-analysis. Perspect. Psychol. Sci. **7**(4), 325–340 (2012)

10. Asimakopoulos, S., Asimakopoulos, G., Spillers, F.: Motivation and user engagement in fitness tracking: heuristics for mobile healthcare wearables. Informatics **4**(1), 1–16 (2017). https://doi.org/10.3390/informatics4010005

11. Schaffarczyk, L., Ilhan, A.: Healthier life and more fun? users' motivations to apply activity tracking technology and the impact of gamification. In: Paper Presented at the International Conference on Human-Computer Interaction, pp. 124–136 (2019)

12. Kerner, C., Goodyear, V.: The motivational impact of wearable healthy lifestyle technologies: a self-determination perspective on Fitbits with adolescents. Am. J. Health Educ. **48**(5), 287–297 (2017). https://doi.org/10.1080/19325037.2017.1343161

13. Teixeira, P.J., Carraça, E.V., Markland, D., Silva, M.N., Ryan, R.M.: Exercise, physical activity, and self-determination theory: a systematic review. Int. J. Behav. Nutr. Phys. Act. **9**(1), 1–30 (2012)

14. Silva, M.N., et al.: Using self-determination theory to promote physical activity and weight control: a randomized controlled trial in women. J. Behav. Medi. **33**(2), 110–122 (2010). https://doi.org/10.1007/s10865-009-9239-y

15. Shin, G., Feng, Y., Jarrahi, M.H., Gafinowitz, N.: Beyond novelty effect: a mixed-methods exploration into the motivation for long-term activity tracker use. JAMIA Open **2**(1), 62–72 (2019). https://doi.org/10.1093/jamiaopen/ooy048

16. Butryn, M., Arigo, D., Raggio, G., Colasanti, M., Forman, E.: Enhancing physical activity promotion in midlife women with technology-based self-monitoring and social connectivity: a pilot study. J. Health Psychol. **21**(8), 1548–1555 (2016)

17. Etkin, J.: The hidden cost of personal quantification. J. Consum. Res. **42**(6), 967–984 (2016). https://academic.oup.com/jcr/article/42/6/967/2358309

18. Randriambelonoro, M., Chen, Y., Pu, P.: Can fitness trackers help diabetic and obese users make and sustain lifestyle changes? Computer **50**(3), 20–29 (2017)

19. Ajana, B.: Personal metrics: users' experiences and perceptions of self-tracking practices and data. Soc. Sci. Inf. **59**(4), 654–678 (2020)

20. Saunders, M., Lewis, P., Thornhill, A.: Research Methods for Business Students, 8th edn. Pearson Education Limited (2019)

21. Peters, D., Calvo, R., Ryan, R.: Designing for motivation, engagement and well-being in digital experience. Front. Psychol. **9**, 1–15 (2018)

22. Hair, J., Ringle, C., Sarstedt, M.: PLS-SEM: indeed a silver bullet. J. Mark. Theory Pract. **19**(2), 139–152 (2011). https://doi.org/10.2753/MTP1069-6679190202
23. Sarstedt, M., Ringle, C., Hair, J.: Partial least squares structural equation modeling, pp. 1–40. Springer International Publishing. Cham (2017). https://doi.org/10.1007/978-3-319-05542-8_15-1

Pandemic

Who's the Bigger Brand After COVID-19 Pandemic? An Assessment of Fan Engagement During Euro 2020

Vishal Mehra[1,2], Prabhsimran Singh[1,2(✉)], Yogesh K. Dwivedi[3,4], Gurpreet Singh[1,2], and Ravinder Singh Sawhney[2]

[1] Department of Computer Engineering & Technology, Guru Nanak Dev University, Amritsar, India
mehravishal1992@gmail.com, {vishalcet.rsh, prabhsimran.dcet}@gndu.ac.in, prabh_singh32@yahoo.com, gurisingh0504@gmail.com
[2] Department of Electronics Technology, Guru Nanak Dev University, Amritsar, India
sawhney.ece@gndu.ac.in
[3] School of Management, Emerging Market Research Center (EMaRC), Swansea University, Swansea, UK
y.k.dwivedi@swansea.ac.uk
[4] Department of Management, Symbiosis Institute of Business Management, Pune & Symbiosis International (Deemed University), Maharashtra Pune, India

Abstract. Post COVID-19 pandemic, sports events and sports activities have been severely affected. The mega sports events were either postponed or held in the absence of live audience. Through this study we investigate the progressive use of social media by fans and other stakeholders to express their support to favorite sports teams, athletes, coaches, sports organizations, sponsors and more during COVID-19. UEFA Euro 2020 was conducted across 12 countries with an intent to show unity and bring normalcy in sports business during the third wave of COVID-19. Hashtag analysis and mention analysis have been performed to find sports teams, athletes or other stakeholders that were directly being discussed about by the fans. We also focused on tweet context annotations that provide entities as pairs of domain and entity collected from tweets' text. Our results indicated that hashtags and mentions alone cannot substantially justify the popularity of any entity. Thus, from the point of view of identifying any athlete, team, organization or any sponsor as a brand, tweet context annotations can be valuable from the perspective of E-Branding, E-Marketing and E-Commerce.

Keywords: COVID-19 · Digital media · Euro 2020 · Social media · Sport branding · Sport management · Twitter

1 Introduction

Sports is an integral part of human life. The ideas and phenomena responsible for evolution and development of humans over the generations are long-established in sports

S. Papagiannidis et al. (Eds.): I3E 2022, LNCS 13454, pp. 391–402, 2022.
https://doi.org/10.1007/978-3-031-15342-6_30

(Sustainable Development Goals Fund 2018). As sports have evolved over the time, certain terminologies have also developed that are most commonly used to identify the entities of sports such as fans, athletes, sports persons, sports teams, coaches, broadcasters, sports journalists and sport-media as brands in the domain of sports business and management (Gibbs et al. 2014; Singh et al. 2019, June; Fenton et al. 2021; Mehra et al. 2021). Relying on Internet as the backbone all the latter stated entities of sports have cherished the power of social media to expand the reach to the global audience (Hopkins 2013). Twitter is one such social media tool that has found acceptance amongst diverse audience all over the world as it provides an immersive information sharing experience amongst fans, athletes, sport marketers and sport organizations (Wang 2021).

After the COVID-19 was declared pandemic by WHO on March 11, 2020 (Kato 2021) nationwide lockdowns were imposed and restrictions were imposed on outdoor activities such as sports and entertainment across the globe (Singh et al. 2020; Mehra et al. 2021). All forms of sports and sport related activities were either postponed or cancelled. It was for the first time in history that Olympics event was postponed for over a year. UEFA Euro 2020 and Copa America were postponed till 2021 (ESPN News Services 2020, March 23; Al Jazeera 2020, September 20). Many of the football players such as Pedri Gonzalez, Ferran Torres, Gavi Paez, Ousmane Dembele, Sergino Dest, Philippe Coutinho, Abde Ezzalzouli, Lionel Messi were reported to be infected with COVID-19 (Desk 2022).

With time as the COVID-19 progressed all over the world, the Twitter emerged as an effective medium of communication to disseminate information for fans, athletes, sports journalists, sports organizations and social bots (Mattei et al. 2021; Mehra et al. 2021). The research fraternity actively participated in identifying the relevance of Twitter as a social media tool by presenting studies of diverse nature that can be broadly categorized to include (a) role of athletes in maintaining a connection with fans during the pandemic (Bowes et al. 2021; Sharpe et al. 2020; Mehra et al. 2021; Smith 2021) (b) exchange of views and conversations among fans/spectators (Chehal et al. 2021; Garcia and Berton 2021; González et al. 2021; Mattei et al. 2021; Mehra et al. 2021) (c) efficiency of sports organizations to maintain healthy fan engagement with favorite teams and athletes (Bond et al. 2020; Sharpe et al. 2020; Bond et al. 2021) and (d) the idea to continue certain sports during pandemic (Bingaman 2020; Davidson et al. 2020).

Thus, it becomes imperative to identify the class of athletes, fans, sports teams, sports organizations and sponsors who actively participated and stayed on toes for successful completion of Euro 2020, during the third wave of COVID-19. Euro 2020 the mega sports event that is endorsed by multitude of stakeholders was delayed for over a year to avoid the spread of COVID-19 as health of citizens and athletes was the top priority (Lee Ludvigsen 2021). This study aims to find the answers to following research questions:

RQ1: Who was the fan-favorite during Euro 2020?

Fans express their support towards athletes, teams or events through hashtags or mentions. Analysis of hashtags and mentions a part of social media analytics is crucial to any study to estimate the popularity of related entity (Singh et al. 2020, Mehra et al. 2021).

RQ2: Identify the entities that grabbed most attention during the course of Euro2020?

Tweet Context Annotations contain the micro-information in the form of keywords identified by Twitter across more than 50 domains (Twitter, n.d.). To find an answer to RQ2 we rely on these annotations.

2 Literature Review

Over the years social media, a potent tool for information dissemination has experienced immense growth across various sectors such as sports, education, healthcare, financial sector, industrial sector, public administration and many more (Stieglitz et al. 2014; Rathore et al. 2017; Stieglitz et al. 2018; Singh et al. 2019; Mehra et al. 2021). During the ongoing COVID-19 pandemic as well the social media played a crucial role in disseminating the vital information (González et al. 2021) to analyze sports across diverse fields such as *entrepreneurship* (Hammerschmidt et al. 2021), *brand communities* (Fenton et al. 2021), *fan engagement* (Bingaman 2020; Davidson et al. 2020; Majumdar and Naha 2020; Bond et al. 2020; Bond et al. 2021; Stavros et al. 2021), *women's sports* (Bowes et al. 2021; Doyle et al. 2021), *promotion of digital platforms* (Westmattelmann et al. 2020; Manoli 2020; Areiza-Padilla et al. 2021; Hedenborg et al. 2022), *athletes and sports organizations as role models* (Sharpe et al. 2020; Elliott et al. 2021; Smith 2021), *brand involvement* (Pan and Phua 2020; Russo and Tallarita 2021; Su et al. 2021) and *sport management* (Ratten and Jones 2020; Smith and Skinner 2021). In this section, we put light on the related works to the forementioned fields that resulted in their rise, relevance and importance in sports.

2.1 Brand Communities, Brand Involvement and Promotion of Digital Platforms

The brand is one of the most valuable assets of any sports entity. Athletes and sports organizations are such entities that have made the most of social media platforms to increase their brand values through the digital connections with fans, teams, sponsors and other stakeholders across the globe. The digital platforms and environment indeed play an important role in managing sports brands by collecting behavioral data such as content linking, merchandise and ticket purchases and more that help to extract meaningful insights and make proper decisions to maintain a healthy connection with the fans (Kunkel and Biscaia, 2020; Pan and Phua, 2020; Fenton et al. 2021; Su et al. 2021). The sports brands were ready to hone the power of E-commerce channels by branding on the backbone of well-being, optimism, resilience and entertainment but delivery timelines and hygiene standards were the major concerns of consumers. In India, E-commerce websites such as Amazon and Flipkart were discussed the most over Twitter (Chehal et al. 2021; Russo and Tallarita 2021). To further strengthen the bond with the consumers, sports brands shared empowering content, fulfilling social and civic responsibility. This shared value created by sports brands made the fans to perceive togetherness and themselves to be benefitted towards broader societal good and involvement during the period of COVID-19. (Su et al. 2021). To promote acceptance and increase the brand value via social media the concepts of E-Loyalty, E-Brand Image, E-Customization and E-Purchase Intention need to be capitalized by athletes, sports teams, sports organization and sponsors (Areiza-Padilla et al. 2021) as COVID-19 forced the individuals, groups and nations to increase the investment in digital tools and digital infrastructure while promoting the consumption of sports through social media and other forms of media thus, deepening the roots of media in sports (Manoli et al. 2020; Westmattelmann et al. 2020; Hedenborg et al. 2022).

2.2   Fan Engagement, Athletes and Sports Organizations as Role Models

Fans, athletes, sports organizations, sport brands and many other entities have used Twitter as the favorite social media platform during this ongoing pandemic for spreading the information to promote good health (Bingaman 2020; Sharpe et al. 2020; Chehal et al. 2021; Davidson et al. 2020; González et al. 2021; Garcia and Berton 2021; Mattei et al. 2021; Mehra et al. 2021; Priyadarshini et al. 2021). Fans were concerned about physical performance of athletes and presented grief over demise of athletes due to covid. Marketing of sports goods and other stuff such as masks found a place on Twitter. On the other hand, sports organizations promoted physical activities and digital/online exercise programs through campaigns on Twitter (Bond et al. 2020; Bond et al. 2021; González et al. 2021). Football clubs, NBA franchises and players provided social and economic help to fight against COVID-19 (Sharpe et al. 2020). Football athletes were seen portraying diverse roles over social media through hashtags such as #StayHomeSaveLives (Mesut Ozil), #nevergiveup #countingdownthedays (Tim Krul), #Apartbuttogether (John Egan), #lockdownsaturdays #stayhome #savelives (Theo Walcott), #GymDone (Andy Carroll) (Smith 2021; Stavros et al. 2021). COVID-19 has provided an opportunity to the sports broadcasters to test and apply newer ideas to enrich fan experience with more creative content, such as the use of Spidercam to perform live interview of any player during the event over a particular achievement. (Bond et al. 2020; Bond et al. 2021; Majumdar and Naha 2020).

2.3   Entrepreneurship, Sport Management and Women's Sports

Dynamic nature of sport makes it a natural setting for entrepreneurship. Sport entrepreneurship can be identified at individual level (athletes, coaches and managers) and organizational level (sports teams and sports organizations) (Ratten and Jones 2020). At the time of crisis, the companies with entrepreneurial profile are supposed to survive as they possess the characteristics of risk-taking and innovation. Despite most of the professional football clubs lacked the skills for crisis management, they did not suffer any cash crunch. It was stated that making ample amount of money and creating reserves were disadvantageous as the profits would be taxed. (Hammerschmidt et al. 2021). Women's sports need special attention for its revival. After facing financial crisis, mental and social isolation, women need equity in brand endorsements and brand sponsorships to achieve economic gains, so that they can invest in health equipment and other sports products or goods (Bowes et al. 2021; Doyle et al. 2021; Smith and Skinner 2021).

2.4   COVID-19, Euro 2020

Hosting Euro 2020 was a great challenge so it was postponed to 2021 where it witnessed the third wave of covid (Heese et al. 2022). But COVID-19 forced the UEFA to perform unimaginable and never happened task of hosting Euro 2020 among 12 European nations. At the time where nations were facing financial losses and hosting mega sport events was being criticized, Euro 2020's format was completely new and was purposed to demonstrate cultural togetherness and fluidity within Eurozone. Fans were affected the most by this multi-nation format as they had to bear high travel costs and tickets for a game clearly a logistical obstacle (Lee Ludvigsen 2021).

In Germany, only 20% seats were available for booking for all the matches. In Munich the COVID-19 infected cases were reported during several matches amongst Portugal-Germany, Germany-Hungary, Belgium-Italy, despite the cases were reported to be wearing masks all the time and few of them were vaccinated. The Euro 2020 is supposed to have increased the risk of transmission of novel coronavirus (Heese et al. 2022). The cases were found in Scotland, Finland and Moscow as well despite all the recommended measures were strictly enforced (Marsh et al. 2021).

3 Methodology

For the purpose of collecting data, we used tweepy API. As the tweets were to be collected from June 11, 2021 to July 12, 2021, we used the Twitter API V2 for academic research to fetch historic data. Twitter API V1.1 for basic users does not provide this feature (Roesslein, n.d.). To fetch the data, we used the hashtags for example, #TURvsITA OR #ITAvsTUR OR #TURvITA OR #ITAvTUR. Each nation in the hashtag is represented by the three-letter abbreviation as proposed by FIFA. The final match between England and Italy received highest number of tweets 42850 and the match between North Macedonia and Netherlands received only 180 tweets.

A total of 3,36,310 tweets in English language were collected from 1,08,585 unique users globally. The data contained a lot of noise in form of punctuations, stop words, web links, special characters, emojis, whitespaces (extra blank spaces between the words or sentences) were eliminated. in order to keep the focus on the meaningful words in the sentence. Once the data was ready various programming techniques were applied to gain the meaningful insights from the data (Singh et al. 2018; Singh et al. 2020, Singh et al. 2020; Mehra et al. 2021).

4 Results and Discussions

In RQ1, we try to analyze the support given by fans to their favorite teams and athletes through social media. For this we analyzed the hashtags and mentions in the Twitter data (See Table 1). As expected, the #EURO2020 was the most used hashtag with a variation in the form of #Euro2020. This shows the behavior of social media users to more often use capital letters in hashtags for the purpose of highlighting the topic they are very keen to discuss about. #Euro2021 was also famous amongst fans as the event was being held in 2021. #ENGvsGER for England vs Germany was second in the list presenting it as the most followed and one of the most discussed matches amongst fans. Apart from England other nations that received huge support from fans through digital media were Scotland, Croatia, Portugal, France, Switzerland and Hungary.

It was interesting to note that amongst athletes, teams, coaches, sport managers or sport brands none was at the top in the list of mentions. The Twitter users with user names Urban Pictures, Simon London, Otto English and Boris Reitschuster, and Twitter handles @Urban_Pictures, @slondonuk, @Otto_English and @reitschuster respectively were found to be mentioned the most by the Twitter users. This clearly shows that independent journalists are cherished amongst the masses in comparison to the conventional well-established media such as British Broadcasting Corporation (BBC-with sports specific Twitter handle @BBCSport), ITV News (@itvnews) and Talkradio (@talkRADIO) as they lagged behind by a huge difference. Amongst the athletes Cristiano Ronaldo (@Cristiano) was received highest mentions, followed by English professional football players Jack Grealish (@JackGrealish) and Raheem Sterling (@sterling7). Fans also mentioned former English footballer David Seamen (@thedavidseamen) in their tweets.

Table 1. Top-20 hashtags and mentions during Euro 2020

Hashtags	Count	Mentions	Count
#EURO2020	84,090	@Urban_Pictures	9,230
#ENGvsGER	32,863	@slondonuk	5,024
#ENGvSCO	22,814	@IamHappyToast	4,421
#ENG	19,422	@JamieAndrew99	3,247
#SCOvCZE	18,060	@Otto_English	2,318
#EngvsCro	13,269	@England	2,316
#ENGSCO	10,357	@ugames_uk	1,856
#Euro2021	6,951	@reitschuster	1,471
#Euro2020	6,756	@itvnews	1,443
#EnglandvGermany	6,503	@BorisJohnson_MP	1,366
#GERvsPOR	6,232	@SonySportsIndia	1,012
#FRAvSUI	5,754	@GarethSouthgate	935
#Kane	5,481	@Cristiano	914
#pride	5,171	@JackGrealish	819
#BLM	5,048	@ScotlandNT	786
#mycaptain	5,027	@BBCSport	779
#SCO	4,718	@sterling7	683
#England	4,689	@thedavidseaman	625
#HUNvsFRA	4,453	@talkRADIO	599
#ENGvCRO	4,258	@Iromg	595

The availability of keywords derived through the analysis of tweets' text in the pairs of domain and entity can be very helpful for the researchers who are novice at programming and find it difficult to build sophisticated codes for performing named entity recognition (NER) (Twitter, n.d.; Nasar et al. 2021). To answer RQ2, dataset for Euro 2020, revealed tweet annotations across 43 domains. The domain names that were highly important and useful from the perspective of this research were selected named "Sports Event", "Sports Team", "Sports League", "Athlete", "Sports Personality", "Journalist", "Brand", "Sport", "Coach" and "Fan Community". The forementioned domain names were uniquely analyzed and top-20 entity names were derived from the tweet annotations as listed in Table 2. As the dataset has been fetched for Euro 2020, for the domain name Sports League the entity UEFA European Championship stood at the top with 2,66,278 annotations count followed by the topic of International Soccer with the count of 1,87,172 and Europe – Soccer with count 187163. WWE, NFL, FIFA Men's World Cup, Copa América, ICC World Test Championship were also being discussed but their count was comparatively negligible. This clearly states that fans are more focused towards the sport. The behavior was same for entity Soccer with count of 26,257 identified in the domain of Sport. Diverse forms of games were being discussed along with Euro 2020 such as cricket, rugby, basketball, combat sports and more at a very miniscule level.

Team England (49,712) was the fan favorite team followed by Germany (15,016), Portugal (10,834), Scotland (9,336), France (9,163) to name a few. Vis-à-vis Sports Events/matches in which England participated such as England vs Germany (3,60,111), England vs Scotland (12,869) and England vs Croatia (19,257) were at the top and as a match England vs Germany was the fan-favorite.

Although in the analysis of hashtags Cristiano Ronaldo gathered the top spot followed by Jack Grealish and Raheem Sterling, tweet annotations revealed a completely different story. As the tweet annotations are derived from tweet text, results indicated that sports fans were presenting higher engagement in context of Raheem Sterling (3,652) followed by Jack Grealish (3,499) and Cristiano Ronaldo (3,168) at the third spot. The fans presented enthusiasm towards Euro 2020 by supporting many other athletes as listed in Table 2. Former professional football players such as Gary Lineker (329), Darren Fletcher (215), Alan Shearer (212), John Barnes (128) received a huge support from fans along with many football managers, sports commentators, young professional football players listed under the domain of Sports Personality. Gareth Southgate (3,536) the coach of England's football team turned out to be the most discussed Coach during Euro 2020. Coaches of other teams such as Steve Clarke (218), Senol Gunes (194), José Mourinho (147) and Joachim Low (116) were amongst the top-5 most discussed football coaches.

The entities identified as brands were broadly categorized as TV/ Movies related, Online Site, Online Services, Beverage, Sports, Gas/Oil, Financial Services, Auto Manufacturer, Telco, Non-Profit and more. Amongst these BBC (162) topped the list of domain name Brand. Sony (651), global online gambling company William Hill (536), Twitter (487) and Coca-Cola (415) were top-5 most supported brands. ESPN (328) an American international sports channel, Gas/Oil brands such as Mobil1 (247) and Exxon-Mobil (245), Telco brands named Hisense (213) and Apple (149), Online Site such as Instagram (96) and Youtube (81), Auto Manufacturer such as Volkswagen (65) and Beverage named Heineken (123) along with Coca-Cola (415) were amongst the top-20 brands being discussed amongst the fans.

Table 2. Sports specific tweet annotations during Euro 2020.

	ENTITY NAMES								DOMAIN NAMES								
Sports Event		**Sports Team**		**Sports League**		**Athlete**		**Sports Personality**		**Journalist**		**Brand**		**Sport**		**Coach**	
Name	Count	Name	Count	Name	Count	Name	Count	Name	Count	Name	Count	Name	Count	Name	Count	Name	Count
England vs Germany	36011	England	49712	UEFA European Championship	266278	Raheem Sterling	3652	Gary Lineker	329	Darren Fletcher	218	BBC	1621	Soccer	26257	Gareth Southgate	3536
England vs Scotland	22869	Germany	15016	International Soccer	187172	Jack Grealish	3499	Darren Fletcher	215	Alex Scott	179	Sony	651	Combat Sports	532	Steve Clarke	218
England vs Croatia	19257	Portugal	10834	Europe - Soccer	187163	Cristiano Ronaldo	3168	Alan Shearer	212	Clive Tyldesley	113	William Hill	536	American Football	498	Senol Gunes	194
Scotland vs Czech Republic	18754	Scotland	9336	WWE	517	Christian Eriksen	2667	Alex Scott	178	Gabby Logan	94	Twitter	487	Rugby	320	José Mourinho	147
Portugal vs Germany	9521	France	9163	Premier League	509	Kylian Mbappe	2426	John Barnes	128	Dam Walker	61	Coca-Cola	415	Cricket	246	Joachim Low	116
Denmark vs Finland	8902	Leicester City	8645	NFL	466	Harry Kane	1792	Clive Tyldesley	113	Victoria Derbyshire	48	ESPN	328	Racing	197	Jurgen Klopp	95
France vs Switzerland	8432	Denmark	7163	UEFA Champions League	360	Kalvin Phillips	1740	Ian Wright	87	Ian Payne	37	Mobil1	247	Basketball	135	Frank James Lampard Jr.	91
Belgium vs Portugal	5559	Croatia	5773	Copa América	214	Paul Pogba	1463	Martin Keown	82	Martin Tyler	33	ExxonMobil	245	Hockey	111	Andriy Shevchenko	82
Hungary vs France	5268	Wales	5214	Formula 1	183	Romelu Lukaku	953	Roy Keane	66	Kelly Somers	24	Hisense	213	Netball	78	Fernando Santos	73
Turkey vs Italy	5263	Belgium	3768	FA Cup	156	David Beckham	915	Taylor Twellman	51	Sam Matterface	21	Republic	174	Baseball	59	Gennaro Gattuso	64
Croatia vs Spain	5187	Spain	3579	South America - Soccer	151	Patrick Schick	816	Kenny Dalglish	39	Robert Peston	19	Apple	149	Cycling	52	Ole Gunnar Solskjaer	46
Czech Republic vs England	5015	Czech Republic	3486	UEFA Europa League	127	Karim Benzema	791	Martin Tyler	34	Laura Woods	15	Heineken	123	Diving	47	Pep Guardiola	43
France vs Germany	4663	Switzerland	3031	FIFA World Cup Men's	123	Joachim Low	763	Alex Ferguson	29			PlayStation	114	Boxing	28	Hansi Flick	41
Croatia vs Scotland	4486	Hungary	2758	NBA	119	Phil Foden	629	Micah Richards	27			Fiverr	110	Olympic Rugby	25	Robert Page	38
Sweden vs Ukraine	3889	Finland	2699	UEFA Nations League	115	Kai Havertz	547	Jim White	27			Instagram	96	Rugby League	25	Roberto Mancini	37
Portugal vs France	3654	Italy	2645	Indian Premier League	106	Luka Modric	541	Danny Murphy	26			BBC News	83	Olympic Archery	24	Fatih Tarim	32
Italy vs Wales	3210	Ukraine	2516	NHL	100	Danny Ward	520	Jeff Stelling	26			YouTube	81	Olympic Soccer	23	Sam Allardyce	27
Germany vs Hungary	2509	Turkey	2467	ICC World Test Championship	69	Luke Shaw	518	Michel Platini	23			Xbox	72	Rugby Union	23	Frank De Boer	25
Denmark vs Belgium	2247	Sweden	1823	ICC World Test Championship 2019-21	65	Gareth Bale	505	Daniel Levy	10			IKEA	70	Rowing	14	Zinedine Zidane	22
Wales vs Denmark	2215	Netherland	1470	Bundesliga	62	Kevin De Bruyne	436	Steffi Graf	5			Volkswagen	65	Bowling	10	Emma Hayes	20

5 Limitations and Recommendations for Future Work

The present study is focused on the in-depth analysis of the text data generated over social media that is generally ignored. Still there are certain limitations of this study that can be met in future studies. Various social media analytics techniques such as sentiment analysis and network analysis can be performed in conjunction with tweet annotations to find how the communities are formed in real time based on sentiments towards the identified entities. Location based entities in tweets can also be capitalized to get an idea about the locations where sports fans present maximum engagement. Twitter does not provide names of diseases as part of tweet context annotations. They need to be collected through custom NER model.

The scope of this study can be broadened by incorporating other social media platforms such as Instagram, Facebook, Youtube and more. As there was a huge gap in the count of tweets retrieved for the matches amongst England and Italy and North Macedonia and Netherlands, multilingual studies need to be promoted and performed to identify the reason for such huge difference.

6 Conclusions

Post-covid the acceptance and use of digital devices and digital media witnessed a massive jump. Fans, athletes, sports teams, sports organizations all on social media for sharing information during the initial period of COVID-19. Effective and affective engagement of fans and athletes is integral for any sport event to be considered successful. After the COVID-19 sports and its related activities have been severely affected. Marketers, brands, sponsors, events, teams, organizations and athletes all witnessed an unexpected and unforeseen disruption that not only affected every entity individually, in terms of mental, social and physical well-being but also resulted in economic losses through loss of jobs, pay cuts or brand values. To mitigate such adverse effects Euro 2020 was planned and conducted across 12 nations to avoid monetary pressure and curb the spread of COVID-19.

Through this study it was found that sports event of Euro 2020 was the priority and the most important brand amongst fans and spectators all around the world. Whereas the coach Jack Grealish was most discussed coaches and team England was the favorite team as a brand. We also found that hashtags alone cannot be the deciding factor to assess the popularity of an athlete, journalist or any other brand. Tweet context annotations provide the entities mentioned in text that are overlooked during analysis of hashtags thus, the results to estimate popularity through hashtags may be ambiguous. It can be inferred that tweet context annotations should be given importance by the researchers to broaden the scope of studies and perform better correlation of topics as in case of sport branding and sport management.

References

Al Jazeera.: Coronavirus: what sporting events are affected by the pandemic? Coronavirus pandemic. https://www.aljazeera.com/sports/2020/9/20/coronavirus-what-sporting-events-are-aff ected-by-the-pandemic. Accessed 15 March 2022

Areiza-Padilla, J.A., Galindo-Becerra, T., del Río, M.C.: Social networks and e-loyalty: a new means of sports training during COVID-19 quarantines. J. Theor. Appl. Electron. Commer. Res. **16**(7), 2808–2823 (2021). https://doi.org/10.3390/jtaer16070154

Bingaman, J.: Australian football in America during COVID-19. Int. J. Sport Commun. **13**(3), 533–540 (2020). https://doi.org/10.1123/ijsc.2020-0217

Bond, A.J., Widdop, P., Cockayne, D., Parnell, D.: Prosumption, networks and value during a global pandemic: lockdown leisure and COVID-19. Leis. Sci. **43**(1–2), 70–77 (2020). https://doi.org/10.1080/01490400.2020.1773985

Bond, A.J., Widdop, P., Cockayne, D., Parnell, D.: Sport prosumer networks: exploring prosumption value in Twitter conversations during COVID-19. Manag. Sport Leis. 1–17 (2021). https://doi.org/10.1080/23750472.2021.1970615

Bowes, A., Lomax, L., Piasecki, J.: A losing battle? Women's sport pre- and post-COVID-19. Eur. Sport Manag. Q. **21**(3), 443–461 (2021). https://doi.org/10.1080/16184742.2021.1904267

Chehal, D., Gupta, P., Gulati, P.: COVID-19 pandemic lockdown: an emotional health perspective of Indians on Twitter. Int. J. Soc. Psychiatry **67**(1), 64–72 (2021)

Davidson, N.P., Du, J., Giardina, M.D.: Through the perilous fight: a case analysis of professional wrestling during the COVID-19 pandemic. Int. J. Sport Commun. **13**(3), 465–473 (2020). https://doi.org/10.1123/ijsc.2020-0224

Desk, S.: Coronavirus disrupts sports again: full list of matches cancelled or postponed and players affected. The Indian Express (2022). https://indianexpress.com/article/sports/sport-others/coronavirus-sports-events-players-latest-news-7694545/. Accessed 15 March 2022

Doyle, J.P., Kunkel, T., Kelly, S.J., Filo, K., Cuskelly, G.: Seeing the same things differently: exploring the unique brand associations linked to women's professional sport teams. J. Strateg. Mark. 1–15 (2021). https://doi.org/10.1080/0965254x.2021.1922489

Elliott, S., Drummond, M.J., Prichard, I., Eime, R., Drummond, C., Mason, R.: Understanding the impact of COVID-19 on youth sport in Australia and consequences for future participation and retention. BMC Public Health **21**(1) (2021). https://doi.org/10.1186/s12889-021-10505-5

ESPN News Services. List of sporting events canceled because of the coronavirus. ESPN (2020). https://www.espn.in/olympics/story/_/id/28824781/list-sporting-events-canceled-coronavirus. Accessed 15 March 2022

Fenton, A., Keegan, B.J., Parry, K.D.: Understanding sporting social media brand communities, place and social capital: a netnography of football fans. Commun. Sport (2021). https://doi.org/10.1177/2167479520986149

Garcia, K., Berton, L.: Topic detection and sentiment analysis in Twitter content related to COVID-19 from Brazil and the USA. Appl. Soft Comput. **101**, 107057 (2021). https://doi.org/10.1016/j.asoc.2020.107057

Gibbs, C., O'Reilly, N., Brunette, M.: Professional team sport and Twitter: gratifications sought and obtained by followers. Int. J. Sport Commun. **7**(2) (2014)

González, L.M., et al.: The Impact of COVID-19 on sport in Twitter: a quantitative and qualitative content analysis. Int. J. Environ. Res. Public Health **18**(9), 4554 (2021). https://doi.org/10.3390/ijerph18094554

Hammerschmidt, J., Durst, S., Kraus, S., Puumalainen, K.: Professional football clubs and empirical evidence from the COVID-19 crisis: time for sport entrepreneurship? Technol. Forecast. Soc. Chang. **165**, 120572 (2021). https://doi.org/10.1016/j.techfore.2021.120572

Hedenborg, S., Svensson, D., Radmann, A.: Global challenges and innovations in sport: effects of Covid-19 on sport. Sport Soc. 1–4 (2022). https://doi.org/10.1080/17430437.2022.2038878

Heese, H., et al.: Results of the enhanced COVID-19 surveillance during UEFA EURO 2020 in Germany. Epidemiol. Infect. **150** (2022). https://doi.org/10.1017/s0950268822000449

Hopkins, J.L.: Engaging Australian rules football fans with social media: a case study. Int. J. Sport Manag. Mark. **13**(1–2), 104–121 (2013)

Kato, T.: Opposition in Japan to the olympics during the COVID-19 pandemic. Humanit. Soc. Sci. Commun. **8**(1), 1–9 (2021)

Kunkel, T., Biscaia, R.: Sport brands: brand relationships and consumer behavior. Sport Mark. Q. **29**(1), 3–17 (2020). https://doi.org/10.32731/smq.291.032020.01

Lee Ludvigsen, J.A.: Mega-events, expansion and prospects: perceptions of Euro 2020 and its 12-country hosting format. J. Consum. Cult. (2021). https://doi.org/10.1177/146954052110 26045

Majumdar, B., Naha, S.: Live sport during the COVID-19 crisis: fans as creative broadcasters. Sport Soc. **23**(7), 1091–1099 (2020). https://doi.org/10.1080/17430437.2020.1776972

Manoli, A.E.: COVID-19 and the solidification of media's power in football. Manag. Sport Leis. **27**(1–2), 67–71 (2020). https://doi.org/10.1080/23750472.2020.1792802

Marsh, K., Griffiths, E., Young, J.J., Gibb, C.A., McMenamin, J.: Contributions of the EURO 2020 football championship events to a third wave of SARS-CoV-2 in Scotland, 11 June to 7 July 2021. Eurosurveillance **26**(31) (2021). https://doi.org/10.2807/1560-7917.es.2021.26.31. 2100707

Mattei, M., Caldarelli, G., Squartini, T., Saracco, F.: Italian Twitter semantic network during the Covid-19 epidemic. EPJ Data Sci. **10**(1), 1–27 (2021). https://doi.org/10.1140/epjds/s13688-021-00301-x

Mehra, V., Sarin, P., Singh, P., Sawhney, R.S., Kar, A.K.: Impact of COVID-19 pandemic on e-participation of fans in sports events. In: Dennehy, D., Griva, A., Pouloudi, N., Dwivedi, Y.K., Pappas, I., Mäntymäki, M. (eds.) Responsible AI and Analytics for an Ethical and Inclusive Digitized Society, vol. 12896, pp. 692–703. Springer, Cham (2021). https://doi.org/10.1007/978-3-030-85447-8_57

Nasar, Z., Jaffry, S.W., Malik, M.K.: Named entity recognition and relation extraction: state-of-the-art. ACM Comput. Surv. (CSUR) **54**(1), 1–39 (2021)

Pan, P.L., Phua, J.: Connecting sponsor brands through sports competitions: an identity approach to brand trust and brand loyalty. Sport Bus. Manag.: Int. J. **11**(2), 164–184 (2020). https://doi. org/10.1108/sbm-01-2019-0003

Priyadarshini, I., Mohanty, P., Kumar, R., Sharma, R., Puri, V., Singh, P.K.: A study on the sentiments and psychology of Twitter users during COVID-19 lockdown period. Multimedia Tools Appl. **81**, 1–23 (2021). https://doi.org/10.1007/s11042-021-11004-w

Rathore, A.K., Kar, A.K., Ilavarasan, P.V.: Social media analytics: literature review and directions for future research. Decis. Anal. **14**(4), 229–249 (2017). https://doi.org/10.1287/deca.2017. 0355

Ratten, V., Jones, P.: New challenges in sport entrepreneurship for value creation. Int. Entrep. Manag. J. **16**(3), 961–980 (2020). https://doi.org/10.1007/s11365-020-00664-z

Roesslein, J.: Tweepy documentation—tweepy 4.7.0 documentation. https://docs.tweepy.org/en/ stable/. Accessed 24 March 2022

Russo, G., Tallarita, L.: Sports brands communication in the 'COVID' age: strategies, representations, identity and consumption. Ital. Sociol. Rev. **11**(5S), 653–671 (2021)

Sharpe, S., Mountifield, C., Filo, K.: The social media response from athletes and sport organizations to COVID-19: an altruistic tone. Int. J. Sport Commun. **13**(3), 474–483 (2020)

Singh, P., Dwivedi, Y.K., Kahlon, K.S., Pathania, A., Sawhney, R.S.: Can Twitter analytics predict election outcome? An insight from 2017 Punjab assembly elections. Gov. Inf. Q. **37**(2), 101444 (2020). https://doi.org/10.1016/j.giq.2019.101444

Singh, P., Dwivedi, Y.K., Kahlon, K.S., Sawhney, R.S., Alalwan, A.A., Rana, N.P.: Smart monitoring and controlling of government policies using social media and cloud computing. Inf. Syst. Front. **22**(2), 315–337 (2019). https://doi.org/10.1007/s10796-019-09916-y

Singh, P., Kahlon, K.S., Sawhney, R.S., Vohra, R., Kaur, S.: Social media buzz created by #nanotechnology: insights from Twitter analytics. Nanotechnol. Rev. **7**(6), 521–528 (2018). https:// doi.org/10.1515/ntrev-2018-0053

Singh, P., Kaur, H., Kahlon, K.S., Sawhney, R.S.: Do people virtually support their favorite cricket team? Insights from 2018 Asia cup. In: Proceedings of the Third International Conference on Advanced Informatics for Computing Research, pp. 1–8 (2019)

Singh, P., Singh, S., Sohal, M., Dwivedi, Y.K., Kahlon, K.S., Sawhney, R.S.: Psychological fear and anxiety caused by COVID-19: insights from Twitter analytics. Asian J. Psychiatr. **54**, 102280 (2020)

Smith, A.C.T., Skinner, J.: Sport management and COVID-19: trends and legacies. Eur. Sport Manag. Q. **22**(1), 1–10 (2021). https://doi.org/10.1080/16184742.2021.1993952

Smith, D.C.V.: Footballers' citizenship during COVID-19: a case study of Premier League players' community support. Int. Rev. Sociol. Sport (2021). https://doi.org/10.1177/101269022110 45679

Staff, R.: Impact of COVID-19 pandemic on sports events around the world. CN (2020). https://cn.reuters.com/article/health-coronavirus-sport-idINKBN23I1WL. Accessed 15 March 2022

Stavros, C., Smith, A.C., Lopez-Gonzalez, H.: A mediasport typology for transformative relationships: enlargement, enhancement, connection and engagement beyond COVID-19. Eur. Sport Manag. Q. **22**(1), 72–91 (2021). https://doi.org/10.1080/16184742.2021.1925723

Stieglitz, S., Dang-Xuan, L., Bruns, A., Neuberger, C.: Social media analytics. Bus. Inf. Syst. Eng. **6**(2), 89–96 (2014). https://doi.org/10.1007/s12599-014-0315-7

Stieglitz, S., Mirbabaie, M., Ross, B., Neuberger, C.: Social media analytics – challenges in topic discovery, data collection, and data preparation. Int. J. Inf. Manag. **39**, 156–168 (2018). https://doi.org/10.1016/j.ijinfomgt.2017.12.002

Su, Y., Du, J., Biscaia, R., Inoue, Y.: We are in this together: sport brand involvement and fans' well-being. Eur. Sport Manag. Q. **22**(1), 92–119 (2021). https://doi.org/10.1080/16184742. 2021.1978519

Sustainable Development Goals Fund. The Contribution of Sports to the achievement of Sustainable Development Goals: A Toolkit for Action (2018). https://www.sdgfund.org/sites/default/files/report-sdg_fund_sports_and_sdgs_web_0.pdf

Twitter (n.d.). Docs|Twitter Developer Platform. https://developer.twitter.com/en/docs/twitter-api/annotations/overview. Accessed 30 March 2022

Walkowiak, M.P., Walkowiak, J.B., Walkowiak, D.: COVID-19 passport as a factor determining the success of national vaccination campaigns: does it work? The case of Lithuania vs Poland. Vaccines **9**(12), 1498 (2021). https://doi.org/10.3390/vaccines9121498

Wang, Y.: Building relationships with fans: how sports organizations used Twitter as a communication tool. Sport Soc. **24**(7), 1055–1069 (2021)

Westmattelmann, D., Grotenhermen, J.G., Sprenger, M., Schewe, G.: The show must go on - virtualisation of sport events during the COVID-19 pandemic. Eur. J. Inf. Syst. **30**(2), 119–136 (2020). https://doi.org/10.1080/0960085x.2020.1850186

Online Shopping Behaviour in South Africa During the COVID-19 Pandemic

Margaret Cullen[1] , Andre P. Calitz[2]([✉]) , and Joseph Shati[1]

[1] Business School, Nelson Mandela University, Port Elizabeth, South Africa
{Margaret.Cullen,S219111154}@Mandela.ac.za
[2] Department of Computing Sciences, Nelson Mandela University, Port Elizabeth, South Africa
Andre.Calitz@Mandela.ac.za

Abstract. Traditional brick-and-mortar stores have had to endure competition the past years from various shopping channels, particularly online shopping, which is driven by mobile technologies and more recently, the COVID-19 pandemic. Consumers, restricted by COVID-19 lockdown regulations, had to increasingly make use of online shopping. The aim of this exploratory study was to determine how the COVID-19 pandemic influenced the online shopping behaviour of South African consumers and if the behaviour would continue in the post COVID-19 period. Factors were identified from literature that influence consumer's online shopping behaviour. A national survey was conducted, using mixed methods research and the data from 673 respondents were statistically analysed.

The findings indicate that only 12% of the respondents shopped online for the first time, due to the COVID-19 pandemic and 87% indicated they shop online monthly. Sixty-eight percent indicated they will continue shopping online and 65% think online shopping is a safer option. The products purchased most during the pandemic period were fast foods and clothing and the preferred delivery method was receiving the goods at home. The factors that affected online shopping during the COVID-19 period most were Personal Experience of Online Shopping, Interaction with products and the Current impact of Covid-19 on shopping. The findings suggest that customers in South Africa will continue to make use of online technologies to purchase goods and services.

Keywords: Online shopping · Shopping behaviour · COVID-19 · South Africa

1 Introduction

The development of the Internet and mobile devices has transformed shopping patterns from the monopoly of the traditional brick-and-mortar store channel to an array of platforms [1]. The various platforms enabled consumers to shop through catalogues, websites, mobile applications and physical stores. Some consumers enjoy the convenience offered by online platforms to investigate their future purchases and complete the purchase instore where they prefer the physical contact with the product [2]. This has led to retailers initiating multi-channel strategies to attract multi-channel consumers trying

S. Papagiannidis et al. (Eds.): I3E 2022, LNCS 13454, pp. 403–415, 2022.
https://doi.org/10.1007/978-3-031-15342-6_31

to exploit benefits associated with multi-channel use [3]. Despite the rapid development of the various shopping platforms, brick-and-mortar is still the preferred purchasing platform in South Africa [1].

The dominance of brick-and-mortar stores has been attributed to self-gratification and in-person judgement that is associated with instore shopping, lack of human interaction and fear of security posed by online shopping [1]. Consumers have maintained their instore loyalty despite the convenience offered by online shopping platforms. Brick-and-mortar stores' unique location next to other services provide consumers with an opportunity to accomplish more on a single trip increasing their efficiency, which influences the consumers' channel choices [4]. Shopping habits are generally stable and slow to change unless distorted by a major life event [5, 6].

The factors that influence peoples' online shopping behaviour include previous online exposure, access to the Internet, income and exposure to modern technologies, including mobile technologies. The COVID-19 pandemic has had a drastic impact on human behaviour, including people's shopping habits during the lockdown periods. The pandemic has obligated consumers to employ drastic measures, such as social distancing and working from home. Social distancing in particular has led to spikes in online shopping, by both old and new customers, as consumers battle to avoid dense supermarkets [5, 7]. The fear of the virus engendered dread of populated areas, enforcing social distancing, which consequently boosted online shopping [6].

The aim of this exploratory study was to determine how the COVID-19 pandemic had influenced the online shopping behaviour of consumers in South Africa and whether the behaviour will continue post COVID-19. The factors that affect the online purchasing behaviour of South African consumers have been investigated in this study. This paper provides preliminary insights into online shopping behaviour of South African consumers during the past COVID-19 period. The results highlight the factors which influence online shopping behaviour in South Africa and consumers' online shopping behaviour, during the post COVID-19 period.

The layout of the paper is as follows: the background of the study is highlighted in Section one. Literature on online shopping is discussed in Sect. 2, including the factors that influence the online shopping behavior of consumers. The research design is presented in Sect. 3. The Online shopping survey results are presented in Sect. 4. Managerial recommendations are provided in Sect. 5 and conclusions and future research are presented in Sect. 6.

2 Literature Review

Online shopping is the transacting of goods or services over the Internet in exchange for value [8]. Rudansky-Kloppers [9] views online shopping as a platform that enables customers to search for and select products or services online, choose a delivery method and pay for them. Online shopping's adoption is dependent on the availability of information technologies' infrastructure in a society [10]. Products or services listed online are described either through text or pictures or the combination of the two to enable customers to shop with minimum assistance.

The advent of the Internet enabled and disrupted many aspects of consumers' lives, particularly the search and purchase of products [10]. The Internet conveniently allowed consumers to move to online shopping by providing flexible and personalised access [11]. Companies recognised the Internet's potential and this sparked the establishment of online shopping platforms [12]. The online platforms brought about hassle-free shopping with a global reach [13]. Retailers recognised that online shopping affords them the opportunity to lower the cost of doing business and expand their footprint [14]. It is noteworthy, that although online shopping has made indelible strides, it is still in a nascent stage [12] with many people still unfamiliar with the concept, particularly in developing countries [15].

2.1 South African Online Shopping Behaviour

In the South African context, which exhibits traits of both a developed and a developing economy, online shopping has been characterised by early adoption by high-income earners and laggard adoption by the rest of the population, typical of a developing nation [10]. Online shopping is increasing in South Africa but still lags behind Western and some Eastern countries [9]. The differences are influenced by economic development and cultural factors [16]. The high mobile penetration has significantly shifted consumers' buying behaviour towards online shopping in South Africa [17]. The nation is economically dichotomous, with access to technology, a strong private sector and financial institutions, at the same time with a large percentage of the population still living below the poverty datum line [10]. This is attributed as the reason online shopping is still in its infancy despite having been around since 1996.

The COVID-19 pandemic forced nations to implement drastic measures, such as lockdowns, social distancing and restrictive physical access to certain products to curb the spread of the virus [18, 19]. As part of social distancing to curb the spread of the deadly virus, non-essential employees were instructed to work from home, travel restrictions were imposed, some businesses had to close and previously dense shopping centres became restrictive on the number of people allowed at a given time [5, 20]. The periods of lockdowns or self-isolation were long enough that they changed the way consumers behave [21]. The preventive measures put in place brought about a shift in societal attitudes accelerating a structural move to online shopping [22].

The pandemic drastically shifted previously stable shopping habits [5, 6], obliging some consumers to hastily move to online shopping to access various shops [15], resulting in online shopping becoming the shopping mainstream [23]. The COVID-19 pandemic has upended shopping behaviour, which has seen most people migrating their lives to laptops and mobile devices [24].

2.2 Acceptance of Technologies

The earlier phase of the lockdowns saw agile businesses promptly moving to provide easy access to consumers through mobile or website online shopping platforms to sustain their businesses [13], connecting with a large number of people who had adopted new habits [24]. The restrictive lockdowns and social isolating measures disrupted and forced businesses to reassess their strategies to reach some of their loyal brick-and-mortar consumers in the digital space.

Businesses aggressively expanded their digitisation strategies, strengthening their competitive position in the market [25]. This has seen companies expanding their multi-channel distribution systems and investing in online shopping infrastructure, which include the expansion of the workforce, improving delivery quality and payment security [26]. COVID-19 accelerated the technological investments of businesses despite the pandemic inducing financial constraints [22]. The measures to curb the spread of the virus rapidly moved both business and social interactions to online media [20, 26], which considerably improved the use of online services [13], accelerating diffusion of technologies amongst ordinary people enhancing the intention to shop online [27].

2.3 Communication

Dannenberg et al. [26] and Koch et al. [18], partly attribute the online shopping surge to sensation media that reported the pandemic akin to a horror scenario portraying escaping to digitisation as the only shopping alternative. The media sensation led to consumers flocking to online platforms as if it was the only remaining platform open to supply the consumers' needs and assist in supporting the economy [18, 23]. The shift is also attributed to how online shopping has kept the socio-economic systems running during the pandemic, showing its worth and why more consumers should adopt it [26]. However, in developing nations like South Africa, online shopping faced obstacles such as limited technology infrastructure and unreliability of telecommunications [10], which will play a role in the behavioural shift towards maintaining online shopping post the pandemic [24].

2.4 Products Purchased Online

Online shopping has also allowed retailers to expand their range of products, drawing customers exclusively to their online shopping platforms [24]. This has afforded previously niche businesses a platform to find potential new markets [22], suggesting that the switch has performed positively in many categories and that consumers will see no benefit from switching back to in store shopping, despite encountering a few obstacles. Industry experts have also suggested that consumers will be more inclined to shun products or services associated with detrimental environmental and social impact to diminish chances of any future pandemics [18].

2.5 Methods of Payment and Delivery

Consumers, especially the older population sheltered at home, swiftly accepted technology and dispelled fears regarding payment security and the invasion of privacy during the pandemic, shifting towards online shopping [21, 26]. Online security involves payment and private information security and the businesses' credibility. If not adequately addressed it turns away potential customers [28]. Online fraud has been a major concern that deters consumers from online shopping, however secure payment options have been developed, which has enduced a change in behaviour because the options are trusted. This behaviour change, favouring online purchases, was aided by the convenience and prompt delivery of purchased goods [29]. Reduced delivery costs are abetting the move to local producers, increasing the number of customers moving to online platforms that connect local businesses [26]. The local platforms receiving most traffic are those of well-known brands, demonstrating care and concern for their staff, with limited supply chain challenges, enabling them to reliably deliver despite the surging demands during the pandemic [29]. The ability of online platforms to satisfactorily cope with consumers' delivery demands will ensure that consumers remain shopping online post the pandemic [29].

2.6 Effect of COVID-19 on Online Shopping

A number of factors have an influence on online shopping and its growth. The earlier phase of the lockdowns saw agile businesses promptly moving to provide easy access to consumers through mobile or website online shopping platforms to sustain their businesses [13], connecting with a large number of people who had adopted new shopping habits [24]. The fact that people were under lockdown with limited movement forced them to shop online. Selecting a channel from the available options is driven by the consumers' behaviour, which can be divided into either hedonic or utilitarian motives [1]. Consumers driven by utilitarian motives want to complete shopping in an efficient way that prioritises saving monetary resources, time and effort. Girard et al. [30] suggest that such consumers are inclined to at least use convenient online channels to cost effectively acquire current information on prices and product offerings before making a purchase. Contrarily, the hedonic motivated consumers consider entertainment as a primary prerequisite of choosing a channel [1]. The chosen channel must stimulate happiness, enjoyment and sensuality in the consumer. Girard et al. [30] theorise that consumers who wish to enjoy shopping are more likely to go to a shopping mall rather than buying online.

2.7 Working from Home

Working from home, which is saving companies' overhead costs, is mainly concentrated among high income workers stationed in high income geographies [5]. Yahya and Sugiyanto [11] consider high income earners to be more likely to shop online, driving the surge in online shopping. Zwanka and Buff [31] predict that working from home among high income earners will remain a permanent shift based on the desired productivity experienced by companies during the pandemic translating to a permanent shift towards online shopping. Nielsen [29] also attributes the surge of online shopping to unemployment and furloughing, which has significantly curtailed the consumers' spending power, which has seen consumers surf online, searching for prices and promotions to match their reduced spending ability without incurring travel costs. Working from home has made online shopping a convenience, which has resulted in a behavioural shift of people not having to visit shops and malls because they can shop from the comfort of their home. All major retail grocery stores in South Africa have provided mobile shopping Apps for ordering goods and provide motorbike delivery services.

Online shopping will be sustained in areas with a well-developed delivery infrastructure and affluent population who were hardly impacted economically by the pandemic

[21]. The surge will also be maintained among the majority of urban dwellers and the millennials who have embraced online shopping to save time and shop at their convenience [13]. Elderly consumers who previously resisted migrating to online platforms, were now forced to by the pandemic and are boosting online sales and profit [25].

3 Research Design

This study followed a positivist paradigm and gathered quantitative and qualitative data from South African online consumers. An online questionnaire was developed from literature and a pilot study was conducted amongst 8 MBA participants. The questionnaire, included items associated with the factors identified in literature and was assessed using a 5-point Likert scale, where 1 = Strongly Disagree to 5 = Strongly Agree. The final questionnaire was updated and distributed using the survey tool, Questionpro. The target population was the South African online shopping community of all ages.

The selected participants, who were Business School post graduate students, were requested to forward the questionnaire to other prospective respondents, resulting in snowball sampling. Snowball sampling adds to the representativeness of the findings [32]. This approach used was to collect data using a relatively reliable research tool, in a cost-effective manner, easy to administer, less time consuming and safe, particularly during the COVID-19 pandemic [10]. The online study investigated whether there has been shift to online shopping during the COVID-19 period.

The data were statistically analysed by the university statistical consultant, using Statistica and included Exploratory Factor Analysis (EFA). A conceptual model was derived from literature and was initially designed to test the various factors that contribute to online shopping The seven independent factors identified from literature were *Shopping Behaviour, Acceptance of Technologies, Communication, Product Variety, Methods of payment, Delivery and the impact of COVID-19*. The dependant variable was *Online Shopping Behaviour*. The EFA identified eight independent factors, namely *Personal Experience of Online Shopping, Interaction with products, Interaction with people, Shopping Behaviour, Product variety, Acceptance of Technologies, Current impact of Covid-19 on shopping and Covid-19 and shopping*. The updated conceptual model after the EFA is illustrated in Fig. 1. Ethics approval was obtained from the University Ethics Committee.

3.1 Academic Theory

In order to gain a better understanding of the intention to adopt and continue using online shopping, the adoption of technology, based on the technology acceptance model was used (TAM). The TAM theory, a framework for understanding the adoption of technology [33], posits that people's attitude, intention and feeling towards adopting technology is predicated by the people's perceived usefulness and ease of use of the technology [34] and subsequent acceptance and use [33]. The perceived usefulness and perceived ease of use influences the consumers' intention to engage in online shopping subsequently determining the shoppers' behaviour [36].The updated conceptual model incorporating the TAM is presented in Fig. 1.

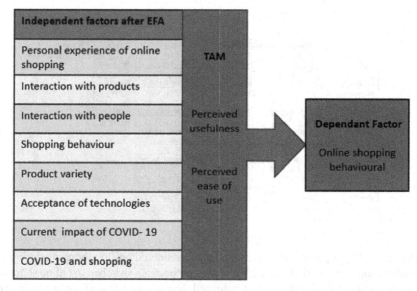

Fig. 1. Updated conceptual model

4   Online Shopping Survey Results

The demographic profiles of the respondents (n = 673) are presented in Table 1. The household income of the respondents is a factor influencing online shopping [8]. At least 85% (n = 573) of the respondents earn a monthly income of over R10 000, living above the poverty datum line, which enhances their chances of shopping online [30]. Ninety two percent of the respondents were either self-employed or employed. This is representative of the online shoppers' profile, people that have means to earn an income. The employed or self-employed groups also dominantly shop online, because of its convenience and flexibility as a way to balance between working and shopping time [12]. The majority of the respondents were from the Eastern Cape (60%, n = 255), Gauteng (20%, n = 84), Western Cape (9%, n = 40) and the remainer from the other six provinces in South Africa.

The survey also questioned whether the respondents shop online or not. The results indicated that 84% (n = 565) shopped online and 16% (n = 108) did not. The majority of the respondents shopped online less than once a month (45%, n = 251), 42% (n = 238) and 12% (n = 67) weekly. The majority rated their shopping experience as good to excellent (87%, n = 587), 97% (n = 649) rated their Internet access as good to excellent and 91% (n = 609) had Internet access at home and 99% Internet access on their phone. The preferred payment method was Credit/Debit card (43%, n = 291) and EFT (33%, n = 219). Eighty-one percent (n = 545) had their goods delivered at home and 12% (n = 71) 'click and collect'.

The items included for the factor COVID-19 and online shopping are presented in Table 2. The responses for Strongly Disagree/Disagree and Agree/Strongly Agree have been combined for reporting purposes. The results indicate that the majority of the respondents (80%, n = 536) did not shop online for the first time due to the COVID-19

Table 1. Demographic profiles

Education	Matric and <	Certificate	Diploma	Degree	PG degree
	64 (10%)	43 (6%)	130 (19%)	195 (29%)	241 (36%)
Age	18-29 years	30-39 years	40-49 years	50+ years	
	171 (25%)	311 (46%)	131 (20%)	60 (9%)	
Household monthly income	< R10 000	R10 000-R29 999	R30 000-R49 999	R50 000 +	
	104 (15%)	235 (35%)	209 (31%)	125 (19%)	
Province	Eastern Cape	Gauteng	Western Cape	Other	
	255 (60%)	84 (20%)	40 (10%)	42 (10%)	
Employment status	Employed	Self employed	Without work/ retired		
	550 (82%)	65 (10%)	58 (8%)		
Marital status	Living together/ married	Single	Divorced/widowed		
	357 (53%)	285 (42%)	31 (5%)		
Gender	Male	Female	Total		
	249 (37%)	424 (63%)	673 (100%)		

pandemic. Forty-six percent of the respondents considered on-line shopping during the COVID-19 pandemic period. Only 27% of the respondents switched to online shopping during the period. Sixty-eight percent indicated they will continue shopping online and 65% think online shopping is a safer option.

The respondents indicated that the majority (84%; n = 565) shopped online at most once a month. This aligns with the respondents being paid monthly. The collected data also showed that almost all respondents (99.4%; n = 669) have access to the Internet, which is representative of the target population, online shoppers' characteristics, as online shopping requires Internet access.

A correlation coefficient r is statistically significant at the 0.05 level for n = 673 if $|r| > = .082$ and practically significant, if $|r| > = .300$. The correlations of the independent factors and the dependent factor, Online-Shopping in general, indicated that all the independent factors had a negative or positive medium to strong correlation with the dependent factor, as all correlations were both statistically and practically significant if $|r| > = .300$ (Table 3).

The results show that eight independent factors with a p-value <.0005 are statistically significant with the dependent factor, *Online shopping. Interaction with people, interaction with products* and *shopping behaviour* have a low negative correlation with Online shopping, which is statistically significant. *Acceptance of Internet technologies, Current impact of COVID-19 on shopping, COVID-19 and shopping* and *Products bought online* have a low to medium positive correlation with Online shopping. The factors that ranked most important for online shopping were *Personal Experience of Online Shopping, Interaction with products and Current impact of Covid-19 on shopping.*

The ANOVA results indicated that the demographical variable, Marital status (f-value = 8,24, D.F. = 1;656, p = 004, Cohen's d = 0,20) showed a statistical significance and a small practical significance with online shopping in general. In addition the *Preferred method of payment* (f-value = 8,32, D.F. = 2;591, p < .0005, Cohen's d = 0,38) showed a statistical significance and a small practical significance with online shopping for consumers paying cash versus customers using a credit card or EFT.

Table 2. COVID-19 online shopping

Items	Disagree		Neutral		Agree	
	n	%	n	%	n	%
I bought online for the first time because of COVID-19	536	80%	52	8%	85	12%
COVID-19 has made me consider online shopping	237	35%	127	19%	309	46%
COVID-19 has made me switch to online shopping	316	47%	176	26%	181	27%
The COVID-19 lockdown forced me to buy online	322	48%	126	19%	225	33%
I prefer to buy online since COVID-19	244	36%	171	25%	258	39%
I will continue to buy online post COVID-19	88	13%	127	19%	458	68%
I trust online delivery services safety precautions for COVID-19	112	17%	238	35%	323	48%
Buying online is a safer option because of COVID-19	75	11%	159	24%	439	65%
In store experiences are risky with COVID-19	72	11%	155	23%	446	66%
Physical stores pay attention to the COVID-19 health and safety measures	78	12%	245	36%	350	52%

5 Managerial Recommendations

The reviewed literature suggests that age, income, education, gender and employment status have an influence on online shopping [37]. The research findings from this study indicate that *Marital status* and *Method of payment* were the demographical variables that influenced online shopping during the COVID-19 period. The demographics in this study show that in South Africa, online shoppers are generally urban, tertiary educated, employed with access to Internet and an income above the poverty datum line.

Based on the findings, it is recommended that companies maintain and ensure excellent online shopping services and continue to improve the offerings and technologies,

Table 3. Cronbach Alpha Coefficients and correlations with dependent factor (n = 673)

Independent factors	μ	S.D.	Alpha	Reliability	p-value	Correlation
Personal experience of online shopping	3,67	0,73	0,76	Good	<.0005	,478
Interaction with products	3,40	0,78	0,79	Good	<.0005	−,308
Interaction with people	2,81	0,90	0,74	Good	<.0005	−,345
Shopping behaviour	3,11	0,73	0,67	Acceptable	<.0005	−,377
Acceptance of technologies	3,32	0,69	0,86	Excellent	<.0005	,525
Current impact of Covid-19 on shopping	3,61	0,80	0,82	Excellent	<.0005	,435
Covid-19 and shopping	3,17	0,74	0,56	Acceptable	<.0005	,310
Products bought online	2,01	0,66	0,82	Excellent	<.0005	,437

specifically the use of mobile Apps. The use of timely and efficient home delivery services is an important requirement. Marketers need to embrace this channel because of its popularity. Most of the respondents shopped once a month, it is therefore, recommended that companies run promotions on online platforms that align with the majority of the consumers' pay days. Most of the consumers based in the study had access to the Internet through mobile devices, meaning businesses must flight adverts and provide shopping platforms that are compatible with mobile devices. Most online consumers agree that post-COVID-19, they will remain shopping online. It is recommended that while consumers are still shopping online due to the pandemic, companies must provide excellent customer experience to ensure that post the COVID-19 pandemic, the consumers will remaining loyal to the business and online shopping. Excellent customer experience will determine whether they will maintain the behaviour post the pandemic.

6 Conclusions and Future Research

The two factors that influence an individual's intention to use new technology, the perceived ease of use and the perceived usefulness are confirmed in this study. More people are preferring online shopping over traditional shopping because of the ease and comfort [36]. Marketers and retailers need to segment their market appropriately to focus on this channel in addition to the normal retail channels. The findings profile an online shopper as a high-income earner and relatively educated individual who can confidently use technology. The results demonstrate that as explained by the TAM theory, the perceived usefulness and ease of use for consumers enabled them to access goods and services online during the pandemic, which led to the adoption of preventative behaviours and prevailing norms such as online shopping to curb the risk of contracting COVID-19. This exploratory study provides useful information to businesses operating and those planning to move to online platforms on how to entice consumers to initiate and continue to frequently shop online. Online retailers must adopt different strategies to persuade customers to shop online.

The findings indicate that online products purchased included fast foods (42%), clothing and other apparel (29%) and home appliances (22%). Limited alcohol (4%) was purchased due to the COVID-19 lockdown regulations in South Africa. The most important factors identified in this study were *Personal Experience of Online Shopping, Interaction with people and products* and the *Current impact of Covid-19 on shopping*. Working from home will be a world-wide trend that will remain in place for the foreseeable future. The findings allow companies, marketers and other researchers to gain insight into the online shopping factors influencing South Africans and provide a foundation for further related research. The limitations of the study are that the majority of the respondents (60%) were from the Eastern Cape province. Future research needs to be conducted to include a more representative sample of the South African population and to determine any consumer online behavioural change in the post COVID-19 period.

References

1. Kim, E., Libaque-Saenz, C.F., Park, M.-C.: Understanding shopping routes of offline purchasers: selection of search-channels (online vs. offline) and search-platforms (mobile vs. PC) based on product types. Serv. Bus. **13**(2), 305–338 (2018). https://doi.org/10.1007/s11 628-018-0384-7
2. Kaufman-Scarboroug, C., Lindquist, J.D.: E-shopping in a multiple channel environment. J. Consum. Mark. **19**(4), 333–350 (2002). https://doi.org/10.1108/07363760210433645
3. McKinsey: The future of shopping: connected, virtual and augmented. McKinsey & Company, pp. 1–33 (2019). https://www.mckinsey.com/business-functions/marketing-and-sales/solutions/periscope/our-insights/surveys/the-future-of-shopping-connected-virtual-and-aug mented
4. International council of shopping centers. Mixed-use properties: a convenient option for shoppers (2019). https://www.icsc.com/uploads/t07-subpage/Mix_Use_Convenience_Con sumerSeries.pdf
5. Yoon, E.: 3 behavioral trends that will reshape our post-Covid world. Harvard Bus. Rev. (2020)
6. Yuen, K.F., Wang, X., Ma, F., Li, K.X.: The psychological causes of panic buying following a health crisis. Int. J. Environ. Res. Public Health **17**(10), 3513 (2020). https://doi.org/10.3390/ijerph17103513
7. Hasanat, M.W., Hoque, A., Shikha, F.A., Anwar, M., Hamid, A.B.A., Tat, H.H.: The impact of coronavirus (COVID-19) on e-business in Malaysia. Asian J. Multi. Stud. **3**(1), 85–90 (2020). https://asianjournal.org/online/index.php/ajms/article/view/219
8. Akram, M.S.: Drivers and barriers to online shopping in a newly digitalized society. TEM J. **7**(1), 118–127 (2018). https://doi.org/10.18421/TEM71-14
9. Rudansky-Kloppers, S.: Investigating factors influencing customer online buying satisfaction in Gauteng. South Africa. Int. B. Econ. **13**, 1187–1198 (2014)
10. Swiegers, L.: Perceived Risk Barriers to Online Shopping: Experiences of Technologically Enabled Generation y Consumers. Stellenbosch University, South Africa (2018). https://doi.org/10.1109/robot.1994.350900
11. Yahya, S., Sugiyanto, C.: Indonesian demand for online shopping: revisited. J. Indonesian Econ. Bus. **35**(3), 188–203 (2020). https://doi.org/10.22146/jieb.55358
12. Nielsen: Connect commerce: connectivity is enabling lifestyle evolution. Nielsen Company, pp. 1–19 (2018). https://www.nielsen.com/pt/pt/insights/report/2019/connected-commerce-connectivity-is-enabling-lifestyle-evolution/

13. Ali, B.: Impact of COVID-19 on consumer buying behavior toward online shopping in Iraq. Econ. Stud. J. **18**(3), 267–280 (2020)
14. Zaveri, B., Amin, P.: A conceptual framework to understanding online consumer buying behavior. Int. J. Online Mark. **3**(1), 47–58 (2013)
15. Handayani, P.W., Nurahmawati, R.A., Pinem, A.A., Azzahro, F.: Switching intention from traditional to online groceries using the moderating effect of gender in Indonesia. J. Food Prod. Mark. **26**(6), 1–15 (2020). https://doi.org/10.1080/10454446.2020.1792023
16. Ayob, A.H.: E-commerce adoption in ASEAN: who and where? Future Bus. J. **7**(1), 1–11 (2021). https://doi.org/10.1186/s43093-020-00051-8
17. Mapande, F.V., Appiah, M.: The factors influencing customers to conduct online shopping: South African perspective. In: 2018 International Conference on Intelligent and Innovative Computing Applications, ICONIC 2018, p. 5. (2019). https://doi.org/10.1109/ICONIC.2018.8601257
18. Koch, J., Frommeyer, B., Schewe, G.: Online shopping motives during the COVID-19 pandemic—Lessons from the Crisis. Sustainability **12**(10247), 1–20 (2020). https://doi.org/10.3390/su122410247
19. Pham, V.K., Do Thi, T.H., Le Ha, T., H.: A study on the COVID-19 awareness affecting the consumer perceived benefits of online shopping in Vietnam. Cogent Bus. Manag. **7**(1), 1–16 (2020). https://doi.org/10.1080/23311975.2020.1846882
20. Yan, Z.: Unprecedented pandemic, unprecedented shift, and unprecedented opportunity. Hum. Behav. Emerg. Technol. **2**(2), 110–112 (2020). https://doi.org/10.1002/hbe2.192
21. Fabius, V., Kohli, S., Veranen, S.M., Timelin, B.: Meet the Next-Normal Consumer. McKinsey & Company, pp. 1–9 (2020)
22. Jacobides, M.G., Reeves, M.: Adapt your business to the new reality. Harvard Bus. Rev. **98**, 74–82 (2020)
23. Chang, H., Meyerhoefer, C.: COVID-19 and the demand for online food shopping services: empirical evidence from Taiwan (2020). https://www.nber.org/system/files/working_papers/w27427/w27427.pdf
24. McKinsey: 2020 Holiday season: Navigating shopper behaviors in the pandemic. (2020). https://www.mckinsey.com/business-functions/marketing-and-sales/solutions/periscope/our-insights/surveys/2020-holiday-season-navigating-shopper-behaviors-in-the-pandemic
25. Narayandas, D., Hebbar, V., Li, L.: Lessons from Chinese companies' response to Covid-19. Harvard Bus. Rev. (2020)
26. Dannenberg, P., Fuchs, M., Riedler, T., Wiedemann, C.: Digital transition by COVID-19 pandemic? The German food online retail. Tijdschr. Econ. Soc. Geogr. **111**(3), 543–560 (2020). https://doi.org/10.1111/tesg.12453
27. Yohn, D.L.: The pandemic is rewriting the rules of retail. Harvard Bus. Rev. 2–6 (2020). https://hbr.org/2020/07/the-pandemic-is-rewriting-the-rules-of-retail%0A. https://hbr.org/2020/07/the-pandemic-is-rewriting-the-rules-of-retail?ab=hero-main-text
28. Vaitkevicius, S., Mazeikiene, E., Bilan, S., Navickas, V., Savaneviciene, A.: Economic demand formation motives in online-shopping. Eng. Econ. **30**(5), 631–640 (2019). https://doi.org/10.5755/j01.ee.30.5.23755
29. Nielsen: China's shifting retail lanscape signals the permanence of change post-Covid-19 (2020). https://nielseniq.com/global/en/insights/analysis/2020/chinas-shifting-retail-landscape-signals-the-permanence-of-change-post-covid-19/
30. Gunday, G., Karabon, M., Kooij, S., Moulton, J., Omeñaca, J.: How European Shoppers will Buy Groceries in the Next Normal. McKinsey & Company, pp. 1–10 (2020)
31. Girard, T., Korgaonkar, P., Silverblatt, R.: Relationship of type of product, shopping orientations, and demographics with preference. J. Bus. Psychol. **18**(1), 101–120 (2003)

32. Zwanka, R.J., Buff, C.: COVID-19 generation: a conceptual framework of the consumer behavioral shifts to be caused by the COVID-19 pandemic. J. Int. Consum. Mark. 1–10 (2020). https://doi.org/10.1080/08961530.2020.1871646

33. Cassim, L.: Guidelines on how to Write a Thesis and Research Report. Johannesburg (2017)

34. Ha, S., Stoel, L.: Consumer e-shopping acceptance: antecedents in a technology acceptance model. J. Bus. Res. **62**(5), 565–571 (2009). https://doi.org/10.1016/j.jbusres.2008.06.016

35. Sukendro, S., et al.: Using an extended technology acceptance model to understand students' use of e-learning during Covid-19: Indonesian sport science education context. Heliyon **6**(August), e05410 (2020). https://doi.org/10.1016/j.heliyon.2020.e05410

36. Olivier, X.R.: An Investigation into the Antecedents and Outcomes of the M-Shopping Experience. Stellenbosch University, South Africa (2016)

37. Daroch, B., Nagrath, G., Gupta, A.: A study on factors limiting online shopping behaviour of consumers. Rajagiri Manag. J. **15**(1), 39–52 (2021). https://doi.org/10.1108/RAMJ-07-2020-0038

Technology Legitimation and User Resistance: The NHS COVID-19 App

Carlos Ferreira(✉) ⓘ, Maureen Meadows ⓘ, and Evronia Azer ⓘ

Coventry University, Coventry, UK
{ab6859,ac3495,ad3008}@coventry.ac.uk

Abstract. Innovative technologies often face acceptance challenges. This is especially true when they constitute disruptive innovations. Disruptive innovations can forcefully alter the way things are done in the economy and society and have differential impacts for social groups. Legitimacy – the fit between an innovation, and society at large – is an important explanatory factor of the success of disruptive technologies. The micro-judgements of legitimacy that individuals make with regards to a technology, can help understand why some innovations succeed or fail. Likewise, users' actions when using said innovations may indicate how acceptable the technology is to users. This paper analyses how users judge, and use, the NHS COVID-19 Test & Trace app. Preliminary findings suggest that individuals' micro-legitimacy judgements are strongly related to the decision to use the app or not, and that users have adopted a number of workaround behaviours to resist or compensate for the app's functionality.

Keywords: Legitimacy · Legitimation · Technology acceptance

1 Introduction

This paper analyses how users judge, and use, the NHS COVID-19 Test & Trace app. The COVID-19 pandemic caused widespread changes to individuals' behaviour. The need to reduce contagion led to the imposition of social distance mandates, lockdowns and the shuttering of business and other organisations. The collection and analysis of data about individuals' contacts was presented as a mechanism to address the social and economic impact of the pandemic, helping reduce infection rates while allowing society to continue to operate, albeit in managed ways [1]. Mobile phone data collection and analysis frameworks were developed to estimate proximity between users and the extent of time of contact. The UK National Health Service (NHS) developed and implemented one such application, the NHS COVID-19 Test & Trace app, which was promoted by the UK government as part of the country's Test and Trace system.

Innovative technologies often face challenges. This is especially true when they constitute disruptive innovations. In the traditional sense, disruptive innovation is characterised as strategic actions taken by companies, which give them an advantage over competitors in the same market; the extent of the disruption confined to the market

© IFIP International Federation for Information Processing 2022
Published by Springer Nature Switzerland AG 2022
S. Papagiannidis et al. (Eds.): I3E 2022, LNCS 13454, pp. 416–421, 2022.
https://doi.org/10.1007/978-3-031-15342-6_32

segment in which the disruptor and disrupted operate [2]. Recent scholarship takes a broader view of the extent to which disruption can have an impact: the discontinuity caused by disruptive innovations can reverberate across social systems [3]. Systems suffer disruption when a significant portion of agents in that system must reformulate their strategies in order to survive an innovation [4]. Disruptive innovations can forcefully alter the way things are done in the economy and society, challenge social contracts, affect social mores and norms, and have differential impacts for social groups [5]. For this reason, legitimacy – the fit between an innovation, and society at large [6] – is an important explanatory factor for the success – or otherwise – of disruptive technologies. Specifically, the micro-judgements of legitimacy that individuals make with regards to a technology, can help understand why some innovations succeed or fail [7]. Likewise, users' actions when using said innovations – for example, resisting the requirements of the technology – may indicate how acceptable the technology is to users [8].

This paper approaches the acceptability of the NHS COVID-19 Test & Trace app from the user/evaluator perspective, to address three research questions:

1. Which dimensions of legitimacy are more important for users and non-users of the NHS COVID-19 app?
2. Do users of the NHS COVID-19 app engage in workarounds or resistance behaviours?
3. Is there a relationship between users' reported need for legitimacy and user behaviour?

2 Literature Review

2.1 Legitimacy

Legitimacy consists of "a generalized perception or assumption that the actions of an entity are desirable, proper, or appropriate within some socially constructed system of norms, values, beliefs, and definitions" [6]. Based on a legitimacy-as-perception perspective, individuals' judgements are not aggregated in uniform groups, but are regarded as single individuals making their own judgements or adopting judgements from others. Legitimacy is, therefore, a multi-level phenomenon that can be studied at the collective level (macro) and individual level (micro) [9]. This paper focuses on micro-level legitimacy judgements [10], analysing how individual users take active roles in evaluating the legitimacy of a technology [7]. These judgements are underpinned by disparate behaviours, depending on the type of legitimacy involved [11].

Four distinct types of legitimacy can be identified: regulatory, pragmatic, moral and cultural-cognitive legitimacy [12]. Regulatory legitimacy is associated with a perception that the entity being evaluated follows existing rules. This establishes a 'baseline' legitimacy, ascertaining that the entity is legal. The second type of legitimacy is pragmatic legitimacy. This requires an entity being evaluated to demonstrate that it can deliver on claims associated with the measurable performance of its products or services, aligning with the evaluator's interests. The third type, moral legitimacy, relates to values. To achieve this level of legitimacy, an entity must demonstrate that it follows socially valued purposes and goals. The final dimension, known as cultural-cognitive legitimacy, involves demonstrating the fit between an entity and the evaluator's mental and cultural models and meaning systems [6].

Individual users play a distinctive role in legitimising innovations. This individual level legitimation is distinct from societal level legitimacy [9]. It is possible to assess individuals' judgements of a new technology in terms of expected utility (pragmatic legitimacy), their normative evaluations of it (moral legitimacy), and their cognitive assessments of its comprehensibility and taken-for-grantedness about the technology. These micro-judgements and perception of an innovation guide individuals' behaviours, which in turn help produce the collective perfection of legitimacy within a group [7, 11]. But innovations can be disruptive to social systems, in which case users may modulate their behaviours accordingly. The next section describes how users can sometimes choose to resist innovative technologies.

2.2 User Resistance

One of the most prominent models in the literature on acceptance of technology is the Unified Theory of Acceptance and Use of Technology (UTAUT), an evolution of the earlier Technology Acceptance Model (TAM). The model consists of a multi-level framework of technology acceptance which combines higher-level contextual factors and individual-level contextual factors with the original TAM main affects. These factors result in higher or lower acceptance and use of technology [13]. The model has since been subject to a wide variety of extensions, which have improved its ability to predict behaviour [14]. However, the UTAUT model has been criticised for taking a narrow view of technology acceptance, as it focuses on beliefs, perception and usage intention. The model may also be approaching the limits of its contribution to knowledge, as it focuses only on the individual user, and assumes a direct relationship between intention and actual behaviour. [15]. One area which UTAUT struggles to explain is user resistance to the technology. User resistance has been identified as a salient reason for the failure of innovative technologies, especially in cases of information systems implementation [16]. A variety of reasons for user resistance have been pointed out, including cynicism among users [17], a bias towards the status-quo [16] and users' personality traits [18].

Beyond the causes of user resistance, it is relevant to understand the forms which resistance can take – the behaviours individuals will engage in to resist an innovative technology. Users' responses can be functional – signalling the existence of problems with the technology or its effects; or dysfunctional – preventing the adoption of a technology, or generating conflict or ill-will [19]. This suggests that user resistance can be a positive force – highlighting aspects of the technology which do not work as expected or have unintended or negative consequences. In addition, users can develop workaround behaviours – a mismatch between the expectations of technology and actual working practice [8]. In their typology, Ferneley and Sobreperez [8] identify harmless workarounds (which do not significantly affect workflow or data accuracy). These may be a positive act of resistance (enhancing working practices) or a negative act of resistance (if they aim to oppose or challenge the system). In hindrance workarounds, subsequent actions are avoided. These can be positive (if the system is badly designed) or negative (if the action is required by colleagues or management). Finally, essential workarounds are actions necessary to complete the task at hand, and constitute positive resistance.

Users' behaviours when confronted with an innovative, possibly disruptive, technology are impacted by their micro-judgements of legitimacy (Sect. 2.1). This paper will ascertain if resistance behaviours may be related to the salience of specific types of legitimacy.

3   Methodology

The study chose the NHS COVID-19 Test & Trace app as a salient case for study of disruptive technology acceptance and user behaviour, via a 3-stage methodology. Phase 1 involved asking a group of users to keep diaries of their interactions with the NHS COVID-19 app over a four-week period, and reflect on their experiences and opinions of the NHS Test & Trace system. Users were assured that all data collected would be anonymised, and that no behaviours would be reported. They were asked to write down any notifications they received from the app; their feelings and actions in relation to those notifications; and any wider relevant thoughts and opinions, for example relating to news items about Test & Trace, conversations with friends or family members, etc.

Phase 2 involved a number of online Focus Groups with the participants in Phase 1. Phase 3 involved a series of online Focus Groups with non-users of the app, as the researchers were keen to explore whether any behaviours or opinions (such as privacy concerns relating to sharing personal data) might differ between users and non-users. All Focus Groups were recorded, and the discussions were transcribed. The Focus Groups followed a structure protocol.

4   Preliminary Findings

4.1   Legitimacy of the App, and How It Relates to Adoption and Non-adoption

- Users' reasons for adoption relate to the app's pragmatic legitimacy (access to public places which required checking in or traveling abroad) and moral legitimacy ("doing the right thing" to help address the pandemic).
- Non-users' reasons for rejecting the app relate to a perception that it lacks moral legitimacy (the app violates users' rights to choose what to do) and cultural-cognitive legitimacy (questions about data collection, data storage and privacy; and perception that the app's use is not widespread enough for it to be useful).
- The last point – that there would need to be a critical mass of users for the app to be useful - was also noted by users. It affects both the app's cultural-cognitive legitimacy and its pragmatic legitimacy.

4.2   Usage and Workaround Behaviours

- Users report that the app had limited functionality, and would like to see more features. They perceived that the app was not working, or not properly developed.
- False and unclear notifications led to a perception that the app was not fit for purpose. Users were perplexed by the reasons for some notifications, and chose to turn the app off in situations where they believed it might produce false positives (essential workarounds).

- Individuals chose not to use the app, either because it did not work properly (positive hindrance workarounds), or because nobody else was seen to be using it (negative hindrance workarounds).

4.3 Next Steps

The next steps of the analysis involve detailing the responses to research questions 1 and 2, and addressing research question 3 – relating legitimacy micro-judgements to workarounds and resistance behaviours. This will contribute to an inter-disciplinary understanding of how acceptance or rejection of an information system relates to its perceived legitimacy.

References

1. Ferreira, C., Merendino, A., Meadows, M., Simkin, L.: Learning, leading, linking: managing digital disruption. Centre for Business in Society, Coventry University, Coventry (2022)
2. Christensen, C.M.: The Innovator's Dilemma: When New Technologies Cause Great Firms to Fail. Harvard Business Review Press, Boston (1997)
3. Millar, C., Lockett, M., Ladd, T.: Disruption: technology, innovation and society. Technol. Forecast. Soc. Chang. **129**, 254–260 (2018). https://doi.org/10.1016/j.techfore.2017.10.020
4. Kilkki, K., Mäntylä, M., Karhu, K., Hämmäinen, H., Ailisto, H.: A disruption framework. Technol. Forecast. Soc. Chang. **129**, 275–284 (2018). https://doi.org/10.1016/j.techfore.2017.09.034
5. Ferreira, C., Merendino, A., Meadows, M.: Disruption and legitimacy: big data in society. Inf. Syst. Front. https://doi.org/10.1007/s10796-021-10155-3
6. Suchman, M.C.: Managing legitimacy: strategic and institutional approaches. Acad. Manag. Rev. **20**, 571 (1995). https://doi.org/10.2307/258788
7. Bunduchi, R., Candi, M.: Technology legitimation: a product-level examination across the technology lifecycle. Br. J. Manag. (2021). https://doi.org/10.1111/1467-8551.12562
8. Ferneley, E.H., Sobreperez, P.: Resist, comply or workaround? An examination of different facets of user engagement with information systems. Eur. J. Inf. Syst. **15**, 345–356 (2006). https://doi.org/10.1057/palgrave.ejis.3000629
9. Tost, L.P.: An integrative model of legitimacy judgments. Acad. Manag. Rev. **36**, 686–710 (2011). https://doi.org/10.5465/AMR.2011.65554690
10. Bitektine, A., Haack, P.: The "macro" and the "micro" of legitimacy: toward a multilevel theory of the legitimacy process. AMR **40**, 49–75 (2015). https://doi.org/10.5465/amr.2013.0318
11. Bitektine, A.: Toward a theory of social judgments of organizations: the case of legitimacy, reputation, and status. Acad. Manag. Rev. **36**, 151–179 (2011). https://doi.org/10.5465/amr.2009.0382
12. Deephouse, D.L., Bundy, J., Tost, L.P., Suchman, M.C.: Organizational legitimacy: six key questions. In: Greenwood, R., Oliver, C., Lawrence, T., Meyer, R. (eds.) The SAGE Handbook of Organizational Institutionalism. SAGE, Thousand Oaks (2017)
13. Venkatesh, V., Morris, M.G., Davis, G.B.: User acceptance of information technology: toward a unified view. MIS Q. **27**, 425 (2003). https://doi.org/10.2307/30036540
14. Venkatesh, V., Thong, J., Xu, X.: Unified theory of acceptance and use of technology: a synthesis and the road ahead. JAIS **17**, 328–376 (2016). https://doi.org/10.17705/1jais.00428

15. Shachak, A., Kuziemsky, C., Petersen, C.: Beyond TAM and UTAUT: future directions for HIT implementation research. J. Biomed. Inform. **100**, 103315 (2019). https://doi.org/10.1016/j.jbi.2019.103315

16. Kim, K.: Investigating user resistance to information systems implementation: a status quo bias perspective. MIS Q. **33**, 567 (2009). https://doi.org/10.2307/20650309

17. Selander, L., Henfridsson, O.: Cynicism as user resistance in IT implementation: cynicism as user resistance in IT implementation. Inf. Syst. J. **22**, 289–312 (2012). https://doi.org/10.1111/j.1365-2575.2011.00386.x

18. Laumer, S., Maier, C., Eckhardt, A., Weitzel, T.: User personality and resistance to mandatory information systems in organizations: a theoretical model and empirical test of dispositional resistance to change. J. Inf. Technol. **31**, 67–82 (2016). https://doi.org/10.1057/jit.2015.17

19. Rivard, L.: Information technology implementers' responses to user resistance: nature and effects. MIS Q. **36**, 897 (2012). https://doi.org/10.2307/41703485

The Impact of Improvisational and Dynamic Capabilities on Business Model Innovation During COVID-19: A Composite-Based Approach

Rogier van de Wetering[1]([✉]), Joshua Doe[2], Ronald van den Heuvel[1], and Hussam Al Halbusi[3]

[1] Faculty of Science, Open University, Heerlen, The Netherlands
rogier.vandewetering@ou.nl
[2] Marketing Department, Central University, Accra, Ghana
[3] Department of Management, Ahmed Bin Mohammed Military College, Doha, Qatar

Abstract. Dynamic capabilities embody various capabilities that drive the organization's adaptiveness and are studied from management and information systems perspectives. However, the impact of specific dynamic and organizational capabilities, i.e., management system adaptability and improvisational capabilities, on business model innovation under tumultuous times still has to be unfolded. Therefore, this study investigates the role of these capabilities during the COVID-19 crisis. This study presents the results of analyses on obtained survey data (N = 105) from Ghana and shows that these two strategic capabilities significantly influence business model innovation. Also, this study shows that business model innovation positively influences organizational performance under COVID-19. These results extend the current knowledge base of dynamic and organizational capabilities while offering implications for practice. We also offer various practical recommendations that help overcome business model innovation challenges during tumultuous times.

Keywords: Management system adaptability · Improvisational capabilities · Dynamic capability · Business model innovation · Organizational performance under COVID-19 · Composite-based SEM

1 Introduction

At the beginning of the COVID-19 pandemic, many organizations faced a downturn due to multiple challenges. Some notable adverse effects of this downturn include shareholder distress, a substantial drop in customer and consumer demand, an increase in the cost of capital in tightening credit markets, and even a decline in asset value due to a lack of visibility when employees do not come to locations as much as before. Under these tumultuous conditions, organizations typically focus on improving plans and actions on tactical or functional levers [1].

© IFIP International Federation for Information Processing 2022
Published by Springer Nature Switzerland AG 2022
S. Papagiannidis et al. (Eds.): I3E 2022, LNCS 13454, pp. 422–433, 2022.
https://doi.org/10.1007/978-3-031-15342-6_33

However, many organizations miss substantial business opportunities through structural complexity reduction and effective and innovative business model use [2].

Business models depict the content, structure, and governance of transactions designed to create value by exploiting business opportunities [3, 4]. Each organization has a business model [5]. Some, however, have not clearly articulated and documented this. Typically, a business model describes the organization's value propositions (products/services, offerings), profit formula, the organization's key resources (e.g., people, process, technology, and support) the processes needed for execution and collaboration [6]. In essence, business models can be considered a driving force in the organization's business operations that are in line with what customers want, how people can do their work most efficiently and with the proper behavior [7].

It is well known that different levels of innovation ambition require different people, motivational factors, and organizational support systems [8, 9]. A key focal point in innovation concerns business model innovation [10]. Business model innovation allows firms to address down-turn events by changing their core value proposition to customers and their underlying operating model [3]. The degree to which an organization's business model innovation is being rolled out can be boldly classified into three levels of ambition. The first is the primary 'creation' of incremental enhancement of products and services. The second is adjacent 'sustaining innovation,' which focuses on leveraging offerings and value propositions into a new space. Finally, the third one is the 'transformational' level that embraces the development of new offers to customers and possibly even new businesses to serve markets and customer needs that may not yet exist [6].

Many organizations cannot achieve business benefits from their business model innovation when they re-balance the innovation portfolio from core to fundamental and subsequently to the transformational level. One reason why this is so is that these firms lack essential organizational resources, capabilities, and key processes to be truly transformative in their business model [4, 6, 10]. Hence, we argue that organizations capable of orchestrating their organizational resources and addressing down-turn events by changing their core value proposition will successfully achieve business model innovation and high levels of organizational performance.

To this end, we embrace the suitable dynamic capabilities view (DCV) as a lens to investigate this particular claim [11]. Moreover, Teece [4] argues that it is crucial to understand the contribution of dynamic capabilities to achieving business model innovation, as current scholarly contributions are predominately theoretical.

Hence, this study investigates the key role of two particular organizational capabilities, i.e., management system adaptability, as dynamic capability [12, 13] and improvisational capabilities [3, 14], as drivers of business model innovation. These crucial capabilities enable a firm's offerings and competitive position, and these capabilities are created through configurations of assets and activities where processes and people (professionals) are combined, controlled, and interconnected. These organizational capabilities bridge the firm's strategic objectives, ambitions, and day-to-day activities.

Against this background, we define the main research question: *"To what extent do management system adaptability and improvisational capabilities influence business model innovation, and what is the subsequent impact on organizational performance under COVID-19?"*.

This paper is organized as follows. First, we outline the theory and position the framework with associated hypotheses. Then, we outline the methods, after which we present the core results of this study. Finally, the current paper ends with a discussion, including theoretical and practical contributions.

2   Theory and the study's Framework

2.1   Capability Perspective, Dynamic and Improvisational Capabilities

We ground this study in the DCV. This theory provides scholars and leaders with insights into how to adapt firms under turbulent conditions and adjust their operating base with processes and technologies in line with the market demands [4, 14]. This theory starts with the notion of a 'capability.' A capability can be regarded as aggregating several underlying elements that refer to tangible and intangible assets firms use to develop and implement the business strategy [15]. Think, for instance, about competencies (i.e., individual employee skills), business processes that produce a particular output, knowledge systems, and partnerships (i.e., the interfaces with key participants an organization needs to produce outputs) [15, 16].

The combination of these individual aspects gives an organization a particular capability. However, unfortunately, there is often confusion between capabilities and competencies. This is because capabilities are always associated with the organizational level; competencies and skillsets, in essence, describe an individual.

In this research context, we focus on specific capabilities, i.e., dynamic and improvisational capabilities. Hence, we follow Wang and Ahmed [17] and define dynamic capabilities as '...the firm's behavioral orientation constantly to integrate, reconfigure, renew and recreate its resources and capabilities and, most importantly, upgrade and reconstruct its core capabilities in response to the changing environment to attain and sustain competitive advantage.' A crucial unique dynamic capability is the firm's adaptive capability (next to, for instance, absorptive capacity and innovation capability) which is considered the ability of a firm to reconfigure resources, coordinate processes, and effectively address changes in the business environment [4, 13, 18–20].

This research focuses on a specific dimension of adaptive capability, namely the management system adaptive capability [13]. Hence, this particular capability is essential for firms as it encourages employees and managers to challenge outmoded practices across the organization and allows a firm to respond to changes in the market adequately [13, 21].

The extant literature distinguishes between dynamic capabilities and improvisational ones [14]. Hence, improvisational capabilities denote repetitively engaging in improvisational actions without formal planning by building innovative products and solutions to enhance operational and competitive benefits [3, 22]. Improvisational capabilities operate as a "third hand," according to Pavlou and El Sawy [14], next to 'planned' dynamic and operational (zero-order) capabilities—that drive the present business operations—as a driver of change, adaption, and innovation during tumultuous times [23].

2.2   Hypotheses Development

We adopt a complementarity and ambidexterity perspective, claiming that the simultaneous execution of two seemingly opposing capabilities, i.e., improvisational and dynamic capabilities, complement each other to collectively achieve business model innovation during crises. This idea resonates well with Mintzberg's 'intended' versus 'emerging' strategy [24].

Consistent with prior research on innovativeness that shows that dynamic capabilities drive the use the new technological innovations and enable business process innovations [25–28], we now argue that management system adaptability, as a dynamic capability, drives the firm's business model innovation. It does so by actively reducing inefficient coordination and control mechanisms across the organization and encouraging communication and information flow among the organization's teams and employees [13, 21]. In this regard, organizations that have managerial systems that are flexible and adaptive can better challenge outmoded traditions and practices, respond faster to shifts in the market and harness the organization-wide skills and competencies necessary to innovate [13, 21, 25]. Moreover, management systems adaptability is especially crucial during sudden disruptions, like the COVID-19 pandemic, as firms must react and adapt to changing customer demands and behaviors, seize business and technological opportunities and embrace new service innovations [20, 25, 26, 29].

Based on the above, we define the following:

Hypothesis 1 (H1): *Management systems adaptability positively impacts business model innovation during COVID-19.*

The nature of improvisational capabilities is different from dynamic capabilities. First, they are 'emergent' and enable firms to take action spontaneously rather than based on rigorous planning. Pavlou and El Sawy [14] summarize this well as they argue that these capabilities help firms to "….spontaneously reconfigure existing resources to build new operational capabilities to address urgent, unpredictable, and novel environmental situations." Second, under conditions of high uncertainty where there is no time for organizational resource planning, these capabilities are crucial as they offer firms the reflexive instincts and needed improvisational activities to adapt and respond to the problems using the resources available [22, 30, 31]. Hence, improvisational capabilities provide firms with the necessary skillset to adapt the firm's products, propositions and services, delivery channels, and technological platforms and support the way customer transactions are done [3, 4, 14, 22].

Management systems adaptability and improvisational capabilities collectively allow organizations to foresee trends, developments clearly, and market disruption, deeply understand market dynamics, and adjust accordingly. Furthermore, they enable firms to use combinations of resources (people, processes, technology) for new business operations, allowing firms to quickly respond to market and business changes and drive business model innovation [3, 13, 14, 21]. Synthesizing from the above, we define the following hypothesis:

Hypothesis 2 (H2): *Improvisational capabilities positively impact business model innovation during COVID-19.*

Deducting from our theoretical framework, we argue that business model innovation is a crucial antecedent to achieving high levels of organizational performance. For example, business model innovation is a key enabler for organizations to efficiently deliver excellent services, offerings, and value to their customers through new digital technologies and online channels [5, 6]. In addition, especially during times of high uncertainty, customers want mobility in product and service delivery and a seamless service experience that ultimately results in high customer satisfaction [32, 33].

Business model innovation allows firms to address down-turn events like COVID-19 by changing their core propositions to customers and the firm's underlying operating model [3, 34]. Also, business model innovation drives an organization's growth ambitions (e.g., high profitability, increased market share) by transforming the organization's (go-to) markets and segments and the way the business operations can be scaled and deliver high-quality personalized services [4, 6, 35, 36]. The organization can accelerate new revenue streams through business model innovation so that opportunities can be capitalized cost-effectively [29–32, 37, 38].

In addition, research has shown that business model innovation will substantially impact the firm's competitiveness and value-creation processes for the organization [8, 39]. Finally, we define:

Hypothesis 3 (H3): *Business model innovation positively impacts organizational performance during COVID-19.*

3   Methods and Composite-Based Analyses

We used an online survey anonymously and conveniently distributed it among SMEs in Ghana through our professional and educational network. In addition, we targeted senior business practitioners, like chief executive officers, chief information officers, chief digital officers, and IT managers. The data collection process was performed between 8th April and 20th May 2020. After removing incomplete and inadequate responses, our sample size was 105 SMEs.

We adopted previously empirically validated measures for all constructs of the framework. We adopted four items from [3] to measure the firm's capability to engage in improvisational actions without formal planning, i.e., improvisational capabilities, and three items from [12, 13] to measure the firm's management system adaptability.

In addition, we used nine indicators from [3, 9] to measure business model innovation. Finally, we adopted five measures from [23, 40] to measure organizational performance during COVID-19 and evaluate performance from a broad and balanced perspective. All measures are included in the Appendix.

We used structural equation modeling (SEM) as the preferred analysis method to test the hypotheses. Specifically, we use composite-based SEM, a variance-based approach that uses weighted linear combinations of measurable items as proxies for underlying theoretical conceptualizations [41]. This approach to SEM handles both emergent variables (composite-formative measurements) and latent variables (reflective measurement and common factor model) [42]. Therefore, it is considered a full estimator to SEM used in various types of research, including exploratory research and relationship assessment between different proxies, confirmatory research, and predictive research [43]. Furthermore, composite-based SEM works well with relatively small sample sizes, as in our work, has less strict requirements concerning multivariate normality, and offers model specification and requirement flexibility [44, 45]. Finally, composite-based SEM allows scholars to extend existing theory by examining the model's ability to predict instead of establishing model fit only, as in covariance-based SEM [45, 46].

We use ADANCO 2.3 as the analysis tool [41], and all constructs are operationalized as latent variables, thus representing (reflective) common factor models. Moreover, compared to other composite-based tools like SmartPLS or WarpPLS, ADANCO offers the possibility to assess the overall goodness of fit [42, 47].

4   Empirical Results and Interpretation

Before we tested the core hypotheses of this work, we assessed the model fit. Table 1 outlines the key results of this assessment. Using ADANCO, model fit is assessed through three related metrics [42]. The first one is SRMR (Standardized root mean squared residual). This metric describes how the empirical correlation matrix differs from a model-implied correlation matrix. In addition, the software provides bootstrap-based outcomes for HI95 and HI99 percentiles. So, if the SRMS goes beyond these two values, it is improbable that the model is true. The other two metrics, dULS (unweighted least squares discrepancy) and dG (geodesic discrepancy), are other metrics to unfold the extent to which the empirical correlation matrix differs from the model-implied variant.

As can be seen from the Table beneath, all obtained values are below HI99-values, suggesting an appropriate model fit. The hypotheses can now be tested.

Table 1. Goodness of fit assessment

Goodness of model fit (saturated model)

	Value	HI95	HI99	Conclusion
SRMR	0.0688	0.0631	0.0690	Supported
d_{ULS}	1.0946	0.9196	1.1007	Supported
d_G	0.8037	0.8573	0.9965	Supported

Figure 1 shows the outcomes of the structural model assessment using ADANCO. This Figure includes the software's obtained beta coefficients (i.e., estimates from the regression analyses), t-values (i.e., the coefficient divided by the associated standard error and also showing the importance of the construct in the model), and coefficient of determination (R^2), that shows the amount of variation in the respective outcomes (dependent variables).

As the Figure shows, all hypotheses can be accepted as the beta coefficients were significant. We also controlled these outcomes by including "size" and "industry" in the model. These variables had no significant impact on the outcomes (size: $\beta = -0.004$ $t = 0.353$, $p = 0.93$) and "industry" ($\beta = -0.056$, $t = 0.204$, $p = 0.58$).

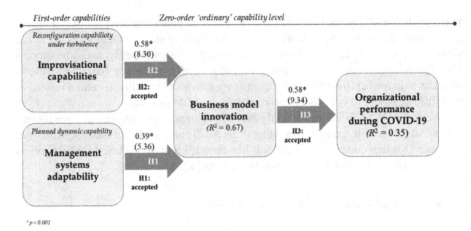

Fig. 1. Results of the structural models.

5 Discussion

It goes without saying that under tumultuous times, firms must reframe how they position their offerings in the marketplace and how they interact with customers. This work tried to unfold whether or not two strategic capabilities collectively drive the firm's business model innovation that serves as the foundation for achieving high levels of organizational performance under COVID-19. Outcomes of this work using a composite-based approach showcased that both improvisational capabilities and management systems adaptability are critical drivers of business model innovation. We also showed that business model innovation positively influences organizational performance under COVID-19. These outcomes have several theoretical and practical implications, which will be discussed next.

Building upon the foundations of the DCV, we argued that two strategic capabilities could profoundly impact organizational success. This study proposed that planned (management systems adaptability) and improvisational capabilities positively impact business model innovation. We found evidence for the study's main proposition and thereby extended work by [14] by showing the collective impact that planned and improvisational capabilities can have on business model innovation. However, based on this work's outcomes, it is evident that improvisational capabilities have a more substantial impact than management systems adaptability. It could be that the planned dynamic capabilities' effect is weaker under highly tumultuous conditions like the current COVID-19 pandemic, whereas the effect of improvisational capabilities is more substantial, as argued by Pavlou and Sawy [14]. With these outcomes, we also adhere to the call by Teece [4] that scholars should investigate the contributions of dynamic capabilities to business model innovation.

We also add the body of knowledge on innovation and managing down-turn events [4, 6, 10, 21]. Specifically, this work now shows how business model innovation driven by strategic capabilities can drive high levels of organizational performance during a global pandemic like COVID-10. Hence, we stress that organizations capable of orchestrating their organizational resources and addressing downturn events by making specific changes to their core value proposition will successfully achieve business model innovation and high levels of organizational performance.

Next to theoretical contributions, we also outline some implications of this work for practice. Hence, we argue that organizations that excel in their business model innovation should embrace a strategic approach using an integrative process of project management and dynamic resource allocation; and an organizational model that establishes the right capabilities, metrics, incentives, decision rights, and responsibilities.

Also, decision-makers should develop dynamic capabilities to proactively identify, manage, and evaluate a wide range of new businesses, projects, opportunities, and risks.

Moreover, these capabilities enable the organization to challenge the status quo and leave outmoded traditions and practices. Also, firms should actively engage in improvisational activities and allow a firm to respond quickly to changes in the market. Hence, business model innovation and its subsequent impact on performance must start with and be guided by a clear set of choices that connect to the overall firm and even department and business unit strategies.

This study has several limitations that future work could address. First, we currently only collected data from Ghana, possibly inhibiting the generalization of these outcomes to developed countries, even though we expect that the outcomes will be generalizable to other emerging countries. Second, the theoretical model only included dynamic and improvisational capabilities as an antecedent of business model innovation.

Apart from the discriminant validity tests, showing the distinctiveness of each construct, Pavlou and El Sawy [14] argue that planned and dynamic capabilities can have different relationships with their antecedents (e.g., IT system support or flexibility), their outcomes (consequences), and possible moderating constructs like the technological or market turbulence. Future work could investigate these particular relationships.

Third, we only focused on a particular dimension of adaptive capability: the management system adaptability [13]. The DCV embraces various capabilities, including sense and respond capabilities, knowledge processes, digital dynamic capability, and strategic flexibility [13, 20, 21, 48–51]. Thus, future work can also unravel the contributions of organizational capabilities to business model innovation.

Appendix A: Measurement items

Improvisational Capabilities
(7-point Likert Scale, 1 = Strongly disagree, 7 = Strongly agree)
*   To what extent do you agree with the following statements?*

IMP1: We apply combinations of business and IT resources at hand to pursue new strategic initiatives such as entering a new market
IMP2: We apply combinations of resources at hand for new business operations
IMP3: We apply combinations of resources at hand for expansion
IMP4: We apply combinations of resources at hand to create new products or services

Management System Adaptability
(7-point Likert Scale, 1 = Strongly disagree, 7 = Strongly agree)
To what extent do you agree with the following statements?

MSA1:The management systems in this organization encourage people to challenge outmoded traditions/practices/sacred cows
MSA2: The management systems in this organization are flexible enough to allow us to respond quickly to the current changes in our markets
MSA3: The management systems in this organization evolve rapidly in response to shifts in our business priorities

Business Model Innovation
(7-point Likert Scale,, 1 = Strongly disagree, 7 = Strongly agree.
Please indicate your firm's capabilities relative to competition for each of the following:

BMI1: Our business model offers new combinations of products, services, and information
BMI2: Our business model attracts a lot of new customers
BMI3: Our business model attracts a lot of new suppliers and partners
BMI4: Our business model bonds participants together in novel ways
BMI5: Our business model links participants to transactions in novel ways
BMI6: We frequently introduce new ideas and innovations into our business model
BMI7: We frequently introduce new operational processes, routines, and norms into our business model
BMI8: We are pioneers of the business model
BMI9: Overall, our business model is novel

Organizational Performance During COVID-19
(7-point Likert Scale,, 1 = Strongly disagree, 7 = Strongly agree)
For the past few weeks, our company, relatively to our main competitors in the same industry (for non-competing governmental agencies, you could also read competitors as 'other ministries or departments'), has been able to maintain or increase:

OP1:Customer satisfaction
OP2: Business brand and image
OP3: Customer loyalty
OP4: Market share
OP5: Profitability

References

1. Crittenden, V.L., Crittenden, W.F.: Building a capable organization: the eight levers of strategy implementation. Bus. Horiz. **51**(4), 301–309 (2008)

2. Bock, A.J., Opsahl, T., George, G., Gann, D.M.: The effects of culture and structure on strategic flexibility during business model innovation. J. Manage. Stud. **49**(2), 279–305 (2012)
3. Guo, H., Su, Z., Ahlstrom, D.: Business model innovation: the effects of exploratory orientation, opportunity recognition, and entrepreneurial bricolage in an emerging economy. Asia Pac. J. Manag. **33**(2), 533–549 (2015). https://doi.org/10.1007/s10490-015-9428-x
4. Teece, D.J.: Business models and dynamic capabilities. Long Range Plan. **51**(1), 40–49 (2018)
5. Chesbrough, H.: Business model innovation: it's not just about technology anymore. Strategy Leadersh. **35**(6), 12–17 (2007)
6. Christensen, C.M., Bartman, T., Bever, D.V.: The hard truth about business model innovation. MIT Sloan Manag. Rev. **58**(1), 31–40 (2016)
7. Lindgardt, Z., Reeves, M., Stalk, G., Deimler, M.S.: Business model innovation. When the Game Gets Tough, Change the Game. The Boston Consulting Group, Boston, MA 118 (2009)
8. Anwar, M.: Business model innovation and SMEs performance—does competitive advantage mediate? Int. J. Innov. Manag. **22**(07), 1850057 (2018)
9. Zott, C., Amit, R.: Business model design and the performance of entrepreneurial firms. Organ. Sci. **18**(2), 181–199 (2007)
10. Chesbrough, H.: Business model innovation: opportunities and barriers. Long Range Plan. **43**(2–3), 354–363 (2010)
11. Rachinger, M., Rauter, R., Müller, C., Vorraber, W., Schirgi, E.: Digitalization and its influence on business model innovation. J. Manuf. Technol. Manag. **30**(8), 1143–1160 (2018)
12. Gibson, C.B., Birkinshaw, J.: The antecedents, consequences, and mediating role of organizational ambidexterity. Acad. Manag. J. **47**(2), 209–226 (2004)
13. Akgün, A.E., Keskin, H., Byrne, J.: Antecedents and contingent effects of organizational adaptive capability on firm product innovativeness. J. Product Innov. Manag. **29**, 171–189 (2012)
14. Pavlou, P.A., El Sawy, O.A.: The "third hand": IT-enabled competitive advantage in turbulence through improvisational capabilities. Inf. Syst. Res. **21**(3), 443–471 (2010)
15. Ray, G., Barney, J.B., Muhanna, W.A.: Capabilities, business processes, and competitive advantage: choosing the dependent variable in empirical tests of the resource-based view. Strateg. Manag. J. **25**(1), 23–37 (2004)
16. Ismail, A.I., Rose, R.C., Uli, J., Abdullah, H.: The relationship between organisational resources, capabilities, systems and competitive advantage. Asian Acad. Manag. J. **17**(1), 151–173 (2012)
17. Wang, C.L., Ahmed, P.K.: Dynamic capabilities: a review and research agenda. Int. J. Manag. Rev. **9**(1), 31–51 (2007)
18. Zhou, K.Z., Li, C.B.: How strategic orientations influence the building of dynamic capability in emerging economies. J. Bus. Res. **63**(3), 224–231 (2010)
19. Van de Wetering, R.: The impact of artificial intelligence ambidexterity and strategic flexibility on operational ambidexterity. In: Proceedings of the Pacific Asia Conference on Information Systems (PACIS) 2022, Taipei/Sydney Virtual Conference (2022)
20. Van de Wetering, R.: Understanding the Impact of enterprise architecture driven dynamic capabilities on agility: a variance and fsQCA study. Pac. Asia J. Assoc. Inf. Syst. **13**(4), 32–68 (2021)
21. Tuominen, M., Rajala, A., Möller, K.: How does adaptability drive firm innovativeness? J. Bus. Res. **57**(5), 495–506 (2004)
22. Senyard, J., Baker, T., Davidsson, P.: Entrepreneurial bricolage: towards systematic empirical testing. Front. Entrepreneurship Res. **29**(5), 1–14 (2009)
23. Van de Wetering, R.: Enterprise Architecture Resources, Dynamic Capabilities, and their Pathways to Operational Value. In: Proceedings of the Fortieth International Conference on Information Systems (ICIS), AIS (2019)

24. Mintzberg, H.: The strategy concept I: five Ps for strategy. Calif. Manage. Rev. **30**(1), 11–24 (1987)
25. Van de Wetering, R., Hendrickx, T., Brinkkemper, S., Kurnia, S.: The impact of EA-Driven dynamic capabilities, innovativeness, and structure on organizational benefits: a variance and fsQCA perspective. Sustainability **13**(10), 5414 (2021)
26. Van de Wetering, R., Besuyen, M.: How IT-enabled dynamic capabilities add value to the development of innovation capabilities, In: Mehdi Khosrow-Pour, D.B.A. (eds.) Encyclopedia of Organizational Knowledge, Administration, and Technology, pp. 999–1016. IGI Global: Hershey, PA, USA (2021)
27. Teece, D., Leih, S.: Uncertainty, innovation, and dynamic capabilities: an introduction. Calif. Manage. Rev. **58**(4), 5–12 (2016)
28. Schoemaker, P.J., Heaton, S., Teece, D.: Innovation, dynamic capabilities, and leadership. Calif. Manage. Rev. **61**(1), 15–42 (2018)
29. Jiang, Y., Stylos, N.: Triggers of consumers' enhanced digital engagement and the role of digital technologies in transforming the retail ecosystem during COVID-19 pandemic. Technol. Forecast. Soc. Chang. **172**, 1–19 (2021)
30. e Cunha, M.P., Gomes, E., Mellahi, K., Miner, A.S., Rego, A.: Strategic agility through improvisational capabilities: implications for a paradox-sensitive HRM. Hum. Resour. Manag. Rev. 30(1), 100695 (2020)
31. Baker, T., Miner, A.S., Eesley, D.T.: Improvising firms: bricolage, account giving and improvisational competencies in the founding process. Res. Policy **32**(2), 255–276 (2003)
32. Keiningham, T., et al.: Customer experience driven business model innovation. J. Bus. Res. **116**, 431–440 (2020)
33. Clauss, T., Kesting, T., Naskrent, J.: A rolling stone gathers no moss: the effect of customers' perceived business model innovativeness on customer value co-creation behavior and customer satisfaction in the service sector. R&D Manag. **49**(2), 180–203 (2019)
34. Clauss, T., Breier, M., Kraus, S., Durst, S., Mahto, R.V.: Temporary business model innovation–SMEs' innovation response to the COVID-19 crisis. R&D Manag. **52**(2), 294–312 (2022)
35. Johnson, M.W., Lafley, A.G.: Seizing the white space. In: Business Model Innovation for Growth and Renewal. Harvard Business School Press, Boston, MA (2010)
36. Amit, R., Zott, C.: Business model innovation: creating value in times of change. IESE Business School of Navarra, Barcelona. IESE Working Paper, No. WP-870 (2010)
37. Pohle, G., Chapman, M.: IBM's global CEO report 2006: business model innovation matters. Strategy Leadersh. (2006)
38. Ucaktürk, A., Bekmezci, M., Ucaktürk, T.: Prevailing during the periods of economical crisis and recession through business model innovation. Procedia-Soc. Behav. Sci. **24**, 89–100 (2011)
39. Amit, R., Zott, C.: Creating value through business model innovation. Strategy in changing markets: new business models. MIT Sloan Manag. Rev. 53(310), 36–44 (2012)
40. Chen, J.-S., Tsou, H.-T.: Performance effects of IT capability, service process innovation, and the mediating role of customer service. J. Eng. Tech. Manage **29**(1), 71–94 (2012)
41. Dijkstra, T.K., Henseler, J.: Linear indices in nonlinear structural equation models: best fitting proper indices and other composites. Qual. Quant. **45**(6), 1505–1518 (2011)
42. Henseler, J.: Composite-based structural equation modeling: analyzing latent and emergent variables. Guilford Publications (2020)
43. Henseler, J.: Partial least squares path modeling: quo vadis? Qual. Quant. **52**(1), 1–8 (2018). https://doi.org/10.1007/s11135-018-0689-6
44. Hair Jr, J.F., Sarstedt, M., Ringle, C.M., Gudergan, S.P.: Advanced issues in partial least squares structural equation modeling. SAGE Publications (2017)

45. Petter, S., Hadavi, Y.: With great power comes great responsibility: the use of partial least squares in information systems research. ACM SIGMIS Database DATABASE Adv. Inf. Syst. **52**(SI), 10–23 (2021)
46. Hair, J.F., Risher, J.J., Sarstedt, M., Ringle, C.M.: When to use and how to report the results of PLS-SEM. Eur. Bus. Rev. **31**(1), 2–24 (2019)
47. Tsao, W.-C., Hsieh, M.-T., Lin, T.M.: Intensifying online loyalty! the power of website quality and the perceived value of consumer/seller relationship. Ind. Manag. Data Syst. **116**(9), 1987–2010 (2016)
48. Wetering, R.: Achieving digital-driven patient agility in the era of big data. In: Dennehy, D., Griva, A., Pouloudi, N., Dwivedi, Y.K., Pappas, I., Mäntymäki, M. (eds.) I3E 2021. LNCS, vol. 12896, pp. 82–93. Springer, Cham (2021). https://doi.org/10.1007/978-3-030-85447-8_8
49. Teece, D.J., Pisano, G., Shuen, A.: Dynamic capabilities and strategic management. Strateg. Manag. J. **18**(7), 509–533 (1997)
50. Zhou, K.Z., Wu, F.: Technological capability, strategic flexibility, and product innovation. Strateg. Manag. J. **31**(5), 547–561 (2010)
51. Van de Wetering, R., Versendaal, J.: Information technology ambidexterity, digital dynamic capability, and knowledge processes as enablers of patient agility: empirical study. JMIRx Med **2**(4), e32336 (2021). https://doi.org/10.2196/32336

The Ephemeral and Information Systems Research: Conceptualizing Ephemerality in a Post-pandemic World

Ronan Doyle[1,2]([✉]) [iD], Kieran Conboy[1,2] [iD], and David Kreps[1,2] [iD]

[1] National University of Ireland, Galway, Ireland
r.doyle28@nuigalway.ie
[2] Lero, the Science Foundation Ireland Research Centre for Software, Limerick, Ireland

Abstract. The Covid-19 pandemic has accelerated business use of digital technology with ephemeral functionality. However, ephemerality as a concept is not well defined in the information systems (IS) literature, making application and operationalization challenging. We conduct an interdisciplinary review of the temporal and material qualities of the ephemeral. We then conduct a standalone review of ephemerality in IS. Based upon our reviews, we propose a definition for ephemeral and develop a framework of ephemeral characteristics. We outline incongruence between this framework and IS conceptualization of ephemerality.

Keywords: Ephemeral · Information Systems · Conceptualization

1 Introduction

History shows that pandemics can catalyze extraordinary socioeconomic, cultural, and political change (Griffin and Denholm 2020). In the Covid-19 context, one such change seems to be the accelerated adoption of digital technology (Carroll and Conboy 2020; Dwivedi et al. 2020). Specific to this article, the pandemic is accelerating business use of digital technology with ephemeral functionality (Goldberg and Prive 2022). Conferencing app Zoom, with 10 million pre-pandemic 'daily participants' in December 2019, reported 300 million daily participants by May 2020 (theverge.com). 'Ephemeral' is dictionary defined as 'lasting or used for a very short time' (*Oxford English Dictionary* 2004). The nature of, and global response to, Covid-19 has highlighted the ephemerality of, for instance, sociopolitical, organizational, and strategic knowledge, of digital information and its circulation, and of popular culture, media, and market trends. In the information systems (IS) context, while computerized information is traditionally characterized more by durability than ephemerality (Kallinikos 2009), ephemerality is now emerging as an intentional design choice (Xu et al. 2018) in areas like privacy (He et al. 2021), blockchain (Carvalho et al. 2020), and social media (Morlok et al. 2018).

The problem is that the concept of ephemerality is not well defined in the literature. The word 'ephemeral' is routinely applied in IS with little qualification (e.g.: ephemeral

© IFIP International Federation for Information Processing 2022
Published by Springer Nature Switzerland AG 2022
S. Papagiannidis et al. (Eds.): I3E 2022, LNCS 13454, pp. 434–455, 2022.
https://doi.org/10.1007/978-3-031-15342-6_34

online communities (Quintarelli et al. 2019), ephemeral blockchain concepts (Carvalho et al. 2020), and ephemeral design knowledge (vom Brocke et al. 2021). Yoo's (2010) impactful and insightful experimental computing paper notes ephemerality as one of three characteristics of digital but does not delineate what ephemeral means. In such cases, IS researchers are informed only by the dictionary definition for ephemeral and the context of the individual study (DDC). If digital is the future of IS (Burton-Jones et al. 2021) and ephemerality partially characterizes digital, we believe that a broader and deeper understanding of ephemerality will benefit all IS stakeholders.

Broader and deeper conceptualisation of the ephemeral can augment theorization of digital. As Taylor (2007, p. 4/5) puts it, 'digital technologies... further ask us to reformulate our understanding of... the ephemeral.' The challenge for IS researchers, therefore, is to determine not only how digital *is* ephemeral, but also how digital is *reformulating the ephemeral*. IS researchers are well positioned to provide new theoretical perspectives on, for example, the ephemerality of digital transformation boundaries (Sandberg et al. 2020), of information and knowledge (Salovaara and Tuunainen 2015; Alavi and Leidner 2002), and of organizations (Prester et al. 2019), as well as the ephemeral nature of the sociomaterial and processual (Orlikowski and Scott 2008; Mousavi Baygi et al. 2021). Enhanced understanding can also contribute to disentangling the ephemeral from associated (and similarly elusive) digital-related concepts such as social acceleration (Fichman et al. 2014) and fluidity (Malhotra and Majchrzak 2021).

On the other hand, lack of conceptual depth stymies development of normative principles around ephemerality, raising potentiality for ephemerality-related risk (McPeak 2017; Shein 2013). Ephemerality highlights, for example, regulatory and corporate compliance concerns around the technical preservation of knowledge (Kelly and Baron 2021). Ephemerality-based social media[1] are already implicated in US election interference (Mueller 2016). Uber has directed employees to no longer use such platforms for Uber-related business. And JPMorgan have been fined $200 m for failing to archive employee business communication via third-party apps. While ephemeral functionality can help address concerns around storage constraints, data persistence, and 'authentic' digital communication (Giallorenzo et al. 2019), we will not adequately regulate for the consequences of digital ephemerality without better understanding what ephemerality implies. Enhanced understanding may also help disentangle the ephemeral from issues like privacy, anonymity, and trust (Welsh 2020; Schlesinger et al. 2017).

However, despite noteworthy IS reference to the ephemeral, to the best of our knowledge no extant IS research delineates the concept in depth. Ephemerality is receiving attention in other fields. In the humanities and social sciences, the ephemeral informs interpretations of modernity and postmodernity (e.g.: Simmel 1900; Harvey 1989; Castells 1996; Bauman 2000; Rosa 2019). There is a rich lineage of ephemerality as a concept in the performance arts (Reason 2006) and in media studies (Grainge 2011). Philosophers (e.g.: Bergson 1911, 1946; Buci-Glucksmann 2014; Grosz 2013), artists (e.g.: Purpura 2009), and urban planners (e.g.: Crane 2015; Vera and Mehrotra 2015)

---

[1] Examples of 'ephemerality-based platforms' (Morlok et al. 2018) include Snapchat, Telegram, Wickr, Clubhouse, and Confide. Other apps are also adding ephemeral functions to their platforms, such as Facebook and Instagram Vanish Mode, TikTok Stories, WhatsApp View Once, and Twitter Spaces. Web-tools like TweetDelete enable automatic deletion of tweets.

have been inspired by the ephemeral. Ephemerality is also a feature of studies in philosophy of science (Glennan 2010), organization studies (e.g.: Bakker et al. 2016; Elkjaer 2017; Sydow 2017), computer science (e.g.: Schlesinger et al. 2017), consumer research (Bardhi and Eckhardt 2017), cyberpsychology (Utz et al. 2015), marketing (e.g.: Belanche et al. 2019), and communication (Bayer et al. 2015; Kaun and Stiernstedt 2004). The contexts of digitalization are common to most recent studies.

Digital technology is supporting the response to the Covid-19 pandemic (Doyle and Conboy 2020). Whether changes forced by this crisis endure or are themselves ephemeral remains to be seen (Bentata 2019). Ephemeral communication may prevail in business settings (Goldberg and Prive 2022), just as 'ephemeral ICU beds' may be standardized in health settings (Lefrant et al. 2021). The pandemic has also brought into focus the ephemeral nature *of* digital technologies. We suggest that the IS perspective on ephemerality should be widely and uniquely informative, not least because ephemerality is seen to challenge both social and technical norms (Haber 2019; McRoberts et al. 2017). The aim of this research, therefore, is to contribute toward overcoming the issues and realizing the benefits outlined above by providing a rich definition and conceptualization of the ephemeral based upon an interdisciplinary literature review of the term.

The remainder of this article is structured as follows: in Sect. 2, we discuss the theoretical background relevant to the review; in Sect. 3, we outline our methodological approach; in Sect. 4, we present our interdisciplinary review of the ephemeral; in Sect. 5, we present a standalone review of the ephemeral in IS; in Sect. 6, we propose a definition for ephemeral and develop a framework of ephemeral characteristics; in Sect. 7, we outline incongruence between this framework and IS conceptualization.

2 Theoretical Background

As per *Merriam-Webster* (2022), the etymological roots of 'ephemeral' are in the Greek word *ephēmeros* from the stems *epi-* (meaning 'on' or 'in') and *hēmera* (meaning 'day'), yielding the adjective *ephemeron* (meaning 'lasting (only) a day'). It is not until the 1800s, however, that an increase is noted in the use of the adjectival form *ephemeral* through its 'application to transitory objects and abstract ideas' (Young 2003).

'Ephemeral' thus emerges in the nineteenth century as a 'signifier' of modernity (Marcus and Saka 2006). Baudelaire (1964), characterizing modernity (in part) as 'the ephemeral, the fugitive, the contingent,' worries about 'a riot of [ephemeral] details'. As such, the task is to 'distill the eternal from the transitory' (*ibid.*), which sets an antagonistic and dualistic template of sorts, particularly in Western thinking, for the modernist relationship with ephemerality. In modernity, the ephemeral is 'that which is resistant to meaning' (Doane 2002, p. 11). For Marx, Dostoevsky, and Goethe, the ephemeral must be 'confronted' and, as is possible, 'dealt with' (Harvey 1989). This negative, acutely modernist sense of the ephemeral is borne not only of its problematic 'representability' (Doane 2002, p. 11), of our inability to fix and quantify ephemeral value, but also of an emergent sense of the implications of ephemerality for stable societal structures, processes, and relations. In ephemeral digital contexts, for example, where the ephemeral has 'commonly [been] seen more as a problem than as a solution' (Cotta et al. 2015), 'fixing' the ephemeral remains the predominant objective.

The ephemeral is perhaps most directly confronted in postmodern thinking. Given its basis in a "weak' ontology of *becoming'* (Chia 1995), postmodernism 'wallows' in 'total acceptance of... ephemerality' (Harvey 1989, p. 27). By challenging the logic of language and organizing, the postmodernist aims to more adequately express 'the ephemeral aspects of process' (Chia 1995). It is not surprising then that the ephemeral receives particular attention in research traditions that, firstly, are significantly defined by their relation to the transitory and, secondly, wrestle with postmodern perspectives. For example, Artieri and colleagues (2021) note that ephemerality is a core focus in performance studies (e.g.: Phelan 1993) and in media studies (e.g.: Grainge 2011). On one level, the primary research challenge of the ephemeral is to 'write time' (Reason 2006). However, time is not the only concern when considering ephemerality.

Across the literature, two dimensions of the ephemeral reflect dictionary definitions: the temporal and the material. The temporal refers, as per standard definition (*ephemeral*), to experiences or perceptions of short duration: the perception of a rainbow, the experience of verbal interaction, the brief timeline of an ephemeral digital text. The material refers, as per standard definition (*ephemera*), to objects or things of time-limited and insubstantial value: train tickets, event programs, the content of an ephemeral digital text. As will be developed in Sects. 4, 5, 6, and 7, however, the ephemeral is not merely time-bound, singular, and insubstantial: the unstable ephemeral is also repetitive, recombinatory, and durable, with agency and meaning distributed in time.

3 Methodological Approach

Motivated by an interdisciplinary IS review (Smith et al. 2012) of another 'hard-to-fix' concept (privacy), we follow the three-stage, concept-centric review approach proposed by Webster and Watson (2002). First, we performed a broad search spanning the information systems, social sciences, philosophy, humanities, marketing, management, and organization theory literatures. Secondly, working backward to broaden the scope (*ibid.*), we reviewed citations for articles identified in step one, identifying literature of potential interest in other disciplines, including performance and media studies. Finally, we used Web of Science to work forward (*ibid.*), identifying further candidate articles citing the key articles previously identified. 156 articles and 18 books were selected.

4 Interdisciplinary Review of the Ephemeral

Sub-Sects. 4.1 through 4.4 present our interdisciplinary review of the ephemeral.

4.1 Short-Lived: Speed, Compression, Limitation

Ephemeral timespans range from split seconds, through minutes, weeks, and months, to years (Doring et al. 2013; Datry et al. 2017; Vidal-Abarca et al. 2020). Nevertheless, in any specific context, the ephemeral always seems relatively short-lived (Schneider and Foot 2004), always conveys 'connotations of brevity and evanescence' (Grainge 2011, p. 3). For example, ephemeral products (such as hygiene products (López-Forniés and Sierra-Pérez 2021) or digital products, like Snapchat (Villaespesa and Wowkowych 2020) are 'short-term oriented' (Janssen et al. 2014). Ephemeral 'briefness', however, is not only defined in terms of duration. The short-lived quality of the ephemeral is also shaped by interrelated forms of speed, compression, and limitation.

Firstly, social theorists describe ephemeral in terms of an accelerating pace of change (e.g.: Bauman 2000; Urry 2000; Rosa 2013). Ephemeral speed is evident in turnover of technologies, products, labor processes, ideas, and images (Urry 1995, p. 177); the 'high-speed temporality' of social media (Arda 2021); speed of access to consumption (Bardhi and Eckhardt 2017), and ephemeral organizations 'quickly convert[ing] decision into action' (Lanzara 1983). However, for Chun (2008) we must 'think beyond speed' because 'flow and segmentation do not quite encompass digital media's ephemerality.'

Secondly, the ephemeral compresses perceptual boundaries of value to timeframes localised to the present. This compressed relationship of the ephemeral and the present time reinforces its short-lived nature. That the ephemeral 'inhabits the present' (Chun 2016, p. 160) and is perceivable in the 'here and now' is 'essential for [its] effectiveness' (Grudin 2001, citing Toda 1999). Social theory abstractions like 'time-space compression' (Harvey 1989), 'timeless time' (Castells 1996), 'instantaneous time' (Urry 2000), and 'liquid modernity' (Bauman 2000), theorize this ephemeral quality. Liquid modernity, for example, describes change so short-lived, quickly changing, and present-oriented that effective stabilization of societal structures is no longer feasible. Eckhardt and Bardhi (2020), drawing from Bauman to develop a framework of 'liquid consumption' around three constructs (one being ephemerality (Bardhi and Eckhardt 2017), note that the ephemeral refers to 'the expiration date of value increasingly shortening'.

Thirdly, the short-lived ephemeral is limited. 'Anchored in the present' (He and Kivetz 2016), ephemeral time is 'fundamentally perishable' (Reason 2006) and the ephemeral moment materially 'constrained' (Bayer et al. 2015). Ephemeral live performance is an example (Barba 1992). Dance, for instance, is said to exist at a 'perpetual vanishing point' (Siegel 1972). Phelan (1993) and Auslander (1999) note ephemeral live performance is based upon disappearance; ephemeral organizations 'are there to disappear' (Lanzara 1983); for Grainge (2011), the ephemerality of web content means that 'digital materials are always under threat of disappearing'; and digital texts can be materially and temporally restricted to a specific number of views or a pre-determined span of viewing time (Chen and Cheung 2019; Vazquez-Herrero et al. 2019).

In sum, the short-lived (durational) quality of the ephemeral is characterized by speed (of change), compression (of space, time, agency, experience, value, and/or relevance), and limitation (of space, time, agency, experience, value, and/or relevance).

4.2 Repetitive: Anticipated, Varied

Ephemeral time is a time 'of repetitions and variations' (Buci-Glucksmann 2012). Performance scholars illuminate ephemeral repetition through the logic that 'ephemerality [is] repeated each night of a repeated live performance' (Reason 2006). TV programs are 'ephemeral in the sense of being both fleeting and repeated', with the *most repeated* programs particularly ephemeral (Uricchio 2011, p. 28–31). The ephemeral is also cyclically repetitive. Brassley (1998) notes ephemeral cycles in the study of landscapes, ranging from twice-daily (i.e.: tide movement) to progression of the seasons. And for Vera and

Mehrotra (2015), the cyclically celebrated event in the ephemeral city of Kumbh Mela expresses 'a range of ephemeral configurations.' In such places – and others, like humanitarian camps, work settlements, and music festivals – the life cycle of the ephemeral object (be it city, camp, settlement, or festival environment) – aligns with the duration of the activity so that objective start and end times are predictable.

Ephemeral repetition, therefore, not only infers orientation to the ephemeral 'past' but also anticipation of the ephemeral 'future'. Anticipation can range from the relative certainty of '*anticipated ephemera*' (Brassley 1998) to the uncertainty of the ephemeral as 'a space of projective anticipation' (Crane 2015). For example, 'anticipation of the future embodied actions and activities', or *how* ephemerality *might* be repeated, is an important feature in ephemeral work settings (Hindmarsh and Pilnick 2007). Drawing from Lefebvre (2003), Crane (2015) describes the ephemeral urban space as one of 'projective anticipation', where 'groups take control of spaces for expressive actions and constructions, which are soon destroyed' (Lefebvre 2003, p. 130). Covid-19 virus-testing and vaccination clinics are illustrative instantiations of ephemeral urban space. The ephemerality of such spaces is characterized not only by being short-lived but also by the anticipation that the ephemeral will be repeated *in* the space.

Ephemeral repetition is evident in the habituation of ephemeral actions. Consider the ephemerality of a mouse-click or the ease with which the ephemeral is enacted through taps and swipes on mobile platforms. In this sense, following Bergson and Deleuze, repetition through habit enables forms of stability 'in a universe in which nothing truly repeats' (Grosz 2013). For Deleuze (1994), to repeat 'is to behave in a certain manner, but in relation to something unique or singular.' Referencing festivals, Deleuze notes repetitions 'do not add a second and a third time to the first, but carry the first time to the 'nth' power.' Hindmarsh and Pilnick (2007) reflect this understanding in their study of ephemeral workteams in surgical settings, where actors '*(re)produce* the routine or normative character of activities *for the first time again*.' In repetition, the ephemeral orients to the past to stabilize the present in a variation of that past, and, simultaneously, anticipates the future in repeated and varied forms of the ephemeral present.

For Phelan (1993), repetition marks the repeated as 'different'. Ephemerality repeats in ephemeral ways: there is always some variation in repetition of the ephemeral.

4.3 Recombinatory: Multiple Possibilities

The ephemeral is recombinatory. Recombination repurposes the 'old' ephemeral artifact, action, space, or experience in a 'new' ephemeral present. The ephemeral city is dismantled, its material components 'recycled or repurposed' (Vera and Mehrotra 2015). Or 'old' ephemeral media texts are recombined in 'new' ephemeral sequences and contexts (Urricchio 2011, p. 28). Digital technology intensifies the capacity for ephemeral recombination. For example, the ephemeral recombination of prodigious volumes of diverse and ephemeral digital texts (Grainge 2011, p. 3; Chun 2008) is endemic in the copying, cutting, pasting, splicing, and (re)circulation *of* ephemeral digital texts.

We distinguish the ephemerally repetitive from the ephemerally recombinatory in two interrelated ways. Firstly, where the meaning or knowledge gained from the ephemerally repetitive is sufficiently *similar* to the past or 'first' ephemeral, the meaning or knowledge gained from the ephemerally recombined is sufficiently *different*. The roof of a food stall in the ephemeral city is recombined as one wall of a dwelling in a work settlement. Or the rerun of a television series recombines the ephemeral meaning of the artifact for both returning and first-time viewers (Urricchio 2011, p. 28).

And secondly, where the ephemerally repetitive *anticipates* the future, the ephemerally recombinatory opens up the future in *multiple possibilities*. Lefebvre (2003) defines the urban ephemeral space as 'multifunctional, polyvalent, transfunctional' (Crane 2015). In the ephemeral city, there are 'infinite possibilities for recombination' (Vera and Mehrotra 2015). In ephemeral organizations, the 'possibilities for action and response are multiplied' (Lanzara 1983). In the examples cited, however, there remains a sense of linearity and succession, which the ephemeral is also theorized to disrupt.

In its future orientation, recombination is more fragmented and disjointed than repetition. For Castells (1996), 'timeless time' disorders succession and fosters simultaneity, creating what he terms 'structural ephemerality' (Castells 2004, p. 57). For example, remote and non-linear work-day models (Gibbs et al. 2021; Dong et al. 2002) disorder the traditional segregation and linear flow of the working day. In a similar vein, media scholars note that as the digitized file can be recombined (Kompare 2002, p. 1), it disorders the traditional, linear logic of broadcast flow (Williams 1974). In cultures organized around systems of electronic media, the various forms of 'ephemeral symbolic communication' (Castells 2000) become a productive constituent of ephemeral 'timeless time' (Castells 1996). Fundamental to these systems, through digitalization and recurrent communication, is their recombinatory ability (Castells 2004, p. 12).

In sum, while the ephemeral is relatively short-lived, recombination of ephemeral experience, space and/or artifact enables repurposing *of* the ephemeral *from* the ephemeral in fragmented, disjointed ways that opens up the future in multiple possibilities.

4.4 Unstable, Durable

The ephemeral is unstable. Ephemerality is associated with organizational instability (Bechky 2006; van Marrewijk et al. 2016). Ephemeral computing environments are unstable, ever-changing (Cotta et al. 2016) and ephemeral time is 'unstable time, made up of fragments' (Guillaume and Huysmans 2018). In processual terms, 'ephemeral emergence' (Sawyer 2005, p. 210–214) cannot be known in advance as it occurs within 'episodic interactive encounters' (Tsoukas 2016). In postmodern terms, the ephemeral 'is interested in following traces, glimmers, and specks of things' (Munoz 1996, p. 10).

Ephemeral instability underpins the modernist challenge of 'fixing' the ephemeral. Archivists struggle to categorize, store, and define ephemera (Young 2003). The 'stage detritus' concept highlights the 'unstable' state of live performance (Reason 2006, p. 54) and the ephemeral is used to signify 'moving image detritus' (Grainge 2011, p. 2), such as outdated TV sets (Hastie 2007). Finally, the ephemeral as a concept is somewhat passed over in the processual literature, where reality is ephemerally unstable and stability must be accounted for (Chia and Nayak 2017). The Bergsonian sense of duration applies in processual thinking, where 'temporariness' is 'centerstage' (Bakker et al. 2016) and 'the ephemeral and dynamic becomingness of human experience as a continuous flow of creative action' is the focus (Garud et al. 2015).

However, the short-lived, unstable ephemeral is also durable. The ephemeral is 'embodied or materialized in durable objects' (López-Bertran 2019). And ephemeral objects of value are 'the durable material of cultural resilience and continuity' (Lepani 2012, p. 75), with the short-lived limitation of such objects catalyzing their durability (MacCarthy 2017). Digital technology intensifies ephemeral durability, complicating 'any clear division between technology as *either* permanent *or* ephemeral' (Evans 2011, p. 157). Media scholars note that although the 'configuration of space/time constructed through online media' is unstable and fragmented, the ephemeral fragments 'are so abundant as to be inexhaustible' and 'connect us into a network' (Grainge 2011, p. 224). In this network, the ephemeral is 'made to endure' (Chun 2008).

Durability attunes us to the anticipation and possibility *in* the ephemeral and distributes the ephemeral in time. The past of an ephemeral text (e.g.: a TV program) is 'reactivated' through 'knowledge that has since been acquired' (Uricchio 2011, p. 29/30) or the 'affective ephemera of likes and comments' (Haber 2019) stimulate what has objectively passed, regenerating fresh ephemeral agency, meaning, and durability.

Durability also guides us toward the idea that the ephemeral is not only short-lived but 'eternal' (e.g.: Castells' 'eternal ephemerality' (2000, p. 497). In a landmark new media paper, Chun (2008) suggests digital technology originates non-linear temporalities that move 'simultaneously towards the future and the past', proliferating 'enduring ephemerals'. The modernist tension inherent to the ephemeral no longer seems a dualism but a duality: the ephemeral is fleeting *and* persistent (van Nimwegen and Bergman 2019), old *and* new (Chun 2008), 'open-ended *and* constrained' (Tsoukas 2016), short-lived *and* durable (Pimlott 2011; Gale 2009). We are given a sense of this perspective in Prado and Sapsed's (2016) study of ephemeral innovations in project-based organizations, where 'permanence is only realized through activation in the temporary.'

Finally, Husserl emphasizes that no experience is ephemeral merely in the sense of being short-lived or momentary (Moran 2011). Rather, lived experience and 'the objective moment constituted in it, may become "forgotten"; but for all this, it in no way disappears without a trace... it has merely become latent' (Husserl 1948/1973, p. 122). Husserlian traces are afforded material and temporal durability in the digital network. The short-lived, unstable ephemeral, in ephemeral ways, endures.

5   A Review of the Ephemeral in IS

Sub-Sects. 5.1 through 5.8 outline a review of the ephemeral in the IS literature. The review is categorized into eight representative IS research contexts.

5.1   The Nature of IS/IT

Reviewed IS research recognize ephemerality as a characteristic of both the IS "core", nature, or identity (Lyytinen and King 2004; Lim et al. 2007) and the IS research focus (Niederman et al. 1990; El Sawy 2003; Desouza et al. 2006). Dictionary definition and study context (DDC) primarily inform adjectival application of the term.

5.2 Digital/Digitalization

Ephemeral a characteristic of digital material (Yoo 2010; Kallinikos et al. 2010; Urquhart and Vaast 2012; Lehmann and Recker 2019; Von Briel et al. 2018; Lyytinen 2021) and experience of digital technology (Yoo 2010; Bødker 2014; 2017). DDC primarily applies. Ephemeral associated with change (Von Briel et al. 2018; Mousavi Baygi 2021), editability (Kallinikos et al. 2010; 2013), malleability (Yoo 2010; von Briel et al. 2018), fluidity (Malhotra and Majchrzak 2021), and forgetting (Bannon 2006).

5.3 Information and Knowledge

Ephemerality a characteristic of knowledge (Salovaara and Tuunainen 2015; Vaast et al. 2006; Alavi and Leidner 2002), design knowledge (vom Brocke et al. 2021), and knowledge in dynamic environments (Peterson et al. 2002). For Alavi and Leidner (2002), 'some knowledge' is ephemeral. For Salovaara and Tuunainen (2015), ephemerality of knowledge refers to 'temporal fluctuation in its relevance'. Here, the ephemerality of knowledge is a temporal variable and is typically contrasted with *stable* or *kernel* knowledge. DDC primarily applies. For Kallinikos (2009), all information is time-bound and ephemeral. Here, data production intensifies information ephemerality.

5.4 Organisation

Ephemerality of organizations (Prester et al. 2019) identified in organisational politics (Beath 1991), forms and structures (Lee 1993; Ahuja and Choudhury 1999; Truex et al. 2000; Carstensen 2004), and the boundaries distinguishing organization, ICTs, and environment (Holmström and Truex 2003; Hovorka and Germonprez 2011; Mousavi Baygi et al. 2021). DDC primarily applies. IS/IT is driving emergence of ephemeral organisational structures (Truex et al. 2000; Carstensen 2004) and forms (Ahuja and Choudhury 1999). Association with organizational fluidity (e.g.: Prester et al. 2019).

5.5 Online Groups, Communities, Teams

Ephemerality is a characteristic of online groups, communities, and teams (Sarker and Sahay 2003; Bernstein et al. 2011; Butler et al. 2014; Fuller and Summers 2017; Quintarelli et al. 2019). DDC typically applies. Ephemeral groups characterized in opposition to 'persistent' groups (Quintarelli et al. 2019). Sarker and Sahay (2003) adopt Castells' (1996) perspective, characterizing virtual teams as both 'eternal' and 'ephemeral'.

5.6 Social Media

Ephemerality a characteristic of social media (Xu et al. 2018; Cavalcanti et al. 2017; Morlok et al. 2017; 2018; Browne et al. 2017; Wakefield and Wakefield 2018; Sibona et al. 2020). DDC primarily applies. For example, a three-second Snapchat 'snap' is more ephemeral than a ten-second 'snap' (Morlok et al. 2018). Ephemerality characterized as a technically controllable feature (Cavalcanti et al. 2017; Morlok et al. 2017; Wakefield and Wakefield 2018) and refers to social media content not easily digitally saved or stored, and/or only available for a limited time (Cavalcanti et al. 2017; Morlok et al. 2018). The ephemeral typically conceptualized in opposition to persistence or durability (Xu et al. 2018; Marabelli et al. 2016; Morlok et al. 2017; Faik et al. 2020).

5.7 Blockchain Technology

Ephemerality a characteristic of specific technical functions (e.g.: redactable blockchain; ephemeral 'trapdoor keys' and 'wallets') that may enhance blockchain privacy and security (Courtois and Mercer 2017; Henry et al. 2018; Tedeschi et al. 2018; Ashritha et al. 2019; Huang et al. 2019). DDC exclusively applies.

5.8 Miscellaneous Contexts

Ephemeral identified as a characteristic of communication (Ljungberg and Sorensen 1998; Burke and Chidambaram 1999; Kakihara and Sorensen 2001; Kakar et al. 2012), contemporary relationships (Smith and McKeen 2012; Orman 2015), after-hours work (Chen and Karahanna 2018), moods and emotions (Zhang 2013), and of how engagement with digital technology feels (Bødker and Jensen 2017). DDC primarily applies.

6 Defining and Characterizing Ephemerality

Based upon our reviews, we propose the following definition for 'ephemeral':

the ephemeral refers to unstable times, spaces, artifacts, and actors that are both relatively short-lived and repetitive, recombinatory, and durable.

Below, we characterize the ephemeral through the four dimensions of Yoo's (2010) schematic for experiential computing: space, time, artifacts, and actors. We consider the schematic appropriate for three reasons. Firstly, experiential computing is concerned with 'computing in everyday life experiences' (*ibid.*). The ephemeral is fundamentally concerned with that which is processed and encountered in the everyday (Guillaume and Huysmans 2018). Secondly, experimental computing describes a spatiotemporal context 'that is temporary and unfolds over time' (Yoo 2010). The material and temporal ephemeral is both short-lived and distributed in time. Thirdly, we consider the schematic an appropriately broad structure for conceptualizing the ephemeral in IS research.

Table 1. Conceptual framework of ephemeral dimensions and characteristics

Ephemeral dimensions	Ephemeral characteristics			
	Short-lived	Repetitive	Recombinatory	Unstable, Durable
Time	*Speed:* of change *Compression:* of and to the present time *Limitation:* by transience, disappearance	*Repetitive:* recycling past in repetition; ephemera-lity increased in repetition. *Anticipated:* looks to future repetition. *Varied:* present is stabilized in variation of the past	*Recombinatory:* repurposing of past in present; repurposed present sufficiently different to past; repurposed time disordered. *Multiple possibilities:* future is open, uncertain	*Unstable:* emergent, volatile, non-linear, fragmented, fleeting temporal traces. *Durable:* duality of ephemeral time as short-lived *and* durable/ 'eternal'
Space	*Speed:* of spatial transformation *Compression:* of space and the present time *Limitation:* of spatial value, use, and relevance	*Repetitive:* recycling of space; ephemerality increased in repetition. *Anticipated:* ephemeral will be repeated in the space. *Varied:* present space stabilized in similar variation of past	*Recombinatory:* repurposing of space that is sufficiently different to past use or form of the space. *Multiple possibilities:* future ephemerality of the space is open, uncertain	*Unstable:* short-lived spatial limitations. *Durable:* ephemeral materialized and extend-ed in space through repetition and/or recombination; endurance catalyzed by *being* short-lived
Artifact	*Speed:* of material production, circulation, and consumption. *Compression:* of material value, use, relevance. *Limitation:* of social and technical functions	*Repetitive:* recycling of artifact; ephemerality increased in repetition. *Anticipated:* ephemeral will be repeated in artifa-ct. *Varied:* artifact stabilized in variation of past	*Recombinatory:* repurposing of artifact sufficiently different to past use or form of the artifact. *Multiple possibilities:* future ephemerality of the artifact is open, uncertain	*Unstable:* short-lived material limitations. *Durable:* ephemeral materialized and extended through repetition and/or recombination; endurance catalyzed by *being* short-lived
Actor	*Speed:* of perception, experience, agency *Compression:* of perception, experience, agency to the present time *Limitation:* of perception, experience, agency to the present time	*Repetitive:* recycling of agency, experience; ephemerality increased in repetition. *Anticipated:* future repetition of agency, experience. *Varied:* present agency, experience stabilized in variation of the past	*Recombinatory:* repurposing perception, experience, agency sufficiently different to past perception, experience, agency. *Multiple possibilities:* future ephemerality of perception, experience, agency is open, uncertain	*Unstable:* short-lived limitations of perception, experience, agency. *Durable:* ephemeral embodied, extended in perception, experience, agency through repetition and/or recombination; endurance catalyzed by *being* short-lived

7 Ephemeral Characteristics: IS Congruence/Incongruence

Table 2 outlines congruence and incongruence between the ephemeral characterized in Table 1 and in IS research (Sect. 5), briefly noting the consequences of incongruence.

Table 2. Ephemeral characteristics: IS congruence/incongruence and consequences

Ephem. charac	IS conceptual congruence	Conceptual incongruence and consequences (and/or implications)
Short-lived (fast, compressed, limited)	Short-lived DDC conceptualization is predominant; duration and limitation emphasized[a]; speed noted (e.g.: Marton et al. 2013; vom Brocke et al. 2020); compression *implicitly* noted in two reviewed studies (Sarker and Sahay 2003; Jones et al. 2008)	*DDC consequences:* ephemeral technically controllable (e.g.: Morlok et al. 2018; Wakefield and Wakefield 2018); ephemerality an assumption (Morlok 2017). *DDC implication:* digital *more* ephemeral than physical and/or material (Yoo 2010; von Briel et al. 2018)
Repetitive (anticipated, varied)	*Implicit reference only:* short innovation contexts with 'determinate ephemeral life cycles' (Malhotra and Majchrzak 2021); repeatability and digital ephemera (Marabelli et al. 2016); system retrieval of ephemeral knowledge and 'fluctuation of [knowledge] relevance' (Salovaara and Tuunainen 2013; 2015)	No explicit reference to ephemeral repetition. *Consequences:* downgrading of ephemeral value and/or relevance; missed opportunity for study of ephemeral (e.g.: new ephemeral patterns; describing the ephemeral past and future); inaccurate theory development and design; increased risk
Recombinatory (multiple possibilities)	*Implicit reference only:* ephemeral links 'formed, broken, and reformed' (Ahuja and Choudhury 1999); ephemeral disrup-ting communication sequencing (Rennecker and Godwin 2008); data growth inc-reasing info. ephemerality (Kallinikos 2009); digital editability (Kallinikos et al. 2013) congruent with recombination	No explicit reference to ephemeral recombination. *Consequences:* downgr-ading ephemeral value and/or relevan-ce; missed opportunity for study of ep-hemeral (e.g.: material, temporal eph-emeral editability; identifying ephemeral combinations); inaccurate theory development, design; increased risk

(*continued*)

Table 2. (*continued*)

Ephem. charac	IS conceptual congruence	Conceptual incongruence and consequences (and/or implications)
Unstable	DDC applies but explicit association of ephemeral with continual change and environmental contextualization, dyna-mism, emergence, and liquidity (e.g.: Truex et al. 2000; Peterson et al. 2002; Avital 2004; Carstensen 2004; Vaast et al. 2006; Mousavi Baygi et al. 2021)	*Consequences*: DDC and instability reinforce 'negative' ephemeral conceptualization (e.g.: Alter 2003; 2012; Lim et al. 2007; Kreps 2018) and the IS/'technological' aim to 'capture' the ephemeral (e.g.: Urquhart and Vaast 2012; Ives et al. 2016)
Durable	Sociomaterial moving away from dualistic accounts (e.g.: collapsing division between material and social (Hovorka and Germonprez 2011) and digital ephemera afforded temporal depth (Marabelli et al. 2016) – but DDC still typically applies (e.g.: Hedman et al. 2013; Hafermalz and Riemer 2015). Two reviewed studies note ephemeral 'eternality' (Sarker and Sahay 2003; Jones et al. 2008)	General incongruence. *Consequences*: ephemeral set against conceptual opp-osite[b]; durability is sidestepped (e.g.: ephemeral as 'perception' (Rennecker et al. 2008; Morlok et al. 2017), delineation of ephemeral and 'recalled' (Oja and Galliers 2011), and ephemeral leaving 'no persistent trace' (Ljungberg and Sørensen 1998)); DDC assumptions put research focus on user characteristics and experience at the expense of the ephemeral concept

[a] E.G.: Alavi and Leidner 2002; Bannon 2006; Desouza 2006; Smith and McKeen 2012; Wakefield and Wakefield 2018; Xu et al. 2018; Sibona et al. 2020; Browne et al. 2017; Morlok et al. 2017; 2018; Urquhart and Vaast 2012; Carvalho et al. 2020; He et al. 2021
[b] E.G.: Kakihara and Sørensen 2001; Bernstein et al. 2011; Ives et al. 2016; Morlok et al. 2017; Xu et al. 2018; Wakefield and Wakefield 2018; Quintarelli et al. 2019

8   Conclusion

In this article, we define and conceptualize the ephemeral as not only short-lived and unstable but also repetitive, recombinatory and durable. In future studies, we hope to further develop, refine, and test our definition and framework in IS contexts, such as digitalization, social media, and knowledge and information management.

Acknowledgement. "This work was supported with the financial support of the Science Foundation Ireland grant 13/RC/2094 and co-funded under the European Regional Development

Fund through the Southern and Eastern Regional Operational Programme to Lero - the Science Foundation Ireland Research Centre for Software (www.lero.ie)".

References

Ahuja, M., Choudhury, V.: Evolution of virtual organizations over time: an empirical examination. AMCIS Proc. **209** (1999)

Alavi, M., Leidner, D.E.: Review: Knowledge management and knowledge management systems: conceptual foundations and research issues. MIS Q. **25**(1), 107–136 (2002)

Alter, S.: The IS core - XI: sorting out the issues about the core, scope, and identity of the IS field. Commun. Assoc. Inf. Syst. **12**(41) (2003)

Alter, S.: Exploring the temporal nature of sociomateriality from a work system perspective. Business Analytics and Information Systems. Paper 23 (2012)

Arda, B.: Ephemeral social media visuals and their picturesque design: interaction and user experience in Instagram stories. Sapientiae, Film and Media Studies **19**, 156–175 (2021). https://doi.org/10.2478/ausfm-2021-0010

Arner, D.W., Barberis, J.N., Walker, J., Buckley, R.P., Dahdal, A.M., Zetzsche, D.A.: Digital finance and the COVID-19 crisis (2020). https://ssrn.com/abstract=3558889

Ashritha, K., Sindhu, M., Lakshmy, K.V.: Redactable blockchain using enhanced chameleon hash function. In: 5th International Conference on Advanced Computing and Communication Systems (ICACCS) (2019)

Artieri et al., 2021. Artieri, G., Brilli, S., Zurovac, E.: Below the radar: private groups, locked platforms, and ephemeral content—introduction to the special issue. Social Media and Society (2021)

Auslander, P.: Liveness: Performance in a Mediatized Culture. Routledge, London (1999)

Bakker, R., DeFillippi, R., Schwab, A., Sydow, J.: Temporary organizing: promises, processes, problems. Organ. Stud. 1–17 (2006). https://doi.org/10.1177/0170840616655982

Bannon, L.J.: Forgetting as a feature, not a bug: the duality of memory and implications for ubiquitous computing. CoDesign **2**(1), 3–15 (2006)

Bauman, Z.: Liquid Modernity. Polity Press, Cambridge (2000)

Barba, E.: Efermaele: "that which will be said afterwards." Drama Rev. **36**(2), 77–80 (1992)

Bardhi, F., Eckhardt, G.: Liquid consumption. J. Consum. Res. **44** (2017). https://doi.org/10.1093/jcr/ucx050

Baudelaire, C.: The Painter of Modern Life and Other Essays. Trans. Mayne, J. Phaidon, London (1964)

Bayer, J.B., Ellison, N.B., Schoenebeck, S.Y., Falk, E.B.: Sharing the small moments: ephemeral social interaction on Snapchat. Inf. Commun. Soc. **19**(7), 956–977 (2015)

Beath, C.: Supporting the information technology champion. MIS Q. (1991)

Bechky, B.: Gaffers, gofers, and grips: role-based coordination in temporary organizations. Organ. Sci. **17**(1), 3–21 (2006)

Belanche, D., Cenjor, I., Pérez-Rueda, A.: Instagram stories versus Facebook wall: an advertising effectiveness analysis. Span. J. Mark. - ESIC (2019)

Bentata, Y.: COVID 2019 pandemic: a true digital revolution and birth of a new educational era, or an ephemeral phenomenon? Med. Educ. Online **25**(1) (2020). https://doi.org/10.1080/10872981.2020.1781378

Bergson, H.: Time and Free Will. George Allen and Unwin, New York (1911/2005)

Bergson, H.: Creative Evolution. Random House Modern Library, New York (1946/1992)

Bernstein, M., Monroy-Hernandez, A., Harry, D., Andre, P., Panovich, K., Vargas, G.: 4chan and /b/: an analysis of anonymity and ephemerality in a large online community. In: Association for the Advancement of Artificial Intelligence (2011)

Bødker, M.: Walking, sensing, participation: three meditations for experiental computing. In: Proceedings of the European Conference on Information Systems (ECIS). Israel, 9–11 June (2014)

Bødker, M.: "What else is there...?": reporting meditations in experiential computing. Eur. J. Inf. Syst. **26**(3), 274–286 (2017). https://doi.org/10.1057/s41303-017-0041-6

Bødker, M., Jensen, T.B.: Sounding out IS? Moods and affective entanglements in experiental computing. In: Proceedings of the 25th European Conference on Information Systems (ECIS), Portugal, pp. 3003–3012 (2017)

Brassley, P.: On the unrecognized significance of the ephemeral landscape. Landsc. Res. **23**(2), 119–132 (1998). https://doi.org/10.1080/01426399808706531

Browne, O., O'Reilly, P., Hutchinson, M.: Ephemeral returns: social network valuations and perceived privacy. In: ICIS Proceedings, pp. 1–10 (2017)

Buci-Glucksmann, C.: Esthétique de l'éphémère, Paris, Galilée, quoted in: Denoit, N. (2014) "Showing: Time": the Ephemeral Made Sublime. Hybrid [Online], p. 13 (2003). https://doi.org/10.4000/hybrid.115

Buci-Glucksmann, C.: Time spirals: from the immemorial to the ephemeral. Translator: Jonathan Pollock (2012). http://dombis.com/wp-content/uploads/2012/11/CBG_Time-spirals.pdf

Buci-Glucksmann, C., Quinz, E.: "Ephemeral Heritages", for an aesthetics of the ephemeral. Interview with Christine Buci-glucksmann. Trans. Heft, S. Hybrid, n° 1 (2014)

Burke, K., Chidambaram, L.: How much bandwidth is enough? A longitudinal examination of media characteristics and group outcomes. MIS Q. **23**(4) (1999)

Burton-Jones, A., Butler, B., Scott, S., Xu, S.: Next-generation information systems theorizing: a call to action. MIS Q. **45**(1), 301–314 (2021)

Butler, B., Bateman, P., Gray, P., Gray, E.: An attraction-selection-attrition theory of online community size and resilience. MIS Q. **38**(3), 699–728 (2014)

Camacho, D., Lara-Cabrera, R., Merelo-Guervós, J.J., et al.: From ephemeral computing to deep bioinspired algorithms: new trends and applications. Future Gener. Comput. Syst. (2018)

Carroll, N., Conboy, K.: Normalising the "new normal": changing tech-driven work practices under pandemic time pressure. Int. J. Inf. Manage. (2020). https://doi.org/10.1016/j.ijinfomgt.2020.102186

Carstensen, P.H.: Developments in WIS development. ECIS Proc. **43** (2004). http://aisel.aisnet.org/ecis2004/43

Carvalho, A., Sambhara, C., Young, P.: What the history of Linux says about the future of cryptocurrencies. Commun. Assoc. Inf. Syst. **46** (2020). https://doi.org/10.17705/1CAIS.04602

Cavalcanti, L.H.C., Pinto, A., Brubaker, J.R., Dombrowski, L.S.: Media, meaning, and context loss in ephemeral communication platforms: a qualitative investigation on snapchat. In: CSCW, pp. 1934–1945 (2017). https://doi.org/10.1145/2998181.2998266

Castells, M.: The Information Age: Economy, Society and Culture. 2nd edn. Blackwell, Oxford (1996/2010)

Castells, M.: Materials for an exploratory theory of the network society. Br. J. Sociol. **51**(1), 5–24 (2000)

Castells, M.: Informationalism, networks, and the network society: a theoretical blueprint. Castells, M. (ed.) The Network Society: A Cross-Cultural Perspective. Edward Elgar, Northampton (2004)

Chen, A., Karahanna, E.: Life interrupted: the effects of technology-mediated work interruptions on work and nonwork outcomes. MIS Q. **42**(4), 1023–1042 (2018)

Chen, K-J., Cheung, H.: Unlocking the power of ephemeral content: the roles of motivations, gratification, need for closure, and engagement. Comput. Hum. Behav. (2019)

Chia, R.: From modern to postmodern organizational analysis. Organ. Stud. **16**, 579 (1995). https://doi.org/10.1177/017084069501600406

Chia, R., Nayak, A.: Circumventing the logic and limits of representation: otherness in east–west approaches to paradox. In: Smith, W., Lewis, M., Jarzabkowski, J., Langley, A. (eds.) The Oxford Handbook of Organizational Paradox. Oxford University Press (2017)

Chun, W.: The enduring ephemeral, or the future is a memory. Crit. Inquiry **35**(1), 148–171 (2008)

Chun, W.: Updating to Remain the Same: Habitual New Media. MIT Press (2016)

Cotta, C., Fernandez-Leiva, A., et al.: Ephemeral computing and bioinspired optimization, challenges and opportunities. In: Proceedings of the 7th International Joint Conference on Computational Intelligence (IJCCI 2015), pp. 319–324 (2015)

Cotta, C., et al.: Application areas of ephemeral computing: a survey. In: Nguyen, N., Kowalczyk, R., Filipe, J. (eds) Transactions on Computational Collective Intelligence XXIV. LNCS, vol. 9770. Springer, Berlin, Heidelberg (2016). https://doi.org/10.1007/978-3-662-53525-7_9

Courtois, N., Mercer, R.: Stealth address and key management techniques in blockchain systems. In: Proceedings of the 3rd International Conference on Information Systems Security and Privacy (ICISSP), pp. 559–566 (2017). https://doi.org/10.5220/0006270005590566

Crane, S.: Rewriting the battles of Algiers: ephemeral tactics in the city at war. Space Cult. **18**(4), 387–410 (2015)

Datry, T., et al.: Flow intermittence and ecosystem services in rivers of the Anthropocene. J. Appl. Ecol. (2017). https://doi.org/10.1111/1365-2664.12941

Deleuze, G.: Difference and Repetition. Trans. Paul Patton. Athlone, London (1994)

Desouza, K., El Sawy, O., Galliers, R., Loebbecke, C., Watson, R.: Beyond rigor and relevance towards responsibility and reverberation: information systems research that really matters. Commun. Assoc. Inf. Syst. **17**(1), 16 (2006). https://doi.org/10.17705/1CAIS.01716

Doane, M.A.: The Emergence of Cinematic Time. Harvard University Press (2002)

Dong, R., Wu, H., Ni, S., Lu, T.: The nonlinear consequences of working hours for job satisfaction: the moderating role of job autonomy. Curr. Psychol. 1–22 (2021). https://doi.org/10.1007/s12144-021-02463-3

Doyle, R., Conboy, K.: The role of IS in the covid-19 pandemic: a liquid-modern perspective. Int. J. Inf. Manage. (2020). https://doi.org/10.1016/j.ijinfomgt.2020.102184

Dwivedi, Y.K., et al.: Impact of COVID-19 pandemic on information management research and practice: transforming education, work and life. Int. J. Inf. Manage. **55**, 102211 (2020)

Eckhardt, G., Bardhi, F.: The value in de-emphasizing structure in liquidity. Mark. Theory **20**(4), 573–580 (2020)

Elkjaer, B.: Organizations as real and ephemeral. Zeitschrift für Weiterbildungsforschung **40**(1), 53–68 (2017). https://doi.org/10.1007/s40955-017-0086-0

El Sawy, O.: The IS core IX: the 3 faces of IS identity: connection, immersion, and fusion. Commun. Assoc. Inf. Syst. **12**, 39 (2003). https://doi.org/10.17705/1CAIS.01239

Evans, E.-J.: 'Carnaby Street, 10 a.m.': KateModern and the ephemeral dynamics of online drama. In: Ephemeral Media: Transitory Screen Culture from Television to YouTube. Palgrave Macmillan (2011)

Faik, I., Barrett, M., Oborn, E.: How does information technology matter in societal change? An affordance-based institutional logics perspective. MIS Q. (2020)

Fichman, R., Dos Santos, B., Zheng, Z.: Digital Innovation as a fundamental and powerful concept in the information systems curriculum. MIS Q. **38**(2), 329–353 (2014)

Fuller, R., Summers, J.: The impact of virtual team consistency on individual performance and perceptual outcomes over time. In: Proceedings of the 50th Hawaii International Conference on System Sciences (2017)

Gale, T.: Urban beaches, virtual worlds and 'the end of tourism'. Mobilities **4**(1), 119–138 (2009). https://doi.org/10.1080/17450100802657996

Garud, R., Simpson, B., Langley, A., Tsoukas, H.: How does novelty emerge? In: The Emergence of Novelty in Organizations. Perspectives on Process Organization Studies, pp. 1–24. Oxford University Press, Oxford (2015)

Glennan, S.: Ephemeral mechanisms and historical explanation. Erkenn. **72**, 251–266 (2010). https://doi.org/10.1007/s10670-009-9203-9

Giallorenzo, S., Montesi, F., Safina, L., Zingaro, S.P.: Ephemeral data handling in microservices. In: IEEE International Conference on Services Computing (SCC) (2019). https://doi.org/10.1109/SCC.2019.00048

Gibbs, M., Mengel, F., Siemroth, C.: Work from Home and Productivity: Evidence from Personnel and Analytics Data on IT Professionals. Becker Friedman Institute, University of Chicago (2021)

Gisdakis, S., Manolopoulos, V., Tao, S., Rusu, A., Papadimitratos, P.: Secure and privacy-preserving smartphone-based traffic information systems. IEEE Trans. Intell. Transp. Syst. (2014)

Goldberg, H., Prive, J.: And just like that, it was gone—the discoverability of ephemeral communications. https://www.law.com/thelegalintelligencer/2022/02/04/and-just-like-that-it-was-gone-the-discoverability-of-ephemeral-communications/. Accessed 14 April 2022

Grainge, P.: Ephemeral Media: Transitory Screen Culture from Television to YouTube. Palgrave Macmillan (2011)

Griffin, D., Denholm, J.: This isn't the first global pandemic, and it won't be the last. Here's what we've learned from 4 others throughout history. https://theconversation.com/this-isnt-the-first-global-pandemic-and-it-wont-be-the-last-heres-what-weve-learned-from-4-others-throughout-history-136231. Accessed 14 April 2022

Grosz, E.: Habit today: Ravaisson, Bergson Deleuze and us. Body Soc. **19**(2–3), 219 (2013)

Grudin, J.: Group dynamics and ubiquitous computing. Commun. ACM **45**(12), 74–78 (2001)

Guillaume, X., Huysmans, J.: The concept of 'the everyday': ephemeral politics and the abundance of life. Coop. Confl. (2018)

Haber, B.: The digital ephemeral turn: queer theory, privacy, and the temporality of risk. Media Cult. Soc. (2019)

Hafermalz, E., Riemer, K.: The question of materiality: mattering in the network society. ECIS 2015 Completed Research Papers. Paper 66 (2015)

Harvey, D.: The Condition of Postmodernity: an Enquiry into the Origins of Cultural Change. Blackwell, Cambridge (1989)

Hastie, A.: Detritus and the moving image: ephemera, materiality, history. J. Vis. Cult. **6**(2), 171–174 [1470–4129] (2007)

He, D., Kivetz, R.: Blink and you'll miss it: the consequences of ephemeral messaging. In: Moreau, P.M., Puntoni, S., Duluth, M.N. (eds.) NA - Advances in Consumer Research. USA: Association for Consumer Research, pp. 470–471 (2016)

He, Y., Xu, X., Huang, N., Hong, Y., Liu, D.: Preserving user privacy through ephemeral sharing design: a large-scale randomized field experiment in online dating. In: ICIS 2021 Proceedings (2021)

Hedman, J., Srinivasan, N., Lindgren, R.: Digital traces of information systems: sociomateriality made researchable. In: Thirty Fourth International Conference on Information Systems, Milan (2013)

Henry, R., Herzberg, A., Kate, A.: Blockchain access privacy: challenges and directions. Co-published by the IEEE Computer and Reliability Societies (2018)

Hindmarsh, J., Pilnick, A.: Knowing bodies at work: embodiment and ephemeral teamwork in anaesthesia. Organ. Stud. **28**(09), 1395–1416 (2007)

Holmstroem, J., Truex, D.: Social theory in IS research: some recommendations for informed adaptation of social theories in IS research. In: AMCIS Proceedings (2003)

Hovorka, D.S., Germonprez, M.: Towards an informatively account of design research. All Sprouts Content 452 (2011). http://aisel.aisnet.org/sprouts_all/452

Huang, K., Zhang, X., Mu, Y., Rezaeibagha, F., Du, X., Guizani, N.: Achieving intelligent trust-layer for IoT via self-redactable blockchain. IEEE Trans. Industr. Inform. (2019). https://doi.org/10.1109/TII.2019.2943331

Husserl, E.: Experience and Judgment, Investigations in a Genealogy of Logic. Northwestern University Press (1948/1973)

Ives, B., Rodriguez, J.A., Palese, B.: Enhancing customer service through the internet of things and digital data streams. MIS Q. Exec. 15(4), 5 (2016)

Jones, M., Munir, K., Orlikowski, W., Runde, J.: About time too: online news and changing temporal structures in the newspaper industry. In: ICIS Proceedings 156 (2008). http://aisel.aisnet.org/icis2008/156

Janssen, C., Vanhamme, J., Lindgreen, A., Lefebvre, C.: The Catch-22 of responsible luxury: effects of luxury product characteristics on consumers' perception of fit with corporate social responsibility. J. Bus. Ethics 119(1), 45–57 (2013). https://doi.org/10.1007/s10551-013-1621-6

Kakar, A.K., Hale, J., Hale, D.: Social traps of agile methods. In: AMCIS 2012 Proceedings (2012). http://aisel.aisnet.org/amcis2012/proceedings/SystemsAnalysis/1

Kakihara, M., Sorensen, C.: Expanding the 'mobility' concept. ACM SIGGROUP Bull. 22(3) (2001)

Kallinikos, J.: The making of ephemeria: on the shortening life spans of information. Int. J. Interdiscip. Sci. 4(3) (2009)

Kallinikos, J., Aaltonen, A., Marton, A.: A theory of digital objects. First Mondays (2010)

Kallinikos, J., Aaltonen, A., Marton, A.: The ambivalent ontology of digital artifacts. MIS Q. 37(2), 357–370 (2013)

Kaun, A., Stiernstedt, F.: Facebook time: technological and institutional affordances for media memories. New Media Soc. 16(7), 1154–1168 (2004)

Kelly, T., Baron, J. The rise of ephemeral messaging apps in the business world. Natl. Law Rev. XI(249) (2021)

Kompare, D.: Flow to files: conceiving 21st century media. In: Conference Paper, Media in Transition 2, Cambridge, MA (2002)

Kreps, D.: Infomateriality. In: Thirty Ninth International Conference on Information Systems, San Francisco, USA (2018)

Lanzara, G.F.: Ephemeral organizations in extreme environments; emergences, strategy, extinctions. J. Manage. Stud. 20(1), 71–95 (1983)

Lee, A.S.: Electronic mail as a medium for rich communication: an empirical investigation using hermeneutic interpretation. In: ICIS 1993 Proceedings, p. 52 (1993)

Lefebvre, H.: The Urban Revolution. University of Minnesota Press (1970). Trans. Bononno, R. (2003)

Lefrant, J.-Y., Benhamou, D., Dureuil, B., et al.: ICU bed capacity during COVID-19 pandemic in France: From ephemeral beds to continuous and permanent adaptation. Anaesthesia Crit. Care Pain Med. 40, 100873 (2021)

Lehmann, J., Recker, J.: Offerings that are "ever-in-the-making": post-launch continuous digital innovation in late-stage entrepreneurial ventures. In: ICIS 2019 Proceedings, p. 11 (2019)

Lepani, K.: Islands of Love, Islands of Risk: Culture and HIV in the Trobriands. Vanderbilt University Press, Nashville (2012)

Lim, J., Rong, G., Grover, V.: An inductive approach to documenting the "core" and evolution of the IS field. Commun. Assoc. Inf. Syst. 19, 32 (2007). https://doi.org/10.17705/1CAIS.01932

Ljungberg, F., Sorensen, C.: Are you "pulling the plug" or "pushing up the daisies"? In: Proceedings of 31st Annual Hawaii International Conference on System Sciences (1998)

López-Bertran, M.: Ephemeral art. In: Encyclopedia of Global Archaeology (2019). https://doi.org/10.1007/978-3-319-51726-1_2825-1

López-Forniés, I., Sierra-Pérez, J.: Ephemeral products: opportunities for circularity based on ideation for reuse. An experience. In: Rizzi, C., Campana, F., Bici, M., Gherardini, F., Ingrassia, T., Cicconi, P. (eds.) ADM 2021. Lecture Notes in Mechanical Engineering, pp. 365–372. Springer, Cham (2021). https://doi.org/10.1007/978-3-030-91234-5_37

Lyytinen, K.: Innovation logics in the digital era: a systemic review of the emerging digital innovation regime. Innovation **24**, 13–34 (2021). https://doi.org/10.1080/14479338.2021.1938579

Lyytinen, K., King, J. Nothing at the center?: academic legitimacy in the information systems field. J. Assoc. Inf. Syst. **5**(6), 8 (2004). https://doi.org/10.17705/1jais.00051

MacCarthy, M.: Doing away with Doba? Women's wealth and shifting values in Trobriand mortuary distributions. In: Hermkens, A.-K., Lepani, K. (eds.) SINUOUS OBJECTS, Revaluing Women's Wealth in the Contemporary Pacific. Australian National University Press (2017)

Malhotra, A., Majchrzak, A.: Hidden patterns of knowledge evolution in fluid digital innovation. Innovation. **24**, 35–46 (2021). https://doi.org/10.1080/14479338.2021.1879653

Marabelli, M., Newell, S., Galliers, R.: The materiality of impression management in social media use: a focus on time, space and algorithms. In: Thirty Seventh International Conference on Information Systems (2016)

Marcus, G., Saka, E.: Assemblage. Theory, Culture and Society. Sage Publishing (2006)

Marton, A., Avital, M., Blegind, J.T.: Reframing open big data. In: ECIS 2013 Completed Research, p. 146 (2013). http://aisel.aisnet.org/ecis2013_cr/146

McPeak, A.: Self-destruct apps: spoliation by design? Akron Law Rev. **51**(3), 749 (2017)

McRoberts, S., Ma, H., Hall, A., Yarosh, S.: Share first, save later: performance of self through snapchat stories. In: CHI 2017, 06–11 May 2017, Denver, CO, USA (2017)

Merriam-Webster.com (2022). https://www.merriam-webster.com/dictionary/ephemeral

Moran, D.: Edmund Husserl's phenomenology of habituality and habitus. J. Br. Soc. Phenomenol. **42**, 53–77 (2011)

Morlok, T., Schneider, K., Matt, C., Hess, T.: Snap. Share. (Don't) care? ephemerality, privacy concerns, and the use of ephemeral social network sites. In: Proceedings of Twenty-third Americas Conference on Information Systems (2017)

Morlok, T., Constantiou, I., Hess, T.: Gone for better or for worse? Exploring the dual nature of ephemerality on social media platforms. In: ECIS Completed Research Papers. Paper 15 (2018)

Mousavi Baygi, R., Introna, L.D., Hultin, L.: Everything flows: studying continuous socio-technological transformation in a fluid and dynamic digital world. MIS Q. **45**(1) (2021)

Mueller, R.: Report on the investigation into russian interference in the 2016 presidential election (2019). https://www.justice.gov/storage/report.pdf

Muñoz, J.E.: Ephemera as Evidence: introductory notes to queer acts. Women Perform. J. Feminist Theory **8**(2), 5–16 (1996). https://doi.org/10.1080/07407709608571228 (1996)

Niederman, F., Brancheau, J., Wetherbe, J.: Information systems management issues for the 1990s. MIS Q. (1991)

Oja, M-K., Galliers, R.: Affect and materiality in enterprise systems usage: setting the stage for user experience. In: ECIS 2011 Proceedings, p. 13 (2011)

Orman, L.V.: The design of trust networks. Commun. Assoc. Inf. Syst. **37**(41) (2015). https://doi.org/10.17705/1CAIS.03741

Orlikowski, W.J., Scott, S.V.: Sociomateriality: challenging the separation of technology, work and organization. Acad. Manag. Ann. **2**(1) (2008)

Oxford English Dictionary (OED) Oxford: Clarendon Press; Oxford University Press (2004)

Peterson, R., Parker, M., Ribbers, P.: Information technology governance processes under environmental dynamism: investigating competing theories of decision making and knowledge sharing. In: ICIS 2002 Proceedings, p. 52 (2002). http://aisel.aisnet.org/icis2002/52

Phelan, P.: Unmarked: The Politics of Performance. Routledge, London (1993)

Pimlott, H.: 'Eternal ephemera' or the durability of 'disposable literature': the power and persistence of print in an electronic world. Media Cult. Soc. **33**(4), 515–530 (2011)

Prado, P., Sapsed, J.: The anthropophagic organization: how innovations transcend the temporary in a project-based organization. Organ. Stud. **37**(12), 1793–1818 (2016). https://doi.org/10.1177/0170840616655491

Prester, J., Cecez-Kecmanovic, D., Schlagwein, D.: Becoming a digital nomad: decentered identity work along agentic lines. In: 11th International Process Symposium (2019)

Purpura, A.: Framing the ephemeral. African Arts **42**(3), 11–15 (2009). https://doi.org/10.1162/afar.2009.42.3.11

Quintarelli, E., Rabosio, E., Tanca, L.: Efficiently using contextual influence to recommend new items to ephemeral groups. Inf. Syst. **84**, 197–213 (2019)

Reason, M.: Documentation, Disappearance, and the Representation of Live Performance. Palgrave Macmillan, London (2006)

Rennecker, J., Godwin, L.: Theorizing the unintended consequences of instant messaging for worker productivity. All Sprouts Content **49** (2008)

Rennecker, J., Dennis, A.R., Hansen, S.: 'Invisible whispering': instant messaging in meetings. All Sprouts Content, p. 110 (2008). http://aisel.aisnet.org/sprouts_all/110

Rosa, H.: Social Acceleration: A New Theory of Modernity. Columbia University Press, New York (2013)

Rosa, H.: Resonance: A Sociology of Our Relationship to the World. Polity, Cambridge (2019). Trans. J. Wagner

Salovaara, A., Tuunainen, V.: Software developers' online chat as an intra-firm mechanism for sharing ephemeral knowledge. ICIS (2013)

Salovaara, A., Tuunainen, V.: Mediated sharing as software developers' strategy to manage ephemeral knowledge. ECIS Completed Research Papers. Paper 158 (2015)

Sandberg, J., Holmström, J., Lyytinen, K.: Digitization and phase transitions in platform organizing logics: Evidence from the process automation industry. MIS Q. **44**(1), 129–153 (2020). https://doi.org/10.25300/MISQ/2020/14520

Sarker, S., Sahay, S.: Understanding virtual team development: an interpretive study. J. Assoc. Inf. Syst. **4**, 1 (2003)

Sawyer, K.: Social Emergence. Cambridge University Press, Cambridge (2005)

Schlesinger, A., Chandrasekharan, E., Masden, C.A., Bruckman, A.S., Edwards, W.K., Grinter, R.E.: Situated anonymity: impacts of anonymity, ephemerality, and hyper-locality on social media. In: Proceedings of the 2017 CHI Conference on Human Factors in Computing Systems, Denver, CO, USA (2017)

Schneider, S., Foot, K.: The web as an object of study. New Media Soc. **6**(1), 114–122 (2004). https://doi.org/10.1177/1461444804039912

Shein, E.: Ephemeral data. Commun. ACM. **56**(9), 20–22 (2013)

Sibona, C., Walczak, S., White, E.: A guide for purposive sampling on Twitter. Commun. Assoc. Inf. Syst. **46**, 22 (2020). https://doi.org/10.17705/1CAIS.04622

Siegel, M.: At the Vanishing Point: A Critic Looks at Dance. Saturday Review Press, New York (1972)

Simmel, G.: *The philosophy of money*. London: Routledge. (1900/2004)

Smith, H.J., Dinev, T., Xu, H.: Information privacy research: an interdisciplinary review. MIS Q. **35**(4), 989–1016 (2011)

Smith, H.A., McKeen, J.D.: Enabling collaboration with IT. Commun. Assoc. Inf. Syst. **28**(16) (2012). https://doi.org/10.17705/1CAIS.02816

Sydow, J.: Temporary organizing – the end of organizations as we know them? Rutgers Bus. Rev. **2**(2) (2017)

Taylor, D.: The Archive and the Repertoire. Duke University Press (2007)

Tedeschi, P., Piro, G., Boggia, G.: When blockchain makes ephemeral keys authentic: a novel key agreement mechanism in the IoT world. IEEE (2018)

theverge.com (2020). https://www.the-verge.com/2020/4/23/21232401/zoom-300-million-users-growth-coronavirus-pandemic-security-privacy-concerns-response. Accessed 14 June 2020

Toda, M.: The urge theory of emotion and social interaction. Unpublished manuscript. Chukyo University (1999)

Truex, D.P., Baskerville, R., Travis, J.: Amethodical systems development: the deferred meaning of systems development methods. Account. Manag. Inf. Technol. **10**, 53–79 (2000)

Tsoukas, H.: Don't simplify, complexify: from disjunctive to conjunctive theorizing in organization and management studies. J. Manag. Stud. **54**(2), 132–153 (2016)

Uricchio, W.: The recurrent, the recombinatory and the ephemeral. In: Grainge, P. (ed.) Ephemeral Media: Transitory Screen Culture from Television to YouTube. Palgrave Macmillan (2011). https://web.mit.edu/uricchio/Public/pdfs/pdfs/The%20Recurrent.pdf

Urquhart, C., Vaast, E.: Building social media theory from case studies: a new frontier for is research. In: Thirty Third International Conference on Information Systems (2012)

Urry, J.: Consuming Places. Routledge (1995)

Urry, J.: Sociology Beyond Societies: Mobilities for the Twenty-First Century. Routledge (2000/2012)

Utz, S., Muscanell, N., Khalid, C.: Snapchat elicits more jealousy than Facebook: a comparison of Snapchat and Facebook use. Cyberpsychol. Behav. Soc. Netw. **18**(3), 141–146 (2015)

Vaast, E., Boland, R., Davidson, E., Pawlowski, S., Schultze, U.: Investigating the "knowledge" in knowledge management: a social representations perspective. Commun. Assoc. Inf. Syst. **17**(15) (2006). https://doi.org/10.17705/1CAIS.01715

van Marrewijk, A., Ybema, S., Smits, K., Clegg, S., Pitsis, T.: Clash of the titans: temporal organizing and collaborative dynamics in the panama canal megaproject. Organ. Stud. **37**(12), 1745–1769 (2016)

van Nimwegen, C., Bergman, K.: Effects on cognition of the burn after reading principle in ephemeral media applications. Behav. Inf. Technol. **38**, 1060–1067 (2019)

Vázquez-Herrero, J., Direito-Rebollal, S., López-García, X.: Ephemeral journalism: news distribution through instagram stories. Soc. Media + Soc. (2019)

Vera, F., and Mehrotra, R.: Temporary Flows and Ephemeral Cities. Room One Thousand 3 (2015). https://escholarship.org/uc/item/18f9p6np

Vidal-Abarca, M.R., Gómez, R., Sánchez-Montoya, M., Arce, M., Nicolás, N., Suárez, M.: Defining dry rivers as the most extreme type of non-perennial fluvial ecosystems. Sustainability **12**, 7202 (2020). https://doi.org/10.3390/su12177202(2020)

Villaespesa, E., Wowkowych, S.: Ephemeral storytelling with social media: snapchat and instagram stories at the brooklyn museum. Soc. Media + Soc. **1**(13) (2020)

vom Brocke, J., Winter, R., Hevner, A., Maedche, A.: Special issue editorial – accumulation and evolution of design knowledge in design science research: a journey through time and space. J. Assoc. Inf. Syst. **21**, 9 (2021)

von Briel, F., Recker, J., Davidsson, P.: Not all digital venture ideas are created equal: implications for venture creation processes. J. Strategic Inf. Syst. (2018). https://doi.org/10.1016/j.jsis.2018.06.002

Wakefield, L., Wakefield, R.: Anxiety and ephemeral social media use in negative eWOM creation. J. Interact. Mark. **41**, 44–59 (2018)

Webster, J., Watson, R.: Analyzing the past to prepare for the future: writing a literature review. MIS Q. **26**(2), xiii–xxiii (2002)

Welsh, S.: Ephemerality as Data Prevention: Values for an Ethics of Ephemeral Mobile Media. Mob. Media Commun. 1–17 (2020)

Williams, R.: Television: Technology and Cultural Form. Fontana, London (1974)

Xu, B., Chang, P., Welker, C., Bazarova, N., Cosley, D.: Automatic archiving versus default deletion: what snapchat tells us about ephemerality in design. CSCW Conference on Computing Support Coop Work. Author manuscript; Available in PMC 2018 (2018)

Yoo, Y.: Computing in everyday life: a call for research on experiential computing. MIS Q. **34**(2), 213–231 (2010)

Young, T.G.: Evidence: toward a library definition of ephemera. RBM J. Rare Books Manusc. Cult. Heritage **4**(1) (2003). https://doi.org/10.5860/rbm.4.1.214

Zhang, P.: The affective response model: a theoretical framework of affective concepts and their relations in the ICT context. MIS Q. **37**(1), 247–274 (2013)

Modelling User Experience, Emotions and Concerns for Predicting Firm Response-the Case of Low-Cost Carriers During Pandemic

Shagun Sarraf[1]([✉]) [iD], P. Vigneswara Ilavarsana[2] [iD], Agam Gupta[2], and Arpan Kumar Kar[2] [iD]

[1] Bharti School of Telecommunication Technology and Management, Indian Institute of Technology Delhi, New Delhi, India
Shagun.Sarraf@dbst.iitd.ac.in

[2] Department of Management Studies, Indian Institute of Technology Delhi, New Delhi, India

Abstract. The customers use social media platforms to share their grievances and unresolved concerns about a product or service. This behaviour was rampant during the ongoing pandemic, COVID-19. The airline industry could not handle the uncertainties and manage the customer distress. The extant research on how airlines could address social media grievances needs further enrichment. The present paper presents a model of low-cost carriers (LCCs) response to social media customer complaints. It uses content analysis, followed by logistic regression for the model verification. Results highlighted that the type of complainer, emotions, lockdown situation, complain text, and complain concerns can impact the firm's response. The paper contributes to understanding firms' responses to social media customer complaints.

Keywords: Low-cost carriers · COVID-19 · Customer complains · Social media

1 Introduction

Past research has attested that effective customer complaint management can impact customer satisfaction and business performance. [1] has outlined, that organisations have a substantial stake in understanding the harms a dissatisfied customer can cause to the brand. A dissatisfied customer can impact the organisation's brand image, leaving the firm unsure of responding to public criticism, as its marketer's number one fear [2].

The airline companies in India are currently bearing a heavy load of consumer complaints on their shoulder regarding their negligent services, especially low-cost carriers (LCC) are striving to survive the crisis [3]. [4] highlighted that the customer complaints have increased to a rate of 11.75 per 100000 customers in 2022 from 1.06 in 2019. Most of such grievances have been raised due to their debatable policy related to air travel and flight cancellations due to COVID-19 [5]. According to the airlines, the major causes of grievances are staffing, reservation agent and industry analysts [6].

© IFIP International Federation for Information Processing 2022
Published by Springer Nature Switzerland AG 2022
S. Papagiannidis et al. (Eds.): I3E 2022, LNCS 13454, pp. 456–467, 2022.
https://doi.org/10.1007/978-3-031-15342-6_35

The basic premise of all the past studies is to address the complaints by the final customers on the social media platforms and the actions that the LCC takes to resolve the customer complaints. However, there is insufficient literature on how organisations deal with customer complaints during a crisis, i.e., COVID-19. Based on this, the present study aims to understand the complaint management strategies of LCC at the time of the COVID crisis. The following research questions direct our study:

RQ1: Which factors determine a firm response to the customer social media complaints?
RQ2: How do these factors causes a firm response to the customer social media complaints?

The following is the structure of the paper: Sect. 2 presents a literature review and hypothesis development, tracked by research methodology in Sect. 3. Section 4 outlines the study results, followed by a discussion and implications in Sect. 5. Lastly, Sect. 6 represents the conclusion of the study.

2 Literature Review and Hypothesis Development

We followed a thorough approach in the literature review for the hypothesis development. It also highlighted the services of the LCCs in India and the firm response to social media customer complaints.

2.1 Low-Cost Carriers (LCCs) Services in India

The introduction of LCCs has changed the entire air travel perception. It is reshaping the highly competitive airline industry. [7] presented in their reports that from 2013 to 2020, the LCCs have captured 82% of the market. [8] introduced the market share of LCCs in 2020, where Indigo has 48.2%, SpiceJet 15.6%, Go Air 10.8%, Air Asia India 6.7% and Air India Express 0.1%. LCCs provide essential air travel services with no frills and even at lower costs; on average, the fare is 40%−60% lower than the full-service carriers' fare [9]. However, with growing customer aspirations, their customer service quality expectations also increase.

2.2 Types of Complainers

Past research has made a valuable contribution to the study of customer complaints. [10] the type of complainers can broadly be divided into three categories. Firstly, early squabbles, where the customer organisation relationship might be in danger, but the customer has still committed its ties with the organisation. Secondly, the rock seems imminent, where the customer has not decided to exit the organisation. Lastly, the exes are the angry customers who actively terminate their relationship with the organisation. The companies should implement varied strategies with the customers, i.e., eliminate, develop, and retain while ensuring organisations' long-term interest [11]. Therefore, the organisation should terminate relationships with low-value customers to increase the firm's performance [12]. Thus, we hypothesised:

H1a: Complaints posted by early squabbles are more likely to result in a firm response than the exes.

H1b: Complaints posted by the rock are more likely to result in a firm response than the exes.

2.3 Emotions of the Customers

The past studies have conceptualised the specific emotions involved in customer complaining [13]. Emotion plays a significant role in how the complaint has made, and the text used. The valence-based approach has distinguished it between positive and negative emotions [14]. Positive emotion represents a hopeful customer, calmly explaining the problems and looking for solutions. The negative emotions create a displeasing situation considering the brand is not on their side. During the COVID times, users understood the aviation industry's crisis, thus maintaining a positive notion towards their complaints. Therefore, we propose the following hypothesis:

H2: Positive emotions expressed in the customer complaint posts are more likely to result in a firm response.

2.4 Type of Complain Text

The role of complaining text, which the complainers use on the social media platform to air their grievances, can be broadly categorised into three categories. General, specific, and higher-order text focus on the service provider's help, with questions or requests threatening the brand. In general, complaint texts highlight a customer's broad concerns; the customer is not specific, only requesting the service provider to help. Problems are mentioned in specific text complaint texts, i.e., a request or a specific question. The higher-order text highlights the customer's intention to threaten the brand. Here customers are determined to their problems' solutions; the text can also include a direct threat to the brand [15]. [16] outlined that an airline responds to only half of the thousands of mentions that it receives online. Therefore, we propose the following hypothesis:

H3a: General complaint texts are more likely to result in a firm response than higher order complaint texts.

H3b: Specific complaint texts are more likely to result in a firm response than higher order complaint texts.

2.5 Complain Concerns

Customers' complaint posts highlight the post-consumption concerns. Past researchers have highlighted a few concerns that are highlighted in customer complaints. It includes financial concerns, technical concerns, and other concerns. Financial concerns highlight the economic waste. Technical concerns highlight improper product functionality or its defects. At the same time, other concerns include psychological, physical, and social concerns. Psychological concerns include emotional suffering, physical concerns include health-related issues, and social concerns have when a dispute with an individual becomes more important than a product [17]. Therefore, we propose the following hypothesis.

H4a: Financial concerns expressed in customer complaint posts are more likely to result in a firm response.

H4b: Technical concerns expressed in customer complaint posts are more likely to result in a firm response.

H4c: Other concerns expressed in customer complaint posts are more likely to result in a firm response.

2.6 Complaints During Pandemic

COVID 19 lockdown around the globe has led to a challenging phase for the entire economy. Social media platforms of US-based airlines experienced a 965% surge in customer complaints [18]. The airlines face losses and challenging times by cutting their workforce by 90% [19] and asking the government to salvage the industry. Therefore, these unforeseen circumstances have made the complaint handling process difficult during the lockdown.

During the lockdown period, ambiguity about the cancellation, credit shell, and government reimbursement guidelines was not reshared by the airlines. Taking advantage of the situation, the airlines were exploiting the passengers. A credit shell is provided to the customers for their cancelled flights which the same passenger could utilise within a year for the same journey. This caused disappointment amongst users about who qualified for the refund. Due to COVID19, conventional channels were closed. This led to customers bombarding the social media pages of the airlines. While during the unlock phase, the apex court came to the rescue while asking the government and the airlines to work on the modalities of the refund and credit shell [20]. Thus, we hypothesized:

H5: Customer complaints posted on social media during the unlocking phase are more likely to result in a firm response than posted in the lockdown phase.

2.7 Firm Response

Dissatisfied customers negatively evaluate companies. To restore a positive brand image, the organisations need to take proactive actions like an apology, compensation, or corrective actions [21]. The firm response categories are action and no action. The action involves a defensive response that highlights the firm response as putting organisational interest first, including shifting the blame, attacking the accuser, or denying the responsibility. The other actions could be accommodative, focusing on putting complainers' concerns first, including compensations, corrective actions, or apology [21]. Also, no action category has been included, where organisations maintain silence by separating themselves from any adverse events [21]. However, the organisation's silence is only acceptable to the customers who have favourable feelings towards the brand. Thus, no action strategy could be damaging to the organisation's reputation.

3 Research Methodology

To understand customer complaints and firm responses of LCCs, we conducted a quantitative content analysis. Researchers have highlighted that content analysis is a feasible method to understand multiple aspects of the content and the new phenomenon [22]. Followed by logistic regression for statistical analysis.

3.1 Content Analysis

Researchers have widely used quantitative content analysis to make inferences about the communication messages. The quantitative content analysis includes sampling texts, selecting the relevant unit of research, and learning the conceptualisation [23]. It is employed in this study as its helpful in understating the holistic qualities of the text.

Sampling
For the study, the customer complaints posted on the LCCs' official Facebook pages are the unit of analysis. There are 5 LCCs in India, i.e., Air India Express, Air Asia India, Indigo, Go Air and SpiceJet. We considered English comments only.

Data collection and analysis were conducted from March 25 to June 10, 2020. The Facebook pages of the airlines were accessed on 12 June 2020, and the first 60 complaints with some texts were extracted. [24] suggests that 60 is adequate for any quantitative analysis using inferential statistics. In all, we used 300 complaints in the study. To locate relevant posts, we accessed the official Facebook pages of popular LCCs in India. We did a general screening of the comments on the post related to the pandemic. The specific period (Table 1) consists of COVID-19 phases of lockdown imposed by the Govt of India.

The period for data collection was chosen for the following reasons:

a) COVID19 restrictions in the country halted the airline's operations. Only medical evacuation flights, off-shore helicopters, cargo operations, or the flights with DGCA approval were operational [25].
b) All international commercial passenger services were closed till 1830 h GMT off 3 May 2020. However, the restriction did not apply to international all-cargo operations and flights specifically approved by DGCA [26].
c) Airlines were refrained from booking tickets till 3 May 2020.
d) If a passenger has booked a ticket during the first lockdown period (25 March 20-14 April 20) and the airline has received the payment for booking of the air ticket during the first lockdown for domestic or international air travel during the same time or for the period of (15 April 20-3 May 20). Then airlines were supposed fully refund the cancellation charges within three weeks of the requested cancellation [27].

Coding Procedure
Two researchers manually coded the content based on prior coding [28] and the defined categories before the analysis. For the study, we created an excel sheet using the following column headings: text of customer complaints, lockdown/Unlock, type of the text,

Table 1. Lockdown phases and government guidelines

S. No	Lockdown period	Related instruction	Announcement date
1	Lockdown1 (25 March 20 - 14 April 20)	Air travel suspended, However, Cargo Flights, Special Flights, medical evacuation flights authorised by aviation regulator DGCA - Permitted	24 March 2020
2	Lockdown 2 (15 April 20 - 3 May 20)	Air travel suspended, However, Cargo Flights, Special Flights, medical evacuation flights are authorised by aviation regulator DGCA – Permitted.	14 April 2020
3	Lockdown 3 (4 May 20 - 17 May 20)	Air travel suspended, However, Cargo Flights, Special Flights, medical evacuation flights authorised by aviation regulator DGCA - Permitted	1 May 2020
4	Lockdown 4 (18 May 20 - 31 May 20)	Domestic Flights restarted in a calibrated manner from 25th may, announced by Union Minister Hardeep Singh Puri	17 May 2020
5	Unlock (1 June 20 - 30 June 20)	International Travel Prohibited Interstate and Intra-State – Allowed	31 May 2020

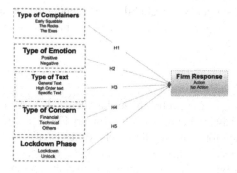

Fig. 1. Research model

emotions, complaint concerns, type of the complainer and firm response. Followed by logistic regression.

As categorical independent variables can't be directly entered in regression analysis, we introduced dummy variables and coded [29]. Dummy variables are quantitative variables that are dichotomous—typically representing 1 for the presence of a qualitative attribute and 0 means absence. The response of the airlines is treated as a dependent variable.

The firm response was coded as action = 1 and no action = 0. For instance, for a complaint, the response was, "Please share your PNR so we may check." It was coded as 1. The emotions were coded as Positive = 1 and negative = 0. Also, lockdown situations are coded as unlock = 1 and lockdown = 0. The type of text was coded with respect to higher-order text and where '1' if the text is General text or '0' otherwise and '1' if the text is Specific text or '0' otherwise. The area of concern has been coded with respect to others (psychological, social and physical), where '1' if the text is technical or '0' otherwise; '1' if the text is financial or '0' otherwise and '1' if the text is both (Technical and financial) or '0' otherwise. Finally, the type of complainers concerning the rock was '1' if the text is Early Squabbles or '0' otherwise and '1' if the text is the exes or '0' otherwise.

For instance, a passenger complained, "Not to book SpiceJet as its service is only to embezzle public money by hook or crook in the name of credit shell, but you do not find any amount in credit shell nor get any response as all the staff are in the auto mood. So the response is the same all the time". Emotion was coded as 1, airline as 0, lockdown phase as 0, general text, financial concern and the rock as a complainer.

A few other complaints text from the users reads "I want a refund, why you all harassing people who have a good faith on Spice jet, do you really think these people will again deal with you??"; "I'm going to court for complaint, because we are not giving refunds", etc.

Inter Coder Reliability

We conducted intercoder reliability to test the data's manual coding validity. This ensures uniformity in coding and reduces ambiguity [30]. Specifically, two coders independently coded the user complaints. After coding the data, the authors met to discuss and resolve any disagreements. The inter-coder reliability tests conducted on each answer indicated Cohen's kappa scores ranged from 0.882 to 0.978. This meant a very high inter-coder reliability [31].

3.2 Logistic Regression

We used logistic regression as a probabilistic classifier [32]. As per our research hypothesis, the dependent variable is dichotomous, i.e., binary [33]. Past researchers have widely used logistic regression for analysing firms' choice decisions [34]. For the analysis, we used the SPSS package, which is used to examine the effect of various independent variables on the probability of firms' response to customer complaints posted on social media platforms (Fig. 1). The binary logistics regression model is as follows:

$$\log\left(\frac{\pi}{1-\pi}\right) = \beta_0 + \beta_1 \textit{ Type of compaliner} + \beta_2 \textit{ Type of text}$$
$$+ \beta_3 \textit{ Emotions} + \beta_4 \textit{ Type of concern}$$
$$+ \beta_5 \textit{ Lockdown Phase}$$

where π, indicates the probability of firm response, $\beta 0$ constant intercept and $\beta 1, \beta 2 \ldots \beta 5$ regression coefficients.

4   Results

In this section, the finding of the study has been presented. Prior to logistic regression, we accessed the correlation of the variables; all values are less than 0.35. Further, we also performed a VIF test to examine multicollinearity. The results highlighted that the values are less than 2, highlighting multicollinearity absence [34].

Then we performed logistic regression; the Omnibus test of the model coefficient showed the chi-square value of 121.76 (p < 0.05), highlighting that model's statistical significance. The Chi-square value highlighted in the Hosmer and Lemeshow test is 2.469 (p = 0.96), highlighting a complete extraction of current data and ensuring the model's goodness of fit. In this model, we can say that 70.7% of changes in the dependent variable can be due to the dependent variables in the model. The model correctly classified 82.1% of cases overall and with a sensitivity of 94.7%.

The logistics results have highlighted that early squabble complainers would experience a reduction of 45% in the odds of receiving a firm response compared to the exes complainers (p < 0.05). In the case of the rocks complainers, the odds of receiving a firm response is 1.89 times higher than the exes complainers (p < 0.05). Hence, supporting hypotheses 1a and 1b. The study outlined that the odds of complaints highlighting positive emotions would experience a 39% reduction in firm response compared to negative emotions (p > 0.05). Hence, it does not support hypothesis 2. In the case of complaint texts, the general text would experience a 46% of firm response reduction (p > 0.05); however, in the case of a specific text, the odds of receiving a firm response are 1.29 times higher than the higher-order texts (p < 0.05). Hence, not supporting hypothesis 3a and supporting hypothesis 3b. The complaint concerns have highlighted that financial and technical concerns would experience 1.76 and 1.65 times of firm response than the complaint highlighting both the concerns, i.e., financial, and technical (p < 0.05). However, in the case of other complaint concerns, the odds of receiving a firm response would experience a reduction of 43%, (p > 0.05). Thus, supporting hypotheses 4a and 4b, but 4c. The complaints posted during the unlocking period have 1.55 times higher odds of receiving a firm response than complaints posted in the lockdown period (p < 0.05). Hence supporting hypothesis 5 (Table 2).

Table 2. Logistics regression result

Influencing Factors	Reference Category	p	Exp (B)	95% CI Lower	95% CI Upper
Complainers Type					
Early Squabble	The exes	0.016	0.55	0.3457	0.90002
The rocks		0.0075	1.89	1.1858	3.0358
Lockdown Situation	Lockdown	0.0117	1.55	0.3430	0.8749
Unlock					
Emotions	Negative				
Positive		0.537	0.61	0.771	1.1485
Complain Text	High Order				
General		0.3963	0.54	0.3387	0.886
Specific		0.0142	1.29	0.7156	2.328
Complain Concerns	Both				
Financial		0.0196	1.76	1.0947	2.8373
Technical		0.0244	1.65	0.8891	3.0973
Other		0.1115	0.57	0.3574	0.9315

5 Discussion

This study has contributed to exploring the nature of customer complaints on social media during a pandemic and how the LCCs responded to it. Social media plays a critical role in crisis response in the context of customer complaints. Past studies have highlighted that customer complaints handling lacked commitment to handling complaints, a slow complaint handling process and a reactive approach to the complaints [35]. However, the studies have not highlighted the attributes of the text that contributes to firm response. This study highlights that the emotions of the complainers don't solely hinge on the response of the airlines. Instead, concern types, text type, lockdown period and type of complainers are the significant factors responsible for LCCs' response.

The study has identified that early squabble complainers and the rocks complainers are more likely to receive firm responses that the rock complainers. In the case of emotions, the texts expressing the negative emotions are more likely to receive firm response. The type of text also plays an important role in the firm response where higher-order text is more likely to receive firm response that general text; and specific text complaints are more like to receive firm response than higher-order text. The study attested that the complaints posted during unlock phase concerning financial and technical concerns are more likely to receive a firm response.

6 Implications for Practice

The study highlighted the type of the complainer's results in a firm response, where the firms need to identify the type of customer they are dealing with and the best way to respond. For early squabble complainers, thank the customers and politely resolve the situation. In the case of rock, complainers acknowledge the problem and are respectful. Lastly, the exes complainers should be responded to while maintaining composure and apologising. Findings encounter a list of complaints concerning financial and technical concerns of the passengers are the concerns that are more likely to be addressed by the airlines first. Majorly the passengers had financial concerns with the airline. These situations deeply distressed passengers.

Type of complain text and complain concerns describe that depending on the information involved, the firm should clearly understand the issues that can be addressed privately or publicly. The study outlined; specific complaints are more likely to receive a firm response. Hence, specific complaints must be handled confidentially. The organisation needs to understand the multifaced phenomena of complaint management rather than oversimplifying it with a single complaint response strategy for the complaints.

7 Conclusion

Social media has the potential to reach a wider audience; customers are widely expressing their satisfaction and dissatisfaction over multiple social media platforms. Around the nation, the airlines are following a well-developed grievance redressal mechanism. For the study, the data chosen is from social media platforms to understand the LCCs response to customer complaints. While emphasising in the time of pandemic where the customers face inconvenience, the callous practices of the providers are worsening the situation. The providers need to have a dedicated team for complaint management and constructive criticism, which would push the airlines towards excellence with customer satisfaction.

8 Limitations and Future of Research

In this paper factors concerning factors influencing LCCs response to customer complaints on social media platforms and verified using social media data. The platform used for the study was only Facebook, however, other platforms could also be explored like Twitter, Instagram, etc. Further, in this paper, we have focused on extracting the factors influencing firm response but not its interrelation between the elements. Also, LCCs considered are from India with major market share, other carriers could also be considered. The study has only considered the time for pandemic, future research can also do a longitudinal study to understand the pattern of LCCs response to customer complaints.

References

1. Fornell, C., Wernerfelt, B.: Defensive marketing strategy by customer complaint management: a theoretical analysis. J. Mark. Res. **24**(4), 337–346 (1987). https://doi.org/10.1177/002224 378702400401
2. Gillin, P.: Secrets of social media marketing: how to use online conversations and customer communities to turbo-charge your business! (2008)
3. Vinod, B.: The COVID-19 pandemic and airline cash flow. J. Revenue Pricing Manag. **19**(4), 228–229 (2020). https://doi.org/10.1057/s41272-020-00251-5
4. McCoy, D.: Airline report: customer complaints skyrocketed in 2020 during COVID-19. Wichita Bus. J. (2021). https://www.bizjournals.com/wichita/news/2021/05/03/customer-complaints-aqr.html. Accessed 03 Jun 2022
5. Taub, E.A.: The continuing confusion over airline travel credits. The new york times (2021). https://www.nytimes.com/2021/07/06/travel/airline-travel-credits-questions-answers.html
6. Murphy, H.: 275 minutes on hold: why airline customer service still can't keep up. The New York times (2021). https://www.nytimes.com/2021/11/12/travel/airline-customer-service-covid.html. Accessed 03 Jun 2022
7. Statista, Market share of low cost carriers across India from financial year 2013 to 2020 (2020). https://www.statista.com/statistics/1043630/india-low-cost-carrier-market-share/#:~:text=. The market share of low, from rail to air transport
8. Statista, Market share of airlines across India in financial year 2020, by passengers carried (2021). https://www.statista.com/statistics/575207/air-carrier-india-domestic-market-share/
9. Kim, Y.K., Lee, H.R.: Customer satisfaction using low cost carriers. Tour. Manag. **32**(2), 235–243 (2011). https://doi.org/10.1016/j.tourman.2009.12.008
10. Melancon, J.P., Dalakas, V.: Consumer social voice in the age of social media: segmentation profiles and relationship marketing strategies. Bus. Horiz. **61**(1), 157–167 (2018). https://doi.org/10.1016/j.bushor.2017.09.015
11. Reinartz, W., Krafft, M., Hoyer, W.D.: The customer relationship management process: its measurement and impact on performance. J. Mark. Res. **41**(3), 293–305 (2004). https://doi.org/10.1509/jmkr.41.3.293.35991

12. Feng, H., Morgan, N.A., Rego, L.L.: The impact of unprofitable customer management strategies on shareholder value. J. Acad. Mark. Sci. **48**(2), 246–269 (2020). https://doi.org/10.1007/s11747-019-00686-2
13. Tronvoll, B.: Negative emotions and their effect on customer complaint behaviour. J. Serv. Manag. **22**, 111–134 (2011). https://doi.org/10.1108/09564231111106947
14. Schoefer, K., Diamantopoulos, A.: The role of emotions in translating perceptions of (in)justice into postcomplaint behavioral responses. J. Serv. Res. **11**, 91–103 (2008). https://doi.org/10.1177/1094670508319091
15. Kasnakoglu, B.T., Yilmaz, C., Varnali, K.: An asymmetric configural model approach for understanding complainer emotions and loyalty. J. Bus. Res. **69**(9), 3659–3672 (2016). https://doi.org/10.1016/j.jbusres.2016.03.027
16. Josephs, L.: Between five minutes and five hours : How long airlines take to respond to your complaint on Twitter. CNBC (2018). https://www.newslikethis.com/2018/01/09/between-five-minutes-and-fivehours-how-long-airlines-take-respond-your-complaint-twitter. Accessed 05 Apr 2022
17. Jacoby, J., Kaplan, L.B.: The components of perceived risk. Adv. Consum. Res., 82–393 (1972 January)
18. Airlines, F., Agents, O.T.: Latest data reveals a dramatic surge in consumer complaints against airlines. PR Newswire (2020). https://www.prnewswire.com/news-releases/latest-data-reveals-a-dramatic-surge-in-consumer-complaints-against-airlines-301088933.html. Accessed 12 Jan 2022
19. Donthu, N., Gustafsson, A.: Effects of COVID-19 on business and research. J. Bus. Res. **117**, 284–289 (2020). https://doi.org/10.1016/j.jbusres.2020.06.008
20. Online, F.: Refunds for cancelled air tickets : SC comes to the rescue of flyers, asks airlines to allow passengers to use credit shells for 2 years. Financial express (2020). https://www.financialexpress.com/lifestyle/travel-tourism/refunds-for-cancelled-air-tickets-sc-comes-to-the-rescue-of-flyers-asks-airlines-to-allow-passengers-to-use-credit-shells-for-2-years/1989496/
21. Lee, Y.L., Song, S.: An empirical investigation of electronic word-ofmouth: informational motive and corporate response strategy. Comput. Human Behav. **26**(5), 1073–1080 (2010). https://doi.org/10.1016/j.chb.2010.03.009
22. Morehouse, J., Saffer, A.J.: Promoting the faith: examining megachurches' audience-centric advertising strategies on social media. J. Advert. **50**(4), 408–422 (2021). https://doi.org/10.1080/00913367.2021.1939202
23. Krippendorff, K.: Content Analysis: An Introduction to Its Methodology. Sage, CA (2018)
24. Merriam, S. B.: Qualitative Research: A Guide to Design and Implementation, vol. 2 (2009)
25. Government of India, Issue/extension of Airworthiness reeview certificate during lockdown phase of COVID19, Director genral of civil aviation (2020). https://www.dgca.gov.in/digigov-portal/jsp/dgca/homePage/covid19.jsp. Accessed 01 Apr 2021
26. Government of India, Travel and visa restrictions relateed to covid-19, Directorate general of civil aviation (2020). https://www.dgca.gov.in/digigov-portal/jsp/dgca/homePage/covid19.jsp. Accessed 01 Apr 2021
27. Government of India, refund of air fare during the lockdown period, suspending domestic and international flight operations. directorate general of civil aviation (2020). https://www.dgca.gov.in/digigovportal/jsp/dgca/homePage/covid19.jsp. Accessed 01 Apr 2021
28. Oyner, O., Korelina, A.: The influence of customer engagement in value co-creation on customer satisfaction: searching for new forms of co-creation in the Russian hotel industry. Worldw. Hosp. Tour. Themes **8**(3), 327–345 (2016). https://doi.org/10.1108/WHATT-02-2016-0005
29. te Grotenhuis, M., Thijs, P.: Dummy variables and their interactions in regression analysis: examples from research on body mass index, pp. 1–22 (2015). http://arxiv.org/abs/1511.05728

30. O'Connor, C., Joffe, H.: Intercoder reliability in qualitative research: debates and practical guidelines. Int. J. Qual. Methods **19**(2020). https://doi.org/10.1177/1609406919899220
31. Landis, J.R., Koch, G.G.: The measurement of observer agreement for categorical data. Biometrics 33(1), 159 (1977 Mar). https://doi.org/10.2307/2529310
32. Sugiyama, M., Hachiya, H., Yamada, M., Simm, J., Nam, H.: Least-squares probabilistic classifier: a computationally efficient alternative to kernel logistic regression. In: International Workshop on Statistical Machine Learning for Speech Processing (IWSML), vol. 1, no. x, pp. 1–10 (2012). http://www.ism.ac.jp/IWSML2012/r2.pdf
33. Sreejesh, S., Mohapatra, S., Anusree, M.R.: Binary Logistic Regression (2013)
34. Jain, A., Lawrence, E.R.: Asset quality comparison of subchapter s banks and credit unions. Int. J. Financ. **26**(3), 344–359 (2014). https://ejwl.idm.oclc.org/login?url=http://search.ebs cohost.com/login.aspx?direct=true&db=bth&AN=108558635&site=ehost-live
35. Metwally, D.: Complaint handling in the airline industry: the way to enhance customer loyalty. Mediterr. J. Soc. Sci. **4**(10), 299–311 (2013). https://doi.org/10.5901/mjss.2013.v4n10p299

Privacy, Trust and Security

Toward a GDPR Compliant Blockchain Governance Framework

Hasan Mahmud[1] (ID), A. K. M. Najmul Islam[1] (ID), Bilal Naqvi[1] (ID),
and Matti Mäntymäki[2(✉)] (ID)

[1] LUT University, 53850 Lappeenranta, Finland
{hasan.mahmud,najmul.islam,syed.naqvi}@lut.fi
[2] Turku School of Economics, University of Turku, 20014 Turku, Finland
matti.mantymaki@utu.fi

Abstract. Recent research has highlighted multiple incompatibilities between blockchain technology and the General Data Protection Regulation (GDPR) regarding data controller and data deletion. Such incompatibilities impede the adoption of blockchain technology on a larger scale. This paper aims to resolve these incompatibilities, exploring the issues that need to be considered while developing a GDPR compliant blockchain governance framework. We collected data using 20 semi-structured interviews and discussions from 18 different IT companies involved in blockchain-based service development. We analyzed the data using the Gioia approach. We identified three major governance dimensions that must be considered for GDPR compliant blockchain services, namely community, blockchain protocol, and compliance; each of which has several sub-dimensions. Our study extends prior governance frameworks, suggesting the guidelines to comply with GDPR requirements. This guidelines might help organizations to build a GDPR compliant blockchain business model. Based on our findings, we also put forward directions for future inquiry.

Keywords: Blockchain · Blockchain governance · Compliance · GDPR · Off-chain storage

1 Introduction

Blockchain, a distributed ledger technology, allows participants of the network who may or may not trust each other to agree on a decision without the intervention of any central authority [1, 2]. The inherent features of blockchain technology such as immutability, removal of middlemen, decentralized decision-making, and anonymity [2, 3] have allured many organizations around the world to adopt and experiment with blockchain, paving the way for the emergence of the blockchain economy [2]. Later, the development of smart contracts, algorithms that run automatically without risk of downtime, censorship, or fraud, following the rules enacted in the contract, has further facilitated the adoption of blockchain across different industries [2]. Despite the increasing public

© IFIP International Federation for Information Processing 2022
Published by Springer Nature Switzerland AG 2022
S. Papagiannidis et al. (Eds.): I3E 2022, LNCS 13454, pp. 471–484, 2022.
https://doi.org/10.1007/978-3-031-15342-6_36

interest and technological developments, governance of business and industry applications of blockchain is not well understood [2]. Prior research suggests that the lack of an appropriate governance model is challenging the widespread adoption of blockchain technology [4, 5].

The General Data Protection Regulation (GDPR) has a significant impact on blockchain implementation. The implementation of the GDPR has raised several tensions regarding security, privacy, and the protection of personal data related to blockchain technology [5]. Among these, two overarching factors identified by the European Parliamentary Research Service (EPRS) are as follows.

- There shall be at least one central data controller who is responsible for ensuring data integrity and compliance with the GDPR [6]. GDPR requires data controllers and processors to obtain unambiguous consent of data subjects for their data to be processed [7]. This provides data subjects a right to know about what data is being collected and for what purposes. This also obligates data controllers and processors to remove the data that are no longer relevant [7]. It renders full control of data back to the data owners [8]. On the contrary, blockchain is a decentralized platform having no central data controller. Therefore, there is a lack of consensus among the practitioners and scholars of blockchain regarding who should be considered data controller or owner [6].
- Data must be modified or deleted when necessary [6]. Contrary to this, due to immutability by design, blockchain is an append-only ledger to which data can only be added. Deletion or removal of data from the blockchain is contradictory to blockchain design principles [6].

These two tensions play a critical role in the widespread adoption of blockchain. Organizations are struggling to find way(s) to design blockchain-based services, and to comply with these regulations. However, given the pervasive impacts of these tensions, scholars have attempted to suggest several approaches to tackle them. For example, to resolve the paradox of the data controller, scholars suggest defining participating nodes as controllers [9], miners as processors [10], joint controllers for federated blockchain [11], and developers as processors for smart contracts [12]. Similarly, to overcome the tension between data deletion and modification, scholars identified three methods [13]. First, storing personal data off-chain, storing a hash of personal data in the blockchain, and finally creating a link between them. Second, define a consensus mechanism to delete blocks. Third, using smart contracts to revoke access. Although scholars suggest a few techniques to comply with the GDPR requirements, they did not provide any guidelines on what needs to be considered while implementing these techniques. Thus, existing literature lacks GDPR compliant blockchain governance framework. Furthermore, our literature review indicates that there are few empirical studies on how organizations are adapting GDPR requirements with their blockchain design [14]. As such, blockchain governance frameworks suggested in existing literature [1, 2, 5, 15] fundamentally ignore the necessity of a separate governance framework to tackle the unique requirements of GDPR.

Therefore, this paper is guided by the research question (RQ): *What are the issues organizations must consider while developing a GDPR compliant blockchain governance framework?* To answer the above RQ, we conducted 20 semi-structured interviews among 18 different IT companies operating in Finland. After analyzing the interview data, we identified three main dimensions that the organizations must consider when developing the GDPR compliant governance framework: community, protocol, and compliance. The community comprises various issues related to stakeholders, communication, development, and decision rights. The protocol comprises issues related to consensus algorithms, incentives, and off-chain storage. Finally, compliance includes issues related to roles and responsibilities, accountability, and data collection and consent management. With these findings, we contribute to the existing literature on blockchain governance [1, 2, 5, 15] by including GDPR requirements.

The rest of the paper is organized as follows. Section 2 describes the background on blockchain and blockchain governance. Section 3 presents our research method whereas Sect. 4 discusses the identified dimensions and sub-dimensions that a GDPR compliant blockchain governance framework should consider. Section 5 illustrates the theoretical and practical implications. Finally, Sect. 6 concludes the paper.

2 Blockchain Governance

Blockchain governance refers to "the means of achieving the direction, control, and coordination of stakeholders within the context of a given blockchain project to which they jointly contribute" [1]. Research demonstrates that despite widespread interest in blockchain among researchers and practitioners, the adoption of blockchain is thwarted by the lack of governance models [5, 16]. Therefore, recently researchers have begun to develop blockchain governance frameworks, identifying different facets of blockchain and borrowing themes from different disciplines such as IT, management, and social science [5]. For example, Beck et al. [2] proposed a blockchain governance framework identifying themes from the Information Technology (IT) governance framework. They identified three dimensions of blockchain governance: decision rights, accountability, and incentives. Decision rights concern the generation and implementation of decision proposals, as well as the ratification and monitoring of decisions [2]. Accountability refers to which degree actors are responsible for their actions and decisions. Finally, incentives entail what motivates stakeholders to behave responsibly.

Again, observing the multitude of similarities between blockchain and Open-source Software (OSS), Pelt et al. [1] proposed a blockchain framework governance invoking OSS literature. They identified six dimensions of blockchain governance: (i) *formation and context* highlight the relevant background information (purpose, license) of blockchain (ii) *roles* define the roles of stakeholders in different layers (iii) *incentives* capture the motivational factors (iv) *membership* denotes the participation and management of the membership (v) *communication* focuses on the different formal and informal way of communication between stakeholders (vi) *decision making* describes how decisions are made, monitored, and controlled. Additionally, they discussed all these dimensions from the perspective of three layers: (i) *Off-chain community* includes a wider community of a blockchain, and governance mechanism focuses on the ties of the community (ii) *Off-chain development* includes the governance of the software development process and the protocol maintenance (iii) *On-chain protocol* consists of all the governance mechanisms taking place in the blockchain. For example, the decision-making process, consensus protocol, and rules of interaction. Furthermore, utilizing the concept from social science, Tan et al. [5] categorized nine blockchain governance decisions into three groups: (i) *micro-level* focuses on blockchain infrastructure, modularity, and standards in building, upgrading, and adoption of the blockchain. Micro-level governance defines infrastructure and application architecture and interoperability (ii) *Meso-level* deals with the governance of collective decision-making and actions. It includes the mechanisms related to decision-making, incentive, and consensus (iii) *Macro-level* governance concerns the rules and norms that are specific to a particular constitution, culture, history, and legal foundations. The decision domain consists of the organization of governance, accountability of governance, and control of governance.

However, though it is clear that there are some studies on blockchain governance, research on GDPR compliant blockchain governance is still lacking. In this current study, considering the multiple tensions between blockchain and GDPR and based on the different existing blockchain governance frameworks, we propose some issues/agendas for developing a blockchain governance framework that is GDPR compliant.

3   Research Method

3.1   Data Collection

We collected data using 20 semi-structured interviews and discussions from 18 different IT companies in Finland. All these companies were running blockchain-related projects when we conducted these interviews. The interviews had three major themes: 1) the importance of blockchain for the companies, 2) challenges the companies face with blockchain-based solutions, and 3) the GDPR-related specific challenges they face and how do they comply with the GDPR requirements. The interviewees had diverse backgrounds not just limited to technical but included interviewees from business and legal domains. The major roles of the interviewees include CEO, CTO, head of research, software developer, service designer, and legal expert. The interviews lasted approximately one hour on average. Due ethical concerns were considered including seeking permission from the interviewees. Notes were also taken during the interviews.

3.2   Data Analysis

We used the Gioia method [17] to analyze the interview data. In typical inductive research, data collection and analysis processes are partially overlapped. This was also the case in our study. However, certain steps can be recognized in our data analysis process, which we discuss next. There were three stages in our analysis. In the first stage, we went through the interview data several times and assigned codes to describe different segments of the content. Table 1 shows the codes that were generated at this stage with the associated quotes from the data. In the second stage, we categorized the related codes to develop more abstract concepts, which are also known as second-order

Table 1. Key concepts and associated codes with examples

2nd order Concept	Example code/1st order concept	Example quotes
Many stakeholders in a blockchain system	Developers, smart contract developers, validators or miners, investors, and end-users	"Blockchain-based systems can have various entities. For example, if you think about blockchain-based healthcare data storage, different branches of hospitals, patients and doctors can be part of the networked system." "Well, the participants in any blockchain-based system differ in different domains."
Communication is the key to further development	Online discussion forums, offline events, formal and informal interactions	"We understand that frequent communication is important for the community. We will arrange regular workshops and events so that everyone can be up to date." "Informal interactions can happen in different blogs and forums as well. The community members can start a discussion using the facility."
Development ideas are described in the community	Development team, anyone can propose ideas	"Any stakeholder can propose ideas for development. Then it is agreed within the community." "A process needs to be in place in deciding which development ideas to be implemented."
Decision rights belong to key stakeholders	Core developers or lead developers, the data subject, miners, validators	"The data belong to the data subject. They should be able to decide what to do with it." "The validators can be the participating organizations in the network. They can manage necessary decision making inside the network."

(*continued*)

Table 1. (*continued*)

2nd order Concept	Example code/1st order concept	Example quotes
Data validation happens using consensus algorithms	PoW, PoS, PoA, PBFT, or any combination	"When a data is entered into the block, the validation happens with consensus algorithm." "Well, there are different consensus algorithms, and a blockchain can have combinations of multiple for validating the data."
Incentives are needed for the stakeholder's	Validators or miners need incentives	"We can use reputation allocation for the participants." "The participants who have validated most blocks are rated as honest validators"
Off-chain storage for GDPR compliance	Off-chain data can be removed or updated when necessary	"We store the personally identifiable information and other types of metadata in the off-chain. Hash and signature of the metadata are stored in the on-chain." "Managing the access rights in off-chain is important. We have used traditional storage like access mechanism for the off-chain."
Roles and responsibilities in accordance with GDPR	Data controller, processor, data protection officer	"Data controller can be the experts from the company who understands the data and how it can be used." "Though we have not yet decided who can be the data processors, it is certainly needed in blockchain-based organizations."

(*continued*)

Table 1. (*continued*)

2nd order Concept	Example code/1st order concept	Example quotes
Accountability in accordance with GDPR	The data controller makes sure that GDPR requirements are fulfilled	"We use smart contact to validate the data controllers' roles and any data loss." "As a financial aid institution, we use a blockchain-based system so that the money spent and where it's coming from is transparent. The responsible person can be easily identified in case of any problem arises." "If the data management lifecycle and data collection volume is lower, the accountability is easier to manage. Hence, we have taken the approach of less data collection to avoid the case of accountability."
Data Collection and Consent Management	The organization collects user data and consent as well	"We will try to collect as minimal data as possible. Data that is not related to our work, we don't collect that." "We only collect purposeful data." "The consents are stored in the archive until the user revokes it."

concepts. Finally, in the third stage, we aggregated the second-order concepts into three broader themes or dimensions: community, blockchain protocol, and compliance toward building a GDPR compliant blockchain governance framework. The derived dimensions along their corresponding sub-dimensions have been depicted in Fig. 1.

4   Towards a GDPR Compliant Blockchain Governance Framework

Our interview data revealed several sub-dimensions, which we grouped under three main dimensions as presented in Fig. 1. Next, we elaborate on these dimensions.

4.1   Community

The decentralized nature of the blockchain system is characterized as a community of various interest groups. To manage and coordinate this entire community toward a common goal, it is important to have a governance mechanism that defines the roles of different stakeholders, their ways of communication, shared development ideas and implementation responsibilities, and the authority and rights to make the decisions. Lacking any proper governance system may jeopardize the success of the blockchain ecosystem.

Our data analysis revealed that a blockchain ecosystem consists of various actors such as blockchain developers, smart contract developers, data controllers, validators or miners, investors, and end-users. Stakeholders possess a substantial influence on the functioning of the system and, at the same time, they are affected by it [18]. This is because the stakeholders shape the blockchain protocol rules and once the rules are implemented, the blockchain protocol shapes stakeholders' activities [19]. Therefore, a

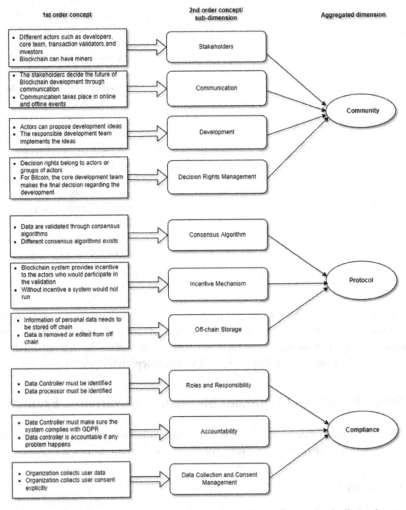

Fig. 1. GDPR compliant blockchain governance dimensions and sub-dimensions

blockchain governance framework needs to highlight the definitions of all stakeholders, their inclusion criteria, their roles and responsibilities, and their modus operandi. One of the challenges concerning stakeholders is the data portability that is possessed by different participants of distributed systems. So, it is also important to have guidelines about the information creation, sharing, and availability outside the blockchain (even before its creation) in the governance model.

After defining the stakeholders, it is important to set rules and norms to be followed by the stakeholders while communicating in the community. The governance framework may include the tools to be used for discussions related to community or development, how the discussion will be coordinated, and how to reach an agreement about the discussion [1]. Again, in the community, especially the open-source community, any actor can propose development ideas. It is unlikely that all ideas are implementable. Therefore, there is a need for a mechanism to choose the best idea to be implemented. Besides, regular maintenance and updates are required for the smooth functioning of the system. Regular monitoring also helps to identify potential threats, which in turn helps to ensure the safety of the system. As such, monitoring and maintenance should come under the purview of the governance framework.

Finally, decision-making rights should be entrusted to a particular actor or group of actors. Blockchain governance is the placement and enactment of decision rights [20]. It includes a set of officially granted rights and obligations to make decisions, give orders, and take certain actions independently in the system [2]. The governance framework should highlight how decisions are made, implemented, and controlled. Some of the key decision areas to be included are the voting mechanism, consensus mechanism, personal data protection, dispute resolution, and the development of the blockchain network.

4.2 Protocol

The protocol specifies the rules and regulations for managing the blockchain network. Our interview data revealed three sub-dimensions of the protocol that needs to be considered in the blockchain governance framework: consensus algorithms, incentive mechanisms, and off-chain storage. Consensus algorithms are used to validate data and add the data to the blockchain. It is a fault-tolerant technique used to establish an appropriate agreement across the blockchain network. Various consensus algorithms exist such as Proof of Work (PoW), Proof of Stake (PoS), and Proof of Authority (PoA). In PoW, participating nodes constantly try to validate the block, using their computing power. This mechanism is often criticized for its extensive consumption of energy [21]. On the other hand, PoS is an energy-efficient alternative to PoW, in which consensus is reached by the nodes with a larger proportion of stake in the network. PoA is used in permissioned and private blockchains [22]. In PoA, a set of trusted entities known as validators are responsible to add new blocks to the network. This provides comparatively better performance as it requires fewer validators and less computational power. Respondents of our interview suggest that a blockchain system can use multiple consensus algorithms considering scalability, performance, and security issues.

Network participants should be incentivized for contributing to the network. Incentive mechanisms can also be part of the consensus algorithms. Without the incentive, a blockchain system would not be successful. Participants can be rewarded with pecuniary or non-pecuniary incentives or both. The governance framework should determine how incentives will be provided for the roles accomplished by the participants such as developers, miners or validators, off-chain contributors, etc. Besides, it is also important to underscore what factors motivate the community members and why node operators want to contribute [1].

The last sub-dimension of protocol that has emerged from the interview data is the maintenance of off-chain storage for storing personal data. This off-chain storage has been suggested by the experts as a way to comply with the GDPR requirements of personal data modification and deletion. In the off-chain storage, data can be deleted, modified, and added. The idea is that all personal data, as deemed by the user, will be stored in off-chain storage. After storing data, a hash value will be generated by algorithms. The generated hash value will then be tagged and synched with the corresponding on-chain network. As a result, when users need to modify or add any personal data, they will be able to do so in the off-chain storage, which will in turn be updated in the on-chain database also. Again, if the users want to delete all their data, then the concerned hash value index will be removed from the off-chain storage, which ultimately will make users' records traceless in the on-chain. To manage the off-chain storage, the governance framework should have guidelines regarding who will be the owner or controller of the off-chain storage, who will be responsible for maintaining this storage, and what would be the process of data modification and deletion, and the responsibility of the user thereon.

4.3 Compliance

Our final theme is directly related to GDPR compliance, which emphasizes defining the roles and responsibilities of the stakeholders and their accountabilities, consent management, and data minimization. GDPR requires appointing a data controller (Article 24, 26), data processor (Article 28), and data protection officer (Article 37) to protect personal data. According to the GDPR, *a data controller* is responsible to implement suitable measures to protect the data subject's rights and to ensure that the data is being processed duly by the data processor. If there is more than one entity responsible for decision-making, a joint controller should be defined. Data controllers ensure the protection of users' data. The *Data processor* processes the data under the supervision of the data controller. *The data protection officer* informs and advises the data controller or the processor and monitors the compliance of GDPR. By *accountability*, GDPR requires that organizations take appropriate technical and organizational measures to protect personal data and be able to justify the effectiveness of those measures if the necessity arises to do so. *Consent* refers to the data subject's wishes that signify agreement to process personal data. Before the collection of personal data, users' consent should be obtained, explicitly mentioning what personal data will be collected, why the data will be processed, and how long the data will be stored. Data needs to be collected as minimally as possible.

GDPR compliant blockchain governance guidelines need to devise who will be the data controller, data processor, and data protection officer, what would be their qualifications and job responsibilities, to whom they will be accountable, what technical and organizational measures should be taken to protect personal data and how those can be implemented, what would be the controlling mechanisms, and what would be the consequence of a failure of data protection. Regarding consent management, the governance framework may indicate how users' consent will be obtained, how users will be informed about the type of data, the purpose of data collection, and storing periods, and how they can revoke their given consent, etc.

5 Discussion

5.1 Theoretical Implications

Our paper has three major theoretical contributions. First, to the best of our knowledge, our paper on toward developing a blockchain governance framework is the first to accommodate GDPR requirements. The governance frameworks proposed by prior studies are mainly centered on identifying various governance dimensions drawing on different theories and expert interviews without considering GDPR or other regulatory requirements. For example, Beck et al. [2] discussed blockchain governance for blockchain economy—decentralized autonomous organizations (DAO)—drawing on dimensions from IT governance literature: decision rights, accountability, and incentives. Again, Pelt et al. [1] proposed a blockchain governance framework, consisting of six dimensions: formation and context, roles, incentives, membership, communication, and decision making, and three layers: off-chain community, off-chain development, and on-chain protocol. They based their findings on expert interviews, case studies, and an open-source software governance framework. More recently, Goldsby and Hanisch [15] have proposed a blockchain governance model, highlighting the coordination and control challenges faced in blockchain governance contexts and their coping strategies. However, these prior studies did not consider the tensions between GDPR and blockchain design. In our paper, we underscore the possible ways of overcoming those tensions. Therefore, our study extended prior governance frameworks [1, 2, 15] by adding GDPR requirements.

Second, our research identified major concepts related to GDPR compliance of blockchain. Under these concepts, we have identified three dimensions namely community, protocol, and compliance. We have also described what kinds of considerations should be taken concerning these dimensions. Especially, under compliance, we described the roles, responsibilities, and accountabilities of different actors such as data controllers and data processors.

Third, in contrast to prior literature [e.g., 1], we have identified that off-chain storage is a part of the blockchain protocol to be compliant with GDPR. For example, under the off-chain storage sub-dimension, we described how off-chain storage could be used to accommodate the GDPR requirements of data modification and deletion. Our results also reveal that many issues must be considered when governing such off-chain.

5.2 Practical Implications

Our study has several practical implications. First, our interview with the expert revealed that the adoption of blockchain is hindered by the lack of a GDPR compliance governance framework. They are struggling with GDPR requirements while using blockchain technology. We provided a list of considerations that might help organizations to build a GDPR compliant blockchain business model. Second, understanding how blockchains are governed and how GDPR requirements are met is imperative for policymakers [23]. Our findings will help them in setting standards and practices to expedite the adoption of blockchain technology.

Third, our findings highlight the need for a GDPR-centric blockchain design approach. With this, we suggest blockchain architects proactively consider GDPR requirements and include the GDPR design requirements in the system architecture. This echoes what EPRS [6] suggested by noting that "blockchain architects need to be aware of this [challenge] from the outset and make sure that they design their respective use cases in a manner that allows compliance with European data protection law". The findings of our paper would help blockchain architects while considering how to proactively include GDPR requirements in the system architecture.

6   Limitations and Future Research Directions

The present study has limitations that also guide to spur future research. First, the study is based on industry experts from Finland. Future research could be benefited by considering a more extensive set of experts from different industries and different countries. Second, we proposed different dimensions and considerations in developing a GDPR compliant blockchain by considering the viewpoints of the interviewees who were involved in different cases. With this approach, we managed to identify the key issues that are valid for multiple cases. However, for a more in-depth understanding, future scholars may pursue to validate our recommendations through in-depth case studies.

7   Conclusion

To address the current gap in blockchain governance literature, we attempted to answer the question of how blockchain can be designed that also comply with GDPR requirements. In this regard, we interviewed industry experts who are using blockchain in their organizations. Upon scrutinizing the interview data using the Gioia method, we derived three core dimensions and ten sub-dimensions. We underscored that the organizations could overcome the tensions between GDPR and blockchain by following our recommendations in designing their blockchain.

Acknowledgment. This study was financially supported by the Foundation for Economic Education (www.lsr.fi).

References

1. van Pelt, R., Jansen, S., Baars, D., Overbeek, S.: Defining blockchain governance: a framework for analysis and comparison. Inf. Syst. Manag. **38**, 21–41 (2020). https://doi.org/10.1080/105 80530.2020.1720046

2. Beck, R., Müller-Bloch, C., King, J.: Governance in the blockchain economy: a framework and research agenda. J. Assoc. Inf. Syst. **19**, 1 (2018)
3. Zheng, X.R., Lu, Y.: Blockchain technology–recent research and future trend. Enterp. Inf. Syst. 1–23 (2021). https://doi.org/10.1080/17517575.2021.1939895
4. Janssen, M., Weerakkody, V., Ismagilova, E., Sivarajah, U., Irani, Z.: A framework for analyzing blockchain technology adoption: integrating institutional, market and technical factors. Int. J. Inf. Manage. **50**, 302–309 (2020)
5. Tan, E., Mahula, S., Crompvoets, J.: Blockchain governance in the public sector: a conceptual framework for public management. Gov. Inf. Q. **39**, 101625 (2022). https://doi.org/10.1016/J.GIQ.2021.101625
6. EPRS: blockchain and the general data protection regulation can distributed ledgers be squared with European data protection law? (2019). https://doi.org/10.2861/535
7. Tankard, C.: What the GDPR means for businesses. Netw. Secur. **2016**, 5–8 (2016)
8. Truong, N.B., Sun, K., Lee, G.M., Guo, Y.: GDPR-Compliant personal data management: a blockchain-based solution. IEEE Trans. Inf. Forensics Secur. **15**, 1746–1761 (2020). https://doi.org/10.1109/TIFS.2019.2948287
9. Bayle, A., Koscina, M., Manset, D., Perez-Kempner, O.: When blockchain meets the right to be forgotten: technology versus law in the healthcare industry. In: Proceedings - 2018 IEEE/WIC/ACM International Conference on Web Intelligence, WI 2018, pp. 788–792 (2019)
10. Jambert, A.: Blockchain and the GDPR: a data protection authority point of view. In: Blazy, O., Yeun, C.Y. (eds.) WISTP 2018. LNCS, vol. 11469, pp. 3–6. Springer, Cham (2019). https://doi.org/10.1007/978-3-030-20074-9_1
11. Dutta, R., Das, A., Dey, A., Bhattacharya, S.: Blockchain vs GDPR in collaborative data governance. In: Luo, Y. (ed.) CDVE 2020. LNCS, vol. 12341, pp. 81–92. Springer, Cham (2020). https://doi.org/10.1007/978-3-030-60816-3_10
12. Kondova, G., Erbguth, J.: Self-sovereign identity on public blockchains and the GDPR. In: Proceedings of the ACM Symposium on Applied Computing, pp. 342–345 (2020)
13. Haque, A.B., Islam, A.K.M.N., Hyrynsalmi, S., Naqvi, B., Smolander, K.: GDPR compliant blockchains-a systematic literature review. IEEE Access. **9**, 50593–50606 (2021)
14. Rieger, A., Lockl, J., Urbach, N., Guggenmos, F., Fridgen, G.: Building a blockchain application that complies with the EU general data protection regulation. MIS Quart. Executive **18**, 263–279 (2019). https://doi.org/10.17705/2MSQE.00020
15. Goldsby, C., Hanisch, M.: The boon and bane of blockchain: getting the governance right. Calif. Manag. Rev. **64**(3), 141–168 (2022). https://doi.org/10.1177/00081256221080747
16. Batubara, F.R., Ubacht, J., Janssen, M.: Challenges of blockchain technology adoption for e-government: a systematic literature review. In: ACM International Conference Proceeding Series (2018). https://doi.org/10.1145/3209281.3209317
17. Gioia, D.A., Corley, K.G., Hamilton, A.L.: Seeking qualitative rigor in inductive research: notes on the gioia methodology. Organ. Res. Methods **16**, 15–31 (2013). https://doi.org/10.1177/1094428112452151
18. Allen, D.W.E., Berg, C., Markey-Towler, B., Novak, M., Potts, J.: Blockchain and the evolution of institutional technologies: implications for innovation policy. Res. Policy **49**, 103865 (2020). https://doi.org/10.1016/J.RESPOL.2019.103865
19. Rossi, M., Mueller-Bloch, C., Thatcher, J.B., Beck, R.: Blockchain research in information systems: current trends and an inclusive future research agenda. J. Assoc. Inf. Syst. **20**, 1388–1403 (2019). https://doi.org/10.17705/1jais.00571
20. Ziolkowski, R., Miscione, G., Schwabe, G.: Decision problems in blockchain governance: old wine in new bottles or walking in someone else's shoes? J. Manag. Inf. Syst. **37**, 316–348 (2020). https://doi.org/10.1080/07421222.2020.1759974
21. O'dwyer, K.J., Malone, D.: Bitcoin Mining and its Energy Footprint (2014)

22. Singh, P.K., Singh, R., Nandi, S.K., Nandi, S.: Managing smart home appliances with proof of authority and blockchain. In: Lüke, K.-H., Eichler, G., Erfurth, C., Fahrnberger, G. (eds.) I4CS 2019. CCIS, vol. 1041, pp. 221–232. Springer, Cham (2019). https://doi.org/10.1007/978-3-030-22482-0_16
23. Wright, A., de Filippi, P.: Decentralized blockchain technology and the rise of lex cryptographia. SSRN Electron. J. (2015).https://doi.org/10.2139/SSRN.2580664

Voice Assistants: (Physical) Device Use Perceptions, Acceptance, and Privacy Concerns

Ali Farooq[1] 🆔, Debora Jeske[2](✉) 🆔, Paul van Schaik[3] 🆔, and Michael Moran[4] 🆔

[1] University of Turku, 20500 Turku, Finland
[2] University College Cork, Cork T23 K208, Republic of Ireland
d.jeske@ucc.ie
[3] Teesside University, Middlesbrough TS1 3BA, UK
[4] Atlantic Technological University, Galway H91 T8NW, Republic of Ireland

Abstract. Using UTAUT2 model and privacy concerns, the study identifies the factors that predict users' and non-users' behavioral intention to continue or start using physical voice assistant devices in the future as their prominence is increasing significantly in both work and home locations. Users and non-users of voice assistants were recruited via an online survey in both Ireland and Finland. The final sample ($N = 119$) included 54 users and 65 non-users of voice assistants. Group differences and predictive effects were investigated using independent samples t-tests, analysis of covariance, and multiple regression. Users differed significantly from non-users on a number of UTAUT2 model variables such as effort expectancy, social influence, facilitating conditions, hedonic motivation, private value, and privacy concern. Users' behavioral intention to continue using voice assistants was stronger than non-users' behavioral intention to start using such voice assistants. Multiple regression results show that, for non-users, both effort expectancy and privacy concerns appear to impact their intention to adopt voice assistants – in contrast to participants who are already users. However, social influence, facilitating conditions, price value, effort, and performance expectancy were not significant predictors of behavioral intention. The findings suggest that the continued or future use of voice assistants can be predicted by assessing both users' and non-users' expectations regarding the degree to which they are or expect to become habituated to the use of voice assistants, and enjoyment and value derived from these devices. The findings add to the emerging evidence-base about users' and non-users' perceptions, acceptance, and concerns regarding using voice assistants and highlights the importance of context in the adoption, acceptance, and perceptions of both user groups.

Keywords: Voice assistants · UTAUT2 · Performance expectancy · Effort expectancy · Smart speaker · Behavioral intention

1 Introduction

Many recent articles focus on user acceptance of a number of different voice assistant tools (e.g., Burbach et al. 2019). These are known under names such as smart speaker

© IFIP International Federation for Information Processing 2022
Published by Springer Nature Switzerland AG 2022
S. Papagiannidis et al. (Eds.): I3E 2022, LNCS 13454, pp. 485–498, 2022.
https://doi.org/10.1007/978-3-031-15342-6_37

assistants (Brause and Blank 2020), smart voice assistant speakers (Lee et al. 2020), smart home devices, smart home hubs (Chhetri and Motti 2019), intelligent and digital personal assistants (De Barcelos Silva et al. 2020), artificial intelligence-based voice assistant systems (Lee et al. 2021), intelligent personal assistants (Liao et al. 2019), and in-home or home voice assistants (Lucia-Palacios and Pérez-López 2021; McLean and Osei-Frimpong 2019; Pal et al. 2020). Indeed, the market for such devices with speaker functions and speaker compatibility has increased as these devices become more well-known and find wider acceptance in various settings and countries. Current popular devices include many well-known devices such as Amazon's Echo, Google Home, Wing (Chhetri and Motti 2019), Insteon's Hub (2021), or Xiao Ai, a voice assistant that is part of the Mi AI speaker by Xiaomi (Tan 2021). It is important to note that many computers and smartphones now offer preinstalled and integrated voice assistant functions (e.g., Siri, GoogleAssistant, Cortana, and OpenSource assistants such as Mycroft and Rhasspy Voice Assistant). In this paper, we are particularly interested in exploring user and non-user perceptions of voice assistant devices that are visible as devices in the home or workplace (rather than integrated into devices that existed before voice assistants came about, such as smart phones, computers, or smart watches). Good examples include Amazon Echo, Alexa, and Google Home, as these are physical devices in their own right that are usually placed within the users' and non-users' line of sight, often in private and shared premises such as office spaces. The guiding theoretical framework in this research is the unified theory of acceptance and use of technology (UTAUT) (Venkatesh et al. 2003) and its successor (UTAUT2; Venkatesh et al. 2012) as both models have been used to explore consumers' adoption of new, intelligent assistant devices (e.g., Liao et al. 2019; Sohn and Kwon 2020).

The goal of the current quantitative research presented in this paper is to examine users and non-users' behavioral intention to use voice assistants as a function of a number of different perceptions related to the performance of those efforts, the expectations people have regarding the use of such devices, but also aspects such as facilitating conditions and social influence. We focus here on the use of these physical devices in both home and work as voice assistants have become more common in both locations, particularly as many employees now increasingly started working from home due to the Covid-19 pandemic (e.g., Jeske 2022). An example statistic backs up this trend: according to Juniper Research, up to 55% of American households are expected to own voice assistants such as smart speakers (Dee 2021).

2   Recent Work on Voice Assistants

The interest in voice assistants has grown significantly over the last five years. This is in part due to the interplay of many stakeholders (Pal et al. 2020), concerns about data leakages and surveillance (Ford and Palmer 2019; Frick et al. 2021), and malware-induced misperception attacks (attacks that involve the delivery of manipulated content via voice assistants; Sharevski et al. 2021). Major stakeholders include the manufacturers, users, non-users (as they are essentially bystanders whose interactions with users may also be captured), government and other agencies, third-party application developers and cloud service providers (Chhetri and Motti 2019; Pal et al. 2020; Pfeifle 2018). In recognition of these dynamics, more and more studies focus on multiple stakeholders.

Nevertheless, while the research around voice assistants is expanding rapidly, a number of questions remain: is the adoption, acceptance, and use of these (physical vs. virtual) devices influenced by the same characteristics and concerns when they are used in public or private spaces (e.g., see work on virtual voice assistants by Burbach et al. 2019)? Can we consider workspaces truly public venues when they are actually located in our homes (see also virtual voice assistant work by Easwara Moorthy and Vu 2015)? Does digital competitiveness and societal adoption play a potential role in affecting privacy concerns in different countries? What privacy or additional features may be particularly desirable and attractive for current users (and non-users), such as the option to select a 'home-zone' forget mode when the home office is again used for private activities rather than work? The current study is making an attempt to add to our current knowledge of voice assistants in the hope of contributing to a meta-analysis in the future on how context influences (physical) voice assistant adoption and usage.

In this study, we specifically consider the perceptions of both users and non-users of physical voice assistants in work and home settings. Even individuals who are not users are affected by the popularity of these devices in their homes, office, and public spaces (Pal et al. 2020). Studying both groups is an approach that has been taken by a number of other authors as well. Lau et al. (2018) similarly studied in their qualitative study the perceptions and factors that would predict the adoption of voice assistants by users and non-users in their homes, but not in work settings. Liao et al. (2019) considered the perspective of users and non-users working for a US university regarding intelligent personal assistants in a quantitative study. However, these authors focused on smartphone users where voice assistants are an integrated feature, rather than a visible physical device. No information was provided about the context of use, such as the home and/or the workplace. The current research therefore includes both users and non-users as important stakeholders, in both home and work settings. The following section provides a more detailed overview of recent work on voice assistants and an overview of our hypotheses and research model.

2.1   Performance and Effort Expectancy

We therefore define performance expectancy as the extent to which users as well as non-users might believe that using a system or electronic tool such as a voice assistant will help them to accomplish certain tasks or achieve a certain level of performance (Venkatesh et al. 2003). In our context, effort expectancy is the extent to which users and non-users feel that they find voice assistants to be easy to use (Venkatesh et al. 2003). This is a particular concern for many who use devices set up in different languages (which is often the case with voice assistants) or devices that they have had little or no experience. Past research by Dwivedi et al. (2019) demonstrated that both performance and effort expectancy are positive predictors of behavioral intention to use information systems and technology devices. Liao et al. (2019) similarly found evidence that perceived performance and effort expectancy influenced users' decision to adopt phone-based intelligent personal assistants in a sample of US users and non-users. This leads us to propose the following two hypotheses:

H1: Performance Expectancy is a positive predictor of intention to use voice assistants.

H2: Effort Expectancy is a positive predictor of intention to use voice assistants.

2.2   Social Influence and Facilitating Conditions

The degree to which both users and non-users form the intention to perform a behavior (e.g., Venkatesh et al. 2003), such as using a voice assistant, may vary due to the user's experience, expectations, the supportive conditions as well as the encouragement they receive from their social environment. Social conditions reflect circumstances in that users and non-users may be exposed and encouraged by people in their social environments to use certain devices, which – in turn – constitutes social influence in the current study. The degree to which other individuals around a user or non-user believe that such devices ought to be used is also likely to drive the adoption as well as continued use of voice assistants. Evidence on the intention and use of information systems and technology information has linked social influence as well as facilitating conditions significantly and positively to behavioral intentions (Dwivedi et al. 2019). The social benefits have also been studied in relation to voice assistants (McLean and Osei-Frimpong 2019). This leads us to propose the following hypothesis:

H3: Social Influence is a positive predictor of the intention to use voice assistants.

The increase in interconnectivity in the home and at work has supported the adoption of many tools such as voice assistants. In addition, such devices are becoming increasingly popular gifts from family members and friends to one another (Liao et al. 2019). Facilitating conditions thus capture the resources, knowledge, and technological compatibility of devices. In some cases, they are also likely to be potentially socially supported as well. These circumstances increase the presence of such devices in various locations, while the organizational and technical infrastructure such as wireless access further creates facilitating conditions that will support the use of such devices (Venkatesh et al. 2003). We, therefore, propose that:

H4: Facilitating conditions are a positive predictor of the intention to use voice assistants.

2.3   Hedonic Motivation, Price Value, and the Importance of Habitual Use

Past evidence based on a South Korean sample of 378 survey respondents suggested that purchase intentions of AI-based intelligent products tested using UTAUT2 are higher when they expected to enjoy these products (Sohn and Kwon 2020). In the context of UTAUT2 (Venkatesh et al. 2012), hedonic motivation thus captures the extent to which a person finds using a specific technology enjoyable and entertaining. Lee et al. (2020) reported that hedonic motivation predicted satisfaction with voice assistants. Furthermore, the context in which voice assistants may also matter, as McLean and Osei-Frimpong (2019) reported that hedonic benefits would only motivate users in smaller households to use voice assistants, which suggests that the social environment plays a role in terms of how users use such devices. Despite this mixed picture regarding the effect of hedonic motivation on behavioral intention to use various tools, we propose the following hypotheses:

H5: Hedonic motivation is a positive predictor of the intention to use voice assistants.

Price value, together with design and brand value, has been shown to positively influence users' perceived benefits in relation to smart speakers in a South Korean study (Park et al. 2018). Perceived value thus captures the degree to which individuals find that certain devices are reasonably priced and represent good value (see also Venkatesh et al. 2012). Lau et al. (2018) also reported that price, together with convenience, motivate the decision to use and adopt smart speakers among both users and non-users. When users feel that they paid a good price for their device and it will add value to their interactions, they may also be more likely to use voice assistants in the future. Accordingly, we propose that:

H6: Price value is a positive predictor of the intention to use voice assistants.

The routine use of voice assistants may also foster the habitual use of voice assistants over time. Habit in relation to UTAUT2 (Venkatesh et al. 2012) thus refers to the extent to which individuals get first used to a device, use it regularly, and over time automatically resort to using this device over others as a matter of habit. The development of a habit – in the home or at work – of voice assistants may therefore also increase the intention among users and non-users to use voice assistants in the future. Lee et al. (2020) reported that habit formation also predicted the continuous use of voice assistants in their sample. Furthermore, habit operated as a mediator between satisfaction with the voice assistant and the continuous use of the assistants. This suggests a positive association. We, therefore, hypothesize that:

H7: The habitual use is a positive predictor of the intention to use voice assistants.

2.4 The Role of Privacy Concerns

Privacy concern captures the perceptions of users regarding the extent to which virtual and physical voice assistant devices are safe to use, help to support or undermine a user's privacy (Burbach et al. 2019), and the extent to which data shared with such devices are safeguarded appropriately (see also study by Kim et al. 2011). While privacy concerns are absent from the UTAUT2 model, these concerns are particularly likely when users and non-users are concerned about the security of their data as there is evidence that voice assistants and other smart devices are hacked or compromised (e.g., Park et al. 2018; Sharevski et al. 2021; Yan et al. 2021). For example, Chhetri and Motti (2019) identified various user concerns in user reviews, including aspects such as tracking, storage of conversations, lack of data security, and potential hacking risks. This leads us to propose the following:

H8: Privacy concerns are a negative predictor of the intention to use virtual assistants.

3 Method

3.1 Data Collection and Sample

Data collection took place in two countries: Ireland and Finland. These countries were selected because they both ranked among the top 20 in the world in 2020 and 2021 in terms of their digital competitiveness (IMD 2021). Both countries also share a lot of similarities in terms of the size of their populations and economies, while both countries are also known as international tech hubs (Gallagher 2022). Students are digital natives who tend to use various electronic gadgets (including voice assistants; Farooq et al. 2019). We, therefore, expected that familiarity with and the use of physical voice assistants would be likely in the general and student populations.

A cross-sectional research design was used, with data collection in two educational institutions in Ireland and one in Finland. Ethics was obtained from both Irish institutions for this study. Data collection started in July 2020 and concluded in May 2021. All participants were asked to give consent. The two surveys ran separately (one in Ireland and one in Finland) and 145 individuals moved past the consent page. The final dataset includes 119 participants who completed at least 80% of the survey. This included 75 participants from Ireland (63%) and 44 participants (37%) from Finland. Research participants in both countries had the option to register after the study for a raffle (via a separate form not connected to the original survey).

3.2 Participant Description

The sample size of 119 participants included 63% males, 37% females with an average of 25.15 years (SD = 7.75, range 18 to 69). At the time of the study, 47% of respondents were students of bachelor, 10% of masters and PhD, and 3% were pursuing non-degree qualifications (another 30% of respondents opted out to provide information about their educational level). Among the respondents, 45% (n = 54) had used a voice assistant previously at home (n = 51), the workplace (n = 12), or both places (n = 9). In terms of participants' work experience, we should note that a significant proportion of the sample was working while studying. In terms of the Irish sample, an estimated 70–80% of students contacted for this survey were working while studying, while 30–40% of students in the Finnish sample – based on Turku statistics – are working while studying.

3.3 Measures

For this study, we used established scales from the previous studies, which we adapted in relation to voice assistants. All UTAUT-related constructs were measured on a 5-points Likert scale (1 = strongly disagree, to 5 = strongly agree). Some of the original response options were reduced cognitive load. In addition, we added a few questions to learn more about our participants' past experiences and demographics. The data from current users and non-users were combined (N = 119).

Prior Experience Using a Voice Assistant. Participants were asked "Please tell us if you have experience with Amazon Echo, Apple's HomePod or Alexa and other voice assistants/smart speakers". In addition, we asked if they used them at home, at work, or both which was the case for 54 participants (45.4%).

Performance Expectancy. This variable was measured using three questions from the perceived usefulness scale adapted from Davis (1989) and Venkatesh et al. (2003). We asked both users and non-users (M = 3.22., SD = 1.02 α = .88). An example statement for a current user of voice assistants is: "Being able to use voice assistants enables me to accomplish tasks more quickly at home/at work". A non-user was presented with a slightly amended statement: "Being able to use voice assistants will enable me to accomplish tasks more quickly at home/at work".

Effort Expectancy. We used four items from the perceived ease of use scale presented in Davis (1989), which were also featured in Venkatesh et al. (2012). The items were slightly adapted in relation to voice assistants. All four were used in the final composite (M = 3.22, SD = 1.02, α = .88). Current users would receive an item such as this: "Learning to use voice assistants/smart speaker is easy for me" while non-users were presented with this item: "Learning to use voice assistants/smart speaker would be easy for me". Higher scores indicate more positive ease of use perceptions.

Social Influence. This measure featured three items Anderson and Agarwal (2010). We focused on assessing participants' perceptions of descriptive social norms, in particular, as to what other people do (M = 2.36., SD = 1.10, α = .90). Both users and non-users were presented with identical items, for example, the statement "I believe people who are important to me use voice assistants/smart speakers".

Facilitating Conditions. This was measured using four items adapted from Venkatesh et al. (2012), again adapted in relation to voice assistants (M = 4.21, SD = 0.58, α = .57). Both users and non-users were asked to respond to items such as: "I have the resources necessary to use voice assistants/smart speakers".

Hedonic Motivation. This was also measured using three items by Venkatesh et al. (2012), also called "perceived enjoyment" in TAM research (M = 3.85, SD = 0.92, α = .92). For example, all participants were asked to respond to items such as "Using voice assistants/smart speakers is enjoyable".

Price Value (Price Motivation). We used the three items by Venkatesh et al (2012). The original items asked about internet costs and were amended in relation to voice assistant (M = 3.43, SD = 0.98, α = .88). In order to give non-users an idea of the cost estimates of such devices for 2020, we included a price range (60–100 Euro).

Habit (Habitual Use of Voice Assistants). We also wanted to assess the extent to which participants would expect that their use of voice assistants is (in the case of users) or could be (in the case of non-users) become a habit, using three items from Venkatesh et al. (2012). An example demonstrates this. Users were asked "The use of voice assistants/smart speakers has become a habit for me" while non-users were asked "The use of voice assistants/smart speakers could become a habit for me", followed by the 5-point Likert response scale as with the other scales (M = 3.01, SD = 1.17, α = .85).

Behavioral Intention (to Use Voice Assistants in the Future). This was assessed with three items from Venkatesh et al. (2012), again adapted in reference to voice assistants

(M = 2.93, SD = 1.21, α = .91). Both users and non-users were asked, for example, "I intend to use voice assistants in the future". The same response scale options were applied as above. The composite of the three items represented our outcome variable in this study.

Privacy Concern. We included privacy concerns using four items which were slightly adapted in reference to voice assistants from Kim et al. (2011; M = 2.57, SD = 1.04, α = .87) with five answering options (1 = strongly disagree, to 5 = strongly agree). An example item was "In general, using voice assistants/smart speakers is risk-free". Higher scores indicate lower privacy concern.

Control Variables (Demographics). We also asked respondents about their gender, age, educational level, the educational discipline they were studying (as we recruited cross-sectionally).

4 Results

4.1 Group Comparisons and Correlations

As expected, users ($n = 54$) and non-users ($n = 65$) differed in some respects when we explored the two groups using independent samples t-tests. Please note that due to a sampling error, performance expectancy was only recorded in the Irish data (for 73 participants) but not in the Finnish data. As a result, the analysis of group differences for Performance Expectancy was excluded as the ratio was 8 to 65 users vs. non-users.

Users reported lower effort expectancy than non-users ($M_u = 2.22, SD = 1.13; M_n = 4.28, SD = 0.63; t(117) = -12.51, p < .001$), more social influence ($M_u = 2.85, SD = 1.09; M_n = 1.95, SD = 0.92; t(117) = 4.86, p < .001$), and greater hedonic motivation ($M_u = 4.09, SD = 0.66; M_n = 3.65, SD = 1.05; t(117) = 2.71, p = .008$). Other significant differences emerged: users scored higher on price value ($M_u = 3.79, SD = 0.87; M_n = 3.13, SD = 0.97; t(117) = -3.88, p < .001$), privacy concern ($M_u = 2.82, SD = 0.95; M_n = 2.36, SD = 1.07; t(117) = 2.48, p = .015$) and intention to continue using voice assistants in the future than non-users ($M_u = 3.56, SD = 1.01; M_n = 2.41, SD = 1.22; t(117) = 5.87, p < .001$). No significant differences ($p < .05$) were observed in relation to habit development ($p = .065$) and facilitating conditions between users and non-users ($p = .123$). Most of the scale composites for the combined sample correlated weakly to moderately, as expected; there was little evidence of multi-collinearity (Table 1).

4.2 Main Analysis and Hypothesis Testing

We first examined the predictive effects of the UTAUT variables on behavioral intention for users and non-users (as separate samples) using the forced-entry method in multiple regression. Country was only a significant control variable in the case of non-users. In the case of users ($n = 54$), the seven predictors collectively explained 60% of the variance in behavioral intention ($R^2_{adj} = .60, F(7,46) = 12.15, p < .001$). The results for non-users

Table 1. Correlations for the combined sample ($N = 117$)

Constructs	PE	EE	HU	SI	FC	HM	PV	PC	BI
PE	1								
EE	.12	1							
HU	.67**	.27**	1						
SI	.43**	−.28**	.17	1					
FC	.23*	−.09	.13	.23*	1				
HM	.71**	−.04	.40**	.24**	.36**	1			
PV	.36**	−.25**	.33**	.27**	.27**	.42**	1		
PC	.37**	−.07**	.26**	.28**	.03	.23**	.34**	1	
BI	.71**	−.29	.57**	.44**	.19*	.61*	.53**	.39**	1

Note. ** p < .01, * p < .05. PE = Performance Expectancy (n = 73), EE = Effort Expectancy, HU = Habit Development/Habitual Use, SI = Social Influence, FC = Facilitating Conditions, HM = Hedonic Motivation, PV = Price Value, PC = Privacy Concern, and BI = Behavioral Intention.

($n = 65$) indicated that the seven variables explained 64% of the variance in behavioral intention ($R^2\Delta = .64$, $F(7,56) = 17.40$, $p < .001$). Only two predictors were significant: hedonic motivation (H5, $\beta = .26$, $p = .022$ in the case of users; $\beta = .43$, $p < .001$ for non-users) and habit development (H7, $\beta = .63$, $p < .001$ in the case of users; $\beta = .50$, $p < .001$ for non-users). In an exploratory analysis, we also controlled for privacy concern in the first step (rather than having it as a regular predictor at the end, following the other UTAUT variables). In this case, privacy concerns (H8) had both a marginally significant effect in the case of users ($p = .084$) and a significant effect for non-users ($p = .004$). Furthermore, given this constellation, effort expectancy (H2) appeared to play more of role for non-users alone ($\beta = -.19$, $p = .052$), but not users ($\beta = -.06$, $p = .538$). The negative coefficient suggests that non-users expect that the use of voice assistants will require more effort for them, in line with H2.

Please note that in the earlier analyses, we excluded performance expectancy (H1) due to the missing cases. In a final analysis with the 73 cases for which we had performance expectancy information, we examined the extent to which this variable predicts behavioral intention when we control for the three UTAUT predictors (effort expectancy, habit development, and hedonic motivation) while simultaneously excluding country and privacy concerns as control variables. In that case, all variables were significant ($p < .001$). Performance expectancy, however, only had a marginal significant and positive effect on behavioral intention (H1, $\beta = .18$, $p = .098$), possibly due to suppression effects through shared variance with other UTAUT variables (see correlations in Table 1).

5 Discussion

The goal of the current study was to provide more insights to the emerging research base around user and non-user concerns about voice assistants, intentions to purchase and use voice assistants, and factors that increase users' and non-users' intention to the adoption of such devices in the home and at work. What is more, the research aimed to provide further evidence regarding the extent to which UTAUT2 model variables and privacy concern are significant predictors of users' and non-users' behavioral intention to continue or start using voice assistants in the future.

The group differences suggested that users differed significantly from non-users in relation to a number of UTAUT2 model variables when we examined these individually (group comparisons). However, the picture is not as clear-cut and should be interpreted with caution as most of these differences disappeared when we analyzed the effect of all variables together in multiple regression analyses. Our regression results indicated that only hedonic motivation (H5) and habit development (H7) significantly predicted behavioral intention among users and non-users alike. This is also in line with research that showed that enjoyment predicts purchase intentions regarding voice assistants (Sohn and Kwon 2020) and the work by Lee et al. (2020), which showed that habit could positively increase the intention to continue using voice assistants. The case for the effect of effort expectancy (H2) is much weaker as it only emerged as a marginally significant effect for non-users, while performance expectancy (H1) had a very small and only marginally significant effect on behavioral intention in a much smaller sample once other UTAUT variables such as hedonic motivation, habit development and effort expectancy were entered in the first step before performance expectancy.

However, a number of predictors did not have the expected effects on behavioral intention. This included social influence (H3) and facilitating conditions (H4), in contrast to Dwivedi et al. (2019) and the findings regarding social benefits in McLean and Osei-Frimpong (2019). In contrast to our prediction, privacy concern (H8) did not have a direct effect on behavioral intention to use voice assistants in our study as proposed when it was examined as a predictor together with other UTAUT variables (H8). However, privacy concern did seem to play a role when it was entered as a control variable in the first step before all other UTAUT variables. This might be due to suppression effects.

More research in this area may be helpful to understand the role of conflicting beliefs and the way users as well as non-users evaluate the pros and cons of adopting tools when they report strong, moderate, or weak privacy concerns. For example, the interactivity of voice assistants has been shown to reduce the perceived intrusiveness via brand trust, which in turn has a positive influence on performance expectancy (see Lucia-Palacios and Pérez-López 2021). These findings might also explain why we see no direct effects of privacy concern, but an indication that privacy is possible to interact with performance expectancy in relation to behavioral intention.

5.1 Practical Implications

Several resources exist to help users of smart home devices such as voice assistant identify more privacy-enhancing solutions (e.g., Chhetri and Motti 2019) and the different privacy concerns of various stakeholders involved in the use of voice assistants (Pal et al. 2020). Clear communication, interactivity features (that offer more information and communication), and privacy-enhancing defaults may go a long way to build a trusting relationship between users and device manufacturers (see Lucia-Palacios and Pérez-López 2021). Such steps may also alleviate the privacy concerns of current users and prospective non-users (Pal et al. 2020) and make performance expectancy a more influential predictor of behavioral intention, as our results suggest.

5.2 Limitations

Some methodological and procedural limitations apply. First, we used self-reports and a student sample (although a significant proportion of our participants were working while studying). However, it is worth noting that the two groups – users and non-users – would have different reference points for their self-reports: users have experience using voice assistants to consult, while non-users are more likely to report on their perceptions rather than experience (although it is not definite that they are not passive users or bystanders, Pal et al. 2020). Second, we explored the behavioral intentions of our participants rather than actual use. The second would be preferable, but was a limitation of the design. Future research may wish to consider more longitudinal work similar to the diary study by Lau et al. (2018).

And third, we would like to acknowledge the limitations of using such a cross-sectional, educational, and international sample and outline some suggestions to consider cross-cultural factors in future research sections. However, other researchers also run certain analyses on combined samples of users and non-users (e.g., Liao et al. 2019) or users who are single users of voice assistants or sharing these devices (Lee et al. 2020). Future data collection efforts may need to increase sampling sizes in order to create the statistical requirements for multi-group analysis. And fourth, past research has shown that brand names can also influence trust, as some brand names may be more trusted than others (Park et al. 2018; Frick et al. 2021), leading users and non-users to be potentially more accepting of data collection via these brand devices (Chavanne 2018). In our case, we used well-known brand names (HomePod, Alexa, and Echo) as examples of physical voice assistants that are not incorporated into other devices. This suggests that the use of those brand names may also have impacted our results, a potential limitation to be confirmed in future work.

5.3 Future Research

Future research may wish to consider the role of user attitudes in relation to behavioral intention to use voice assistants. Attitudes related to trust, malicious attacks via voice assistants and therefore risk management, resistance, intentionality of device ownership (intentional vs. unintentional, e.g., in the case of preinstalled devices or the cases where voice assistants are given as gifts to users), and data sharing may be important areas for investigation in future studies regarding voice assistants as well (see also Hong et al. 2019; Michler et al. 2019; Sharevski et al. 2021; Yan et al. 2021). We would propose that future research may consider whether users and non-users have different privacy perceptions depending on the use of voice assistants in private as well as shared spaces.

A number of privacy theories such as the privacy calculus theory may serve as useful starting points. In addition, it may be worthwhile to explore additional theories – in addition to the well-established UTAUT – in the exploration of how, why, and when non-users decide to adopt certain physical and integrated devices in their everyday usage in the workplace and at home. We would also like to make two further suggestions. One, it would be interesting to see a meta-analysis on voice assistants that explored effects given certain context factors (public, private, multi-purpose environments; voluntary vs. involuntary adoption in shared spaces). Two, it would be interesting to see more theoretical frameworks and work in this area in order to move the research further and beyond both UTAUT and the focus on mostly virtual voice assistants.

In addition, we observed some country differences in relation to effort expectancy and facilitating conditions between participants in Finland vs. Ireland. More research on cultural variables could explain some of these findings. And lastly, the possible effects of voice assistants being used or misused, manipulated or compromised, and their use by various users in one environment (e.g., in the home or at work) are certainly worthy of more exploration (see also Lee et al. 2020; Sharevski et al. 2021).

5.4 Conclusions

In our study, the predictors of the acceptance of voice assistants were predominantly intrinsic (hedonic motivation) and habitual (habitual voice assistant use). However, contextual factors (facilitating conditions, social influence, privacy concern) were not predictors, nor did performance or effort expectancy predict behavioral intention to use voice assistants. Our results, therefore, suggest that predominantly individual factors rather than social factors drive the acceptance of voice assistants in users and non-users. Through experimental manipulation, future research may investigate the conditions under which privacy is a driver as well, such as specific contexts (e.g., private vs. public spaces at work and at home, multi-purpose locations such as home offices, shared and personal spaces in the home). This work may also validate the relative importance of drivers of voice assistant acceptance through experimental research.

References

Anderson, C.L., Agarwal, R.: Practicing safe computing: a multimedia empirical examination of home computer user security behavioral intentions. MIS Q. **34**(3), 613–643 (2010)

Brause, S.R., Blank, G.: Externalized domestication: smart speaker assistants, networks and domestication theory. Inf. Commun. Soc. **23**(5), 751–763 (2020)

Burbach, L., Halbach, P., Plettenberg, N., Nakayama, J., Ziefle, M., Valdez, A.C.: "Hey, Siri", "Ok, Google", "Alexa". Acceptance-relevant factors of virtual voice-assistants. In: 2019 IEEE International Professional Communication Conference (ProComm), pp. 101–111 (2019)

Chavanne, D.: Generalized trust, need for cognitive closure, and the perceived acceptability of personal data collection. Games **9**(2), 1–18 (2018)

Chhetri, C., Motti, V.G.: Eliciting privacy concerns for smart home devices from a user centre perpsective. In: Taylor, N., Christian-Lamb, C., Martin, M., Nardi, B. (eds.) iConference 2019. LNCS, vol. 11420, pp. 91–101. Springer, Cham (2019). https://doi.org/10.1007/978-3-030-157 42-5_8

Davis, F.D.: Perceived usefulness, perceived ease of use, and user acceptance of information technology. MIS Q. **13**(3), 319–340 (1989)

De Barcelos Silva, A., et al.: Intelligent personal assistants: a systematic literature review. Expert Syst. Appl. **147**(6), 1–13 (2020). Article 113193

Dee, C.: Voice search: the latest statistics and trends for 2022 and beyond. Algolia, 15 November 2022 (2021). https://www.algolia.com/blog/product/voice-search-the-latest-statistics-and-trends-for-2022-and-beyond/. Accessed 18 June 2022

Dwivedi, Y.K., Rana, N.P., Jeyaraj, A., Clement, M., Williams, M.: D: Re-examining the unified theory of acceptance and use of technology (UTAUT): Towards a revised theoretical model. Inf. Syst. Front. **21**(3), 719–734 (2019)

Easwara Moorthy, A., Vu, K.P.L.: Privacy concerns for use of voice activated personal assistant in the public space. Int. J. Hum.–Comput. Interact. **31**(4), 307–335 (2015)

Farooq, A., Ndiege, J.R.A., Isoaho, J.: Factors affecting security behavior of kenyan students: an integration of protection motivation theory and theory of planned behavior. In: 2019 IEEE AFRICON, pp. 1–8. IEEE (2019)

Ford, M., Palmer, W.: Alexa, are you listening to me? An analysis of Alexa voice service network traffic. Pers. Ubiquit. Comput. **23**(1), 67–79 (2018). https://doi.org/10.1007/s00779-018-1174-x

Frick, N.R.J., Wilms, K.L., Brachten, F., Hetjens, T., Stieglitz, S., Ross, B.: The perceived surveillance of conversations through smart devices. Electron. Commer. Res. Appl. **47**(5/6), 1–16 (2021). Article ID: 101046

Gallagher, C.: Ireland and Finland: similar countries with vastly different security approaches. The Irish Times, 26 February 2022. https://www.irishtimes.com/news/ireland/irish-news/ireland-and-finland-similar-countries-with-vastly-different-security-approaches-1.4812357. Accessed 18 June 2022

Hong, A., Nam, C., Kim, S.: What will be the possible barriers to consumers' adoption of smart home services? Telecommunications Policy **44**(2), 1–15 (2019). Article ID 101867

IMD: IMD World Digital Competitiveness Ranking 2021 (2021). https://www.imd.org/globalassets/wcc/docs/release-2021/digital_2021.pdf. Accessed 18 June 2022

Insteon: Insteon. Superior Smart Lighting and Electrical Control. https://www.insteon.com. Accessed 6 Nov 2021

Jeske, D.: Remote workers' experiences with electronic monitoring during Covid-19: Implications and recommendations. Int. J. Workplace Health Manag. **15**(3), 393–409 (2022)

Kim, M.J., Chung, N., Lee, C.K.: The effect of perceived trust on electronic commerce: Shopping online for tourism products and services in South Korea. Tour. Manage. **32**(2), 256–265 (2011)

Lau, J., Zimmerman, B., Schaub, F.: Alexa, are you listening? Privacy perceptions, concerns and privacy-seeking behaviors with smart speakers. Proc. ACM Hum.-Comput. Interact. **2**(CSCW), 1–31 (2018). Article ID: 102

Lee, K., Lee, K.Y., Sheehan, L.: Hey Alexa! A Magic Spell of Social Glue?: Sharing a Smart Voice Assistant Speaker and Its Impact on Users' Perception of Group Harmony. Inf. Syst. Front. **22**(3), 563–583 (2020)

Lee, K.Y., Sheehan, L., Lee, K., Chang, Y.: The continuation and recommendation intention of artificial intelligence-based voice assistant systems (AIVAS): the influence of personal traits. Internet Res. **31**(5), 1899–1939 (2021)

Liao, Y., Vitak, J., Kumar, P., Zimmer, M., Kritikos, K.: Understanding the role of privacy and trust in intelligent personal assistant adoption. In: Taylor, N.G., Christian-Lamb, C., Martin, M.H., Nardi, B. (eds.) iConference 2019. LNCS, vol. 11420, pp. 102–113. Springer, Cham (2019). https://doi.org/10.1007/978-3-030-15742-5_9

McLean, G., Osei-Frimpong, K.: Hey Alexa… examine the variables influencing the use of artificial intelligent in-home voice assistants. Comput. Hum. Behav. **99**(10), 28–37 (2019)

Michler, O., Decker, R., Stummer, C.: To trust or not to trust smart consumer products: a literature review of trust-building factors. Manag. Rev. Q. **70**(3), 391–420 (2019). https://doi.org/10.1007/s11301-019-00171-8

Pal, D., Arpnikanondt, C., Razzaque, M.A., Funilkul, S.: To trust or not-trust: privacy issues with voice assistants. IT Prof. **22**(5), 46–53 (2020)

Park, K., Kwak, C., Lee, J., Ahn, J.H.: The effect of platform characteristics on the adoption of smart speakers: empirical evidence in South Korea. Telemat. Inform. **35**(8), 2118–2132 (2018)

Lucia-Palacios, L., Pérez-López, R.: Effects of home voice assistants' autonomy on instrusiveness and usefulness: direct, indirect, and moderating effects of interactivity. J. Interact. Mark. **56**(11), 41–54 (2021)

Pfeifle, A.: Alexa, what should we do about privacy? Protecting privacy for users of voice-activated devices. Wash. Law Rev. **93**(1), 421–458 (2018)

Tan, Y.: Talking smart. The World of Chinese, 11 March 2021. https://www.theworldofchinese.com/2021/03/chinese-smart-speakers-market/. Accessed 6 Nov 2021

Sharevski, F., Jachim, P., Treebridge, P., Li, A., Babin, A., Adadevoh, C.: Meet Malexa, Alexa's malicious twin: Malware-induced misperception through intelligent voice assistants. Int. J. Hum.-Comput. Stud. **149**(May), 1–13 (2021). Article ID: 102604

Sohn, K., Kwon, O.: Technology acceptance theories and factors influencing artificial Intelligence-based intelligent products. Telemat. Inform. **47** (2020). Article 101324

Venkatesh, V., Morris, M.G., Davis, G.B., Davis, F.D.: User acceptance of information technology: toward a unified view. MIS Q. **27**(3), 425–478 (2003)

Venkatesh, V., Thong, J.Y., Xu, X.: Consumer acceptance and use of information technology: extending the unified theory of acceptance and use of technology. MIS Q. **36**(1), 157–178 (2012)

Yan, C., Zhang, G., Ji, X., Zhang, T., Zhang, T., Xu, W.: The feasibility of injecting inaudible voice commands to voice assistants. IEEE Trans. Dependable Secure Comput. **18**(3), 1108–1124 (2021)

Correction to: Artificial Intelligence Ambidexterity, Adaptive Transformation Capability, and Their Impact on Performance Under Tumultuous Times

Rogier van de Wetering, Patrick Mikalef, and Denis Dennehy

Correction to:
Chapter "Artificial Intelligence Ambidexterity, Adaptive Transformation Capability, and Their Impact on Performance Under Tumultuous Times" in: S. Papagiannidis et al. (Eds.):
The Role of Digital Technologies in Shaping the Post-Pandemic World, **LNCS 13454,**
https://doi.org/10.1007/978-3-031-15342-6_3

The last name "Mikalef" of the chapter author "Patrick Mikalef" name was unfortunately published with a typo error. The initially published version has now been corrected.

The updated original version of this chapter can be found at
https://doi.org/10.1007/978-3-031-15342-6_3

Author Index

Printed in the United States
by Baker & Taylor Publisher Services